# CLIO FROM THE RIGHT

Essays of a Conservative Historian

Edward S. Shapiro
Seton Hall University

UNIVERSITY
PRESS OF
AMERICA

Copyright © 1983 by

**University Press of America, Inc.**

P.O. Box 19101, Washington, D.C. 20036

All rights reserved
Printed in the United States of America

ISBN (Perfect): 0-8191-3034-6
ISBN (Cloth): 0-8191-3033-8
LCN: 82-25615

973.91
S 529 c

83-6623

To Daryl Who Made It All Possible

## ACKNOWLEDGMENTS

I am grateful to the following journals for allowing me to reprint the essays in this volume:

"Progressivism and Violence" first appeared in the North Dakota Quarterly, (Spring, 1978).

"Robert A. Woods and the Settlement House Impulse," first appeared in the Social Service Review, (June, 1978) and is reprinted by permission of the University of Chicago Press.

"The 1960s Revisited" first appeared in Midstream, (December, 1981).

"Of Kennedys and Kings" is to appear in Modern Age.

"Robert F. Kennedy and His Times" first appeared in the St. Croix Review, (June, 1978).

"The Return of Conservatism" first appeared in the Virginia Quarterly Review, (Spring, 1978).

"George Will" first appeared in the American Spectator, (March, 1979).

"George Will and American Conservatism" first appeared in the St. Croix Review, (August-September, 1982).

"History Through the Eyes of Irwin Unger" first appeared in the Conservative Historians Forum, (January, 1980).

"Decentralist Intellectuals and the New Deal" first appeared in the Journal of American History, LVIII (March, 1972), 938-957.

"American Conservative Intellectuals, the 1930's, and the Crisis of Ideology" first appeared in Modern Age, (Fall, 1979).

"Catholic Agrarian Thought and the New Deal" first appeared in the Catholic Historical Review, (October, 1979).

"The Catholic Rural Life Movement and the New Deal's Agricultural Policies" first appeared in the American Benedictine Review, (Fall, 1977).

"Walter Prescott Webb and the Crisis of a Frontierless Democracy" is to appear in Continuity.

"The Southern Agrarians, H. L. Mencken, and the Quest for Southern Identity" first appeared in American Studies, (Fall, 1972).

"The Southern Agrarians and the Tennessee Valley Authority" first appeared in the American Quarterly, (Winter, 1970), and is reprinted by permission of the University of Pennsylvania (Copyright 1970, Trustees of the Universith of Pennsylvania).

"Donald Davidson and the Tennessee Valley Authority" first appeared in the <u>Tennessee Historical Quarterly</u>, XXXIII (Winter, 1974), no. 4.

"Frank L. Owsley and the Defense of Southern Identity" first appeared in the <u>Tennessee Historical Quarterly</u>, XXXVI (Spring, 1977), no. 1.

"Pearl Harbor" is to appear in <u>Modern Age</u>.

"Roosevelt the Diplomat" first appeared in the <u>American Spectator</u>, (October, 1979).

"The Military Options to Hiroshima" first appeared in the <u>Naval War College Review</u>, (Spring, 1978) and <u>Amerika Studien</u>, (1978).

"Responsibility for the Cold War" first appeared in the <u>Intercollegiate Review</u>, (Winter, 1976-77).

"The Perjury of Alger Hiss" first appeared in the <u>Intercollegiate Review</u>, Fall-Winter, 1980).

"Revisionism R.I.P." first appeared in the <u>Intercollegiate Review</u>, (Fall-Winter, 1981).

"The War Among the Jews" is to appear in the <u>Intercollegiate Review</u>.

"American Jews and the Business Mentality" first appeared in <u>Judaism</u>, (Spring, 1978).

"The Golden Door" first appeared in the <u>American Jewish Historical Quarterly</u>, (March, 1977).

"City College and the Jewish Poor" first appeared in <u>American Jewish History</u>, (March, 1982).

"German and Russian Jews in America" first appeared in <u>Midstream</u>, (April, 1979).

"An Orthodox Recrudescence" first appeared in <u>Midstream</u>, (June-July, 1981).

"New Jersey's Jews" first appeared in Barbara Cunningham, ed., <u>The New Jersey Ethnic Experience</u> (1977).

"American Jewry and the State of Israel" first appeared in the <u>Journal of Ecumenical Studies</u> (Temple University), vol. 14, no. 1 (Winter, 1977), 1-16.

The following essays appeared or will appear in <u>Congress Monthly</u>:

"'The Unknown War': Fairy-Tale Version" (December, 1978).

"Liberalism and Jewish Survival" (June, 1978).

"Jewish Socialism in the United States" (May, 980).

"The Jewish Poor" (September-October, 1981).

"American Anti-Semitism Reconsidered" (January, 1980).

"The American Jewish Academic" (September-October, 1978).

"Does Conservative Judaism Have a Future?" (June, 1982).

"More Bintel Brief" (forthcoming).

## CONTENTS

| | | |
|---|---|---|
| ACKNOWLEDGMENTS | | v |
| PREFACE | | xiii |
| Part I | LIBERALISM AND CONSERVATISM | |
| | Progressivism and Violence | 1 |
| | Robert A. Woods and the Settlement House Impulse | 9 |
| | The 1960s Revisited | 21 |
| | Of Kennedys and Kings | 25 |
| | Robert F. Kennedy and His Times | 29 |
| | The Return of Conservatism | 37 |
| | George Will | 41 |
| | George Will and American Conservatism | 45 |
| | History Through the Eyes of Irwin Unger | 53 |
| Part II | THE NINETEEN THIRTIES | |
| | Decentralist Intellectuals and the New Deal | 57 |
| | American Conservative Intellectuals, the 1930s, and the Crisis of Ideology | 77 |
| | Catholic Agrarian Thought and the New Deal | 89 |
| | The Catholic Rural Life Movement and the New Deal's Agricultural Policies | 107 |
| | Walter Prescott Webb and the Crisis of a Frontierless Democracy | 133 |
| Part III | THE SOUTHERN AGRARIANS | |
| | The Southern Agrarians, H. L. Mencken, and the Quest for Southern Identity | 155 |

|  |  |  |
|---|---|---|
| | The Southern Agrarians and the Tennessee Valley Authority | 173 |
| | Donald Davidson and the Tennessee Valley Authority: The Response of a Southern Conservative | 189 |
| | Frank L. Owsley and the Defense of Southern Identity | 205 |
| Part IV | DIPLOMACY AND THE COLD WAR | |
| | Pearl Harbor | 225 |
| | Roosevelt the Diplomat | 233 |
| | The Military Options to Hiroshima: A Critical Examination of Gar Alperovitz's *Atomic Diplomacy* | 241 |
| | Responsibility for the Cold War: A Bibliographic Review | 255 |
| | The 'Unknown War': Fairy-Tale Version | 263 |
| | The Perjury of Alger Hiss: Icon of the Cold War | 269 |
| | Revisionism R.I.P. | 281 |
| | The Lessons of Tehran | 287 |
| Part V | THE AMERICAN JEWISH CONDITION | |
| | American Jews and the Business Mentality | 291 |
| | Liberalism and Jewish Survival | 299 |
| | Jewish Socialism in the United States | 305 |
| | The Golden Door | 311 |
| | City College and the Jewish Poor | 315 |
| | The War Among the Jews | 319 |
| | The Jewish Poor | 341 |
| | German and Russian Jews in America | 347 |

| | |
|---|---|
| The Jews of New Jersey | 357 |
| American Anti-Semitism Reconsidered | 377 |
| The American Jewish Academic | 385 |
| Does Conservative Judaism Have a Future? | 391 |
| An Orthodox Recrudescence | 401 |
| More Bintel Brief | 405 |
| American Jewry and the State of Israel | 409 |
| ABOUT THE AUTHOR | 425 |

PREFACE

The early 1960's, when I first began the serious study of American history and culture, was not hospitable to someone like myself with right-of-center ideas and a conservative temperament. John F. Kennedy had just been elected President, the stuffiness and lethargy of the 1950s had been replaced by social commitment and political idealism, and a new national agenda had been laid down. My discomfort itensified when the liberalism of the New Frontier with its wars on poverty, peace corps, and alliances for progress was supplanted by the radicalism of the post-1964 years. The war in Southeast Asia, racial conflict, and campus turmoil spawned new academic gurus, including C. Wright Mills, Herbert Marcuse, Franz Fanon, Paul Goodman, William A. Williams, and Eldridge Cleaver. Only one who had been in academic during these years can appreciate the extent to which dissenting voices were intimidated, and presumably dispassionate and independent scholars, fearful of being reproached as warmongers, racists, and reactionaries, caved in before the new academic orthodoxy.

During the 1970's and early 1980's I published a series of essays and reviews questioning many of the assumptions and conclusions of liberal and radical historiography. I, of course, was not along since the 1970's witnessed a decided move to the right by the general population and the intelligentsia. Indicative of this shift was the transformation of _Commentary_ magazine, the growth of the _American Spectator,_ the founding of _Continuity_ by a caucus of young conservative historians, and the creation of several foundations sponsoring research by conservative scholars. By 1982, I believed, the time was appropriate to bring the essays and reviews together in one volume.

This collection is divided into five parts, each encompassing a different area of my research and interest. The first section makes my political and social commitments (and biases) clear. They include a preference for social continuity and class reconciliation, a distaste for the reformist mentality as exhibited by the Kennedys, an admiration for the conservatism of the columnist George Will, and a rejection of the dominant liberal interpretation of American history.

The second section contains the results of my research in the intellectual history of the 1930s which had first appeared in embryonic form in my dissertation on "The American Distributists and the New Deal" (Harvard, 1968). These essays attempt to rectify what certainly is one of contemporary American conservatism's greatest weaknesses, its lack of historical awareness.

American conservatives are usually ignorant of the fact that there is such a thing as an American conservative tradition, and that a conservative intellectual does not want to restore chivalry, the divine right of kings, or slavery. The research of dozens of reputable non-liberal and nonradical historians is currently providing American conservatives with what Henry Steele Commager has called a "usable past". Conservatism, after all, was not born yesterday.

The third section analyzes the Southern Agrarians, that most distinctive and important of all American conservative groupings of the Twentieth Century. It is impossible to understand American conservatism without understanding the South, the most conservative of our regions, and it is impossible to understand the South without understanding the Agrarians. No other group of American intellectuals have presented in the Twentieth Century such a fundamental and comprehensive challenge to "modernism" as the Southern Agrarians, and no other group has so profoundly defended regionalism, religion, decentralization, and individualism.

Section four discusses certain aspects of American foreign relations during the past forty years, and the manner in which they have been presented by historians and the mass media. The emergence of "revisionism" among our diplomatic historians has influenced, for good or ill, the way in which our relations with the Soviet Union and other adversaries is viewed. Perhaps in no other area is their greater need for the insights of conservatism than in diplomacy. As I am writing this preface the citizens of New Jersey are considering whether to follow the advice of Ed Asner, Jane Fonda, and other authorities on American foreign policy to recommend to the White House and the Kremlin a mutual freeze on the development of nuclear weapons.

The last section discusses that area of American life which is closest to my heart. A Jewish conservative must be gratified by the emergence of a conservative Jewish intelligentsia, the growing number of Jews who are more committed to, and more knowledgeable about their faith, the increasing role of Israel as a bulwark of sanity, stability, and American interests in the Middle East, and the dramatic decline of American anti-Semitism since the end of World War II. Jewish liberism is, in my opinion, a threat to the interests of American Jewry. The Jewish interest is with those who, loosely classified as conservatives, wish to strengthen the traditional structure of marriage and the family, reject the hedonism and materialism of our consumer culture, support a stronger American posture in world affairs, favor international stability and oppose

"third world" radicalism, uphold private enterprise and
the sanctity of private property, and defend the private
sector against the aggressive designs of the government
and quasi-public agencies.

# 1
# Progressivism and Violence

▶The wave of revisionist literature on early Twentieth Century American history has had an unsettling effect on the interpretation of the Progressive movement. Historians, impressed by the complexity and diversity of the movement, have used such terms as "paradox" and "dilemma" to describe it, and have expanded the composition of the Progressives to include a whole host of different interest groups such as urban workers, new immigrants, populists, status conscious WASP lawyers, old Mugwumps, and elitist technocrats. Indeed, Peter Filene has concluded that the very concept of Progressivism itself is a mirage. In each of its aspects, he writes, "goals, values, membership and supporters — the movement displays a puzzling and irreducible incoherence." Filene suggests that, unless a new synthesis can be developed, historians should drop the idea that there ever was such a thing as the Progressive movement since they have so far been unable to organize the historical data of the period in any logical manner.[1]

And yet in spite of Filene's justified caveat, eliminating the term "Progressivism" from our historical lexicon would be akin to throwing out the baby with the bath water. Despite their differences in economic, social, and geographic backgrounds and despite their differences on political issues, the Progressives shared a mood of desperation stemming from the belief that American society was being torn apart by economic, class, and ethnic rivalries engendered by industrialization, urbanization, and immigration. Other Americans also feared the United States was liable to explode at any moment, but the Progressives were distinguished by their faith that the country's social, economic, and ethnic divisions could be bridged through a variety of social, philanthropic, and political institutions.

[1] Peter G. Filene, "An Obituary for 'The Progressive Movement'," *American Quarterly*, XXII (Spring, 1970), 31-34; David M. Kennedy, "Overview: The Progressive Era," *Historian*, XXXVII (May 1975), 453-68; G. Edward White, "The Social Values of the Progressives: Some New Perspectives," *South Atlantic Quarterly*, LXX (Winter 1971), 62.

Progressives were acutely conscious of the fact that American industrialization had been accompanied by increasingly violent and bloodstained struggles between labor and management. Sensible and well-meaning persons were terrified by the prospect of a cataclysmic class war between the dispossessed working-class of the factory towns and large cities and the newly spawned industrial and financial plutocracy. "The time has come when forbearance has ceased to be a virtue," the liberal Protestant minister Lyman Abbott declared in 1894 during the Pullman strike. "There must be some shooting, men must be killed, and then there will be an end of this defiance of the law and destruction of property. . . . The soldiers must use their guns. They must shoot to kill." The pastor William H. Garwardine feared that "we as a nation are dividing ourselves, like ancient Rome, into two classes, the rich and the poor, the oppressor and the oppressed." The Pullman strike had been preceded by the violent year of 1877, the appearance of the Molly Maguires, the use of Pinkerton detectives, the Haymarket riot of 1886, the violence in Couer d'Alene, Idaho in 1892, and the Homestead strike of 1892, and was followed by Coxey's Army, the assassination of President William McKinley, the appearance of violent anarchist groups, the founding of the Industrial Workers of the World in 1905, and the Ludlow, Colorado massacre of 1914. The fear of industrial violence led to the creation of the Industrial Relations Commission in 1910 by the federal government. The commission's task, noted Walter Lippmann, was "explaining why America, supposed to become the land of promise, has become the land of disappointment and deep-seated discontents."[2]

Americans responded to growing industrial strife and to the presence of large numbers of immigrants from southern and eastern Europe by emphasizing the importance of patriotism, civic duty, and tradition. They established hundreds of patriotic and genealogical societies, required public schools to teach American history and civics, created a quasi-religious cult devoted to the worship of the American flag, listened to the rousing patriotic music of John Philip Sousa, read historical novels, embarked on overseas imperialistic adventures, and made the jingoist Theodore Roosevelt the most popular political figure of the era.[3]

The new economic, social, and ethnic divisions existed in their starkest forms in the large cities. Here the very rich and very poor lived in close

---

[2] Abbott quoted by Richard M. Abrams, "The Failure of Progressivism," in Abrams and Lawrence W. Levine, eds., *The Shaping of Twentieth Century America: Interpretative Essays* (Boston: Little, Borwn, 1972), 209-10; Garwardine quoted by Frederic C. Jahar, *Doubters and Dissenters: Cataclysmic Thought in America, 1885-1918* (New York: Macmillan, 1964), 43; Lippmann quoted by Graham Adams, Jr., *The Age of Industrial Violence, 1910-1915: The Activities and Findings of the United States Commission on Industrial Relations* (New York: Columbia University Press, 1966), 50. See also John Braeman, "Seven Progressives," *Business History Review*, XXXV (Winter 1961), 583-84; Samuel P. Hays, *The Response to Industrialism: 1885-1914* (Chicago: University of Chicago Press, 1957), 37-43; and Samuel Rezneck, "Unemployment, Unrest, and Relief in the United States During the Depression of 1893-1897," *Journal of Political Economy*, LXI (August 1953), 333-39, 344-45.

[3] Wallace E. Davies, *Patriotism on Parade: The Story of Veterans' and Hereditary Organizations in America, 1783-1900* (Cambridge: Harvard University Press, 1955), 44-49; Merle Curti, *The Roots of American Loyalty* (New York: Columbia University Press, 1946), 180-200.

proximity and mutual hostility, large immigrant communities seemingly resisted Americanization, and social dissolution and communal fragmentation had progressed the furtherest. The contemporary image of the city as reflected in such books as Ward McAllister's *Society as I Found It* (1890), Jacob Riis' *How the Other Half Lives* (1890), Benjamin O. Flower's *Civilization's Inferno* (1893), Josiah Strong's *The Challenge of the City* (1907), and Robert A. Woods' *The City Wilderness* (1898) was of growing class and ethnic chasms and the increasing likelihood of urban violence. Vida D. Scudder's semiautobiographical novel appropriately entitled *A Listener in Babel* (1903) described Boston at the turn of the century as a "cleavage of classes, cleavage of races, cleavage of faiths! an inextricable confusion. And the voice of democracy, crying aloud in our streets: 'Out of all this achieve brotherhood! achieve the race to be.'"[4]

This sense of urban crisis was deepened by the realization that the frontier period of American history had ended or was rapidly drawing to a close. Growing urban discontent and the increasing violence of labor-management relations was attributed by some to the diminishing supply of free land out west. With the end of the frontier Americans could look forward to the growth of an urban proletariat and the emergence of the social and economic problems prevalent in Europe. The economist Francis A. Walker wrote in 1892, one year before Frederick Jackson Turner published his seminal essay on the frontier in American history, that "reluctant as we may be to recognize it, a labor problem is at last upon us. No longer can a continent of free virgin lands avert from us the social struggle which the old world has known so long and so painfully." Other Americans predicted that a large standing army would now be needed to keep down the urban rabble and prevent "social disturbances of grave significance."[5]

The fear of urban violence and the desire to strengthen the forces of social harmony lay behind virtually every urban reform of the Progressive era. The social gospel movement and the institutional church of Protestantism hoped to replace the conflict of urban life with Christian brotherhood. Protestant seminaries introduced courses in "Christian sociology" stressing religious reconciliation in contrast to the individualism and competitiveness of social Darwinism. Protestant ministers emphasized the need for the rich and poor to worship together, believing this would overcome their mutual hostility.[6]

[4] Scudder quoted by Arthur Mann, *Yankee Reformers in the Urban Age* (Cambridge: Harvard University Press, 1954), 1. See also, Herbert G. Gutman, "Work, Culture, and Society in Industrializing America, 1815-1919," *American Historical Review*, LXXVIII (June 1973), 576; Frederic C. Jaher, "The Boston Brahmins in the Age of Industrial Capitalism," in Jaher, ed., *The Age of Industrialism in America: Essays in Social Structure and Cultural Values* (New York: Free Press, 1968), 204-213; and Richard Sennett, "Middle-Class Families and Urban Violence: The Experiences of a Chicago Community in the Nineteenth Century," in Tamara K. Haraven, ed., *Anonymous Americans: Explorations in Nineteenth Century Social History* (Englewood Cliffs: Prentice-Hall, 1971), 281-89.

[5] Walker quoted by Richard Hofstadter, *The Progressive Historians: Turner, Beard, Parrington* (New York: Alfred A. Knopf, 1968), 59-60; Lee Benson, *Turner and Beard: American Historical Writing Reconsidered* (Glencoe, Ill.: Free Press, 1960), 70-89.

[6] Aaron I. Abell, *The Urban Impact on American Protestantism, 1865-1900* (Hamden, Conn.: Archon, 1962), 57-58, 69-87; Charles Howard Hopkins, *The Rise of the Social Gospel in American Protestantism, 1865-1915* (New Haven: Yale University Press, 1940), 24-32, 67-73, 94-96, 272-87.

The Progressive quest for urban social harmony influenced John Dewey's movement to reform the country's schools. Modern urban education, Dewey claimed, was neither breaking down the barriers of nationality and class among children nor training them to live in a democratic community. Dewey envisaged the Progressive school's major function as inculcating democracy, service, and cooperation among its students who then would go on to create a "worthy, lovely, and harmonious" society. Other Progressive educationists believed one way to counteract ethnic and class divisions and to create a sense of unity and order was for schools to enlarge their responsibilities by becoming social centers. The centers would provide a place where persons of diverse ethnic and social background could meet one another and develop a sense of community similar to that found in rural America. Edward J. Ward of Rochester, New York, the most enthusiastic spokesman for the social center movement, contended that it could create "the community interest, the neighborly spirit, the democracy that we knew before we came to the city." Some Progressive social reformers, such as Joseph Lee of Boston, believed playgrounds were the answer to the problem of urban disorder. Playgrounds, it was argued, could instill in the young a sense of loyalty to teams and schools which could later be applied in the teaching of citizenship and the inculcation of loyalty to the city and the nation.[7]

The social settlement movement was the most important effort of Progressive social reformers to prevent urban violence. The founders of the social settlements wished to heal the social lesions stemming from the fragmentation of rural homogeneity and the dissolution of the sense of community resulting from industrialization, urbanization, and immigration. In contrast to Marxists, the settlement workers viewed conflict as abnormal and unnatural, as something to be eliminated rather than exploited. Cooperation and love, rather than hatred and rivalry, were the most basic human impulses. Unfortunately modern urban society was sharply divided into competing economic groups and warring ethnic communities, and the settlement reformers saw their own task as helping restore a pre-industrial, pre-urban social order free from social strife. "The social organism has broken down through large districts of our great cities," Jane Addams declared. Nevertheless, settlement workers "are bound to regard the entire life of their city as organic, to make an effort to unify it, and to protect against its over differentiation."[8]

The model for the settlement movement was the small town where

---

[7]Dewey quoted by Lawrence A. Cremin, *The Transformation of the School: Progressivism in American Education, 1876-1957* (New York: Alfred A. Knopf, 1961), 117-22; Ward quoted by Edward W. Stevens, Jr., "Social Centers, Politics, and Social Efficiency in the Progressive Era," *History of Education Quarterly*, XII (Spring 1972), 22-23; K. Gerald Marsden, "Philanthropy and the Boston Playground Movement, 1887-1907," *Social Service Review*, XXXV (March 1961), 48-58.

[8]Jane Addams, "The Subjective Necessity for Social Settlements," in *Philanthropy and Social Progress* (Boston: T. Y. Crowell, 1893), 4-6; Clarke A. Chambers, *Seedtime of Reform: American Social Service and Social Action, 1918-1933* (Ann Arbor: University of Michigan Press, 1963), 14-15, 112; Daniel Levine, *Varieties of Reform Thought* (Madison: State Historical Society of Wisconsin, 1964), 16-21; Nathan I. Huggins, *Protestants Against Poverty: Boston's Charities, 1870-1900* (Westport, Conn.: Greenwood, 1971), chs. i. and vii.

everybody knew each other, where sharp economic and class distinctions did not exist, and where personal communication was a vital aspect of daily life. The settlements believed they could instill a sense of community in their neighborhoods. Addams termed it "salvation by acre". This sense of community would, it was hoped, supersede ethnic, religious, and class loyalties and unify the disparate populations of the metropolis. Seth Low, one of the founders of University Settlement in New York City, was especially concerned about the potential for strife between labor and capital. The "laboring man knows as little about the educated and rich people of New York as the latter knows about the laboring men. Out of this mutual ignorance is bred mutual suspicion and mutual distrust," he feared. Settlement houses, by enabling workers to become acquainted with representatives of the employing class on equal terms, dissipates class antagonisms and makes "the life of our city better in all its aspects." Arthur C. Holden, a leading interpreter of the goals of the settlement movement, maintained that the movement "deprecates class distinctions and class limitations. It makes use of class consciousness and group consciousness only as a means of arousing the dulled and senseless members of society to a consciousness of their social entity and of awakening them to a realization of group relationships to society as a whole." The struggle for urban social justice, Holden claimed, "is a spiritual battle, not a class war."[9]

This shrinking from class conflict and violence continually manifested itself among settlement workers. Jane Addams was a pacifist and the first woman to win the Nobel Prize for peace. Virtually all the settlement workers favored the settling of labor-management disputes through arbitration boards and conciliation rather than through strikes which could lead to violence. Because of its doctrine of class conflict, socialism was anathema to the settlement workers. They preferred to believe that education and the accumulation of data from the social sciences would enable disinterested experts to resolve industrial clashes peacefully, equitably, and scientifically. Jane Addams, in particular, had an excessively optimistic view of the power and role of education in resolving economic disputes. In rejecting class conflict, the settlement workers argued that classes were dependent on each other, and that each class should be motivated by a desire to serve the broader social good. According to Arthur Holden, the major contribution of the settlement movement had been to emphasize "the mutual interdependence of the different parts of the social structure."[10]

The work of the leading sociologists and psychologists of the Progressive era mirrored the emphasis of the settlement pioneers on social unity as well as their distrust of conflict. Rejecting the individualism and

[9]Law quoted by Arthur C. Holden, *The Settlement Idea: A Vision of Social Justice* (New York: Macmillan, 1922), 16-17; Holden quoted in *ibid.*, 89-90, 180; Allen F. Davis, *Spearheads for Reform: The Social Settlements and the Progressive Movement, 1890-1914* (New York: Oxford University Press, 1967), 75-76; George E. Peterson, *The New England College in the Age of the University* (Amherst: Amherst College Press, 1964), 190-92; Robert A. Woods, "The University Settlement Ideal," in *Philanthropy and Social Progress*, 91.

[10]Holden, *The Settlement Idea*, 87-88; John C. Farrell, *Beloved Lady: A History of Jane Addams' Ideas on Reform and Peace* (Baltimore: Johns Hopkins Press, 1967); Davis, *Spearheads for Reform*, 108-12.

naturalism of social Darwinism, the Progressive social scientists stressed the social nature of man and the decisive influence of society in the development of personality. A person's normal growth, wrote James Mark Baldwin, "lands him in essential solidarity with his fellows, while . . . the exercise of his social duties and privileges advances his highest and finest individuality." For Charles H. Cooley, life was characterized by reciprocity and interaction. He wrote in his *Social Process* (1920) that "the central fact of history from the psychological point of view is the gradual enlargement of social consciousness and rational cooperation", while Henry Demarest Lloyd in *Man the Social Creator* (1906) spoke of "the attraction of men for each other as the gravitating force which explains the position, motion and relations of the social atoms and the social masses." All social problems, Lloyd claimed elsewhere, "are problems of union."[11]

This quest for unit was a central motif in the journalism of the Progressive era, especially in that most important of all Progressive magazines, *The New Republic*. Herbert Croly, Walter Weyl, and Wlater Lippmann, the three founders of the journal, categorically rejected class conflict as an instrument of social melioration. Croly's *The Promise of American Life* argued that social regeneration would remain incomplete "until the conviction and feeling of human brotherhood enters into possession of the human spirit." For *The New Republic*, the midwife of a new social order was to be education which, by disseminating an ideology stressing reconciliation and nationalism, would counteract the centrifugal forces engendered by industrialization and urbanization.[12]

The Progressives' ideal of social solidarity, their desire to transcend economic and social conflict by creating centers of social cohesion, their faith in the social nature of man, their longing for a middle-class society without extreme variations of wealth and status, their conviction that education and expertise could resolve class and ethnic conflicts stamped them as enlightened conservatives. Their social outlook never completely recovered from the shock of World War I. The war challenged the belief of Progressive intellectuals that conflict and violence were mere transitory aspects of history which were being gradually eliminated through the application of reason and science. The war showed that violence was far more deeply imbedded in human nature than John Dewey, Jane Addams, and the other Progressive intellectuals had ever imagined. Indeed, for some American intellectuals the war destroyed any faith at all in man's goodness and social nature, and they became convinced that Hobbes and Calvin, rather than Locke, had more clearly recognized the true nature of man.

The chaos and violence of the Great War strengthened the Progressive quest for order, harmony, cooperation and unity. The answer to Arthur S.

[11]Baldwin quoted by Fay Berger Karpf, *American Social Psychology: Its Origins, Development, and European Background* (New York: McGraw-Hill, 1932), 269-91; Cooley quoted by David W. Noble, "The Religion of Progress in America, 1890-1914," *Social Research*, XXII (Winter 1955), 433; Lloyd quoted in *ibid.*, 422, and in Daniel Aaron, *Men of Good Hope: A Story of American Progressives* (New York: Oxford University Press, 1951), 163-64.

[12]Croly quoted by David W. Noble, *The Paradox of Progressive Thought* (Minneapolis: University of Minnesota Press, 1958), 66. See also, Charles B. Forcey, *The Crossroads of Liberalism: Croly, Weyl, Lippmann, and the Progressive Era, 1900-1925* (New York: Oxford University Press, 1961).

Link's query of 1959, "What Happened to the Progressive Movement in the 1920's?", is to be found in part in the emergence of the industrial sociology of Elton Mayo and his disciples. Influenced by Emile Durkheim and Vilfredo Pareto, Mayo believed western civilization to be on the verge of collapse due to the constant and disruptive change fostered by modern industrialization and urbanization, and this could be averted only by an elite of social scientists capable of restoring social equilibrium and harmony. For Mayo the good society was the pre-industrial agrarian society in which social solidarity rather than alienation predominated. As he wrote in his *Social Problems of an Industrial Civilization* (1945), "patriotism is not enough; we must have no hatred or bitterness toward anyone."[13]

Mayo based his industrial sociology on the belief that man was a social animal who preferred harmony to conflict. He denied that conflict between management and labor might be rooted in objective economic circumstances. Rather, the structure of the modern factory encouraged conflict instead of cooperation and confused laborers as to their best interests. The future of American industry depended, Mayo argued, on the ability of human relations experts to convince workers to accept the goals of management. His work at Western Electric's Hawthorne plant at Chicago convinced him that management could secure this by persuading the working force that they were important, that they were participating in something valuable, and that they were part of a team. Ordway Tead, a prominent advocate of industrial sociology, clearly stated its objectives in his 1935 work *The Art of Leadership*. "We should never forget that people love to be led," Tead wrote. "They can become identified with a strong force outside themselves into which with others they can pour their own increasing energy and thus feel a harmony of oneness with a power bigger than themselves."[14]

For Mayo, any negative attitudes labor might have toward management could be overcome by improving communications. His assumptions that conflict was unnatural and unnecessary, that workers really wanted to cooperate with management, that hostility toward management was irrational and unfounded, and that workers should be fitted to the job rather than the job to the workers were profoundly elitist. Harmony and cooperation, rather than social justice, were Mayo's ultimate objectives, and for him the key to happiness was social solidarity.

Frederick Winslow Taylor, the founder of scientific management, shared Mayo's distate for conflict and his passion for order and cooperation. Taylor wanted wage rates, hours of work, and working conditions determined by scientific expertise rather than by the struggle between labor and management. By accurately discovering the economic functions best suited

---

[13]Arthur S. Link, "What Happened to the Progressive Movement in the 1920's?" *American Historical Reivew*, LXIV (July 1959), 833-51; Mayo quoted by Henry S. Kariel, *The Decline of American Pluralism* (Stanford: Stanford University Press, 1961), 174-75.

[14]Tead quoted by R. Alan Lawson, *The Failure of Independent Liberalism, 1930-1941* (New York: G. P. Putnam's, 1971), 52-54; William H. Whyte, Jr., *The Organization Man* (Garden City: Anchor Books, 1957), 39-42; J. A. C. Brown, *The Social Psychology of Industry: Human Relations in the Factory* (Baltimore: Penguin Books, 1954), 69-85; Reinhard Bendix, *Work and Authority in Industry: Ideologies of Management in the Course of Industrialization* (New York: Harper & Row, 1963), 308-19.

for each individual, scientific management could usher in a golden age of high productivity and social harmony. As Daniel J. Boorstin has written, Taylor possessed "an evangelical belief in the healing, harmonizing powers of efficiency." Taylor was confident that industrial conflict was giving way to cooperation resulting from the acceptance by labor and management of the dictates of scientific management. "We are now on the threshold of the coming era of true cooperation," he wrote, "the time is coming when all the great things will be done by the cooperation of many men in which each man performs that function for which he is best suited."[15]

The Progressive intellectuals' emphasis on social harmony, as well as their renunciation of conflict and violence, stemmed in large part from the importance they attributed to the sociological, rather than the economic or political, sources of America's domestic ills. They believed that, even more than anti-trust legislation, pure food and drug laws, and crusades against political bosses, the nation needed a restoration of a sense of rural community, an increase in face-to-face communication, and an end to alienation. The Progressives' underscoring of the primacy of alienation and the quest for community resembled, in crucial respects, the stress the great European conservative thinkers of the late Eighteenth and early Nineteenth Centuries, such as Edmund Burke, Louis de Bonald, and Robert de Lamennais, placed on the socially disintegrating impact on European society of the French Revolution, modern nationalism, and secularism.

Viewed from the perspective of the 1970's, it is easier to comprehend the essential conservative message of the Progressives, and the wide gulf which separates them from a modern radical such as Saul Alinsky who believed it necessary to "rub raw the sores of discontent" to achieve meaningful social change. The chaos in the cities and on the campuses during the 1960's sensitized Americans to the question of "law and order" and directed their attention to the sociological roots of student discontent and urban disorder. A society which has produced the McCone, Kerner, and Scranton Commissions and has flocked to such vigilante movies as "Death Wish" and "Shaft" perhaps can appreciate the Progressives' pervasive fear of violence and social dissolution.

[15]Daniel J. Boorstin, *The Americans: The Democratic Experience* (New York: Random House, 1973), 363-64; Bendix, *Work and Authority*, 274-87; Samuel Haber, *Efficiency and Uplift: Scientific Management in the Progressive Era, 1890-1920* (Chicago: University of Chicago Press, 1964), chs. i and ii.

# 9
# Robert A. Woods and the Settlement House Impulse

The South End House, established in 1891, was Boston's first social settlement house. Its founding and early history reflected the dismay of Boston's intellectual, social, and religious elite regarding the city's growing cultural heterogeneity and the increasing potential for ethnic and religious conflict and communal disintegration. Its primary goal of restoring communal harmony was conservative and resulted in part from the nostalgic feelings for the small New England town of Boston's leadership, which hoped the South End House could become an urban counterpart of the New England town meeting hall. The South End House, by attempting to become the focus for the social and communal loyalties of the South End's inhabitants, initially was viewed with great suspicion by the Roman Catholic church. Its emphasis on social reconciliation and the restoration of a sense of community were popular themes among American intellectuals of the late nineteenth and early twentieth centuries.

Boston's rapid economic and demographic growth during the late nineteenth century greatly troubled the city's social and intellectual leadership. They believed immigration and industrialization had destroyed the city's ethnic and cultural homogeneity, had sharply divided the city into hostile classes, and had increased the likelihood of violent economic and ethnic conflict.[1] Vida D. Scudder's semiautobiographical novel, appropriately entitled *A Listener in Babel*, described Boston at the turn of the century as a "cleavage of classes, cleavage of races, cleavage of faiths: an inextricable confusion."[2]

One element of the city's elite recoiled from this growing ethnic and social differentiation by retreating to a golden age of cultural homogeneity which supposedly existed prior to the disrupting impact of modern industrialization and immigration. Their stress on the colonial, and hence English, roots of Boston and New England society led to an emphasis on genealogy, the establishment of preparatory schools along English lines, and an increased popularity of Anglo-Catholicism. Other Bostonians responded to the threat of communal disintegration by founding a host of charitable and civic institutions which would, it was hoped, inculcate a sense of community transcending class and ethnic loyalties and restore social harmony.

Joseph Lee, for instance, argued that playgrounds could instill in Boston's youth a sense of loyalty to teams and schools which later could be broadened to include loyalty to the city and the nation. Mary Parker Follett, the leader of Boston's community-center movement, believed neighborhood centers could overcome civic apathy, further mutual understanding among diverse ethnic, economic, and religious groups, and overcome the fragmentation of modern life. Edwin D. Mead, Albert Bushnell Hart, and Edward Everett Hale hoped that the books, pamphlets, and lectures sponsored by the Massachusetts Society for Promoting Good Citizenship could teach the immigrants and their children proper American political principles and counteract their supposed affinity for violence and corruption. The fear of social dissolution and ethnic conflict was, in part, responsible for the founding of the Immigration Restriction League of Boston in 1894 by Charles Warren, Robert DeCourcey Ward, and Prescott Farnsworth Hall. The desire for social reconciliation and a strengthening of a sense of community among Boston's various population groups also shaped the early history of the South End House, the city's first settlement house.[3]

Founded in 1891 by Robert A. Woods, the South End House was located in a neighborhood which had clearly seen better days. Retrieved from the tides around 1850, the South End had rapidly grown into an area of wide avenues, tree-shaded squares and parks, and red-brick and brownstone houses. But by 1873 its period of prosperity had ended. The depression of 1873—accompanied by the foreclosures on many South End mortgages, the expansion of downtown business into the neighborhood, the infiltration by the Irish, and, most important, the reclamation of the Back Bay—all contributed to the South End's decline.[4] It was shortly after the end of the Civil War that Thomas Apley, George Apley's father, spied one of his South End neighbors in shirt-sleeves. "The next day he sold his house for what he had paid for it and . . . moved to Beacon Street. . . . [He] had sensed the approach of a change; a man in his shirt sleeves had told him that the days of the South End were numbered."[5] The erection of elevated railroad tracks along Washington Street in 1900 was the final blow to any hope of arresting the area's deterioration.[6]

After the departure of the Yankee, the South End rapidly degenerated into a lodging-house and tenement district of approximately 45,000 persons of whom 28,000 lived in 2,500 lodging houses. The lodgers were mostly unmarried native Americans drawn from rural New England and New York by the opportunities, both real and imagined, of the Boston economy, particularly the demand for white-collar workers. The lodging houses also contained 6,000 Canadians who had left the farms and fishing villages of Nova Scotia, Newfoundland, New Brunswick, Ontario, and Labrador to try their luck in the big city. The lodging-house population was extremely transient, with a residential turnover of 50 percent per year.[7] The lodgers' disordered social life was responsible for the many "clairvoyants, palmists, astrologers, magnetic and inspirational healers, psychometric readers, and mahatmas" in the South End,[8] while "the absence of all semblance of home ties, of companionship and friendship, and for hundreds of young men and women, even of mere acquaintances" led to prostitution and even, at times, suicide.[9]

In contrast, the tenements housed mostly immigrants, with the Irish making up 60 percent and the Jews 20 percent. The remainder consisted of Italian, British, and German newcomers. Most of the immigrants were unskilled laborers who worked in coal slips, lumberyards, piano factories, steam laundries, woodworking establishments, and the many retail stores in the South End. There were also 2,800 blacks living on its outer fringes. The immigrants exhibited some of the classic symptoms of social dislocation, including a high rate of alcoholism and lower standards of sexual morality. Perhaps even more important to outside observers was the inhabitants' loyalty to local Irish political bosses, which seemingly indicated little civic pride.[10]

By 1900 the South End had become, according to Edward Everett Hale, "the most charitied acre in Christendom."[11] Boston's communal leadership and social workers focused their energies on the South End because here existed, in their starkest forms, the things which were most troubling the New England conscience: alienation from any sense of community, ethnic pluralism, the potential for conflict and violence, and evidences of social dissolution. If they had been merely interested in the alleviation of suffering and the dispensing of charity they would have concentrated on the North End, Boston's poorest section. The fact that the South End was not populated by the very poor was especially attractive since the area did not yet exhibit the irreversible social disintegration characteristic of a slum. Boston's leaders believed neighborhood rehabilitation could be achieved among the working poor and lower middle-class of the South End. At least this was the hope of Robert A. Woods when he came to the South End in 1891.

Woods, who had been raised in Pittsburgh, had graduated from Amherst College in 1886 and then had spent three years at the Andover Theological Seminary, the bastion of New England Congregationalism. While at Amherst he was deeply influenced by the social gospel espoused by William Jewett Tucker, a professor of pastoral theology. Encouraged by Tucker, Woods left for England in 1890 in order to study the social settlement movement with the intention of ultimately establishing a settlement in Boston. While in London he resided at Toynbee Hall, England's first social settlement.[12]

Established in 1884 in London's East End, Toynbee Hall annually attracted some fifteen to twenty university students as residents. They came to Toynbee Hall in order to help bridge the gap between England's social classes, the East End then being one of the worst slums in all of England. The residents were, however, more impressed by the spiritual than the material poverty of the East End's settlers. As J. A. R. Pimlott, the historian of Toynbee Hall, has written, what distinguished the inhabitants of the East End "so conspicuously from the poor of other industrial cities was . . . their isolation. Amongst this conglomeration of nearly a million people there was no communal life."[13] Toynbee Hall responded to this social vacuum by undertaking an ambitious program of adult education, cultural uplift, entertainment, charity, and civic betterment.[14]

Woods's stay in England reinforced his view of social work as decentralized social reconstruction. The English social settlements were intimately connected to the local parishes. The head of Toynbee Hall, for example, was a vicar, Samuel A. Barnett. Woods realized America's religious diversity would doom social settlements closely tied to any specific religious structure or denomination. Instead, his model was the American small town, especially the New England village. There was in Woods, as well as in the other American settlement pioneers, an intense distaste for the impersonality, anonymity, and heterogeneity of big cities and a longing for the social harmony and face-to-face relationships supposedly characteristic of rural life. They argued that social settlements could overcome artificial class, religious, and ethnic differences and imbue urban neighborhoods with the social cohesion and sense of community found in small towns. "The settlements," Woods wrote, "are able to take neighborhoods in cities, and by patience bring back to them much of the healthy village life, so that people shall know and care for each other."[15] Other settlement workers also praised the neighborhood ideal. For Graham Taylor, neighborhoods were "the source of civic strength for progress," while Mary Simkhovitch contended that the task of the settlement was elaborating "the methods by which a neighborhood may become a consciously effective group."[16] Jane Addams often talked in terms of "salvation by acre."

Woods's view of the role of the settlement house resulted from the emphasis he placed on man's social and organic nature and the necessity of establishing institutions enabling people to interact socially in spite of religious, economic, and ethnic differences. Industrialization, however, had divided society into hostile economic groups, had fostered the emergence of a revolutionary, class-conscious socialism, and had led the nation to the brink of "disintegration." The challenge of socialism could be answered only through a democratic philosophy and institutions such as social settlements which appreciated "common human loyalties" and overcame the "isolation of classes and nationalities."[17] Woods believed that the social cohesion which Henry Adams had discovered among the gothic cathedrals of medieval France could be created in Boston's South End through a settlement house.

As Boston's most prominent social worker during the 1890s and early twentieth century and as the interpreter of the settlement-house impulse to his wealthy Yankee financial backers, Woods realized that a major barrier to implementing his social vision was the vast economic and social gulf separating the South End and the Back Bay. In England he had seen hostile social classes, influenced by the settlement movement, "coming together, seeking a unity of interest, each learning to render to the other . . . what it has received."[18] In Boston, however, the Yankees had retreated to the "emptiness" of the Back Bay and the North Shore.[19] The Yankees and the immigrants needed each other, he cried out. People "become tired of being shut in with a single class in society; so tired that they may seek some unmistakable way of escape."[20] Boston's social settlements could be "bits of neutral territory where the descendants of the Puritans may meet the chosen leaders among the immigrants from Italy, Russia, and the Levant,"[21] and usher in a new era of social reconciliation in which "hatred of class, and race and sect will begin to melt away. The new day will begin when—underneath and above all group loyalties—we shall have our great common songs, processions, holidays."[22]

Upon Woods's return to the United States from England plans were immediately launched to establish a Boston settlement house. Tucker was especially eager to see such an institution and was influential in rallying Brahmin financial support for the project. According to Tucker, a Boston settlement house would foster "a true social unity . . . (and) the acknowledgement of neighborhood which realizes that fine social ideal—the community."[23] In October 1891 the Andover House Association was founded with Tucker as chairman of its executive council and Woods as resident head. In order to eliminate any sectarian religious connotation and to identify the settlement more closely with the community, the settlement soon changed its name to the South End House. The association almost immediately attracted a membership of approximately 200 whose annual dues of three dollars and other benefactions went to the support of the settlement's activities and the purchase of a sixteen-room mansion at 6 Rollins Street in 1891. The settlement opened on January 1, 1892, and its goals were clearly put forth in the organization's "Articles of Association": "To bring into friendly and helpful relations with one another the people of the neighborhood in which the House is situated. To serve as a medium between the different social elements of the city for bringing about a more intelligent and systematic understanding of their mutual obligations."[24]

The building housed young men, mostly recent college graduates, who wished to become part of the growing social settlement movement and to take part in the social rehabilitation of the South End. The settlement benefited from annual scholarships given to graduates of Amherst, Dartmouth, and Harvard for a year's residence and study of the South End. Initially it was not anticipated that the majority of residents would devote themselves full time to settlement activities. Most would pursue their careers and in the evenings and on weekends would participate in the life of the neighborhood and aid in the slow and unobtrusive uplifting of the area. It was hoped that the residents would "create a thousand ripples of good influence which shall interact and re-enforce [sic] one another so as to affect families as families, the village groups found in particular blocks and streets, the loyalties, political, industrial and moral, which hold neighborhood people together."[25]

The settlement at first downplayed its institutional and philanthropic character, refusing in the beginning even to place a sign on its door to identify itself. With the accumulation of a substantial endowment and the expansion of its work, the settlement's initial approach would later be modified. It would then hire professional social workers and encourage the area's inhabitants to congregate at the settlement, especially when the settlement purchased a hall on Harrison Avenue in 1902 at a cost of $43,000. The settlement also acquired a female residence house during the first decade of the twentieth century.[26]

The activities of the settlement's residents were of a dual nature. Some of them produced scholarly monographs analyzing Boston's social problems, including studies of the Boston Negro, tenement life, the adolescent girl, the city's ethnic composition, and the lodging-house problem. Woods believed that the problems afflicting the South End were found in varying degrees throughout the country, and he encouraged the residents to view the settlement as a social science laboratory through which they could accumulate necessary information prior to embarking on a meaningful program of local and national social reconstruction.[27]

Most of the residents preferred working directly with the area's inhabitants and sharing their life with them to publishing scholarly studies of the South End. They quickly concluded that one of the keys to neighborhood rehabilitation was the young. It was often the child who interpreted American life to his immigrant parents, and it was through him that the South End House hoped to draw the immigrant family within the orbit of the settlement. The settlement organized for the youth of the area a diverse number of clubs involved in cultural, charitable, and social activities. It supplemented the clubs with classes in dancing, arts and crafts, music, and manual and industrial training, as well as with summer camps, a kindergarten, and an art center. These activities not only provided wholesome recreation for the young but also "brought a larger number of families into closer relationship with the South End House and . . . added several new families to its sphere of influence."[28] The settlement gained the confidence of the parents because of its work with the young. Once this occurred, the settlement maintained constant contact with the immigrant families by having the residents continually visit their homes. At times the residents were making over 300 calls per week. Each resident cared for a small group of families and they, in turn, looked to him as an "adviser and helper."[29]

The settlement was also involved in a myriad of activities to improve the civic, economic, and moral tone of the community. It took the lead in organizing a neighborhood improvement society, a rooming-house association, a room registry, a savings bank, a babies' clinic, and a pawnshop. It provided a reading and recreation room for adults and also furnished instruction in English and prenatal counseling for the immigrants. The South End House gradually came to see itself as the civic voice of the South End, particularly with the purchase of the hall on Harrison Avenue.[30]

The acquisition of the hall, the association maintained, put "in the midst of a tenement neighborhood something which answered in present-day terms to the town hall in the New England village." It was the "centre not only for the settlement but of the neighborhood."[31] For Woods, the new building was the means by which the democratic and social cohesion of the New England village could be recreated in the midst of the tenements and lodging houses of Boston's South End. The hall was frequently used as an auditorium for labor unions and other organizations of the area. Lecture series and conferences presenting diverse opinions were often held there, thereby enabling the South End House to fulfill its role as a "neutral territory" on which the various elements of the community could meet and mediate their differences.[32] In addition, because of their interest in reconciling conflicting economic and social interests, their dismay regarding the prospect of industrial violence, and their commitment to communal welfare, the settlement's residents were frequently called upon to arbitrate strikes.[33]

The settlement also articulated the needs of the South End to the broader community. Residents testified before committees of the state legislature regarding the South End's problems; lobbied before the municipal government on behalf of public baths on Dover Street, a branch of the Boston public library, and a public gymnasium and playground; and worked with other charitable societies such as the Better Dwellings Society, the Associated Charities, and the Helping Hand Reform Club.[34] They also endeavored to educate the South End's inhabitants on "American political ideas and American national loyalties"[35] and to destroy the "inveterate sectionalism" of municipal politics,[36] by which they meant the fragmenting of politics along ethnic and religious lines. For Woods, the political future of polyglot areas such as the South End depended on the transformation of local ethnic political bosses into leaders representing "a distinctively local kind of public spirit."[37]

The South End House disdained mere almsgiving and instead attempted to change fundamentally the social outlook of the South End's inhabitants. By becoming their friend, adviser, and confidant, the settlement hoped it would eventually become the spokesman for their interests. As the settlement happily noted, club leaders frequently visited members of the community in their homes and were often "called in upon occasions of domestic joy or sorrow."[38] This caused a backlash on the part of the city's Roman Catholic hierarchy who viewed the South End House as a rival for the loyalties of the approximately 40 percent of the South End's population which was Catholic.

Prior to 1892 the Catholic church had done little in the way of social amelioration in the South End except for the work of the St. Vincent de Paul Society. This indifference to social and economic conditions reflected the conservatism of the primarily Irish hierarchy who believed the church's attitude toward social inequities should be an otherworldly passivity and who viewed the secular and Protestant philanthropies as ungodly. The establishment of the South End House, the increasing scope and intensity of work of the many Protestant charities in the South End, and the ascension of William Henry O'Connell as archbishop of Boston upon the death of John Joseph Williams in 1907 resulted in an outburst of Catholic charitable activities in the South End. Archbishop Williams had been a saintly prelate but a deficient administrator and fund raiser and had left the archdiocesan charitable organizations in complete shambles and near bankruptcy.[39] O'Connell believed one of his major responsibilities was to expand the work of these organizations and to put them on a firmer financial basis, especially in view of the threat posed to Catholic souls by the Protestant philanthropies. For O'Connell, non-Catholic charity was "essentially defective, and must, whatever its external appearance or pretence, finally resolve itself into another form of egotism." Only Catholic charities, the archbishop claimed, were sufficiently permeated with Christianity to counter the selfishness and "egotism" characteristic of modern life.[40] O'Connell, accordingly, embarked upon a vigorous program to expand the archdiocese's charitable program and within twenty-five years both the number and worth of Boston's Catholic charitable institutions had doubled.[41]

The settlement movement was of particular concern to the Catholic church in Boston. At first Catholics in the South End were warned by their parish priests to avoid the South End House, largely because of fears that it was a Protestant proselytizing institution.[42] Two years after O'Connell became archbishop, the archdiocesan newspaper condemned the settlement workers. "These social regenerators have begun their task at the wrong end," the *Pilot* noted. "True reformation begins from within, and as these workers have little to offer in religion nor obtain for their suppliants spiritual strength, their labors will be without lasting results."[43]

This suspicion of the South End House combined with the increasing emphasis on charity within the Boston archdiocese led to the establishment in 1907 of a settlement for girls at 1472 Washington Street by the Ladies' Catholic Club of the Cathedral of the Holy Cross. Its purpose was "to provide instruction, religious and secular, and amusement for girls whose homes and home-life do not afford them such advantages."[44] This Catholic settlement was short lived, in part because the Boston hierarchy gradually dropped its opposition to the settlement movement. Even O'Connell eventually shed his initial apprehension regarding the South End House and became a supporter of the institution when he recognized that it was not an evangelical agency and posed no threat to the church. Woods, of course, had always realized that the religious pluralism of Boston's South End precluded religious work. The model for the South End House was, after all, not the English parish but rather the New England town.

The primary goals of Tucker, Woods, and the supporters of the South End House were social reconciliation and the restoration of a sense of community. For them the major problems resulting from rapid immigration, industrialization, and urbanization were more social than economic. They echoed the emphasis that such contemporary American social thinkers as Robert Park, Jane Addams, Charles H. Cooley, James Mark Baldwin, Richard T. Ely, John Dewey, Josiah Royce, Edward A. Ross, William Allen White, Frederic Howe, Franklin Giddings, and Henry Demarest Lloyd placed on the restoration of social solidarity—the revival of face-to-face relationships, and an increase in communication. Lloyd, for instance, argued that the significance of the settlement movement lay in its attempt to "re-establish union in communities grown so large that all social connections are endangered, domestic as well as civic."[45]

The South End House attempted to reduce the alienation, anonymity, and rootlessness associated with rapid economic and social change. Woods even once recommended the restoration of social cohesion by returning to the medieval guild system. "The settlement has been engaged for a generation with ... a guild experiment in terms of the local community," he maintained. "The neighborhood guild has remarkable capacity for being universal. It crosses all the lines of social stratification within its borders."[46]

The South End House was not a radical venture. It was less a "spearhead for reform" than a conservative response to cultural diversity and social fragmentation. The South End House embodied the nostalgia of *fin de siècle* Bostonians brought face to face with the more unseemly aspects of urbanization, industrialization, and immigration. It would take several more decades before they were finally convinced that cultural and ethnic heterogeneity were to be permanent rather than transitory aspects of Boston's development and that the New England village could not serve as a model for Boston's future.

# Notes

1. Nathan Irving Huggins, *Protestants against Poverty: Boston's Charities, 1870–1900* (Westport, Conn.: Greenwood Press, 1971), chaps. 1, 7.
2. Arthur Mann, *Yankee Reformers in the Urban Age* (Cambridge, Mass.: Harvard University Press, 1954), p. 1.
3. K. Gerald Marsden, "Philanthropy and the Boston Playground Movement, 1887–1907," *Social Service Review* 35 (March 1961): 48–58; Jean B. Quandt, *From the Small Town to the Great Community: The Social Thought of Progressive Intellectuals* (New Brunswick, N.J.: Rutgers University Press, 1970), pp. 36–50; Barbara Miller Solomon, *Ancestors and Immigrants: A Changing New England Tradition* (Cambridge, Mass.: Harvard University Press, 1956), chap. 5; Frederic Cople Jaher, "The Boston Brahmins in the Age of Industrial Capitalism," in *The Age of Industrialism in America: Essays in Social Structure and Cultural Values* (New York: Macmillan Publishing Co., 1968), pp. 204–13.
4. Walter Muir Whitehill, *Boston: A Topographical History* (Cambridge, Mass.: Harvard University Press, 1959), p. 122; John W. Putnam, "Neighborhood Organization in the South End of Boston," South End House Papers (South End House Library, Boston), p. 1 (hereafter South End House Papers); Robert A. Woods, ed., *The City Wilderness: A Settlement Study by Residents and Associates of the South End House* (Boston: Houghton Mifflin Co., 1898), p. 31.
5. John P. Marquand, *The Late George Apley: A Novel in the Form of a Memoir* (New York: Robert Hale, 1937), p. 26.
6. *Boston Globe* (May 7, 1950).
7. Allen D. Albert, "South End House," South End House Papers; Albert B. Wolfe, *The Lodging-House Problem in Boston* (Boston: Houghton Mifflin Co., 1906), passim.
8. Woods, p. 219.
9. Wolfe, pp. 109, 112, 135, 140–45.

10. Woods, pp. 56–57, 83–85; John Daniels, *In Freedom's Birthplace: A Study of the Boston Negroes* (Boston: Houghton Mifflin Co., 1914), p. 145; Robert A. Woods and Albert J. Kennedy, eds., *Young Working Girls: A Summary of Evidence from Two Thousand Social Workers* (Boston: Houghton Mifflin Co., 1913), p. 4.

11. Robert A. Woods Scrapbook, Robert A. Woods Papers, Houghton Library, Harvard University, Cambridge, Mass. (hereafter Woods Papers).

12. Mann, pp. 115–17.

13. J. A. R. Pimlott, *Toynbee Hall, Fifty Years of Social Progress: 1884–1934* (London: J. M. Dent & Sons, 1935), pp. 5–6.

14. Ibid., pp. 48–50.

15. Robert A. Woods, "The University Settlement Idea," in *Philanthropy and Social Progress* (Boston: Thomas Y. Crowell Co., 1893), pp. 57–59.

16. Allen F. Davis, *Spearheads for Reform: The Social Settlements and the Progressive Movement, 1890–1914* (New York: Oxford University Press, 1967), pp. 75–76.

17. Robert A. Woods and Albert J. Kennedy, *The Settlement Horizon: A National Estimate* (New York: Russell Sage Foundation, 1922), pp. 39–41, 60–68.

18. Robert A. Woods, *English Social Movements* (New York: Charles Scribner's Sons, 1891), p. 263.

19. Woods to William Jewett Tucker, February 18, 1892, Woods Papers.

20. Woods to Anna Dawes, December 20, 1892, Woods Papers.

21. Solomon, p. 143.

22. Robert A. Woods, "University Settlements: Their Point and Drift," *Quarterly Journal of Economics* 14 (October 1899): 4. See also, *South End House Eighth Annual Report* (1900), Widener Library, Harvard University, Cambridge, Mass., pp. 7–8 (hereafter cited as Widener); Woods, Notes for Speeches, n.d., Woods Papers.

23. William Jewett Tucker, "The Work of the Andover House in Boston," *Scribner's Magazine* 13 (March 1893): 361–62.

24. Andover House Association, "Articles of Association" (1891), South End House Papers; see also, *Boston Herald* (October 19, 1891).

25. "South End House Fourteenth Annual Report" (1906), Widener, p. 20.

26. *Boston Evening Transcript* (July 9, 1902).

27. Mann, p. 122.

28. "South End House Sixth Annual Report" (1898), Widener, p. 15.

29. Andover House Association, *Report for the Year 1892–93* (1893), Widener, pp. 3–4; see also, Esther G. Barrows, *Neighbors All: A Settlement Notebook* (Boston: Houghton Mifflin Co., 1929), p. 13.

30. Barrows, passim.

31. "South End House Twentieth Annual Report" (1912), Widener, p. 15.

32. Solomon, p. 143.

33. Woods, *City Wilderness*, p. 276.

34. Barrows, p. 112; Andover House Association, "Circular Number Nine," South End House Papers.

35. Woods, *City Wilderness*, p. 307.

36. "South End House Fourteenth Annual Report" (1906), Widener, p. 4.

37. Robert A. Woods, *The Neighborhood in Nation Building: The Running Comment of Thirty Years at the South End House* (Boston: Houghton Mifflin Co., 1923), pp. 67–71.

38. "South End House Seventh Yearly Report" (1899), Widener, p. 7.

39. Robert D. Cross, *The Emergence of Liberal Catholicism in America* (Cambridge, Mass.: Harvard University Press, 1958), pp. 106–12; Robert H. Lord, John E. Sexton, and Edward T. Harrington, *History of the Archdiocese of Boston in the Various Stages of Its Development, 1604–1943*, 3 vols. (Boston: Pilot Publishing Co., 1945), 3:358, 531; *A Brief Historical Review of the Archdiocese of Boston, 1907–1923* (Boston: Pilot Publishing Co., 1925), pp. 5–10.

40. William Cardinal O'Connell, *Sermons and Addresses of His Eminence William Cardinal O'Connell, Archbishop of Boston*, 11 vols. (Boston: Pilot Publishing Co., 1938), 3:150, and 6:239.

41. *A Brief Historical Review of the Archdiocese of Boston*, pp. 9–10.

42. Woods, *Neighborhood in Nation Building*, p. 267; "South End House Twentieth Annual Report" (1912), Widener, p. 10.

43. *Boston Pilot* (February 6, 1909).

44. Ibid. (March 7, 1908).
45. Daniel Aaron, *Men of Good Hope: A Story of American Progressives* (New York: Oxford University Press, 1951), pp. 163–64; see also, Quandt, *From Small Town to the Great Community*, passim; R. Jackson Wilson, *In Quest of Community: Social Philosophy in the United States, 1860–1920* (New York: John Wiley & Sons, 1968), passim; Park Dixon Goist, "City and 'Community': The Urban Theory of Robert Park," *American Quarterly* 23 (Spring 1971): 46–59; David Noble, *The Paradox of Progressive Thought* (Minneapolis: University of Minnesota Press, 1958), passim; Fay Berger Karpf, *American Social Psychology: Its Origins, Development, and European Background* (New York: McGraw-Hill Book Co., 1932), pp. 225–327.
46. Woods, untitled speech, n.d., Woods Papers.

# The 1960s Revisited

*Fire in the Streets: America in the 1960s*, by Milton Viorst. Simon and Schuster. New York. 591 pages, $14.95.

The 1960s delivered a rude shock to believers in the idea of progress. At the beginning of the decade social activists of all sorts looked forward to an era of creative social change. The launching of the sit-in movement of blacks in the South and the election of John F. Kennedy indicated that America had finally emerged from the lassitude and mediocrity which supposedly marked the Eisenhower years. American youth were praised for rejecting the privatism and careerism of the 1950s in behalf of social involvement and political engagement. Surely poverty, racial injustice, and urban decay would be conquered during the upcoming years.

And yet the promise of the 1960s soon degenerated into such aimless anti-intellectualism, widespread violence, and pervasive cultural nihilism and vulgarity that the historian Richard Hofstadter described the decade as an "age of rubbish." A Gresham's law of social developments seemed to be operating whereby the Rap Browns replaced the Martin Luther Kings, the riots of Detroit and Newark supplanted the sit-ins of Durham and Greensboro, the Beatles gave way before the Rolling Stones, and Tom Hayden and the founders of the Students for a Democratic Society were succeeded by Bernardine Dohrn, Mark Rudd, and the bomb-throwers. The decade began with the sit-ins in Greensboro, North Carolina on February 1, 1960. It ended with the Woodstock rock festival of August 16, 1969, the "Days of Rage" in Chicago in October, 1969, the Rolling Stones' concert at Altamont, California, the arrest of Charles Manson in December, 1969, and the killings at Kent State University in May, 1970. Somehow the beneficent political and cultural impulses which were to awaken America from its lethargy and smugness had been sidetracked. Little wonder, then, that the social activists of the 1960s were followed by the "me" generation of the 1970s, that the most important intellectual development of the 1970s was the emergence of an articulate and persuasive "neo-conservatism," or that the past decade was marked by an exhaustion of political and social ideas.

Milton Viorst attempts to make sense of the turbulence of the 1960s by examining the lives of 14 key personalities associated with the decade including Allard Lowenstein, Bayard Rustin, Stokely Carmichael, Joseph Rauh, Tom Hayden, and Allen Ginsberg. Unfortunately *Fire in the Streets* is reluctant to probe beneath the surface to unravel the sociological, cultural, intellectual, and economic factors impelling the mass agitation of the 1960s. Nor is Viorst especially anxious to allocate blame for the degeneration of the decade's turbulent passions, in part because he shares many of the assumptions of the protestors. Thus he contends that during the 1950s, Americans "lived beneath a blanket of conformity, scarcely aware that it was suffocating." Only a few brave souls were "gasping for air" and open to new currents of thought that "would ultimately permit Americans to breathe more freely." Among these were Allen Ginsberg, one of the gurus of the counterculture. Ginsberg's breath of fresh air included homosexuality, drugs, and a withdrawal from social and political responsibility. Most Americans would view Ginsberg as depraved. For Viorst, however, he was a spokesman for "material abnegation, spiritual liberation, inner peace, total truth."

Because of its sentimental gullibility, *Fire in the Streets* will not satisfy those of us who were deprived of political innocence during the 1960s, nor will it provide any guidelines for the 1980s.

Viorst has an extremely stereotyped view of the young. He contrasts the committed college generation of the sixties with its predecessor who, "nurtured on McCarthyism and social orthodoxy," was "neatly combed and showed respect for its elders." This will surprise those who attended university during the 1950s. We certainly did not show respect for our elders, did not consider ourselves old fogies, and did not support the junior Senator from Wisconsin. Viorst, however, correctly notes that the rebellious instincts of the 1960s were most likely to be found among youths with the least to complain about. While car mechanics, waitresses, and beauty parlor operators were notable for their absence in the Movement, the offspring of affluent professionals and businessmen gravitated to the endless marches, sit-ins, and protests. The dissidents, Viorst writes, "had little need to earn money, few mundane responsibilities and plenty of leisure time. Unburdened by commonplace worries, they were free to cultivate their individuality and inflate their grievances." Jews in particular were an important part of the New Left until it revealed a virulent strain of anti-Semitism and anti-Zionism.

It seems clear now that the psychology and sociology of the protestors furnishes a more adequate explanation for the campus turmoil of the sixties than any supposed social, political, or economic failings of the nation. Bored and restless, they responded to persons and events which provided a significance to their aimless lives. They were attracted to the cause of American blacks both for its own sake and as a means to imbue their future with direction and purpose. Thus Mario Savio, the leader of the Free Speech Movement at Berkeley in 1964-65, described middle-class life as "flat and stale," a "wasteland." "Society," Savio claimed, provided no challenge. "It is a bleak scene, but it is all a lot of us have to look forward to. . . . American society is simply no longer exciting." Tell this to the Haitians, Cubans, Russian Jews, and various other refugee groups who are doing everything in their power to live in the middle-class society for which Savio and other dissidents had only contempt. The student movement was never afflicted with a proper sense of proportion, nor did it exhibit any sense of history.

The boredom and emptiness felt by the students was best revealed at Berkeley during 1946-65. Clark Kerr, then president of the University of California, noted in his book *The Uses of the University* that undergraduates at large universities felt neglected, insecure, deprived of a sense of identity, and fearful that they were being manipulated by an impersonal academic machine. Protestors paraded around the campus with signs proclaiming "Shut This Factory Down," "My Mind is Not the Property of the University of California," and "I Am a UC Student: Do Not Fold, Bend or Mutilate."

The discontent of the young was elevated to cosmic importance by C. Wright Mills, a radical sociologist at Columbia University and author of *The Power Elite*. Mills' influential essay "Letter to the New Left" established him as one of the seminal personalities within the Movement. "Letter to the New Left" argued that the "Victorian Marxism" of Marx and other 19th-century Socialist thinkers naively romanticized the working class, attributing to it imaginary revolutionary tendencies. Mills claimed that only a radicalism which looked to the young intelligentsia as an engine for social change could succeed. Only the young had not been corrupted by American materialism and recognized the necessity for revolution. "Never trust anyone over 30," the saying went. Certainly there was something fundamentally wrong in a revolutionary ideology which saw its salvation in half-educated adolescents.

The quest for excitement afflicted the civil rights movement which during the decade saw its peaceful sit-ins replaced by shoot-outs, looting, and riots. Blacks were as insecure and frustrated as the students and they lashed out in a similar irrational fashion. Black social and economic expectations had been heightened by television and inflated political rhetoric to the point that many assumed the good things of material America should be theirs simply for the taking. The pilfered color television set became the symbol of the black protest movement when it turned violent. The Harvard urbanologist Edward Banfield described it as rioting for "fun and profits." One young Watts resident surprised Bayard Rustin by claiming the Los Angeles riot had been a Watts victory. When Rustin dissented, saying it had been black homes, stores, and institutions that had been destroyed, the young man responded, "We won because we made the whole world pay attention to us." When a child behaves this way it is called a temper tantrum.

One of the more disturbing aspects of the sixties was the extent to which the mass media accepted at face value the dissidents' description of their objectives and motivations. Indeed, the mass media have absorbed many of the underlying assumptions of the New Left. Its distrust of private enterprise and business, its lionizing of Ralph Nader, its belief in the unsullied idealism and righteousness of the young (except if they are part of the majority of American youths who do not attend college), and its conviction that personal honesty and individuality are more important than social responsibility and prudence are part of the legacy of the 1960s.

Another part of this legacy is the argument that anti-Communism is an anachronism. The Port Huron Statement of June, 1962, the most important exposition of New Left ideology, claimed that anti-Communism "leads not only to the perversion of democracy and to the political stagnation of a warfare society, but it also has the unintended consequence of preventing an honest and effective approach to the issues." Anti-Communism, the document concluded, mistakenly assumes the Soviet Union to be expansionist, thereby rationalizing the military domination of American society. Forty years ago Norman Thomas was saying the same thing about Nazi Germany and the opponents of isolationism.

The intellectual immaturity of the New Left is revealed in this abrupt dismissal of the Soviet challenge. Recent developments in Africa and the Middle East should convince anyone that Soviet expansionism is not a fantasy hatched in the febrile imagination of Dr. Strangelove.

The Scranton Commission, appointed in the wake of the Kent State killings, predicted that the student culture's self-righteousness, its distrust of the slow processes of democracy, and its impatience with behavioral restraints would continue to generate problems for America. It noted that, as a nation, "we are not in grave danger of losing what is common among us through growing intolerance of opposing views on issues and of diversity itself." Actually, as Viorst points out, the protests of the 1960s ended "with a thirteen-second fusillade in a small Ohio town." After Kent State even the concept of an independent student culture disappeared. Some of its practices and values died out while others were adopted by the general society.

The rapid eclipse of the protests was due in part to the gradual deescalation of the American commitment in Vietnam as well as to the dead-end in which the civil rights movement found itself. In addition, the public had finally become bored and, one suspects, the young embarrassed at the Movement's flouting of social norms. Viorst writes that "a society can function at a feverish emotional pitch for only so long, and Americans, after ten years of it, were tired." Most Americans were grateful for a little peace and quiet.

Viorst, in contrast, elegizes the 1960s, lamenting the fact that "our ideas became timid, our leaders drab, our concerns self-centered." "It was," he writes, "as if the country suddenly went into sedation, its passions, removed from the streets, taken home and locked in a closet." And yet one must ask what major works in history, politics, sociology, literature, and philosophy emerged from the Movement? Which of its representatives led lives worthy of emulation? Nobel Prizes are, after all, given to Mother Theresas and Alfred Schweitzers, not to Stokely Carmichaels.

Allard Lowenstein and Jerry Rubin are two of the 14 persons whose lives are examined in *Fire in the Streets*. Lowenstein, leader of the 1967-68 dump Lyndon Johnson movement, was murdered in 1980 by a former disciple named Dennis Sweeney who somehow blamed Lowenstein for his own difficult personal affairs. Rubin fared differently. The self-appointed leader of the Yippies, Rubin revealed the tendency of the protest movements of the sixties to descend into sheer zaniness. Unfortunately Rubin was not untypical of many Jewish youths, although not too many went the full distance with him into nihilism, exhibitionism, and foolishness. Rubin mastered the art of exploiting the potentialities of television, satisfying its interest in the prurient and in buffoonery. Rubin and other New Left leaders illustrated the truth of the statement by the radical activist James Mellen that, according to the protestors, "the political effectiveness of an act was less important than the demonstration of one's own character." The question one must ask is what did the acts of the radicals reveal about their character? Certainly the characters of Sweeney and Rubin leave much to be desired.

**V**iorst concludes *Fire in the Streets* with a short description of the lasting impact of the sixties. Besides rock music and marijuana, there was an emphasis on individual rights. The civil rights movement, after securing the end of legal segregation, moved into a new phase stressing reverse discrimination, busing, and racism under the rubric of affirmative action. Women, homosexuals, convicts, and the handicapped demanded, and partially secured, various "rights." Personal freedom ("doing your own thing") led "to the abolition of the draft, access by women to legal abortions, social acceptance of unmarrieds living together, the proliferation of bizarre religious and semireligious cults." This was not done without serious misgivings, misgivings that were politically manifested in Miami, Detroit, and elsewhere. The Movement's hopes for a liberating lifestyle, a resurgence of political radicalism, and the creation of a participatory democracy all fell by the wayside, leaving us with what Viorst terms a "national propensity to self-indulgence." Viorst would welcome a rebirth of the spirit of protest of the sixties without its anti-intellectualism, its attack on academic freedom, its nihilism and vulgarity, and its social disorder.

One can legitimately ask, however, whether the sense of community, the political realism, and the prudent diplomacy required by the United States could ever be furnished by an American Left given over to sentimentality, self-righteousness, emotionalism, and knee-jerk contempt for America's friends. ■

OF KENNEDYS AND KINGS

Of Kennedys and Kings: Making Sense of the Sixties, by Harris Wofford. New York: Farrar Straus Giroux, 1980.

In 1950, when he was only twenty-four, Harris Wofford and his wife published India Afire which, among other things, suggested that American civil rights leaders adopt the tactics and strategy of Mahatma Gandhi. This support for the civil rights movement and the "emerging nations" would dominate virtually all of Wofford's political activities during the 1960's which he has now chronicled in this memoir. When the black boycott of the busses of Montgomery, Alabama began in 1955, Wofford became a staunch ally of the boycott's leader, Martin Luther King, assisted King in writing Stride Toward Freedom, and helped arrange King's 1957 trip to India. In the late 1950's Wofford was counsel to the Rev. Theodore Hesburgh on the Commission on Civil Rights. According to Arthur M. Schlesinger, Jr., "this experience convinced Wofford "that the untapped sources of executive action offered the best immediate hope for new civil rights progress."

Wofford's interest in India brought him into close collaboration with Chester Bowles, the former American ambassador to India and an influential voice in the liberal wing of the Democratic Party. Bowles vigorously advocated reshaping the nation's diplomacy away from preoccupation with the Soviet Union and the Cold War and towards a greater interest in the underdeveloped regions of Latin America, Asia, and Africa. Bowles supported the presidential candidacy of John Kennedy, while Wofford became a speechwriter for the future president and edited The Strategy of Peace, a collection of Kennedy's speeches on foreign policy.

Kennedy's election gave Wofford the opportunity to further the civil rights movement and transform American diplomacy. He had organized and coordinated the civil rights section of Kennedy's campaign and after the election was appointed Special Assistant to the President for Civil Rights. He helped establish the Peace Corps and in 1962 moved to Addis Ababa to become the Peace Corps' Special Representative for Africa and director of its Ethiopian program. "The Peace Corps," Wofford writes, "had from the beginning seemed to me the liveliest embodiment of the New Frontier." (More sceptical observers would reserve that distinction for the far livelier Vietnamese War which also reflected the crusading spirit of the New Frontier.) Wofford returned to Washington after Kennedy's assassination as the Peace Corps' associate director and had a hand in establishing the Office of Economic Opportunity which conducted the war on poverty. This quintessential New Frontiersman resigned from the Peace Corps in 1966 and, appropriately enough, became president of a new experimental college in Old Westbury, Long Island.

Of <u>Kennedys and Kings</u> is more than a mere recounting of its author's involvement in the New Frontier and the Great Society. It is also a passionate defense of Wofford's two political lodestars, the civil rights movement and the "third world". Thus Martin Luther King is the black hero of the book, while its white heroes are Sargent Shriver and Chester Bowles rather than John Kennedy and Lyndon Johnson. Wofford is not a partisan of Kennedy, largely because the president did not share his anti-militarism and crusading enthusiasms. Thus he faults Kennedy for not pushing the Peace Corps concept, for not being more vigorous in supporting the civil rights campaign, for authorizing the Bay of Pigs invasion, and for firing Bowles as Undersecretary of State in the "Thanksgiving Massacre" of 1961. Kennedy's failure to make better use of Bowles, Wofford claims, "demonstrated a flaw in the President's own intelligence at least as great as the failure of the outside intelligence provided him by the CIA, the Pentagon, or the State Department. He badly needed someone close to him who had 'a basic moral reference point.'"

Throughout <u>Of Kennedys and Kings</u> there is a persistent distaste for the macho image projected by the Kennedys. Wofford surmises that this might have come back to haunt the Kennedys because of their support of C.I.A. efforts to murder Fidel Castro. Kennedy's assassination, Wofford speculates, could have been a reprisal to this inane plan. (Wofford also believes the F.B.I. might have been implicated in the killing of Martin Luther King.) In any case, Wofford contends, Robert Kennedy held himself personally responsible for his brother's death, and his subsequent efforts to end the Vietnamese war and revitalize domestic reform impulses were related to this sense of guilt. Wofford was a zealous supporter of the "new" Robert Kennedy, welcomed his call for the creation of a new politics, and described him as "one of the most appealing and promising men in the history of American politics." "I wanted him to be President more than anyone I had ever supported," he concludes.

Wofford, it is clear, has never left the 1960's. For him it was "an extraordinary time of social invention and constructive politics" marked by deStalinization in the Soviet Union, reform within the Roman Catholic Church, and a Peace Corps and a war on poverty in the United States. Americans witnessed "a surge in the spirit of national service, with people in surprising numbers really interested in what they could do for their country." A more balanced view of the decade, however, would take into consideration the fact that those who migrated to the banks of the Potomac in the hope of doing good ended up by doing very well indeed in terms of fat government salaries and perquisities, while the rest of the country was saddled with higher taxes, onerous regulations, and social programs of dubious value.

Wofford would have us believe that, for the first time in many years, "talent and intelligence were widely enlisted to work on the nation's problems." And yet the efforts of the "best and the brightest" were no more successful in the domestic realm than they were in managing our affairs in Southeast Asia. The test of any policy lies in its impact and not in the education or the intelligence of its sponsors. It is typical of defenders of the New Frontier and Great Society, Wofford included, to take the reformist goals of the 1960's at face value without investigating their effect in the real world.

He is also nostalgic about the Sixties because it was "a time of peaceful competition and cooperation in the exploration of space, when man first set forth toward the moon and nuclear tests in the atmosphere were finally banned." Wofford argues that the Cold War has sidetracked the United States from its responsibility of aiding the "third world", that America should identify with the forces of social and economic change in the underdeveloped nations (he quotes John Kennedy's absurd statement in the 1960 campaign that "this world-wide revolution which we see all around us is part of the original American revolution"), that the impulse to propose military solutions to political and diplomatic problems is invariably mistaken, and that the United Nations continues to be the last best hope of mankind.

Wofford's dream of a new American diplomacy were, he laments, shunted aside by the militarization of foreign policy under Kennedy and Johnson. Instead of asking fundamental questions about the direction of American policy, the two administrations generally focused on the mechanics of leadership. This too frequently lead to the use of military means as in Cuba, the Dominican Republic, and Vietnam. Wofford is probably correct in arguing that American diplomacy of the Sixties suffered from a surfeit of CIAism and militarism. In contrast, the recent impotence of the United States has stemmed in part from the decay of its armed forces as well as the reluctance of its leaders even to consider military options, both part of the legacy of the Vietnam conflict. One would not expect Wofford to be displeased by this. As Edmund Burke once remarked, "It is a general error to suppose the loudest complainers for the public to be the most anxious for its welfare."

*Robert F. Kennedy and His Times*, by Arthur M. Schlesinger, Jr., Houghton Mifflin, Boston, 1978, 1066 pp., $19.95.

Over ten years have passed since the assassination of Robert Kennedy, that enfant terrible of American politics of the 1960s. Arthur M. Schlesinger, Jr.'s thick and beautifully constructed volume of liberal hagiography bids us to remember Kennedy as the tribune of the dispossessed who responded to the turbulence of that decade "more directly and sensitively than any other political leader of the era." Kennedy, according to his biographer, was a representative figure in the Emersonian sense who embodied the consciousness of his age and sensed the possibilities for creative change. "Robert Kennedy's message of commitment to the desolate and the disinherited is rarely sounded in the 1970s," Schlesinger laments, "but the problems about which he cared so much remain." Any evaluation of Robert Kennedy's life thus must focus on his role in the politics of the 1960s and on the quality of his ideas, as well as those of his acolyte because it is often difficult to separate the two. Here perhaps lies the key to the mystery which puzzled Kennedy to his death: why he was so intensely disliked and unable to shake completely the image of self-righteousness, arrogance, and ruthlessness which had first surfaced in the mid-1950s.

There was always something of the outsider about Kennedy, and his identification with Chicanos, blacks, Indians, and the poor was probably more visceral than reasoned. As an outsider himself he could empathize with the outcasts of American society. From the very beginning he felt that he was in a competition with his older brothers Joseph, Jr. and John, a competition which he could not win. He attended Milton Academy outside of Boston where his fervent Roman Catholicism made him stand out at this elitist WASP prep school. Then on to Harvard where his academic performance could be charitably described only as mediocre at best. Kennedy was far more interested in football than books. He was able to compensate for his lack of athletic ability by a pugnaciousness which often bordered on foolhardiness. His first major job was on the staff of Senator Joseph McCarthy, another outsider who during his career took on both major political parties, the United States Army, Dwight Eisenhower, and American Protestantism. After the election of 1954 Kennedy became counsel to the Senate Permanent Subcommittee on Investigations headed by John McClellan of Arkansas. Kennedy now became a national figure because of his zealous pursuit of union racketeering in general, and Dave Beck and Jimmy Hoffa of the Teamsters in particular. As an outsider, Kennedy was particularly disgusted by the abuse of power and corruption of union leaders, especially since they were at the expense of anonymous and powerless union members. Kennedy's discovery of widespread corruption in the labor movement did not, however, make him sympathetic to business. Kennedy believed businessmen to be just as dishonest, if not more so, than the union moguls. "These corrupt businessmen are still sitting down to luncheon and dinner meetings with business groups across the country," Kennedy decried in *The Enemy Within*, "and they are getting encouragement and admiration—not censure." Kennedy's zealousness, his sense of righteousness, and his hatred for those who betray the trust of others made him an exceedingly effective investigator, and the public saw in him a Twentieth Century Torquemada in search of the malefactors of great power. Added to this was a quirk in Kennedy's personality which prevented him from relaxing and enjoying the spectacle of men's imperfections.

Unfortunately Kennedy's sympathy for the dispossessed was not accompanied by a solid grounding in economics and sociology which could have tempered his moralistic tendency to divide the population between "them" and "us." Schlesinger quotes Richard Boone of the Ford Foundation: "Bobby best understood things by feeling and touching them. He did feel and he did touch and he came to believe and to understand." One might legitimately question, in view of the history of many of the New Deal's and Great Society's programs, whether understanding based on sympathy and intuition is sufficient, and whether something else is needed for successful legislation besides good intentions. Kennedy's knee-jerk empathy with society's outcasts often lead him astray. Thus in August, 1963, while Attorney-General, he lamented that half of Spanish-speaking Americans earned less than the average per capita income. Unfortunately, empathy and intuition alone does not inform one that it is the nature of every average to mark the point where half the sample is below. Kennedy lacked those virtues of scepticism and restraint which could have moderated his undisciplined compassion and humanitarianism and made him a more effective public servant.

Kennedy's idealism characterized his approach to foreign policy. "Innovations, imagination, yes, even revolutionary concepts are essential," he told his brother in 1962. John Paton Davies, Jr., a wise diplomat who had been hounded out of the State Department in the 1950s because of his realism regarding China, was a leading critic of this romantic stance towards diplomacy. "Crusading activism touched with naivete," Davies noted in 1964, "seldom welcomes warnings of pitfalls and entanglements."

In November, 1965 Kennedy and his wife Ethel traveled to South America. In Lima he told a group of university students that revolution in Latin America was inevitable, though he hoped it would be peaceful. Kennedy's stop in Brazil was also marked by verbal fireworks. He was horrified by the low pay of Brazilian sugar cane workers and became an instant advocate of the Brazilian minimum wage law. In Natal he told a crowd, "Every child an education! Every family adequate housing! Every man a job!" Though a guest in Brazil for less than week, Kennedy felt impelled to lecture the country's president on the merits of a minimum wage, the advantages of which have escaped most American economists, as well as to criticize the nation's business leaders for their social failings. Schlesinger believes Kennedy's purpose in going to Latin America was to promote a liberal revolution American style. It was, he writes, "a quixotic venture uncommon in history." The trip logically resulted from the dominant assumption of the New Frontier's Latin American policy that only the non-Communist left could save the southern part of the hemisphere from Castroism. It is obvious today that social lethargy and traditionalism were far more powerful than the romantic ideologues of the New Frontier ever imagined. Revolution, it scarcely needs to be said, was inevitable neither in the 1960s or the 1970s.

Back in the United States, Kennedy gave a major speech in the Senate in May, 1966, on his Latin American journey. "There is a revolution now going on down there," he said, "and we must identify ourselves with that revolution." One can only speculate on what Kennedy would have done had he been elected president in 1968. The African and Middle East policies of our current administration do not indicate that compassion, idealism, and activism are necessarily the most important, or even the most desirable, traits of a successful foreign policy.

In many ways Robert Kennedy was the opposite of his brother John. John Kennedy, Schlesinger writes, was "urbane, objective, analytical, controlled, contained, masterful, a man of perspective," while his brother was "more open, exposed, emotional, subjective, intense, a man of commitment." John Kennedy, unlike his brother, distrusted passion. "Reason was John Kennedy's medium; experience was Robert's." Robert Kennedy, Schlesinger argues, "began as a true believer." Perhaps this explains his popularity with college students. They responded to his simplistic approach to reality, and shared his belief that life should not be unfair and that new policies and different leaders could right the wrongs of a cruel world. The dispossessed also responded to him because, being remote from power, they also had a simplistic understanding of the nature of power and an equally naive view of the source of their problems. They focused their anger at a wicked white power structure, or evil grape growers, or the unenlightened people running the Bureau of Indian Affairs, and Kennedy shared their anger. The contrast between Kennedy and the current occupant of his seat, Daniel P. Moynihan, could not be sharper. Chastened by the failures of the Great Society, Moynihan is one of the nation's most astute social thinkers and a leading advocate of prudence and restraint. Kennedy's description of Moynihan was characteristic. "He knows all the facts, and he's against all the solutions."

Kennedy's social activism, his commitment to change, his empathy with outsiders especially marked the last two years of his life. He spoke in increasingly apocalyptic terms of a nation divided between the world of the affluent white middle-class and the world of the discontented and hungry. He told one journalist during the campaign of 1968 that his strategy for defeating Eugene McCarthy and Hubert Humphrey for the Democratic presidential nomination and then triumphing in the general election was to forget about the labor unions and the South, to create a new coalition based upon the young, poor whites, and the minorities, and to emphasize the issue of poverty. Kennedy, Schlesinger contends, "was rallying the unrepresented to recapture and reconstruct the nation." One can hardly think of a political formula more doomed to failure than this one. Not surprisingly, Humphrey and not Kennedy was the choice of the majority of registered Democrats, even after Kennedy's amazing victory in the Indiana primary. And if the 1972 election is any indication, the nomination of Kennedy would have resulted in a crushing Democratic loss. The nation, as Richard Scammon and Ben Wattenberg have reminded us, is unpoor, unblack, and unyoung. One can legitimately ask whether Kennedy's frantic drive for the nomination in the spring of 1968 was serious or whether it was another act in the politics of theater which marked the latter half of the 1960s.

Politics was very important for Kennedy but not the type of politics involving legislation. Schlesinger does not mention any legislative accomplishments of Kennedy during his tenure in the Senate. Kennedy was far more interested in the theatrics of politics than in its mechanics. "There aren't ten politicians in the whole state I like and trust," he told Jack Newfield of the *New York Village Voice*. One can imagine that these feelings were reciprocated. Increasingly he turned to the reform Democrats and Liberals of New York City for support.

Schlesinger does not discuss Kennedy's economic training, his economic advisors, or his economic views. He read widely but there is no mention of his having read anything in economics. Thus it is not surprising that he tended to ignore economics. In responding to the riot in the Watts ghetto of Los Angeles in 1965, Kennedy contended that the source of the trouble was bad housing, inferior education, and inadequate employment opportunities. The solution would come only when the blacks could "acquire and wisely exercise political power in the community, only when they establish meaningful communication with a society from which they have been excluded." One cannot imagine a more superficial analysis of the racial problem of the 1960s. Black mayors have not been able to reverse the downward trend in cities such as Newark, Gary, and Detroit.

An expanding economy is the key to improving the status of the poor, but it works slowly and without fanfare. Anyone listening to Kennedy's analysis of the race problem would have been totally unprepared for the 1970 census finding that over fifty percent of America's blacks had achieved middle-class status. Schlesinger shares Kennedy's myopia regarding the benefits accruing from American capitalism. The last fifteen years have witnessed a sharp decline in the number of Americans classified as poor as well as a quantum increase in welfare payments of all sorts to the poor, and yet Schlesinger can contrast Robert Kennedy's vision with that of the reality of contemporary America, anticipating that "the time will surely come again when the richest nation of earth will overcome its indifference to the degradation of its citizens."

Kennedy's grounding in sociology was also weak. He was vulnerable to the latest sociological fad. As Peter Maas remarked, Kennedy "continually embraced new things." The new thing of the 1960s was race. Kennedy became a prime instigator of the mood of guilt and pessimism which swept over the nation, a mood which was willing to excuse and overlook the most outrageous acts and rhetoric if done in the name of racial uplift. In August, 1965, for instance, Kennedy attacked former President Eisenhower's criticism of the perpetrators of the Watts' riot. "There is no point in telling Negroes to obey the law," Kennedy argued. "To many Negroes the law is the enemy." After a particularly brutal session with black militants in Oakland during the California 1968 primary campaign, Kennedy stated: "after all the abuse the blacks have taken through the centuries, whites are just going to have to let them get some of these feelings out if we are all really ever going to settle down to a decent relationship."

In the mid-1960s many began to speak of "participatory democracy," of the need for blacks to take part in decisions affecting their own interests, of the necessity for rebuilding a sense of community within urban communities. Kennedy embraced such thinking, contending that there was no more important urban task than overcoming the impersonality and anonymity of the metropolis. He responded by proposing a whole host of new government programs to create economically self-sufficient black communities through community development corporations. Kennedy seemed to have a congenial belief that every social problem required a political solution and that every human need required a government agency. And yet as Robert A. Nisbet has argued in his brilliant *The Quest for Community*, the powerful centralized modern state has preempted many of the traditional responsibilities of the family, religion, and other voluntary associations and is responsible for the anomie and rootlessness of much of modern western society. The modern state is not the answer to the need for community but rather its cause.

Charles Spalding, a close friend of the Kennedys, noted, "Jack has traveled in that speculative area where doubt lives. Bobby does not travel there." RFK was impatient with those who did not see it his way, with social and economic conditions which did not immediately yield to good intentions, with a political system which did not respond promptly to generous sentiments. He had a rashness and impetuousness, Schlesinger describes it as "reckless impulsiveness," which pushed him to taking extreme positions. A fervent critic of the war in Vietnam, he once asked an audience, "Don't you understand that what we are doing to the Vietnamese is not very different from what Hitler did to the Jews?" These rhetorical flights of fancy revealed a radical, and at times revolutionary, streak. He described Che Guevera as "a revolutionary hero." Richard Goodwin believed Kennedy really belonged "in the hills, leading some guerrilla army, without speeches or contaminating compromise, fighting to translate the utmost purity of intention into the power to change a nation or a world." Kennedy, he thought, was drawn naturally "to motion and to turmoil." Robert Kennedy was an American Cromwell bent on slaying the comfortable and lethargic. A man of intense moral certainty, he was reluctant to give his opponents the benefit of the doubt (a vice shared by his biographer) and concluded that his foes were either defending their selfish interests or were intellectually unreedemable.

Kennedy had the ability to arouse great passion among his supporters as well as strong opposition among the nonbelievers. He personified for the latter the attack on highly valued aspects of American life: law and order, due process and the merit principle, and patriotism (during the height of the war Kennedy came out in favor of sending blood to North Vietnam). Much of this antipathy to Kennedy was based on a misreading of the man. Kennedy himself was mystified by the antagonism he aroused. "Why do people hate me so?" he once asked Dorothy Schiff of the *New York Post*. And yet there was in Kennedy a thinly veiled contempt for the white middle class, a class which was comfortable in its affluence, a class which does not do brave things or think bold thoughts, a class which would never be invited to Hickory Hill to rub shoulders with the beautiful people, the athletes, movie personalities, and other celebrities whom Kennedy attracted. There was in

Kennedy, in other words, an element of the "radical chic" which Tom Wolfe described in his devastating portrait of Leonard Bernstein's cocktail party for the Black Panthers.

The white middle class is the great fact of American politics. Unwilling to climb the mountain with a Robert Kennedy (or a George McGovern), it has also refused to descend into the swamp with a George Wallace or a Joseph McCarthy. When confronted with depression its choice was neither a Stalin nor a Hitler but a Roosevelt. The problems and discontents of the American middle class are every bit as real, although not as palpable, as the afflictions of the outsiders of the 1960s. They send their children to schools which seemingly do not educate, they are controlled by governments whose appetite for tax dollars is evidently insatiable, and they live in families which are weakening before their very eyes. This middle class has not yet found its Robert Kennedy.

# THE RETURN OF CONSERVATISM

*The Superfluous Men: Conservative Critics of American Culture, 1900-1945.* Edited by Robert M. Crunden. Texas. $14.95.

After a hiatus of nearly two decades, interest in American conservatism is back in fashion. During the 1950's Clinton Rossiter, Peter Viereck, Russell Kirk, and Robert Nisbet, among others, had created a mini-academic industry for the analysis and, at times, dissemination of the "new conservatism." The prominence of radicalism and the "New Left" during the 1960's as well as the national political triumph of liberalism, however, made the American academy a most inhospitable place for any serious investigation of conservatism, much less its propagation. During this decade conservatism was viewed as exotic, reactionary, anachronistic, and irrelevant. The academy, nevertheless, to a certain extent does follow the election returns, and during the past several years there has been a growing interest in American conservatism. John Diggins's 1975 book *Up From Communism*, a study of the thought of Will Herberg, Max Eastman, James Burnham, and John Dos Passos, as well as George Nash's comprehensive *The Conservative Intellectual Movement in America* (1976), for example, exhibit a willingness to take recent American conservatism seriously. Robert M. Crunden's edition of some pre-1945 writings of American conservatives is another indication that the intellectual community will once again have to confront a conservative challenge to the liberal and radical orthodoxy which has been dominant during the past several decades.

The reasons for this renewed interest in conservatism are, as Crunden points out in his introduction, both simple and complex. It is perhaps impossible to explain fully the reasons for the shift in mood within a nation, but there are at least some obvious reasons for the growing popularity of conservatism during the 1970's which has even carried along some elements within the intelligentsia and made the study of American conservatism a fit topic once more for investigation. The disenchantment with the "best and the brightest's" Vietnam War, the evident failure of many of the social programs spawned during the Johnson years, the social excesses of the 1960's, and the exorbitant growth of government during the past 15 years have led many Americans to question whether liberalism itself isn't seriously flawed. The growing disenchantment with liberalism has coincided with a more positive view of the 1950's, a decade without any Ralph Naders leading crusades to have the federal government eliminate all the foibles and petty vices of mankind, nor was it a time when we were supposed to consider a Mark Rudd, a Rap Brown, or a Staughton Lynd serious social critics.

What is perhaps most interesting about Crunden's book is the hints it gives regarding possible future interpretations of American conservatism. For Crunden, the importance of pre-1945 American conservatism lay in its critique of culture. Its politics, he claims, was completely irrelevant. Crunden, a professor of history and American civilization at the University of Texas, believes American conservatism of this period was best represented by a person such as Albert Jay Nock, about whom Crunden published an excellent study in 1964. Conservatives, he would have us believe, valued religion, the classics, agriculture, leisure, and elitist educational institutions. Conversely, they opposed materialism, capitalism, industrialization, urbanization, plutocracy, utilitarianism, and mass democratic politics. His selection of essays and excerpts from books of George Santayana, Ralph Adams Cram, Albert Jay Nock, H. L. Mencken, Donald Davidson, Frank L. Owsley, Irving Babbitt, Paul Elmer More, Allen Tate, John Crowe Ransom, and Walter Lippmann is designed to show that these conservatives were, with the exception of Lippmann, "superfluous." First of all, they were cultural elitists alienated from contemporary mass society and with nothing to say of practical value for, or interest to, the American public. Secondly, except for Lippmann, they were not interested in politics, and, according to Crunden, the essence of their conservatism lay in the belief that the most important things in life could not be obtained through politics and that governmental activity interfered with the enjoyment of culture and the articulation of cultural values. "They often made excellent debating points," he writes, "but they were generally and perhaps rightly ignored by most Americans because what they said often had little bearing on the actual daily processes of government." Evidently, Crunden believes the role of conservative intellectuals should not be to exercise power but rather to criticize from the sidelines the activities of liberals and collectivists and to yearn for another society, whether it be classical Greece, medieval France, or the antebellum South, in which tradition, authority, religion, art, and the social graces were highly valued. To Crunden, it is precisely the superfluous political character of the conservatives which enabled them to have been important cultural critics of American life.

One can seriously question Crunden's interpretation of pre-1945 American conservatism while recognizing the value of collecting within one volume some of the most important statements of early 20th-century cultural conservatism. His error is in believing that cultural conservatism was the only variety of conservatism worth taking seriously. Another editor could just as easily have selected essays demonstrating the importance and relevance of political conservatism. One pre-1945 conservative who immediately springs to mind is the historian, essayist, and journalist Herbert Agar. Agar's essays, "Private Property or Capitalism" and "The Task for Conservatism," both published in 1934, were brilliant attempts to resuscitate American conservatism based on the principle of the widespread distribution of property. There was also the important collection of articles entitled *Who Owns America?*

A *New Declaration of Independence*, edited by Agar and Allen Tate in 1936, which attempted to formulate a conservative economic, political, and social program involving the repudiation of both Marxism and plutocracy, the encouragement of economic and political decentralization, the revival of small-scale farming and small business, and the widespread distribution of productive property.

The warnings of the pre-1945 politically conservative intellectuals regarding the growth of political centralization, the continuing dispossession of the farming and shopkeeping classes, the growing dependence of many Americans on remote economic and political bureaucracies, and the debasement of political discourse by zealous reformers are not merely of antiquarian interest. If modern American conservatives are often politically inarticulate, it is in part because they are generally unfamiliar with the writings of those who should be their mentors. American conservative intellectuals of the first half of the 20th century were not, as Crunden believes, solely morose and snobbish aesthetes pining for a past golden age. Instead, many were doing their best to reconcile conservative social values with modern industrialization and urbanization. That they have not been widely remembered should not detract from the importance of their effort.

# GEORGE WILL

<u>The Pursuit of Happiness, and Other Sobering Thoughts</u> by George F. Will. New York: Harper & Row, 1978.

George F. Will is perhaps America's most thoughtful and important conservative columnist. His semi-weekly column for the <u>Washington Post</u>, begun in 1973 and now appearing in approximately 300 newspapers, and his biweekly contributions to <u>Newsweek</u> won for him the 1977 Pulitzer Prize for distinguished commentary. He is also the luminary of "Martin Agronsky and Company," a weekly TV round table of comment and controversy by leading Washington journalists. The son of Frederick L. Will, a professor of philosophy at the University of Illinois for nearly four decades, George Will was born in 1941 and educated at Trinity College (Connecticut), Oxford, and Princeton, where he received a Ph.D in political science in 1964. He taught at Michigan State and the University of Toronto in the 1960s, and then served as an assistant to Senator Gordon Allott of Colorado and as the Washington editor of <u>National Review</u>.

The key to Will's thinking is provided by his doctoral dissertation, "Beyond the Reach of Majorities: Closed Questions in the Open Society." In it he criticized the contemporary liberal arguments for political tolerance, contending that they stemmed from a mistaken skepticism regarding the ability to arrive at substantive knowledge about what is politically desirable and undesirable. Will claimed that every open society must have a public philosophy, which proclaims its commitment to fundamental moral and political precepts, as well as an "economy of intolerance," which rejects the legitimacy of some beliefs. This economy of intolerance reflects the community's underlying value system. Thus intolerance of political organizations preaching racism, communism, or fascism demonstrates a society's commitment to equality and democracy. Will argued that the ultimate rationale for an open society is the encouragement it gives to the intellectual and moral growth of its citizens. Laws that deny the ballot to anti-democratic movements educate the citizenry in the community's public philosophy.*

* This questioning of the liberal case for tolerance has been a staple of postwar conservatism, and the subject of major works by William F. Buckley, Jr., Richard Weaver, and Willmoore Kendall, among others.

Will's belief that a government must be concerned with the values of its citizens is the central theme of this collection of 138 columns published over the last several years. Politics, Will writes in the introduction, "should be about the cultivation and conservation of character." He is concerned not with whom is currently wielding power in Washington, but rather with the principles (or lack of principles) motivating the powerful. Without principles "nations, like individuals, are guided by vagrant impulses and imperious appetites." His own principles, he argues, constitute "a coherent conservative philosophy."

Will's conservatism is in the classic tradition of 19th- and 20th-century European conservatism, which has been more concerned with preserving ethical and religious values than with conserving the wealth of the affluent. "Conservatism that does not extend beyond reverence for enterprise," Will states, "is unphilosophic, has little to do with government and conserves little."

> True conservatism, on the other hand, distrusts and tries to modify the social forces that work against the conservation of traditional values. But for a century the dominant conservatism has uncritically worshiped the most transforming force, the dynamism of the American economy. No coherent conservatism can be based solely on commercialism, but this conservatism has been consistently ardent only about economic growth, and hence about economies of scale, and social mobility. These take a severe toll against small towns, small enterprises, family farms, local governments, craftsmanship, environmental values, a sense of community and other aspects of humane living.

Such words do not sit well with other self-proclaimed conservatives who Will contends are spokesmen for "a radically anti-political ideology, decayed Jeffersonianism characterized by a frivolous hostility toward the state, and lacking the traditional conservative appreciation of the dignity of the political vocation and the grandeur of its responsibilities." Thus Allan Ryskind and Kevin Phillips have virtually read Will out of the conservative movement because he hasn't remained faithful to the party line of anti-statism, evangelical anti-Communism and militarism, contempt for the poor, and freedom for businessmen to destroy the landscape in the name of private enterprise. Will has also committed the cardinal sin of writing in the Washington Post.

Liberals, on the other hand, attack Will because of his commitment to the proposition that politics must concern itself with values and public virtue. For Will, the standard by which politics should be judged is the extent to which it fosters virtue and what he calls "conduct in its moral aspect" or "manners." Liberals, by contrast, seek justice and individual freedom (although often at the expense of creating a leviathan-like state). While Will emphasizes duties and responsibilities, liberals stress rights and privileges. In an essay in the New York Review of Books, Ronald Dworkin suggests that Will is wrong to expect a people which, by Will's own addmission, is materialistic, avaricious, and influenced by institutions inculcating "instant gratification of immoderate appetites," to elect philosopher-kings who will then establish a framework for encouraging virtue. Criticizing Will as an elitist, Dworkin believes the true task of government to be justice and not virtue. "Civilization is possible without justice," he writes, "but it then becomes, like slaves at Monticello, only a profound embarrassment, and a disgrace."

Will believes civility is under siege in a society in which condoms can be huckstered over television, in which the sole remaining growth industry in the country's largest city is pornography, in which a sizeable portion of the population believes that the community should be morally indifferent to homosexuality, and in which abortion (Will calls it "discretionary killing") is openly practiced and widely praised. Will also refuses to bow down before the altar of the young, instead attributing the campus turmoil of the 1960s to "prolonged adolescence." Nor does he take the easy way out by relating urban violence and riots to economic and social maladjustments. The United States, Will writes, "has within its urban population many people who lack the economic abilities and character traits necessary for life in a free and lawful society."

Just as Henry Adams was uncomfortable in the era of the dynamo, so George Will is ill at ease in the age of Madison Avenue and Hugh Hefner. The twentieth century, he avows, "is not a gentlemen's century." Richard Nixon, Robert Dole, Spiro Agnew, and Jimmy Carter have inhabited a Washington once reserved for Washington, Madison, Adams, and Jefferson. Bella Abzug and Larry Flynt both stalk the land polluting the atmosphere. "One must have a heart of stone," Will laments, "to feel no pang of regret about the vanishing of Jefferson's Republic."

Will's belief that politics is something more than who gets what, when and where, his argument that a mature society governs rather than is governed by its appetites, his use of the words "public philosophy" and civility," and his concern for the debasement of contemporary politics resulting from a mass electorate being influenced by the mass media remind one of Walter Lippmann, and especially of Lippmann's conservative classic, Essays in the Public Philosophy (1955). Lippmann also spoke of a public interest and criticized the Benthamite belief that the public interest was merely the sum total of the private interests of individuals; he also was skeptical of democratic politicians who appealed to the populace's appetites; and he also feared that "the democracies are ceasing to receive the traditions of civility in which the good society. . . originated and developed."

Only time will tell whether Will is to become another Lippmann. At the very least, he has helped to rescue conservatism from those who believe that conservatism is more a matter of profits than principles. As Meg Greenfield, the deputy editor of the Washington Post's editorial page, noted, "He's got an interesting Tory mind." For this we should be grateful.

# GEORGE WILL AND AMERICAN CONSERVATISM

Meg Greenfield once described her *Washington Post* colleague George Will as having "an interesting Tory mind." This mildly disparaging, if not patronizing, characterization has now been wryly and openly adopted by Will in his recently published collection of *Newsweek* and *Washington Post* essays, *The Pursuit of Virtue and other Tory Notions*. So strongly does Will feel about the word "Tory" that he even contemplated using it as a nickname for his daughter Victoria to whom he has dedicated his new volume. His wife strongly dissents, perhaps recalling Sam Johnson's *Dictionary* definition of Tory: "A cant term, derived, I suppose, from an Irish word, signifying savage."

Will's designation of himself as a Tory locates him within the corpus of conservative ideology. He is, of course, a conservative, and is rumored to be the president's favorite columnist. His essays provoke a splenetic response among American leftists. Thus Benjamin Demott of Amherst College, writing in the *Nation*, the Avis of American leftist weeklies, attacked Will for being a quintessential American, a defender of Mormon social values, a supporter of the status quo, and an admirer of Ray Kroc of McDonald's restaurants. His book, DeMott remarked, despite its "vaguely bookish air," lacks seriousness and independence. DeMott concluded that America needs a "real right," not the ersatz provided by Will, as well as "clarity about the difference between challenge and charm, conscience and its counterfeits—the pursuit of virtue and the pursuit of something else." Demott reflects, of course, the intellectual bankruptcy of contemporary leftism, which must depend on name-calling, as well as its amazement that anyone could be conversant with Gladstone, Emerson, Wilde, and Jefferson and still call himself a conservative.

Benjamin Disraeli once declared that, "a man who is not a Liberal at sixteen has no heart; a man who is not a Conservative at sixty has no head." Will did not have to wait until three score years to discover the true faith. Rather, one suspects, he was a conservative virtually from birth, partially through the influence of his father, a professor of philosophy at the University of Illinois, but more importantly because early in life he fell within the orbit of the Chicago Cubs.

Being a devoted fan of the Cubs in the 1940s and 1950s instilled in Will the basic conservative truths which have remained with him to this very day: that progress is a figment of the imagination and bears no relationship to the realities of life, including those occurring in Wrigley Field; that man is imperfect and corrupted by original sin, particularly the sin of passed balls, strike-outs, dropped fly balls, and missed signals; that life is not fair, as the long-suffering fans on Chicago's North Side well know; that good intentions, in and of themselves, are unable to accomplish anything, especially without good pitching and hitting; that pessimism regarding man's future and the participants in the World Series is a mark of the educated man; that mankind is a most gullible creature, ignoring the lessons of experience and following pied pipers predicting eternal salvation, permanent prosperity, and National League pennants; that people are most intractable, refusing to be molded by the ukases of commissars, social welfare bureaucrats, and third-base coaches; that no amount of social engineering can overcome inadequate schooling, a weak family structure, and lack of athletic ability; that change is not the same as improvement whether it be in academia, the family, or the front office; that achievement and not affirmative action should determine one's place in education, the economy, and on the diamond; and that standards of excellence save us from confusing momentary pleasure with happiness and the three-game winning streak with a pennant drive. Will's beloved Cubs correspond to Elbert Hubbard's definition of a conservative: "a man who is too cowardly to fight and too fat to run."

Central to Will's Toryism is the conviction that conservatism and capitalism are like oil and water. For Will, the term "libertarian conservative" is an oxymoron. Conservatism, rightly understood, stresses responsibilities rather than prerogatives, and the calls of conscience rather than the demands of ambition and avarice. Capitalism, Will writes, is "a marvelous producer of material blessings, but capitalism itself is a mixed blessing; it is an inflamer of appetites, an enlarger of expectations, a diminisher of patience." Left-wing critics of capitalism will be disappointed, however, if they assume Will is a comrade-in-arms.

Will is no Nineteenth Century Tory socialist repulsed by the vulgarity and ugliness of modern industrialism. For him capitalism is the worst social and economic system in the world, with the exception of those which have been proposed to replace it. Modern liberal reformers of capitalism, as typified by a Ted Kennedy, advocate a progressive tax system which inhibits productivity; an obtrusive government which increases social regulations, redistributes wealth, and encourages racial quotas; the multiplication of various entitlement programs which diminish individual responsibility and undermine fiscal solvency; and a foreign policy which weakens military preparedness, magnifies the failings of America's allies, and misjudges the magnitude of the Soviet threat. And since socialists have long ago given up their belief in the necessity of public ownership of the means of production and distribution, socialism is merely modern liberalism made more ubiquitous and noxious. Will thus does not believe that the failings of American capitalism can be rectifed by those with little understanding of the dynamics of economic growth or such little respect for the ability of Americans to solve their problems without the aid of Washington's guidelines and largesse.

Will, just like Walter Lippmann before him, looks to an enlightened political leadership to provide the citizen an interpretation of his responsibilities more expansive than the pursuit of private goals. Despite his interest in cultural matters, Will is at heart a political commentator who admires politicians, emphasizes the importance of governing, and defends the dignity of the political vocation. The success of a democracy, he writes, "depends on what is in the heads of the citizens." The statesman's responsibility is to see to it that these are ideas which reinforce those habits of thought and behavior necessary for the proper functioning of a republic.

For Will, Franklin D. Roosevelt and John Kennedy exemplify the type of leadership indispensable to a democracy. Kennedy's strongest beliefs "were about the dynamics and importance of national morale and prestige." Will's barometer for the decline of American politics during the 1960s and 1970s is the contrast between Kennedy and Jimmy Carter. While Kennedy challenged the public, Carter offered it bromides emphasizing earnestness and sincerity, and justified the failures of his administration by drawing attention to the difficulties of presidential governing. Reagan, Will believes, provides a refreshing contrast to his predecessor, possessing "a potent constellation" of conservative ideas, a faith in the continuing greatness of the country, a Tory impulse toward "progressive change," and a sympathy for that majority of Americans dismayed by the politics of cultural protest of the last decade and a half.

It is Will's position on cultural politics which most clearly sets him off from his critics on the left. They argue that the private and public realms are two distinct entities, and that the government should not regulate private behavior among consenting adults (as long as the behavior does not touch on economic relationships, otherwise the government is obliged to step in with minimum wage laws, licensing requirements, and other restrictions on individual freedom). Will, in contrast, believes statecraft ultimately involves "soulcraft," and that social and cultural anxieties find their way into a society's political agenda." It is ludicrous, he claims, for a democracy, which demands a virtuous citizenry, to be oblivious of behavior and ideologies which undermine the "manners" of the populace.

Will believes the abuse of freedom of speech and press which allows pornographers to hawk their wares in Times Square, Nazis to march in Skokie, Illinois, and doctors to abort on demand can be traced to liberalism's confusing of truth with popularity. Thus Oliver Wendell Holmes, Jr. claimed that the test of the truth of any idea is its ability to win support in the competition of the marketplace. Since all ideas have the right to compete, all ideas have the right ultimately to triumph. "So the logic of liberalism is that it is better to be ruled by Nazis than to restrict them." Will rejects totally the liberal rationale for tolerance.

First of all, he denies that liberalism is really neutral regarding the uses that people can make of their freedom. Abortion-on-demand, for example, is concerned less with providing freedom of choice for women, and more with enacting into law the feminist view of the family, the role of women, and the responsibilities of parenting. Secondly, Will rejects the argument that the First Amendment sanctions all varieties of expression, and that a democracy cannot make value judgments between speech which is compatible and speech which is incompatible with civilized behavior and the country's political system.

This dissent from the liberal view of toleration was fully developed in Will's 1968 Princeton Ph.D. dissertation, "Beyond the Reach of Majorities: Closed Questions in the Open Society." The events of the seventies only strengthened his conviction that the process of determining truth and error in political matters differs radically from the manner whereby we decide which tube of toothpaste to purchase, even though a commercial society might deny the distinction. The dissertation argued that, contrary to the scepticism permeating modern liberal political thought, political philosophy can arrive at substantive knowlege regarding political goods and evils, knowledge which can then serve as the basis for intolerance toward antidemocratic ideologies.

Every society, Will noted, even a democratic one, has certain bedrock principles and practices which are not subject to dispute. A political system which is totally neutral before all ideas simply does not take itself seriously and is unworthy of support. Complete political nihilism is impossible for any society committed to its own survival. It is therefore permissible, and at times mandatory, for a democracy to proscribe totalitarian or racist political movements. This repression has the added benefit of educating the citizens regarding the underlying values of their society, and of inculcating an attitude of moral seriousness toward the nation's public philosophy.

Will's Toryism—his scepticism regarding capitalism, his praise of strong political leadership, his restricted view of permissible social and political behavior, his conviction that America's public philosophy is something other than the pursuit of private ends—is poles apart from the libertarian, free-market outlook which many believe to be the sole voice of modern American conservatism. Will does share the libertarian fear of the modern state as a threat to private property, individualism, and Burke's "little platoons." In the taxonomy of American conservatism, however, he belongs more with the "new" conservatism, particularly that of Robert Nisbet and Leo Strauss.

In Nisbet's *The Quest for Community* Will discovered a "deeper, richer" conservatism than the free-market variety, one embodying "the major theme of Western conservatism: the defense of society against the political state; the preservation, to the extent feasible, of the autonomy of social groups against politicized control." One can question whether this support of "society against the political state" can be harmonized with Will's warm memories of the New Frontier. His faith in heroic leadership is, however, balanced by an appreciation for that political prudence which has always accompanied great conservative statesmanship. In an eloquent tribute to Harold Macmillan, Will quotes the former prime minister's response when he was once asked to provide the British with "a sense of purpose." "If people want a sense of purpose they can get it from their archbishops."

Strauss, a professor of government at the University of Chicago during the 1950s and 1960s, was the most influential conservative political scientist of the post-war era. A zealous exponent of classical political thought, Strauss attacked the emphasis of political philosophy since the time of Thomas Hobbes on natural rights rather than justice and natural law. In *The Political Philosophy of Hobbes* and *Natural Right and History* Strauss called for a return to the classical interpretation of natural law, to Aristotle's view of man as a social being, and to the classical emphasis on reason and the duties of citizenship. These Straussian themes resonate in Will's distaste for the multiplication of "rights" and entitlements, his belief that reason can arrive at objective political truth, his opposition to excessive individualism, his rejection of ethical relativism and the unwillingness to make value judgments, and his opinion that energetic governments should attempt to inculcate virtue in the body polis. Will is undoubtedly Strauss's best known, if not necessarily his most influential, disciple.

The influence of Strauss, of course, extends beyond Will. Irving Kristol, one of the gurus of "neo-conservatism," acknowledged his own debt to Strauss in his 1972 *On the Democratic Idea in America*. Here he lamented the growing reluctance of Americans to exercise that self-discipline over their appetites necessary for popular government. Kristol denied that "the actions of self-serving men will coalesce into a common good," or that "the emancipation of the individual from social restraints will result in a more perfect community." Kristol agreed with Will that a democracy must foster virtue and discourage corruption among the citizenry. "If you care for the quality of life in our American democracy," he concluded, "then you have to be for censorship."

Will's stature within American journalism (he won the Pulitzer Prize in 1977 for distinguished commentary) and his popularity among the general public indicates that his appeal is due to more than, as Benjamin DeMott would have us believe, his "charm." Will has tapped a widespread discontent among Americans regarding the seeming precipitate rush toward hedonism and the dissolving of the bonds of social convention. Americans are also disturbed by the acquiescence of the educational, cultural, and intellectual "leaders" in this pernicious ethical relativism. How refreshing it is to read Will's description of the *New York Times* (its "spacious skepticism extends to all values except its own"); his sketch of Walter Cronkite ("What does Walter Conkiete do? ... primarily he 'does' Walter Cronkite: the punctuating eyebrows, the inflections of a very papal Pope, the slightly lurching cadence of an engine with a cold curburetor"); his view of televised decadence ("Television in the 1970s vindicated the wit who said that life would be tolerable were it not for its amusements"); and his analysis of what Americans are fond of describing as "higher education" ("A society that thinks the choice between ways of living is just a choice between equally eligible 'life styles' turns universities into academic cafeterias offering junk food for the mind.") Will, it can be argued, has become a Strauss for the masses.

The real question for readers of Will is whether the American "soulcraft" has already deteriorated beyond any hope of recovery. The election of Ronald Reagan would argue otherwise. And yet there are enough indications that the corrosive influence of the welfare state, incessant advertising, and the dissolving of educational standards have encouraged a cult of instant material gratification inimical to sound statecraft. Athletics remains one of the few activities in which standards of excellence are taken seriously, in which there is a direct relationship between effort and achievement, and in which affirmative action is ignored (witness, for example, the predominance of white faces in tennis and of black faces in basketball). Athletics, alas, is also the supposed realm of the Chicago Cubs.

Readers of George Will will not be surprised if America has passed its zenith or the Cubs fail to appear in the World Series. We have, after all, been warned. And yet history teaches us that where there's a "Will" there's a way, and that "Will" power rather than fate determines destiny. Wrigley Field might yet be an exciting place this October. As any conservative knows, life's mysteries defy rational analysis.

# History Through the Eyes of Irwin Unger

Each semester I join hundreds of other idealistic historians in a never-ending crusade to instruct college-university students in the mysteries of the American past. As most of my readers know, schools on the semester plan generally slice the "U.S. Survey" into two segments, with the second portion (these are the sections which are assigned to me) devoted to the post-Civil War period. Such a course generally spans fourteen or fifteen weeks, the students being required to read a textbook and several paperbacks. My usual approach has been to leave the reading of the textbook to the students on the premise that they are literate enough to understand it and conscientious enough to read it without the prodding of quizzes, class recitations, or weekly essays. Increasingly, of late, I have been proved wrong.

The end of the academic boom of the 1960's brought a fiscal crisis for many universities, including my own. Faced with diminishing enrollments, colleges have been forced to hustle for students, accepting in the process a gradual dilution of academic standards. In addition, the search for warm bodies among the "disadvantaged" has brought to the campus students unaccustomed to reading and writing. Finally, the younger generation, which pandering politicians a few years back were calling the best educated and most idealistic in our nation's history, has been inculcated with a gospel of instant gratification and pleasure courtesy of television and advertising. Work, preparation, and care have become outmoded in an era in which one's fondest sexual aspirations can be achieved by changing mouthwash or deodorant, and in which the fountain of youth and heavenly bliss is just two hours away via Eastern Airlines.

After several frustrating semesters during which the students successfully resisted my efforts to impart some knowledge to them, I reluctantly decided that my academic standards were too high. Somehow I would have to reach them by descending to their level without giving up all pretense of being an employee of what is rather loosely described as "an institution of higher learning." Besides reducing the number of paperbacks and increasing the showing of movies, I decided to have our thrice-weekly classes devoted to a close examination of the textbook. In this way I would force the students to read the text (although this later proved to be more of a pious wish), and an "intellectual dialogue" could develop between students and teacher. The textbook I chose, Irwin Unger's *These United States*, Volume II, consists of fourteen chapters, the exact number of weeks in our semester. Thus each Monday—I hoped—the professor and his acolytes would start afresh examining another phase of our country's historical development.

This game plan forced me to do something which I had managed to avoid during a decade and a half of university teaching: to give the assigned text a careful and complete reading. I had not previously paid much attention to textbooks, presuming that they were all fairly similar and of the same deadly literary quality. (Compared to most textbooks, the Manhattan telephone book reads like a Robert Ludlum novel.) I believed I had better things to do with my time than to examine in depth the numerous textbooks sent to me by publishers eager to sell their wares, most of which eventually end up in my children's school library. My choice of text was generally determined by length (five hundred pages was the limit), the number of photographs and photographic essays (the more the better), and its availability in a paperback edition (or else the students might not purchase it).

My practice was to read the assigned chapter in *These United States* a few days before our class of the week and to jot down its most important and controversial points. These would then be reviewed in class along with any items the students cared to discuss. I soon discovered that this textbook was anything but a dry and neutral chronicling of facts, dates, names, and events. Instead the book was permeated by a liberal ideology which was grist for the mill of my conservative instincts. As for the students, they too were being confronted with something new. The teacher was actually criticizing the textbook, showing its egregious errors of omission and interpretation! Never again, I hoped, would my students assume that something must be correct just because it is written down. In my wildest fantasies I even imagined they might approach books assigned by their other professors with a more critical eye. My excitement was dampened, however, by the suspicion that the orientation of *These United States* could probably be found in virtually all other textbooks used in American universities. The American historical profession, despite its professed tolerance and addiction to unorthodox ideas, is dominated by those who would sooner admit to being embezzlers and voyeurs than question the beneficence of the social security system or the sainthood of John F. Kennedy. Could the willingness of Americans to accept big government and its interference in our private social and economic affairs, I asked myself, be due in part to the interpretation of American history conveyed by the textbooks they had read in college?

Irwin Unger is one of the doyens of American history. A professor at New York University, he won the 1965 Pulitzer Prize in History for *The Greenback Era: A Social and Political History of American Finance, 1865-1879*. He is also the author of *The Movement: A History of the American New Left, 1959-1972* and the editor of *Beyond Liberalism: The New Left Views American History*. His own orientation could be described as liberal and egalitarian, although his professional standards are much higher than those of many like-minded historians. In the July 1967 issue of the *American Historical Review* he criticized certain New Left historians for excessive present-mindedness, an attitude which "suggests a contempt for pure history, history that has not enlisted in the good fight....Clio at their behest has donned a uniform and does battle for social virtue." Radical historians, he warned, are frequently ill-tempered and extreme, allowing "the tone of the picket line and the handbill to invade their professional work." The sum and character of Unger's work, however, clearly establishes him as a member of the American left. From the perspective of the 1960's, he wrote, "the United States began to look like anything but an unmitigated success." Replete with agonies and injustices, evasions and unfinished revolutions, American history does "not include total exemption from the ills that societies are heir to." Even conservative historians, of course, might agree with some parts of these statements, especially if the latter point means to suggest that societies are, by their very nature, subject to "ills" which resist even aggressive and sweeping "reforms." Other interpretations and attitudes found in *These United States*, however, place considerable distance between Unger's camp and ours.

For instance, Unger has a knee-jerk sympathy for the poor and working class which, at times, leads him astray. A particularly noteworthy example is his discussion of the conditions of the wage earner at the turn of the nineteenth century. He mentions that the sweatshop workers of the New York garment industry were "exploited by their employers," though the very same sentence admits that the employers themselves "had to struggle hard to keep alive." Unger laments the status of the agricultural workers who were as "badly underpaid as were day laborers of every sort." In the same chapter, however, Unger discusses the economic difficulties of the American capitalist farmer, difficulties which were responsible for drawing him into the various agrarian movements of the late nineteenth century. One must ask, therefore, who were exploiting the garment workers and the farm laborers if the clothing manufacturers and capitalist farmers were not prospering themselves? Actually the low wages of garment workers and farm laborers were not due to "exploitation"; each group labored in one of the most competitive industries of the day. Had a garment manufacturer or a farmer decided to pay his employees more than market wages, his expenses would have spiralled and he would have soon been bankrupt. Low wages were caused by the underdeveloped state of the economy, not by capitalist "exploitation." Professor Unger is implying that since poverty is unfortunate, someone must be at fault. Despite his warnings regarding New Left historiography, he exhibits a similar tendency to moralize.

Unger's picture of industrial working conditions emphasize low wages, grueling and unhealthy jobs, the lack of job security, frequent periods of sustained unemployment, and the absence of pensions or social security for the elderly. He includes in the text the photograph of a worker who lost an arm in an industrial accident. For the unskilled, Unger writes, "life was not only precarious but meager and harsh....Life was getting better, but there was still a long way to go before people at the base of the wage pyramid could say that America had fulfilled its traditional promise of abundance." Working people "found life all too much like Thomas Hobbes' description of life in a state of nature: 'solitary, poor, nasty, brutish, and short.' "

The major problem with this interpretation is that it doesn't take into consideration the outlook of the workers themselves. If things were so bad under American capitalism, how can the massive immigration of Europeans to the industrial areas of America be explained? Similarly, why did millions of Americans voluntarily desert the countryside and move to the factory cities? Europeans and many of the rural Americans who chose to migrate to the industrial heartland were voting with their feet. Life in Pittsburgh or Toledo in the 1890's seems to have been preferable to remaining in Lodz, Palermo, or Forgotten Corners in the Heartland of America. Unger's argument that industrial labor was under-paid is meaningless. Under-paid in relation to what? The wages were certainly low compared to today, but they were higher than wages in contemporary Europe and rural America. The Italian farm laborer who migrated to New York City found working conditions safer, salaries higher, and hours shorter. Although the streets of America were not paved with gold, European immigrants experienced change for the better. At least this is what they told their countrymen who had remained behind, and this is one reason why the immigration from Europe accelerated during the late nineteenth and early twentieth centuries.

Social and economic mobility was a reality, not a myth, for the American working force at the turn of the century. The increase in home ownership, the movement from the unskilled into the semi-skilled and skilled trades, and the opportunity for children to continue their education were due to the economic benefits of a burgeoning economy. America was not then afflicted with the debilitating effects of social welfare legislation and monopolistic trade unions, nor were we burdened with government licensing regulations or social movements advocating the "improvement of life" at the expense of productivity. Immigrants improved their lives and enhanced their welfare by working long hours at unskilled jobs, knowing this was the only way they could accumulate the capital and skills to better the lives of their families. Paradoxically, many of their grandchildren would have the opportunity to sneer at American capitalism from the safety of academia and suburbia.

Unger's dislike of private enterprise is also revealed in his description of the overcrowded housing conditions in the cities during the late nineteenth century. The problem, he claims, was the urban dweller had little protection from the "predatory profit motive." Unger praises the outlawing of the "dumbbell" tenement in New York City and the establishing of stringent minimum housing guidelines in New York City and Chicago. He fails to mention, however, that the effect of such regulations was to reduce housing density and to make the construction of additional housing more expensive, thereby driving up rents. The "predatory profit motive" provided cheaper housing for the urban poor than the efforts of various housing philanthropists, and cheaper housing is precisely what the urban poor wanted. This is not the first or last time that the efforts of various social reformers adversely affected the interests of those whom they were attempting to aid. The establishment of rent control in New York City after World War II, for instance, was done supposedly in behalf of the city's poor and lower-middle class, but it has driven up the price of rental units by diminishing the city's housing stock and decreasing the number of apartments turned over every year.

Unger's faith in government planning is brought out in his discussion of the rise of radio during the 1920's and its effect on small town life and entertainment. Unger laments the fact that radio was placed under a minimum of government control. Instead, radio became a private industry dependent on revenue from advertising. "Advertisers who paid the bills and naturally wished to attract the largest audiences," he writes, "were far more inclined to pay for 'Roxy and His Gang' or 'Amos 'n Andy' than for serious discussion or the Metropolitan Opera." The result was that commercial broadcasting "surrendered a great opportunity to elevate public taste." Unger criticizes radio because, in giving people what they want, it has been responsive to the free market and not the small elite which enjoys the Metropolitan Opera. One could well disagree with Unger on this issue, however. The very fact that the mass media in America has remained relatively immune from government dictation has made possible a diversity of programming which would not have occurred under government ownership. One has only to contrast the mass media in America with that in most of the rest of the world to realize how fortunate we are in this respect.

Unger's complaint over the supposed reluctance of advertisers to pay for such broadcasts as the Metropolitan Opera is singularly inappropriate, considering that the Texaco Corporation has been sponsoring Saturday broadcasts of the Met for almost four decades! In fact, this is the longest continuing sponsorship of any radio or television program. That the National Broadcasting Company was privately owned did not prevent it from establishing the NBC Symphony Orchestra in 1937 with Arturo Toscanini as conductor, a move which CBS—in the finest tradition of free enterprise—countered with its own concert series. Actually, one could argue that free enterprise radio is more "democratic" than state-owned or state-controlled systems. Under the latter, everyone's taxes are used to subsidize *Hamlet* (or whatever) whereas under free enterprise Texaco chooses to sponsor the Met hoping that its high-brow listeners, in gratitude, will buy that brand of gasoline. One should also recall that, under the "mixed" system which has actually developed in this country, a good part of the revenues which support educational radio and television come from taxes levied on business.

Unger is predictably partial to the New Deal. Because of the reforms of the 1930's, he holds, the American people would never again be completely vulnerable to "the uncertainties of a freewheeling economy modified only in favor of powerful business groups." The Social Security Act, the Fair Labor Standards Act of 1938, and farm price supports, he claims, have made another depression less likely. Viewed from the perspective of the 1970's, however, this evaluation of the New Deal seems rather unsophisticated and outdated. The Social Security System is in deep trouble, with its rates continually rising and its actuarial future shrouded in darkness. A major effect of the minimum wage laws has been to increase teenage unemployment, especially among blacks. The farm price support program has helped to reduce the farm population while farm prices have increased, taxes have risen to pay farmers not to plant, and vast farm surpluses were created.

Unger does chide FDR, however, for failing to do more "to reduce the inequalities of wealth and power" through a more rigorous system of progressive taxation and a more comprehensive welfare program. In contrast to the liberal 1930's, Unger sees the post-World War II era as a time in which "every step forward [sic !] in reducing inequalities of income and status and expanding the safeguards against life's mischances would be hard fought." Unger regrets the removal of wartime price controls and he attacks President Truman for not vigorously backing an "improved" bill so that "middle and lower-income consumers could be protected against runaway prices." For Unger, American politics is a morality play. On one side are the good guys who favor egalitarianism, government regulation and the welfare state; on the other side are conservatives and reactionaries who seek to restrain the forces of progress and enlightenment. Social welfare measures are described as "significant" and " progressive," while conservative political impulses are labelled "timid." Along with other liberals, Unger accepts reformist rhetoric at face value without bothering to consider the actual impact of liberal reforms. The road to hell, we need not be reminded, is paved with good intentions. The fact that liberal hearts are in the right place is no guarantee that their minds are also.

Richard Nixon presents a problem for Unger. While hardly sympathetic toward Nixon, Unger does praise the former president for not being completely opposed to "domestic reform or new ideas," particularly environmentalism. Although not as staunch a defender of the environment as Ralph Nader "whose young researchers regularly attacked the large corporations for polluting air and water and contaminating the food that Americans consumed," Nixon did approve three environmental measures during his first term. This is the sum total of Unger's discussion of the recent ecology movement. He fails to include the more unfortunate side effects of the environmental craze, such as price increases at a time when our number one domestic problem is raging inflation, or a ballooning government regulation of industry which has served to decrease productivity while slowing down our rate of technological innovation.

Unger praises Nixon's 1971 economic departure. The president's rejection of the conservative gospel of balanced budgets and fear of inflation in favor of a program for reducing unemployment and accelerating growth through increased government spending plus price, wage, and rent controls was, according to Unger, "constructive" and evidence that Nixon was "capable of learning." Actually, Nixon's price fixing was disastrous, as Milton Friedman has clearly demonstrated, and the refusal of the Carter administration to institute mandatory wage and price controls is due in part to their failure during the Nixon era.

Unger's antipathy toward free enterprise is also reflected in his discussion of Nixon's China policy. He notes that the triumph of the Chinese Communists in 1949 had resulted in a "a new society in China, giving the Chinese people a new sense of pride and unity, and modernizing the country's economy." In contrast, we are told, Chiang Kai-shek's regime on Taiwan "had settled down to modest prosperity." Actually, capitalist Taiwan has one of Asia's most dynamic economies, while Red China's "modernization" is largely mythical and the so-called People's Republic remains a shockingly primitive country.*

The liberal definition of virtue is clearly brought out in Unger's description of President Ford. Although he was "a stolid conservative," Professor Unger writes, Ford was "nevertheless an open, decent, and generous person." Is one to assume from this that conservatives are by nature narrow-minded, cruel, and ungenerous? Ford, he claims, was "an unabashed conservative" in domestic matters, and thus a failure. But he was not a "die hard" and, to his credit, did see the necessity for Keynesian countercyclical measures when the economy went into a tailspin. Such is Unger's fairy tale.

Every writer is entitled to his opinions and has the right to compose any type of book he wants, but the author of a textbook to be read by first and second year college students has a unique obligation to his readers. He must not, it seems to me, present his ideology and opinions as "fact" to be accepted in full by unsophisticated students who are accustomed to viewing textbooks as impartial. I fear that innocent undergraduates (are there any other kind?) will not recognize that Unger's prejudices are simply that— prejudices, especially since their professors will probably share the same leftist outlook as the book.

Those on the American right should be disturbed by the domination of the American history textbook market by books such as *These United States*. I am unaware of any major American history text written from an anti-collectivist, pro-free enterprise point of view. We have radical texts, texts emphasizing blacks and other minorities, texts stressing "anonymous" Americans, and texts reflecting virtually every new methodological and literary approach. And yet where can one find an American history textbook which does not take liberal rhetoric at face value, which does not contrast noble leftist goals with grubby conservative reality, which does not characterize opponents of egalitarianism and big government as stodgy, mean-spirited, and troglodytic? A right-wing American history textbook might find a market and, in the process, earn its authors a few dollars (as well as glory and gratitude). This would only be fair since conservatives are supposed to believe in the free market and economic incentives.

# Decentralist Intellectuals and the New Deal

ALMOST a decade ago William E. Leuchtenburg noted that the full intellectual history of the 1930s has yet to be written.[1] The earliest treatments of the Roosevelt era were primarily the work of historians sympathetic with economic and political collectivism. Their studies have largely shaped historical understanding of the intellectual history of the New Deal era. Their emphasis was upon intellectuals such as John Dewey and Reinhold Niebuhr and journals such as *New Republic*, *Nation*, and *Common Sense*. Their work virtually ignored intellectuals and journals with other interpretations of the economic crisis of the 1930s. Especially unfamiliar to many historians is a small group of intellectuals who, calling themselves "agrarians," "distributists," and "decentralists," argued in behalf of a peaceful, middle-class revolution leading to the widespread distribution of property, the decentralization of economic and political authority, and the decentralization of the city.

The decentralist intellectuals included Southern Agrarians, historian and journalist Herbert Agar, contributors to *Who Owns America? A New Declaration of Independence* and *Free America*, and members of the Catholic rural life movement. The Southern Agrarians were famous for *I'll Take My Stand: The South and the Agrarian Tradition*, published in 1930 in order to dramatize the plight of southern agriculture, and for their opposition to big business and the rapid industrialization of the South. Agar, perhaps the most important of the decentralist intellectuals, had been influenced by the English Distributist movement of Hilaire Belloc and G. K. Chesterton while living in England during the late 1920s. After returning to the United States, he was instrumental in the publication of *Who Owns America?*, a collection of articles by agrarian and non-agrarian decentralists

---

Edward S. Shapiro is associate professor of history in Seton Hall University.

[1] William E. Leuchtenburg, *Franklin D. Roosevelt and the New Deal, 1932-1940* (New York, 1963), 361. The argument of this paper is more fully presented in Edward S. Shapiro, "The American Distributists and the New Deal" (doctoral dissertation, Harvard University, 1968).

eager to formulate a political program acceptable to all varieties of decentralist thought, and in the founding of *Free America*, the first magazine devoted exclusively to the dissemination of decentralist ideas. The most significant statements of Catholic rural, social, economic, and political thought were made by John A. Rawe, Edgar Schmiedeler, and contributors to *Catholic Rural Objectives* published in 1935, 1936, 1937, and 1944.[2]

The decentralist intellectuals were primarily concerned with reversing the trend toward large-scale industrialization for which they blamed the dispossession of the propertied middle class of shopkeepers and small manufacturers, the creation of a depersonalized and propertyless working class, and the centralization of economic and political power into fewer hands. They feared economic giantism was leading to an oligarchic or a socialistic state which would carry economic centralization and the dispossession of the middle class to their logical conclusion. Moreover, they believed that the federal government's policies toward big business during the 1920s, especially high tariffs and rigged prices, had created an imbalance between production and consumption which was responsible for the Depression.[3]

Decentralists predicted that liberal reformers who wished to retain the basic structure of large-scale industrialization while meliorating some of its more unfortunate effects would eventually either be coopted by the plutocracy or become more radical upon recognizing the superficiality of their reforms. For the decentralist intellectuals, even Marxism was essentially palliative. As Allen Tate, one Southern Agrarian, wrote to literary critic Malcolm Cowley, "From my point of view . . . you and the other Marxians are not revolutionary enough: you want to keep capitalism with the capitalism left out." Tate claimed that only a program looking to a return to the widespread ownership of property had a chance to overthrow capitalism and "create a decent society in terms of American history."[4]

[2] Virginia Rock, "The Making and Meaning of *I'll Take My Stand*: A Study in Utopian Conservatism, 1925-1939" (doctoral dissertation, University of Minnesota, 1961); Herbert Agar, *Land of the Free* (Boston, 1935); Raymond Witte, *Twenty-Five Years of Crusading: A History of the National Catholic Rural Life Conference* (Des Moines, 1948).

[3] Herbert Agar, "Introduction," Herbert Agar and Allen Tate, eds., *Who Owns America? A New Declaration of Independence* (Boston, 1936), vii; John Crowe Ransom, "What Does the South Want?" *ibid.*, 83-84; Herbert Agar, "Private Property or Capitalism," *American Scholar*, III (Autumn 1934), 396-403; Luigi G. Ligutti and John C. Rawe, *Rural Roads to Security: America's Third Struggle for Freedom* (Milwaukee, 1940), 41; John Gould Fletcher, *The Two Frontiers: A Study in Historical Psychology* (New York, 1930), 297; Andrew N. Lytle, "The Backwoods Progression," *American Review*, I (Sept. 1933), 434. The Southern Agrarians, concerned over the threat of industrial communism, considered calling their book "Tracts Against Communism." Rob Roy Purdy, ed., *Fugitives' Reunion: Conversations at Vanderbilt, May 3-5, 1956* (Nashville, 1959), 207.

[4] Daniel Aaron, *Writers on the Left* (New York, 1961), 352-53, 458. See also Herbert Agar, "The Ideal We Share," *New Masses*, XIX (April 7, 1936), 27; Herbert Agar, "John

The other major threat to a propertied society, the decentralist intellectuals argued, was urbanization. For them the distinctive features of the metropolis were a dispossessed working class controlled by demogogic political bosses, the popularity of ideologies emphasizing collectivism and class conflict, and the monopolization of private property by a financial and business plutocracy. Catholic decentralists asserted that urbanization was responsible for increasing secularism among Catholics, the declining number of persons entering religious vocations, and the growing discrepancy between the birthrate of American Catholics who were primarily urban and the higher birthrate of the moral, rural-oriented Protestants.[5]

The post Civil War growth of factories and cities had, according to decentralists, sharply divided American society into opposing factions. While one faction, centered in the Northeast, admired economic centralization and generally voted Republican, the other faction, strong among the farmers and small businessmen of the South and Middle West, cherished the diffusion of property and looked to the Democrats as "the party of rural America, of the farmer, the shopkeeper, the artisan." Decentralists emphasized the pervasiveness of conflict between urban-industrial America and rural America. The agrarian poet John Gould Fletcher declared America could never fulfill her spiritual and cultural destiny without rejecting "the mock cosmopolitan Europeanism" of the East, turning its stance westward, and becoming "provincial, rooted in the backwoods, solitary and remote, as were Thoreau and Hawthorne." The Southern Agrarians stressed the tendency of the Northeast to transform other sections of the country into economic colonies. "It is the nature of industrial enterprise, corporate monopoly and high finance," Donald Davidson wrote, "to devour, to exploit, to imperialize...." John Crowe Ransom proposed in 1929 a political alliance between the South and West since both sections "desire to defend home,

Strachey, Marx, and the Distributist Ideal," *American Review*, V (May 1935), 168-84; and Herbert Agar, "The Marxian Myth: A Reply to Mr. Corey," *Free America*, I (March 1937), 11-12. Marxists replied that decentralist intellectuals were hopeless middle-class reactionaries for believing large-scale industrialism could be destroyed and the United States could return to a bourgeois economy in which most people owned productive property. Granville Hicks, *The Great Tradition: An Interpretation of American Literature Since the Civil War* (New York, 1935), 282; Bern Brandon, "Metaphysics of Reaction," *Marxist Quarterly*, I (Jan.-March 1937), 125-33.

[5] Agar, *Land of the Free*, 13-20; Troy J. Cauley, *Agrarianism: A Program for Farmers* (Chapel Hill, 1935), 191; Donald Davidson, review of *Faith in Living, Free America*, IV (Oct. 1940), 19; John Donald Wade, "Of the Mean and Sure Estate," Agar and Tate, eds., *Who Owns America?* 254-57; Edgar Schmiedeler, *A Better Rural Life* (New York, 1938), 1-12, 218-21, 234, 238, 246; Witte, *Twenty-Five Years of Crusading*, 1-6; Martin E. Schirber, "American Catholicism and Life On the Land," *Social Order*, 12 (May 1962), 201; Robert D. Cross, "The Changing Image of the City among American Catholics," *Catholic Historical Review*, XLVIII (April 1962), 33-52.

stability of life, the practice of leisure, and the natural enemy of both is the insidious industrial system."[6]

The decentralist intellectuals did not believe they were economically impractical and technologically reactionary for espousing the cause of small business and rural America during the 1920s and 1930s. On the contrary, they strongly contended that their goals and ideas harmonized with the dominant tendencies of modern technology. They pointed to the substitution of electricity for steam power. Electricity, decentralists predicted, would lead to the dispersal of industry because there was no longer any need for factories to remain concentrated close to sources of coal, and because electricity could easily be adapted to the requirements of small factories and home industries. Electricity also promised to make farm life less onerous and more attractive and, thus, help stem the drift of farmers to the cities. As one enthusiast proclaimed, electricity offered an opportunity "to make possible a sweeping program of decentralized regional development in terms of the most advanced science." In addition, decentralists claimed the introduction of the automobile allowed men to move out of the city, to acquire land and even engage in part-time farming, and to commute to their urban jobs.[7]

The nomination and election of Franklin D. Roosevelt in 1932 encouraged decentralists. They hoped to see an administration embark upon a comprehensive program of economic and demographic decentralization and aid for rural America. This expectation resulted from Roosevelt's well-known opposition to monopolies, Wall Street, and the decreasing economic independence of the small businessman and the farmer, as well as his at-

[6] Herbert Agar, *What Is America?* (London, 1936), 240-43; Fletcher, *Two Frontiers*, 178; Donald Davidson, *The Attack On Leviathan: Regionalism and Nationalism in the United States* (Chapel Hill, 1938), 127; John Crowe Ransom, "The South Defends Its Heritage," *Harper's Magazine*, 159 (June 1929), 117; Andrew Nelson Lytle, "The Hind Tit," *I'll Take My Stand: The South and the Agrarian Tradition* (New York, 1930), 201-45; John Donald Wade, "Old Wine in a New Bottle," *Virginia Quarterly Review*, XI (April 1935), 246; David Cushman Coyle, *The Irrepressible Conflict: Business vs. Finance* (Geneva, N. Y., 1932), 12; David Cushman Coyle, *Roads to a New America* (Boston, 1938), 18-19. For the widespread prevalence of the colonial economy idea among southern social scientists and politicians, see George Brown Tindall, *The Emergence of the New South, 1913-1945* (Baton Rouge, 1967), 594-99.

[7] Peter Van Dresser, "Will Electricity Decentralize Us?" *Free America*, II (Nov. 1938), 15; David Cushman Coyle, *Electricity: Achievements of Civilization* (New York, 1939), 14; David Cushman Coyle, "Inefficient Efficiency," *Virginia Quarterly Review*, XIV (Summer 1938), 368-79; Herbert Agar, *Pursuit of Happiness: The Story of American Democracy* (Boston, 1938), 50; Herman C. Nixon, *Forty Acres and Steel Mules* (Chapel Hill, 1938), 72, 77-78; Donald Davidson, "Agrarianism for Commuters," *American Review*, I (May 1933), 240-41; Donald Davidson, "'Southern Agrarians' State Their Case," *Progressive Farmer and Southern Ruralist*, LI (June 1936), 5; Cauley, *Agrarianism*, 70; Ralph L. Woods, *America Reborn: A Plan for Decentralization of Industry* (New York, 1939), 81-99, 104-34.

tempts to improve rural life while governor of New York and some of his 1932 campaign promises. Moreover, Roosevelt in the 1932 campaign vowed, if elected, to provide relief for farmers, to discipline Wall Street, and to "systematically eliminate special advantages, special favors, special privileges wherever possible, whether they come from tariff subsidies, credit favoritism, taxation or otherwise."[8]

The major initial acts of the New Deal, however, were far different from the reforms proposed by the decentralist intellectuals. They had suggested helping the small businessman and the consumer by lowering tariffs, strengthening the government's antitrust program, and withdrawing all political favors given big business and high finance since the Civil War. The National Industrial Recovery Act (NIRA) of 1933 instead authorized the suspension of antitrust laws so as to permit industry-wide economic planning. The decentralists predicted that permitting industrialists to establish production quotas would lead to higher prices and profits, diminished competition, lower consumer purchasing power, a cartelized economy, and the "political, moral, and intellectual slavery of the individual" resulting from the economic and political planning necessary to administer such a law.[9]

The farmer could best be aided, decentralists argued, through the prohibition of land ownership by banks, insurance companies, and other corporations; the heavy taxation of land owned by absentee landlords; low-interest loans; meliorating landlord-tenant relations in behalf of the tenants; rural electrification; and the encouragement of farm cooperatives. The keystone of the early New Deal farm program was the Agricultural Adjustment Act (AAA) of 1933, which proposed to raise farm incomes by limiting pro-

[8] John Crowe Ransom to Andrew Nelson Lytle, Nov. 16, 1932, Andrew Lytle Papers (Tennessee State Library and Archives); Lytle to Allen Tate, Feb. 23, 1933, Allen Tate Papers (Princeton University); Herman C. Nixon to Donald Davidson, March 17, 25, 1931, Donald Davidson Papers (Vanderbilt University); Frank L. Owsley, "Scottsboro, the Third Crusade: The Sequel to Abolition and Reconstruction," *American Review*, I (June 1933), 274; Daniel R. Fusfeld, *The Economic Thought of Franklin D. Roosevelt and the Origins of the New Deal* (New York, 1956), 84-86, 123-30, 203-05, 227-38, 245-46; Frank Freidel, *F. D. R. and the South* (Baton Rouge, 1965), 6-18, 64-66; R. G. Tugwell, "The Sources of New Deal Reformism," *Ethics*, LXIV (July 1954), 266; R. G. Tugwell, "The Preparation of a President," *Western Political Quarterly*, I (June 1948), 132-33; Franklin D. Roosevelt, "Growing Up by Plan," *Survey Graphic*, LXVII (Feb. 1, 1932), 483-84; Franklin D. Roosevelt, "Back to the Land," *Review of Reviews*, LXXXIV (Oct. 1931), 63-64; Franklin D. Roosevelt, "Actualities of Agricultural Planning," *America Faces the Future*, Charles A. Beard, ed. (Boston, 1932), 331-38.

[9] James Truslow Adams, *The Living Jefferson* (New York, 1936), 382; Coyle, *Irrepressible Conflict*, 13-16; David Cushman Coyle, "The Twilight of National Planning," *Harper's Magazine*, 171 (Oct. 1935), 562-65; Herbert Agar, "The Task for Conservatism," *American Review*, III (April 1934), 10-12; Cauley, *Agrarianism*, 197-98; Davidson, *Attack On Leviathan*, 40; Frederick P. Kenkel, "Throwing the Small Fry to the Lion," *Central-Blatt and Social Justice*, XXVI (Nov. 1933), 241.

duction and providing benefit payments to participating farmers. Decentralists claimed AAA would curtail farming at the very time the government should be encouraging an expansion of the farm population and, by making farmers wards of the state, dangerously centralize political power in Washington. According to Andrew Nelson Lytle, AAA was a "road to agricultural servility; it is up to us to divert him [Roosevelt] towards the more stable agrarian life." Decentralists traced the source of the New Deal's agricultural program to a mistaken belief that farmers were rural businessmen who, just like other businessmen, needed a boost in income. They contended, however, that the farmers most needed a more secure land tenure and a greater degree of economic self-sufficiency rather than more cash. No solution to the farm problem, Davidson wrote, could ever be achieved in "terms of the industrial economics now being applied by the Tugwells and Ezekiels of the Roosevelt Administration." Even those decentralists who recognized that, as long as industry had its tariffs and other subsidies, AAA benefit payments were necessary to compensate the farmer and to create a balanced and stable economy, believed AAA to be no substitute for guaranteeing land ownership and reducing farm tenancy. Decentralists agreed with Davidson that the early New Deal, by legislating benefit payments and ignoring the problem of dispossession, had "done more to pacify the farmers than to save them."[10]

This lack of enthusiasm for NIRA and AAA extended as well to the Trade Agreements Act of June 1934. This law authorized the President to enter into reciprocal tariff agreements with other nations which could eventually result in the lowering of tariffs by as much as 50 percent. Some decentralists, disappointed that tariffs were not to be cut even more, claimed the industrial Northeast was still exploiting farmers and consumers. David-

[10] John Crowe Ransom, "Happy Farmers," *American Review*, I (Oct. 1933), 534-35; Ransom, "What Does the South Want?" Agar and Tate, eds., *Who Owns America?* 189; Herbert Agar, "Just Why Economics?" *North American Review*, 240 (Sept. 1935), 200-05; Herbert Agar, "What Is the New Deal?" Louisville *Courier-Journal*, April 22, 1936; Herbert Agar, "Why Help the Farmer?" *ibid.*, Aug. 14, 1939; John C. Rawe, "Agrarianism: An Economic Foundation," *Modern Schoolman*, XIII (Nov. 1935), 18; John C. Rawe, "Agrarianism: The Basis for a Better Life," *American Review*, VI (Dec. 1935), 188-92; Cauley, *Agrarianism*, 94-103, 180-211; Frederick P. Kenkel, "Rural Economic Welfare in the Light of Present Conditions," *Central-Blatt and Social Justice*, XXVI (Nov. 1933), 236; Edgar Schmiedeler, *Balanced Abundance* (New York, 1939), 21-25; David Cushman Coyle, *Uncommon Sense* (Washington, 1936), 77-79, 97-101; Lytle to Seward Collins, May 17, Aug. 25, 1933, Seward Collins Papers (Beinecke Library, Yale University); John Gould Fletcher to Frank L. Owsley, March 2, 1935, Frank Owsley Papers (in possession of Mrs. Frank L. Owsley, Nashville, Tennessee); Allen Tate, "The Problem of the Unemployed: A Modest Proposal," *American Review*, I (May 1933), 135; Donald Davidson, "The Restoration of the Farmer," *American Review*, III (April 1934), 100; Donald Davidson, "A Case in Farming," *ibid.* (Sept. 1934), 530.

son argued that, despite the trade act, the goal of the New Deal was national self-sufficiency which could "ruin the South's export trade in cotton and tobacco and reduce the Southern States to the condition of pensioners upon a socialized America." Frank L. Owsley, a fellow Southern Agrarian, agreed with Davidson, and in 1935 demanded subsidies for the South and West on the export of their agricultural products should the New Deal continue to temporize on the tariff issue. Other decentralists, however, feared that lowering of tariff barriers would increase trade in staple crops and strengthen commercial farming at the expense of subsistence agriculture. Agar and economist Troy J. Cauley proposed that tariff reduction be combined with the fostering of subsistence farming in order that both regional and industrial exploitation and commercial farming could be diminished.[11]

The redeeming features of the early New Deal for the decentralist intellectuals were the creation of the Tennessee Valley Authority (TVA) in 1933 and the Rural Electrification Administration (REA) in 1935. The electricity flowing from TVA and REA, they predicted, would slow down the movement of population to the cities by making rural life more comfortable, encourage the founding of small-scale and owner-operated rural industries, facilitate the movement of businesses into rural areas, break the stranglehold of Wall Street holding companies over southern power companies, and by bolstering the rural economies of the West and South help restore economic balance to the nation. Decentralists approved TVA's resettling of farmers on better land, establishing demonstration farms, producing cheap fertilizers, developing inexpensive farm machinery, and teaching the most recent methods of soil conservation. All of these, they felt, promoted family farming and the individual ownership of land. They also commended TVA's emphasis on decentralized decision making and grassroots democracy which they favorably compared to the centralization and bureaucratization found in many of the other New Deal agencies. They pointed out that the setting of prices and production quotas by NIRA and AAA had resulted in a vast expansion of the political bureaucracy, while TVA merely established an economic and social framework within which private enterprise could function more effectively. Herman C. Nixon

[11] Donald Davidson, "Where Regionalism and Sectionalism Meet," *Social Forces*, 13 (Oct. 1934), 28-29; Davidson, *Attack On Leviathan*, 203-04, 283; Frank L. Owsley, "The Pillars of Agrarianism," *American Review*, IV (March 1935), 533, 541-47; Herman C. Nixon, *Possum Trot: Rural Community, South* (Norman, 1941), 84-96; H. Clarence Nixon, "The New Deal and the South," *Virginia Quarterly Review*, XIX (Summer 1943), 333; Schmiedeler, *Balanced Abundance*, 8-9; Agar, *Land of the Free*, 272-73; Herbert Agar, "International Trade and Cotton," Louisville *Courier-Journal*, Sept. 20, 1935; T. J. Cauley, "The Integration of Agrarian and Exchange Economies," *American Review*, V (Oct. 1935), 587-602.

termed TVA "the strongest card in the New Deal. . . . The nation needs a series of the grand projects of the TVA type . . . but it seems fortunate that the eroded South became the scene of the first experiment."[12]

The decentralist intellectuals were disappointed throughout Roosevelt's first term by the New Deal's failure to develop into the radical economic movement they had originally expected. In August 1933, Owsley looked forward to Roosevelt reducing "the plutocrats to ranks as far as control of the government goes. New York is to be trimmed of its complete financial control if he has his way." Fletcher, bemused by the Hundred Days, complimented the President for "putting the speculators where they belong—in the wastebasket (many of them belong on lamp-posts)," and anticipated eagerly further attacks on Wall Street. The economist David Cushman Coyle hopefully described the New Deal in 1934 as "the quest of the American people for a way to free themselves from the octopus of finance that has been strangling their free business for several generations." But the inability of the New Deal to destroy completely and quickly the power of high finance disillusioned the decentralists. They accused the New Dealers of temporizing and leaving the power of plutocracy untouched. The "standpat Rooseveltians," Fletcher complained in 1934, seem "to be accomplishing little beyond beclouding the real issues." Despite taking the country off the gold standard, passing two major acts regulating the stock

[12] Fletcher to Davidson, July 27, 1933, Davidson Papers; Frank L. Owsley, "Mr. Daniels Discovers the South," *Southern Review*, IV (Spring 1939), 670; David Cushman Coyle, *Land of Hope: The Way of Life in the Tennessee Valley* (Evanston, 1941); David Cushman Coyle, *Electric Power on the Farm: The Story of Electricity, its usefulness on farms, and the movement to electrify rural america* (Washington, 1936); David Cushman Coyle, "Planning Is a Fighting Word," *Harper's Magazine*, 192 (June 1946), 555-56; Woods, *America Reborn*, 233-36, 306-12; Ralph L. Woods, review of *God's Valley, Free America*, III (July 1939), 19-20; Herbert Agar, "TVA and Socialism," Louisville *Courier-Journal*, June 9, 1937; Herbert Agar, "A Boost for Democracy," *ibid.*, March 7, 1939; R. F. Bessey, "National Planning and Decentralization," *Free America*, VII (Summer 1943), 14; Thomas Haile, "Agriculture and The TVA," *ibid.*, V (Nov. 1941), 3-6; Ransom, "What Does the South Want?" Agar and Tate, eds., *Who Owns America?* 189; Charles Rumford Walker, "The Farmer Harnesses the Kilowatt," *Free America*, IV (June 1940), 3-5; Ligutti and Rawe, *Rural Roads to Security*, 183, 309; Edgar Schmiedeler, *The Rural South: Problem or Prospect?* (New York, 1940), 7; Nixon, *Forty Acres and Steel Mules*, 80-81. For a criticism of TVA, see R. G. Tugwell and E. C. Banfield, "Grass Roots Democracy—Myth or Reality?" *Public Administration Review*, X (Winter 1950), 47-55. For a decentralist criticism of TVA, see Davidson, "Where Regionalism and Sectionalism Meet," *Social Forces*, 25-27; Donald Davidson, "That This Nation May Endure: The Need for Political Regionalism," Agar and Tate, eds., *Who Owns America?* 124-25; Donald Davidson, "Regionalism as Social Science," *Southern Review*, III (Autumn 1937), 219-20; Donald Davidson, "On Being in Hock to the North," *Free America*, III (May 1939), 4; Donald Davidson, "Political Regionalism and Administrative Regionalism," *Annals of The American Academy of Political and Social Science*, 207 (Jan. 1940), 138-43; Donald Davidson, *The Tennessee: The New River-Civil War to TVA* (New York, 1948), ii; Donald Davidson, "Regionalism," *Collier's 1954 Year Book*, William T. Couch, ed. (New York, 1954), 509.

exchanges, and enacting legislation divorcing investment banking from commercial banking, Agar defined the New Deal as "finance-capitalism with its rewards more firmly distributed, and its knavery curtailed."[13]

Decentralists regretfully concluded that the New Dealers believed they could restore prosperity without destroying industrial and financial centralization. This was attributed to a naïve faith in tinkering. The New Deal, Agar wrote, was evidently "mere crisis legislation, mere extemporizing in the hope that something . . . will turn up." Tate blamed Roosevelt for the New Deal's degeneration into a diffuse humanitarianism: the President was "an honest man, but horribly simple; the best he can do is to think the whole problem will be solved when a little of the big income is restored and all men have enough to eat." Other decentralists, however, ascribed the New Deal floundering to a collectivistic philosophy rather than to any pragmatic, non-ideological outlook. The example of NIRA and the presence of Rexford G. Tugwell and other collectivists within the New Deal caused Davidson to accuse the New Dealers of merely seeking "to repair our faltering economic system and to guarantee a modicum of comfort to the human casualties of our false way of life. But they are doing nothing to repair the false way of life. Rather they seem to want to crystallize it in all its falsity." Evidently the New Deal did not accept the decentralist's contention that permanent economic recovery and lasting social reform could come only with economic dispersal and the widespread ownership of property.[14]

[13] Owsley to Davidson, Aug. 5, 1933, Davidson Papers; Fletcher to Henry Bergen, Aug. 18, Nov. 15, 1933, May 11, 12, July 5, 13, Nov. 19, Dec. 3, 1934, Henry Bergen Papers (in possession of Eugene Haun, Ann Arbor, Michigan); Fletcher to Tate, July 22, 1934, Tate Papers; David Cushman Coyle, "Recovery and Finance," *Virginia Quarterly Review*, X (Oct. 1934), 489-93; Coyle, *Uncommon Sense*, 123-34; John Crowe Ransom, "A Capital for the New Deal," *American Review*, II (Dec. 1933), 142; Lytle, "The Backwoods Progression," 431; Troy J. Cauley and Fred Wenn, "A Debate: Resolved: That the United States Should Return to the Gold Standard," *Bulletin of Emory University*, XX (June 1934), 59-61; Richard B. Ransom, "The Private and Corporate Economies," *American Review*, VI (Feb. 1936), 392-99; John C. Rawe, "Agriculture and the Property State," Agar and Tate, eds., *Who Owns America?* 46-48; Agar, "The Task for Conservatism," 10-11.

[14] Herbert Agar to Tate, Nov. 7, 1933, Tate Papers; Herbert Agar, "Private Property or Capitalism," *American Scholar*, III (Autumn 1934), 397; Tate to Agar, Nov. 17, 1933, Tate Papers; Richard B. Ransom, "New American Frontiers: A Plan for Permanent Recovery," *American Review*, V (Sept. 1935), 386-90; Andrew Nelson Lytle, "John Taylor and the Political Economy of Agriculture," Part III, *American Review*, IV (Nov. 1934), 96. T. J. Cauley criticized the New Deal stock market legislation as "probably well conceived within its limits," but "essentially directed against symptoms rather than fundamental causes. It will prosper accordingly." Cauley, "Integration of Agrarian and Exchange Economies," 602. Donald Davidson, " 'I'll Take My Stand': A History," *American Review*, V (Summer 1935), 320-21; Edd Winfield Parks, "On Banishing Nonsense," *American Review*, I (Oct. 1933), 574-76; Frederick P. Kenkel, "New Deals, Past and Present, V," *Central-Blatt and Social*

In 1935, the course of the New Deal shifted. The Public Utility Holding Company Act, the Wealth Tax Act, the establishment of the Resettlement Administration, and the Banking Act and Revenue Act of 1936 reflected a change from cooperation between government and business and the acceptance of consolidation and planning to an emphasis on the free market and a distrust of concentrated economic and political power.[15] The decentralist intellectuals welcomed this reversal in New Deal strategy. As Agar wrote Tate, "for the first time in a long time we have friends in high places." The New Deal was at last "seeking to find how to make us once more a nation in which the average man is a small proprietor, owning his farm, shop, or business." And yet they remained dissatisfied with the New Deal, complaining, for example, that the Wealth Tax Act should have graduated taxes even more sharply. "America will not start to recover its lost freedom," Coyle stated, "until it can enact and enforce upper bracket tax rates that will stop the growth of great fortunes and make them start to shrink away." As a result of political timidity, the "tax policies of the New Deal have been wavering and uncertain." And Lyle H. Lanier claimed that, after four years of the New Deal, the nation was still afflicted with "economic fascism."[16]

Many decentralists would have voted Republican in 1936 had the Republicans nominated a prominent progressive such as Senator William E. Borah of Idaho. The nomination of Alfred M. Landon, however, confirmed their distrust of the Republicans as the party of big business, and they supported Roosevelt in the hope that a decisive Democratic victory would lead to a showdown with plutocracy. Tate summarized for the *New Republic* the sentiment of the decentralists.

I shall vote for Roosevelt.... There are very few of the President's policies that I like, but he has been aware that a crisis exists, and there is at least a strong probability that he will take firmer and more coherent ground, in his second administration, against privilege and Big Business. Should Landon be elected he would certainly bring on a revolution of violence in his efforts to restore the good

*Justice*, XXVII (June 1934), 77; Rawe, "Agrarianism: The Basis for a Better Life," *American Review*, 176-88.

[15] Arthur M. Schlesinger, Jr., *The Politics of Upheaval* (Boston, 1960), 385-95.

[16] Agar to Tate, Sept. 29, 1935, Tate Papers; Herbert Agar, "Share-Our-Wealth," Louisville *Courier-Journal*, Aug. 16, 1935; Herbert Agar, " 'A Cockeyed Tax?' III," *ibid.*, Oct. 21, 1936; David Cushman Coyle, *Why Pay Taxes* (Washington, 1937), 79-80, 91-96; David Cushman Coyle, "Map of the New Deal," *Scribner's Magazine*, XCIX (April 1936), 224; David Cushman Coyle, "The Fallacy of Mass Production," Agar and Tate, eds., *Who Owns America?* 11; Rawe, "Agriculture and the Property State," *ibid.*, 49-51; Richard B. Ransom, "Corporate and Private Persons," *ibid.*, 77-79; Lyle H. Lanier to Tate, Dec. 7, 1936, Tate Papers.

old days of finance-capitalism. If I were a Communist, I think I should vote for Landon.[17]

Roosevelt's overwhelming victory encouraged decentralists, and they anxiously anticipated the New Deal accelerating its campaign against rural poverty. For decentralists, rural poverty, especially as it pertained to dispossession and the growth in farm tenancy, was the most important social and economic problem of the 1930s. They believed that it was responsible for the creation of a mobile farm proletariat lacking personal initiative and social responsibility, the erosion of human and natural resources, the rise of rural political demagoguery, and the general spirit of hopelessness and degradation permeating wide portions of the rural South. The New Deal's attack on rural poverty had begun in 1933 with a program establishing 25,000 families on subsistence homesteads. Decentralists strongly endorsed farm colonization, arguing that it enlarged the rural population, reduced industrial unemployment, decreased the amount of money spent for relief, and did not necessarily have to lead to an increase in political centralization. They were critical, nevertheless, of a program aiding only 25,000 families at a time when millions of Americans were unemployed. As Lytle asserted, the subsistence homesteads "are a move in the right direction, but how timid and coy are their steps. . . . Our hope for the betterment of country life demands that these casual experiments be turned into a real offensive." Decentralists also disliked the New Dealer's paternalistic control over the homesteads, and they were greatly dismayed when Tugwell's Resettlement Administration absorbed the homestead program in 1935.[18]

The Resettlement Administration's operation of the subsistence homesteads reflected Tugwell's opposition to the back-to-the-land movement, his belief that the family farm was a technological anachronism which would inevitably give way to the factory farm, and his distrust of individualism and political and economic decentralization. It encouraged commercial and mechanized agriculture, introduced progressive schools in order to aid in

[17] Agar to Collins, Dec. 10, 1934, Collins Papers; Herbert Agar, " 'Blind Mouths'—Notes on the Nominating Conventions," *Southern Review*, II (Autumn 1936), 231-33; John C. Rawe, "Corporations and Human Liberty: A Study in Exploitation—II. Regaining the Rights of the Individual," *American Review*, IV (Feb. 1935), 481; Allen Tate, "How They Are Voting: IV," *New Republic*, LXXXVIII (Oct. 21, 1936), 304-05.

[18] James A. Byrnes, "Foreword," *Catholic Rural Life Objectives*, II (1936), 3-6; Edgar Schmiedeler, "A Review of Rural Insecurity," *ibid.*, III (1937), 51-52; John Crowe Ransom, "The State and the Land," *New Republic*, LXX (Feb. 17, 1932), 8-10; Andrew Lytle, "The Small Farm Secures the State," Agar and Tate, eds., *Who Owns America?* 239; Woods, *America Reborn*, 297-302; *Free America*, V (April 1941), 2, 11; Ligutti and Rawe, *Rural Roads to Security*, 171-73, 255-56; William H. Issel, "Ralph Borsodi and the Agrarian Response to Modern America," *Agricultural History*, XLI (April 1967), 159-64.

the transition from a competitive to a cooperative society, and attempted to reform the homesteaders along collectivist lines. All of this was, of course, anathema to decentralists who saw Tugwell as the prime example of those New Dealers who "use the terminology of industrial economists and neglect to emphasize the human values of an unincorporated agrarian system. They would control production in the field in the same way as in the factory, establish homesteads only by way of temporary relief, and allow the further capitalization of joint-stock interests in extensive land holdings."[19] Troubled by Tugwell and the very modest New Deal approach to rural poverty and agrarian dispossession, decentralists became increasingly more vocal in demanding "a public policy that will transform the family-farm operator into a farm owner instead of transforming owners into tenants or day laborers on a corporation farm." Ransom and others who had supported AAA as a stopgap measure to tide farmers over until a program dealing with dispossession could be developed were especially disappointed and disturbed.[20]

The growing discontent of farmers, the threat of socialist agitation among tenants and sharecroppers in the South, and the decisive Democratic victory in 1936 focused attention on the problem of farm tenancy and the Bankhead proposal. This was a bill introduced by Senator John H. Bankhead of Alabama providing long-term loans at low interest to enable sharecroppers and tenants to become farm owners. Bankhead maintained passage of his bill would enlarge the yeoman class, rectify in part the population imbalance between country and city, and reduce relief payments.[21] The

[19] Joseph Dorfman, *The Economic Mind in American Civilization* (5 vols., New York, 1959), V, 502-15; Arthur M. Schlesinger, Jr., *The Coming of the New Deal* (Boston, 1958), 369-71; Paul K. Conkin, *Tomorrow a New World: The New Deal Community Program* (Ithaca, 1959), 186-213. In 1930, Rexford Tugwell defined a farm as "an area of vicious, ill-tempered soil with a not very good house, inadequate barns, makeshift machinery, happenstance stock, tired, overworked men and women—and all the pests and bucolic plagues that nature has evolved . . . a place where ugly, brooding monotony, that haunts by day and night, unseats the mind." Sidney Baldwin, *Poverty and Politics: The Rise and Decline of the Farm Security Administration* (Chapel Hill, 1968), 88; Rawe, "Agrarianism: An Economic Foundation," *Modern Schoolman*, 18.

[20] Edwin V. O'Hara, "A Spiritual and Material Mission to Rural America," *Catholic Rural Life Objectives*, I (1935), 6; H. Clarence Nixon, "Farm Tenancy to the Forefront," *Southwest Review*, XXII (Oct. 1936), 11-12; Nixon, *Forty Acres and Steel Mules*, 56-57; Chard Powers Smith, "Something to Do Now," *Free America*, I (Feb. 1937), 8; Coyle, *Uncommon Sense*, 97-101; Ransom, "Happy Farmers," *American Review*, 522-23; and John Crowe Ransom, "Sociology and the Black Belt," *American Review*, IV (Dec. 1934), 153-54.

[21] John H. Bankhead, "The One Way to Permanent National Recovery," *Liberty*, X (July 22, 1933), 18. Owsley believed the Southern Agrarians had been one of the formative influences behind the introduction of the Bankhead bill. Frank L. Owsley, "The Agrarians Today," *Shenandoah*, III (Summer 1952), 27; Bankhead to Owsley, March 15, 1935, Owsley Papers.

Bankhead bill quickly became the major political concern of decentralists. Owsley claimed it was the best proposal so far brought forth during the New Deal. "Most of the other Roosevelt legislation has dealt with the distribution of income; this is the distribution of capital." Decentralists predicted the Bankhead bill would invigorate New Deal soil conservation programs by giving farmers a personal stake in the land and, by increasing the number of economically independent families, undercut the attempts of Norman Thomas and other radicals to win over the dispossessed rural class of the South and West. In addition, it would be cheaper than farm relief since the loans would be paid back, and the recipients would not become dependent on the state as had occurred under AAA. The Bankhead bill was not another palliative, decentralists claimed; it was an effort to solve the most fundamental social and economic problem of the twentieth century, the drastic decline in property ownership. *Commonweal*, then under the editorship of Michael Williams, recommended the Bankhead measure to everyone who desired "the reestablishment of the principle of private property, and of the principle of personal and family liberty—which is dependent for its practical realization upon the possession of real personal property in land by great numbers of individuals, and not upon the possession of vast holdings in land, and great wealth of other sorts, by a small minority of the nation."[22]

The Bankhead bill became law in 1937 and a new agency, the Farm Security Administration (FSA), was established to administer a multi-faceted program of land purchasing by tenants and sharecroppers, retirement of submarginal land, and rural rehabilitation of needy farm families through short-term loans and grants for the purchase of livestock, equipment, and supplies. Will Alexander was appointed head of FSA succeeding Tugwell, who had opposed the Bankhead Act, as chief of the New Deal rural poverty program. Tugwell did not believe the land could absorb a significant number of the urban unemployed, nor did he believe the preservation of the family farm should be an object of public policy. The Bankhead Act, he warned, would create little more than "a contented and scattered peasantry."[23] The decentralist's evaluation of the Bankhead Act was diametri-

[22] Owsley to Marvin M. Lowes, March 16, 1935, Collins Papers; John C. Rawe to Edward Day Stewart, Feb. 7, 1937, Owsley Papers; Fletcher to Owsley, May 25, 1935, Owsley Papers; Herbert Agar, "A Substitute for 'Share-Our-Wealth,' " Louisville *Courier-Journal*, Aug. 20, 1935; Nixon, "Farm Tenancy to the Forefront," *Southwest Review*, 12-15; Coyle, *Uncommon Sense*, 97-101; *Free America*, I (Aug. 1937), 5; "In Support of the Bankhead Bill," *Commonweal*, XXI (April 26, 1935), 719.

[23] Schlesinger, *Coming of the New Deal*, 380; Bernard Sternsher, *Rexford Tugwell and the New Deal* (New Brunswick, 1964), 306.

cally opposed to Tugwell's assessment. Primarily they objected to the appropriation of only $50 million for FSA. As *Free America* remarked, "The thing should be attacked in terms of billions of dollars. Then only can the drift into tenancy and degradation be stopped and reversed."[24]

Decentralists attributed the meekness of the New Deal's approach to rural poverty to its insistence on saving a diseased agricultural economy in order to achieve economic recovery. Tinkering with farm subsidies and acreage limitations, they argued, had resulted in the nation "paying through the nose to perpetuate a system of commercial agriculture which might better be allowed to fall of its own weight." They emphasized that the New Deal had not reformed the tax structure so as to weigh most heavily on absentee landlords, had not enacted legislation ending land speculation or guaranteeing basic rights to tenants, and had not started a large land purchase program. Although the New Deal had possibly increased farm income and helped rectify the imbalance between agriculture and industry, it had been at the expense of pushing many poor farmers off the land and keeping the remaining farmers tightly controlled by a distant bureaucracy.[25]

The decentralist intellectuals claimed the New Deal response to widespread industrial unemployment exhibited the same superficiality as its farm program. "Relief through charitable doles," Ransom had observed in 1932, "may be humanitarian but it is not economic . . . this month's dole is of no effect in preventing next month's." Decentralists realized that, even though individual initiative might be undermined and relief recipients become dependent on the state, temporary relief measures and government jobs were needed to prevent widespread suffering. This was the price the nation had to pay for not being a decentralized and propertied society. But alongside these there should be other measures designed to make the unemployed economically independent, and it was the lack of the latter which made the New Deal's relief program appear increasingly artificial and inadequate. As *Free America* editorialized in 1937, "At the outset the government had no alternative but to care for the immediate needy. . . . But all that should now be replaced by other measures tending to make the citizens

[24] *Free America*, I (March 1937), 7; *ibid.*, I (May 1937), 3-4; Edgar Schmiedeler, *Our Rural Proletariat* (New York, 1939), 22-25; T. J. Cauley, "The Public Interest in the Use of Rural Land," *Southwestern Social Science Quarterly*, XXX (March 1950), 252.

[25] Frank Money, "Agricultural Paradox," *Free America*, I (Aug. 1937), 1; *ibid.*, III (Aug. 1939), 2, 7; Ralph Borsodi, "Democracy, Plutocracy, Bureaucracy," *ibid.*, III (Aug. 1939), 11; Donald Davidson, review of *Agriculture in Modern Life*, *ibid.*, III (Dec. 1939), 18; Thomas H. Haile, "Free Men and the Market," *ibid.*, V (June 1941), 12; Frank L. Owsley, "Pellagra Diet," *Southern Review*, VI (Spring 1941), 751-53; John C. Rawe, "The Home on the Land," *Catholic Rural Life Bulletin*, II (Feb. 20, 1939), 24; Edgar Schmiedeler, *Vanishing Homesteads* (New York, 1941), 23-25.

self-reliant and responsible." Agar questioned the long-range implications of the New Deal's public works agencies hiring millions of the unemployed.

Great public works, carried forward by the state in periods when unemployment in private business is high, may become a permanent part of the economy. They may prove a blessing, and a solution to the problem of unemployment. They will never prove a solution to the problem of liberty. The men who work for the state can only remain free if a determining majority of their fellow citizens do not work for the state but keep their own power over their own will in the only way it can be kept: by earning their own security. The citizens who work for themselves can see to it that the citizens who work for the state are not deprived of free will. They can guard the guardians; they can watch the watchmen. But if the time comes when the big majority, or the whole, is working for the state, liberty is dead.[26]

Decentralists approached the Social Security Act of 1935 and the Fair Labor Standards Act of 1938 in the same ambivalent manner as they did relief measures. They recognized that an overly centralized industrial society contained persons unable to provide for their old age and unemployment, and yet they feared a federal social security program would further concentrate political authority and make the people look to the state, rather than to themselves, for security. The 1935 act would be unnecessary, of course, in a propertied society. Accordingly, Agar justified the Social Security Act as something to temporarily tide the nation over until property could be widely distributed. He believed the New Deal actually wanted "a defense of American freedom in the only way it can be defended—by the preservation of real property."[27]

The Fair Labor Standards Act established maximum hours and minimum wage standards and was the major New Deal factory measure. Factory legislation, decentralists contended, was a makeshift alternative for the more basic reforms. They argued that, although the employees of large-scale factories must be protected against economic hazards, "the greater the need for such protection the deeper the illness of the society." Such legislation was merely palliative and could lead to a paternalistic state. Davidson declared

---

[26] Ransom, "The State and the Land," 9-10; *Free America*, I (Sept. 1937), 4; Ralph Borsodi, "Planning: For What?" *ibid.*, III (Dec. 1939), 16-18; Cauley, "Integration of Agrarian and Exchange Economies," 587; Tate, "The Problem of the Unemployed," 130-32, 135; Herbert Agar, *A Time for Greatness* (Boston, 1942), 252.

[27] Herbert Agar, "Every Man a King," Louisville *Courier-Journal*, Aug. 14, 1935. Several decentralists criticized the Social Security Act's failure to include farm laborers and farm tenants within its provisions. They accused the New Deal of needless discrimination against rural America, particularly the South with its large agrarian proletariat. David Cushman Coyle, *Roads to a New America* (New York, 1937), 335-43; Herman C. Nixon, *Social Security for Southern Farmers* (Chapel Hill, 1936), 6-7; Schmiedeler, *A Better Rural Life*, 249-64.

the Fair Labor Standards Act illustrated the New Deal's desire to retain, while reforming, centralized industrialism. Evidently the New Deal had chosen "to leave social and economic tendencies as they are, and apply a certain amount of humanitarian correction from above, to make the results of those tendencies easier to bear."[28]

For the decentralist intellectuals, the major importance of factory legislation was its effect on economic decentralization rather than the amelioration of the working conditions of the industrial laborer. Coyle, in particular, feared that many small businesses would go bankrupt because of inability to pay the minimum wage and that the 1938 act would impede the movement of industry from the Northeast to the low-wage areas of the South and West. *Free America*, although suspicious of the Fair Labor Standards Act, did anticipate some good coming from it. The magazine believed close supervision was needed over businesses such as utilities and railroads unable to decentralize. Perhaps this act would be the prelude to democratic control over such property, and perhaps businesses not wishing to fall under its provisions would voluntarily decentralize. *Free America* proposed:

the government meddle all it likes with big nation-size industry, industry so large that responsibility between employer and employee is impossible. But let it keep its hands off little industry serving only a few hundred men and in which personal contact between employer and worker is not only possible but unavoidable.[29]

Decentralists denied that the urban and industrial worker could ever secure economic and social justice within a centralized industrial economy. Even labor unions could not gain for him the economic security and personal independence which would be his if he owned a piece of land or controlled a small business. Labor unions, they asserted, were simply necessary evils under modern working conditions. "If we cannot alter the conditions for the better, if we cannot get ahead in our race with collectivism," *Free America* commented, "then we cannot complain that the workers proceed in a theoretically collectivist direction." New Deal efforts to aid the labor movement, although desirable in order to create a countervailing force to oppose big business, failed to answer the more pressing need of economic

---

[28] John C. Rawe, "The Agrarian Concept of Property," *Modern Schoolman*, XIV (Nov. 1936), 4; Donald Davidson, "Where Are the Laymen? A Study in Policy-Making," *American Review*, IX (Oct. 1937), 478; Richmond Croom Beatty, *Lord Macaulay: Victorian Liberal* (Norman, 1938), 286.

[29] Coyle, *Roads to a New America*, 292-95; *Free America*, I (July 1937), 3-5; Davidson, *Attack On Leviathan*, 282. Nixon and Agar, in contrast, favored wage and hour legislation because it would prevent a rapid and ruthless industrialization of the South. Nixon, *Possum Trot*, 155-56; Herbert Agar, "The New Carpetbaggers, I," Louisville *Courier-Journal*, April 9, 1937.

decentralization. Legislation such as Article 7 (a) of NIRA and the National Labor Relations Act of 1935 was an "irrelevant matter of great interest [to the workers] but only a source of confusion in the more vital struggle to rearrange the economic machinery so that it would not jam."[30]

The National Housing Act of 1937 disturbed decentralists more than any other New Deal measure with the possible exception of NIRA. This act authorized the United States Housing Authority to extend long-term, low-interest loans to local public agencies to clear slums and build housing projects. Decentralists argued that building housing on the sites of old slums merely encouraged people to remain in the city and offered no incentive for industry to decentralize. And to make matters worse, there was nothing in the act providing for home ownership. "Outside of giving a few people more decent living quarters," *Free America* complained, "nothing is to be done toward translating our ever-increasing, expropriated, dependent proletariat into an independent and responsible citizenry." Public housing appeared to be a gigantic subsidy to urbanized industry since it enabled urban labor to be decently housed without having industry pay for it through higher wages. Decentralists proposed that, if possible, public housing be single dwellings, that suburban building be given priority, that each separate dwelling include an acre of tillable land, and that the occupants be educated in the principles of subsistence agriculture.[31]

The decentralist intellectuals were thus generally disappointed with the various New Deal programs to reform industrial and urban life. For them, relief, social security, and public housing left untouched economic centralization, financial aggrandizement, and dispossession. There were, nevertheless, some measures during Roosevelt's second term which bore more directly on the issue of economic centralization. In March 1938, Thurman Arnold was appointed attorney general in charge of the Antitrust Division of the Department of Justice, and he soon became the most active trustbust-

[30] *Free America*, I (Feb. 1937), 3-5; *ibid.*, I (July 1937), 5-6; Coyle, "Twilight of National Planning," 557-62; Beatty, *Lord Macaulay*, 286; Rawe, "Agrarian Concept of Property," 4; Allen Tate, "A View of the Whole South," *American Review*, II (Feb. 1934), 418-19; Graham Carey, "Sufficiency, Security and Freedom," *Free America*, III (Feb. 1939), 10-11; Ligutti and Rawe, *Rural Roads to Security*, 38-39; Herbert Agar, "Farm Owners or Farm Unions?" Louisville *Courier-Journal*, Sept. 28, 1936.

[31] *Free America*, I (Sept. 1937), 7; *ibid.*, I (April 1937), 4; *ibid.*, I (Aug. 1937), 9; Ralph L. Woods, "Defense and Decentralization," *Free America*, IV (Sept. 1940), 3-5; "These Men: The Biggest Little Mayor in the World," *Free America*, IV (Nov. 1940), 6-8; Ligutti and Rawe, *Rural Roads to Security*, 109-11; John C. Rawe, "The Modern Homestead: A Vital Economic Institution," *Modern Schoolman*, XV (Jan. 1938), 34-35; Davidson, "Regionalism as Social Science," 224. Agar was almost apologetic for supporting public housing. Herbert Agar, "Federal Housing, II," Louisville *Courier-Journal*, March 27, 1939; Herbert Agar, "Free and Independent," *ibid.*, Feb. 8, 1938.

er in American history. One month later, Roosevelt requested funds for an investigation of monopolies which resulted in the three-year inquiry by the Temporary National Economic Committee. There was also the selection of Hadan Alldredge of Alabama, a vigorous foe of regional railroad rate differentials, as a commissioner of the Interstate Commerce Commission (ICC), and the passage of the Transportation Act of 1940, empowering ICC to aid farmers by reducing railway rates on agricultural products.

Decentralists hailed these modest successes,[32] but they remained convinced the New Deal had not tamed plutocracy. Tate, who in 1936 looked forward to the New Deal attacking "privilege and Big Business," described the United States in 1938 as a "plutocratic regime masked as a democracy." Agar, who in 1936 predicted that Roosevelt intended to push the struggle against plutocracy "through to a conclusion," asserted in 1938 the New Deal had been a failure because it had tried merely to ameliorate the worst effects of modern capitalism—"the result has been a permanent crisis of unemployment and a ten-year-long depression." Coyle, who in 1936 saw the New Deal as "the early stage of the final effort of the American economic and political system to throw off the shackles of big business," continually called for more vigorous attacks on economic centralization during the late 1930s. The growth of political centralization also dismayed the decentralist intellectuals, a development they saw as unnecessary since it had not resulted in the disciplining of big business or the creation of a propertied society. According to the utopian agrarian Ralph Borsodi, the New Deal had made it "virtually impossible for anyone to own property, to engage in business small or large, without paying constant and obsequious tribute to bureaucracy."[33]

Decentralist's criticisms of the New Deal for merely tinkering

[32] Nixon, "New Deal and the South," 329-33; Davidson, "On Being in Hock to the North," 5; Joseph L. Nicholson, "The Place of Small Business," *Free America*, IV (June 1940), 9; Herbert Agar, "Roosevelt and Collectivism," Louisville *Courier-Journal*, May 7, 1938; Agar, *A Time for Greatness*, 171, 176; Ellis W. Hawley, *The New Deal and the Problem of Monopoly: A Study in Economic Ambivalence* (Princeton, 1966), 439.

[33] Allen Tate, review of *Pursuit of Happiness*, *Free America*, II (Oct. 1938), 16-18; Herbert Agar, "Mr. Roosevelt and a Free Economy," Louisville *Courier-Journal*, June 29, 1936; Herbert Agar, "Pump-Priming, II," *ibid.*, Aug. 3, 1938; Herbert Agar, "Dorothy Thompson and the New Deal, II," *ibid.*, Aug. 13, 1938; Herbert Agar, "The Right to Private Property," *Free America*, III (June 1939), 7; Coyle, "Map of the New Deal," 220-21; Coyle, "Inefficient Efficiency," 376-78; Borsodi, "Democracy, Plutocracy, Bureaucracy," 11; Ralph Borsodi, "Decentralization," *Free America*, II (Feb. 1938), 12; Graham Carey, "Sufficiency, Security, and Freedom," *ibid.*, III (Jan. 1939), 5; Beatty, *Lord Macaulay*, 371; Chard Powers Smith, "In Defence of Democracy," *Free America*, I (April 1937), 5-7; Francis P. Miller, "Democracy: A Way of Life," *ibid.*, I (Nov. 1937), 1-2; Stoyan Pribichevich, "Modern Leviathan," *ibid.*, II (Aug. 1938), 13; Frank L. Owsley, review of *The Social Philosophy of John Taylor of Caroline*, *ibid.*, IV (Feb. 1940), 18-19; Ligutti and Rawe, *Rural Roads to Security*, 255-56.

with capitalism and for failing to recognize the need for drastic reforms were surprisingly similar to the complaints of collectivist intellectuals. *Common Sense, Nation,* and *New Republic*, the three major journals of liberals and collectivists in the 1930s, all criticized the New Deal for attempting to patch up capitalism rather than moving toward collectivism. According to *Common Sense*, the New Deal was "whirligig reform" led by a President "more renowned for his artistic juggling than for robust resolution." Max Lerner, an editor of *Nation*, attributed the New Deal's errors to Roosevelt's lack of "a clearly articulated social philosophy," and predicted he would be "better remembered for his inadequacies than for his achievements." The historian Charles A. Beard censured the New Deal for not nationalizing the banks and railroads, and for not accepting his vision of an integrated economy directed by government planners. "At the end of the depression, if it ever ends," he grumbled in 1935, "the concentration of wealth in the United States will doubtless mark a new high point in the evolution of American economy." The problem for the Marxist historian Louis M. Hacker was "not how to sustain an edifice whose foundation is slipping and which has displayed vital flaws in most of the parts of its superstructure: not where to continue patching farther or even what to salvage, but what to substitute." By calling a truce to class conflict in the hope purchasing power could be restored, the New Deal had been unable to effect any "enduring changes in the class relations in American economic society." The English socialist Harold J. Laski also disliked Roosevelt's reluctance to diagram a long-range collectivist program. Laski regretfully concluded that Roosevelt simply did not recognize that "the social system in America today is bankrupt."[34]

The weaknesses of the New Deal, according to decentralist intellectuals, stemmed from the pragmatic spirit and intellectual flabbiness of American liberalism. Refusing to contemplate fundamental social and economic change, the New Deal had merely attempted to ameliorate the worst aspects of large-scale capitalism through welfare programs and federal spending. The basic problems of dispossession, sectional imperialism, and economic centralization, decentralists claimed, had remained relatively untouched

---

[34] Frank A. Warren, III, *Liberals and Communism: The "Red Decade" Revisited* (Bloomington, 1966), 41-42; George Wolfskill and John A. Hudson, *All but the People: Franklin D. Roosevelt and His Critics, 1933-39* (London, 1969), 135-36; Max Lerner, "Roosevelt and History," *Nation*, CXLVI (May 7, 1938), 534; Charles A. Beard, "National Politics and War," *Scribner's Magazine*, XCVII (Feb. 1935), 69-70; Louis M. Hacker, "The New Deal Is No Revolution: Well, Then: What Next?" *Harper's Magazine*, 168 (Jan. 1934), 121-33; Harold J. Laski, "On America," *Living Age*, CCCLXVIII (Aug. 1935), 554; Harold J. Laski, "What Is Vital in Democracy?" *Survey Graphic*, XXIV (April 1935), 179.

during the 1930s. This critique largely agrees with the analysis of the New Deal by radicals during the 1930s and by many contemporary radical historians. Although approaching the New Deal from differing intellectual perspectives, they also emphasize the inadequacies of the Roosevelt administration, especially its failure to redistribute significantly the national income and its acceptance of capitalism and private property. This perhaps reveals the moderate nature of the New Deal. It disappointed both critics and defenders of private property. When contrasted with the European reform movements of the 1930s, the New Deal increasingly appears to be a cautious, middle-of-the-road program which satisfied neither decentralist readers of *Free America* nor the radical and socialist readers of *Nation* and *New Republic*.

# American Conservative Intellectuals, the 1930's, and the Crisis of Ideology

EDWARD S. SHAPIRO

THE TRIUMPH of the New Deal in 1932, the seemingly inexorable trend toward economic and political collectivism during the 1930's, and the accompanying discrediting of conservative ideas among much of the American intelligentsia were all a severe challenge to American conservative intellectuals.[1] Put on the defensive by the growing popularity of radical ideologies and forced by the pressure of events to defend ideas which many Americans considered irrelevant, anachronistic, and even fascist, American conservative thinkers were compelled to rethink their premises and to redefine the meaning of "conservatism." This ferment within American conservative circles brought to the surface a fundamental schism among conservative intellectuals over the very definition of conservatism and the stance conservative intellectuals should take toward contemporary developments in the United States and Europe. Nothing better illustrates this crisis within American conservatism during the 1930's than the founding of the journal the *American Review* in 1933 and the establishing four years later of a rival magazine *Free America*. The quarrel between these two magazines is important not only for what it reveals about the thinking of those American intellectuals who dissented from what appeared to be the almost inevitable trend toward political radicalism and economic collectivism during the 1930's, but also for what it reveals about the modern effort to define conservatism, perhaps the most ambiguous of all political terms. This is especially relevant today when the United States is experiencing a revival of conservative ideas and a simultaneous comprehensive challenge to reigning political and intellectual liberal orthodoxies.

The guiding personality behind the *American Review* was Seward Collins, a New Yorker with journalistic ambitions. Educated at the Hill School and Princeton University, Collins had become publisher and editor of the *Bookman* in the late 1920's. The *Bookman's* largely literary fare did not satisfy his desire to become a significant force in American politics and social thought, and so in 1933 Collins transformed it into the *American Review*. Throughout its four years of existence the *American Review* would reflect Collins' idiosyncratic outlook and his attempt to forge disparate elements into a conservative force which, he hoped, would counter "the well-nigh universal liberalism, radicalism, and false conservatism of our organs of opinion."[2] Collins' own outlook was a curious melange of medievalism, Jeffersonianism, and authoritarianism which he attributed to the influence of Hilaire Belloc's *The Servile State*. "I'm not Catholic at all," he once proclaimed, "I just want to see the end of Communism and capitalism and a return to the life of the Middle Ages."[3] Unfortunately, Collins was also an admirer of European fascism and an anti-Semite to boot.

Collins originally intended the *American Review* to disseminate the ideas of the English

Distributism of G. K. Chesterton and Belloc, the neo-Scholasticism of Christopher Dawson and Martin C. D'Arcy, the New Humanism of Irving Babbitt and Paul Elmer More, and the Southern Agrarianism of John Crowe Ransom, Allen Tate, and Donald Davidson. Of the four groups, only the Distributists and the Agrarians contributed frequently to the new review. The Agrarians published more than sixty articles and reviews in the *American Review*. Only Stark Young, Lyle H. Lanier, Henry B. Kline and Herman C. Nixon of the original twelve contributors to *I'll Take My Stand: The South and the Agrarian Tradition* never published in the *American Review*. In fact, prior to launching his new magazine Collins had met with the Agrarians in Tennessee to win their support. Although they would have preferred that Collins establish an exclusively agrarian journal, they were initially quite enthusiastic about his plans. The founding of the *American Review*, Davidson later wrote, indicated not only an increasing "insistence of the regions of the hinterland upon their point of view, but a thoughtful insurgence on the part of the Old Northeast against the growing clamor of the parties represented in such Marxian periodicals as *The New Masses*." Collins had been the first editor of a magazine published in a large city to throw his influence "to the side of the pluralistic forces of the various regions rather than to the monistic and centralizing forces of the metropolis."[1]

Herbert Agar was another important American conservative intellectual who wrote for the *American Review*. The winner of the Pulitzer Prize in history in 1934 for *The People's Choice*, a chronicle of the presidency, Agar had been the London correspondent for the Louisville *Courier-Journal* between 1929 and 1933, and in 1933 had become press adviser to the American embassy in London when Barry Bingham, publisher of the *Courier-Journal*, was appointed ambassador to the Court of St. James. While in England Agar was deeply impressed by the social thought of Belloc and Chesterton. Agar learned from the two leading English distributists of the danger posed to democracy by plutocracy and that the widespread distribution of property was essential to democracy. Power follows property, Agar frequently noted, and American democracy was threatened unless the tendency toward economic centralization and dispossession could be reversed.[5]

Agar returned to the United States hopeful of taking part in, and perhaps even leading, a political movement of farmers and small businessmen supporting the restoration of property and opposing the power of Wall Street and big business. America, Agar argued, was at a political crossroads. She could choose to alleviate the chaos brought on by the depression by opting for radical solutions dependent upon the expansion of centralized economic and political planning. This would result in the creation of a centralized totalitarian bureaucracy and the loss of individual freedom. Or America could decide to return to the traditional principles of economic individualism, the widespread distribution of property, and political decentralization. Anything less would lead eventually to a slave state. Collins figured prominently in Agar's plans. The *American Review* could provide a national organ of opinion for the spreading of decentralist and distributist ideas. Agar also hoped to convince Collins to become an editor, along with Tate and himself, of a weekly decentralist-distributist magazine which would provide a conservative alternative to the *Nation* and the *New Republic*. Finally, Agar wanted to use the offices of the *American Review* as a mailing address for his decentralist-distributist political movement, at least in its early stages.[6]

In their initial enthusiasm for the *American Review*, Agar and the Agrarians were willing to overlook Collins' failings as an editor. He refused to respond to correspondence, he procrastinated an infuriatingly long time before paying his contributors, and he opened up the pages of the *American Review* to writers with very little sympathy for Jeffersonian principles of political and economic decentralization. The Agrarians shelved their own plans to establish an agrarian weekly, convinced that Collins had provided them with a national outlet for the spread of agrarian economic and political ideas. The Agrarians, Davidson wrote Tate, owed Collins "endless gratitude."[7] Collins, for his part, described himself to the Agrarians as a supporter of agrarian and distributist principles, and he told them to view the *American Review* in large measure as their own magazine and to use it for anything they might wish to say.[8] The early relationship between Agar and Collins was also quite cordial. Collins published Agar's important essay "The Task for Conservatism" in April, 1934 shortly after Agar had returned to the United States, while Agar expressed complete confidence in Collins' "grand intellectual honesty" and looked forward to a fruitful collaboration.[9]

This expectation was, however, shattered in 1936 by what proved to be the most significant cause célèbre in American intellectual conservatism during the 1930's. The occasion was the publication of an interview with Collins by the left-wing novelist Grace Lumpkin in the February, 1936 issue of the radical magazine *Fight*. Collins began by affirming the similarity in economic objectives between himself and the Agrarians. Asked by Lumpkin whether he favored destroying factories, Collins responded, "certainly. We would have only individual craftsmen working. We would also distribute the land . . . give each person his own piece of land." Lumpkin pointed out that this resembled "forty acres and a mule." Even more embarrassing was Collins' discussion of education. Rejecting general education, he argued that only the fit should be schooled. "Education doesn't make people happy. It is unimportant." Lumpkin then asked Collins whether he was a fascist. "Yes, I am a fascist," he responded. "I admire Hitler and Mussolini very much. They have done great things for their countries." When asked about Hitler's persecution of the Jews, Collins replied, "It is not persecution. The Jews make trouble. It is necessary to segregate them." Collins also contended that the Negro must be segregated, although he should be given land to support himself. Lumpkin concluded the interview by querying Collins about his medievalism and his desire to restore the guilds. Not only did Collins state that he wished to introduce a nobility into America complete with kings, nobles, and dukes, but he supported abolishing the automobile and going back to the horse.

Q. You wish to do without conveniences?
Mr. Collins: Yes.
Q. Without bathtubs?
Mr. Collins: I never use a bathtub.
Q. You don't bathe?
Mr. Collins (dignified): I use a shower.
Q. Then you would want a shower?
Mr. Collins: I could rig up a shower.

Lumpkin commented at the end that the interview had shown "only the superficial aspects of the movement which Mr. Collins and the Southern Agrarians represent," and that among the Southern Agrarians and the contributors to the *American Review* was "the beginning of a group that is preparing the philosophical and moral shirt-front for Fascism."[10]

Agar and Tate were horrified when they heard of the Lumpkin interview. Despite Collins' disclaimer that he had replied only in jest to Lumpkin's questions, Agar and Tate feared that the Agrarians and Distributists would be identified with Collins' zany ideas. Agar immediately suggested to Collins that he sue Lumpkin and issue a statement disassociating himself from fascism.[11] Tate believed the Agrarians had to make clear their disagreement with Collins, and he suggested that Donald Davidson draft an agrarian manifesto outlining their differences. Failure to act would result in the Agrarians' being charged with fascism and medievalism. Although Collins had been valuable, "we can't let him make us Fascists when the big plank in our platform is that we are offering the sole alternative to Fascism," Tate told Davidson, "we've got to seize this occasion to clear up all the nonsense that has been said about us."[12]

Tate and Agar prayed that the interview would not become more widely known. Unfortunately, it received national attention when the *New Republic* mentioned it in its May 27, 1936 issue. The magazine also printed in the same issue an open letter from Tate to Lumpkin strongly protesting being bracketed with Collins, disclaiming any intention of seeking to restore the Middle Ages, and denying any sympathy for fascism. "I hold the political views that I do hold," Tate exclaimed, "because they alone seem to me to stand between us and the Fascist State. . . . I am so deeply opposed to fascism that I should choose communism if it were the alternative to it." Lumpkin responded by noting that there was sufficient evidence in the writings of the Agrarians, including Tate's, to justify identifying the Agrarians with fascism and Collins. "Any kind of honest examination of the theoretical basis of fascism by you and your group should make you uncomfortable at the similarity," she told Tate and the *New Republic's* readers.[13]

Two weeks later the *New Republic* printed a letter from Collins denying the accuracy of the now famous interview and avowing that, from his view at least, the entire interview was a spoof. Collins, nevertheless, proclaimed his support for fascism and declared that his interpretation of fascism differed from Tate's. While Tate believed fascism to be a plutocratic movement, Collins claimed it was a petty bourgeois crusade "tending toward an agrarian and distributist society." The *New Republic's* editors ended the discussion over the Lumpkin interview by asking Tate to consider carefully the point made by both Lumpkin and Collins that "some theories of the Southern Agrarians are quite close to part of Hitler's and Mussolini's programs. . . . The danger is that the American fascists, now completely lacking in intellectual respectability, will seize hold of Mr. Tate's ideas and some of his associates also."[11]

While Agar had not been mentioned by name in the Lumpkin interview as Tate had been, he also felt the need to publicly repudiate Collins. The forum he chose was the *Marxist Quarterly*. The winter, 1937 issue of the journal contained a letter from Agar describing his break with Collins and the *American Review* over the fascist question. "I would not, now that its politics have become unmistakably clear, write a piece for the *American Review*, if it were the last publication left in America—as it might become if America goes fascist," Agar stated.[15] Agar had been publishing a biweekly political column for the Louisville *Courier-Journal* since July, 1935, and he naturally feared his budding career as a political commentator could be destroyed by guilt through association with Collins. In addition, Agar and Tate were bringing out an important symposium in 1936 entitled *Who Owns America? A New Declaration of Independence*. This was to be a full statement of agrarian-distributist thinking on culture, politics, and economics. Any possibility of the book making a "real dent on public opinion" would be jeopardized if the Agrarian-Distributists became identified with Collins.[16] When the book was published, Agar distributed copies to Roosevelt, Harold Ickes, Cordell Hull, Henry Wallace, and Senator William Borah of Idaho in order to open up lines of communication with the New Dealers so that the administration could be pushed in a distributist-agrarian direction during its second term. Perhaps, he speculated, the Agrarians and Distributists could become the philosophers of a reformed New Deal. Agar was heartened by Roosevelt's speech accepting the Democratic nomination for a second term which, he claimed, "came directly out of *Who Owns America?* Now let him act on it!"[17]

*Who Owns America?* argued that the United States could continue to drift along toward economic giantism and political centralization. This would eventually result in fascism or communism. Or the nation could rediscover its traditional agenda of democracy, individualism, and the widespread distribution of property. The response to the book was mixed. John Chamberlain, not surprisingly, described it as nostalgic, reactionary, and tending toward fascism, while Lewis Gannett dismissed it as impractical. The socialist Broadus Mitchell, while praising the good intentions of the symposium's contributors, charged that they were utopians since "they do not take account of the vitality of the forces which oppose them. They repeatedly lapse into mere wishful thinking." The

Catholic journal *Commonweal*, on the other hand, believed the book to be very noteworthy, and the Harvard historian Crane Brinton praised its realism and relevance. Interestingly enough, the most laudatory review was by Seward Collins in the October, 1936 issue of the *American Review*, several months after Tate and Agar had expressed their dissatisfaction with Collins. *Who Owns America?*, Collins wrote, was simply "the most significant American book produced by the depression. It contains more sanity and penetration, more sense of American realities and American history, more grasp of economic fundamentals, more enlightened moral passion" than all the other depression books put together.[18]

*Who Owns America?* was one aspect of the Agrarian-Distributist effort to define and win support for a decentralist-agrarian program. Another was the meeting in early June, 1936 at Nashville, Tennessee of Agrarians and Distributists which created the Committee for the Alliance of Agrarian and Distributist Groups. The origins of the Nashville meeting can be traced back to early 1936 when a group known as "Independent Americans" began meeting periodically at the New York apartment of the lawyer, paleontologist, and poet Chard Powers Smith. Taking part in these discussions were several varieties of economic decentralists, including disciples of the homestead experiments of Ralph Borsodi, leaders of the cooperative movement, and religious advocates of a return to the soil. Smith suggested to Agar that he call a national convention of political and economic decentralists to be held during the summer of 1936 somewhere in the Mississippi Valley. He proposed inviting representatives from Borsodi's School for Living in Suffern, New York, the cooperative movement, the Southern Agrarians, the National Committee on Small Farm Ownership, the Catholic rural life movement, the Southern Policy Association, and other like-minded organizations. Smith believed such a meeting could establish a permanent organization which could then publicize the case for the widespread distribution of property and lay the groundwork for a major convention of decentralists to be convened in 1937. "I believe that you have started a great revival that has long been potential in the blood of America," Smith told Agar. "I hope it will go farther than you at present intend, perhaps farther even than you have dreamed."[19]

Smith's suggestion for a national meeting coincided with Agar's own desire to have the advocates of property become politically more visible. After conferring with the Southern Agrarians, Agar called for a meeting which took place on June 4th and 5th. Those attending included Tate, Borsodi, Smith, Agar, Davidson, Robert Penn Warren, John Crowe Ransom, Cleanth Brooks, Lyle Lanier, John Donald Wade, Frank Owsley, Charles Pipkin, and Father John C. Rawe, S. J. The delegates approved a statement of principles strongly condemning fascism, plutocracy, and communism, praising the decentralization of ownership in industry, agriculture, and trade, calling for the revival of family farming, and arguing that liberty was being threatened in America by the growth of giant corporations, the decline in proprietorship, and excessive urbanization. "In politics we are losing our freedom. In economics we are losing our independence. In life we are losing our proper sense of values." The document opposed the substitution of governmental collectivism for the economic collectivism of the large corporation, and called for a "distributed responsible ownership."[20]

One of the recommendations to come out of the Nashville meeting was the founding of a decentralist-agrarian weekly magazine. "The need of such a publication to represent our program in the South and West is overwhelming," a committee of Agrarians and Distributists declared. ". . . we could publish a weekly that would capture within two or three years a large portion of the audience that reads *The Nation* and *The New Republic* because it cannot get anything else."[21] This suggestion was opportune, coming during the height of the aftermath of the Lumpkin interview with Collins. Plans to establish a magazine proceeded intermittently during the rest of 1936 and then, with the financial backing of

Chauncey Stillman, *Free America* appeared in January, 1937.

The eight original editors of *Free America* were Agar, Borsodi, Smith, Stillman, Richard Merrifield, George F. Havell, Bertram Fowler, and Katherine Gauss Jackson. From the very beginning the new monthly stressed that it would offer a decentralist-distributist-agrarian alternative to the economic and political collectivism and deracination pervading *The Nation* and *The New Republic*, as well as an alternative to the fascism of the *American Review*. In the first article of the first issue Agar explained why *Free America* had been established. Thanking Collins for the aid he had initially given to the Agrarians and the Distributists, Agar regretfully noted that Collins had also become "a defender of certain aspects of the fascist point of view, a fact which has finally made it impossible for us to collaborate with him. We owe a debt to the *American Review*. It has given generous support to agrarian-distributist principles. Yet because of its fascist tendencies it cannot give support to democracy, which *Free America* feels to be the spirit and final justification of these principles." Agar predicted that *Free America* would build on the work of the Southern Agrarians, the Borsodi homestead movement, the "Independent Americans" of New York, the National Catholic Rural Life Conference, the cooperative movement, and the survivors of the Henry George single-tax crusade in order to "express the reborn desire of our people to save democracy."[22] Beginning in July, 1937, every issue of *Free America* contained the following statement:

> *Free America* stands for individual freedom and believes that freedom can exist only in societies in which the great majority are the effective owners of tangible and productive property and in which group activity is democratic. In order to achieve such a society, ownership, production, population, and government must be decentralized. *Free America* is therefore opposed to finance-capitalism, fascism, and communism.

From the beginning, *Free America* attempted to articulate a social and political alternative to liberalism, fascism, and communism, and to rehabilitate conservatism by severing it from any association with the Liberty League mentality. This clearly reflected the influence of Agar. Stillman, in fact, had decided to subsidize *Free America* because of Agar's role in it. A recent graduate of Columbia University's school of architecture, Stillman had been enormously impressed by Agar's defense of traditional Jeffersonianism in his 1935 book *Land of the Free*. Agar described himself as a Jeffersonian conservative. Continually quoting James Madison's aphorism that a voter without property was "the instrument of opulence and ambition," Agar argued that only a revival of subsistence farming, the decentralization of manufacturing in small shops and factories, and a resuscitation of small business in which ownership and control were not separated could insure the preservation of liberty. Denying that "conservatism" and private enterprise were identical, Agar maintained that it was private enterprise which in fact had been responsible for the dispossession of much of the American middle-class. Private enterprise would have to be restrained in order to preserve private property, while American conservatives would have "to redefine the historic purpose of America, to scotch forever the association of this purpose with the obscenities of Big Business, and to show how it can be attained in politics."[23]

Agar had little sympathy with reformers on the American left. He charged that Huey Long and Charles Townsend wrongly emphasized the redistribution of money and possessions rather than property, while most liberals and New Dealers wished to patch up the old system and provided no alternative to the servile state toward which the nation was heading. Liberals and Liberty Leaguers alike, Agar claimed, merely wished to restore prosperity without considering whether prosperity alone, without the freedom, responsibility, and dignity which come from the ownership of property, would make the United States a good place in which to live.[21]

The dispossession and proletarianization of

the middle-class were responsible, Agar argued, for the growth of European fascism. Fascism was simply low-wage capitalism and would soon be superseded by communism since it was "too bad to be endured."[25] There was no reason, however, why Americans had to choose between fascism-plutocracy and communism. There always remained the middle-way alternative of economic decentralization, the widespread distribution of property, and democracy. The choice for America was between Distributism-Agrarianism and collectivism, whether of the Huey Long, *New Republic*, fascist, or communist variety.

Despite numerous attacks on fascism by Agar, the Southern Agrarians, and *Free America*, the small band of American fascist intellectuals argued that the Distributists and Agrarians were objectively fascistic in outlook. It was impossible, American fascists claimed, to achieve the agrarian and distributist goals within a liberal political framework and by the normal constitutional means of compromise, interest group competition, and log-rolling. Only through a strong leader who was "above faction and beyond public interest" could an anti-plutocratic society of widely distributed property be established.[26] Collins also tended to discount the anti-fascism of Agar and the Southern Agrarians, preferring to believe that the founding of *Free America* was due more to Agar's political ambitions and his having gone leftist, than to any fundamental differences over the meaning of conservatism.[27] American Marxists agreed with the fascists that, while the Agrarians and Distributists talked the democratic game, their attempt to turn back the clock to the nineteenth century was, in essence, fascistic.[28]

*Free America* never became the major decentralist-distributist-agrarian journal Agar desired, although it did acquire a respectable circulation by the outbreak of World War II. Part of the monthly's early problems was due to a quarrel during the magazine's first year between Chard Smith and Agar over Agar's demand that Smith moderate his editorial criticisms of the New Deal. Smith refused and soon resigned as an editor. A more serious rift was between Agar and the Southern Agrarians, including Tate, who had refused to follow the example of Agar and break with Collins over the issue of fascism. This was not because they were sympathetic to fascism. "I am opposed to Fascism as an ultimate goal," Frank Owsley wrote the American fascist Geoffrey Stone, "and unless the situation becomes more desperate, that is, unless nothing can be accomplished under the 'Democratic process,' I shall remain opposed to Fascism as an instrument, as a means to an end, in as much as it might become the end in itself."[29] John Gould Fletcher declared that, under fascism, Germany had become "utterly the property of one single super-financier, and therefore governed by a dictatorship . . . more purely mercenary in motive than the worst form of dictatorship that governed the decadent Roman Empire."[30] The Agrarians refused to boycott the *American Review* because they remained grateful to Collins for opening up the pages of his review to them. Davidson, for his part, was prepared to break with Agar if it came down to a choice between Collins and Agar.[31]

Despite Agar's fervent entreaties, no Agrarian ever became officially associated with *Free America* except for Tate who, for a few months in 1939 and 1940, was book review editor. When plans for the journal were first formulated in 1936, the Agrarians believed Tate had promised them that theirs would be the dominant voice in the magazine, and that they would share control over the magazine's content with the New York group of Jackson, Havell, Smith, and Stillman. Anything else, they feared, would result in the Agrarians being swallowed up into a potpourri of decentralist thinking with the distinctive agrarian message being lost in the process. "I cannot see our position as a single contribution to a more inclusive position," Tate explained to Agar, for "we are the center to which other various movements must be drawn. If democracy means anything to us, it means the position that we have defined and developed; it doesn't mean that position plus the other movements which seem to me to be useful approximations of what we want." Tate predicted that, unless the Agrarians had their way, the magazine would shortly degenerate into "an organ of eclectic liberal opinion, and if we are in the organization agrarianism will die a quiet death."[32] The Agrarians were extremely bitter over what they believed to be Agar's reneging on his promises. They attributed this to the baneful influences of the New Yorkers. New York City, in effect, had triumphed over Nashville. They also feared that Agar wished to tie the agrarian tail to the kite of his own political ambitions.[33]

Agar sympathized with the Agrarians' fear that locating *Free America* in New York City would inevitably distort its agrarian and decentralist message. He favored moving it from "the evil associations of New York," but believed that was impossible in the immediate future for financial reasons, particularly the journal's dependence on Stillman's largesse. Agar also tried unsuccessfully to convince the Agrarians of the unworkability of an editorial board, half of whose members would live hundreds of miles from New York. He reassured the Agrarians that, while they would not dominate the magazine, it would be far closer to an agrarian journal than anything else in the country.[34]

The refusal of the Agrarians to lend their full weight to *Free America* was an important reason why the magazine never achieved any significant intellectual distinction. Agar constantly asked Tate to become an editor, once complaining that "the literary tone of the magazine is low, and it needs new ideas, new editorial creativeness, and the quality which you above all could give it." *Free America* had tried to develop a distributist-agrarian position without the full cooperation of the Agrarians, "the leading exponents of our ideas in the country, and if the magazine is to become permanent that state of affairs has got to stop."[35] As Tate had predicted, *Free America* developed into an eclectic journal featuring articles on do-it-yourself homesteading, home gardening, conservation, consumer cooperatives, small business, and demographic decentralization. Ironically, *Free America* was a victim in part of the geographical decentralization (*i.e.*, Nashville vs. New York) which was one of the magazine's most important tenets. It was never able to unite the various decentralist movements throughout the country into a viable political movement, nor did it ever find a charismatic national political leader who could unite the South and West behind a program of redistributing property. *Free America* ended publication in 1947, ten years after Collins had closed down the *American Review* as a result of what he termed "the ill-fated interview."[36]

The quarrel between *Free America* and the *American Review* ultimately involved the attempt to develop a relevant conservatism for the America of the 1930's. Collins looked to Europe for inspiration, believed that a worldwide conflict was taking place between fascism and communism, and contended that conservatism could triumph in the United States only in the guise of fascism and monarchism. As he told Lumpkin during the interview, he knew very little about America, and his kind words for Mussolini and Hitler revealed a gross ignorance of American conditions and sensibilities. Tate and Agar, on the other hand, believed that a conservatism revolving around the widespread distribution of property would be able to win support among the many persons who still valued traditional American economic and political teachings. Interestingly enough, a similar debate over the nature of radicalism took place in the United States during the 1930's. While many American leftists looked to the European ideology of Marxism for salvation, Alfred Bingham and his magazine *Common Sense* argued in behalf of a home grown radicalism purged of the Marxian contempt for the middle class and its romanticizing of the proletariat.

The fascist question reappeared in 1949 when Ezra Pound was awarded the Bollingen Prize by the Fellows of the Library of Congress in American Literature. Among the Fellows were Robert Penn Warren and Allen Tate. The poet Robert Hillyer vehemently criticized the award, describing the Fellows as a clique of New Critics who have "pooled their separate timidities and frustrations, gaining strength from each others' weakness, and have succeeded in an age unprepared by education against unpretentious cheek." Hillyer professed to see in the Bollingen flap the emergence of "clouds of a neo-Fascism." Hillyer's charges appeared in the *Saturday Review of Literature*. The magazine's editors seconded Hillyer's accusations, and denied the relevance of any aesthetic doctrine which separated art from politics.[37]

Tate and Warren were outraged by this attack, and Tate drew up a one-page statement entitled "A Personal Statement on Fascism" which circulated as part of *The Case Against the 'Saturday Review of Literature.'* In it he denied any sympathy with fascism which he described as revolutionary, nihilistic, and tyrannical. Opposing both fascism and communism, Tate praised the distributist and agrarian program of widely distributed property. The Distributists and Agrarians of the 1930's, Tate claimed, had believed that in America "the choice between communism and fascism was an unreal one: we sought an American solution which would circumvent both."[38]

The controversy over the Bollingen Prize heated up with the publication of Robert Gorham Davis' essay, "The New Criticism and the Democratic Tradition," in the winter, 1949-1950 issue of the *American Scholar*. Davis, a professor of literature at Smith College, charged that the literary quarterlies had been captured by the New Critics. According to Davis the New Criticism valued authority, hierarchy, tradition, dogma, and absolutes. He traced the origin of these ideas back to the New Humanists, the agrarian manifestos *I'll Take My Stand* and *Who Owns America?*, the literary criticism of Allen Tate and Yvor Winters, John Crowe Ransom's *God Without Thunder*, T. S. Eliot, and "Seward Collins' Catholic-distributivist (*sic!*) *American Review* for which Donald Davidson and Allen Tate wrote for even after it had become openly pro-Franco- and profascist."[39] Tate, once again, defended the Agrarians and Distributists against the fascist canard. He claimed to be a Jeffersonian, and denied that the New Criticism had any political relevance. "It is not the part of the man of letters or of imagination to order the political life," he claimed. Pound's mistake had been "to identify certain values with a contemporary political movement.... He was convinced of certain values of the moral and spiritual life, and he tried to translate them into immediate action."[40]

The issue of fascism highlighted once more the problem of defining conservatism, a problem which had become more important with the postwar emergence of the "New Conservatism." Indeed, as George H. Nash has written, "the very quest for self-definition" has been one of the most notable themes of recent American conservative intellectuals. "Behind what principles and aspirations could they coalesce?," Nash asked. "What intellectual legitimacy did the conservative movement have?"[41] What, in other words, made an American conservative a conservative. Certainly the postwar conservative intellectual movement has lacked precision and agreement on basic principles. While the eminent political philosopher Leo Strauss, for example, looked to the classic political thought of Plato, Aristotle, and Cicero, Russell Kirk believed Edmund Burke to be the fount of American conservative wisdom, Peter Viereck wrote admiringly of Metternich, and Robert Nisbet praised Lamennais and Tocqueville. The postwar conservative intellectuals were also split between libertarians emphasizing liberty, free enterprise, individualism, and self-assertion and traditionalists stressing order, morality, truth, virtue, and self-restraint. Frank S. Meyer was the most prominent of the limited band of postwar conservative intellectuals who articulated a philosophy of "fusionism" integrating free market and Burkean conservatism. Finally, some nonconservatives even questioned whether the very concept of conservatism had any relevance to America at all. Was Louis Hartz, for instance, correct in claiming in his *The Liberal Tradition in America* that the lack of a feudal past had imprisoned the United States within a Lockean-liberal consensus?[42]

Part of the conservative difficulty lay in the

dominant view of the 1930's as a conservative wasteland, a decade in which liberal and radical ideas supposedly dominated serious discourse. Conservative thinkers were forced to go back beyond the Roosevelt era in their quest for authentic American conservative ideas and heroes, back to the Adamses, Calhouns, John Taylors, and John Randolphs. American conservatives have not yet appreciated the extent to which American conservative intellectuals during the depression decade seriously confronted such issues as government aggrandizement and agrarian and commercial dispossession. A clearer understanding of the efforts of Herbert Agar and Allen Tate to provide an alternative to the political and economic collectivism of the 1930's would not only provide American conservatism the historical continuity which any intellectual movement needs, and especially a conservative one, but it would also answer the accusation that conservatism has no legitimate place in American life since it lacks a native tradition. Finally, it would help shift the focus on conservative interest to where it should always have been and where the battle with liberalism has been joined—over the issues of demographic centralization, political collectivism, and economic dispossession. For this writer, any American conservatism which claims to be both American and conservative should envision, as its central core, a concern for the widespread distribution of productive property and the decentralization of political and economic decision-making.[43] While it is clear that there would be general agreement among conservatives on the desirability of political decentralization, any economic decentralization which involved "economic levelling" (or any other kind of "levelling") would no doubt be the source of considerable and continuing dispute.

[1]The research for the essay was financed by a grant from the Faculty Research Council of Seton Hall University. [2]Seward Collins, "The American Review's First Year," *American Review*, III (April, 1934), 118. An excellent account of Collins and the *American Review* is the essay by Albert E. Stone, Jr., "Seward Collins and *The American Review:* Experiment in Pro-Fascism, 1933-37," *American Quarterly*, XII (Spring, 1960), 4-19. [3]Quoted in John Roy Carlson, *Under Cover: My Four Years in the Nazi Underworld of America* (New York: E. P. Dutton, 1943), p. 202. [4]Donald Davidson, *The Attack on Leviathan: Regionalism and Nationalism in the United States* (Chapel Hill: University of North Carolina Press, 1938), pp. 77-78. For the meeting of Collins with the Agrarians, see Davidson, *Southern Writers in the Modern World* (Athens: University of Georgia Press, 1958), p. 61; Rob Roy Purdy, ed., *Fugitives' Reunion: Conversations at Vanderbilt, May 3-5, 1956* (Nashville, Tenn.: Vanderbilt University Press, 1959), p. 219; W. S. Knickerbocker, "Tactics in Tennessee," *Westminster Magazine*, XXIII (Winter, 1935), 225-26. Collins invited the Agrarians to participate in the *American Review* on March 8, 1933. Seward Collins to Davidson, March 8, 1933, Collins Papers (Yale University). For the Agrarians' enthusiastic response to Collins' offer, see Davidson to Collins, March 12, 1933, Allen Tate Papers (Princeton University); Davidson to Tate, March 16, 1933, and April 5, 1933, *ibid.*; Davidson to Collins, March 18, 1933, Davidson Papers (Vanderbilt University); Davidson to John Gould Fletcher, April 7, 1933, Davidson Papers; Fletcher to Collins, April 21, 1933, Collins Papers; John Crowe Ransom to Collins, October 16, 1933, Collins Papers. Clinton Rossiter described the *American Review* as "a rich repository of conservative musings of every possible variety: distributism, agrarianism, monarchism, neo-Scholasticism, guildism, crypto-Fascism, traditionalism, antique republicanism, feudalism, and, unfortunately, Francoism." Clinton Rossiter, *Conservatism in America* (New York: Alfred A. Knopf, 1956), p. 312. [5]"Agar Named Editor of Courier-Journal," Louisville *Courier-Journal*, November 17, 1939; Virginia J. Rock, "The Making and Meaning of *I'll Take My Stand:* A Study in Utopian Conservatism, 1925-1934," (unpublished Ph.D. dissertation, dep't. of modern language and literature, University of Minnesota, 1961), pp. 388-91. [6]Herbert Agar to Collins, December 10, 1934, Collins Papers; Agar to Tate, January 15, 1935, Tate Papers. [7]Davidson to Tate, February 15, 1934, Tate Papers. The Agrarians were especially grateful for the publishing outlet provided by the *American Review* since in 1935 they had a very serious disagreement with the *Virginia Quarterly Review*. Edward S. Shapiro, "The Southern Agrarians, H. L. Mencken, and the Quest for Southern Identity," *American Studies*, XIII (Fall, 1972), 83-87. [8]Collins to Davidson, March 8, 1933, Collins Papers. [9]Agar to Tate, January 29, 1935, Tate Papers. [10]Grace Lumpkin, "'I Want a King,'" *Fight*, (February, 1936), 3, 14. [11]Stone, "Seward Collins and *American Review*," 16-17. [12]Tate to Davidson, February 23, 1936, Davidson Papers. Actually Collins had made his pro-fascist and pro-monarchy views known well before 1936. In May, 1933 he praised Hitler for ending the threat of communism in Germany, and called Mussolini "the most constructive statesman of our age" since he saw most clearly the need for monarchy and had "joined it to a sound moral system." Collins, "The Revival of Monarchy," *American Review*, I (May, 1933), 251-53. One year later Collins defined fascism as "the revival of monarchy,

property, the guilds, the security of the family and the peasantry, and the ancient ways of European life." Collins, "American Review's First Year," 124. Collins was thus a little bewildered by Agar and Tate's belated discovery of his sympathy for fascism, Collins to Agar, December 23, 1936, Tate Papers. Davidson never had any doubt where Collins stood regarding fascism. Davidson to Collins, May 27, 1936, Collins Papers. [13]"Fascism and the Southern Agrarians," New Republic, LXXXVII (May 27, 1936), 75-76. [14]"The Sunny Side of Fascism," New Republic, LXXXVII (June 10, 1936), 131-32. This same issue of the New Republic contained a letter from Grace Lumpkin in which she took leave of Allen Tate "with genuine regret and sadness as he goes about with his butterfly net busily recapturing Southern traditions." [15]This letter was in a footnote in Bern Brandon, "Metaphysics of Reaction," Marxist Quarterly, I (January-March, 1937), 129 fn. [16]Stone, "Seward Collins and American Review," 16-17, quoting Agar. [17]Agar to Chard Powers Smith, June 30, 1936, Smith Papers (Williamstown, Massachusetts). For Agar's distributing copies of Who Owns America?, see Davidson to Tate, April 24, 1936, Tate Papers. For Agar's political hopes for the Agrarians-Distributists, see Agar to Smith, April 13, 1936, Collins Papers. [18]Collins, "Three Important Books," American Review, VII (October, 1936), 603; John Chamberlain, "Agrarianism, American Style," Saturday Review of Literature, XIV (July 25, 1936), 17; Broadus Mitchell, "'O Time in Your Flight,'" Nation, CXLII (June 24, 1936), 813-14; "To Make America Free," Commonweal, XXIV (May 8, 1936), 29-30; Crane Brinton, "Who Owns America?" Southern Review, II (Summer, 1936), 15-21. [19]Smith to Agar, April 8, 1936, Tate Papers. Smith had published a few pro-distributist essays. See, for instance, Smith, "Cartwright vs. America," Scribner's Magazine, XCI (June, 1932), 330-34. [20]The statement of principles was published as "The Agrarian Concept of Property," Modern Schoolman, XIV (November, 1936), 4-5. [21]"Minutes of Convention Held by the Committee for the Alliance of Agrarian and Distributist Groups at Nashville, Tennessee, June 4-5, 1936," Andrew Nelson Lytle Papers (Vanderbilt University). [22]Agar, "Free America," Free America, I (January, 1937), 1-2, 14-16. [23]Agar, "The Task for Conservatism," American Review, III (April, 1934), 4, 10; Agar, "Private Property or Capitalism," American Scholar, III (Autumn, 1934), 396-403. [24]New York Herald-Tribune, January 14, 1935, p. 11. [25]Agar, "But Can It Be Done?" Who Owns America? A New Declaration of Independence, eds. Herbert Agar and Allen Tate (Boston: Houghton Mifflin; 1936), 97-107; Agar, What is America? (London; Eyre and Spottiswoode, 1936), p. 218. [26]Alan McCausland, "Democracy: The Ideal and the Institution," Examiner, II (Winter, 1939), 48; Paul Sweet, "Fascism and Agrarianism," ibid., I (Spring, 1938), 189-204; E. W. Swody, Review of The Attack on Leviathan, by Donald Davidson, ibid., I, (Summer, 1938), 329-30. [27]Collins to G. R. Elliott, January 15, 1937, Collins Papers; Collins to Graham Carey, March 7, 1937, ibid. [28]Brandon, "Metaphysics of Reaction," 129-33; V. F. Calverton, "The Bankruptcy of Southern Culture," Scribner's Magazine, XCIX (May, 1936), 298. [29]Frank L. Owsley to Geoffrey Stone, May 24, 1938, Owsley Papers (Vanderbilt University). [30]John Gould Fletcher, "A 'Century of Progress'," American Review, IV (January, 1935), 382-83. [31]Davidson to Collins, December 20, 1936, Collins Papers; Tate to Agar, January 7, 1937, Tate Papers. [32]Tate to Agar, December 9, 1936, Tate Papers. [33]Lyle H. Lanier to Tate, December 8, 1936, Tate Papers; Davidson to Tate, December 20, 1936, ibid. [34]Agar to Lytle, December 16, 1936, Lytle Papers; Agar to Tate, December 22, 1936, Tate Papers; Agar to Tate, February 15, 1937, ibid.; [35]Agar to Tate, May 17, 1939, Tate Papers. [36]Stone, "Collins and American Review," 14. [37]Robert Hillyer, "Poetry's New Priesthood," Saturday Review of Literature, XXXII (June 18, 1939), 7-9, 38; Editorial, ibid., XXXII (June 11, 1949), 20-21. [38]Tate, "A Personal Statement on Fascism," Tate Papers. [39]Robert Gorham Davis, "The New Criticism and the Democratic Tradition," American Scholar, XIX (Winter, 1949-1950), 9-11. [40]Tate, et. al., "The New Criticism," American Scholar, XX (Spring, 1951), 225-29. [41]George H. Nash, The Conservative Intellectual Movement in America: Since 1945 (New York: Basic Books, 1976), xiv. [42]Louis Hartz, The Liberal Tradition in America: An Interpretation of American Political Thought Since the Revolution (New York: Harcourt, Brace, 1955); Nash, Conservative Intellectual Movement, chs. 5-8. [43]For the response of the Agrarians-Distributists to the political and social issues of the 1930's, see Edward S. Shapiro, "Decentralist Intellectuals and the New Deal," Journal of American History, LVIII (March, 1972), 938-57; Shapiro, "The Southern Agrarians and the Tennessee Valley Authority," American Quarterly, XXII (Winter, 1970), 791-806; and Shapiro, "Catholic Agrarians and the New Deal," Catholic Historical Review, in press.

# CATHOLIC AGRARIAN THOUGHT
## AND THE NEW DEAL

The study of American Catholic social and political thought during the 1930's has so far largely focused on the Catholic response to the industrial and urban problems engendered by the economic collapse of 1929. Historians have viewed the program of industrial democracy and urban reforms of Monsignor John A. Ryan and his supporters, most notably Fathers Francis J. Haas and Raymond A. McGowan, as embodying the most relevant and important aspects of Catholic social consciousness during the depression decade. As a result, other elements within American Catholicism with differing political and economic orientations have been slighted.[1]

Especially is this true of the Catholic rural life movement which, during the Roosevelt era, articulated a comprehensive and coherent reform program. While Ryan and his colleagues at the Catholic University of America were chiefly concerned with the difficulties of the urban working class, the Catholic ruralists were mainly interested in the tribulations of rural America, and their analysis of the crisis facing the United States differed significantly from that of the "social democratic" wing of American Catholicism.[2] Although the American

---

[1] David J. O'Brien, *American Catholics and Social Reform: The New Deal Years* (New York, 1968), pp. 97, 121; Aaron I. Abell (ed.), *American Catholic Thought on Social Questions* (Indianapolis, 1968), pp. xv, xxv, xlvii; Neil Betten, "Social Catholicism and the Emergence of Catholic Radicalism in America," *Journal of Human Relations*, XVIII (Winter, 1970), 710 ff.; Francis L. Broderick, *Right Reverend New Dealer: John A. Ryan* (New York, 1963), pp. 277-279; George Q. Flynn, *American Catholics and the Roosevelt Presidency, 1932-1936* (Lexington, Kentucky, 1968), p. 7.

[2] It is characteristic that O'Brien's book *American Catholics and Social Reform*, the finest analysis of American Catholic social thought during the 1930's, contains a twenty-nine-page chapter devoted to Ryan while the index contains only one reference to Father Edgar Schmiedeler, O.S.B., Executive Secretary of the National Catholic Rural Life Conference from 1931 to 1934 and head of the Rural Life Bureau of the Social Action Department of the National Catholic Welfare Conference during the 1930's.

Catholic rural movement was a product of uniquely American conditions, it had counterparts in many European countries, particularly in Great Britain where Eric Gill, Father Vincent McNabb, G. K. Chesterton, and Hilaire Belloc advocated a "distributist" society based on the widespread distribution of property, the revival of agriculture, and the restoration of the artisan to his previous position of importance.[3]

The message of the Catholic rural movement was spread by, among others, the membership of the National Catholic Rural Life Conference, many midwestern Benedictine monks, especially those of St. John's Abbey in Collegeville, Minnesota, and even by elements within the Catholic Worker movement. Claiming to represent the approximately twenty-five per cent of America's Catholics who lived in rural areas during the 1930's, the Catholic agrarians were especially influential in the Midwest, where the bulk of Catholic farmers lived. Not only did the Rural Life Bureau of the Social Action Department of the National Catholic Welfare Conference (NCWC), which was headed by a leading Catholic ruralist, influence the NCWC's position on agriculture, but also several Catholic rural leaders, such as Aloisius J. Muench and Edwin V. O'Hara, were prominent bishops and helped to shape the thinking of the Church's hierarchy regarding rural matters. In addition, Catholic agrarians through an avalanche of books and articles in the Catholic press strongly argued that the future welfare of both the American Church and the nation depended primarily upon a strengthening of the nation's rural economy and culture, and they disseminated a reform program which they claimed most accurately reflected the social teachings of the popes.

The differences between the urban and rural wings of American Catholic social thought during the 1930's were of degree rather than of kind. Both groups supported the establishment of a vocationally organized society along the lines proposed by Popes Leo XIII and Pius XI. The ruralists, for their part, recognized the need to succor the urban victims of the economic crisis through unemployment compensation, minimum wage legislation, and public works. The urbanists, on the other hand, realized the necessity of increasing farm income, diminishing farm tenancy, and broadening the ownership of productive property. Where the ruralists differed from the urbanists was in their greater interest in agrarian than in industrial problems,

[3] For English Catholic "distributist" thought, see Hilaire Belloc, *The Restoration of Property* (New York, 1936).

in their belief that large-scale industrialization and large cities should gradually be reduced, in the absolute priority they placed on the widespread distribution of property, in their advocacy of the "agrarian myth," and in their interpretation of the papal encyclicals *Rerum Novarum* and *Quadragesimo Anno*.[4]

Whereas the Catholic advocates of industrial democracy naturally focused on those parts of the two encyclicals stressing the obligations of capital toward labor, the right of workers to organize their own unions, and the maintenance of a just social order through state intervention, the Catholic ruralists emphasized statements in the encyclicals regarding the sanctity of private property, the danger in the growth of a dispossessed rural proletariat, and the desirability of increasing the number of independent farmers. For the Catholic ruralists the greatest evil of modern capitalism was the proletarianization of large sectors of the population and the transformation of erstwhile property owners, such as shopkeepers and especially farmers, into wage earners, agricultural workers, and farm tenants. They maintained that only the widespread distribution of property, particularly of land, could alleviate the alienation, uprootedness, and insecurity of the American urban and rural proletariat, and they found in *Rerum Novarum* and *Quadragesimo Anno* a model for a middle-class society of property owners. The papal pronouncement most frequently quoted by American Catholic ruralists was Leo XIII's argument in *Rerum Novarum* that,

> If working people can be encouraged to look forward to obtaining a share in the land, the result will be that the gulf between vast wealth and deep poverty will be bridged over, and the two orders will be brought nearer together. . . . Men always work harder and more readily when they work on that which is their own; nay, they learn to love the very soil which yields in response to the labor of their hands, not only food to eat, but an abundance of the good things for themselves and those that are dear to them.[5]

Catholic ruralists also heartily approved of the political "middle-way" of Leo XIII and Pius XI and the popes' condemnation of both political inaction in the face of social misery and excessive centralization of governmental powers. Permanent prosperity and political

---

[4] O'Brien, *op. cit.*, pp. 129-130; Flynn, *op. cit.*, pp. 238-239; R. A. McGowan, Review of *Who Owns America? A New Declaration of Independence*, ed. Herbert Agar and Allen Tate, *Commonweal*, XXIV (June 12, 1936), 191-193.

[5] *Five Great Encyclicals* (New York, 1939), pp. 22-23.

freedom could be achieved, the agrarians argued, only through the economic independence resulting from the widespread distribution of productive property, and not through socialism with its elimination of private property and its centralization of economic and political authority.[6]

In addition to their commitment to papal social teachings, American Catholic ruralists were also fervent supporters of Jeffersonian agrarianism. Only in an agrarian society, they claimed, were private property, economic democracy, and political freedom secure. Fully accepting the "agrarian myth" and the superiority of rural to urban life, they argued that only in the countryside could be found the "initiative, prudence, thrift, courage, and other priceless virtues" which make for "the promotion of simple but wholesome and rugged living."[7] "It seems that Christ Himself wished to emphasize the dignity" of agriculture, a Wisconsin priest incongruously named Urban Baer wrote. "For He was born . . . on the very land itself, in an old stable, surrounded by beasts of burden, and first visited by shepherds who were the farmers of those days. Our Lord's parables and teachings abound with references to the soil. . . . Since Christ taught so much of things pertaining to the land how pardonably proud should not the farmer be of his calling and of his trust."[8]

American Catholic agrarians contended not only that a stronger countryside was beneficial to the entire nation, but also that the augmenting of the Catholic rural population would be of particular value to the Church in its struggle for survival in a largely Protestant country. The Catholic rural life movement had originally been established because of the fears of the Reverend Edwin V. O'Hara and others that the predominantly urban character of American Catholicism was a threat to the Church. The unnatural mechanistic urban environment was, they emphasized, not conducive to the perpetuation of religious values and practices among the three-fourths of American Catholics who happened to be urban. Furthermore, Catholic rural advocates were extremely troubled by the impact of the city upon the

[6] John C. Rawe and Luigi G. Ligutti, *Rural Roads to Security: America's Third Struggle for Freedom* (Milwaukee, 1940).

[7] Aloisius J. Muench, "Introduction," in *Manifesto on Rural Life* (Milwaukee, 1939), p. vi.

[8] Urban Baer, *Farmers of Tomorrow* (Sparta, Wisconsin, 1939), p. 39. See also J. M. Campbell, "In the Country," *Commonweal*, XV (February 3, 1932), 378-380, and Virgil Michel, "Agriculture and Reconstruction," *Commonweal*, XXIX (January 13, 1939), 317-318.

family, and especially on its birth rate. They were impressed by statistics showing that the urban birth rate was appreciably smaller than the rural birth rate. This meant that, since American Protestantism was still largely rural, the percentage of Americans who were Catholic would gradually decline unless the demographic character of the Church was drastically changed now that immigration of Catholics from Europe had practically ceased.[9]

The Catholic rural enthusiasts viewed recent American history as a falling away from the golden age of the pre-Civil War period when agriculture and small business predominated, property was widely distributed, and Americans were not beholden to business tycoons, labor bosses, or government bureaucrats. They blamed the triumph of big business in the post-bellum period for the recent social and economic degradation of large segments of the population, the series of depressions which were slowly dispossessing farmers and small businessmen, the exploitation of the countryside by the city, the growth of an arrogant financial plutocracy, the increasing intensity of class conflict, and the growing popularity of radical ideologies. They were convinced that, as a result of the 1929 depression, the United States stood at a decisive point in its history.[10]

One possibility was that the country would continue drifting into complete plutocratic control. A more likely alternative was that Americans, thoroughly disillusioned with big business and high finance, would look toward economic and political collectivism for deliverance from their economic misery. In contrast to the plutocracy of the right and the socialism of the left, the agrarians offered a third option having as its basis the revival of traditional American beliefs in the importance of yeoman farming, the desirability of widespread distribution of property, and the fear of centralized economic and political power. "Governmental collectivism is not a cure for the collectivism of private joint-stock corporations and their destructive social economy," the Jesuit John C. Rawe wrote, "There is but *one*

[9] Muench, "The Catholic Church and Rural Welfare," *Catholic Rural Life Objectives*, III (1937), 17; Edwin V. O'Hara, *The Church and the Country Community* (New York, 1927), p. 71; Edgar Schmiedeler, *The Threat of American Decline* (Washington, D.C., n.d.); Robert D. Cross, "The Changing Image of the City Among American Catholics," *Catholic Historical Review*, XLVIII (April, 1962), 38-43; Raymond Philip Witte, *Twenty-Five Years of Crusading: A History of the National Catholic Rural Life Conference* (Des Moines, 1948).

[10] Baer, *op. cit.*, ch. iv; James A. Byrnes, "A Manifesto on Rural Life," *American Catholic Sociological Review*, I (March, 1940), 29-31.

solution for this nation and that is a new Declaration of Independence and a return to the Jeffersonian concept of the Constitution through widespread ownership and co-operation under a general freehold tenure of property."[11]

The Catholic agrarians contended that meaningful economic recovery and permanent prosperity could not occur without rectifying the economic imbalance between the countryside and the cities and this would require extensive political reforms including lower tariffs, the elimination of monopolies, and significant aid for farmers. "Will we use the years immediately ahead to stem the persistent drift downward," Father Edgar Schmiedeler, head of the Rural Life Bureau, pondered in 1935, "or will we blithely and unconcernedly drift on until actual decline has come upon us?"[12]

Catholic ruralists did not believe the Republican Party, which had been controlled for decades by northern financiers and industrialists, would aid farmers and small-businessmen. Instead they supported the election of Franklin D. Roosevelt in 1932, and hoped that the New Deal would reverse the tendency toward the concentration of economic power and the dispossession of the agrarian class. They were particularly pleased by statements made by Roosevelt during the campaign favoring an increase in farm income, especially his speech on September 14, 1932, at Topeka, Kansas, approving in broad outlines the domestic allotment proposal. The board of directors of the National Catholic Rural Life Conference in October, 1932, passed a resolution supporting domestic allotment as a desirable means for raising farm income. This, they maintained, would help restore economic balance between the country and city and would conform to Pius XI's plea in *Quadragesimo Anno* for "a reasonable relationship between the prices obtained for the products of the various economic groups, agrarian, industrial, etc."[13] Schmiedeler, however, voiced a caveat which would become increasingly prominent as the New Deal farm program unfolded. Domestic allotment, he declared, "may play the part of a much needed 'shot in the arm,' but it is not a fundamental remedy for the economic situation. It is high time that far more

[11] John C. Rawe, "Agriculture and the Property State," *Who Owns America?* pp. 49-50.

[12] Schmiedeler, "The Shadow of American Decline," *Homiletic and Pastoral Review*, XXXVI (October, 1935), 40.

[13] O'Hara, "Concern of the Church in the Rural Problem," *Catholic Action*, XIV (November, 1932), 4; O'Hara, "Voluntary Domestic Allotment Plan," *Catholic World*, CXXXVI (March, 1933), 642-646; Flynn, *op. cit.*, p. 67.

effective steps be taken in behalf of the American farmer, for if he be dispossessed, the nation will pay dearly in the loss of its staunch and sturdy yeomanry, in the loss of the choicest fruits of its fields."[14]

The keystone of the early New Deal's farm program was the 1933 Agricultural Adjustment Act which provided for government payments to farmers who agreed to restrict the production of such crops as wheat, cotton, and tobacco. The payments to the farmers were supposed to restore "parity" between the prices of farm products and industrial goods. The Catholic agrarians generally welcomed the AAA since it would introduce "balance" into the economy by providing agriculture the equivalent of the protective tariff which industry had long enjoyed. The AAA, Schmiedeler declared, was "a charter of economic equality with the city."[15] The agrarians also welcomed the fact that the administration of the AAA was supposed to be on a decentralized and democratic basis. And yet, despite the fact that the AAA evidently had temporarily increased farm income and had checked the wave of despair and pessimism which had swept through the countryside during the early 1930's, many Catholic agrarians were profoundly disturbed by its operations and implications.[16]

They feared that, if the benefit payments of the AAA were to become permanent aspects of federal agricultural policy, the farmers would become regimented, collectivized, and wards of a bloated political bureaucracy. They were also concerned that the philosophy of scarcity embodied in the AAA defeated the very purpose of economic activity which, according to Catholic social principles, was the providing of goods and services for as large a number of persons as possible. Some of the agrarians also feared that the New Dealers were more committed to augmenting the income of a diminishing number of farmers than to increasing the size of the farm population. They realized that one of the effects of the AAA had been to push many marginal farmers off the land. Was there any future for family farming, they asked, when the government had as its goal a reduction in the number of acres under cultivation?[17] The New Deal farm experts, Rawe complained, "use the terminology of city-bred industrial eco-

[14] Schmiedeler, *Why Rural Life* (National Catholic Welfare Conference, 1933), p. 15.

[15] Quoted in "Rural Life Conference Begins Second Decade of Rural Catholic Action," *Catholic Action*, XV (November, 1933), 5.

[16] Raymond J. Miller, "The 'Quadragesimo Anno' and the Reconstruction of Agriculture," *Catholic Rural Life Objections*, II (1936), 52-53; Flynn, *op. cit.*, pp. 71-72.

[17] Frederick P. Kenkel to L. P. Herron, September 30, 1933, Kenkel Papers, Uni-

nomists and neglect to emphasize the human values of an agrarian system. They would control production in the field in the same way as in the factory, establish homesteads only by way of temporary relief and allow the further capitalization of joint stock interests in extensive land holdings. Meanwhile we cannot safely say whether their philosophy is industrial or agrarian."[18] The AAA benefit payments had undoubtedly improved the cash income of some farmers, but, the agrarians asked, had they freed farmers from the exactions of the commercial economy? "Is it not time for us as a nation" to consider, asked Father W. Howard Bishop in his presidential address to the National Catholic Rural Life Conference in 1934, "long-range programs of a permanent nature. . . ?"[19]

The basic problem with the AAA, according to the agrarians, was that it was only at best a temporary expedient for dealing with farm surpluses and the decline in farm income, and that it ignored the most important of all farm problems, the rapid increase in farm tenancy, sharecropping, and dispossession. Two years after the passage of the AAA Bishop O'Hara declared that, "Our most pressing need is a public policy that will transform the family-farm operator into a farm owner instead of transforming owners into tenants or day laborers on a corporation farm."[20]

Other aspects of the early New Deal agricultural program held out more hope for the Catholic ruralists for an agrarian restoration. They particularly welcomed the Farm Credit Administration (FCA) which was empowered to refinance farm mortgages and to establish a system of regional banks to make mortgage, production, and marketing loans and to provide credits to agricultural co-operatives. The FCA, they anticipated, would undoubtedly help stem the tide of farm foreclosures as well as encouraging the farmers' efforts to help themselves through the establishing of co-operatives. As Schmiedeler noted, the FCA "has done an exceptional piece of work for the farmer." But

---

versity of Notre Dame Archives; *Manifesto on Rural Life*, p. 64; Vincent J. Ryan, "State and Reconstruction," *Catholic Rural Life Objectives*, IV (1944), 35; John Thomas and James McShane, "Farmers Must Reform Methods of Farming," *Catholic Rural Life Bulletin*, IV (November 20, 1941), 103, 106; Flynn, *op. cit.*, p. 70.

[18] Rawe, "Agrarianism: The Basis for a Better Life," *American Review*, VI (December, 1935), 181.

[19] W. Howard Bishop, "Presidential Address," National Catholic Rural Life Conference, *Proceedings of Twelfth Annual Convention* (St. Paul, 1934), pp. 28, 31-32.

[20] O'Hara, "A Spiritual and Material Mission to Rural America," *Catholic Rural Life Objectives*, I (1935), 6.

while thankful for the FCA, the Catholic agrarians believed that its activities were largely "palliative" and that something more fundamental was required. Thus the delegates to the 1934 convention of the National Catholic Rural Life Conference, while praising the Roosevelt administration's efforts to bring debt relief to the farmer, resolved that,

> It is time the government should turn the main force of its depression activities toward the permanent rehabilitation on the land of as large a portion of the unemployed in our cities, and of the several types of stranded, tenant farmers in the country as have the desire and ability to settle permanently on small farms which they will come to own by easy annual payments at a low rate of interest over a period of years.[21]

Steps had been taken along these lines in 1933 with the creation of the Subsistence Homestead Division in the Department of the Interior and the Rural Rehabilitation Division in the Federal Emergency Relief Administration, and in 1935 with the establishment of the Resettlement Administration. These agencies financed subsistence homesteads, the resettlement and rehabilitation of poverty-stricken farmers, and the retirement of submarginal land, and they embodied the back-to-the-land strain in the early New Deal. Catholic agrarians approved of the work of these New Deal agencies, but believed it to be too tentative and limited to deal in a meaningful way with the problems of farm tenancy and rural poverty. They were heartened, however, in 1935 by indications that the government was finally on the verge of launching a comprehensive attack on agrarian dispossession and destitution.[22]

In that year Senator John H. Bankhead of Alabama introduced a bill to help tenants, sharecroppers, and farm laborers become independent farmers by providing them one billion dollars in low-interest loans for the purchase of land, farm implements, and stock. For the Catholic agrarians this was unquestionably the most important piece of legislation presented during the 1930's. Not only was it the only

---

[21] Schmiedeler, "A Review of the Year," *Proceedings of Twelfth Annual Convention*, pp. 36-37; "1934 Convention Resolutions," *ibid.*, p. 23. See also Baer, *Farmers of Tomorrow*, p. 124, and John A. Kavanaugh, "Credit Relief for the American Farmer," *Catholic Rural Life Bulletin*, I (May 20, 1938), 10.

[22] Arthur M. Schlesinger, Jr., *The Coming of the New Deal* (Boston, 1959), pp. 361-381; Paul K. Conkin, *Tomorrow a New World: The New Deal Community Program* (Ithaca, New York, 1959); Schmiedeler, "The Rochester Rural Life Meeting," *Catholic Action*, XVII (December, 1935), 25; Raymond P. Duggan, *A Federal Resettlement Project: Granger Homesteads* (Washington, D.C., 1937).

type of alternative they could envisage to continued urban unemployment, greater expenditures for relief payments, and growing dependence of the destitute upon the government, but it also perfectly harmonized with papal statements on the desirability of the widespread ownership of land, especially Leo XIII's assertion that the law "should favor ownership, and its policy should be to induce as many people as possible to become owners." And yet when the Bankhead proposal became law in 1937 and the Farm Security Administration (FSA) was created to administer it, the agrarians were deeply disappointed. Its appropriations had been so whittled down that for its first two years it could spend only thirty-five million dollars. As a result, the FSA in its early years was able to provide loans to only two per cent of the nation's tenants. Schmiedeler expressed the dominant sentiment among the agrarians when he described the monies set aside for the FSA as "nothing less than ridiculous."[23]

Thus by the end of the 1930's the Catholic agrarians were chagrined by the course the New Deal agricultural program had taken. Commendable as the New Deal measures were, wrote Father Baer, "they are at best palliatives. They are not far reaching enough."[24] The New Deal had failed to realize that tinkering with the existing agricultural economy was not enough and that an all-encompassing campaign against rural poverty and insecurity of tenure was still desperately needed. The New Deal farm program "is an effort to float a rotting ship," complained Emerson Hynes of St. John's University of Minnesota in 1940. "It does not meet the fundamental problem."[25] Some of the agrarians attributed the New Deal's failings to its viewing agriculture as simply another industry in need of help, rather than as a distinct way of life with its own values. As Professor Willis D. Nutting of the University of Notre Dame wrote, although the New

---

[23] *Five Great Encyclicals*, p. 22; Schmiedeler, *Our Rural Proletariat* (New York, 1939), pp. 22-25; James A. Byrnes, "Foreword," *Catholic Rural Life Objectives*, II (1936), 3-6; "In Support of the Bankhead Bill," *Commonweal*, XXI (April 26, 1935), 719-721; *Manifesto on Rural Life*, pp. 10-12; John LaFarge, "Catholic Agrarians Swing Into Action," *America*, LVI (November 14, 1936), 130; Luigi G. Ligutti, "What's Wrong With Farmers," *America*, LXIX (April 24, 1943), 67; Vincent J. Ryan, "A Statement by the President," *Catholic Rural Life Bulletin*, III (November 20, 1940), 18; Witte, *op. cit.*, pp. 218-219; Sidney Baldwin, *Poverty and Politics: The Rise and Decline of the Farm Security Administration* (Chapel Hill, North Carolina, 1968), pp. 145-148; Flynn, *op. cit.*, pp. 74-75.

[24] Baer, *Farmers of Tomorrow*, p. 140.

[25] Emerson Hynes, "Agriculture in the Next Decade," *Catholic Rural Life Bulletin*, III (February 20, 1940), 4-5.

Deal farm programs might raise the farmer's standard of living and provide him with more creidt, "they *will not* give him independence, economic or otherwise. They *will not* build a real rural culture."[26] Father Rawe believed that the mistakes of the New Deal's farm policies could be traced to the New Dealers' excessively commercial and urban perspective. "We elect to pay a subsidy for reduction of crops, and we even think that several years of widespread drought fits in nicely in the commercial program of agricultural scarcity," he lamented. "Somehow we fail to teach land use for subsistence, an agrarian economy with its sane production program for home requirements first, enabling each farm in a greater or less degree to escape commercial exploitation in the food industries."[27]

The Catholic agrarians were correct in recognizing the gulf separating them from the New Deal. While certain New Dealers, most notably the President himself, paid tribute to the Jeffersonian ideal, the administration was largely concerned with raising the income and morale of large commercial farmers. Reforming the social and economic structure of the countryside and reversing what seemed to be an inevitable tendency toward larger and larger farm units using modern technology and factory methods of production, appeared to most New Deal farm bureaucrats to be unrealistic, if not anachronistic.

The Catholic agrarians' major criterion for evaluating the New Deal's nonagricultural programs was the degree to which they encouraged the widespread distribution of property and undermined the power of high finance and big business, while avoiding government paternalism. They did not wish to exchange the economic collectivism of plutocracy for the political collectivism of Washington, but they were willing to contemplate a greater temporary role for the federal government if it would result in a more equitable distribution of property and the elimination of monopolies, if it would encourage demographic decentralization, if it would strengthen the middle class, and if it would foster voluntary actions by various private groups. They naturally looked to the industrial guild system advocated by

[26] Willis D. Nutting, "Foundations of a Rural Christian Culture," *Catholic Rural Life Bulletin*, II (February 20, 1939), 1-2.

[27] Rawe, "Life, Liberty and the Pursuit of Happiness in Agriculture," A Paper Presented to the National Catholic Rural Life Conference (St. Paul, 1936), pp. 39-40; see also Joseph H. Fichter, "Is Our Form of Land Tenure Best Fitted for Modern Needs?" *America*, LXI (November 1, 1941), 96.

Leo XIII and Pius XI as a means of aiding the industrial victims of the depression. Catholic agrarians believed that guilds along with producer and consumer co-operatives and credit unions were the type of self-help organizations the New Deal should assist if the nation was to avoid the tyranny of Wall Street and the dictatorship of big government.[28]

The National Industrial Recovery Act of 1933, for instance, was initially welcomed as a step toward the vocational organization of American industry. Very shortly, however, many agrarians became disenchanted with it because of fears that the act was causing an inordinate growth of bureaucracy and an excessive centralization of power in Washington. This "wielding of the big stick by a sort of benevolent dictatorship," the membership of the Central Verein claimed, conflicted with papal teachings. In addition, some agrarians feared the NIRA's major effect would be the bolstering of the existing economic structure, with the middle class continuing to be pushed to the wall.[29]

As far as the New Deal's relief and social security legislation were concerned, the Catholic agrarians recognized the need for government assistance to the unemployed, the aged, and the dependent. But they also claimed that this should be supplemented by government programs encouraging the destitute to become economically self-sufficient, thereby eliminating the necessity for dependence on politicians. As Father Rawe exclaimed, New Deal bureaucrats were quite generous with "doles, taxes, borrowed money, charitable donations, but they had very little knowledge of teaching people to help themselves."[30] Professor Nutting agreed. While recognizing that there existed "innumerable cases of dire poverty and cruel exploitation which

---

[28] Aloisius J. Muench, *The New Social Order* (Lenten Pastoral, 1941), pp. 11-18; Colman J. Barry, *American Nuncio, Cardinal Aloisius Muench* (Collegeville, Minnesota, 1969), p. 45; John LaFarge, "The Agrarian Crisis and the Catholic Church," *Catholic Rural Life Objectives*, III (1937), 24; Virgil Michel, *Christian Social Reconstruction: Some Fundamentals of the Quadragesimo Anno* (Milwaukee, 1937), pp. 76-90.

[29] Catholic Central-Verein of America, *Official Report of the 78th General Convention* (St. Paul, 1933), pp. 91-93; LaFarge, "Agriculture and Vocation," *Commonweal*, XXVIII (July 1, 1938), 262; Muench, "Unemployment, Old Age, and Health Insurance," *Homiletic and Pastoral Review*, XXXV (June, 1935), 980; Schmiedeler, "Beyond the NRA," *Commonweal*, XVIII (September 22, 1933), 485.

[30] Rawe, "Agriculture: An Airplane Survey," *Catholic Rural Life Bulletin*, III (February 20, 1940), 1.

must be remedied immediately by first aid measures," he also argued that "these measures must not be thought to be a cure for the real ills of society."[31] Similarly, while the agrarians believed the government must step in and regulate the relations between capital and labor, the real solution to the "labor problem" was the elimination of the propertyless proletariat through the distribution of property. Legislation such as the Fair Labor Standards Act of 1938 establishing minimum wage and maximum hour standards merely dealt with the symptoms of the American crisis. The United States government, Father Leo R. Ward wrote, "cannot rescue and finally redeem a large unemployed and pauperized minority; the best a government can do is to make this minority officially pauper."[32]

The attitude of the agrarians toward the New Deal's social reforms is clearly brought out by their response to the National Housing (Wagner-Steagall) Act of 1937. While favoring the amelioration of urban living conditions, they contended that the building of public housing projects in the large cities inhibited the movement of population from urban to rural areas and were thus "subsidies to maintain congestion." Furthermore, urban public housing fostered small families, weakened property ownership, and encouraged the perpetuation of slums. Such housing would not appeal to any "self-reliant American families" desiring to preserve their liberty and security "since they do not give any opportunity, even in a small degree, for any measure of economic self-sufficiency through family enterprise and cooperation."[33]

A more sensible method of providing housing than the renting of urban apartments from the government would be for Washington to subsidize the construction of houses in rural areas where the poor could actually become landowners and even engage in part-time farming. Only this type of housing program would strengthen the American family and invigorate the nation's social fabric. As Rawe maintained, "every housing program should be a homestead program. Nothing prevents the successful combination of industrial wage earn-

---

[31] Nutting, *Reclamation of Independence* (Nevada City, California, 1947), pp. 60-61.

[32] Leo R. Ward, "Land. Decentralization and Democracy: Notes on Recent Publications," *Review of Politics*, 1 (October, 1939), 477-478. See also Ligutti, *For This We Stand* (Des Moines, 1946), p. 1, and Rawe and Ligutti, *Rural Roads to Security*, pp. 11, 28.

[33] Rawe and Ligutti, *Rural Roads to Security*, pp. 12, 109-111.

ing and part-time farming today save a certain spirit of narrow urban industrialism . . . and a want of democratic vision."[34]

As the 1930's progressed the Catholic agrarians increasingly concluded that the New Deal had not brought the United States significantly closer to being a propertied society. The status of big business and high finance had been left relatively undisturbed. The high tariff system had been modified to some extent by the various reciprocal tariff agreements, but there had not been a meaningful antitrust campaign and the discriminatory railroad freight rate schedules which favored the industrialized and urbanized Northeast at the expense of the South and West had been untouched. The New Deal agencies were "perhaps a trifle more effective and some of the more obvious abuses and the more intolerable injustices were checked," Father Schmiedeler wrote. "But all in all, the framework of the system remained."[35]

That the New Deal had been so ineffective in decentralizing property was seen as particularly unfortunate in view of the fact that the 1930's had experienced a vast increase in Washington's power. Events in Europe had made the Catholic agrarians quite sensitive to political centralization, and by the end of the decade they were virtually unanimous in condemning the paternalism and regimentation which they claimed had been fostered by the Roosevelt administration. Thus Bishop Muench of Fargo, one of the staunchest Catholic agrarian defenders of the New Deal, warned in 1941 that "governmental control and regimentation are winding their octupus [sic] tentacles tighter and tighter around every phase of our national life. American democracy is developing into totalitarian democracy."[36] The alternative, according to Fathers Rawe and Luigi G. Ligutti, was learning "to solve our own economic problems independent of government regimentation. Government regimentation has opened the way to much graft and exploitation, excessive taxation and gen-

[34] Rawe, "The Modern Homestead: A Vital Economic Institution," *Modern Schoolman*, XV (January, 1938), 34-35. See also George Weller, "Decentralized City Homesteads," *Commonweal*, XXVIII (July 22, 1938), 341-344.

[35] Schmiedeler, "A Silent Revolution," *Catholic World*, CXLIII (June, 1936), 283. See also Michel, "Agriculture and Reconstruction," p. 317; Rawe, "Agrarianism: Basis for a Better Life," pp. 176-189; Vincent J. Ryan, "State and Reconstruction," *Catholic Rural Life Objectives*, IV (1944), 33; *Rural Life in a Peaceful World* (Des Moines, 1944), p. 10.

[36] Muench, "Leadership for the New America," *Catholic Mind*, XXXIX (October 8, 1941), 3.

eral loss of true liberty." They queried whether there was not "a better program for producing a desirable society than that which centralizes every aspect of life under the domination of remote economic planners and public officials?"[37]

The agrarians attributed the failure of the New Deal to divest plutocracy of its power partially to the fact that, not being sufficiently permeated with decentralist and agrarian principles, it could not envisage an economic and social structure much different from the existing one. The government, Father Rawe complained, "forgetting its agrarian past, continues to protect an all too privileged industrial class and sinks its hopes deeper and deeper in stocks and bonds, industrial giants, falsified values, and quack nostrums."[38] While the Catholic agrarians had stressed the need for radical measures in behalf of the middle class, the New Dealers had temporized and been satisfied with achieving social justice within the existing system. "The liberals," Nutting wrote, "have done good first aid work but they have made no progress in effecting a cure of social ills."[39] The basic problem with the New Deal, the Catholic agrarians asserted, was that it was seemingly more interested in economic recovery than with fundamental economic and social reform along agrarian and decentralist lines.[40]

The disillusionment of the Catholic agrarians with the halfway measures of the New Deal was inevitable considering that, while the New Dealers had to operate in a pragmatic political environment in which a premium was placed on compromise and improvisation, the agrarians could evaluate the New Deal on the basis of how closely it approximated their Catholic and Jeffersonian social ideology. What for the Roosevelt officials was politically necessary, was for the agrarians inconsistency, superficiality, and an overemphasis on urban and industrial problems at the expense of historic American principles.

---

[37] Rawe and Ligutti, *Rural Roads to Security*, pp. 30, 199-202, 262. See also Baer, *Farmers of Tomorrow*, pp. 186-187, 195-196; J. M. Campbell, "Wanted: Catholic Leaders," *Christian Front*, II (December, 1937), 173-174; *Manifesto on Rural Life*, p. 67; Nutting, "The Road Back to Freedom," *Ave Maria*, XLIX (February 11, 1939), 163-164.

[38] Rawe, "Agrarianism: Basis for a Better Life," p. 188.

[39] Nutting, *Reclamation of Independence*, pp. 175-176.

[40] "To Make America Free," *Commonweal*, XXIV (May 8, 1936), 30; Muench, "Agrarianism in the Christian Social Order," *Catholic Rural Life Bureau*, I (May 20, 1938), 2-3; Rawe and Ligutti, *Rural Roads to Security*, p. 283; Leo R. Ward, "The Social Significance of Cooperation," *Review of Politics*, III (October, 1941), 448-449.

While the agrarians had serious misgivings about the New Deal, they certainly were not economic "conservatives." They, in fact, favored more radical economic and social reforms and were more opposed to big business than the "liberals" of the Catholic University of America.[41]

For most American historians John A. Ryan has virtually personified American Catholic social consciousness during the 1930's. While unable to accept Ryan's claim that "the only adequate and effective leadership both in education and in social problems that exist in this country derives from the Catholic University,"[42] still they have tended to view the "social democratic" aspect of Catholic social thought as its most significant and prominent element during the depression decade. David J. O'Brien, for instance, has argued that during the 1930's "Catholic social actions leaders were preoccupied with labor problems."[43] The sympathy for and interest in the collectivist and urban wing of Catholic social thought by modern Catholic historians is virtually inevitable since most are products of a working class, urban culture. Conversely, they tend to view the agrarian and decentralist side of Catholic social thought as anachronistic and reactionary.

The danger in writing American Catholic intellectual history from an almost exclusively "liberal" and "social welfare" perspective is twofold. Not only is Catholic social thought unduly simplified, and hence distorted, but also the value judgments lying behind the writing of such history often go unrecognized. Indeed, one can make a case that in some respects the Catholic proponents of demographic, economic, and political decentralization were more in the mainstream of American history and more perspicacious than their collectivist coreligionists.

The Catholic agrarians, for example, were not wrong in affirming the continuing validity of the "agrarian myth." Well before the onset of the Great Depression the growth of America's largest cities had slowed down and there had begun the trek to the suburbs, perhaps the most important social development in contemporary America. Al-

[41] For analyses of other decentralist and agrarian intellectuals of the 1930's, see Edward S. Shapiro, "Decentralist Intellectuals and the New Deal," *Journal of American History*, LVIII (March, 1972), 938-957, and *idem*, "The Southern Agrarians and the Tennessee Valley Authority," *American Quarterly*, XXII (Winter, 1970), 791-806.

[42] Quoted in Broderick, *op. cit.*, pp. 242-243.

[43] O'Brien, *op. cit.*, pp. vii, 97.

though a response to many social and economic factors, suburbia has reflected the continuing commitment of most Americans to an updated "agrarian myth" and to the thesis that cities are nice places to visit but not to inhabit. Nor were the Catholic agrarians unperceptive in questioning the permanent effects of urban and industrial reforms. Not only has the social welfare and regulatory legislation of the 1930's and 1960's vastly increased the federal bureaucracy, but it has become increasingly clear that much of this legislation not only failed to deliver on its promises but was, in fact, counterproductive. Thus it should be comforting for historians of American social reform, and particularly of American Catholic social thought, to know that the Church's heritage of social concern dating from the 1930's contains other elements besides that of "liberalism," especially at a time when the word "liberal" has fallen on such hard times.

# THE CATHOLIC RURAL LIFE MOVEMENT AND THE NEW DEAL FARM PROGRAM

Although American Roman Catholics in the 1930s were primarily urban and their most prominent spokesmen on social matters were largely concerned with alleviating the plight of the urban working class, there was also a significant Catholic rural population which looked to the Catholic rural life movement and especially to its two most important organizations, the National Catholic Rural Life Conference and the Rural Life Bureau of the Social Action Department of the National Catholic Welfare Conference, for direction on social and political issues during the New Deal era. During the depression decade leaders of the Catholic rural life movement formulated an agrarian program embodying Catholic social principles which provided a standard for evaluating the agricultural policies of the Roosevelt administration. Four factors were of particular importance in determining the shape of this program—the pessimism of Catholic rural leaders regarding the future of American Catholicism; the social teachings of the popes, especially those of Leo XIII and Pius XI in the encyclicals *Rerum Novarum* and *Quadragesimo Anno;* the impact of the "agrarian myth" on American Catholic rural leaders; and the desperate condition of agriculture during the 1930s.[1]

The NCRLC had been founded in 1923 by Fr. Edwin V. O'Hara in large part due to the fears of rural Catholic leaders that the Church's future in the United States was very bleak because of its overwhelming urban character. Impressed by statistics pointing out the great disparity between American urban and rural birth rates and the inability of cities to grow without migration from rural areas, and horrified by the widespread use of birth control techniques among urban Catholics, they concluded that the concentration of Catholics in the large metropolises would lead inevitably to a declining Catholic birth rate and a shrinkage in the percentage of Americans who were Catholic. Profoundly disturbed by these indications of the gradual demographic suicide of American Catholicism, the NCRLC encouraged a variety of social, economic and religious activities in order to make rural life more attractive so that Catholics, particularly the youth, would not desert the countryside. The emphasis Catholic leaders had always attached to increasing the Catholic population had assumed greater importance during the 1920s because of increasing anti-Catholic sentiment as evidenced by the popularity of the Ku Klux Klan and the numerous political and legal attacks on Catholic parochial schools. Feeling beleaguered because of their minority status, Catholic ruralists anticipated the future with dread. "Cities kill," exclaimed Msgr. Luigi G. Ligutti, the executive secretary of the NCRLC, to a Catholic audience. He predicted that, without a major change in the distribution of American Catholics, they would be increasingly afflicted with economic and biological "proletarianism." Catholic ruralists frequently attacked the urban orientation of the American hierarchy. "To build for magnificence only in the city, and forget the Church in the country district," Fr. Joseph M. Campbell warned, "will be to erect monuments of a people that will in time be dead and gone." And Edwin V. O'Hara, the future Bishop of Great Falls, Montana and Kansas City, Missouri, argued that "the future will be with the Church that ministers to the rural population."[2]

---

[2] Luigi G. Ligutti "Cities Kill" *Commonweal* 32 (2 August 1940) 300-301; Joseph M. Campbell "In the Country" *Commonweal* 15 (3 February 1932) 378-380; Edwin V. O'Hara quoted in J. G. Shaw, *Edwin Vincent O'Hara: American Prelate* (NY 1957) pp. 64-68. See also Edwin V. O'Hara, *The Church and the Country Community* (NY 1927); Theodore Maynard "The Lost Land" *Commonweal* 34 (26 September 1941) 533-536; Raymond P. Witte, *Twenty-Five Years of Crusading: A History of the National Catholic Rural Life Conference* (Des Moines,

Catholic ruralists reminded their coreligionists that they had a religious obligation to aid the rural Church and to strengthen the nation's rural life. Both Leo XIII and Pius XI, they pointed out, had spoken in behalf of the amelioration of the economic and social conditions of farmers and had favored the elimination of the farm proletariat. Catholic ruralists continually quoted Leo XIII's statement in *Rerum Novarum* (1891):

If working people can be encouraged to look forward to obtaining a share in the land, the result will be that the gulf between vast wealth and deep poverty will be bridged over, and the two orders will be brought nearer together. Another consequence will be the greater abundance of the fruits of the earth. Men always work harder and more readily when they work on that which is their own; nay, they learn to love the very soil which yields in response to the labor of their hands, not only food to eat, but an abundance of the good things for themselves and those that are dear to them. It is evident how such a spirit of willing labor would add to the produce of the earth and to the wealth of the community. And a third advantage would arise from this: men would cling to the country in which they were born; for no one would exchange his country for a foreign land if his own afforded him the means of living a tolerable and happy life.

They also repeatedly cited Pius XI's concern, as voiced in *Quadragesimo Anno* (1931), for "the immense army of hired rural laborers, whose condition is depressed in the extreme, and who have no hope of ever obtaining a share in the land." "Unless efficacious remedies be applied," the pope warned, this agricultural laboring class "will remain perpetually sunk in the proletarian condition."[3]

AGRARIAN MYTH

Catholic rural life leaders enthusiastically espoused what has come to be known as the "agrarian myth." They argued

IA 1948) and Martin Schirber, O.S.B. "Catholic Rural Life" *The American Apostolate: American Catholics in the Twentieth Century*, ed. Leo R. Ward, C.S.C. (Westminster, MD 1952) pp. 133-148. An invaluable article on American Catholic attitudes toward the city is Robert D. Cross "The Changing Image of the City Among American Catholics" *Catholic Historical Review* 48 (April 1962) esp. pp. 37-43.

[3] *Five Great Encyclicals* (NY 1939) pp. 22-23, 142.

that only in a society dominated by farms and small towns could individualism, independence, cultural stability, the widespread ownership of property, economic freedom, political and social conservatism, a strong family life, and religion flourish. In contrast, they believed that rootlessness, depersonalization, wage slavery, regimentation, pauperization, social and political radicalism, and materialism characterized modern American industrial and urban civilization. "Destroy agriculture, the backbone of a nation," Fr. Urban Baer of Wisconsin warned, "and eventually that very same nation itself will be headed down the Niagara of destruction and dissolution."[4]

A belief in agrarian fundamentalism was at the basis of Catholic ruralist thinking. "For what, after all, is more fundamental in a civilization than a staunch and steadfast yeomanry?" asked Fr. Edgar Schmiedeler, O.S.B., head of the NCWC's Rural Life Bureau during the 1930s. "What is more basic, more primary, than a well balanced and contented people with their roots... in the soil?...what comparison is there between the substantial realities of the country and the many superficial artificialities of the garish gewgaws of the city?" O'Hara agreed. "The farmer pursues the most fundamental, the most dignified profession in the world," he declared. "He is the primal producer.... It is... from the country with its prolific population and its fertile fields that the city must draw both its sustenance and its people."[5]

Catholic agrarians emphasized the political advantages of a large landowning rural population. While the dispossessed proletariat of the metropolis was attracted to socialism and other radical ideologies, rural areas remained steadfast and conservative. The "only cure for communism, the real cure for communism," Msgr. Ligutti told a congressional committee, is "to have every family own a cow." Catholic ruralists

[4] Urban Baer, *Farmers of Tomorrow* (Sparta, WI 1939) pp. xiii-xiv. For the impact of the "agrarian myth" in American history, see Henry Nash Smith, *Virgin Land: The American West as Myth and Symbol* (NY 1959), book three, and Richard Hofstadter, *The Age of Reform, From Bryan to F.D.R.* (NY 1955) ch. 1.
[5] Edgar Schmiedeler, O.S.B., *Why Rural Life* (National Catholic Welfare Conference 1933) p. 3; O'Hara quoted in Witte, *Twenty-Five Years of Crusading*, p. 48.

feared that the United States, in its infatuation with urbanization and large-scale industrialization, was entering an era of class conflict and economic and political collectivism. Democracy and civil liberties would gradually disappear, they believed, since they were dependent upon the widespread distribution of property and could not co-exist with the centralization of economic and political power.[6]

Rural areas were also conducive for the inculcation of strong moral values and for the strengthening of the family. The innocent recreations of the countryside were compared to "the commercialized amusements and feverish streets and artificial gaiety of city life." While cities were rife with crime and immorality, Catholic ruralists contended, rural areas trained children in "the development of self-reliance, initiative, and character." They also compared the family life of the urban proletariat with that of a homestead. Births were fewer and divorces more frequent in the city, they claimed. As Fr. W. Howard Bishop, the founder of the Glenmary Home Missions, declared, in urban areas "families exist statistically but not as institutions which can any longer be depended on either as the prolific sources or as nurseries of human life."[7]

The feature of rural life which was probably the most appealing to Catholic agrarians was its supposed affinity for religion. The claim that large cities were socially disordering and incompatible with religion had become a staple of American sociology during the 1920s, and Catholic ruralists shared this belief. "Catholic life must be a life close to nature," the Benedictine monk, Virgil Michel, wrote, "for the supernatural in the dispensation of God builds on the natural." Whereas

[6] Ligutti testimony in U.S. Congress, Senate, Committee on Appropriations, *Hearings Before the Subcommittee of the Committee on Appropriationes*, 77th Cong., 2nd Sess., 1942, pp. 520-524. Other characteristic expressions of the agrarian myth among Catholic ruralists may be found in Baer, *Farmers of Tomorrow;* John C. Rawe, S.J., and Luigi G. Ligutti, *Rural Roads to Security: America's Third Struggle for Freedom* (Milwaukee 1940); and Schmiedeler, *Vanishing Homestead* (NY 1941).

[7] Edwin V. O'Hara quoted by Witte, *Twenty-Five Years of Crusading*, pp. 52-54; W. Howard Bishop "Agrarianism, the Basis of the New Order" *Catholic Rural Life Objectives* 1 (1935) 50-52.

the excessively mechanized, artificial and materialistic life of industrial urban society cut man off from nature and nature's God, the patterns of rural living conformed to the natural tempo of life. The continued urbanization of the United States would result in the atrophying of the religious spirit in general and the decline of Catholicism in particular. The debate regarding the relative merits of urban and rural life, Fr. Michel contended, "is really a question of restoring the natural basis of Christian living for the greater flourishing of the supernatural Christ-life among men."[8]

One did not have to believe in the superiority of agriculture to have realized that during the 1920s and 1930s American farming was undergoing a catastrophic depression. What distinguished Catholic agrarians from other observers of American agriculture was their analysis of the reasons for the economic debacle. They attributed the post-world War I farm depression as well as the depression of 1929 to the selfishness, materialism and spirit of aggrandizement which they believed permeated American life. The ultimate cause for this was the triumph of capitalism and Protestantism several centuries ago which had undermined the moral restraints that religion previously had been able to exert on economic egotism. The proximate cause was the triumph of industrialism after the Civil War and the subsequent belief of most Americans that the highest priority was the production of goods at all costs. As a result, factories were built which turned out far more products than the American consumers could purchase, and American farmers deserted subsistence agriculture in behalf of large-scale, commercial farming. The American farm was transformed into a factory for the production of food and fiber. Farmers unable to compete either migrated to the cities or else became members of the rural proletariat of farm laborers, tenants and share-croppers.

---

[8] Virgil Michel, O.S.B., to Rev. James A. Byrnes, no date, Michel Papers in Archives, St. John's University, Collegeville, Minnesota. Michel "Timely Tracts: City or Farm" *Orate Frates* 12 (1938) 367-369. For the impact of urbanization on religion as viewed by American sociologists of the 1920s, see Cross "Changing Image of the City Among American Catholics" pp. 38-39.

OBJECTIVES OF AGRARIANS

First and foremost on the social agenda of the Catholic agrarians during the 1930s was eliminating the rural proletariat and augmenting the number of family farmers. Although recognizing the importance of increasing farm income, the Catholic ruralists believed the fundamental problem of American farmers was insecurity of tenure and not low income. They were far more concerned with the rapid increase in the percentage of farmers who did not own their own land than in the precipitous drop in farm income during the 1920s and early 1930s. In 1880, for example, 25% of all farmers had been tenants, while in 1930 over 40% were tenants. By 1930 60% of all American farm real estate was owned by banks, insurance companies and mortgage companies. The figures were particularly bleak regarding southern agriculture. While in 1880 36% of southern farmers had been tenants, in 1930 over 55% owned none of the land they farmed.

The emphasis of the Catholic agrarians on the importance of land tenure was natural since they valued agriculture because of its social, political, cultural and religious influences and not because of its economic benefits. For them farming was a way of life, not merely a way to make a living. Permanent prosperity would never come to American agriculture until the farmers ceased viewing farming as simply another commercial enterprise. State and federal governments would have to protect the farmers not only against the financial and industrial system which had exploited them in the past, but also against their own instincts to commercialize the land. As the Most Rev. Joseph H. Schlarman, Bishop of Peoria, warned in his presidential address to the NCRLC, unless the trend toward corporation farming, absentee landlordism, tenancy and foreclosures was reversed, the nation would have a farm population consisting of "peons or serfs." He also reminded his listeners that "the fundamental history of civilization is the history of the soil."[9]

[9] Howard A. Turner "Farm Tenancy Distribution and Trends in the United States" *Law and Contemporary Problems* 4 (1937) 424-426; Bishop Joseph H. Schlarman "Presidential Address" *Catholic Rural Life Objectives* 4 (1944) 71.

The Catholic ruralists realized that one of the criticisms of their movement was its supposedly "utopian" character, that it was opposing supposedly inevitable economic and social changes. First of all, they refused to accept the argument that social and economic developments were autonomous forces which must not be made to conform to ethical and religious teachings. Secondly, they did not believe there was anything inevitable about factory farming, agrarian dispossession, and the drift from the countryside to the city. They believed there was sufficient evidence that the trend toward dispossession could be reversed with the aid of the government and through the enterprise of the farmers themselves. They pointed to the Scandinavian countries, and Holland and Belgium where, through the use of consumer and producer cooperatives and government programs of land distribution, tenancy had been checked. Even more significant was the Antigonish Co-operative Movement of Nova Scotia where priests from St. Francis Xavier University had revitalized the economic and social life of a depressed rural community. Catholic ruralists did not see any reason why American farmers could not also make use of farm cooperatives, rural savings banks, and modern technology, particularly electricity and the automobile, in alleviating the economic distress and social isolation of rural areas. Catholic agrarians were especially eager to see the growth of the co-operative movement because it would bring the United States closer to the vocational society recommended by Pius XI in *Quadragesimo Anno*. Any hope for an agrarian restoration would also depend upon a more sympathetic government in Washington, and the Catholic ruralists believed they had precisely that with the inauguration of Franklin D Roosevelt in 1933.[10]

HOPE IN ROOSEVELT

The Catholic agrarians would probably have viewed any

---

[10] For the interest of Catholic ruralists in consumer and producer co-operatives, see Schmiedeler, *Cooperation: A Christian Mode of Industry* (Ozone Park, NY 1941). Rawe and Ligutti, *Rural Roads to Security*, ch. 12, refute the argument that the Catholic ruralists' program would result in a lower standard of living and was opposed to modern technology.

Democratic president as a welcome change. The middlemen, food processors, railroad barons, financiers and industrialists who had exploited the farmers in the past were too powerful within the G.O.P. to expect the Republicans to sponsor a program of meaningful aid for agriculture. In addition, Roosevelt had in the past evidenced a sympathy for the type of agrarian program favored by the Catholic ruralists. Roosevelt had publicly proclaimed that America's strength lay in the countryside, and he predicted that continued urbanization would "eventually bring disaster to the United States." "Land," he asserted in 1932, "is not only the source of all wealth, it is also the source of all human happiness." And in an article appropriately entitled "Back to the Land," the future president criticized the more unseemly aspects of modern urbanization, especially "the factory town of the old type, with its miserable tenants and box-like company houses built in grimy rows on dirty streets—abodes of discouragement and misery." While governor of New York Roosevelt attempted to correct the imbalance between urban sprawl and rural stagnation. From the very beginning when he accepted the Democratic nomination for governor in 1928, he voiced concern for the farmers' plight and his desire to see agriculture achieve economic parity with business and manufacturing. During his four years as governor rural taxes were decreased, state aid to rural roads and schools was increased, a public market system was established, and an ambitious program of securing cheaper electricity for rural areas by harnessing the St. Lawrence River was launched. He declared his objective to be to make "country life in every way as desirable as city life, an objective which will from the economic side make possible the earning of an adequate compensation and on the social side the enjoyment of all the necessary advantages which exist today in the cities."[11]

[11] Daniel R. Fusfeld, *The Economic Thought of Franklin D. Roosevelt and the Origins of the New Deal* (Columbia University Press 1956) pp. 84-85, 123-127; Franklin D. Roosevelt "Growing Up By Plan" *Survey Graphic* 67 (1932) 483-484; Roosevelt "Back to the Land" *Review of Reviews* 84 (1931) 63-64. Roosevelt's farm policies while governor of New York are fully covered in Gertrude Almy Slichter "Franklin D. Roosevelt's Farm Policy as Governor of New York State, 1928-1932" *Agricultural History* 33 (1959) esp. pp. 172-173.

One of the benefits FDR anticipated resulting from an improvement of rural life was demographic decentralization. A movement from urban to rural areas would not only help alleviate the urban unemployment problem, but it would also modify the excessive concentration of population in the big cities. He envisaged this as not simply a back-to-the-land movement, but instead he wished to move industries to rural locations as well. He called this "the third and new type of American life," and he believed it could combine the advantages of both rural and urban existence. The decentralization of industry in small cities and towns was, he maintained, both economically and technologically feasible because of better railroad facilities and the development of electricity, the telephone, and the automobile and truck which made it possible for factories to operate in rural areas. FDR envisaged this "third type" of American life having the economic advantages of industrialization, and the space, freedom and opportunity to establish a permanent home characteristic of rural communities.[12]

During the 1932 campaign Roosevelt continually stressed his determination to aid agriculture. He predicted that, if elected, the tariff would be lowered, the wave of farm foreclosures would be checked, farm prices would rise, and farmers would be able to refinance their mortgages at lower interest rates. "If we would get to the root of the difficulty," he said at Topeka, Kansas during the major farm address of his campaign, "we shall find it in the present lack of equality for agriculture. Farming has not had an even break in our economic system."[13]

Catholic ruralists eagerly responded to Roosevelt's cry for a new deal for agriculture. O'Hara purported to hear an echo of the Catholic doctrine of the "just price" in Roosevelt's proposal of a voluntary domestic allotment program which he presented at Topeka. If the domestic allotment plan did suc-

[12] Fusfeld, *Economic Thought of Roosevelt*, pp. 129-130; Roosevelt "Actualities of Agricultural Planning" *America Faces the Future*, ed., *Charles A. Beard* (Boston 1932) pp. 331-338.
[13] Samuel I. Rosenman, ed., *The Public Papers and Addresses of Franklin D. Roosevelt, The Genesis of the New Deal, 1928-1932* (NY 1938) 1. 654-656, 673-711, 756-770, 812-819.

ceed in raising farm prices, it would help fulfill the recommendation of *Quadragesimo Anno* for

> a reasonable relationship between the prices obtained for the products of the various economic groups, agrarian, industrial, etc. Where this harmonious proportion is kept, man's various economic activities combine and unite into one single organism and become members of a common body, lending each other mutual help and service. For then only will the economic and social organism be soundly established and attain its end, when it secures for all and each those goods which the wealth and resources of nature, technical achievement, and the social organization of economic affairs can give.

The board of directors of the NCRLC at its October, 1932 meeting endorsed the voluntary domestic allotment plan as a desirable way to raise farm income. Upon being notified of this, Roosevelt informed the NCRLC of his intention, once elected, of placing agriculture on an equal footing with business by giving it benefits comparable to what business received through the protective tariff. One Catholic agrarian, however, even before Roosevelt was inaugurated, criticized the voluntary domestic allotment plan along lines which would become increasingly important as the Roosevelt administration developed its farm program. The Roosevelt proposal "may play the part of a much needed 'shot in the arm,'" declared Edgar Schmiedeler, director of the Rural Life Bureau of the NCWC, "but it is not a fundamental remedy for the economic situation. It is high time that far more effective steps be taken in behalf of the American farmer, for if he be dispossessed, the nation will pay dearly in the loss of its staunch and sturdy yeomanry, in the loss of the choicest fruits of its fields." Schmiedeler was here voicing the belief of Catholic agrarians that the major problem facing American agriculture was insecurity of tenure and the increase in tenancy, not low income. Some even believed that high farm prices would, in fact, encourage farmers to become even more deeply involved in commercial agriculture.[14]

[14] O'Hara "Concern of the Church in the Rural Problem" *Catholic Action* 14 (1932) 4; *Five Great Encyclicals*, p. 146; Schmiedeler, *Why Rural Life*, p. 15. For the attitude of the NCRLC toward the voluntary domestic allotment plan, see George Q. Flynn, *American Catholics and the Roosevelt Presidency, 1932-1936* (University of Kentucky Press 1968) p. 67.

AGRICULTURAL ADJUSTMENT ACT

The most important of the early New Deal farm measures was the Agricultural Adjustment Act of 1933 which provided for government payments to farmers who restricted production of such crops as wheat, cotton and tobacco. The AAA embodied the dominant philosophy within both the New Deal and the major farm organizations regarding farm relief. Government bureaucrats and farm spokesmen viewed the farmer as essentially a businessman whose most pressing need was to reduce production so that farm prices could rise. The AAA would enable farmers to artificially restrict production just as urban businessmen had done for decades. The major result of this view of agriculture was that the bulk of New Deal farm benefits, whether one is discussing the first AAA or the legislation which followed it, went largely to commercial farmers who had suffered the greatest drop in income during the depression. "New Deal loans and expenditures," wrote Professor Leonard J. Arrington, "were primarily relief-oriented. They were not, at least in their dollar impact, reform-oriented or equality-oriented. The prime goal would seem to have been the restoration of income for individual farmers rather than the achievement of a greater equality."[15]

Since the major purpose of the AAA was economic recovery rather than agrarian reform, it did little for tenants, sharecroppers and farm laborers. Its major impact on the farm proletariat was to push many completely off the land since it was often more advantageous for the farm owner to reduce his acreage under cultivation. In fact, there were some officials within the Agricultural Adjustment Administration who believed there were already too many farmers, and that the inefficient producers should leave the land and migrate to the cities.[16]

---

[15] Leonard J. Arrington "Western Agriculture and the New Deal" *Agricultural History* 44 (1970) 337-352. Similar evaluations of the impact of New Deal farm policies are found in Theodore Saloutos "New Deal Agricultural Policy: An Evaluation" *Journal of American History* 61 (1974) 403-406, and Sidney Baldwin, *Poverty and Politics: The Rise and Decline of the Farm Security Administration* (University of North Carolina Press 1968) pp. 32-37, 45-46.

[16] Richard S. Kirkendall "The New Deal and Agriculture" *The New*

The Catholic agrarians initially welcomed the AAA since its professed goal was to restore balance and "parity" between the prices received by farmers and industrialists for their products. The AAA, Schmiedeler declared, was "a charter of economic equality with the city." In addition, the precarious status of agriculture demanded that something be done immediately to aid the nearly bankrupt farmers. The AAA was adopted while "one of the greatest crises our nation has ever experienced was at its worst, discontent was widespread and growing into despair, and farmers ... were beginning to resort to mass violence," Bishop reminded the 1934 annual convention of the NCRLC. "Something had to be done quickly, and it must be something very drastic." But Bishop also stated that the AAA was merely a stopgap measure and certainly no substitute for more fundamental reforms. Despite the success of the AAA in increasing farm income, Bishop asked, "isn't it time to consider long-range programs of a permanent nature?" He had in mind government encouragement of diversified small-scale family farming rather than commercial one-crop agriculture. He lamented the fact that elements within the New Deal seemingly accepted "the fallacy that there are already too many farmers, and what we want is fewer and better farmers rather than more tillers of the soil of varying degrees of efficiency." He advised the Roosevelt administration to subordinate its emphasis on efficiency and the tendency "to make of farming a closed corporation for the benefit of those who are already in it" and instead to make land available "to our distressed masses on the easiest possible terms of purchase."[17]

The fear of Bishop and other Catholic agrarians that commercial farmers were to be the major beneficiaries of the AAA, a fear later substantiated by historians of New Deal farm policies, accounted for their increasing pressure for alternative government programs to aid poor farmers and to combat dispossession. Some Catholic agrarians also questioned whether

*Deal: The National Level*, eds. John Braeman, Robert H. Bremner and David Brody (Ohio State University Press 1975) pp. 83-96, 105-106.

[17] Schmiedeler statement in "Rural Life Conference Begins Second Decade of Rural Catholic Action" *Catholic Action* 15 (1933) 5; Bishop "Presidential Address" National Catholic Rural Life Conference, *Proceedings of Twelfth Annual Convention* (St. Paul 1934) pp. 28-32.

crop reduction conformed to Catholic economic principles. While admitting that as long as labor unions and big business attempted to limit the supply of labor and goods, farmers had no alternative but to also limit production, they also argued that this led to an economy of scarcity in which there would be fewer farmers. Was there any chance to resurrect an agrarian culture when the government's farm programs were reducing the number of farmers? New Deal farm experts, the Jesuit John C. Rawe complained, "use the terminology of city-bred industrial economists and neglect to emphasize the human values of an agrarian system. They would control production in the field in the same way as in the factory ... and allow the further capitalization of joint stock interests in extensive land holdings. Meanwhile we cannot safely say whether their philosophy is industrial or agrarian."[18]

Another fear of the Catholic agrarians regarding the AAA was that it might presage the regimentation of the American farmer. Some argued that any regimentation would be an unavoidable result of the need to do something drastic to aid agriculture, and they were encouraged that the government had decided to have farmers actively participate in administering the act. Schmiedeler even maintained that the involvement of the farmers was a step toward establishing in agriculture the vocational system championed by Pius XI. "One can readily see in all this," he claimed, "something in the nature of a self-governing economic group system for the American farmers." Others were not so optimistic and feared that the AAA signalled the beginning of the end for the economic independence and personal liberty of the American farmer.[19]

FARM CREDIT ADMINISTRATION

The early New Deal supplemented the AAA with the estab-

---

[18] Rawe "Agrarianism: The Basis for a Better Life" *American Review* 6 (1935) 181. For other criticisms by Catholic ruralists of crop limitations, see Vincent J. Ryan "State and Reconstruction" *Catholic Rural Life Objectives* 4 (1944) 35, and Schmiedeler "This Crop Control" *Commonweal* 26 (1 October 1937) 507-508.

[19] Schmiedeler "Pius XI's New Social Order and Agriculture," *The American Ecclesiastical Review* 103 (1940) 371-377. For an attack on New Deal farm policies for regimentating the farmer, see Bishop Aloisius J. Muench "Religion and Agrarianism" *Catholic Mind* 38 (1940) 443-444.

lishment in 1933 of the Farm Credit Administration which refinanced farm mortgages, encouraged creditors to make reasonable settlements with indebted farmers, and established a system of twelve regional banks to make mortgage, production and marketing loans and to provide credit to cooperatives. For the Catholic agrarians the FCA held out more promise of an agrarian restoration and an end to rural dispossession than did the AAA. More farm credit and at lower interest rates was a *sine qua non* if the family farm was to be preserved. "So far as the general principles underlying it are concerned," Schmiedeler wrote, "the Farm Credit Administration seems reasonably sound. Certainly it is a notable improvement on the system, or lack of system, that went before." The agrarians were particularly heartened by the FCA's encouragement of cooperatives which, in their opinion, could be of decisive importance in the struggle to maintain as wide a distributon of property as possible in the countryside. Catholic agrarians viewed the self-help of farmers organized into cooperatives as an alternative to the dangerous increase in Washington's power. In addition, cooperatives embodied the values of Christian brotherhood and cooperation rather than the competitiveness and individualism of capitalism. Catholic agrarians envisaged cooperatives as the starting point for the reconstruction of society along the lines of the vocational structure recommended by Pius XI in *Quardragesimo Anno*. Cooperatives were, in fact, one of the major panaceas for Catholic agrarian enthusiasts and they eagerly welcomed the aid of the Farm Credit Administration.[20]

Catholic ruralists also favored the creation in 1933 of the Subsistence Homestead Division in the Interior Department. Prior to Roosevelt's inauguration Schmiedeler had testified before the House of Representatives Committee on Labor in behalf of a proposal to establish a government subsistence homestead program, and Catholic agrarians welcomed Roosevelt's statement in his first inaugural address that Americans must "frankly recognize the overbalance of population in our industrial centers and, by engaging on a national scale in a redistribution, endeavor to provide a better use of the land

---

[20] Schmiedeler, *A Better Rural Life*, pp. 111-115.

for those best fitted for the land." Congress responded by providing $25 million in the National Industrial Recovery Act of 1933 for settling 25,000 families on subsistence homesteads. The subsistence homestead program became of particular interest to Catholic ruralists when Ligutti secured a government loan of $200,000 to build a homestead colony in his home town of Granger, Iowa. Ligutti's proposal had the backing of the NCRLC, and when established it was well publicized in the Catholic press.

Granger Homesteads was a test case for the Catholic agrarians in the workability of their rural philosophy. Of the approximately one hundred New Deal community projects, Granger Homesteads most closely reflected the back-to-the-land philosophy. This was largely because of the influence of Ligutti, a zealous proponent of agrarianism. Proletarianism and the widespread distribution of property cannot exist together, Ligutti once told a Senate committee while defending Granger Homesteads. "It ennobles a man when he begins to own a piece of land, begins to own a cow, and owns cows and pigs and chickens." Ligutti's goal for Granger Homesteads was to settle fifty unemployed coal-mining families from the Granger area onto the land. He hoped that the ownership of land and part-time subsistence farming would overcome their demoralization and inculcate in them a sense of community, as well as strengthen their family life. Part-time farming was probably more successful at Granger Homesteads than in any of the other New Deal homestead projects, again mostly because of Ligutti. Not surprisingly, Ligutti was quite anxious for his homesteaders to form cooperatives and they did establish a cooperative for buying, selling and manufacturing, a cooperative for the purchase and maintenance of some heavy farm machinery, and a credit union.[21]

---

[21] Roosevelt statement quoted in Ralph L. Woods, *America Reborn: A Plan for Decentralization of Industry* (NY 1939) pp. 296-297; Ligutti testimony in U.S. Congress, Senate, Committee on Appropriations, *Hearings Before the Subcommittee of the Committee on Appropriations*, 77th Congress., 2nd Sess., 1942, pp. 523-526. For Granger Homesteads, see John LaFarge, S.J. "Granger Prospers on an Iowa Prairie" *America* 68 (31 October 1942) 96-97; Raymond P. Duggan, *A Federal Resettle-*

Catholic agrarians were confident that Granger Homesteads was more likely to succeed than any of the other New Deal subsistence homestead projects since, because of Ligutti's influence, it had a spiritual dimension which the other projects lacked. Granger Homesteads, the Jesuit John LaFarge contended, should be an example to all Catholics interested in the survival of the Church in America. Catholic ruralists did not, however, unqualifiedly support the subsistence homesteads program. Many of the projects appeared to them to be boondoggles with little or no relevance for the agrarian plight. LaFarge, for instance, described the Arthurdale, West Virginia project as merely "rural housing enhanced by a useful garden." Ligutti, relying on his experience with Granger Homesteads, complained about the excessive red tape, centralization of authority, regimentation and denial of local autonomy and responsibility accompanying the government program. "In the past few years the Federal Government has been introduced into private affairs to an extent heretofore unknown," Ligutti declared. "Wherever possible, this tendency ought to be curbed if the democratic ideal is to persevere in America." Catholic agrarians also contended that the homestead projects were too few and did not involve nearly enough people to make a meaningful contribution to an agrarian restoration. Government homestead projects "have been costly experiments," the authors of *Manifesto on Rural Life* lamented, "they can hardly be rated successful, especially if their cost be considered. They can be justified only as laboratory experiments. If settlement projects are to succeed, there must be a larger measure of local autonomy and local responsibility in formulating and in carrying out the plans."[22]

---

ment Project: *Granger Homesteads* (Catholic University of America Press 1937); Paul K. Conkin, *Tomorrow a New World: The New Deal Community Program* (Cornell University Press 1959) pp. 31-32, 294-304. Ligutti described his approach to the depression in "A Plan to Solve Some Social, Economic and Religious Problems by Agriculture," National Conference of Catholic Charities, *Proceedings of Eighteenth National Conference* (Omaha 1932) 75-78.

[22] LaFarge "Agriculture and Vocation" *Commonweal* 28 (1 July 1938) 261; Rawe and Ligutti, *Rural Roads to Security*, pp. 173-174; *Manifesto on Rural Life* (Milwaukee 1939) pp. 15-16, 94.

REXFORD G. TUGWELL

The attitude of the Catholic agrarians toward the subsistence homesteads sharply distinguished them from Rexford G. Tugwell, an advisor to Roosevelt and the first head of the Resettlement Administration which in 1935 absorbed the homestead program. Tugwell completely rejected the back-to-the-land movement, was sceptical of the subsistence homesteads program, and questioned Roosevelt's wish to move industry into the countryside. He furthermore believed that modern technology had destroyed the economic *raison d'etre* of the small farm, and that it had become an anachronism which should be allowed to disappear. He once described a family farm as "an area of vicious, ill-tempered soil with a not very good house, inadequate barns, makeshift machinery, happenstance stock, tired, over-worked men and women—and all the pests and bucolic plagues that nature has evolved... a place where ugly brooding monotony, that haunts by day and night, unseats the mind." Tugwell valued agriculture because it produced food and fiber, and not because it fostered a supposedly superior way of life.[23]

Tugwell did not anticipate that much good would come from the subsistence homestead projects. He predicted they would "function merely as small eddies of retreat for exceptional persons; and that the greater part of our population will prefer to live and work in the more active and vigorous main stream of a highly complex civilization." The projects' major significance was in demonstrating the merit of social and economic collectivism. Progressive schools were established in the projects in order to help in the transition from a competitive to a collectivist society. Tugwell, as Joseph Dorfman wrote, was a born planner. "His philosophical values, as well as his highly developed aesthetic sense, drove him to a dream of order and symmetry." Tugwell believed government planning by technicians and social scientists could insure that the advantages of modern technology and industrialization benefited all the people. A barrier to such planning was the traditional individualism of the farmer which Tugwell believed

[23] Tugwell quoted in Baldwin, *Poverty and Politics*, pp. 87-88.

to be an anachronistic remnant of a pretechnological era. He also held that the only way to give the homestead communities a firm economic basis was through commercial agriculture and mechanized farming. The Catholic ruralists were naturally suspicious of Tugwell's collectivism and the Resettlement Administration's close supervision of the projects which often made the residents feel like guinea pigs. They also feared that the residents were contracting excessive debts because of Resettlement Administration was encouraging them to purchase heavy farm machinery. The government should have attempted instead to educate the residents in production for home use and in the value of family-farming.[24]

Tugwell, in contrast, believed that efforts to preserve the family farm would do little more than create "a contented and scattered peasantry." The real problem of American agriculture was poverty and not dispossession. Farm ownership would be acceptable for some tenants, Tugwell argued in 1936, only "under the right conditions, at their own choice and with a clear view of its costs and after they have demonstrated their ability to rise." Far more important was providing "treatment of disease, better diet for children, a mule, some seed and fertilizer, clothes to lift the shame of going ragged to town, some hope for the future, a friendly hand to help in every farm and home crisis."[25]

Because of New Deal caution and the unsympathetic attitude of some government officials, most notably Tugwell, the Catholic agrarians in the mid-1930s were still waiting for the comprehensive attack on farm poverty and tenancy which they had expected as a result of the 1932 election. This disappointment was prevalent throughout the Catholic rural life movement. Delegates to the 1934 convention of the NCRLC declared that it was high time the government should focus

---

[24] Tugwell quoted in Arthur M. Schlesinger, Jr., *The Coming of the New Deal* (Boston 1959) pp. 369-370; Joseph Dorfman, *The Economic Mind in American Civilization* (NY 1959) 5. 502-515. For a hostile view of Tugwell, see Rawe "The Land and Cooperation" *United for Freedom: Cooperatives and Christian Democracy*, ed. Leo R. Ward (Milwaukee 1945) p. 138.

[25] Tugwell quoted in Schlesinger, *Coming of New Deal*, p. 380, and Baldwin, *Poverty and Politics*, pp. 163-164.

"the main force of its depression activities toward the permanent rehabilitation on the land of as large a portion of the unemployed in our cities, and of the several types of stranded, tenant farmers in the country as have the desire and ability to settle permanently on small farms which they will come to own by easy annual payments at a low rate of interest over a period of years." Bishop O'Hara proclaimed in 1935 that the country's most pressing need was a public policy that "will transform the family farm-operator into a farm owner instead of transforming owners into tenants or day laborers on a corporation farm." The next year Rawe told the NCRLC annual convention that "government abandonment of the distributed freehold property foundation would today be an act of cowardice and virtually amount to the abdication of democracy and constitutional guarantees."[26]

### THE BANKHEAD BILL

In the midst of this growing pessimism Senator John H. Bankhead of Alabama introduced in 1935 a bill to provide one billion dollars in long-term, low-interest loans to sharecroppers and farm tenants to enable them to become farm owners. Bankhead believed his proposal, which had been in the works for several years, would enlarge the yeoman class, increase subsistence farming, reduce relief payments, and shift population from the cities to the countryside. The Bankhead bill immediately became the most important item on the Catholic ruralists' political agenda and, in fact, they believed it to be the most significant piece of legislation introduced during the 1930s and one of the most momentous proposals ever to be considered by Congress.[27]

Catholic agrarians played a significant role in the lobbying effort in support of the Bankhead bill. As early as 1933 Fr.

[26] "Resolutions Adopted at the St. Paul Meeting of the Catholic Rural Life Conference" *Catholic Action* 16 (1934) 23; O'Hara "A Spiritual and Material Mission to Rural America" *Catholic Rural Life Objectives* 1 (1935) 6; Rawe "Life, Liberty and the Pursuit of Happiness in Agriculture" A Paper Presented to the National Catholic Rural Life Conference (St. Paul 1936) p. 40.

[27] John H. Bankhead "The One Way to Permanent National Recovery" *Liberty* 10 (22 July 1933) 18; Baldwin, *Poverty and Politics*, pp. 133-134.

Bishop had informed the White House of the widespread support among Catholic agrarians for Bankhead's land purchase proposal. "Whereas other measures are to remedy a present emergency," Bishop wrote, "this one adds a plan of permanent readjustment and employment for all who will intelligently take advantage of it.... This arrangement is the only salvation for thousands perhaps millions of self respecting unemployed who want to earn their own living and for whom the old jobs will not be open again if and when industry starts up at full speed." Catholic agrarians became closely identified with the land purchase proposal, and it was therefore natural that when Will Alexander established in 1935 the National Committee on Small Farm Ownership to lobby for the Bankhead bill it included three Catholic agrarians, Bishop, Schmiedeler and Frank O'Hara, the brother of Bishop Edwin O'Hara and a professor at Catholic University. Meeting in Washington in April 1935, the committee declared that:

No greater problem confronts our rural community than the persistent growth of farm tenancy. Nearly one-half of all our farmers are now tilling land owned by others, and if the present tendency toward converting the independent farmer into a dependent and propertyless tenant continues, then we must abandon hope of achieving a stable and progressive rural civilization.... we consider the proposed bill for the gradual conversion of the tenant into a landowner as one of the most important and constructive pieces of legislation ever voted upon by the Congress of the United States.... If passed, it will make possible the growth of a secure and prosperous rural community that owns the land it tills and that can develop to the fullest its share of the American heritage.

When the Catholic Rural Life Conference met in October 1935, its members endorsed the Bankhead bill's attempt "to enable tenant farmers, their sons and farm-minded city people to become independent proprietors, and to encourage widespread distribution of land ownership as opposed to landlordism and the perpetuation of tenantry."[28]

[28] Bishop to Marvin H. McIntyre, 6 May 1933, Official File 503 (Roosevelt Library); National Committee on Small Farm Ownership, "Statement on the Bankhead-Jones Farm Tenancy Bill," 19 April 1935, Frank Tannenbaum Papers (Columbia University Archives); Schmiedeler "The Rochester Rural Life Meeting" *Catholic Action* 17 (1935) 25.

The Bankhead bill was so attractive for Catholic agrarians because, as Schmiedeler wrote to Frederick P. Kenkel, it was "so much in accord with the Catholic attitude regarding land ownership." Schmiedeler was probably referring to Leo XIII's famous statement in *Rerum Novarum* that the law "should favor ownership, and its policy should be to induce as many people as possible to become owners." *Commonweal* editorialized that all Americans favoring the principles of private property and individual liberty should support the Bankhead proposal. "Liberty and property are inseparable," the magazine declared, and "the people through their legitimate government must protect themselves in their right to possess private property and, hence, real liberty. For thus they will protect themselves against either monopolistic private tyranny or the tyranny of state socialism." *Commonweal* was perhaps alluding to socialist agitation among southern sharecroppers in its reference to "the tyranny of state socialism." For Catholic agrarians the Bankhead bill was the only realistic alternative to Norman Thomas' Southern Tenant Farmers Union. Even Fr. Rawe, generally the most intransigent of the Catholic agrarians when it came to the growth of government under the New Deal, favored the Bankhead measure. Writing to a fellow Jesuit agrarian, he asked:

Is this a Congressional bill simply because of the fact that we wish to get Government loans for our work? If there were another way to get the necessary funds I think that all of us would agree to advance our work independently of government (with the exception perhaps of securing government prohibition against corporation farming). When we advance further in the field of agrarian education we may find funds in private groups for local work.[29]

The Bankhead bill was bottled up in Congress until after the 1936 election. Fr. LaFarge spoke for all Catholic agrarians in hoping that "with the task of getting re-elected laid upon

---

[29] Schmiedeler to Frederick P. Kenkel, 2 April 1935, Kenkel Papers (Notre Dame University Archives); *Five Great Encyclicals*, p. 22; "In Support of the Bankhead Bill" *Commonweal* 21 (26 April 1935) 719-721; Rawe to Edward Day Stewart, S.J., 7 February 1937, Frank L. Owsley Papers (Vanderbilt University Archives). For the Southern Tenant Farmers Union, see Jerold S. Auerbach "Southern Tenant Farmers: Socialist Critics of the New Deal" *Labor History* 7 (1966) 3-18.

the shelf, the present Administration will give thought to the fact that as yet little has been done to enable a young man to take up farming." When the Bankhead measure did become law in 1937, however, it had undergone drastic changes. It provided for an appropriation of only thirty-five million dollars for the first two years of operation. A new agency, the Farm Security Administration, was established to administer both the new law and the rural poverty programs which had previously been under the Resettlement Administration.[30]

FARM SECURITY ADMINISTRATION

The Catholic ruralists were greatly disappointed by this turn of events. The FSA in its early years could only provide loans to 2% of the nation's tenants. Schmiedeler, who had been anticipating "far-reaching" legislation to reverse the "ominous growth" of tenancy, now exclaimed, "possibly there are some reasons for the exceedingly small appropriation that is provided for. However, on the face of things it seems nothing less than ridiculous."[31]

Although baffled by the paltry sums provided for the Farm Security Administration, the Catholic agrarians nevertheless were staunch supporters of the FSA's land purchase and rural rehabilitation programs, reasoning that half a loaf was better than none and hoping that the government would broaden the scope of the FSA's activities. Fr. Vincent J. Ryan, while praising the FSA in his 1940 presidential address to the NCRLC annual convention, also noted that "unfortunately this program has not been on a scale large enough to achieve noticeable results." Schmiedeler echoed Fr. Ryan. "I think the FSA has proved itself one of the most practical and successful agencies established under the present Administration," he wrote. "Considering the difficulties under which it has labored, the low income groups to which its activities have been restricted, it has made a very good record. Its operations deserve to be

[30] LaFarge "Catholic Agrarians Swing Into Action" *America* 56 (14 November 1936) 130.
[31] Schmiedeler, *Our Rural Proletariat* (NY 1939) pp. 22-25. For the Bankhead Act, see James G. Maddox "The Bankhead-Jones Farm Tenant Act" *Law and Contemporary Problems*, 4 (1937) 434-455.

greatly expanded." When during World War II the FSA became the target of bitter attacks by the American Farm Bureau Federation, the NCRLC quickly sprang to the agency's defense, frequently testifying in its behalf before various Congressional committees. NCRLC spokesmen contrasted the FSA's fostering of property ownership and family farming with the "new feudalism" of the Farm Bureau. They accused the Farm Bureau of wishing to keep farming as "an occupation for a selected few" and of favoring the growth of a large farm proletariat and migratory farm class. Ligutti told Congress that, once the FSA's attempt to maintain "our democratic way of life" became better known, the Farm Bureau will lose the struggle to destroy the agency, and "the proponents of a feudalized system of agriculture in America will lose much of their influence in determining our national policy." Ligutti also wrote to President Roosevelt to protest the "baseless barrage of smearing attacks" on the FSA, and to draw the president's attention to the fact that these attacks emanated from "corporate and speculative farm interests." "The future of agriculture in our nation is involved," he concluded. It is a question of deep concern "to all elements in our population dedicated to the democratic way of living."[32]

Throughout the 1930s the Catholic agrarians had waited expectantly for a comprehensive campaign against farm tenancy and rural poverty. It never came. The New Deal's farm programs, Urban Baer wrote, "do not go deep enough when one considers the significant seriousness of the problem." Catholic agrarians concluded that the New Deal had taken the easy path of tinkering with the farm economy. There had been no long-range solutions to the problems of agrarian insecurity, poverty and dispossession. Palliatives such as farm subsidies were not a permanent answer. "The farmer wants to stand on his own feet," a NCRLC pamphlet declared. "He does not

---

[32] Vincent J. Ryan "A Statement by the President" *Catholic Rural Life Bulletin* 3 (20 November 1940) 18; Schmiedeler "Land Problems and the FSA" *Catholic Rural Life Bulletin,* 3 (20 February 1940) 6-8, 27-28; Ligutti testimony in *Hearings Before the Subcommittee of the Committee on Appropriations,* pp. 532-533; Ligutti, et al., to Roosevelt, 20 June 1942, Official File 1568 (Roosevelt Library).

want to be either a slave of a competitive price system or a client of a dole-dispensing government."[33]

Dissatisfaction with the New Deal was especially pronounced among the "purists" within the Catholic rural life movement. They claimed that the superficiality of the New Deal's farm program was due to its viewing agriculture as simply another business in need of more cash. As a result, American farmers had not been educated in subsistence agriculture. As Professor Emerson Hynes of St. John's University of Collegeville, Minnesota put it, the New Deal's approach to agriculture "does not encourage or increase the farmer's self-sufficiency—which is, after all, his *only* bulwark of safety. On the contrary, it makes for more dependency. Each farmer becomes a spoke in the national wheel.... The salvation of rural society does not lie in a planned economy imposed from above, but in a restoration of the true concept of farming as a way of life." The basic error of the New Deal was failing to view farming from the perspective of Jeffersonian and Catholic rural ideology. New Deal laws might raise farm income, declared Willis D. Nutting of Notre Dame University, but they will not give farmers economic independence. Nor will they "build a real rural culture."[34]

CONCLUSION

Despite the tendency to view the Catholic agrarians as hopeless reactionaries, their evaluation of the New Deal's farm program is not very different from that of many historians. Sidney Baldwin, Richard Kirkendall, Theodore Saloutos, William E. Leuchtenburg and Grant McConnell have also argued that the New Deal did not significantly reduce rural poverty and dispossession. Historians have also agreed with the Catholic agrarians that the New Deal did not fundamentally change the character of American agriculture. The more affluent

[33] Baer, *Farmers of Tomorrow*, pp. 124-140; *Rural Life in a Peaceful World* (Des Moines, IA 1944) p. 10.
[34] Emerson Hynes "Agriculture in the Next Decade" *Catholic Rural Life Bulletin* 3 (20 February 1940) 4-5; Willis D. Nutting "Foundations of a Rural Christian Culture" *Catholic Rural Life Bulletin* 2 (20 February 1939) 1-2.

farmers received the bulk of New Deal benefits, while the poorer farmers were generally ignored. As Kirkendall has pointed out, New Deal farm laws were relief-oriented and largely served the interests of the large commercial farmers.[35]

Virtually all recent analyses of the New Deal have noted, as did the Catholic agrarians, its pragmatism, its tendency to compromise, and its superficiality. Recent commentators have also sympathized with the dispossessed and rural poor of the 1930s. The basic difference between the agrarians and modern historians is not over any specific political proposals of the agrarians but is instead a matter of social ideology. Historians who are products of an industrial and urban society are unsympathetic toward an ideology which proclaims agriculture to be the basis of civilization and democracy. While agrarian fundamentalism has little modern relevance, still there are other aspects of the ideology of the Catholic rural life movement which speak to contemporary America. These include the need to decentralize economic and political decision-making and the priority which should be placed on the widespread distribution of property and the strengthening of the middle class. From the perspective of the 1970s, the Catholic agrarians of the 1930s were not wrong in warning Americans about the growth of political centralization and government bureaucracy, the dispossession of the family farmer and the small businessman, and the increasing tendency for decisions affecting the welfare of individuals to be made by remote industrial, labor and political organizations.

---

[35] Baldwin, *Poverty and Politics*, p. 190; Kirkendall "New Deal and Agriculture" pp. 86-87, 100; Saloutos "New Deal Agricultural Policy" pp. 408-409; Leuchtenburg, *Franklin D. Roosevelt and the New Deal* (NY 1936) p. 141; Grant McConnell, *The Decline of Agrarian Democracy* (University of California Press 1953) pp. 87-88; Edward C. Banfield "Ten Years of the Farm Tenant Purchase Program" *Journal of Farm Economics* 31 (1949) 469, and Arrington "Western Agriculture and New Deal" p. 352, come to similar conclusions.

## WALTER PRESCOTT WEBB AND THE CRISIS OF A FRONTIERLESS DEMOCRACY

The 1930's were not a propitious time to defend American capitalism.[1] The seeming inability of American business and industry to recover from the ravages of the depression demonstrated the need for radical changes in the structure and control of the economy. Thurman Arnold, Adolf A. Berle, Jr., Gardiner Means, Walter Lippmann, and other influential social commentators even questioned the very existence of the modern financial and manufacturing corporation, and criticized many of the benefits it had received through general incorporation laws and favorable judicial decisions. The Texas historian Walter Prescott Webb, Frederick Jackson Turner's most important disciple, joined this attack on the giant corporations. His 1937 tract, Divided We Stand: The Crisis of a Frontierless Democracy, defended small business, the widespread distribution of productive property, and limitations on the economic leviathans of the Northeast. After World War II, however, Webb repudiated much of the thrust of Divided We Stand, becoming an ardent apostle of the corporate organization of the economy.

This metamorphosis in Webb's thinking was common among many southerners and westerners who had initially opposed the large corporation. The rise to national prominence of southern and western corporations, especially in the energy field, and the increase in the standard of living in the South and West accompanying urbanization and industrialization convinced many regional spokesmen that their antipathy to the large-scale corporation had been misplaced. Now they realized that it had not been the modern corporation per se which had been objectionable, but rather its alien character. As a vigorous exponent of the economic and cultural integrity of the hinterland, Webb exemplified the reaction of many of these leaders of heretofore agrarian regions to rapid industrialization. His social thought, in contrast to his historical writings, was not particularly original, profound, or complex. Its significance lies rather in providing a microcosm for examining a widespread response to indigenous economic development.

Divided We Stand was one among many volumes of the inter-war years which analyzed the economic degradation of the South and Southwest. The depression of 1929 and the interest of the Roosevelt administration in southern poverty lead to an unprecedented interest among social scientists, historians, journalists, and politicians in regionalism and regional inequities. Many of those interested in regionalism during the depression were primarily concerned with discovering why the South and West had lagged economically and socially behind the North and East. They refused to believe that Marxism, which was becoming increasingly popular among eastern intellectuals, could explain the poverty of the South and Southwest. The emphasis of Marxism on class conflict, its repudiation of private property, and its attacks on democracy were anathema. The regionalists, in contrast, argued that the problems of the hinterland were due not to any supposed exploitation of the proletariat by the bourgeoisie, but rather to the financial and industrial exploitation by the Northeast which adversely affected all southerners and westerners, whether they be workers, farmers, or businessmen.

Webb's concern with the economic bondage inflicted by the Northeast on the backcountry stemmed not only from the circumstances of the 1930's, but was also a product of his own background. His parents were militant southerners who had migrated to Texas from Mississippi. They installed in their son a healthy suspicion of the Northeast, a suspicion which deepened when he studied under William E. Dodd at the University of Chicago. Dodd emphasized the importance of regionalism and the conflict between business and agriculture in American history, as well as the necessity of grounding democratic institutions and practices in a democratic social and economic setting. Webb's memories of his early life in rural west Texas undoubtedly reinforced the idea that the northern corporations were the source of the South's economic tribulations. His parents were frightfully poor, as were most of the farmers of west Texas at this time, and it certainly made more sense to attribute this to the desolation inflicted upon the South by the Civil War and to the exploitation of the Southwest by the northern corporation, than to any oppression by the bourgeoisie of an imaginary proletariat.[2]

The poverty of his childhood made an indelible impression on Webb. Early in life he decided he wanted out of both west Texas and farming. Webb's first-hand contact with farming did not foster the romantic attachment to agriculture which Richard Hofstadter would later come to call the "agrarian myth". For Webb, social and economic mobility meant a move from the farm to the city via a career in academia. The memories of his poverty-stricken youth never left Webb, and he was never one to denigrate the importance of making money and getting ahead. His lack of funds even forced him to postpone marriage. "I am sick of school work on starvation wages," he wrote his fiance in 1916. "As long as I am alone I can get along. But for your sake, I want money, money, money, money, and I am going to have it."[3] This healthy regard for money remained with Webb throughout his life, and he managed to accumulate a substantial estate through speculating in Austin, Texas real estate. Webb's experiences with poverty, combined with the devastating impact of the depression on the Southwest, convinced him that the major problems facing the Southwest were economic, and that the way to solve them was through urbanization and industrialization.

This distaste for agriculture and his faith in the gospel of urbanization, industrialization, and economic progress did not mean, however, that Webb's interest in the South was solely economic. In fact, he saw himself as a defender of the culture of the trans-Mississippi against its eastern critics, in particular H. L. Mencken and his clique. Webb strongly supported the revival of regionalism, encouraged the study of local history and the preservation of folk art, and defended western novelists against their eastern detractors. His important book of 1931, The Great Plains, resulted, according to Gregory Tobin, from Webb's efforts "to shake himself free from what he saw as Eastern categories and to look at his own world with a fresh perspective," and was part of a regional quest for historical identity.[4] The Great Plains argued that a unique society had arisen west of the Mississippi because of the successful adaptation of the settlers to a region in which water and trees were scarce. The achievements of the western people were, for Webb, every bit as interesting, significant, and monumental as the accomplishments of the seventeenth-century colonists or the industrial barons of the Nineteenth Century.

Despite his parents' background, Webb saw himself as more a westerner than a southerner. His three major historical works, <u>The Great Plains</u>, <u>The Texas Rangers</u>, and <u>The Great Frontier</u> focused on the West rather than on the South. He wore a Stetson rather than a straw hat and purchased a ranch rather than a plantation. And yet Webb was also conscious that as a Texan he was a product of at least three cultures. In 1942 he published an article entitled "Texas: Eternal Triangle of the Southwest" in which he argued that Texas was a meeting point of the three cultures formed by the forest, plain, and desert. Texas, he noted, "may be thought of as an extension of these three environments and cultures."[5] The fact that Webb felt at home both in the South and West was important in shaping <u>Divided We Stand</u>.

He decided to write the book when he learned of the Supreme Court's decision in the Butler case of 1936 invalidating the processing tax on food processors instituted by the Agricultural Adjustment Act of 1933. The tax was used to pay farmers for reducing production of hogs, rice, wheat, corn, cotton, dairy products, and tobacco. Webb was infuriated by the decision, believing it to be blatant discrimination by the court in behalf of the giant food processors at the expense of farmers. He contended that the government had been subsidizing big business for decades through the protective tariff, land grants to railroads, and favorable banking legislation. Now the court had denied the same type of relief to farmers. Working feverishly, he finished the first draft of <u>Divided We Stand</u> in only six weeks. The book's major purpose, Webb wrote Senator Lister Hill of Alabama, was to help create a political alliance between the economically oppressed South and West to combat the power of the northern corporations. In fact, he had originally planned to entitle the volume either "Should the South and West Secede?" or "Oh South, Oh West".[6] He finally settled on "Divided We Stand" which was an ironic allusion to Lincoln's "House Divided" speech. Webb was delighted to be able to use an inversion of Lincoln's words to indict the northern industrialists and financiers who now dominated the Republican Party.

The volume argued that the Great Depression had resulted from the decreasing number of economic opportunities caused by the growth of the giant northern corporations and the closing of the frontier. Influenced by the 1932 book of Berle and Means, The Modern Corporation and Private Property, Webb asserted that the corporations were the means by which the North had come to dominate the South and West. He pointed out that while the North in 1930 had only 21% of the nation's territory, 57% of the population, and 10% of the natural resources, northerners owned or controlled more than 85% of the country's wealth. Interested only in draining the West and South of their cash, the northern corporations had seized control over the natural and financial resources of the hinterland so that "practically every natural person of the South and West is dependent upon them for the necessities of life and the means of livelihood itself." Throughout the South and West people were "paying tribute to someone in the North."[7] While the primary villain was the northern capitalist, northern farmers and laborers shared the blame because they enjoyed the benefits of this regional exploitation although they had not initiated it.

Divided We Stand was more than merely an attack on the northern corporation. It was also an interpretation of American history squarely in the progressive historiographic tradition of Vernon Louis Parrington, Charles A. Beard, Frederick Jackson Turner, and William E. Dodd with its emphasis on conflict between eastern capitalism and western agrarianism. Webb asserted that the United States was divided into three sections, the South, West, and North, each with "its own mores, ways of life, and culture complexes", and that the central thread of American history was the struggle between the regions for supremacy. The North was currently in the saddle owing to its victory in the Civil War. The South's defeat had enabled the North to carry out a three-pronged program of regional exploitation through (1) the protective tariff; (2) pensions to northern veterans of the war financed partially by taxes on southerners; (3) a patent system which concentrated the benefits of technological improvement in the North.[8]

Webb termed this a "feudal system" in which western and southern vassals were forced to pay tribute to an invisible government of northern corporate lords. The source of the corporations' power lay in the liberal charters granted to them by complaisant state governments, and in the decisions of the Supreme Court defining the corporation as an "artificial person" entitled to protection under the fifth and fourteenth amendments. Webb was particularly disturbed by the ability of the corporate leviathans to destroy local businesses, and he dedicated the second edition of <u>Divided We Stand</u> to the "small business man of America, by small business I mean a merchant, manufacturer, or farmer who is not able to keep a lobbyist in Washington." (He had originally planned to dedicate the book to his wife but she demurred when learning of its title.) He feared that, if the power of the giant corporations was not destroyed, the shopkeepers of the hinterland would become employees of northern chain stores, and the spirit of initiative, individualism, and entrepreneurship would slowly disappear. Small businesses "have died, are dying slowly, and die they will," he lamented. "Those who remain independent confine themselves to commodities that are not well adapted to chain business. . . . They live because of their insignificance."[9]

Only the federal government, Webb contended, could rectify the social and economic imbalance created by the modern corporation. Small businessmen, laborers, farmers, and consumers required the strong arm of Washington to create the cohesiveness and organization enabling them to compete on equal terms with the industrial barons. Webb believed Roosevelt's administration recognized the problem and was attempting to do something about it. Unfortunately, whenever the New Deal tried something meaningful "a cry is raised to heaven that the government is crushing rugged individualism, shackling business, violating the sacred principles of <u>laissez faire</u>, wrecking the constitution, ruining the country, and most ludicrous of all - regimenting the farmer."[10]

And yet Webb was ambivalent regarding the prospect of southern and western industrialization. He believed it was vital to encourage manufacturing in the South and West, declaring that the key to resolving the economic crisis was "restoring to all sections and classes of the American democracy a semblance of equal economic opportunity."[11] However he was quite sceptical that this could ever occur. Not only did southern and western entrepreneurs lack the capital and trained personnel necessary for success, but northerners also owned the basic patents on the machinery vital for industrialization, and they would not willingly relinquish this control.

Webb also doubted whether economic recovery and permanent prosperity could ever be achieved under modern mechanization irrespective of which region controlled the major corporations. He admitted that machines were here to stay since they were more efficient than people. But mechanization also increased unemployment and diminished purchasing power, while simultaneously flooding the market with excess goods. "Thousands, yea, even millions, stand outside the gates of labor listening to the distant song of the machine," he wrote. "The source of the music lies to the North."[12] Furthermore, mechanization strengthened the owning class since "in saving labor the machines puts the laborer out of work and transfers the wages that he would have received to the machines that has become his substitute."[13] Mechanization had thus strengthened the tributary relationship of the West and South to the North, but it was difficult to see how the situation would be greatly improved by replacing northern capitalists with southern and western ones. Unemployment would remain high while the imbalance between production and purchasing power would persist. Webb had reached a dead end in his thinking.

Webb also attributed the Great Depression to the end of the boom period associated with the frontier. The absence of frontiers was "the sine qua non of our problem."[14] The belief that the Depression signalled the end of a distinctive period in American history was not unique to Webb. Lewis Corey, Anna Rochester, Curtis Nettels, Stuart Chase, and George Soule, among others, argued that the end of the frontier had destroyed the dream of economic and social opportunity, created new problems, and demanded a new social order. Such thinking influenced many of the New Dealers, particularly Henry Wallace and Harold Ickes. They claimed the closing of the frontier and the end of economic expansion necessitated coordinated economic planning by the national government. Webb agreed.[15]

Not only had the frontier been responsible for the individualism, entrepreneurship, democracy, and laissez faire characteristic of the Nineteenth Century, Webb declared, but it also provided the economic and social opportunities responsible for heavy immigration and previous economic growth. The frontier was "the greatest relief fund ever known."[16] The government had not hesitated to distribute land to farmers, miners, ranchers, and railroads to keep the boom going. The rise of the corporation, however, indicated that the frontier period of American history was over and pointed to the need for a new philosophy of government. The era of political neglect had ended. Washington must now step in to discipline the oppressive power of the corporation as well as to supply the economic opportunities previously produced spontaneously by the frontier. "It is only in recent years that the government of the United States has faced this problem," he wrote. "Objectors have complained that when the government faced this problem and did something about it, it was abandoning the principles upon which the democracy was founded. In providing relief for millions of unemployed the government has not adopted a new policy, but it has merely changed the form in which relief is administered. The method is new, but the act is old."[17]

Thus the emergency America faced during the 1930's was the crisis of a frontierless democracy, a crisis which had been temporarily postponed during the previous decade by the growth of the automotive industry and installment buying. The New Deal, Webb asserted, recognized the nature of the emergency and was attempting to meet it "realistically and peacefully by substituting new forms of relief for the old ones of the frontier. The revolution is . . . a formal recognition that in a frontierless democracy bread and votes must go together."[18] Under the New Deal the government had begun to substitute itself for the frontier.

While sympathetic toward Roosevelt's administration, Webb was rather suspicious of the Democratic Party which, he believed, was still too heavily influenced by big business. He favored the creation of a new political party which would unite the agrarian elements of the South and West, and possibly include the laborers of the North. Such a party might also attract small businessmen throughout the nation. Once in power it could then move to repeal that section of the fourteenth amendment allowing the Supreme Court to define the corporation as a person, to deprive the states of the power to grant charters to interstate corporations, and to encourage locally controlled manufacturing outside the North. This decentralization of industry would occur after overhauling the patent system and revising the railroad freight rate schedule which discriminated against the South and West.

Response to *Divided We Stand* was predictable with southerners and westerners enthusiastic while northerners were rather critical. Congressman Maury Maverick of San Antonio told his wife, "This is the best goddamned book I've read in years." She must have been impressed since she would later become Webb's second wife. Carl Sandburg also praised the volume, describing it as "one of the great American pamphlets." The Southern Agrarians welcomed *Divided We Stand* since it confirmed what they had been arguing ever since the publication of their own manifesto *I'll Take My Stand: The South and the Agrarian Tradition* in 1930. As John Crowe Ransom put it, Webb's book "is a contribution of great importance for our public discussions. . . . I am inclined to think it has prophetic value." Herbert Agar, a leading advocate of economic and demographic decentralization, characterized it as "the wisest and most interesting comment on today's affairs" by a professional historian. Chauncey Stillman, reviewing the volume in the decentralist magazine *Free America*, contended it was an important, remarkable, and memorable book, "a commentary on the anomaly of our country . . . without parallel". Southern newspapers were particularly impressed by *Divided We Stand*. The *Tennessee Appeal* called it a "brilliant analysis", while the *Dallas Morning News* termed it "dynamite".[19]

Northern opinion was something else. The *New York Times*' reviewer believed the regional emphasis of *Divided We Stand* was outmoded. The problem was class and not regional exploitation. The *Christian Science Monitor* also chided Webb for his sectionalism, contrasting it with "that broader and grander concept of Americanism and national unity which neither war, nor adversity, nor political strife can destroy or even lessen." Marxists, of course, totally rejected Webb's argument. Thus the *New York Daily Worker* attacked Webb for being "naive" and playing into the hands of Wall Street. "What is wrong today in the country can be traced to the evils of monopoly capitalism and not to the imaginary domination of the North," the communist journal asserted. The enemy was not the northern capitalist but all capitalists - southern, western, and northern. The regionalism of Webb was a barrier to the unification of the American working class around "progressive principles". "The job of every progressive American," the paper concluded, "is to fight for a united people against the handful of parasitic reactionaries who pillage and loot the country for their vested interests."[20]

Divided We Stand was an alternate selection of the Book-of-the-Month Club and was read by several of Washington's policy makers. Karl A. Crowley, the Post Office's solicitor, gave copies of it to Congressman Maverick, Sam Rayburn, the Democratic majority leader in the House of Representatives, Senator Joseph C. O'Mahoney of Wyoming, Vice-President John Nance Garner, and President Roosevelt.[21] Webb believed it helped influence the President to convene the Conference on Economic Conditions in the South in July, 1938, and to describe the South as "right now the nation's no. 1 economic problem."[22]

In December, 1938 Webb testified in Washington in the Justice Department's investigation of monopoly in the glass industry. Divided We Stand had originally contained a chapter describing the successful attempt of the Hartford Empire Company of Connecticut to crush a fledgling bottle company in Santa Anna, Texas. His publisher Farrar and Rinehart insisted that all references to the Hartford company be dropped because, it claimed, it feared a libel suit, and Webb reluctantly agreed. Webb believed the Hartford company had actually requested the deletion, and that the two companies were related "in a variety of ways."[23] He protested but to no avail since Farrar and Rinehart stated it would not publish the book if the chapter remained. Webb always believed the publisher sabotaged Divided We Stand, failing to adequately publicize it and taking it out of circulation as soon as possible. At one time he even threatened to sue for damages.[24] The chapter entitled "The Story of the Texas Milk Bottle" was ultimately published in 1944 when the tiny Acorn Press of Austin, Texas brought out a second edition of Divided We Stand.

Webb got a measure of revenge on the Hartford Empire Company in 1938 when it, along with the entire bottle manufacturing industry, became the focus of the investigation of the Temporary National Economic Committee into monopoly in the United States. Representatives of the Hartford Empire Company as well as the Knape-Coleman Glass Company of Santa Anna testified. The investigation revealed that Hartford Empire's control of over seven hundred patents for the manufacturing of glass bottles enabled it to destroy potential competitors and to keep the price of bottles artificially high.[25]

Divided We Stand, written at a crossroads in Webb's intellectual development, was a confusing book. His apotheosis to America's small businessmen hearkened back to a world of yeoman farmers, individual entrepreneurs, and corner grocers. And yet he also argued that the modern corporation was a result of the ending of the frontier and the growth of mechanization, neither of which were likely to be reversed. He contended that mechanization resulted in unemployment and depressions, but he also wished to see a new political party encourage modern industrialization in the hinterland. He was a democrat, but could also write that "a frontier is essential to the maintenance of democracy."[26] He lamented the eclipse of individualism and the increase in economic regimentation, and yet seemingly recognized that industrial conglomerates and collectivism were to be permanent aspects of the American landscape. Webb was slowly groping his way toward the collectivist view of modern society which would mark The Great Frontier. It would then become clear that Webb's real target had never been the modern corporation, mechanization, or capitalism, but rather simply poverty.

Soon after completing Divided We Stand Webb happened to read John Dewey's Individualism Old and New which had come out in 1930. Webb was deeply impressed by the book, and it helped clarify his thinking regarding the place of the large corporation in modern society. By emphasizing that frontier individualism was not a necessary element in democracy, Dewey convinced Webb that democracy and economic consolidation could exist simultaneously. Individualism Old and New asserted that America was torn between the old ideas of individualism and freedom and the new economic realities of standardization, mechanization, quantification, and collectivism. Dewey was particularly concerned with the conflict between the commitment to individual private gain and the technological imperatives of machine technology. He contended that the era of trustbusting was over, and the age of the corporation was here to stay. Inevitably this would place limitations on individualism. Dewey welcomed the demise of the old individualism identified with economic freedom and governmental passivity. This, he asserted, had been a product of America's frontier stage during which the pioneer struggled with "the forces of physical nature. The wilderness was a reality and it had to be subdued. The type of character that evolved was strong and hardy, often picturesque, and sometimes heroic. Individuality was a reality because it corresponded to conditions."[27]

The problems of America, however, were now social rather than physical but the influence of the old individualism remained as an obstacle to the complete recognition of the new social, economic, and political imperatives. "The beliefs and ideas that are uppermost" in the consciousness of the American people, Dewey argued, "are not relevant to the society in which they outwardly act and which constantly reacts upon them. Their conscious ideas and standards are inherited from an age that has passed away; their minds . . . are at odds with actual conditions. This profound split is the cause of distraction and bewilderment."[28] Dewey warned, nevertheless, that the demise of the rugged individualism of the Nineteenth Century did not imply that all varieties of individualism were anachronistic and reactionary. Rather, individualism had to be modernized so that it would conform to the exigencies of a collectivist age.

The individualism appropriate to a society of machines, giant corporations, mass production and distribution, and "integration" of all sorts would be quite different than the economic individualism of the Nineteenth Century. It would have to be purged of any association with private economic gain. "A stable recovery of individuality," Dewey claimed, "waits upon an elimination of the older economic and political individualism, an elimination which will liberate imagination and endeavor for the task of making corporate society contribute to the free culture of its members. Only by economic revision can the sound element in the older individualism--equality of opportunity--be made a reality."[29] The major task for Americans was remolding their society to serve the needs of this new individuality. The new individuality would accept science, technology, and economic and social interdependence, while rejecting the false dichotomy between the corporate and individualistic impulses. "Individuality will again become integral and vital when it creates a frame for itself by attention to the scene in which it must perforce exist and develop."[30] Politically, the new individualism would recognize the inevitability of government regulation and ownership of vital economic processes. The difference between the old and new individualism was the difference between "a blind, chaotic and unplanned determinism, issuing from business conducted for pecuniary profit, and the determination of a socially planned and ordered development. It is the difference . . . between a socialism that is public and one that is capitalistic."[31]

Webb found Dewey's argument compelling. He now realized the world of the small businessman could not be restored, and collectivism was here to stay. Indeed, as he wrote Dewey in 1939, the flight toward collectivism was seemingly a worldwide phenomenon as witness the emergence of Nazism and Fascism. That same month Webb even praised chain stores because their economies of scale lead to lower prices.[32] For Webb, the political challenge to Americans was now whether a system of government based on eighteenth and nineteenth-century rural life and the social outlook of the frontier could be sufficiently modified to discipline the modern corporate predators. American democracy is near the end, he declared, "unless it is willing to make the radical readjustments that the situation requires. Then the question will be whether what we have is democracy. Certainly it will not be in the old usage of that term."[33]

This collectivist drift in Webb's thinking is particularly revealed by his attitude toward the Soviet Union. In his unpublished autobiography, "The Texan's Story", written during World War II while Harmsworth professor at Oxford, Webb claimed that, although Russia's methods were different from ours, the United States had nothing to fear from the Soviet Union, and "we should be friendly with her." Stalin's abolition of the Comintern in 1943 indicated he was a Russian nationalist rather than the leader of an ideological movement with global ambitions. Russia had made great strides economically under Lenin and Stalin, and "her political system is no more radical than the Jeffersonian system was at the time it was accepted." Webb based this analysis of the Soviets on Joseph E. Davies' incredible Mission to Moscow. Forsaking the role of a skeptical historian, Webb believed Davies' whitewashing of Stalin and Russian Communism to be an objective view of the Soviet Union.[34]

The Great Frontier, published in 1952, was Webb's most important book. It argued that the European discoveries of the Sixteenth Century had set off a vast European boom because of the sudden acquisition of vast quantities of land and mineral resources. For four hundred years until the closing of the frontier around 1900, Europe, along with her overseas possessions and the United States, had experienced sustained economic growth. The boom had lead to the emergence of distinctive political, economic, and social systems and to the dominance of a democratic, materialistic, pragmatic, and individualistic temper. The individualism and laissez faire appropriate for a frontier, however, were no longer suitable now that the boom had receded with the end of the frontier. Thus the ideas which Webb had first expressed in Divided We Stand and which were reinforced by Dewey's book now became the key to unlocking the mysteries of the global history of the past four centuries.

In the chapter "The Parabola of Individualism" Webb examined the diminishing role of individualism in an age of corporations, labor unions, and centralized government. Modern capitalism, democracy, and individualism would, he predicted, become increasingly irrelevent in the collectivist era which had now supplanted the frontier period. Both the English Beveridge Plan and the New Deal's social security program were "manifestations of the spirit of resignation which seems to be supplanting a former spirit of personal risk-taking and daring."[35] Success would now come through being part of a large corporation or a member of a labor union.

Echoing Dewey, Webb argued that a cultural gap existed because of the conflict between the political and economic necessities of collectivism and the still powerful ideology of economic individualism. The modern corporation, he argued, must become an instrument of public welfare rather than an engine of private greed. "The business corporations are going to find it difficult to give up the profit motive under which they have done so much," Webb wrote. In any case, "a renunciation of the profit motive will come slowly, as it should, partly from within and partly from without, but it seems to be on its way."[36] Webb also anticipated the rise of a new individualism which would not be primarily oriented to pecuniary ends. The problem was to provide outlets for men's creative energies and, at the same time, to recognize that the frontier psychology was an anachronism. Nevertheless, Webb believed the drift toward socialism to be irresistible.

By the 1950's Webb had come a long way from the anticorporate sentiments of Divided We Stand. In The Great Frontier he cited John Kenneth Galbraith's American Capitalism: The Concept of Countervailing Power and Peter F. Drucker's The Concept of the Corporation to show the benefits flowing from the modern corporation. Contemporary corporate leaders, Webb claimed, were more considerate of the public interest and bore little resemblance to their robber baron predecessors.[37]

In June, 1952 the Dupont Company invited a group of educators, including Webb, to be its guests for ten days. The corporation wanted them to see how a large business actually operated, and this experience strengthened Webb's growing admiration for big business. No longer did he believe corporations to be dangerous. The modern corporation, as evidenced by Dupont, paid high salaries and treated its employees well. The corporation had become an indispensable part of American society, "the most dynamic force, the most powerful active factor present in our history since the Civil War."[38] It was the cutting edge of the inevitable trend toward collectivism. During the Dupont visit Webb declared he had become a supporter of the modern corporation although it had been evident for a long time that his sympathies lay with big business and not with small businessmen unable to hire Washington lobbyists.

Webb's belief that centralization was inescapable determined his politics. He gravitated toward politicians who wished to use the federal government for creative purposes. Lyndon B. Johnson was made to order for Webb. Johnson was "an exciting, dynamic figure in Washington," Webb wrote in 1959. "He has something of the audacity of F. D. R. He believes in the future of America, thinks it can afford to be prosperous, and I do too."[39] That same year Webb became a part-time special consultant to the Senate Majority Leader, focusing on the future of the South. Webb believed the South was on the threshold of an unprecedented period of prosperity because of its long shoreline, fertile land, and plentiful supplies of oil, gas, sulphur, and fresh water. The South, and especially Texas, had the basis for a vast petrochemical industry.

By the 1950's Webb was sounding like one of those apostles of the New South creed of the post-bellum years. "I would convince the southern people that their future is brighter than it has ever been in history," he said in 1959. "I would so inspire them that they would get so busy realizing the opportunities ahead that they would forget the misfortune and injustice of the past, drown their bitterness in success, and revenge the past by becoming the prosperous region of the nation tomorrow."[40] In the course of twenty years the South had moved from being the nation's number one economic problem to the country's leading economic opportunity. "The next century," he predicted, "could belong to the South as the first one belonged to the North."[41]

Webb asserted that the South could realize this bright future only if she discarded her agrarian ways and welcomed industrialism with open arms. The South would also have to repudiate racial segregation. Webb's opposition to jim crow did not stem from any enlightened racial attitudes. Indeed, his views toward racial and religious minorities were, as Joe B. Frantz termed them, "a bit barbaric".[42] For Webb, the South had already lost the national debate over racial segregation, and refusal to recognize the unavoidable would merely impede the region's material progress. "The South tried to escape the inevitable once, and has suffered for it ever since," he warned. "It cannot afford to make the same mistake twice. It cannot afford to be diverted by a cause already lost."[43] In the years after the 1954 Brown decision Webb traveled throughout the South, including Mississippi, preaching this message of
material salvation and cautioning that adherence to segregation was shortsighted and futile.

Webb's predictions concerning the South's economic prospects were prophetic. The South is no longer described as the nation's number one economic problem. Current interest in regionalism focuses not on the northern exploitation of the hinterland described in <u>Divided We Stand</u>, but rather on the flight of industry and capital to the sun belt. It is the Northeast, according to New York Senator Daniel P. Moynihan, which is now suffering "economic decline, and actual diminution of economic activity." And just as Webb attributed the economic lag of the South and West to political favoritism, so do northern leaders claim that Washington has been largely to blame for the plight of their section.[44]

Although Webb's prophecy about the economic renaissance of the South and Southwest has come to pass, little else of his social and economic thought has stood the test of time. For example, he pessimistically argued in The Great Frontier that the end of the frontier would lead to the demise of capitalism, democracy, and individualism. Actually, the economic and social structure of the United States has remained relatively intact since the publication of The Great Frontier. The United States has responded to the problems of a vibrant capitalistic economy not by drifting toward socialism as Webb predicted, but rather by enacting pragmatic and middle-of-the-road reforms and regulations. America has remained prosperous without becoming collectivized, while voters in other advanced industrial nations have become disenchanted with socialism. It would seem that the "crisis of a frontierless democracy" never had the cosmic signficance Webb attributed to it. Webb predicted the end of the frontier would diminish the profit motive. In truth, people seem to be merely asking for a larger piece of the action.

Webb contended in Divided We Stand that the economic future of the South and West depended upon the emergence of a political party which could unite the agrarian elements of both sections and appeal to the nation's small businessmen. No such party has yet appeared. Instead, the increasing affluence of the South and West has been accompanied by a growing commitment to the Republican Party which Webb detested. George McGovern failed to capture one southern state in the 1972 presidential election, while Jimmy Carter managed to win only his own state of Georgia in 1980. The more rapidly industrialization and urbanization advances in the South and West, the more the voters have been attracted to the Republican Party, the traditional home of big business.

Schlegel noted two centuries ago that "the historian is a prophet looking backwards." Historians, even great historians such as Webb, have never been noted for their ability to peer into the future. As the author of The Great Plains, The Texas Rangers, and The Great Frontier, Walter Prescott Webb has a secure and respected place in American historiography. Divided We Stand was one of the most important volumes produced by the hinterland during the 1930's in its struggle against northern economic domination. With its emphasis on regional economic and social differences, its distrust of the judiciary, and its conviction that politics ultimately involves fundamental economic conflict, Divided We Stand stands alongside the realistic historical portraits of Charles A. Beard, William E. Dodd, and Vernon Louis Parrington. Divided We Stand thus reflects both the strengths and weaknesses of Progressive historiography.

## FOOTNOTES

[1] Research for this essay was made possible by a grant from the American Philosophical Society.

[2] Joe B. Frantz, "Walter Prescott Webb and the South," in The Walter Prescott Webb Memorial Lectures: Essays on Walter Prescott Webb, eds. Kenneth R. Philp and Elliott West (Austin, Texas: University of Texas Press, 1976), 4-7; Necah Stewart Furman, Walter Prescott Webb: His Life and Impact (Albuquerque, N. M. : University of New Mexico Press, 1976), ch. 2; Walter Prescott Webb, "The South's Future Prospect," in The Idea of the South: Pursuit of a Central Theme, ed. Frank A. Vandiver (Chicago: University of Chicago Press, 1964), 67-68.

[3] Furman, Webb, pp. 64-67.

[4] Gregory M. Tobin, "Landscape, Region, and the Writing of History: Walter Prescott Webb in the 1920s," American Studies International, XVI (Summer, 1978), 7-10; Furman, Webb, ch. 6.

[5] Webb, "Texas: Eternal Triangle of the Southwest," Saturday Review of Literature, XXX (May 16, 1942), 16-17; Webb, "The South and the Golden Slippers," Texas Quarterly, I (Spring, 1958), 11.

[6] Webb to Lister Hill, May 23, 1939, in Webb Papers (Eugene C. Barker Texas History Center, University of Texas, Austin, Texas); Webb, "Art of Writing," unpublished mss., undated, Webb Papers (Texas State Library, Austin, Texas); "Memorandum of Agreement," Webb Papers (Barker Center); Furman, Webb, pp. 118-20.

[7] Webb, Divided We Stand: The Crisis of a Frontierless Democracy (New York: Farrar and Rinehart, 1937), pp. 24-87.

[8] Webb, Divided We Stand, pp. 3-24.

[9] Webb, Divided We Stand, pp. 102-103.

[10] Webb, Divided We Stand, pp. 142, 170-226.

[11] Webb, Divided We Stand, p. 239.

[12] Webb, Divided We Stand, pp. 143-53.

[13] Webb, Divided We Stand, pp. 132-34.

[14] Webb, Divided We Stand, pp. 158-60.

[15] Steven Kesselman, "The Frontier Thesis and the Great Depression," Journal of the History of Ideas, XXIX (April-June, 1968), 253-68.

[16] Webb, Divided We Stand, pp. 174-75.

[17] Webb, Divided We Stand, pp. 165-70.

[18] Webb, Divided We Stand, pp. 215-16.

[19] Ronald Dugger, Our Invaded Universities: Form, Reform and New Starts (New York: W. W. Norton, 1974), p. 67; Carl Sandburg to Webb, December 8, 1937, Webb Papers (Barker Center); John Crowe Ransom, "The Unequal Sections," Saturday Review of Literature, XVII (December 18, 1937), 6-7; Frank L. Owsley, "A House Divided," Sewanee Review, LIII (July-September, 1945), 500-503; Herbert Agar, "'Good Neighbors' At Home," updated review, Webb Papers (Barker Center); Chauncey Stillman, review

of DWS, Free America, I (December, 1937), 13; Eugene Rutland, review of DWS, Tennessee Appeal, December 5, 1937; Sam Acheson, review of DWS, Dallas Morning News, November 21, 1937. Other enthusiastic reviews were in the Amarillo Daily News, November 4, 1937; Dallas Journal, November 5, 1937; Galveston News, November 7, 1937; and Witchita Falls Times, November 21, 1937.

[20]Ralph Thompson, review of DWS, New York Times, November 4, 1937; Christian Science Monitor, November 20, 1937; Edwin Seaver, review of DWS, New York Daily Worker, December 2, 1937.

[21]Karl A. Crowley to Webb, December 16, 1937, Webb Papers (Barker Center); Webb, "History as High Adventure," American Historical Review, LXIV (January, 1959), 276.

[22]Franklin D. Roosevelt, "A Message to the Conference on Economic Conditions of the South, July 4, 1938," in Samuel T. Rosenman, ed., The Public Papers and Addresses of Franklin D. Roosevelt (13 vols., New York, 1938-1950), VII, 421-22. The report is summarized in ibid., 423-26. For the full report, see Report on Economic Conditions of the South (Washington: United States National Emergency Council, 1938).

[23]Webb to Leon Henderson, December 19, 1938 Webb Papers (Barker Center). Henderson was executive secretary of the Temporary National Economic Committee during 1938 and 1939. See also Webb to Professor John L. McKinley, October 31, 1941, ibid.

[24]Webb to Karl A. Crowley, October 12, 1938, Webb Papers (Barker Center); Webb to Philip G. Hodge, October 7, 1940, ibid. Whether because of or in spite of its publisher, Divided We Stand was chosen as an alternate selection of the Book of the Month Club.

[25]U. S. Congress, Temporary National Economic Committee, Hearings, Investigation of Concentration of Economic Power, 75th Congress, 1939, Part 2, 379-667.

[26]Webb, Divided We Stand, p. 195.

[27]John Dewey, Individualism Old and New (New York: Minton, Balch, 1930), p. 92.

[28]Dewey, Individualism Old and New, p. 70.

[29]Dewey, Individualism Old and New, p. 72.

[30]Dewey, Individualism Old and New, p. 146.

[31]Dewey, Individualism Old and New, pp. 119-20.

[32]Webb to John Dewey, March 10, 1939, Webb Papers (Barker Center); Webb to Raymond C. Smith, March 6, 1939, ibid.

[33]Webb to Professor E. E. Dale, February 15, 1939, Webb Papers (Barker Center).

[34]Webb, "The Texan's Story," pp. 221-27, unpublished mss., undated, Webb Papers (Barker Center).

[35]Webb, The Great Frontier (Boston: Houghton Mifflin, 1952), p. 113.

[36]Webb, Great Frontier, pp. 136-38.

[37]Webb, Great Frontier, p. 132.

[38]Webb, "Statement Made at Education Conference at Wilmington, Delaware, June 24, 1952," unpublished speech, Webb

Papers (Barker Center).

[39] Webb to Edith Parker, February 10, 1959, Webb Papers (Barker Center).

[40] Webb, "The South's Call to Greatness: Challenge to All Southerners," *Texas Business Review*, XXXIII (October, 1949), 1, 6-8.

[41] Webb, "The South and the Golden Slippers," 6.

[42] Joe B. Frantz, "His Politics," in *Three Men in Texas: Bedichek, Webb, and Dobie*, ed. Ronnie Dugger (Austin, Texas: University of Texas Press, 1967), 132.

[43] Webb quoted in *Dallas Morning News*, April 20, 1959.

[44] Daniel P. Moynihan, "Politics and Economics of Regional Growth," *Public Interest*, no. 51 (Spring, 1978), 5. See also Horace Sutton, "Sunbelt vs. Frostbelt: A Second Civil War?" *Saturday Review*, V (April 15, 1978), 28-37; James C. Hyatt, "Rethinking the Sunbelt's Rise," *Wall Street Journal*, October 6, 1978; Bernard L. Weinstein and Robert E. Firestine, *Regional Growth and Decline in the United States: The Rise of the Sunbelt and the Decline of the Northeast* (New York: Praeger, 1978); and Kirkpatrick Sale, *Power Shift: The Rise of the Southern Rim and its Challenge to the Eastern Establishment* (New York: Random House, 1975).

# the southern agrarians, h. l. mencken, and the quest for southern identity

The most prominent characteristic of Southern intellectual history during the 1920's and 1930's was the emphasis on regionalism by writers, economists, sociologists, historians and political scientists busy exploring and defining Southern identity. This interest in regionalism was reflected in the founding of regional learned societies such as the Southern Political Association (1929), the Southern Economic Association (1929), the Southern Historical Association (1934) and the Southern Sociological Society (1934), as well as in the establishing of regional journals such as the *Southern Economic Journal* (1933), the *Journal of Southern History* (1935) and the *Journal of Politics* (1939). The most famous and significant publications by Southerners during this period had titles such as "The Central Theme in Southern History" (Ulrich B. Phillips, 1928), *I'll Take My Stand: The South and the Agrarian Tradition* (Twelve Southerners, 1930), *Human Geography of the South* (Rupert B. Vance, 1935), *Culture in the South* (William T. Couch, ed., 1935), *Southern Regions of the United States* (Howard W. Odum, 1936), *A Southerner Discovers the South* (Jonathan Daniels, 1938), *The Mind of the South* (W. J. Cash, 1941) and *Below the Potomac* (Virginius Dabney, 1942).[1]

Part of this concern with regionalism was a natural reaction to what Professor George B. Tindall has appropriately termed the image of the "benighted South." Throughout the 1920's Northern journalists and social scientists pictured the South as a land of bigoted clergy, degraded sharecroppers and Ku Klux Klan supporters. Edwin Mims, Virginius Dabney and other Southern liberals countered by stressing the rapid economic, social and intellectual progress the South had experienced since the Civil War. Other Southerners accepted the validity of the benighted image, believing the amelioration of the South's economic and social conditions depended upon a frank recognition of the South's shortcomings. The Southern Agrarians, however, warmly defended the agrarianism, religiosity and conservatism of the South, traits which had been the most derided by the South's critics. Their counterattack was directed at H. L. Mencken, the major propagator of the benighted image, and reached a climax in 1935 over an article Mencken published in the *Virginia Quarterly Review* mocking the Agrarians.[2]

Surprisingly, prior to 1925 the Agrarians had admired Mencken. His famous essay "The Sahara of the Bozart," first published in 1917, was like a breath of fresh air for young Southern writers, such as the Agrarians, who were dismayed by the smug complacency, provincialism and moonlight-and-magnolia mystique of Southern literature. Below the Mason-Dixon Line, Mencken wrote, "a poet is now almost as rare as an oboe-player, a dry-point etcher or a metaphysician. It is, indeed, amazing to contemplate so vast a vacuity. One thinks of the interstellar spaces, of the colossal reaches of the now mythical ether. . . . In all that gargantuan paradise of the fourth-rate there is not a single picture gallery worth going into, or a single orchestra capable of playing the nine symphonies of Beethoven, or a single theater devoted to decent plays, or a single public monument (built since the war) that is worth looking at, or a single workshop devoted to the making of beautiful things." The Agrarians, later to become the leading critics of Southern industrialization, also welcomed Mencken's attack on Southern philistinism and babbittry. Southern public opinion, Mencken lamented, "is set by an upstart class but lately emerged from industrial slavery into commercial enterprise—the class of 'hustling' business men, of 'live wires,' of commercial club luminaries, of 'drive' managers, of forward-lookers and right-thinkers—in brief, of third-rate Southerners inoculated with all the worst traits of the Yankee sharper." Little wonder, then, that while other Southerners were describing Mencken as a "pestilential nuisance," a "modern Attila," a "brachycephalous Caliban," "the Black Knight of Slander," and "an intellectual Houyhnhnm," were calling for his deportation even though he had been born in the United States, and were offering to send him a two-volume deluxe illustrated set of *The Folklore of Romantic Arkansas* in answer to his attacks on the deficiencies of Southern culture, the Agrarians were using Mencken's comments on the South to promote *The Fugitive*, a poetry journal they had established in 1922.[3]

Mencken's vindictive attacks on the South during and immediately after the 1925 Scopes Trial, however, quickly transformed the Agrarians' initially favorable impressions of the Baltimore journalist. Mencken believed the key to understanding Southern backwardness lay in the hold over public opinion exercised by fundamentalist Baptist and Methodist clerics, and he blamed the Ku Klux Klan, prohibition and all the other ills afflicting the South on the intolerance, anti-intellectualism and egalitarianism of these "grotesque ecclesiastical mountebanks," "vermin of God," "prehensile pastors" and "snakecharmers." Christianity in the

South was a form of "psychic cannibalism," a "vast machine for pursuing and butchering unbelievers." Mencken's response to the Scopes Trial was therefore predictable. "On the one side was bigotry, ignorance, hatred, superstition, every sort of blackness that the human mind is capable of," he reported, while "on the other side was sense." He described the Tennessee fundamentalists as "morons," "yokels," "gaping primates," and an "anthropoid rabble" led by a band of "gibbering baboons." While Mencken's reports of the trial were highly praised in the North, with Sinclair Lewis appropriately dedicating *Elmer Gantry* to him, they were deeply resented throughout the South where they were widely syndicated.[4]

Mencken attributed the South's susceptibility to the rantings of fundamentalist preachers to its lack of big cities. The region was dominated by country towns and "in every country town there is some Baptist *mullah* who rules by scaring the peasantry. The false assumption that his pretensions are sound, that he can actually bind and loose, that contumacy to him is a variety of cursing God—this false assumption is what makes the yokels so uneasy, so nervous, and hence so unhappy." In his essay "The Husbandman" Mencken described the farmer as a "prehensile moron," a "grasping, selfish and dishonest mammal," "a tedious fraud and ignoramus, a cheap rogue and hypocrite, the eternal Jack of the human pack," "a mundane laborer, scratching for the dollar, full of staphylococci, smelling heavily of sweat and dung. . . ." The KKK, the Eighteenth Amendment, fundamentalism and all the other "imbecilities" which had made the United States a laughing-stock in the civilized parts of the world were products of the yokels' "dung-hill" culture. Mencken believed civilization would never develop in America until the cities liberated themselves from "yokel rule," and he was encouraged by indications that the cities were becoming increasingly restive. The urban dweller, he asserted, "is tired of being governed by his inferiors, and has begun to harbor an active desire to throw them off." Even in the South ministers, prohibitionists, peasants and Ku Kluxers were being challenged by an "emerging South" consisting largely of the young and citified. The continuing urbanization and industrialization of the South doomed "yokel" control because it was "plainly incompatible with civilized progress."[5]

The Agrarians were amazed and horrified by these bitter attacks on the South by Mencken and his imitators. Even more shocking was their acceptance by much of the country as an authentic picture of the South. Perhaps for the first time in their lives the Agrarians realized they belonged to a scorned minority and that their own lives and careers were ineluctably enmeshed with the history and future of their region. Relatively uninterested in the South till then, the Agrarians now began their study of Southern history which was to result in Allen Tate's "Ode to the Confederate Dead" (1927) and his biographies of *Stonewall Jackson*

(1928) and *Jefferson Davis* (1929), Robert Penn Warren's *John Brown* (1929), Donald Davidson's "The Tall Men" (1927) and *The Attack on Leviathan* (1938) and Andrew Nelson Lytle's *Bedford Forrest and His Critter Company* (1931). The Agrarians became determined to vindicate the unique character of the South, but their perception of what this was would not become clear until the publication in 1930 of *I'll Take My Stand: The South and the Agrarian Tradition*. It is doubtful whether this, the most militant defense of Southern distinctiveness of this century, would ever have appeared had not Mencken viewed the Scopes Trial as an opportunity to lambast some of his favorite targets. In the meantime, several Agrarians found themselves in the surprising position of defending the fundamentalists against the barbs of Mencken and religious liberals.[6]

John Crowe Ransom was the first of the Agrarians to express support for fundamentalism. The occasion was an effort by Edwin Mims, chairman of Vanderbilt University's English Department and a prominent Southern liberal intellectual, to line up support in 1925 among members of his department for a statement attacking the fundamentalists. The Scopes Trial was a severe embarrassment for Southern liberals and Mims wished to demonstrate that fundamentalism and intolerance was a minority position in Tennessee. Much to Mims' surprise, Ransom refused to go along, arguing that the issue at Dayton was not tolerance versus free inquiry but rather science versus religious mythology. Ransom elaborated this idea in his 1930 work *God Without Thunder: An Unorthodox Defense of Orthodoxy*. Here Ransom argued that the triumph of science had resulted in personal unhappiness and intellectual anarchy by undermining modern man's belief in the stern God of the Old Testament, leaving him with a "God without thunder." The fundamentalists, because they took religion seriously, had developed a mythology which is "practicable and communicable, because it is unitary, consistent, and dogmatic." According to Ransom, the mistake of the fundamentalists had been in joining their mythology to an obviously erroneous astronomy and biology, whereas the error of the scientists who had testified in behalf of John Thomas Scopes had been in combining a correct science with a desiccated religious mythology. Ransom claimed that Mencken's book *Treatise on the Gods* demonstrated that even he, the great sceptic, had been "intimidated" by the effort of organized scientists to discredit religious myth. Writing to Allen Tate, Ransom protested against the whittling down of the Old Testament God into "the Spirit of Science, or the Spirit of Love, or the Spirit of Rotary; and now religion is not religion at all but a purely secular experience like Y.M.C.A. and Boy Scouts." If modern man desired peace of mind and a more humane economic and social order, then he must realize that religion "is fundamental and prior to intelligent (or human) conduct on any plane."[7]

Donald Davidson agreed with Ransom on the mythological value of fundamentalism. In an article which certainly must have surprised the sophisticated readers of the *Saturday Review of Literature*, he described fundamentalism as "a fierce clinging to poetic supernaturalism against the encroachments of cold logic; it stands for moral seriousness." He warned Southerners to take fundamentalism seriously because it expressed qualities which "belong to the bone and sinew" of their nature. He believed it was the responsibility of the Southern writer to give these qualities "a positive transmutation," to purge them of "blind and belligerent ignorance," without destroying their ability to articulate a religious and moral commitment. In another place Davidson speculated that the major contribution of fundamentalism might well turn out to have been its raising the question of how influential the ethical relativism disseminated by science should be in determining one's philosophy of life.[8]

Davidson never changed his opinion of Mencken as an unscrupulous troublemaker and "lowly misanthrope" which had been formed during the Scopes Trial. Davidson's fullest analysis of the trial is in the second volume of his history of the Tennessee River, published nearly a quarter of a century after the event. Here he pictured George Washington Butler, the author of Tennessee's anti-evolution law, as sober, tolerant, and self-educated, whereas he described Mencken and the other reporters as "publicity seekers, extremists, and character assassins" who undermined the good will that should have existed between Tennessee and the states of the North and West. Because of the antics of Clarence Darrow, Mencken, and the agnostic scientists supporting Scopes, the Trial became "the focus of a holy war in behalf of science and liberalism." In 1958 Davidson was still portraying Mencken as a "vulgar rhetorician" who, along with others of his ilk, had been largely responsible for the image of the benighted South taking hold in the popular imagination during the 1920's. He attributed his own commitment "to advance the cause of the South" to the effects of the Trial.[9]

*I'll Take My Stand* may be seen as a direct answer to Mencken's charge that the rural and religious South was a cultural wasteland. The Agrarians, in fact, turned his argument on its head by contending that it was precisely the religious and rural character of the South which was responsible for the South's cultural excellences: her emphasis on leisure and the enjoyment of life, her code of manners, her folklore and arts and crafts, her delight in conversation and good food. According to the Agrarians, it was the industrial and urban North, with her spirit of mechanistic progress, material aggrandizement, and secularism, which was the cultural aberration and in need of the type of criticism which up to then had been mistakenly directed at the South.[10]

Mencken predictably did not think highly of the Agrarian manifesto. Reviewing the book in the *American Mercury*, he noted that it deserved attention, but not for the wisdom of its ideas. There was simply no future for the South if it should reject industrialization and return to agrarianism, and he suggested that the sooner the poor farmers of the South became "proletarians" the better it would be both for themselves and for the South. The real plight of the South stemmed from religion and not industrialization. The Southern mind had been paralyzed by "a debasing mass of superstitions, designed frankly to make its victims hopeless in this world." Southern religion had created "the very sort of dull, shaky, fearful anthropoid who is now the chief obstacle to all true progress in the South, and a shame to all humanity." The Agrarians were "fashioners of Utopia," "sufferers from nostalgic vapors," and ivory-tower pedagogues for believing that a Southern renaissance depended upon a return to the soil. Instead they should redirect their energies toward repealing the Tennessee anti-evolution law, "an insult and disgrace to every self-respecting citizen of the State."[11]

Hostilities resumed in October, 1934, when Davidson attacked Mencken in the *American Review*. Davidson was then formulating a broad interpretation of American cultural history influenced by Frederick Jackson Turner's stress on the clash between the frontier and the eastern seaboard in American development, and by Oswald Spengler's *The Decline of the West*, which contrasted the sophisticated, nihilistic and cosmopolitan "civilization" of the city with the organic, religious and provincial "culture" of the countryside.[12] According to Davidson, a struggle had been taking place since World War I between the large northern cities, especially New York, and the hinterland of the West and South for cultural supremacy. Urban artists and writers, fascinated by Marxism, Freudianism, German Expressionism, French Dadaism and the erotic primitivism of D. H. Lawrence, had popularized the image of the backward and barbaric South with its "lynchings, shootings, chain gangs, poor whites, Ku Kluxers, hookworm, pellagra, and a few decayed patricians whose chief intent is to deprive the uncontaminated, spiritual-singing Negro of his life and liberty." The Middle West had become "a land of morons, boobs, and shoulder-smacking Babbitts," "of lonely farms where men and women drudge away their sterile lives," "of repressions and shams, where tender little Clyde Griffiths's who start out as bell-boys must perforce end up as murderers." The artists and writers of the South and West, however, had rejected the decadence and defeatism of their European-oriented counterparts and had remained faithful to "the living and diverse traditions of their native America."

Davidson naturally pointed to Mencken as a prime example of the cynical "rebel aesthetes" who, possessing a "volatile dissatisfaction with most things indigenously American," were responsible for these absurdly false pictures of the South and West. He bracketed Mencken with Ludwig Lewisohn, Waldo Frank, Granville Hicks and V. F. Calverton as participants "in one of the most ominous chapters in American literary history." Fortunately the provinces stood firm in their determination to defend their cultural identities against the onslaughts of the Menckenites.[13]

Mencken was infuriated by Davidson's piece, especially because Davidson had grouped him with the New York Marxist literary critics, a clique which he had repeatedly condemned. His answer was to come in an article he was then working on for the *Virginia Quarterly Review*. Back in January of 1934 Lambert Davis, the review's editor, had requested a contribution from Mencken, suggesting the literary South as a possible topic since Mencken's essay "The Sahara of the Bozart" had been so controversial and because many considered him to be the father of the South's literary renaissance. Davis also proposed as an alternative subject the folkways, customs and prejudices of the South. "You might resolve in print the paradox," Davis wrote, "that you are the South's severest critic—and a sentimental Southerner at heart."[14]

Mencken's reply was typical. He agreed to do an essay for Davis but it would focus on the South's most prominent problem, the power of the clergy. He anticipated it would be in the form of an address to Southern youth warning them about the threat which evangelical churchmen posed to intellectual freedom. Perhaps nothing better reveals the anachronistic flavor of Mencken's thought than this contention in 1934, during the depths of the Great Depression, that the South's major problem was neither economic nor political but ecclesiastical.[15]

When Davidson's article came out Mencken decided to retain the idea of an address to Southern youth but to center instead on the religious and regional program of the Agrarians. Davidson's essay had provided him with the opportunity to strike a few more blows against agrarianism and Southern religion, as well as against Davidson personally. He immediately wrote to Davis about his change of plans, noting that although there was a core of truth to what the Agrarians were preaching, "like all enthusiasts, they are riding it to death." Davis welcomed this revision because he himself had serious misgivings about the Agrarians' program and wished to see an intelligent refutation of it in his journal. He was pleased when he finally received Mencken's manuscript. "It is a delightfully written piece of work," he told Mencken, "and blows like a clean breeze through a good deal of our swampy thinking."[16]

"The South Astir" described the Agrarians as "a band of earnest young revolutionaries" offering ideas "only a little less absurd than the old balderdash that they seek to supplant." These utopian reformers had become so isolated from the realities of Southern life that they were unable to recognize the permanence of Southern industrialization or that industrialization had been a godsend to the South. Factories, Mencken contended, had increased the South's wealth, had established salutary impediments to political demagoguery and had offered new hope to an already disinherited peasantry. Wherever in the South industrialism was most firmly entrenched, there you would find not only "a higher level of physical well-being than in the agrarian areas, but also a higher tolerance of ideas." Mencken found it difficult to believe the Agrarians were serious. Didn't these "Agrarian Habakkuks" realize that without industry they "would be clad in linsey-woolsey and fed on sidemeat, and [that] the only books they could read would be excessively orthodox"?

Mencken distorted Davidson's *American Review* essay in order to show the "preposterous conclusions" to which Agrarianism led. Davidson's contention that the South should develop its own cultural identity was interpreted by Mencken as a proposal that the South "should cut itself off from the rest of the country altogether." Davidson, he claimed, wished to turn the South into a "cultural Tibet"; his response to outside ideas was "precisely that of the Mayor and City Council of Dayton, Tenn. . . . he simply throws up his hands, and yields to moral indignation." Mencken compared the Agrarians to the "incense-swingers," the nostalgic defenders of the Old South, since both groups had the same "petulance with outside opinion, and the same incapacity for turning it to profit." Fortunately "the high falutin dream stuff" being broadcast by the Agrarians did not appeal to the new breed of young, concerned and educated Southerners. The chief impediment to the spread of this new spirit of realism remained "the curious Southern tolerance of theological buncombe and pretension."

Mencken ridiculed Davidson's complaint that the benighted image of the South had arisen because the Menckenites resented the Southerners' belief in God. The cities of the North, Mencken retorted, were perfectly willing to allow the pious of the South to make fools of themselves if they so desired. The fundamentalists themselves had made Southern religion a joke throughout the rest of the world as Davidson could discover for himself "by going to Capetown, or Samarkand, or Bogota, and telling the first literate man he meets that he is from Tennessee." Davidson should stop worrying about imaginary plots being hatched in the East against the South, and should concern himself with the "hog-wallow superstition and pseudo-intellectualism" of Southern rural religion. The "earnest but somewhat ridiculous" Agrarians would do more good by cleaning up the Daytons in their own back yard than by marching on the North, a region which had not as yet adopted some of the more notable Southern customs such as "the public frying of blackamoors."[17]

Davidson, outraged by Mencken's personal attack upon him and by his sneering references to Agrarianism, demanded an immediate explanation from Lambert Davis of why he had published such a vilification of himself and the other Agrarians. Certainly, he claimed, there had not been anything in his own article warranting such abuse. He previously had assumed the *VQR* was interested in serious discussions of the South and not in backbiting and vulgarity. Did Mencken's essay indicate a change in editorial policy?[18]

Mencken's outburst came as a great surprise to Davidson, partially because his previous relationship with Davis had been quite cordial. He had warmly congratulated Davis the previous February upon becoming editor of the *VQR* and shortly after had praised him for the high quality of the articles appearing in the journal. Davis, for his part, had published Davidson's "Sacred Harp in the Land of Eden" in the April, 1934 issue, had encouraged Davidson to send him future manuscripts and had lauded the Agrarians for having "done more to raise the issue of culture in the South than any one thing in the past 60 years." Davis had also invited Davidson to contribute to a special tenth anniversary number of the *VQR* to be published in April, 1935.[19]

Davis immediately replied to Davidson's indignant letter. He was able, he wrote, to describe his editorial philosophy and the background of Mencken's essay to Davidson because the "special quality of friendliness in your personality . . . makes me feel that I can answer you more personally and frankly than, under ordinary circumstances, I might." He explained that the origin of the Mencken article antedated Davidson's *American Review* essay, and therefore was not designed to furnish Mencken an opportunity to attack Davidson. His first impulse on receiving Mencken's manuscript had been to reject it because it seemed to be a personal attack on Davidson and also a direct response to Davidson's article, and hence really belonged in the *American Review*. Further consideration, however, had convinced him that Mencken's article could be understood without any awareness of Davidson's essay and that it represented "an intelligible point of view—the metropolitan point of view" which deserved a hearing. Instead of obscuring the issues, as Davidson had claimed, Mencken had actually clarified the differences between the Agrarians and the Southern liberals. Davis did not believe Mencken's personal references to Davidson were exceptional since Mencken never wrote in an aloof and detached manner. "No intelligent person," Davis reassured Davidson, "would come to the conclusion that Mencken had come down from Mount Olympian heights to deliver a personal attack on you."

Davis praised the Agrarians for presenting issues which demanded attention. However he also gently chided Davidson and the other Agrarians for defending the entirety of Southern culture merely because it was Southern. Although he had been too extreme, Mencken had been essentially correct in arguing that Southern intellectuals should not protect all aspects of Southern culture merely because they were indigenous. "After all, even Athens borrowed from the barbarians." Davis hoped the *VQR* could contribute to a much needed synthesis of the positions of Mencken and the Agrarians by continuing to publish articles from both camps. He pointed out that it was in this spirit that the journal had published in the same issue Robert Penn Warren's essay "John Crowe Ransom: A Study in Irony." He had originally planned to put Warren's piece in the April, 1935, issue but decided to include it in the January number to balance Mencken's contribution. In conclusion, Davis promised that the *VQR* would remain open to all intelligible points of view, that it would continue to publish articles by the Agrarians defending aspects of Southern culture warranting defense and that he welcomed the opportunity to talk with Davidson personally regarding these matters. "I want you to believe," he told Davidson, "that no malice, and no desire to obscure the issues, led me to publish the Mencken article."[20]

Davis' attempt to mollify Davidson had to overcome several years of strained relations between the Agrarians and the *VQR* dating from the period when Stringfellow Barr, Davis' predecessor, had been editor of the review. Barr had come to the attention of the Agrarians in April, 1929, after publishing "The Uncultured South" in the *VQR*, and they then invited him to contribute to *I'll Take My Stand*. Although Barr viewed himself at this time as an agrarian decentralist and even went so far as submitting an outline of an essay to the Agrarians for approval, he decided against joining the group because he was unable to endorse completely the statement of principles introducing the Agrarian manifesto. Instead he developed his outline into "Shall Slavery Come South?" which appeared in the *VQR* in October, 1930, the same month he became editor of the quarterly. Here he argued that it was absurd to expect the South to reject the material prosperity and comforts resulting from factories and modern technology. He mocked visionary and traditionalist "Neo-Confederates" who, "frightened by the lengthening shadows of the smokestacks, take refuge in the good old days. . . ." Davidson, Ransom, and Tate correctly assumed that Barr had them in mind and publicly protested. George Fort Milton of the *Chattanooga News* suggested a public debate be held between the Agrarians and Barr, the *Richmond Times Dispatch* publicized this idea, and on November 14, 1930, Richmond's "great debate" took place with over thirty-two hundred persons witnessing the clash between Barr and Ransom in the city's Civic Auditorium. Barr's approach, Tate noted, was typically modern: "he thinks if the South gets rich again, it will be the South still. But the South is not a section of geography, it is an economy setting forth a certain kind of life."[21]

These initial misgivings regarding Barr increased when the *VQR* published Gerald W. Johnson's hostile review of *I'll Take My Stand*. Did the Agrarians realize, Johnson asked, that "the obscenities and depravities of the most degenerate hole of a cotton-mill town are but pale reflections of the lurid obscenities and depravities of Southern backwoods communities?" If the Agrarian program should be enacted the South would be "thrust back into the jungle. . . ." The Agrarians, above all, resented Barr's refusal to transform the *VQR* into a militantly pro-Southern journal. " 'Airing the Southern tradition,' " Barr retorted to Tate, "is only one of my purposes. I always prefer to print things by

Southerners—but my taste frequently leads me to print things by other people instead."[22]

The Agrarians thus welcomed Barr's resignation as editor of the *VQR* and hoped that Lambert Davis would be more sympathetic to their point of view. But Davis' conception of the *VQR* as an honest broker between the North and South, a function which he believed to be in keeping with Virginia's historic role as conciliator between the sections, was similar to Barr's and would not win him friends among the Agrarians who were searching for allies and not mediators in their struggle with Northern cultural and economic penetration of the South. Soon they would have reason to view Davis as a traitor to the traditional South and the *VQR* as a Twentieth Century scalawag magazine.[23]

The precipitating incident was Davis' rejection of Davidson's article "*I'll Take My Stand:* A History" which had been submitted for the tenth anniversary number. Davis wrote Davidson that, although initially intending to publish it, he was unable to accept it because the April issue already contained several articles by the Agrarians and their sympathizers, and because this issue was to be devoted exclusively to literature whereas Davidson's paper was historical. Even though professing admiration for the article, Davis also asserted that he did not think it would be appropriate for any future issue of the *VQR* as well. He suggested Davidson edit a collection of Agrarian writings, using the article as an introduction. Despite its friendly tone, Davidson was incensed by Davis' letter. When he later published the essay in the *American Review*, Davidson added a sentence praising this magazine for giving the Agrarians "understanding and hospitality of a sort we have never received . . . from the *Virginia Quarterly Review*."[24]

Davis would have been amazed by the tempest created by his rejection of Davidson's essay had he read the Agrarians' frenzied correspondence of March, 1935. The Agrarians viewed his rebuff to Davidson as an insult to the entire group even though Davis' relations with them up to this point had been most professional and correct. He had made it quite clear when inviting Davidson, Tate, Ransom, Lytle, and John Donald Wade to contribute to the anniversary number that the issue's emphasis would be exclusively literary. Thus his rejection of Davidson's article because of its "historical" nature was in conformity with the general guidelines he had established. Davis' honesty toward the Agrarians is further illustrated by his response to the Mencken article.[25]

Upon hearing from Mencken that he planned to discuss the Agrarians, Davis immediately wrote Lytle informing him of Mencken's plans, and proposing that an essay Lytle was then working on entitled "A Tradition and a Program" might be suitable for inclusion in the same issue as the Mencken piece. Although Davis had previously discouraged Lytle from submitting this essay to the *VQR*, he now believed it imperative that the Agrarians be represented in the January issue. "Under the circumstances," he wrote to Lytle, "it seems to me fair play to let the other side know about it [i.e., the Mencken article]. Of course, this is not a commission, but I think that the chances are good for both sides being heard from in the January number." Davis eventually rejected Lytle's article because, he claimed, it was too broad, oversimplified and inaccurate, criticisms which Lytle accepted in good grace. Davis now substituted Warren's essay on John Crowe Ransom for the Lytle piece. He noted to Warren that he "needed this essay very much in the present makeup . . . there was need of something to set off against Mencken's blast against Davidson. I don't think any discerning reader will miss the point." Davis thought he was being scrupulously fair to the Agrarians. As he confided to Frank L. Owsley, "You will probably be amused at the extent to which the agrarians come in for praise and blame in this issue. . . . Perhaps everybody will be offended all the way round. But that is what an editor has to expect." Amusement was not quite the way the Agrarians responded to the January issue nor were they particularly sympathetic to Davis' broadminded view of his editorial responsibilities. The *VQR* was, after all, supposedly a Southern journal.[26]

The other Agrarians immediately sprang to Davidson's defense when they heard of his difficulties with the *VQR*. Tate protested to Davis the publication of Mencken's article, describing it as sensationalistic and ignorant. He also questioned his refusal to print Davidson's history of the Agrarians: "I suppose it comes down to this: whether you think the history of our group interesting and important enough to be published at this time." Although this comment to Davis does not reveal it, Tate had been quite angered by his rejection of Davidson's essay. John Gould Fletcher, one of the more militant of the Agrarians, without delay wrote to Davidson, Owsley, Warren, Ransom and Tate, demanding that the Agrarians boycott the *VQR*, including the special anniversary number. Fletcher acted partially out of spite at not having been invited to contribute to the anniversary issue, and partially out of his deep commitment to Agrarianism and contempt for critics of the Agrarians, especially Mencken. He had long been suspicious of what he saw as the lukewarm support of the *VQR* for the traditional South, and he had urged Ransom for some time to establish a staunch Southern literary and political journal modeled on the antebellum *Southern Review*. Such a review, he asserted, was absolutely necessary if the Southern Agrarians were ever to have a serious hearing.[27]

While grateful for Fletcher's support, Davidson told him a boycott was obviously impossible because the *VQR*'s April issue was due to come out within a few days and because the contributors had already been paid. In addition, Warren, Ransom and Tate were offended by Fletcher's peremptory tone and his arrogant demand that they submit to what was, in effect, a loyalty oath. The decision where to publish his works must remain with the author, they told him, and his proposed course of action would prevent them from using one of the nation's leading journals to disseminate the Agrarian message. Not even the fire-eating Owsley supported Fletcher's call for an immediate boycott of the *VQR*.[28]

Owsley, along with Davidson, proposed instead a careful investigation of the *VQR* to be followed by a manifesto signed by the Agrarians denouncing this "thoroughly vicious institution." Owsley hoped this would discredit this "scalawag publication" throughout the South. Although Owsley and Davidson never carried through on their investigation, Owsley did answer Mencken. Ignoring Davidson's advice that the only way to deal with a person such as Mencken was to ignore him, Owsley wrote "The Pillars of Agrarianism," perhaps the finest brief defense of Agrarianism, to clear up Mencken's misrepresentations and to give a true picture of the Agrarians. The original draft of this essay contained an extensive attack on Mencken, but Davidson and Ransom convinced Owsley to remove much of this criticism because they feared Mencken would reply in kind. Owsley's comments on Mencken were thus restricted to a few sentences describing "The South Astir" as unworthy of rebuttal, "violent and lacking in restraint," and full of "billingsgate." Mencken's inability to understand the Agrarians, Owsley claimed, was typical of spokesmen for modern technology and industrial civilization.[29]

Lambert Davis, meanwhile, unaware of the fury he had aroused, continued to profess esteem for the Agrarians. "I can say again," he declared to Tate in late March, "that I have the greatest admiration for what you and the agrarians are doing. I think that we must cultivate historicity and the best way we can do it is to examine our past. You and the other agrarians have done a great job in promoting this cause, and you deserve much credit for it." He did, however, realize that his editorial policy had provoked criticism among the Agrarians, and possibly this was the reason he prefaced the special anniversary number with a two-page statement of editorial purpose. The *VQR*, the statement avowed, attempted to promote an interaction of opposing ideas in order to humanize knowledge. Although fully recognizing that it was a Southern magazine, the *VQR* refused to confine itself to regional concerns, and would continue to seek contributors throughout the world who could write about "matters of interest to any intelligent laymen."[30]

In retrospect, the quarrel between the Agrarians and Mencken and the *VQR* should never have occurred. Mencken's extravagant rhetoric and the Agrarians' combatative mood obscured the fact that their views regarding the South and northern criticism of the region were quite similar. Davidson dimly recognized this as late as 1934, when he noted that Mencken "stood suspect of being at heart a romantic southerner. . . ." Mencken was anything but a critic of the traditional agrarian South. "The Sahara of the Bozart" excoriated the modern South not for failing to measure up to northern standards, but rather for falling away from the level reached by the ante-bellum South, "a civilization of manifold excellences—perhaps the best that the Western Hemisphere has ever seen. . . ." Mencken's ideal society, as seen in his panegyric "Maryland, Apex of Normalcy," was not New York, Chicago, or Pittsburgh, but instead colonial Maryland and Virginia. He attributed the South's decline to the displacement of the landed aristocracy by businessmen and industrialists resulting from the southern defeat in the Civil War, "the most calamitous human event since the discovery of America." The Agrarians were the leading Twentieth Century critics of the "New South" spirit about which Mencken complained, and they, as well as he, used the image of the Old South as a foil with which to attack the rapid industrialization and commercialization of the South.[31]

One of the things which attracted Mencken and the Agrarians to the Old South was the absence of large cities. Both were horrified by modern urbanization, especially as exemplified by New York City. Despite his reputation as an urban scoffer and despite his verbal onslaught against "yokels" and peasant "morons," Mencken was actually a provincial Baltimorean who admired the small-town verities and always approached New York as a shy rustic nearing Babylon. His periodic visits to the big city earned him the nickname in Greenwich Village of a "monthly hick." He responded by describing New York as gross and debauched, lacking manners and style, and good only for making money. One questions, he once asked, whether New York City was "American at all. Huge, Philistine, self-centered, ignorant and vulgar, it is simply a sort of free port, a Hansa town, a place where the raw materials of civilization are received. . . . The town is shoddily cosmopolitan, second-rate European, extraordinarily cringing." Identical sentiments were being expressed at the same time by Davidson, Tate, Fletcher, and other Agrarians.[32]

Mencken was at a loss to explain how Davidson could have bracketed him with the New York intellectuals. "Long before Davidson and his friends ever discovered the fraudulence of the Greenwich Village intelligentsia," he wrote to Lambert Davis, "I was denouncing it monthly in the old *Smart Set*." Mencken and the Agrarians were both dismayed by the extent to which the New York intellectuals had separated themselves from anything taking place west of the Hudson River. In fact, Mencken's primary importance in American letters during the 1920's was his encouraging of American writers and artists to cease facing eastward toward New York and Europe, and to look toward the South and the Middle West for their material. The publication of *The American Language*, his patronage of regional writers and artists and his attacks on the expatriates attest to Mencken's cultural nationalism. "I remain on the dock, wrapped in the flag, when the Young Intellectuals set sail," he announced. "Here I stand, unshaken and undespairing, a loyal and devoted American, even a chauvinist . . . contributing my mite toward the glory of the national arts and sciences, enriching and embellishing the national language. . . . ." Mencken was a vital part of the regionalism of the interwar years which Davidson praised as a valuable protest against the "artistic leviathanism of the machine age, symbolized by the dominance of New York during the nineteen-twenties." The revolt of the Agrarians against the cultural preeminence of New York City was preceded, and perhaps made possible, by the rebellion of Mencken during the 1920's and the support he gave to the burgeoning southern literary renaissance.[33]

Certainly Mencken and the Agrarians misunderstood each other. Davidson's article in the *American Review* misinterpreted Mencken's relationship to the New York intelligentsia, while Mencken's "The South Astir" exaggerated the differences between himself and the Agrarians and ignored their wide areas of agreement. Although based on several misconceptions and undoubtedly blown up all out of proportion, the Mencken-Agrarian feud helped reinvigorate the perennial historical quest for the nature of Southern distinctiveness. Their experiences with the *VQR* and Mencken left the Agrarians even more conscious of their own identity as Southerners. This would later be manifested, for example, in Fletcher's *Arkansas* (1947), Owsley's *Plain Folk of the Old South* (1949), Davidson's *Southern Writers in the Modern World* (1958) and Warren's *The Legacy of the Civil War: Meditations on the Centennial* (1961). The Agrarians' militant defense of Southern uniqueness, in turn, provoked others to explore the theme of Southern identity. Although unable to accept the Agrarian explanation of Southern distinctiveness, these later commentators were equally convinced that the South was different from the rest of the nation. These later attempts to locate the source of the Southern ethos have variously emphasized the South's romanticism and inclination to mythologize, her laziness, her heightened historical consciousness, her folk culture, and her sense of guilt, pessimism, frustration and tragedy. The effort to define Southern identity will undoubtedly continue and probably prove to be just as difficult as it had been for Mencken and the Agrarians, for, to quote the late David M. Potter, "the South remains as challenging as it is baffling, which is about as challenging as a subject can be."[34]

## footnotes

1. George B. Tindall, *The Emergence of the New South, 1913-1945* (Baton Rouge, 1967), 575-606; Tindall, "The 'Colonial Economy' and the Growth Psychology: The South in the 1930's," *South Atlantic Quarterly*, LXIV, 4 (Autumn, 1965), 465-66; Tindall, "The Significance of Howard W. Odum to Southern History: A Preliminary Estimate," *Journal of Southern History*, XXIV, 3 (August, 1958), 289-90; Clarence H. Danhof, "Four Decades of Thought on the South's Economic Problems," *Essays in Southern Economic Development*, eds. Melvin L. Greenhut and W. Tate Whitman (Chapel Hill, 1964), 5-7; Earl H. Rovit, "The Regions Versus the Nation: Critical Battle of the Thirties," *Mississippi Quarterly*, XIII, 2 (Spring, 1960), 90-98; Marion Irish, "Proposed Roads to the New South, 1941: Chapel Hill Planners Versus Nashville Agrarians," *Sewanee Review*, XLIX, 1 (Winter, 1941), 1-27; "Industrialism Versus Agrarianism for the South," *University Debaters' Annual*, ed. Edith M. Phelps (New York, 1932); C. Vann

Woodward, "The Search for Southern Identity," *Virginia Quarterly Review*, XXXIV, 3 (Summer, 1958), 321-27.

2. Tindall, "The Benighted South: Origins of a Modern Image," *Virginia Quarterly Review*, XL, 2 (Spring, 1964), 291-93.

3. H. L. Mencken, "The Sahara of the Bozart," *H. L. Mencken Prejudices: A Selection*, ed. James T. Farrell (New York, 1958), 69-74, 79-82; Tindall, "Benighted South," 284-86; William J. Bosch, "Henry L. Mencken's Image of the South" (unpublished seminar paper, Department of History, University of North Carolina, 1963), 5; Edgar Kemler, *The Irreverent Mr. Mencken* (Boston, 1950), 176-78; John M. Bradbury, *The Fugitives: A Critical Account* (Chapel Hill, 1958), 6-7; Alexander Karanikas, *Tillers of a Myth: Southern Agrarians as Social and Literary Critics* (Madison, Wis., 1966), 21-23; John Lincoln Stewart, *The Burden of Time: The Fugitives and Agrarians* (Princeton, 1965), 114; Rob Roy Purdy, ed., *Fugitives' Reunion: Conversations at Vanderbilt, May 3-5, 1956* (Nashville, 1959), 92.

4. Mencken, "In Tennessee," *Nation*, CXXI, 3130 (July 1, 1925), 21-22; Mencken, "The Hills of Zion," *The Vintage Mencken*, ed. Alistair Cooke (New York, 1955), 153-61; Bosch, "Mencken's Image of the South," *passim*; Kemler, *Irreverent Mr. Mencken*, 186-87; William Manchester, *H. L. Mencken: Disturber of the Peace* (New York, 1950), 191-217; Oscar Cargill, "Mencken and the South," *Georgia Review*, VI, 4 (Winter, 1952), 374.

5. Mencken, "The Husbandman," *H. L. Mencken Prejudices*, ed. Farrell, 157-68; Mencken, "The Politician," *ibid.*, 169-71; Mencken, "The Champion," *ibid.*, 210; Malcolm Moos, ed., *H. L. Mencken on Politics: A Carnival of Buncombe* (New York, 1960), 162-71, 197-200.

6. Purdy, ed., *Fugitives' Reunion*, 178, 199, 204-205; Stewart, *Burden of Time*, 109-115; Louise Cowan, *The Fugitive Group: A Literary History* (Baton Rouge, 1959), 208, 240-46; Virginia Rock, "The Making and Meaning of *I'll Take My Stand*: A Study in Utopian Conservatism, 1925-1939" (unpublished Ph.D. dissertation, Department of Modern Language and Literature, University of Minnesota, 1961), 209.

7. Stewart, *Burden of Time*, 114-15; Ransom, *God Without Thunder: An Unorthodox Defense of Orthodoxy* (New York, 1930), 95-107; Ransom to Tate, July 4, 1929, Tate Papers (Princeton University).

8. Davidson, "The Artist as Southerner," *Saturday Review of Literature*, II (May 15, 1926), 783; Davidson, "First Fruits of Dayton: The Intellectual Evolution in Dixie," *Forum*, LXXIX, 6 (June, 1928), 898. For other evidence of the Agrarians' interest in religion, see Tate, "The Fallacy of Humanism," *Hound and Horn*, III (Winter, 1930), 234-57; John Donald Wade, *John Wesley* (New York, 1930); and Robert Penn Warren's poem "August Revival: Crosby Junction," *Sewanee Review*, XXXIII, 4 (December, 1925), 439.

9. John Tyree Fain, ed., *The Spyglass: Views and Reviews, 1924-1930 by Donald Davidson* (Nashville, 1963), 126-31; Davidson, *The Tennessee* (New York, 1948), II, 195-204; Davidson, *Southern Writers in the Modern World* (Athens, Ga., 1958), 31-41; Davidson to Tate, August 15, 1926, Tate Papers.

10. See especially Ransom, "Reconstructed But Unregenerate," *I'll Take My Stand: The South and the Agrarian Tradition* (New York, 1930), 1-27.

11. Mencken, "Uprising in the Confederacy," *American Mercury*, XXII, 87 (March, 1931), 379-81.

12. Davidson, "Sectionalism in the United States," *Hound and Horn*, VI (July-September, 1933), 561-89.

13. Davidson, "Lands That Were Golden. I. New York and the Hinterland," *American Review*, III, 5 (October, 1934), 545-61. John Gould Fletcher was so impressed by Davidson's article that he wrote a similar one entitled "New York Versus American Culture" (unpublished mss., John Gould Fletcher Papers, University of Arkansas); Davidson to Fletcher, October 7, 1934, Fletcher Papers; Fletcher to Davidson, October 9, 1934, December 5, 1934, Davidson Papers (Vanderbilt University); Fletcher to Robert Penn Warren, December 14, 1934, Warren Papers (Yale University).

14. Mencken to Lambert Davis, November 17, 1934, *Virginia Quarterly Review* Editorial Correspondence, *Virginia Quarterly Review* Papers (University of Virginia); Davis to Mencken, January 13, 1934, *ibid.*

15. Mencken to Davis, January 16, 1934, *ibid.*

16. Mencken to Davis, October 13, 1934, October 16, 1934, *ibid.*; Davis to Mencken, October 15, 1934, November 14, 1934, November 16, 1934, *ibid.*

17. Mencken, "The South Astir," *Virginia Quarterly Review*, XI, 1 (January, 1935), 51-60.

18. Davidson to Davis, January 9, 1935, January 23, 1935, Davidson Papers.

19. Davidson to Davis, February 18, 1934, March 25, 1934, September 25, 1934, *VQR* Editorial Correspondence; Davis to Davidson, February 20, 1934, March 14, 1934, March 27, 1934, *ibid.*; Davis to Davidson, September 14, 1934, October 1, 1934, Davidson Papers.

20. Davis to Davidson, January 17, 1935 (misdated January 17, 1934), Davidson Papers.

21. Davidson to Tate, February 21, 1930, February 25, 1930, Tate Papers; Barr, "Shall Slavery Come South?" *Virginia Quarterly Review*, VI, 4 (October, 1930), 481-94; Stewart, *Burden*

*of Time*, 145-47; Rock, "Making and Meaning of *I'll Take My Stand*," 349-57; M. Thomas Inge, "Richmond's Great Debate," *Richmond Times-Dispatch*, December 6, 1970.

22. Johnson, "The South Faces Itself," *Virginia Quarterly Review*, VII, 1 (January, 1931), 155-57; Barr to Tate, December 31, 1931, Tate Papers; Tate to Ellen Glasgow, March 30, 1933, Tate Papers. The *VQR*'s editorial policy, Davidson complained in 1934, was "studiously noncombatant; it touched mildly upon social and economic issues but ignored literary issues." Davidson, "The Trend of Literature: A Partisan View," *Culture in the South*, ed. William T. Couch (Chapel Hill, 1934), 195.

23. For the Agrarians' dislike of Barr's editorial policies, see Tate to Fletcher, March 14, 1935, Tate Papers; Fletcher to Owsley, March 11, 1935, Frank L. Owsley Papers (in possession of Mrs. Frank L. Owsley, Nashville, Tennessee); Davidson to Fletcher, March 6, 1935, March 12, 1935, Fletcher Papers; Davidson to Tate, March 17, 1935, Tate Papers; Fletcher to Barr, January 20, 1935, *VQR* Editorial Correspondence; Owsley to Fletcher, March 16, 1935, Fletcher Papers. For Davis' view of his editorial responsibilities, see Davis to Davidson, January 30, 1935, Davidson Papers.

24. Davis to Davidson, February 28, 1935, Davidson Papers; Davidson, "*I'll Take My Stand*: A History," *American Review*, V, 3 (Summer, 1935), 317. In January, 1935, Davidson had praised the *VQR* along with the *Southwest Review* for making important contributions to cultural and literary regionalism. This leads one to believe that Davidson's reaction to Davis' rejection of his essay was due in part to pique. Davidson, "Regionalism and Education," *American Review*, IV, 3 (January, 1935), 324-25.

25. Davis to Tate, July 3, 1934, Davis to Warren, September 11, 1934, Davis to Lytle, September 11, 1934, Davis to Ransom, September 11, 1934, Davis to Wade, September 10, 1934, *VQR* Editorial Correspondence.

26. Davis to Lytle, October 3, 1934, October 15, 1934, October 19, 1934, November 11, 1934, November 14, 1934, Lytle to Davis, December 3, 1934, Davis to Warren, December 6, 1934, Davis to Owsley, December 20, 1934, *VQR* Editorial Correspondence.

27. Tate to Davis, March 10, 1935, *VQR* Editorial Correspondence; Tate to Davidson, March 5, 1935, Davidson Papers; Fletcher to Davidson, March 5, 1935, March 11, 1935, March 12, 1935, Davidson Papers; Fletcher to Warren, December 14, 1934, December 27, 1934, March 11, 1935, Warren Papers; Fletcher to Tate, March 7, 1935, March 13, 1935, Tate Papers; Fletcher to Owsley, March 13, 1935, Owsley Papers; Fletcher to Stringfellow Barr, January 20, 1935, *VQR* Editorial Correspondence; Davis to Fletcher, January 31, 1935, *ibid.*; Fletcher to Charles Pipkin, June 22, 1934, *Southern Review Collection* (Yale University); Fletcher to Davidson, March 8, 1934, Fletcher Papers. For Fletcher's commitment to the traditional South, see "Is This the Voice of the South?" *Nation*, CXXXVII, 3573 (December 27, 1933), 734-35; "Regionalism and Folk Art," *Southwest Review*, XIX, 4 (July, 1934), 429-34; *Life Is My Song* (New York, 1937), 356-57, 371-79. Fletcher's widow has recounted how he insisted, against the advice of the architect, that his house "Johnswood" be built in such a way that he could sleep facing south. Charlie May Simon, *Johnswood* (New York, 1953), 27.

28. Davidson to Fletcher, March 12, 1935, March 17, 1935, Fletcher Papers; Tate to Fletcher, March 12, 1935, Fletcher Papers; Tate to Fletcher, March 14, 1935, Tate Papers; Tate to Davidson, March 14, 1935, Davidson Papers; Warren to Fletcher, March 20, 1935, Fletcher Papers; Ransom to Fletcher, March 15, 1935, Fletcher Papers; Davidson to Tate, March 17, 1935, Davidson Papers; Fletcher to Davidson, March 25, 1935, Davidson Papers.

29. Owsley to Fletcher, March 12, 1935, March 16, 1935, Fletcher Papers; Davidson to Fletcher, March 6, 1935, March 12, 1935, Fletcher Papers; Owsley, "The Pillars of Agrarianism," *American Review*, IV, 5 (March, 1935), 529-30. Fletcher also answered Mencken in "The Sin of City-Mindedness: A Reply to H. L. Mencken" (unpublished mss., Fletcher Papers). For Davidson's praise of Fletcher's essay, see Davidson to Fletcher, April 14, 1935, Fletcher Papers.

30. Davis to Tate, March 26, 1935, Tate Papers; "The Green-Room," *Virginia Quarterly Review*, XI, 2 (April, 1935), ii-iv.

31. Davidson, "The Trend of Literature: A Partisan View," 196; Mencken, "The Sahara of the Bozart," 70-73; William Nolte, *H. L. Mencken, Literary Critic* (Middletown, Conn., 1964), 178-83; Douglas C. Stenerson, *H. L. Mencken: Iconoclast from Baltimore* (Chicago, 1971), 65; Kemler, *Irreverent Mr. Mencken*, 175.

32. Manchester, *Mencken*, 86; Ernest Boyd, *H. L. Mencken* (New York, 1927), 3-15; Charles Angoff, *H. L. Mencken, a Portrait from Memory* (New York, 1956), 55; Kemler, *Irreverent Mr. Mencken*, 146; Stenerson, *H. L. Mencken*, 206-207; Mencken, "On Living in Baltimore," *H. L. Mencken Prejudices*, ed. Farrell, 206-210.

33. Mencken to Davis, November 17, 1934, *VQR* Editorial Correspondence; Stenerson, *H. L. Mencken*, 10-15, 133, 219-20; Nolte, *Mencken*, 114-18, 230-31; Kemler, *Irreverent Mr. Mencken*, 168-69; Carl Bode, *Mencken* (Carbondale, Ill., 1969), 174-76; Mencken, "On Being an American," *H. L. Mencken Prejudices*, ed. Farrell, 90; Davidson, *The Attack on Leviathan: Regionalism and Nationalism in the United States* (Chapel Hill, 1938), 78-87.

34. T. Harry Williams, *Romance and Realism in Southern Politics* (Baton Rouge, 1966); David Bertelson, *The Lazy South* (New York, 1967); F. Garvin Davenport, Jr., *The Myth of*

*Southern History: Historical Consciousness in Twentieth-Century Southern Literature* (Nashville, 1970); David M. Potter, "The Enigma of the South," *Yale Review*, LI (October, 1961), 150-51; Woodward, "The Search for Southern Identity," 321-38; Potter, "On Understanding the South: a Review Article," *Journal of Southern History*, XXX, 4 (November, 1964), 462; Monroe L. Billington, *The South, a Central Theme?* (New York, 1969).

# The Southern Agrarians and the Tennessee Valley Authority

HISTORIANS HAVE GENERALLY MISUNDERSTOOD THE ATTITUDE OF THE Southern Agrarians toward the Tennessee Valley Authority.[1] Donald Davidson, it is true, consistently opposed the Authority from the late 1930s on, but the five other Agrarians who expressed an opinion were generally favorable to the project and two of them were highly enthusiastic.[2] John Gould Fletcher called the TVA a "success," and desired a similar project for his native Arkansas. Frank L. Owsley described it as

---

[1] Idus Newby, "The Southern Agrarians: A View After Thirty Years," *Agricultural History*, XXXVII (July 1963), 152-53; Thomas L. Connelly, "The Vanderbilt Agrarians: Time and Place in Southern Tradition," *Tennessee Historical Quarterly*, XXII (Mar. 1963), 28 29, 33. Historians and literary critics have usually described the Agrarians as nostalgic reactionaries. See Christopher Lasch, *The New Radicalism in America, 1889-1963: The Intellectual as a Social Type* (New York, 1965), p. 297; John Lincoln Stewart, *The Burden of Time: The Fugitives and Agrarians* (Princeton, 1965), chaps. 3, 4; Charles Rosenberg, "Insurrection," *New Yorker*, XL (Mar. 14, 1964), 169; Gay Wilson Allen, "Criterions for Criticism," *Saturday Review*, XLIX (June 11, 1966), 64-68; George Steiner, "Thought in a Green Shade," *Reporter*, XXXI (Dec. 31, 1964), 36; Wallace W. Douglas, "Deliberate Exiles: The Social Sources of Agrarian Poetics," *Aspects of American Literature*, ed. Richard M. Ludwig (Columbus, Ohio, 1962), pp. 277-300; Robert Gorham Davis, "The New Criticism and the Democratic Tradition," *American Scholar*, XIX (Winter 1950), 9 19; Alexander Karanikas, *Tillers of a Myth: Southern Agrarians as Social and Literary Critics* (Madison, Wis., 1966), *passim*; I have sharply criticized Karanikas' work in *Southern Humanities Review*, I (Summer 1967), 199-201. The most extreme view of the Agrarians as political reactionaries is that of James L. McDonald, who asserts that they "wanted to abolish the twentieth century, called for a return to the life of the antebellum South, and opposed all attempts at modernization." McDonald, "Reactionary Rebels: Agrarians in Defense of the South," *Midwest Quarterly*, X (Jan. 1969), 160. I have shown in my Harvard dissertation, "The American Distributists and the New Deal" (1968), that the Agrarians can be more accurately described as radical Populists than as reactionaries, and that they were closer in political outlook to a Borah than to a Talmadge.

[2] I have been unable to find any written evaluation of the TVA by Lyle H. Lanier, John Donald Wade, Andrew Nelson Lytle, John Crowe Ransom, Stark Young and Robert Penn Warren. Warren told me that he supported the TVA. Interview with Warren, Apr. 19, 1965.

"a great venture in unified public works, planning, and 'pump priming' on a regional development basis." Allen Tate, although dubious about some aspects of the TVA, nevertheless contended that it was "a good thing." Herman C. Nixon asserted that the Authority represented "the most sympathetic use of outside money ... on a large scale the South has ever known. ... It is:making it possible for more people to live with a little more convenience, security, and happiness in 'God's Valley.'" The Authority, he argued, "may be fairly called the strongest card in the New Deal. ... The nation needs a series of the grand projects of the TVA type ... but it seems fortunate that the eroded South became the scene of the first experiment." Henry Blue Kline even worked for the Authority for several years, and during this period wrote an important study on the effect of discriminatory railroad rates on southern industrial development. After leaving the TVA, Kline joined the staff of the St. Louis *Post-Dispatch* where he wrote several editorials defending the TVA and favoring a Missouri Valley Authority modeled on it.[3]

This support for the TVA grew logically out of the Agrarians' social and political thought and their analysis of the causes of the 1929 depression. The essence of Agrarian social thought was their belief that a society, if it was to be free and prosperous, must have a majority of its people owning productive property. The Agrarians hated modern large-scale industrialization because it centralized the ownership of property among a small percentage of the population and created an insecure and subservient proletariat. They also maintained that the class consciousness and bitter social and economic conflict accompanying industrialization were due to the transformation of the stable, conservative and propertied middle class into coupon clippers and wage slaves.[4]

[3] Fletcher to Donald Davidson, July 27, 1933, Davidson Papers (Vanderbilt University); Fletcher, *Arkansas* (Chapel Hill, N.C., 1947), p. 399; Owsley to Davidson, Aug. 5, 1933, Davidson Papers; Owsley, "Mr. Daniels Discovers the South," *Southern Review*, IV (Spring 1939), 670; Owsley, Oliver P. Chitwood and Herman C. Nixon, *A Short History of the American People* (New York, 1948), II, 634-35. Owsley wrote the section on the New Deal in this textbook. Frank L. Owsley Jr. notes that his father "believed that TVA had given much to the prosperity of the area and helped all of the people. With some reservations, he thought the program did much more good than harm." Owsley Jr. to Edward S. Shapiro, June 11, 1965; Chattanooga *Times*, Nov. 4, 1936; Nixon, *Forty Acres and Steel Mules* (Chapel Hill, N.C., 1938), pp. 80-81; Nixon, *Possum Trot: Rural Community, South* (Norman, Okla., 1941), pp. 152-53; Professor Don K. Price of Harvard's political science department worked with Kline in the TVA and believes that he was "a thorough convert to the TVA approach." Price to Shapiro, Apr. 7, 1965.

[4] John Crowe Ransom, "What Does the South Want?" *Who Owns America? A New Declaration of Independence*, eds. Herbert Agar and Allen Tate (Boston, 1936), pp. 83-84; Donald Davidson, "Agrarianism and Politics," *Review of Politics*, I (Apr. 1939), 121-23; Twelve Southerners, "Introduction: A Statement of Principles," *I'll Take My Stand: The South and the Agrarian Tradition* (New York, 1930), pp. xxii-xxv; Tate, "The Problem of

The Agrarians further claimed that the economic centralization occurring under industrialism led to political centralization and autocratic control of the government either by the wealthy or by radicals. They emphasized that both plutocracy and socialism favored economic consolidation, centralized planning and the dispossession of the middle class. Socialism simply carried out the implications of large-scale corporate ownership to their logical conclusion by having the economy controlled by one gigantic public corporation instead of a few private leviathans. As Allen Tate wrote to Malcolm Cowley, "From my point of view ... you and the other Marxians are not revolutionary enough: you want to keep capitalism with the capitalism left out." Only a program which looked to a return to the widespread ownership of property had a chance to overthrow capitalism and "create a decent society in terms of American history."[5]

The Agrarians blamed the 1929 depression on a gap between production and consumption resulting from the holding down of wages by monopoly capitalists and from the pro-big business policies of the government during the 1920s, especially the high protective tariff. Low wages and the tariff, they argued, had reduced the purchasing power of the working class, had forced the consumer to pay artificially high prices and had deprived farmers of foreign markets for their surplus products. This gap had been temporarily bridged in the 1920s by advertising which, according to Donald Davidson, by "persuading the people always to spend

---

the Unemployed: A Modest Proposal," *American Review*, I (May 1933), 143, 149; Tate, "Notes on Liberty and Property," *Who Owns America?*, pp. 80-93; Tate, "What Is a Traditional Society?" *American Review*, VII (Sept. 1936), 386-87. The Agrarians believed that Henry Ford, because of his assembly line and the regimentation of his employees, personified large-scale industrialization. See, for example, Donald Davidson's comments in John Tyree Fain, ed., *The Spyglass: Views and Reviews, 1924-1930* (Nashville, Tenn., 1963), pp. 235-38.

[5]Tate quoted by Daniel Aaron, *Writers on the Left: Episodes in American Literary Communism* (New York, 1961), pp. 352-53, 458; Davidson, "The Agrarians Today," *Shenandoah*, III (Autumn 1952), 17-18; Andrew Nelson Lytle, "The Backwoods Progression," *American Review*, I (Sept. 1933), 434; Owsley, "The Foundations of Democracy," *Who Owns America?*, p. 67; Henry Blue Kline, "Loophole for Monopoly," St. Louis *Post-Dispatch*, Jan. 25, 1946; Ransom, "Shall the South Follow the East and Go Industrial?" Institute for Citizenship, Emory University, *Proceedings of Fourth Annual Session*, Feb. 10-13, 1931 (Atlanta, Ga., 1931), p. 51; the Agrarians believed the liberal attempt to reform large-scale industrialism without extensive socialism was impossible. Government bureaucrats, according to John Crowe Ransom, would be unable to stop at a minimum of direction but "will call for regulation, . . . And the grand finale of regulation, the millenium itself of regulated industrialism, is Russian communism." Ransom quoted by Davidson, *Southern Writers in the Modern World* (Athens, Ga., 1958), p. 49. The Agrarians were so concerned over the threat of industrial communism that they almost entitled their 1930 symposium "Tracts Against Communism." Rob Roy Purdy, ed., *Fugitives Reunion: Conversations at Vanderbilt, May 3-5, 1956* (Nashville, Tenn. 1959), p. 207.

more than they have, and to want more than they get," offered "precisely the same temptations that Satan offered Christ." The 1929 depression was due, then, to economic imbalances caused by large-scale industrialism and its control of the government—an imbalance between workers and owners, an imbalance between agriculture and industry, and an imbalance between the rural South and West and the industrial Northeast.[6]

The struggle between the Northeast, the center of large-scale capitalism, and the decentralized and propertied societies of the West and South was, according to the Agrarians, the key to understanding America's post-revolutionary history. They praised Frederick Jackson Turner's emphasis on sectionalism, and they agreed with him that the most fundamental fissures in American life were along regional, rather than class, lines. The conflicts between Jefferson and Hamilton, Jackson and Biddle, the North and the South during the Civil War, and Bryan and McKinley were all aspects of this basic antagonism between the industrial and financial Northeast and the South and West with their farmers and small businessmen. "There is no other nation in the Western world," Davidson wrote, "in which sectional alignment on major questions so often occurs." Walter P. Webb's book *Divided We Stand: The Crisis of a Frontierless Democracy,* a work highly praised by the Agrarians, confirmed for them the importance of sectionalism. Webb dedicated the book to the "small businessmen of America" who were being slowly crushed by giant corporations. Webb argued that these corporations were the advance guard of an imperialistic and plutocratic northeastern capitalism determined to control the economies of the South and West and to destroy the "traditional principles of American democracy" which were dependent upon the widespread distribution of property. Wherever one went in the South and West, he would find "people in chains and paying tribute to someone in the North."[7]

---

[6]Fain, ed., *The Spyglass,* p. 238; Ransom, *God Without Thunder: An Unorthodox Defense of Orthodoxy* (New York, 1930), pp. 194-95; Ransom, "The State and the Land," *New Republic,* LXX (Feb. 17, 1932), 8-10; Lanier, "Big Business in the Property State," *Who Owns America?,* p. 22; Owsley, Chitwood, Nixon, *Short History* . . . , II, 605-7. For the emphasis which New Deal thought placed upon this concept of "imbalance," see William E. Leuchtenburg, *Franklin D. Roosevelt and the New Deal: 1932-1940* (New York, 1963), p. 35.

[7]Davidson, *The Attack on Leviathan: Regionalism and Nationalism in the United States* (Chapel Hill, N.C., 1938), pp. 24-25; Owsley, "The Foundations of Democracy," pp. 53-54; Lytle, "John Taylor and the Political Economy of Agriculture," *American Review,* III (Sept. 1934), 432; Lanier, "Mr. Dollard and Scientific Method," *Southern Review,* III (Spring 1938), 669-71; Fletcher, *The Two Frontiers: A Study in Historical Psychology* (New York, 1930), pp. 247-48; Robert Penn Warren, "The Second American Revolution," *Virginia Quarterly Review,* VII (Apr. 1931), 282-88; John Donald Wade, "Old Wine In a New Bottle," *Virginia Quarterly Review,* XI (Apr. 1935), 246; Webb, *Divided We Stand. The Crisis of a Frontierless Democracy* (New York, 1937), *passim;* for a typical Agrarian

As Southerners, the Agrarians were especially sensitive to the imperialistic and exploitative character of large-scale industrialism. The idea that the South was in economic thralldom to the capitalistic North was a staple of southern social thought and southern political rhetoric during the 1930s. For Davidson and the other Agrarians, the nature of the Northeast was "to devour, to exploit, to imperialize," to "walk in silk and satin," while the West and South went in "shoddy." They pointed to the taking over of southern banks, factories and national resources by Yankee capitalists during the late 19th century as illustrating the aggrandizing character of northern capitalism. They claimed that the New South movement, which had encouraged this invasion of northern capitalists, had merely benefited the northern worker and capitalist, while the South had been left impoverished and sucking at the "hind tit."[8]

The dominance of the financial-industrial plutocracy, the Agrarians believed, could be traced back to the southern defeat during the Civil War. They accepted the Beardian interpretation of the war as a struggle between an agrarian, conservative South and an industrial, imperialistic North which destroyed the last major barrier to the complete victory of large-scale capitalism. Fletcher wrote of Reconstruction as

> ...the hour
> When Grant and Wall Street linked, began their work
> Which has not ended yet...

After 1865, the Northeast reduced the South and West to "the position of complaisant accomplices and servile dependents," and through the Republican Party enacted a program fostering big business, the centralization of finance, the proletarianization of the middle class and the destruction of agriculture. The Agrarians cited the protective tariff, the Supreme Court's interpretations of the Fifth and Fourteenth Amendments, and discriminatory railroad rates as examples of advantages acquired by northern capitalists because of their control of the national government. They blamed these subsidies and privileges for the postbellum growth of big business and high finance and the creation of "an economic fascism which threatens the essential democratic institutions of America." The Agrarians argued that the only way to check the eco-

---

response to Webb's book, see Ransom, "The Unequal Sections," *Saturday Review of Literature*, XVII (Dec. 18, 1937), 6–7.

[9]George B. Tindall, "The 'Colonial Economy' and the Growth Psychology: The South in the 1930's," *South Atlantic Quarterly*, LXIV (Autumn 1965), 465–77; Davidson, *Attack on Leviathan*, pp. 110-15, 126, 262-92; Fletcher, *Life Is My Song* (New York, 1937), p. 374; Lytle, "The Hind Tit," *I'll Take My Stand*, pp. 202-3; Ransom, "Reconstructed But Unregenerate," *ibid.*, pp. 22-23.

nomic imperialism of the Northeast was through a revival of regional sentiment in the South and West resulting in sectional economic self-determination.[9]

The urbanization of the United States dismayed the Agrarians as much as did industrialization. The anonymity, alienation, loneliness and regimentation of the modern American city contrasted sharply, they believed, with rural values and the rural way of life. In addition, they attributed the urban popularity of radical, anti-democratic political movements to the city's large proletariat and its lack of a large property-owning middle class. Davidson's poem "The Long Street" perhaps best reveals the Agrarian attitude toward the modern city.

> It was different, once, for Orestes Brown. He lived
> In the hill country where the bluegrass turns
> To upland fallows and tobacco barns,
> A land of no strangers. Orestes Brown had known
> Man, woman, child, both white and black, and called
> Folks by their first names from the Cumberland on
> To his own hearthside. But all that was before
> The family trouble that besets our race
> Drove him to wander through a kinless world
> Till he became a function and a number—
> Motorman Seventeen, on the company rolls—
> For whom, by singular principles of bondage,
> Man, woman, child, both white and black, we were turned
> To strangers all, who dropped their seven cents
> Into the cash-box, so becoming fares,
> Then sat or stood, nameless, till they got off.

[9] Fletcher, *South Star* (New York, 1941), p. 42; Lytle, "Principles of Secession," *Hound and Horn*, V (July-Sept. 1932), 688; Davidson, *Attack on Leviathan*, pp. 110-15; Davidson wrote in his history of the Tennessee River that during the Civil War hunting in the Tennessee Valley had greatly decreased and not since pioneer days had there been such a feast of "wild turkey, quail, deer, and fish of the river. This is the only undebatably 'good result' of the Civil War that any historian has recorded." Davidson, *The Tennessee* (New York, 1948), II, 107-17; Warren, *The Legacy of the Civil War: Meditations on the Centennial* (New York, 1961), pp. 13, 42; Lanier, "Big Business in the Property State," p. 18; Kline, *Regional Freight Rates: Barrier to National Productiveness*, U. S. House of Representatives Document No. 137 (Washington: U. S. Government Printing Office, 1943); Owsley, "The Irrepressible Conflict," *I'll Take My Stand*, pp. 85-89; Fletcher, "Cultural Aspects of Regionalism," *Round Table on Regionalism*, Institute of Public Affairs, University of Virginia, July 9, 1931 (mimeographed, 1931), pp. 6-7; Tate to Seward Collins, Dec. 23, 1933, in Seward Collins Papers (Beinecke Library, Yale University). Indicative of the failure to understand the Agrarians is the comment of Thomas J. Pressley that the Agrarians were "individuals of quite conservative political and economic views" who could be contrasted with the followers of Beard and Parrington who "vigorously criticized the 'New South' spirit and program and insisted that the South's economic difficulties were due primarily to its status as an exploited 'colony' of Northeastern business interests." Pressley, *Americans Interpret Their Civil War* (Princeton, 1954), p. 241.

> But he, Orestes Brown, was not content
> That people should go back and forth without
> The pleasure of a name between themselves
> And him; and in the fullness of his heart
> He broke the rules—he talked to sulky boys
> After the school and movies, or old men
> With hound-dog weariness in their eyes, or forms
> That had a country slouch about the shoulders.
> These last would sometimes talk; the rest, not often.
>
> ...............................
>
> But I knew how the Lord said long ago:
> *I have set my face against this city for evil!*
> And the Lord said: *It shall be given
> To the King of Babylon to burn with fire;
> And desolate is Zion's mount where the foxes run!*[10]

The Agrarians pointed to the city's flashy and cosmopolitan artists as proof of its estrangement from traditional American culture. Truly American art, they proclaimed, could be produced only by artists rooted in a provincial and conservative society, such as the South, and not by deracinated and bohemian urbanites who prefer "sophistication over wisdom; experiment over tradition; technique over style; emancipation over morals." New York, "an island of transplanted Europeans anchored off the Atlantic coast," "a spectacular cosmopolitan city of borrowed culture," which attracted "all the celebrities and semi-celebrities of Europe into its orbit," exemplified the metropolis' alienation from the American hinterland.[11]

---

[10]Wade, "Of the Mean and Sure Estate," *Who Owns America?*, pp. 254–60; Ransom, *God Without Thunder: An Unorthodox Defense of Orthodoxy* (New York, 1930), p. 125; Davidson, *The Long Street: Poems* (Nashville, Tenn., 1961), pp. 64–66; see also Fletcher's poem "Twentieth Century" which described the modern metropolis with its "Pinnacles steeper than all Babels of the Past" and "wreathed with Manhattan mobs that will not rest." *Alcestis*, I (Apr. 1935), n.p.

[11]Davidson, *Attack on Leviathan*, pp. 68–100; Fletcher, *Life Is My Song*, p. 299; Fletcher, "Regionalism and Folk Art," *Southwest Review*, XIX (July 1934), 432–34; Fletcher, "The Stieglitz Spoof," *American Review*, IV (Mar. 1935), 589 ff.; Richard Crowder, "John Gould Fletcher as Cassandra," *South Atlantic Quarterly*, LII (Jan. 1953), 89–91; Tate, "A View of the Whole South," *American Review*, II (Feb. 1934), 416; Tate, "What Is a Traditional Society?" pp. 384–85; Warren, "Literature as a Symptom," *Who Owns America?*, pp. 264–79; Stark Young, "History and Mystery," *New Republic*, LXX (Feb. 24, 1932), 46. Davidson and Fletcher believed the Jew, particularly the New York Jew, embodied the materialism, commercialism, radicalism, deracination and cosmopolitanism characteristic of the city dweller. This led both to espouse a mild form of cultural anti-Semitism. Davidson to Seward Collins, Oct. 10, 1934, Collins Papers; Fletcher to Collins, Dec. 10, 1934; Jan. 18, 1935, Collins Papers; Fletcher to Frank L. Owsley, Dec. 12, 1933, in Owsley Papers (in possession of Mrs. Frank L. Owsley, Nashville, Tenn.); Shapiro, "American Distributists and the New Deal," pp. 66–68, 72–77.

The Agrarians' emphasis on regionalism was not unique during the 1920s and 1930s. The art of Thomas Hart Benton, the regional sociology of Howard Odum and Rupert Vance at the University of North Carolina, and the establishment of regional historical journals such as the *New England Quarterly* (1928), the *Pacific Historical Review* (1932), the *Journal of Southern History* (1935) and the *Bulletin* of the American Association for State and Local History (1941) also reflected the increasing importance of regionalism during this period.

The return of America to a propertied, small town, rural society depended, the Agrarians asserted, upon a political coalition between the West and South. Only if these two sections put aside their differences dating from the Civil War and realized that their common enemy was now the Northeast could industrialism, urbanization and high finance be turned back. As John Crowe Ransom put it, both sections "desire to defend home, stability of life, the practice of leisure, and the natural enemy of both is the insidious industrial system." With the overthrow of the urban industrial-financial plutocracy, the nation's attention could then turn to the plight of the small businessman and the farmer.[12]

The condition of agriculture, particularly southern agriculture, greatly interested the Agrarians. Contrary to what Henry Steele Commager and others have written, most of the Agrarians did not idealize ante-bellum plantation life. Rather, they saw the small southern farmers as uniquely possessing such desirable agrarian virtues as economic independence, strong family ties and religious sentiment. The Agrarians were fully aware of the perilous condition of most small southern farmers. Widespread tenant farming and absentee-landlordism, they argued, had led to economic dependence, dispossession, extreme poverty, political demagoguery and a general atmosphere of hopelessness and degradation. They feared that, if something was not done immediately, the entire South would soon come to resemble one vast Tobacco Road. Davidson, politically the most "conservative" of all the Agrarians, bitterly complained of "Southern lands eroded and worn-out," "the devilish one-crop system and the tenant system," the "illiterate and diseased population" and "the fierce despair" and "terrifying apathy" found throughout the South.[13]

[12]Ransom, "The South Defends Its Heritage," *Harper's Magazine*, CLIX (June 1929), 117; Lytle, "Hind Tit," p. 224.

[13]See the essays by Lytle, "The Hind Tit," Wade, "The Life and Death of Cousin Lucius," and Kline, "William Remington: A Study in Individualism" in *I'll Take My Stand*; Nixon, *Forty Acres* . . . , pp. 17-27, 38-49; Fletcher, *Arkansas*, pp. 338-50; Davidson, *Attack on Leviathan*, p. 113. Owsley has been largely responsible for altering the image of the antebellum South as a land of slaves, planter aristocrats and poor whites. Using social science techniques, Owsley conclusively demonstrated that the social structure of the Old South

The belief that economic and political collectivism, urbanization and the decay of agriculture were not inevitable, and that the United States could once again become a nation dominated by small proprietors and farmers determined the Agrarians' approach to the problems of the 1930s. They claimed that the trend toward economic and demographic concentration, which had been artificially stimulated through political subsidies, could be reversed by means of electricity. Electricity, in contrast to steam power, could be transported cheaply over great distances, thereby enabling industry to move out of the metropolis and into rural areas. In addition, electricity could easily be adapted to small-scale manufacturing and agriculture, which would allow industry to decentralize and would improve the condition of farming. An intelligent use of electricity, the Agrarians contended, could foster a widespread distribution of property and help rectify the economic imbalance between the South and West and the Northeast. The considerations uppermost in the minds of the Agrarians when they evaluated the electrification program and other aspects of the Tennessee Valley Authority were: would it inhibit the growth of large-scale industry and aid small business; would it help the South in its struggle with the industrial-financial oligarchy of the Northeast; would it encourage the decentralization of the metropolis; and would it improve the status of the southern farmer?[14]

The TVA, the Agrarians predicted, by providing "the means for a decentralization of productive wealth," would be "a solid contribution to the economic life of the Valley." They anticipated that the TVA's hydroelectric plants would enable the South to industrialize slowly without repeating the mistakes of northern industrialization. Because the South now had a source of power which could be used by small-scale, rural factories, there was no reason why southern industrialization need be accompanied by the urbanization, political centralization and proletarianization which had occurred in the North. And because southern manufacturing could remain small-scale, southern industrialists could probably secure necessary capital from southern sources without having to go to

---

was based upon "a massive body of plain folk . . . neither rich nor very poor," who were mostly small, independent farmers. Owsley, *Plain Folk of the Old South* (Baton Rouge, La., 1949), pp. vii, ix, 7. For a differing interpretation of the Agrarians which emphasizes their admiration for an aristocratic, stratified society, see Anne Ward Amacher, "Myths and Consequences: Calhoun and Some Nashville Agrarians," *South Atlantic Quarterly*, LIX (Spring 1960), 251-64, and Amacher, "Myths and Consequences: Allen Tate's and Some Other Vanderbilt Traditionalists' Images of Class and Race in the Old South" (Ph.D. diss., New York University, 1956).

[14]Nixon, *Forty Acres* . . . , pp. 72, 77-78; Chattanooga *Times*, Nov. 4, 1936; Davidson, Review of *This Ugly Civilization*, by Ralph Borsodi, *American Review*, I (May 1933), 240-41.

New York banks. Control of southern industries would remain in southern hands, industrial profits would stay in the South and could finance further economic development, and the South could begin to free herself from the grip of northern colonialism. Writing in 1943, Henry Blue Kline argued that the TVA had been "a very significant landmark" in the crusade for economic decentralization, and had fulfilled the expectations of the Agrarians.[15]

Herman C. Nixon was especially impressed by the activities of the TVA's Industrial Division in behalf of economic decentralization. This division encouraged small-scale manufacturing by inventing and demonstrating machines and methods of manufacturing suitable for small factories, by taking surveys and engaging in other research looking toward local production, and by teaching how the manufacture of goods could be domesticated. The TVA's creation of a series of navigable lakes and rivers and the establishment of several parks also encouraged Nixon. He reasoned that the future growth in the economy would be largely in service-oriented enterprises, such as recreation, rather than goods-producing industries, and that the TVA's rivers, lakes and parks, combined with the area's mild climate, could transform the Tennessee Valley into a prime tourist attraction. The growth of tourism would result in the establishment of countless small businesses, such as hotels and restaurants, and this would mean, in turn, an increase in the number of independent businessmen and a diffusion of property ownership.[16]

The Agrarians hoped that the TVA's electricity would also destroy the control of northern holding companies over the southern utility industry. These companies, they contended, had exploited the South through a policy of high prices and low consumption. Not only had the South been paying high electricity bills with the profits flowing north into Wall Street, but many areas of the rural South were without electricity because it had not been immediately profitable to service them. Allen Tate, for one, held that southern economic independence from northern capitalistic control was absolutely dependent upon alternative sources of electrical power. The Agrarians' recognition of the effect of the northern holding companies upon southern economic development resulted in their support for the Public Utility Company Act of 1935, which aimed at breaking up

---

[15] *Chattanooga Times*, Nov. 4, 1936; Nixon, "The South After the War," *Virginia Quarterly Review*, XX (Summer 1944), 323; Nixon, *Lower Piedmont Country* (New York, 1946), pp. 153-55; Owsley, Chitwood, Nixon, *Short History* . . . , II, 630-32; Kline, *Regional Freight Rates*, pp. 43-44.

[16] Nixon, *Possum Trot*, pp. 118, 152-53; Nixon, *The Tennessee Valley: A Recreation Domain*, Papers of the Institute of Research and Training in the Social Sciences, Vanderbilt University, Paper No. 9 (Nashville, Tenn., 1945), *passim*; Nixon, *Lower Piedmont Country*, pp. 228-29.

the utility holding company empires. They anticipated that this act, by striking at northern control of southern power, would further encourage economic decentralization and promote southern economic independence.[17]

Kline's efforts while employed by the TVA to change the national railroad freight rate schedule reflected this emphasis on the need for regional economic independence. He believed these rates had discriminated in favor of the Northeast and against the South and West. Discriminatory freight rates, Kline stressed, hampered the industrialization of the South and West, forced these regions to concentrate on extractive industries and to neglect the more profitable fabricating industries, resulted in artificial economic concentration, and, by destroying free competition, inhibited national productivity.[18]

The TVA's electricity, the Agrarians predicted, would benefit the Valley's agriculture as well as its industry. They foresaw electrification of the southern farm lessening much of the monotony, drudgery and long hours of farm labor, thereby helping stem the rural migration to the city by making farming a more attractive occupation. The ownership of machinery by the individual farmer made possible by electrification would increase his standard of living and his economic independence. The farmer would now have the means to process many of his own crops, thus freeing him from dependence on exploitative middlemen. Electrification would also partially end the cultural isolation of farm life by enabling the farmer to enjoy the radio and to read by electric lights. Other aspects of the TVA which Nixon pointed to as beneficial to farmers were the resettling of farmers on more desirable land created as a result of irrigation projects, the establishing of demonstration farms to bring the latest farming techniques to Valley residents, the producing of cheap fertilizers, the developing of inexpensive farm machinery, the teaching of new methods of processing farm products, the investigating of new crops suitable for the Southeast, and the organizing of soil conservation programs.

[17]Chattanooga *Times*, Nov. 4, 1936; interview with Warren, Apr. 19, 1965; Kline, "Utilities vs. Southwest," St. Louis *Post-Dispatch*, June 2, 1946; Kline, "Upholding Public Power Policy," *ibid.*, Aug. 25, 1949; Nixon, *Possum Trot*, pp. 152-53; Owsley, Chitwood, Nixon, *Short History*..., II, 626.

[18]Kline, *Regional Freight Rates, passim*; Kline, *Freight Rates: The Interregional Tariff Issue*, Papers of the Institute of Research and Training in the Social Sciences, Vanderbilt University, Paper No. 3 (Nashville, Tenn., 1942); Kline and Alvin W. Vogtle, *Freight Rates and the South, ibid.*, Paper No. 5 (1943); Kline, "As to Southern-Western Revolt," St. Louis *Post-Dispatch*, Dec. 1, 1946; for Nixon's support of the TVA's work in this area, see "The New Deal and the South," *Virginia Quarterly Review*, XIX (Summer 1943), 331; for a general study of the freight-rate issue, see Robert A. Lively, "The South and Freight Rates: Political Settlement of an Economic Argument," *Journal of Southern History*, XIV (Aug. 1948), 357-84.

The TVA, Nixon wrote in 1938, "is the greatest movement in the South for modernizing agriculture, conserving rural manhood, and facilitating village development. It should prove a godsend to hillbillies." The Agrarians, as might be expected, also strongly supported the Rural Electrification Administration which aided farmers in establishing nonprofit electrical cooperatives in order to build power lines. The REA, they believed, would enhance the farmer's economic position and broaden his cultural outlook, and, by encouraging the decentralization of industry, would help restore economic balance to the nation.[19]

The major misgivings of the Agrarians regarding the TVA were sociological rather than economic. Some Agrarians suspected the TVA of endeavoring to uplift and modernize the inhabitants of the Valley. Allen Tate, for instance, although strongly in favor of the economic impact which the TVA was having in the Valley, nevertheless attacked it for its reformist spirit. "When the TVA tries to go into the mountains and change ways of living followed by the mountaineers for 150 years," he stated, "it is all wrong. It tries to make them play the radio instead of pitching horseshoes. They've been pitching horseshoes for 150 years and they ought to go right on pitching horseshoes." There were also fears that the TVA's newly created lakes were unnecessarily displacing large numbers of subsistence farmers. Nixon attempted to quiet such fears by claiming that the displacement of farmers had been done in such a manner as to disrupt life least, and that only "a small proportion" of the displaced families had been left stranded, dissatisfied and unadjusted. Both Nixon and Kline emphasized that the efforts of the TVA to work closely with the people of the Valley and through their local institutions indicated a democratic and decentralist orientation. For Kline, the TVA was an "experiment in applied democracy."[20]

Donald Davidson registered the only major dissent among the Agrarians regarding the TVA. Because Davidson wrote more about the TVA and over a longer period of time than the other Agrarians, historians have naturally assumed that his views were typical. Even Davidson, however, initially welcomed the TVA, and it wasn't until the mid-1930s, and especially after 1940, that he became critical. In 1940, he accepted a com-

[19]Nixon to George Fort Milton, Aug. 2, 1934, Milton Papers (Library of Congress); Nixon, *Forty Acres* . . . , pp. 74, 80-81; Nixon, *Possum Trot*, pp. 112, 152-53; Ransom, "What Does the South Want?" p. 189; Kline, "Utilities Rampant Again," St. Louis *Post-Dispatch*, July 6, 1946.

[20]Chattanooga *Times*, Nov. 4, 1936; for a criticism of the TVA similar to Tate's by a friend of the Agrarians, see Richmond Croom Beatty, "Mountaineers Are Shakespearean," *Kenyon Review*, III (Winter 1941), 130; Nixon, *Possum Trot*, pp. 152-53; Nixon, "New Deal and the South," p. 322; Kline, "TVA's for Everybody Else?"; Kline, "Wrong Standard, Right Man," St. Louis *Post-Dispatch*, Oct. 29, 1946.

mission to write a two-volume history of the Tennessee River for the Rinehart Rivers of America series, and his work on these volumes deepened and clarified his earlier apprehensions.

In 1934, Davidson claimed that the TVA was an "ideal regional undertaking. It seems to promise a controlled and reasoned development of ways of life and institutions that are adapted to the soil wherein they grow. In principle, it is statesmanlike and highly imagined, and it naturally excites the interest and wins the support of most thinking Southerners." Despite this, Davidson feared the TVA might degenerate into an abstract attempt to reform the South. He warned there was a possibility of the South becoming a laboratory for the social experimentation of TVA bureaucrats and New Deal brain-trusters. He wished to know whether the TVA was "to continue indefinitely under the paternal wing of the federal government, like some gigantic Berea College which distributed humanitarian benefits, but in an external missionary way; or whether it is finally to be integrated with the section of which it is a natural part." Although the heads of the TVA were capable, most of them were not Southerners, and this gave "color to the charge, already current, that the TVA is another Yankee raid into Southern territory." Despite these early misgivings, Davidson believed the TVA to be one of the more hopeful ventures of the New Deal.[21]

By 1936, however, Davidson's attitude toward the TVA had become decidedly negative. Although continuing to believe the TVA manifested a New Deal recognition of the reality of regionalism, he now argued that it was a regionalism which ignored the wishes of the South. The TVA was a foreign body, foisted upon an unwilling South by a distant political bureaucracy. As presently constituted, it was "an irresponsible projection of a planned, functional society into the midst of one of the most thoroughly democratic parts of the United States. It therefore does not guide us very far in our search for the right kind of regionalism." He proposed reforming the Authority so that the South would have effective control over it and could escape the manipulation of its "resources and population by a paternal ... agency."[22]

Davidson, furthermore, predicted that the TVA would lead neither to the decentralization of property, nor to an increase in southern-owned businesses. The TVA was, in reality, a subsidy "to any migrating manufacturers who want to set up shop in the Tennessee Valley, and above all

[21] Davidson, "Where Regionalism and Sectionalism Meet," *Social Forces*, XIII (Oct. 1934), 25-27.
[22] Davidson, "That This Nation May Endure: The Need for Political Regionalism," *Who Owns America?*, pp. 124-25; Davidson, "Regionalism as Social Science," *Southern Review*, III (Autumn 1937), 219-20.

to the great monopolistic northern corporations which have a great many articles to sell to the Tennessee Valley people." There was nothing in the purpose or the operations of the Authority which insured that decentralized and southern-owned industries would be fostered. On the contrary, the TVA intended to open up the Valley "to a rush of Northern industry much as the old Indian Territory of Oklahoma was opened up . . . to rushing land speculators and homesteaders."[23]

The ultimate goals of the TVA were thus completely alien to the rural culture of the Tennessee Valley. The Authority, Davidson asserted, wished to replace an agrarian economy with industrialism. While industrialists and urbanites would benefit, most of the region's population would soon feel "the impact of an exploitative system." Davidson claimed that the TVA, properly understood, was simply another in the long line of subsidies handed out to northern industrialists since the Civil War. Evidence of this was the Authority's failure to do something about the South's colonial relationship with the North.[24]

The second volume of Davidson's history of the Tennessee River, published in 1948, brought these scattered criticisms together into an extremely bitter critique of the TVA. He declared that when Congress established the Authority in 1933 it had in mind such traditional governmental concerns as flood control and navigation; there was no thought of even having the TVA engage in competition with private power companies. Nevertheless, the independence granted the Authority enabled TVA bureaucrats to transform it into an instrument for paternalistic uplift by utopian social scientists. It became another attempt to "civilize" the South, following in the footsteps of the Scopes trial and the Scottsboro case. If these bureaucrats "achieved good," Davidson remarked, "it would be the good that they and their staff of experts had pondered and blueprinted, not the good that might emerge from the various assemblies, nonexpert, discursively democratic, of the people of the valley."[25]

---

[23]Davidson, "On Being in Hock to the North," *Free America*, III (May 1939), 4.

[24]Davidson, "Political Regionalism and Administrative Regionalism," *Annals of the American Academy of Political and Social Science*, CCVII (Jan. 1940), 138-43.

[25]Davidson, *The Tennessee*, II, 217-24. Davidson believed that David E. Lilienthal, one of the three TVA directors, was the prime example of a God-playing bureaucrat. For Henry Blue Kline, Herman C. Nixon and most students of the TVA, Lilienthal has been the symbol of the decentralist and democratic impulses within the Authority. Robert Drake wrote that when Davidson mentioned Lilienthal's name he made it sound "like it was one of the vilest words in the English language" ("Donald Davidson and the Ancient Mariner," *Vanderbilt Alumnus*, XLIX [Jan. Feb. 1954], 21). Davidson fully agreed with President Eisenhower's comment that the TVA was "creeping socialism" ("Regionalism," *Collier's 1954 Year Book*, ed. William T. Couch [New York, 1954], 509); see also Davidson, Review of *Regionalism in America*, ed. Merrill Jensen, *American Literature*, XXIV (Mar. 1952), 95-96.

The displacement of farmers by the lakes created by the TVA exemplified the Authority's paternalistic outlook. Despite the extinguishing of hearth fires, the vanishing of old landmarks and the obliteration of old graveyards, the TVA juggernaut marched on. "There would be tears, and gnashing of teeth, and lawsuits," Davidson wrote. "There might even be feuds and bloodshed. Yet these harms ... weighed less in the TVA scales than the benefits that would accrue, in terms of industrial and social engineering, to the nearby or the distant majority who sacrificed only tax money."[26]

Davidson believed there was a basic and irreconcilable conflict between the TVA's engineers and the farmers of the Valley. If the engineers had their way, the Valley farmer would soon become a cattle raiser, "enslaved to the aching compulsive teats of a herd of cows and to the trucks and price scale of Borden, Pet, Carnation," or he might become "a forester, a mountain guide, an operator of tourist homes and hot-dog stands, a tipped purveyor, and professional friend to tippling fishermen, hunters of ducks unlimited, abstracting artists, tired neurotics, and vacation seekers of all sorts." Davidson blamed the TVA's anti-agrarian bias for the decline of subsistence farming in the Valley and the transformation of many farmers into urban slum dwellers.[27]

Davidson's view of the TVA, despite what some historians have written, was not typical of the Agrarians. This failure to understand the politics of the Agrarians arises out of a belief that reform and liberalism since the 1930s have been a monopoly of the collectivistic left. When collectivistic and urban-oriented historians read that the Agrarians favored the widespread distribution of property, aid for rural America and the destruction of economic, political and demographic centralization, they immediately conclude that Agrarianism was, at best, "conservative," or, at worst an American version of lower-middle-class fascism. In truth, the Agrarians were anti-fascist as well as radical critics of the New Deal. When they criticized the New Deal it was for failing to move more vigorously against high finance and big business, and for neglecting the small businessman and the small farmer.[28]

[26]Davidson, *Tennessee*, II, 236–38, 313.

[27]Davidson, *Tennessee*, II, 289–305; Davidson, "The Agrarians Today," *Shenandoah*, III (Autumn 1952), 20; Drake wrote that it broke Davidson's heart "to think a lot of scientists and sociologists were going to come in and try to make the Valley over again and 'improve it'—people that didn't give a damn about Andrew Jackson or anybody else." Drake, "Davidson and Ancient Mariner," p. 21; see also Louise Davis, "He Clings to Enduring Values," *Vanderbilt Alumnus*, XXXV (Oct.-Nov. 1949), 9.

[28]For Agrarian opposition to fascism, see Tate, "Fascism and the Southern Agrarians," *New Republic*, LXXXVII (May 27, 1936), 75; Davidson to Tate, May 27, 1936, Tate Papers (Princeton University); and Arthur M. Schlesinger Jr., *The Politics of Upheaval* (Boston, 1960), pp. 70–71. For Agrarian criticism of the New Deal for not being

For many American intellectuals the aspirations of rural and small-town America are irrelevant and atavistic. They praise cosmopolitanism and sophistication, and maintain that political and economic centralization and urbanization are inevitable tendencies from which stem the most important and valuable aspects of American culture. The danger of such beliefs is that they alienate the intellectual from the great majority of Americans who do not share his glorification of urbanization and collectivism, and from an America which is not destined to resemble New York, Chicago, Boston and San Francisco. When seen in these terms, the failure to understand the Agrarians, much less appreciate them, reflects the alienation of much of the American intellectual community from the values of their nation.[29]

---

radical enough, see Nixon, *Forty Acres* . . . , pp. 56-60; Owsley, Chitwood, Nixon, *Short History* . . . , II, pp. 663-66; Davidson, "Mr. Babbitt at Philadelphia," *Southern Review*, VI (Spring 1941), 700; Tate, "How Are They Voting: IV," *New Republic*, LXXXVIII (Oct. 21, 1936), 304-5, and Review of *Pursuit of Happiness*, by Herbert Agar, *Free America*, II (Oct. 1938), 16-18; Warren, "Robert Penn Warren," *Twentieth Century Authors*, eds. Stanley Kunitz and Howard Haycraft (New York, 1942), p. 1477; Kline, "Mr. Harriman's Idea," St. Louis *Post-Dispatch*, Jan. 11, 1947; Lanier to Tate, Dec. 7, 1936, Tate Papers.

[29]For the overwhelming preference of Americans for small-town and farm life and their corresponding distaste for cities, see the report of a Gallup Poll in the New York *Times*, Feb. 19, 1970; for the refusal of America to become urbanized, see Daniel J. Elazar, "Are We a Nation of Cities?" *Public Interest*, No. 4 (Summer 1966), pp. 42-58.

# Donald Davidson and the Tennessee Valley Authority: The Response of a Southern Conservative

Of the twelve contributors to the 1930 agrarian manifesto *I'll Take My Stand: the South and the Agrarian Tradition,* none opposed the Tennessee Valley Authority more consistently and fervently than Donald Davidson. Davidson was almost unique among the Agrarians who generally welcomed the Authority as a means of reviving southern rural life and of freeing southern business and industry, particularly southern utility companies, from the domination of northern economic leviathans. Davidson, however, from the very beginning was suspicious of the Authority and the New Deal, and the development of the TVA during the 1930's and 1940's confirmed his initial fears. The publication in 1948 of the second volume of his history of the Tennessee River marked Davidson as a leader of that minority segment of the southern intelligentsia opposing the Authority.[1]

Davidson's attitude toward the TVA grew logically out of his interpretation of American history. An unreconstructed Southerner, he believed the central theme of American history to be a persistent conflict between Northerners seeking control of the federal government in order to pass legislation beneficial to northern business and industry, and Southerners determined to preserve their agrarian society from the rapacious imperialistic designs of the North. He described the rivalry between the Hamiltonian Federalists and the Jeffersonian Republicans during the 1790's, the struggle between Andrew Jackson and Nicholas Biddle over the recharting of the Second Bank of the United States, the Civil War and Reconstruction, and the emergence of Populism in the late Nineteenth Century as phases in this bitter sectional antagonism. According to Davidson, southern political statesmanship reached its peak when men such as John Taylor of Caroline, John C. Calhoun, and Strom Thurmond recognized the aggressive instincts of northern capital-

---

[1] Edward S. Shapiro, "The Southern Agrarians and the Tennessee Valley Authority," in *American Quarterly,* XXII (Winter, 1970), 791-806.

ism, and opposed the centralization of political power in the federal government which, if dominated by northern economic interests, would threaten the very existence of the South's economic and social structure.[2]

Arguing that regionalism rather than Marxism was the key to understanding American history, Davidson attributed southern poverty to northern exploitation rather than to the South being populated by proletarians. This regional clash cut across class lines since all Northerners benefitted from the destitution of the southern farmer, laborer, and businessman. "Does the Northeast exclaim in horror at the spectacle of Southern lands eroded and worn-out, at the devilish one-crop system and the tenant system, at the burnt and cut-over mountain slopes, the illiterate and diseased population, the fierce despair or the terrifying apathy of large districts, rural and urban?" Davidson asked. "Let him never think that these sins against good order were willfully committed or arose from human sloth and malignity alone." Davidson was, of course, not original in emphasizing regionalism. Through the writings of Frederick Jackson Turner, James Truslow Adams, Charles A. Beard, Vernon Louis Parrington, Howard K. Beale, and others, the antagonism between the industrial North and the agrarian South had become a staple of early Twentieth Century American historiography. Davidson's importance lay in the use he made of what Alfred Kazin has called "the highest expression of the Progressive mind," to defend the traditional South and to attack the New Deal and virtually all its works, in particular the Tennessee Valley Authority.[3]

Davidson was at first ambivalent toward the TVA. He, like the other Southern Agrarians, hoped it would ameliorate the condition of southern agriculture, would encourage the decentralization of ownership of productive property in the South, and would destroy the stranglehold northern utility holding companies had over southern sources of electric power. Davidson also welcomed the regional approach of the Authority. Here was an effort to revive

---

[2] Donald Davidson, *The Attack on Leviathan: Regionalism and Nationalism in the United States* (Chapel Hill, 1938), 13-38, 312-38; John Tyree Fain (ed.), *The Spyglass: Views and Reviews, 1924-1930* (Nashville, 1963), 79-80.

[3] Davidson, "That This Nation May Endure: The Need for Political Regionalism," in *Who Owns America? A New Declaration of Independence*, Herbert Agar and Allen Tate (eds.), (Boston, 1936), 113-20; Alfred Kazin, *On Native Grounds: An Interpretation of Modern American Prose Literature* (Garden City, N.Y., 1942), 123-24; Richard Hofstadter, *The Progressive Historians: Turner, Beard, Parrington* (New York, 1968).

an entire region by ignoring artificial state boundaries and by focusing on the social and economic factors binding the area together. Here, seemingly, was a recognition by the Roosevelt administration of the importance of regionalism, a realization that the United States was not homogeneous but instead contained sections with diverse economies. "In principle," Davidson noted in 1934, the TVA "is statesmanlike and highly imaginative, and it naturally excites the interest and wins the support of most thinking Southerners."[4]

This initial enthusiasm for the Authority was, however, balanced by Davidson's concern during the 1930's over the way it had been originally established and was then operating. A decentralized and regionally-oriented agency, which the TVA claimed to be, should work closely with the local population, giving to it a voice in the decision-making process. However, Davidson claimed, Southern experts were not consulted during the planning stages, there were few Southerners in positions of authority within the TVA, and the elected political leaders of the Southeast had little influence within the Authority. Davidson was convinced by the middle of the decade that the TVA had no intention of respecting the wishes of the Valley's inhabitants. He described the Authority in 1936 as "an irresponsible projection of a planned, functional society into the midst of one of the most thoroughly democratic parts of the United States. It therefore does not guide us very far in our search for the right kind of regionalism. . . . It suggests an unwillingness to discover the foundation upon which building may be permanent." He recommended the South be given the authority to administer the TVA. Only this would prevent the manipulation of the South's resources and population by a paternal and "foreign" agency. Davidson feared that, without any local checks, the Authority would become an abstract and centralized sociological experiment of outsiders to uplift the South.[5]

Davidson deeply resented the fact that during the 1920's and 1930's the South had become something of a national joke. The South, he believed, was viewed by most Northerners as an exotic land of white-robed lynchers, hookworm sufferers, fugitives from chain gangs, ranting fundamentalists, oppressed coal miners, and degraded tenant farmers. The South had become the nation's lead-

---

[4] Davidson, "Where Regionalism and Sectionalism Meet," in *Social Forces*, XIII (October, 1934), 25-27.

[5] Davidson, "That This Nation May Endure," 124-25; Davidson, *Attack on Leviathan*, 119; Sheffield (Alabama) *Standard*, May 11, 1934.

ing economic and social problem, while John Dollard, Arthur Raper, and other sociologists travelled through the region diagnosing her sickness and suggesting suitable reforms. The South, Davidson proclaimed, "it not inhabited by guinea-pigs; it is not the colonial dependency of some eastern or northern brain trust." He feared the TVA was part of a national effort to reform the South along northern lines. He demanded to know whether the Authority "is to continue indefinitely under the paternal wing of the Federal government, like some gigantic Berea College which distributes humanitarian benefits, but in an external, missionary way; or whether it is finally to be integrated with the section of which it is a natural part?" He reminded the Roosevelt administration that the Tennessee Valley "is not located in Utopia, but in the South."[6]

This disenchantment with the TVA paralleled Davidson's disillusionment with the New Deal. Although not voting in 1932, he was not displeased by FDR's victory. He hoped the New Deal would bring relief to the South by launching a concerted drive against northern industrial and financial regional exploitation. Roosevelt had, in fact, indicated during the campaign that he was thinking along such lines. It did not take long, however, for Davidson to become disaffected. In 1936 he reluctantly voted for Roosevelt, the last time in his life he voted for a Democratic presidential candidate. In 1940 he supported Wendell Willkie, nominee of the Republicans, the erstwhile party of big business, high tariffs, and Reconstruction.[7]

Possibly, considering Davidson's opposition to political centralization and his deeply conservative social values, no administration which could have been elected during the 1930's would have pleased him. The almost inevitable concentration of political authority in Washington under the New Deal and the support, both tacit and overt, which some New Dealers gave to the industrial labor movement and to the struggle for racial justice were sufficient in themselves to cause Davidson to break with the Roose-

---

[6] Davidson, "Where Regionalism and Sectionalism Meet," 25-27; Davidson, "A Sociologist in Eden," in *American Review*, VIII (December, 1936), 177-204; Davidson, "Gulliver With Hay Fever," in *American Review*, IX (Summer, 1937), 152-72; Davidson, *Attack on Leviathan*, 156-57; Edward S. Shapiro, "H. L. Mencken, the Southern Agrarians, and the Quest for Southern Identity," in *American Studies*, XIII (Fall, 1972), 76-80.
[7] Interview with Donald Davidson, January 25, 1965; Daniel R. Fusfeld, *The Economic Thought of Franklin D. Roosevelt and the Origins of the New Deal* (New York, 1956), 203-205, 227-35.

velt administration. More importantly, there was the failure, in Davidson's view, to end sectional exploitation and the abuses of big business, and in addition, increasing evidence that some elements within the New Deal were antagonistic toward petty capitalism and private property.[8]

The reason why the power of big business remained unimpared during the 1930's, Davidson explained, was because the New Deal accepted the inevitability of large-scale industrialization and merely wished to eliminate its more egregious offenses. The purposes of the New Deal industrial reforms had been to prevent further economic misfortune by stabilizing the economy, and to repair any inequities within the existing system by diverting purchasing power to the laboring classes. Davidson was unable to find within the New Deal any significant attempt to destroy giant industrialism rather than to reform it, to transform factory workers into farmers, craftsmen, and small businessmen instead of making them more comfortable in their degradation, and to relieve regional, in contrast to class, injustice. Large-scale industrialism, the source of the North's exploitation of the South, had been left untouched under the New Deal, Davidson declared in 1941. "In fact, the general mass-production system, benevolently protected against economic disaster, has been able to achieve a good deal of consolidation and extension...."[9]

This acquiescence in and support for economic giantism explained, Davidson contended, the TVA's refusal to recognize that the Tennessee Valley's economic difficulties stemmed from the regional exploitation of large-scale industrialization. This is why the Authority did not encourage the growth of small, decentralized, southern-owned businesses, or why it did not prevent the transformation of wide areas of the South into gigantic sweatshops controlled by northern businessmen. Indeed, the Valley had been opened "to a rush of Northern industry much as the old Indian Territory of Oklahoma was opened up . . . to rushing land speculators and homesteaders." Not only had the Authority virtually

---

[8] Davidson to Allen Tate, March 27, 1937, Tate Papers (Princeton University); Davidson to Seward Collins, July 17, 1936, Collins Papers (Yale University); Davidson, "Agrarianism and Politics," in *Review of Politics*, I (April, 1939), 117-19, 123.

[9] Davidson, "Mr. Babbitt at Philadelphia," in *Southern Review*, VI (Spring, 1941), 700; Davidson, "An Agrarian Looks at the New Deal," in *Free America*, II (July, 1938), 3-4; Davidson, "Regionalism as Social Science," in *Southern Review*, III (Autumn, 1937), 224.

ignored the problem of absentee-landlordism of southern industry, but it had provided the giant northern monopolies with inexpensive electricity as well as an ample supply of cheap labor which had been pushed off the land by the giant lakes created by the TVA. The Authority's true nature had become clear. It was a giant bonanza for northern capitalists, "another subsidy of the exploitative forces which have already set the region at a disadvantage."[10]

Davidson was convinced this was inevitable so long as the TVA was not controlled by Southerners. The Authority would naturally "reflect the psychology, economics and generalized wishes of whatever regional group happens at the moment to possess Federal power," and Davidson believed this to be the large-scale industrialism of the North. Although the Tennessee Valley was essentially agricultural and its inhabitants wished to remain rural, he predicted the TVA would strive to transform the Valley into a replica of a northern industrial area. "The economic imbalance is to be righted in terms of new industries, pay rolls, dividends . . . and in general a typically modern use of natural and human resources." The Valley's people would be "drawn farther away from the agrarian economy and involved more deeply than ever in the chain of increasing purchasing and increasing debts. The program . . . may benefit urban entrepreneurs and selected industrial groups, while the region as a whole feels, at closer range than before, the impact of an exploitative system."[11]

The agrarian South, Davidson claimed, had remained relatively immune to the commercial-industrial-mechanistic outlook of the industrial North with its emphasis on materialism and economic growth. The South had been content with a slower paced life and had delighted in leisure, conversation, and manners. He feared these were now to be sacrificed to the industrial-commercial spirit being spread by the New Deal and the TVA. Decades later Davidson was still grousing over the New Deal's materialism and its belief that the residents of the Tennessee Valley could be improved through material benefits.[12]

---

[10] Davidson, "On Being in Hock to the North," in *Free America*, III (May, 1939), 4; Davidson, "Political Regionalism and Administrative Regionalism," in *Annals of the American Academy of Political and Social Science*, CCVII (January, 1940), 138-43.

[11] Davidson, "Political Regionalism and Administrative Regionalism," 138-43.

[12] Davidson, "*Still Rebels, Still Yankees," and Other Essays* (Baton Rouge, 1957), 194; Davidson, "Regionalism," in *Collier's 1954 Year Book*, William T. Couch (ed.),

Another of Davidson's fears regarding the TVA stemmed from his dislike of big government. He favored a river authority for the Tennessee Valley with clearly defined duties of flood control, soil conservation, and reforestation, all legitimate concerns of Washington. Such an agency would conserve the South's natural resources, strengthen the agrarian character of the Tennessee Valley, and not unduly increase political centralization. The TVA's powers were, however, virtually unlimited and, in addition, the Authority was largely independent of any governmental supervision. Davidson, in particular, opposed its manufacture and distribution of electricity. This, he claimed, was unconstitutional and socialistic, detracted from the TVA's agricultural and conservation activities, and merely aided the industrial giants of the North.[13]

There was no contradiction in Davidson seeing the Tennessee Valley Authority as an instrument of both political collectivism and large-scale industrialism. Despite the supposed incompatability of big business and big government, Davidson and the other Southern Agrarians argued that political centralization was the direct result as well as the logical conclusion of modern capitalism. Big business, so the argument went, had dispossessed hundreds of thousands of small businessmen who were forced into the ranks of the propertyless factory proletariat. Big government merely carried this dispossession one step further by dispossessing the dispossessors. The giant private monopolies would in time be superseded by one gigantic monopoly directed by Washington politicians. The economic collectivism and dispossession begun during industrialization would end with the elimination of all private property under socialism. For Davidson, Roosevelt's New Deal merely carried out the implications of the economic centralization fostered by Rockefeller and Carnegie.[14]

In 1940 Davidson signed a contract with the Rinehart publishing company to write a two-volume history of the Tennessee River in the "Rivers of America" series edited by Hervey Allen and Carl

---

(New York, 1954), 507-508; Davidson to Harvey Broome, April 25, 1948, in Donald Davidson Papers (Vanderbilt University).

[13] Davidson, "Political Regionalism and Administrative Regionalism," 139-43; Davidson, "That This Nation May Endure," 124.

[14] Davidson, Review of *Too Big*, by Morris L. Ernst, in *Free America*, IV (August, 1940), 18; Davidson, "The Agrarians Today," in *Shenandoah*, III (Autumn, 1952), 17; Davidson, "Agrarianism and Politics," 115-21; Davidson, "Where Are the Laymen? A Study in Policy-Making," in *American Review*, IX (October, 1937), 458-59; Davidson, *Attack on Leviathan*, 94-95.

Carmer. This gave him the opportunity to broaden and deepen his analysis of the TVA which took up one hundred and twenty-five pages of the second volume published in 1948. Here again Davidson placed the TVA within a theory of American history emphasizing the conflict between the North and the South. The South, he wrote, had been involved since the Civil War in a momentous struggle to determine its own future. At first the enemy was the agents of the Union League and the Freedmen's Bureau who exacerbated race relations and foisted unrepresentative state governments upon the South during Reconstruction. The instrument of Southern redemption was the Ku Klux Klan, described by Davidson as a popularly based, self-defense movement, "a chivalric and humane institution, designed to protect those who in these terrible years of ruin and humiliation had at least no other recourse."[15]

The Klan was able to deal with the "detestable" social missionaries but found it more difficult to challenge the "more subtle utopians" of the New South who promised economic salvation to the South if only she would embrace capitalism and industrialization. As a result, the South's mineral resources passed into northern hands in the last quarter of the nineteenth century, and any benefits the South received "were but a meager fraction of the wealth that went elsewhere, some of it forever." The northern campaign against the South reached a crescendo during the 1920's and 1930's. First there was the Scopes Trial of 1925 which "brought down upon the unsuspecting valley, in a peculiarly intense and derisive form, the organized wrath of the outside world. The wrath was so condescending and purposeful that it seemed to have the character of deliberate attack." Six years later there occurred the Scottsboro incident which Davidson called "the grimmest episode in southern experience during the years between the two world wars." The attitude of Samuel S. Leibowitz of New York City, lawyer for the defendants, particularly irritated Davidson. Leibowitz, Davidson wrote, "deemed himself a missionary appointed to rescue the persecuted from the baneful clutch of the heathen." The major effect of the Scopes and Scottsboro trials was to poison sectional relations by picturing the Tennessee Valley as a backwash of civilization, peopled by ignorant, bigoted, and degenerate individuals desperately in need of civilizing."[16]

---
[15] Davidson, *The Tennessee,* Vol. II: *The New River, Civil War to TVA* (New York, 1948), 128-29.
[16] *Ibid.,* 146-48, 195-210.

This hostile and patronizing attitude toward the South was reflected in the widespread view that social progress could replace "supposed social depravity through the distribution of government-controlled electric power." The TVA act, both in its general motivation and in its planning sections, thus "owed much to the trials by jury . . . that plagued Tennessee and Alabama during the years preceding 1933." It was characteristic, Davidson thought, that in a decade such as the 1930's which saw materialism as the road to salvation, southern redemption was to occur through economic uplift.[17]

The South, Davidson claimed, had welcomed FDR's victory in 1932 since it promised to allay the sectional antagonisms of the 1920's and early 1930's and to end her exploitation by Northerners. Similarly Southerners had favored Roosevelt's proposal to Congress in April, 1933, to create the Tennessee Valley Authority because they believed it to be a locally controlled, traditional river improvement measure which would not engage in competition with private utility companies by selling power directly to consumers. Southern congressmen "had little conception of how far-reaching the plans of the authority itself might turn out to be. . . . They did not know exactly what they were voting for, and neither did the constituencies they represented in Congress." Davidson surmised that the South would have objected had she realized the TVA would later interfere with private enterprise, or that the Authority's powers extended considerably beyond mere navigation, flood control, and conservation and encompassed authority to oversee the economic and social development and the general welfare of the Tennessee Valley. The South was too Jeffersonian, too fearful of centralized government, to have acquiesced in the establishment of a governmental agency which would be virtually a power unto itself. The three directors of the TVA had the power to do great good, Davidson argued, but if they did so, "it would be the good that they and their staff of experts had pondered and blueprinted, not the good that might emerge from the various assemblies, nonexpert, discursively democratic, of the people of the valley. . . . They were in the position, as one of their own supporters afterwards said, of playing God to the Tennessee Valley."[18]

---

[17] *Ibid.*, 211, 223.
[18] *Ibid.*, 213-24. Davidson's argument that the South was deceived into believing the TVA bill was simply a traditional river improvement proposal, and that the South would have opposed it had she anticipated the TVA's entry into the business

Davidson criticized the decision of the directors to construct a string of high dams in order to produce the greatest amount of power possible. Davidson favored the building of a system of low dams. This would have been cheaper and would have prevented the innundation of large areas of rich valley land, but it would not have supplied the desired power nor would it have sufficiently controlled flooding. He lamented that, as a result of this decision,

> Hearth fires would be extinguished that were as old as the Republic itself. Old landmarks would vanish; old graveyards would be obliterated; the ancient mounds of the Indian, which had resisted both the plow of the farmer and the pick of the curiosity seeker, would go under the water. There would be tears, and gnashing of teeth, and lawsuits. There might even be feud and bloodshed. Yet these harms, inflicted upon a sizable and innocent minority, weighed less in the TVA scales than the benefits that would accrue, in terms of industrial and social engineering, to the nearby or the distant majority who sacrificed only tax money.[19]

The TVA juggernaut rolled on, impervious to the wishes of the Valley's people, and all the while it was enlarging the scope of its activities, innundating more and more acres of fertile bottom land, and displacing more and more farmers.

The TVA was hostile to agriculture, Davidson contended, because of fears that the silt created by the valley's farmers would

---

of selling electricity (pp. 177, 217-20) is on shaky historical grounds. Roosevelt had been a longtime foe of the private utility companies and had made it clear during the 1932 campaign that they could expect, if he was elected, stringent restrictions on their accustomed modes of operation. Furthermore, the struggle in Congress over passage of a bill centered on the question of government production and distribution of power. Thomas K. McCraw, *TVA and the Power Fight, 1933-1939* (Philadelphia, 1971), 26-36; Preston J. Hubbard, *Origins of the TVA: The Muscle Shoals Controversy, 1919-1932* (Nashville, 1961), 311-15. (Roosevelt's major campaign speech on power was at Portland, Oregon, on September 21, 1932, and can be found in Samuel I. Rosenman, *The Public Papers and Addresses of Franklin D. Roosevelt, Vol. I: The Genesis of the New Deal, 1928-1932* (New York, 1938), 727-42.) Similarly, FDR emphasized his intention to go considerably beyond navigation, flood control, and conservation and to uplift the economic and social structure of the Tennessee Valley. In forwarding to Congress the TVA proposal, he suggested it "should be charged with the broadest duty of planning for the proper use, conservation and development of the natural resources of the Tennessee River drainage basin and its adjoining territory for the general social and economic welfare of the Nation. . . . It is time to extend planning to a wider field, in this instance comprehending in one great project many States directly concerned with the basin of one of our greatest rivers." Rosenman, *The Public Papers and Addresses of Franklin D. Roosevelt, Vol. II: The Year of Crisis, 1933* (New York, 1938), 122-23. See also Arthur M. Schlesinger, Jr., *The Coming of the New Deal* (Boston, 1958), 323-25.

[19] Davidson, *Tennessee*, II, 237-38.

fill the TVA's reservoirs and reduce their ability to create electricity. If the TVA engineer had his way farming would be virtually forbidden in the valley. How else could he deal with the "stubborn independent farmers of the Tennessee Valley who, like their English and Scottish forebears, were ever ready to sing 'God speed the plow.' Could he just *make* them stop plowing?" The farmers would become superfluous with the gradual transformation of the Tennessee Valley from an agricultural to a pastoral society. The growing of corn, cotton, and tobacco would give way to the raising of small grains, truck and fruit crops, and cattle and sheep raising. In his spare time the erstwhile farmer could cater to the needs of the hordes of tourists who would flock to the valley to take advantage of the TVA's recreation program.

> The Tennessee farmer would become a cattle raiser, a dairyman enslaved to the aching, compulsive teats of a herd of cows and to the trucks and price scale of Borden, Pet, Carnation. And then he might also become—though . . . he still detested the idea—a forester, a mountain guide, an operator of tourist homes and hot-dog stands, a tipped purveyor and professional friend to tippling fishermen, hunters of ducks unlimited, abstracting artists, tired neurotics, and vacation seekers of all sorts.[20]

What made this particularly disturbing to Davidson was his belief that the TVA's power program was socialistic and unconstitutional. He dismissed the TVA's claim that its rates provided a necessary and desirable "yardstick" against which to measure the fairness of the rates of the private utility companies. TVA was able to provide cheap electricity only because it received many hidden subsidies available to a government agency. He accused the Authority, in attempting to convince the public of the value of its

---

[20] *Ibid.*, Ch. xvii. Robert Drake, one of Davidson's students, recounted that when Davidson said the name "Lilienthal" he made it sound "like it was one of the vilest words in the English language." Drake, "Donald Davidson and the Ancient Mariner," in *Vanderbilt Alumnus*, XLIX (January-February, 1954), 21. David E. Lilienthal, one of the three original directors of the TVA, was a fervent apostle of public power and headed the Authority's power program. Evidently Davidson held him personally liable for the displacement of the farmers forced to leave their lands because of the TVA-created lakes, as well as for the entire power program which Davidson believed to be unwise and unconstitutional. Davidson was essentially correct in arguing that the agricultural, conservation, and navigation aspects of the TVA became subordinated to the Authority's production and distribution of electricity. Nor was he wrong in seeing Lilienthal as the person most responsible for this development. McCraw, *TVA and the Power Fight*, 55-56, 143-44; Schlesinger, *Coming of the New Deal*, 327-33; Arthur M. Schlesinger, Jr., *The Politics of Upheaval* (Boston, 1960), 363-73.

power program, of having "strongarmed" its rivals and of having "propagandized without too nice a regard for facts." Despite the failure of the Supreme Court to declare the TVA unconstitutional during the 1930's, Davidson was hopeful the dissents of Supreme Court Justices James McReynolds and Pierce Butler in the TEPCO decision would have "considerable long-range philosophic and political effect" and "might receive attention from later political regimes."[21]

Finally, Davidson criticized the Authority's paternalistic attitude toward the valley and its elected representatives, especially Senator Kenneth D. McKellar who opposed the building of Douglas Dam in East Tennessee. Davidson interpreted the struggle between the Authority and Senator McKellar as one between a distant bureaucracy and the forces of democracy and localism. He strongly disagreed with David E. Lilienthal, one of the three original TVA directors, that the TVA represented "Democracy on the March" (the title of Lilienthal's study of the TVA). In fact Lilienthal embodied for Davidson the centralizing and bureaucratic tendencies within the Authority. For Davidson, Lilienthal and most of the other TVA bureaucrats were outsiders sent from Washington to remake the valley despite any wishes the residents might have. "Whether TVA's power program, or any other of its programs, was right or wrong, cheap or costly, fair or unfair, it had to be accepted in the valley.... If you were discontented with TVA, to whom did you appeal? TVA was the government. In the Tennessee Valley there was nothing above it."[22]

Although critical of many aspects of the Authority, Davidson's

---

[21] Davidson, *Tennessee*, II, 265-66, 306-13. For the TVA's propaganda efforts, see McCraw, *TVA and the Power Fight*, 148.

[22] Davidson, *Tennessee*, II, 324-33. In describing the first three directors of the TVA, Davidson wrote, "Of the three men, Lilienthal was farthest removed from the ancient, indigenous life of the valley; in fact, in comparison with the other two men, he seemed much more definitely an 'outsider.'" (II, 223.) Other students of the TVA have also been skeptical of the agency's democratic pretensions. McCraw has argued that democracy "is mostly irrelevant to the electric utility business, once a community has made its basic decision for or against public power." McCraw, *TVA and the Power Fight*, 143-44. See also Schlesinger, *Politics of Upheaval*, 372, and Rexford G. Tugwell and Edward C. Banfield, "Grass-Roots Democracy—Myth or Reality?" in *Public Administration Review*, X (Winter, 1950), 47-55. For Schlesinger, Tugwell, and Banfield the democratic impulses within the TVA were not smothered, as Davidson claimed, by a remote bureaucracy oblivious to the needs of the Tennessee Valley. Rather, the TVA willingly accommodated itself to the demands of the strongest local interests within the valley, leaving most of the valley's population, either for economic or racial factors, powerless to influence the Authority's operations.

volume was more balanced than most of his writings of the 1930's and he did point out many worthwhile features of the agency. He himself believed he had bent over backwards to be fair and, if anything, had erred on the side of generosity. Nevertheless, he anticipated the response to his book would be negative, partially because he believed the TVA maintained a virtual espionage system with enough influence on the mass media to practically blacklist any criticism. He was not to be disappointed. Although some reviews praised the volume, most described it as unbalanced, sentimental, romantic, biased, nostalgic, opinionated, odd, myopic, and perverse. As Charles R. Sanders wrote in the *South Atlantic Quarterly* in January, 1949, "Some of the warmer opinions in this book need to be carried to the high mountain sources of the great Tennessee and to be washed there in the clear, pure, cold water." In response, Davidson suggested to his publisher that copies of the book be sent to the right-wing journalists John T. Flynn, Fulton Lewis, Jr., Raymond Moley, George Sokolsky, and David Lawrence.[23]

Davidson continued his private struggle with northern economic aggrandizement and political centralization until his death in 1968. Increasingly, however, the focus of his disquietude was not the Tennessee Valley Authority but rather the civil rights movement, particularly the attempt to integrate the public schools of Tennessee. Davidson had been concerned with the segregation question at least as far back as the early 1930's, seeing it as another of the issues which northern economic and political interests used to their advantage. His fear that the New Deal and the national Democratic party opposed white supremacy within the South was a major reason for his disaffection from Roosevelt's administration and for his support for Strom Thurmond and the Dixiecrats in 1948. He regretted that the Dixiecrat revolt had not occurred earlier,

---

[23] Davidson to Jean Crawford, July 1, 1947, Davidson Papers; Davidson to Donald T. Wright, January 29, 1948, in *ibid.*; Davidson to Harvey Broome, April 25, 1948; in *ibid.*; Davidson to Frederick Rinehart, September 5, 1953, in *ibid.* See the following reviews of Davidson's volume: Charles Richard Sanders, in *South Atlantic Quarterly*, XLVIII (January, 1949), 164-65; Culver H. Smith, in *American Historical Review*, LIV (January, 1949), 449-50; James A. Barnes, in *Mississippi Valley Historical Review*, XXXV (September, 1948), 322-23; Stanley J. Folmsbee, in *Journal of Southern History*, XIV (May, 1948), 231-84; and in *Georgia Historical Quarterly*, XXIII (June, 1949), 187-88; Herman C. Nixon, in *American Political Science Review*, XLIII (June, 1948), 596-97; Ernest Kirschten, in *Nation*, CLXVI (April 17, 1948), 421; Gerald W. Johnson, in *New York Herald Tribune Weekly Book Review*, January 25, 1948, 1-2.

attributing this to the Roosevelt regime's bribing of southern politicians. Davidson became distraught in 1954 when the Supreme Court handed down the Brown decision outlawing racial segregation in the public schools, and he took the lead in organizing the Tennessee Federation for Constitutional Government, serving as its president from 1955 to 1959.[24]

The T.F.C.G. was the most respectable of the anti-integration organizations established in Tennessee in the wake of the Brown decision. Its members included prominent businessmen, writers, artists, and professors. It denounced rabble-rousing and violence, stressed constitutional arguments in defense of segregation, and favored a multifaceted legislative program to prevent any school integration. This included the repeal of the state compulsory school attendance law, withdrawal of public funds from any integrated school, providing of aid to children attending private segregated schools, the licensing of all private and religious schools, making the promotion of integration a misdemeanor, and forbidding athletic teams from Tennessee educational institutions from competition with integrated teams from other states. The T.F.C.G. also advocated the closure of state parks and other recreational facilities rather than have them integrated under court pressure, as well as forbidding the Tennessee National Guard, state police, or city police from enforcement of orders of a federal court.

The organization claimed the Supreme Court had acted unconstitutionally in the Brown decision by distorting the meaning of the Fourteenth Amendment, by usurping legislative authority, and by depriving the states of their sovereign right to administer their own educational systems. The T.F.C.C. endorsed an extreme states'

---

[24] Davidson to Allen Tate, July 21 and July 23, 1930, in Davidson Papers; Davidson to John Gould Fletcher, April 16, 1933, in *ibid.*; Davidson to Editors of the *Nation*, January 5, 1934, in *ibid.*; Davidson to Frank L. Owsley, August 3, 1936, in Owsley Papers (Vanderbilt University); Davidson, "Gulliver With Hay Fever," 152-72; Davidson, "A Sociologist in Eden," 177-204; and especially Davidson, "Preface to Decision," in *Sewanee Review*, LIII (Summer, 1945), 394-412. Davidson believed that, because of his *Sewanee Review* article, he had been blacklisted by the blacks of Nashville and this explained his inability to hire any servants to help around his house. Davidson to William T. Couch, October 13, 1948, in Davidson Papers. For Davidson's attitude toward the Dixiecrat movement, see Davidson to Tate, March 3, 1948, in Tate Papers. For Davidson's reaction to the Brown decision, see Davidson to Editors of *Human Events*, May 27, 1954, in Davidson Papers; Davidson to Frank Chodorov, May 28, 1954, in *ibid.*; Davidson to Jesse Stuart, May 29, 1954, in *ibid.*; Davidson to John Donald Wade, June 8, 1955, in *ibid.* Davidson predicted he might be jailed because of his anti-integration activities. Davidson to Andrew N. Lytle, October 11, 1957, in Lytle Papers, Tennessee State Library and Archives.

rights position and argued that the Ninth and Tenth Amendments gave to the states the right to interpose their authority between their citizens and the power of the federal government. Failure of the Tennessee legislature to declare for interposition during this crisis "would encourage the extinction of all our constitutional rights and liberties by process of judicial amendment or other Federal usurpation." For Tennessee to supinely accept the judicial tyranny of the Supreme Court "would mean nothing less than the beginning of the reduction of Tennessee to the condition of a feeble and compliant satellite and parasite of an all-powerful and socialistic Federal Government." Privately Davidson praised the white citizens' councils, favored closing Tennessee's public schools rather than have them integrated, and proposed a southern economic boycott of northern businesses supporting the desegregation drive.[15]

Davidson attributed the anti-segregation movement to the same northern missionary attitude regarding the South which had resulted in Reconstruction, the Scopes and Scottsboro Trials, and the Tennessee Valley Authority. Unfortunately the communists and socialists, eager to make the South over, could count on the aid of such southern scalawags as Estes Kefauver, Ralph McGill, and the Southern Regional Council in dismantling segregation. School integration, Davidson claimed, was merely the first step, to be followed by other measures designed to completely obliterate southern distinctiveness. He simply could not believe that any loyal Southerner would support integration, just as he found it difficult to believe that any patriotic Southerner could possibly favor the power and planning programs of the TVA.[16]

Since Davidson assumed there was little indigenous support for school integration in the South, he was confident the authentic South would triumph if only she stood firm. Beginning in 1955 he began calling attention to signs indicating the tide had turned

---

[15] *The Crisis in Tennessee: A Message to the Members of the General Assembly of the State of Tennessee Containing Proposals for Legislative Action to Safeguard and Maintain the Sovereign Rights of the State of Tennessee and its People* (Tennessee Federation for Constitutional Government, 1956); Nashville Banner, November 20, 1956; Neil R. McMillen, "Organized Resistance to School Desegregation in Tennessee," in *Tennessee Historical Quarterly*, XXX (Fall, 1971), 323-24; Hugh Davis Graham, *Crisis in Print: Desegregation and the Press in Tennessee* (Nashville, 1967), 81; Davidson to Louis D. Rubin, Jr., September 2, 1955, in Davidson Papers; Davidson to Dick (?), November 23, 1955, in *ibid*.

[16] Davidson to Floyd C. Watkins, June 11, 1956, in Davidson Papers; Davidson to Thomas J. B. Walsh, December 24, 1956, in *ibid*.; Davidson, "The New South and the Conservative Tradition," in *National Review*, IX (September 10, 1960), 141-46.

in the direction of the conservative, states' rights, segregation position. He maintained this despite the ineffectiveness of the T.F.C.G. and the moderate response of Tennessee to the Brown decision.[27]

By the time of his death and with the growing acceptance of integration in the South, Davidson had become intellectually isolated. Bitter to the end, he continued to issue jeremiads against the Supreme Court and Martin Luther King but unfortunately for him few were listening. Indeed, by 1968 the major thrust of southern conservatism had switched from a concern for segregation to a defense of industrialization and business values. To a certain extent Davidson himself reflected this shift. He, who had been the most critical of all the Southern Agrarians regarding the New South spirit of industrialization, now during the 1960's praised the propaganda of the Southern States Industrial Council and became closely identified with the *National Review*, a journal sympathetic to right-wing business interests. One thing is certain and that is the South of the 1970's would have been a strange and perhaps hostile land for Donald Davidson. Indeed, what would he have made of a South in which the Tennessee Valley Authority is a sacred cow, in which southern universities are busily recruiting black quarterbacks and linebackers, in which the portrait of Martin Luther King hangs in the Georgia State Capitol, and in which the most important of all the Southern Agrarians commends the contemporary versions of Henry W. Grady and Daniel A. Tompkins?[28]

---

[27] Davidson to John Donald Wade, August 4, 1955, in Davidson Papers; Davidson to Tom (?), April 24, 1956, in *ibid.;* Davidson, "New South and Conservative Tradition," 143-45.

[28] Davidson to Louis D. Rubin, Jr., January 28, 1961, in Davidson Papers; Davidson to Melvin E. Bradford, May 11, 1963 and April 9, 1967, in *ibid.;* Davidson to Allen Tate, May 30, 1963, in *ibid.*

# Frank L Owsley and the Defense of Southern Identity

Of all the sections of the United States, none has attracted as much attention, criticism, analysis, and notoriety as the South.[1] A small library has been written defending the proposition that the people living below the Potomac and Ohio Rivers are a single entity bearing the ineradical imprint of "southerness". Included are such representative and often seemingly contradictory titles as *The South as a Conscious Minority, The South and the Sectional Image, The South and the Nation,* and *The Southerner and World Affairs; The Southern Heritage* and *Southern Legacy; The Making of a Southerner, The South and the Southerner, The Southerner as American,* and *Southerners and Other Americans: The Militant South* and *The Uncertain South; The Lasting South, Seeds of Southern Change, This Changing South,* and *The South in Continuity and Change; The Old South* and *The New South; The Romantic South, Romanticism and Nationalism in the Old South,* and *Romance and Realism in Southern Politics; The Emerging South* and *The Advancing South; The Everlasting South* and *An Epitaph for Dixie; The Lazy South* and *Southern Tradition and Regional Progress; The Burden of Southern History* and *The Myth of Southern History; A Southerner Discovers the South* and *A Southerner Discovers New England; The Idea of the South, The Mind of the South, The Southern Temper* and *The Southern Mystique; Southern Exposure* and *Look Away From Dixie;* and, of course, *The Great South*. Perhaps the greatest scholarly tribute to the idea of southern distinctiveness is the ten-volume history of the South published by the Louisiana State University press.

For decades now the South has been an exotic, and for some an obscene, curiosity piece, an object both of popular interest and scholarly investigation. The popularity of the movies "Birth of a Nation", "I Was a Fugitive From a Chain Gang", and "Gone With the Wind" attest to the hold which the theme of southern uniqueness has had over the American popular imagination. Scholars and polemicists such as Frank Tannenbaum, John Dollard, Arthur Raper, Robert Coles, and H. L. Mencken have studied the mysteries and afflictions of the South, often with a mordant fascination, seeking to discover the means whereby the South could take her rightful place within the mainstream of national life. No other section has ever been referred to as a problem, much less the country's number one economic problem, as the South was by Franklin D. Roosevelt in the 1930's, and no other section has ever been advised to put on shoes as was suggested by President Roosevelt's Secretary of Labor Frances Perkins.[2]

Despite this abundance of concern with the South, there is still no agreement regarding the factors responsible for the South's supposed distinctiveness. By now the reality of the South has been covered with so many layers of folklore and mythology that it has become difficult, if not impossible, to separate reality from fiction, truth from myth. In 1961 David M. Potter could write an article appropriately entitled "The Enigma of the South" in which he argued that the South has become "a kind of Sphinx on the American land." And Paul Gaston could declare in his book *The New South Creed: A Study in Southern Mythmaking* that the South is distinguished from other parts of the United States by the extent to which "myths have been spawned . . . and have asserted their hegemony over the Southern mind." The quest for "The Central Theme of Southern History" thus remains as valid today as in 1928 when Ulrich B. Phillips published his famous essay of that title. Closely related to the quest for the central theme is the question of which individual or group most fully embodies and reflects the distinctive characteristics of the South. *Who Speaks for the South?* James McBride Dabbs asked in 1964. Is it Senator Claghorn or Jeeter Lester, Billy Graham or Rhett Butler, Tallulah Bankhead or George Wallace, Uncle Remus or Bear Bryant?[3]

---

[2] Edward S. Shapiro, "The Southern Agrarians, H. L. Mencken, and the Quest for Southern Identity," in *American Studies*, XIII (Fall, 1972), 75-92; George B. Tindall, "The Benighted South: Origins of a Modern Image," in *Virginia Quarterly Review*, XL (Spring, 1964), 281-94.

[3] David M. Potter, "The Enigma of the South," *Yale Review*, LI (October, 1961), 142; Paul Gaston, *The New South Creed: A Study in Southern Mythmaking* (New York, 1970), 8; Tindall, "Mythology: A New Frontier in Southern History," in *Myth and Southern History*, edited by Patrick Gerster and Nicholas Cords (Chicago, 1974), 1-15; Monroe L. Billington (ed.), *The South, a Central Theme?* (New York, 1969). George E. Mowry has noted that no regional journal is as influential as the *Journal of Southern History*, and no parochial topic has

For Phillips "the cardinal test of a Southerner and the central theme of Southern history" was the indomitable resolve of southern whites that the South "shall be and remain a white man's country." Two years after the appearance of Phillips' article the twelve Southern Agrarians brought out their manifesto *I'll Take My Stand: The South and the Agrarian Tradition*, the most militant defense of the idea of southern distinctiveness since that of George Fitzhugh. The Agrarians believed the difference between the southern way of life and the American way of life was the difference between agrarianism and industrialism, and they called upon those Southerners "who are being converted frequently to the industrial gospel" to repent and return "to the support of the Southern tradition." Since the publication of *I'll Take My Stand* historians have continued to probe for the source of southern uniqueness, and the region's distinctiveness has been variously attributed to its romanticism, its conservatism, its tendency to mythologize, its lack of commitment to an ethic of social responsibility, its heightened historical consciousness, its militarism and violence, its sexual license, its folk culture, its sultry climate, and its heritage of frustration, failure, and defeat. "In the history of Southern history in America," David L. Smiley has remarked, "the central theme has been the quest for the central theme."[4]

Despite their disagreements as to the sources of southern distinctiveness, most historians have argued that they are to be found in certain unique characteristics of the southern society, economy, or politics, and that the South's defense of its regional differences ineluctably emerged from these peculiarities. Unfortunately no single interpretation, or combination of interpretations, can explain over one hundred and fifty years of history of a region with a population of great social, racial, economic, and geographical diversity stretching from Virginia to Texas. An alternative approach would be to look to the realm of ideas, for, as Professor Smiley has argued, the South "exists only as a controlling idea or belief upon

---

been covered in such depth as the South has been in the ten-volume history of the South published by the Louisiana State University Press, Mowry, *Another Look at the Twentieth Century South* (Baton Rouge, 1973), 3-4.

[4] Ulrich B. Phillips, "The Central Theme of Southern History," in *American Historical Review*, XXXIV (October, 1928), 31; Twelve Southerners, "Introduction: A Statement of Principles," in *I'll Take My Stand: The South and the Agrarian Tradition* (New York, 1930, 1962), xix-xx; David L. Smiley, "The Quest for the Central Theme in Southern History," in *South Atlantic Quarterly*, LXXI (Summer, 1972), 307-25.

which men acted, risked, and died. . . . Those of whatever persuasion or tradition who believed themselves to be Southern are indeed Southern." Of particular importance in defining southern identity are the ideas Southerners have had of the North and their perceptions of northern attitudes toward the South. The North and South have used each other, C. Vann Woodward has written, "not only to define their identity and to say what they are *not*, but to escape in fantasy from what they *are*." There is need, Vann Woodward continues, "for a history of North-South images and stereotypes, of when and how and why they were developed, the shape they took, the uses that have been made of them and how they have been employed from time to time in regional defense, self-flattery, and polemics. . . . All along they have been prolific breeders of regional myth, and their fertility is not yet exhausted." By refocusing the search for the central theme from the southern economy and social structure onto the various defenses which Southerners developed in response to northern attacks, the question of southern identity loses much of its provincial character and becomes a chapter in the history of the relationship between the North and the South. The central theme of southern history thereby becomes part of American national history.[5]

The southern historian Frank L. Owsley is proof against all-encompassing, monocausal interpretations of southern identity. For Owsley the South was a section perennially under seige, but his perception of what was being attacked and what should be defended changed. Owsley was typical of many Southerners whose defense of the southern way of life was shaped more by their visions of northern designs on the South than by any immutable traits of southern society.

Owsley was born in the black belt of Alabama in 1890 and spent much of his childhood on a farm. He received both his B.A. and M.A. degrees from Alabama Polytechnic Institute and then went on for doctoral work at the University of Chicago where he studied under William E. Dodd. Owsley was in graduate school at a time when American historiography was in revolt against the assumptions of the "nationalist" historians of the late Nineteenth Century. John W. Burgess, Hermann Von Holst, and James Ford Rhodes,

---

[5] Smiley, "Quest for the Central Theme," 324-25; C. Vann Woodward, *American Counterpoint: Slavery and Racism in the North-South Dialogue* (Boston, 1971), 6-7; Michael O'Brien, "C. Vann Woodward and the Burden of Southern Liberalism," in *American Historical Review*, LXXVIII (June, 1973), 603-604.

among others, had argued in the decades immediately following the Civil War that the South had been wrong in challenging the national government. Not only had the South been a barrier to the advance of industrialization, but she had also threatened political centralization and national sovereignty. The victory of the North in the Civil War was morally right since it enabled nationalism, industrial progress, and the abolition of slavery to triumph. Any interpretation of American history which, according to Burgess, "does not demonstrate to the South its error will be worthless, simply because it will not be true. . . . The conviction of the South of its error in seccession and rebellion is absolutely indispensable to the establishment of national cordiality."[5]

Frederick Jackson Turner and Charles A. Beard lead the progressive attack on the nationalist school of historians. As was true of most of the leading progressive historians, Turner and Beard came from small towns outside the East and they stressed the importance of the West and South in American development. In *The Significance of Sections in American History*, *Rise of the New West 1819-1829*, and *The United States, 1830-1850: The Nation and Its Sections* Turner argued that American history was essentially the history of sections, not the history of a national organism whose center was in Washington, New York, or Boston. For Turner, sections were natural economic groupings continually competing for economic advantage. Beard in *An Economic Interpretation of the Constitution* and *Economic Origins of Jeffersonian Democracy* saw the struggle over the adoption of the constitution and the political battles of the 1790's as a clash between agrarian and mercantile forces organized along geographic lines. According to Beard, the political history of the late Eighteenth Century provided the key to understanding all of American political history, a history whose major theme was the conflict between agrarian and industrial interests. Turner and Beard rejected the nationalist interpretation of the Civil War as a moral struggle between the forces of freedom and slavery. In their eyes the war was a conflict between two sections with differing economies for control of the national government. Another characteristic of progressive historiography was its tough-mindedness. The progressive historians

---

[*] For Owsley's biography, see *I'll Take My Stand*, 374-75, and Bernarr Cresap, "Frank L. Owsley and *King Cotton Diplomacy*," in *Alabama Review*, XXVI (October, 1973), 238-40.

discounted ideals, and emphasized the hard economic and sectional realities lying behind the politicians' platitudes. Owsley would incorporate in his work both the progressive emphasis on sectionalism and the importance of the hinterland, as well as its stress on the importance of economic interests in explaining political controversies.[7]

Dodd was one of the most vigorous exponents of this new emphasis on sectionalism. Influenced by his own personal background as the son of a small North Carolina farmer, by the Populist ferment at the turn of the century, and especially by Turner, Dodd stressed in his lectures and writings the importance of sectional conflict, particularly that between the industrial Northeast and the agrarian South. Holding rural democracy in high esteem, Dodd believed that industrial America under the aegis of the Republican Party was drifting away from Jeffersonianism and toward a feudalistic plutocracy dominated by the leaders of finance capitalism. For Dodd political and economic democracy were indivisible and he feared that the dispossession of the middle class would be accompanied by a withering away of republican government. As was true of any Southerner born in the late Nineteenth Century, Owsley did not have to be convinced by Dodd of the crucial role of sectionalism in American history. Dodd, in fact, attracted many southern students to the University of Chicago precisely because of his emphasis on sectionalism. Study under Dodd did, however, sharpen Owsley's awareness of its importance. Furthermore, Dodd's Jeffersonianism and the importance he attributed to the small farmer in the antebellum South would later be echoed in Owsley's pioneering work on the plain folk of the old South.[8]

---

[7] Richard Hofstadter, *The Progressive Historians: Turner, Beard, Parrington* (New York, 1970), 99-103; John Higham with Leonard Krieger and Felix Gilbert, *History* (Englewood Cliffs, New Jersey, 1965), 173-79, 200-201.

[8] For Dodd, see Robert Dallek, *Democrat and Diplomat: The Life of William E. Dodd* (New York, 1968), 60-61, 77-78, and Wendell Holmes Stephenson, *The South Lives in History: Southern Historians and Their Legacy* (Baton Rouge, 1955), ch. ii. For the growing interest in southern history in the late nineteenth and early twentieth centuries, see Stephenson, *The South Lives in History*, ch. i, Owsley frequently acknowledged his debt to Turner, Beard, and Dodd. See, for example, Owsley, "The War of the Sections," in *Virginia Quarterly Review*, X (Autumn, 1934), 635; Owsley, "The American Triangle," in *Virginia Quarterly Review*, XI (Winter, 1935), 113; Owsley, "The Historical Philosophy of Frederick Jackson Turner," in *American Review*, V (Summer, 1935), 368-75. The progressive emphasis on economic rather than moral or ideological factors in history is most prominently reflected in Owsley's work in his volume on Confederate diplomacy, *King Cotton Diplomacy*. Here he argued that England's attitude toward the Civil War was primarily shaped by England's economic stake in the war rather than by

Owsley's first major work, *State Rights in the Confederacy*, published in 1925, reflected the burgeoning interest in sectionalism. Here Owsley argued that "the" major reason for the defeat of the Confederacy was the inability of the Confederate state governments to free themselves from the shibboleths of state rights and their refusal to support Jefferson Davis' government. Had the southern state leaders been more concerned with the interests of their section than with the interests of their individual states, Owsley claimed, it would have been impossible for the North to have won the war. The outbreak of the war itself, Owsley contended elsewhere, resulted from the struggle between the North and the South for national domination.[9]

Owsley's sectionalism, his growing commitment to the South, and his teaching at Vanderbilt University during the 1920's naturally drew him into the orbit of Donald Davidson, John Crowe Ransom, Allen Tate, and other future Southern Agrarians. He was asked to write an historical analysis for the Agrarians' symposium *I'll Take My Stand*, and his essay "The Irrepressible Conflict" marked him as one of the most eloquent, although at times extreme, defenders of the traditional South. Owsley's major argument was that, contrary to the views of the nationalist historians such as Rhodes and Von Holst, the Civil War was not a struggle between freedom and slavery, nor was slavery a major cause of the war. The war was due instead to the North's recognition that the South was a barrier to the growth of northern industry and business because of her opposition to protective tariffs, subsidies to shipping interests, banking legislation favorable to the North, and federal aid for internal improvements. "The struggle between an agrarian and an industrial civilization," Owsley maintained, "was the irrepressible conflict, the house divided against itself, which must become according to the doctrine of the industrial section all the one or the other. It was the doctrine of intolerance, crusading, standardizing alike in industry and in life. The South had to be crushed out; it was in the way; it impeded the progress of the machine. So Juggernaut drove his car across the South." The industrial North necessarily caused the Civil War, Owsley con-

---

anti-slavery sentiment. For an analysis of Owsley's book, see Cresap, "Frank L. Owsley and *King Cotton Diplomacy*," 235-51.

[9] Owsley, *State Rights in the Confederacy* (Chicago, 1925); Owsley, Review of *David Wilmot: Free-Soiler*, by Charles Buxton Going, in *Nashville Tennessean*, November 30, 1924.

tended, since industrialization, by its very nature, is aggressive, exploitative, and imperialistic.[10]

Owsley hoped his essay would achieve two goals. The first was to convince the South "that the things for which it stood were reasonable and sound, that its condemnation at the hands of the North had been contemptible, and that for it, at least, the philosophy of the North is the religion of an alien God." The second goal was to show how the idealistic rhetoric of the anti-slavery movement had been used by the industrial-financial plutocracy of the Northeast for its own purposes."[11]

Owsley frequently returned to these themes during the 1930's and 1940's. Indeed, for Owsley the central theme of southern history was the South's efforts to defend herself against the depradations of northern industrial and financial interests cloaked in the garb of idealism and humanitarianism. Behind all the attacks upon the South, whether it be abolitionism, Reconstruction, the Scopes Trial agitation, or the controversy engendered by the Scottsboro case, Owsley argued, were big business and high finance. Abolitionism, he maintained, had been used to separate the regions of corn and cotton and to keep the East in control of the national government. The abolitionists and their financial supporters, he wrote in 1940, threatened "the existence of the South as seriously as the Nazis threaten the existence of England and . . . their language was so violent, obscene, and insulting that not even Dr. Goebbels in all his flights has seldom equaled and never surpassed it." He accused the Republican Party of having an "uncompromising hostility to Southern interests and attitudes," and claimed that this had continued through the 1930's.[12]

Reconstruction, "the most abominable phase barbarism had assumed since the dawn of civilization", was the political program of northern capitalists determined to reap the benefits of their victory in the war by keeping the South in bondage. Prostrate after the end of hostilities, the South was turned over to "half-savage blacks", "some of whom could still remember the taste of human flesh and the bulk of them hardly three generations removed from cannibalism." The newly freed Negroes were not to blame, however,

[10] Owsley, "The Irrepressible Conflict," in *I'll Take My Stand*, 61-91.
[11] Owsley, "Irrepressible Conflict," 67.
[12] Owsley, Review of *Freedom of Thought in the Old South*, by Clement Eaton, in *Journal of Southern History*, VI (November, 1940), 559; Owsley, "American Triangle," 117; Owsley to James H. Kirkland, January 20, 1936, and Owsley to Leo M. Favrot, March 17, 1936, Owsley Papers (Vanderbilt University).

since they were merely the unwitting tools of Charles Sumner, Benjamin F. Butler, and other "fanatical abstractionists". The southern revolt against the "coldly self-righteous and intolerant" Radical Republicans was lead by the Ku Klux Klan which closely resembled "the underground organization of the countries occupied by the armies of Hitler".[13]

For Owsley the fact that the South was being portrayed in the 1920's and 1930's as a benighted land ruled by the Ku Klux Klan, ranting fundamentalist preachers, prohibitionists, and yokel politicians was proof that the financiers and capitalists of the Northeast had not given up their campaign to destroy the southern spirit and to discredit southern opposition to modern large-scale industrialism. As a native of Alabama, Owsley was particularly angered by the Scottsboro trial of 1931. He perceived behind all the supposedly humanitarian northern agitation in behalf of the Scottsboro defendants a strange alliance of finance-capitalists and communists. Both groups, he avowed, were interested less in aiding the accused Negroes than in humiliating the South since they realized that the South was the last remaining bulwark against the complete triumph of large-scale industrialism. The South, Owsley claimed, even after the experience of the Civil War and Reconstruction remained characterized by the widespread distribution of property, by a commitment to small-scale agriculture and petty capitalism, and by an opposition to political and economic collectivism whether of the plutocratic or communist variety. The South, both ideologically and socially, thus continued to be faithful to the Jeffersonian ideal of a middle-class society of property holders. In the North, by contrast, a powerful financial and industrial plutocracy ruled a rapidly growing, dispossessed factory proletariat. According to Owsley the logic of the type of industrialization found in the Detroits, Pittsburghs, and Chicagos of the North lead ultimately to communism.[14]

It was characteristic of Owsley's thinking that his major contribution to American historiography was his effort to show the Jeffersonian character of the antebellum South. In a series of articles and in his important book *Plain Folk of the Old South*

---

[13] Owsley, "Scottsboro, the Third Crusade: The Sequel to Abolition and Reconstruction," in *American Review*, I (June, 1933), 267-68; Owsley, "Irrepressible Conflict," 62; Owsley, Oliver P. Chitwood, and Herman C. Nixon, *A Short History of the American People*, Vol. II (New York, 1948), 10-22, 22-27, 49-59, 101-105.

[14] Owsley, "Scottsboro," 257-58.

Owsley challenged the image of the Old South propagated by Frederick Law Olmsted and others as consisting largely of planter aristocrats, slaves, and poor whites. He conclusively demonstrated that the social structure of the antebellum South rested upon a "massive body of plain folk . . . neither rich nor very poor", who were mostly small and independent farmers. The "Owsley thesis" implicitly denied that the Civil War involved a northern attempt to preserve democracy since the South was undoubtedly far more democratic and egalitarian than the more industrialized North.[15]

Owsley's commitment to the South during the interwar decades increased as he became more aware of the condescending and patronizing attitude of the North toward the South. He was especially disturbed by H. L. Mencken's biting critique of the South's cultural and social failings, and accused the Baltimore scoffer of being a spokesman for the North's bankrupt urban, technological, and industrial civilization. Owsley even proposed the establishment of a secret organization to strengthen agrarianism in the South and to bolster the morale of Southerners in the face of northern attacks on the South. Members of the organization would be required to read *I'll Take My Stand,* Howard K. Beale's *The Critical Year,* Avery Craven's *Edmund Ruffin,* Jesse T. Carpenter's *The South as a Conscious Minority,* and Allen Tate's *Jefferson Davis.* This reading would be supplemented by visits to Confederate cemeteries where graves would be decorated and orations given on the glories of southern life. "I feel that such occasions," Owsley declared, "offer great possibilities to stir the emotions—and that is what we want to stir—along with the imagination." Owsley hoped

---

[15] Owsley, *Plain Folk of the Old South* (Baton Rouge, 1949), pages vii, ix, 7; Owsley, "The Pattern of Migration and Settlement on the Southern Frontier," in *Journal of Southern History,* XI (May, 1945), 147-76; Frank L. Owsley and Harriet C. Owsley, "The Economic Basis of Society in the Late Ante-bellum South," in *Journal of Southern History,* VI (February, 1940), 24-45; Owsley and Owsley, "Economic Structure of Rural Tennessee: 1850-1860," in *Journal of Southern History,* VIII (May, 1942), 161-82; Frank L. Owsley, Review of *Origins of Class Struggle in Louisiana: A Social History of White Farmers and Laborers in Louisiana During Slavery and After, 1840-1875,* by Roger W. Shugg, in *Journal of Southern History,* VI (February, 1940), 116-17. For a critique of the Owsley "thesis", see Fabian Linden, "Economic Democracy in the Slave South: An Appraisal of Some Recent Views," in *Journal of Negro History,* XXXI (April, 1946), 140-89. James C. Bonner places Owsley's analysis of the antebellum South within the context of southern historiography in "Plantation and Farm: The Agricultural South," in *Writing Southern History: Essays in Historiography in Honor of Fletcher M. Green,* edited by Arthur S. Link and Rembert W. Patrick (Baton Rouge, 1965), 155-57. Charles Beard thought very highly of Owsley's work on the antebellum South. Beard to Owsley, May 14, 1940, Owsley Papers.

this organization could spread throughout the South, but he warned that it "should be dignified, restrained, but grim in the purpose of renewing the spirit and self respect of the South."[16]

What is surprising about Owsley's political and social thought during the 1930's was the extent to which this traditional Southerner, who distrusted centralized political power, favored radical and even semi-socialistic means to destroy the power of big business and high finance and to encourage a wider distribution of productive property. Owsley believed only drastic measures could cure the ills brought on by the 1929 depression which, he argued, was due to the fact that the United States had become overindustrialized in terms of available world and domestic markets. Owsley contrasted the experience of largely agricultural France during the 1930's with the more desperate straits of England and the United States as proof for his contention that the economies of the major industrial nations had "matured" and further industrialization would bring only more unemployment and misery. Owsley had accepted the doctrine of the matured economy while a graduate student but it wasn't until the 1930's that its full force was brought home to him. The only lasting and viable solution to the social and economic problems facing the country was the restoration of a propertied society in which small business and especially agriculture had a larger role.[17]

A conservative revolution whose goals were to end the dispossession of the middle-class, to increase the number of independent farmers, and to destroy the power of the industrial-financial plutocracy would, according to Owsley, provide a democratic alternative to fascism and communism. Fascism and communism, in his view, accepted modern industrialization and merely wished to

---

[16] Owsley to John Gould Fletcher, no date, Owsley Papers; John L. Stewart, *The Burden of Time. The Fugitives and Agrarians* (Princeton, 1965), 109-110, 114-15; Rob Roy Purdy (ed.), *Fugitives' Reunion: Conversations at Vanderbilt, May 3-5, 1956* (Nashville, 1959), 204-205. For Owsley's attitude toward Mencken, see the following: Owsley, "The Pillars of Agrarianism," in *American Review*, IV (March, 1935), 529-30; Shapiro, "The Southern Agrarians . . . Quest for Southern Identity," 86-87; Owsley to Robert Penn Warren, January 12, 1935, Warren Papers (Yale University).

[17] Owsley to Donald Davidson, August 24, 1932, Davidson Papers (Vanderbilt University; Owsley to Seward Collins, April 12, 1934, in *American Review* Papers (Yale University); Owsley to John Gould Fletcher, March 11, 1935, Owsley Papers. For the popularity of the "matured economy" thesis, during the 1930's, see Robert F. Himmelberg (ed.), *The Great Depression and American Capitalism* (Boston, 1968), *passim*. For the political and social outlook of other "middle-class radicals", see Edward S. Shapiro, "Decentralist Intellectuals and the New Deal," in *Journal of American History*, LVIII (March, 1972), 938-57.

carry its collectivist implications through to their logical conclusion, while he envisaged a frontal attack on economic giantism and dispossession. "I am opposed to Fascism as an ultimate goal," he wrote to Geoffrey Stone, one of America's leading fascist intellectuals of the 1930's, "and unless the situation becomes more desperate, that is unless nothing can be accomplished in the direction of the restoration of property under the 'democratic process', I shall remain opposed to Fascism as an instrument, as a means to an end, in as much as it might become the end in itself." Communism, however, appeared to Owsley to be the more likely result of large-scale industrialism since it merely transferred to the government commissars the political and economic power previously exercised by the capitalists. Communism would also, as the example of the Soviet Union showed, continue and accentuate the dispossession and exploitation of the farmers and small businessmen begun by the industrialists and financiers."[18]

Only a propertied society, Owsley contended, could be democratic since the political and economic independence necessary for democracy could exist only where productive property was widely dispersed. Communism and fascism would have little appeal in a propertied state since the people, being able to care for themselves, had no need for the economic security promised by potential dictators. Furthermore, there was a basic conflict between the economic decentralization of a propertied state and the political collectivism of fascism and communism. By emphasizing that democracy was more than formal governmental procedures and structures and that democracy must have an economic basis, Owsley was exhibiting the tendency of the Progressive historians to discount political rhetoric and instead to focus on the economic and social realities determining political action.[19]

Owsley welcomed the victory of the Democrats in the 1932 election, and was hopeful that Franklin D. Roosevelt recognized the need for aiding farmers and small businessmen in their struggle for survival. Roosevelt, he wrote Donald Davidson in August, 1933, "is a great leader. He aims, I am convinced, to reduce the plutocrats to ranks as far as control of government goes. New York is to be trimmed of its complete financial control, if he has his

---

[18] Owsley to Geoffrey Stone, May 24, 1938, Owsley Papers; Owsley, "Scottsboro," 278-79.

[19] Owsley, "The Foundations of Democracy," in *Who Owns America?* edited by Herbert Agar and Allen Tate (Boston, 1936), 67.

way.... Roosevelt is conscious that a large part of the population, several millions, will be left unemployed after a normal situation has been restored and that these millions must be put upon the soil. That will be the biggest job he has had." Owsley attributed FDR's triumph to a coalition of the South and West opposed to a continuation of domination by the Northeast, big business, and the Republicans. He eagerly anticipated a concerted and comprehensive New Deal attack upon northern economic interests and the freeing of the South from its status as a colony of northern capitalists. What he particularly wished to see in this regard was a new freight rate schedule for the railroads which would not discriminate against the South, a lowering of the tariffs, an end to monopolies, and a limiting of the powers and prerogatives of large corporations. Without such reforms the South and West, he predicted, would continue to be impoverished and exploited by absentee corporations headquartered in the North.[20]

Owsley could thus agree with left-wing radicals on the need for a vigorous national reform program. He differed from them, however, on the direction this program should take. Whereas they proposed to use Washington to carry out the implications of political and economic centralization to their logical conclusion of complete socialism, he wanted economic and political decentralization to be the thrust of the New Deal. Owsley, in contrast to the leftists, hoped the centralization of power in Washington would only be temporary. Finally, he differed from them regarding the relevance of Marxism to the American situation. Owsley flatly rejected any attempt to analyze the plight of the United States in terms of "class struggle" and the "dictatorship of the proletariat". The exploitation of the South and West by the North rather than the oppression of the working class by the bourgeoisie lay at the heart of the nation's difficulties. The bond resulting from northern workers and capitalists sharing in the benefits of the exploitation of the hinterland, Owsley contended, was far more significant than any ties of class loyalty they might have to their counterparts in the South and West.[21]

This opposition to big business lead Owsley to even contemplate the nationalization of all corporations which could not be broken

---

[20] Owsley, to Davidson, August 5, 1933, Davidson papers; Owsley; "Scottsboro," 274; Owsley to Marvin M. Lowes, December 11, 1935, in *American Review* Papers; Owsley, "Pellagra Diet," in *Southern Review*, VI (Spring, 1941), 754-55.

[21] Owsley to Allen Tate, November 12, 1935, Tate Papers (Princeton University).

up and which operated in such vital areas as transportation, the extracting of natural resources, and the providing of hydroelectric power. Owsley was especially concerned with the electric power industry since he was a resident of Tennessee and hence familiar with the inequitable manner in which northern-owned utility companies had furnished power to the South. He was thus enthusiastic about the establishment of the Tennessee Valley Authority in 1933, and anticipated that the inexpensive electricity provided by the TVA would make rural life in the Southeast economically more viable and socially more attractive. He also hoped the TVA would destroy the monopoly northern capitalists had over southern sources of power.[22]

Owsley also favored extensive government intervention in agriculture if it would diminish the cancerous increase in farm tenancy and agrarian dispossession which he viewed as the major problem facing the nation, particularly the South, in the 1930's. By 1930 over fifty per cent of southern farmers owned none of the land they farmed. For Owsley the augmenting of the agrarian class was the only permanent solution for the overly industrialized American economy, and the only secure bulwark against communism. Unless the southern black and white tenant farmers were provided land, he warned William E. Dodd, they will provide fertile ground for communist propaganda "and when the trouble breaks we shall have enemies within our own camp and without." Owsley was disappointed that the early New Deal farm legislation had generally ignored the question of absentee-landlordism and tenancy and, instead, had focused on increasing farm income. He would have preferred legislation rehabilitating tenants and sharecroppers into farm owners, forbidding land to be sold to banks, real estate companies, and insurance firms, and offering incentives for subsistence farming. It was not until 1935 that Owsley could rejoice that something was finally going to be done about the "distressingly slow and expensive" progress of rural rehabilitation.[23]

---

[22] Owsley to Davidson, August 5, 1933, Davidson Papers; Owsley to Geoffrey Stone, May 24, 1938, Owsley Papers; Owsley to William E. Dodd, April 16, 1935, Dodd Papers (Library of Congress); Owsley, "Mr. Daniels Discovers the South," in *Southern Review*, IV (Spring, 1939), 670; Edward S. Shapiro, "The Southern Agrarians and the TVA," in *American Quarterly*, XXII (Winter, 1970), 791-806.

[23] Owsley to Dodd, April 16, 1935, Dodd Papers; Owsley to Lowes, March 11, 1935, in *American Review* Papers; Owsley, "Pellagra Diet," 752-53; Troy J. Cauley to Owsley, December 27, 1935, Owsley Papers. Owsley to Allen Tate, November 12, 1935, Tate Papers. Owsley's "The Pillars of Agrarianism," in *American Review*,

In that year Senator John H. Bankhead of Alabama introduced a bill providing long-term loans at low interest to sharecroppers and farm tenants to enable them to become farm owners. Bankhead's bill would establish a government corporation known as the Farmers' Home Corporation with power to loan up to one billion dollars per year to tenants and sharecroppers for the purchase of homes, land, supplies, and equipment. Bankhead argued that his proposal would increase subsistence farming, reduce relief payments, and enable some of the urban employed to return to the land. This was precisely the type of legislation Owsley wanted. The Bankhead bill, Owsley maintained, would increase the number of economically independent Americans, would decrease dependence on the government, and would lessen the appeal of radicals among the rural and urban dispossessed. He believed the Bankhead plan to be the most important measure to come forth during Roosevelt's first term since it was the most direct attempt to encourage the wider distribution of property. "We should all get behind that bill," he wrote to another advocate of a middle-class revolution, "it is the best . . . proposition thus far proposed by any official. . . . Most of the other Roosevelt legislation has dealt with the distribution of income; this is the distribution of capital."[24]

Owsley voted for Roosevelt in 1936, the last time he voted for the national Democratic ticket. Owsley's initial disaffection resulted from his fear that the unprecedented centralization of political power during the 1930's had not been accompanied either by a meaningful attack on plutocracy or by a serious attempt to create a propertied society. He blamed this on the fact that the New Dealers were too enamoured of political and economic centralization. "Regulating the hours of production, the hours of labor, fixing minimum wages and minimum prices and all the other strong measures provided for in the recovery legislation," Owsley declared, "are mere palliatives, mere treatment of symptoms when looked at from the long view. The cause of the disease is left intact." Owsley even concluded that the long-range effect of the

---

IV (March, 1935), 529–47, is the fullest statement of Owsley's social and political thought. Senators Hugo L. Black and John H. Bankhead of Alabama and William E. Dodd praised its emphasis on political decentralization and a return to yeoman agriculture. Black to Owsley, March 16, 1935; Dodd to Owsley, March 26, 1935 and May 4, 1935; Bankhead to Owsley, March 15, 1935, Owsley Papers.

[24] Bankhead to Owsley, March 15, 1935, Owsley Papers; Owsley to Lowes, March 16, 1935, in *American Review* Papers; Owsley to John Gould Fletcher, March 11 and March 16, 1935, Owsley Papers.

New Deal had been to increase industrialization in the South as well as absentee industrial and financial landlordism. A key to Owsley's thinking is found in one of his essays where he denied that Jefferson had believed in laissez-faire. Jefferson, Owsley wrote, "found a tremendous amount of government intervention necessary, even in an agricultural society, to prevent men from injuring one another." He "was unafraid of government except when it was in the hands of the enemies of free government." From the late 1930's until his death in 1956 Owsley believed the federal government had fallen into the hands of "the enemies of free government."[16]

The most important factor in Owsley's new view of the federal government was his dread that the power of Washington was going to be used to interfere in the most delicate and sensitive of all southern concerns, relations between the races. The expansion of federal power had already posed a potential threat to the sanctity of southern racial patterns, but it was a tolerable threat as long as Owsley was convinced that the New Deal recognized the necessity for a fundamental redistribution of productive property.

Owsley always accepted the dominant southern attitude regarding the racial question. His description of the southern black as "guileless" reflected the traditional southern image of the Negro as juvenile and irresponsible. For him segregation was a fundamental aspect of southern life and he would not accept any northern tampering with it. The South, he claimed, hadn't been responsible for slavery since the institution had been introduced into the South by yankee merchants. "Let the blood of slavery rest upon the heads of those who had forced it upon the South." Even so, southern race relations would have been harmonious and beneficial both for whites and blacks had it not been for continual northern interference. During the antebellum period,

> The slave possessed a great sense of security. He was cared for until he was old enough to work, well cared for; and when he became too old or ill to work the master and mistress fed, clothed, housed, and nursed him until death, whereupon he was given a Christian burial in the family cemetery, and quite frequently . . . he

---

[16] Herman C. Nixon to Owsley, October 25, 1935, Owsley Papers; Owsley, "Man or Machine?" (unpublished mss., in *American Review* Papers, 1933), 10-11; Owsley, "The Foundations of Democracy," 62-64; Owsley, "Fear May Come too Late," in *Sewanee Review*, LV (Summer, 1947), 514-17.

had a marble slab with affectionate sentiment inscribed upon it placed at the head of his grave.

The consolidation of black political power within the Democratic Party, the support for civil rights legislation voiced by some New Dealers, most notably Eleanor Roosevelt, and the disruptive effect of some of the New Deal legislation on southern racial patterns lead Owsley, as well as many other Southerners, to question the intentions of the Roosevelt administration towards the South.[26]

This change in attitude regarding the New Deal is readily seen in Owsley's response to Roosevelt's 1937 proposal to "pack" the Supreme Court. Owsley had previously accepted the Beardian view of the Constitution and the Supreme Court as tools of northern economic interests. In 1936 he described the court as a "judicial despotism" which exhibited "excessive amiability toward those who possess great wealth and great indifference toward those who own nothing or small private properties." Owsley wrote differently after Roosevelt's attack on the court. He then accused the New Deal of overstepping constitutional boundaries. Under Roosevelt the presidency, "by the use of patronage, relief funds, manipulation of national credit, and other similar methods, has gained ascendancy over the legislative branch of the national government and for the time being over the Supreme Court." The national administration, Owsley charged in 1940, has "destroyed the sovereignty of the people of the United States and made itself sovereign."[27]

Beginning in the late 1930's Owsley also became deeply disturbed by the growth of the labor movement. He did not in principle op-

---

[26] Owsley, "Scottsboro," 261-72; Owsley, "Irrepressible Conflict," 78; Owsley, "The Old South and the New," in *American Review*, VI (February, 1936), 478-79; Owsley, "The Fundamental Cause of the Civil War: Egocentric Sectionalism," in *Journal of Southern History*, VII (February, 1941), 7-9, 16-18. The most complete analysis of the relationship between the New Deal and the South is Frank B. Friedel, *F.D.R. and the South* (Baton Rouge, 1965).

[27] Owsley, "The Foundations of Democracy," 57-58; Owsley, Review of *The Social Philosophy of John Taylor of Caroline*, by E. T. Hodge, in *Free America*, IV (February, 1940), 19. For the opposition of Southerners to the court-packing plan because of its threat to white supremacy, see Monroe Lee Billington, *The Political South in the Twentieth Century* (New York, 1975), 78-79. Owsley came to believe that, as far as the race issue was concerned, the Democratic Party had been in the same position as the Republican Party was during Reconstruction. Thomas B. Alexander to Owsley, October 17, 1944, Owsley Papers. See also Owsley, "The Agrarians Today," in *Shenandoah*, III (Summer, 1952), 24-25. "The New Deal, of course, went far—and continues—in breaking down the Federal principle in our government. . . . A unitary form of government is rapidly replacing the Federal, which, of course, has the effect of placing the social and economic life of the American people under the national government."

pose unions but he did believe they had become far too powerful and had acquired too much political influence. "I have always been *liberal* in my social views," Owsley wrote Allen Tate in 1943. "Not any more, however. Behold in me, sir, not even a *Conservative* but a *reactionary*. On race and on the 'dictatorship of the proletariat' I stand where my friend John C. Calhoun stood one hundred years ago. If I must choose between 'big business' and 'big labor'—a choice I'd always hoped never to be compelled to make—I must choose big business. . . . God help this country, for it is losing at home what the soldiers are being sent abroad to fight for: *the sovereignty of the people as against the sovereignty of government*." Nothing less than the fate of constitutional democracy and "the freedom, integrity and self respect of the Southern white people" were threatened.[28]

Thus by the end of World War II Owsley was more concerned with the growth of big government and the menace this posed to southern racial patterns than with disciplining big business and high finance. Owsley's defense of the white South's position on race was less a matter of white supremacy and more a matter of protecting the integrity of southern culture and the continuity of southern life from external attack. His racial attitudes must be seen within the context of his lifelong struggle in behalf of regionalism. Indeed, Owsley approved of the amelioration of the condition of southern Negroes just as long as it was due to indigenous forces within the South rather than to pressures from the North. Except for the right to vote, Owsley told Tate, "I am willing and anxious to see the negro enjoy equality before the law, equal economic opportunities, equal cultural opportunities—in short *separate* but *equal opportunities* in all matters. . . ." He was certain that most white Southerners felt as he did and that, if left alone, they would insist on alleviating racial tensions. "But they will never be left alone, and men with the conservative race point of view should take the lead away from the Radicals by coming out in the open. . . . We must make it clear what we will *not do*, or

---

[28]Owsley to Tate, November 14, 1943, and August 13, 1944, Owsley Papers. Owsley's bleakest analysis of the state of American politics is in his posthumously published essay, "Democracy Unlimited," in *Georgia Review*, XV (Summer, 1961), 129-43. For a similar move to the right by another of the Southern Agrarians, see Edward S. Shapiro, "Donald Davidson and the Tennessee Valley Authority: The Response of a Southern Conservative," in *Tennessee Historical Quarterly*, XXXIII (Winter, 1974), 436-51.

*permit to be done;* then we should state positively and clearly what we *will do.*"²⁹

Reflecting the cold-war mentality of the immediate post-World War II era, Owsley attributed much of the agitation over southern segregation to a communist conspiracy directed from Moscow to create "well-planned and highly effective campaigns of disruption in the South." The goals of the Kremlin were to breed tension and distrust between economic, racial, and geographic groups, to encourage disorder and violence, to prevent a strong American foreign policy by weakening national unity, and to foster a situation conducive for "an organized and armed minority to take over and open the gates to Russian invasion."³⁰

Owsley's worst fears were realized in 1954 when the Supreme Court declared school segregation unconstitutional. He not only questioned the reasoning of the Court and denied that its decision was in any way sacrosanct, but also claimed that most Southerners, black and white, preferred segregated schools, that school integration would prevent each race from developing its potentialities to the fullest, and that segregated schools were the only means to preserve harmony between the races and to prevent social mixing between the races. The South must, he believed, use all legal means to get the Brown decision reversed. The court's ruling, Owsley wrote to a fellow segregationist, "is a mighty stride toward the monolithic state that our Yankee liberals are creating. . . . What a great boon this Supreme Court decision is to the Communists, who are in the NAACP up to their eye-balls." One wonders what Owsley would have thought of the 1974-75 University of Alabama basketball team which started five blacks. Not only did the university's band substitute the theme from "Shaft" for "Dixie" in its pre-game show, but the predominately white student body cheered the team on with the cry, "Ungawa, Bama's got soul power."³¹

---
²⁹ Owsley to Tate, December 7, 1943, and July 23, 1945, Tate Papers; Owsley, "A House Divided," in *Sewanee Review*, LIII (July-September, 1945), 503.

³⁰ Owsley, "The Chief Stakes of the South in World Affairs Today," (unpublished mss., Owsley Papers, undated, circa, 1950), 9-17; Owsley, "How Communism Wins the Support of the Masses," (unpublished mss., Owsley Papers, undated), 2ff.

³¹ Owsley, "Whither the Citizens Councils?" in *Tuscaloosa (Ala.) News*, March 21, 1954; Owsley to Andrew Nelson Lytle, February 28, 1956, Lytle Papers (Tennessee State Library and Archives); Peter Bonventre, "How Alabama Got Soul," in *Newsweek*, LXXXV (March 10, 1975), 69. Owsley, accepted, although he did not welcome, the admission of Negroes to southern graduate and professional schools since there were not many southern blacks pursuing postgraduate work and since it was better for them to be educated in the South than in the North. Owsley to Lytle, *op. cit.*

The ideological metamorphis of Owsley from the middle-class radicalism of the 1930's to the conservatism of the 1940's and 1950's was typical of the change in many Southerners. His career shows that for some Southerners the essence of southern identity lay neither in the region's conservatism nor in its agrarianism nor in its liberalism. The South was a "conscious minority" prior to the Civil War and remained one after the war ended, and its identity was to be found in a militant defense of whatever southern interest was currently under northern attack. The Southerner was, above all else, pro-South and among all the southern institutions he wished to defend, the most important was white supremacy. With the resistance of the white South to school integration just about destroyed, with white southern football coaches busily combing the ghettos for future all-American linebackers, and with a portrait of Martin Luther King hanging in the Georgia state capitol, will the South continue to be southern, or, at least, will it continue to be southern in the way Frank L. Owsley believed the South to be?[33]

[33] Smiley, "Quest for the Central Theme," 322-23. For a different interpretation of Owsley, see M. E. Bradford, "What We Can Know for Certain: Frank Owsley and the Recovery of Southern History," in *Sewanee Review*, LXXXVIII (October-December, 1970), 667. "On first impression there is a contradiction of thrust or emphasis between Dr. Owsley's warm consideration of temporary federal or state measures for the relief of regional and national economic distress (c. 1930-1936) and his subsequent warnings against government (c. 1955, in the shadow of the Brown decision)," Professor Bradford writes, "However, the trouble is not so much with Owsley as in the rigid and passionate insufficiency of the political idiom to which we are accustomed. From its beginnings the South has spoken with two voices, which voice depending upon the variety and source of the pressure it experienced from without. The English Whig tradition of earned Saxon rights and its preoccupation with individual self-realization through liberty and law provided a language for dealing with George III, Federalist mercantilism, and subsequent 'colonialist' incursions. But the South has also made its Tory noises: in defense of 'peculiar' institutions—spiritual, moral, social, and economic. In truth, the region's political inheritance is a compounding of these two English strains: a syncretism of worked-out equipoise of the best elements from both doctrines, a synthesis doubled in the 'tidewater and frontier' fusion of its literature."

# PEARL HARBOR

*Infamy: Pearl Harbor and Its Aftermath*, by John Toland. Garden City, N. Y.: Doubleday, 1982.

*At Dawn We Slept: The Untold Story of Pearl Harbor*, by Gordon W. Prange, in collaboration with Donald M. Goldstein and Katherine V. Dillon. New York: McGraw-Hill, 1981.

Although the Japanese attack on Pearl Harbor occurred over four decades ago, interest in the circumstances surrounding the most embarrassing American military disaster in history remains high. The two most recent additions to the literature of December 7, 1941, John Toland's *Infamy: Pearl Harbor and Its Aftermath* and Gordon W. Prange's *At Dawn We Slept: The Untold Story of Pearl Harbor*, were commercial successes, while Toland's volume became a minor cause celebre because of its eccentric thesis.

Toland is best known for *The Rising Sun* (1970), a fat book on "the decline and fall of the Japanese empire" from 1936 through 1945 which won the Pulitzer Prize for History. *The Rising Sun* attributed Pearl Harbor to unimaginative military leadership which believed the Japanese were unable and reluctant to launch such an attack, and to "a national unwillingness to face the facts of a world torn from its stable course after World War I by economic and social revolution, fostered by nationalism and racism, and the inevitable realignment of power in both hemispheres." A decade later, Toland was more specific in apportioning out blame for the tragedy. President Franklin Roosevelt, he wrote in *Infamy*, was the culprit. The Japanese success occurred because "Roosevelt and the inner circle had known about the attack" and withheld this information from the military chiefs in Hawaii.

*Infamy* was not, of course, the first attempt to prove Roosevelt culpable. The most famous was Charles A. Beard's 1948 volume *President Roosevelt and the Coming of the War, 1941: A Study in Appearances and Realities*. Beard's book was a rejoinder to the underlying assumption of the International Military Tribunal of the Far East which had tried the Japanese "war criminals". The Tribunal claimed that, prior to December, 1941, the United States had sought peace while Japan had engaged in a conspiracy to enlarge its sphere of influence. Beard, in contrast, believed Roosevelt bore a major share of responsibility for the outbreak of hostilities. Beard claimed that FDR, frustrated in his efforts to get the United States involved in the European war, saw a conflict with Japan as a "back door" for war with Germany. Beard's opus, as well as such pro-Roosevelt volumes as Robert E. Sherwood's Roosevelt and Hopkins: An Intimate History (1948) which were published shortly after the war's end, reflected the intense partisanship surrounding Roosevelt, the New Deal, and the American entry into World War II. These books were dogmatic and highly emotional, and emphasized personalities rather than more impersonal social, political, and economic factors. For Beard, Roosevelt was a devil. For Sherwood, he was an angel.

Beard did not claim, however, as has Toland, that FDR knew a Japanese fleet was approaching Hawaii and refused to alert the proper authorities. There is little in Infamy to substantiate Toland's reckless accusation. Thus, for example, he charged that Americans had intercepted messages from the Japanese fleet which pinpointed its location. Actually, as students of Pearl Harbor have always known, Admiral Nagumo's ships were on strict radio silence. Toland's other claims are equally questionable. David Kahn, the foremost living authority on cryptography, accused Toland of ignoring facts which contradicted his argument and of distorting what limited evidence he had to substantiate his thesis. There is "not one shred of evidence", Kahn wrote, to suggest that Japan was plotting to attack Pearl Harbor. In order for the United States to have anticipated the attack she would have needed spies in the highest levels of the Japanese government, aerial reconnaissance of the Imperial Japanese Fleet, intercept units close enough to Japanese home waters to monitor Japanese naval messages, and a greatly expanded code-breaking operation capable of deciphering the Japanese naval code. None of these existed at the time of Pearl Harbor.

For Roosevelt and his entourage to have engaged in the type of plot suggested by Toland would have required the assistance of dozens of highly placed government officials, not one of whom revealed, either accidentally or purposely, and either before or after December 7, 1941 the Roosevelt conspiracy. The impossibility of covering up Watergate which, compared to what Toland claimed took place in 1941, was a minor incident, highlights the implausibility of his contention. Surely someone with a political ax to grind, or with a guilty conscience, or out of a sense of duty and honor would have come forward to reveal the scheme. In the absence of this, then, Kahn is certainly correct in believing that "There was no plot, no cover-up. . . . At the heart of the Pearl Harbor tragedy lies not conspiracy, but fallibility." It is not difficult to understand the appeal of Toland's thesis. The Watergate affair and a growing suspicion of government have made a portion of the public vulnerable to the most extreme conspiratorial thinking.

In contrast to <u>Infamy</u>, <u>At Dawn We Slept</u> is the finest study of the background to Pearl Harbor. Prange was well prepared to write this book. From 1945 through 1951 he had been Chief of the Historical Section of the Far East Command in Tokyo during the American military occupation of Japan. After 1951 and until his death in 1980 he was an historian at the University of Maryland. His fascination with Pearl Harbor bordered on an obsession, and he became its unquestioned authority. During the thirty-seven years he devoted to studying the attack, he examined literally tons of documents, interviewed countless Americans and Japanese, and composed a manuscript of some thirty-five hundred pages. Two of Prange's former students reduced this unwieldy manuscript to a still hefty and extremely rewarding volume. Surprisingly, in view of its subtitle, <u>At Dawn We Slept</u> adds little to the general outline of Pearl Harbor already familiar to specialists. The book's value lies rather in its immensity of detail, its sparkling historical vignettes, its incisive portraits of the leading American and Japanese figures, its refusal to make easy and cheap accusations, and its understanding of bureaucratic conflict. <u>At Dawn We Slept</u> is as definitive a treatment of Pearl Harbor as is likely to appear in this generation.

<u>At Dawn We Slept</u> is weakest when it leaves the military aspects of December 7, 1941 and speculates on the ultimate responsibility for the American-Japanese confrontation. Japan, Prange contended, had embarked upon a reckless policy of expansionism and militarism which threatened vital American national interests as well as the interests of America's allies, particularly England. Japanese ambitions were

virtually limitless, seeking "all that the traffic would bear." This statement is surprising in view of Prange's admiration for the Japanese people and his unwillingness to demonize the Japanese military. In its justified effort to exonerate the Roosevelt administration from direct military culpability for Pearl Harbor, At Dawn We Slept overlooks its more serious responsibility for the deterioration of American-Japanese relations during 1940 and 1941.

Roosevelt and his advisors had, by 1940, concluded that Germany and not Japan was the greater threat to American security. The "Germany first" decision declared that, in the event of a two-ocean war, the United States would conduct a defensive strategy in the Pacific while most of its resources would be channeled into the European conflict. This most fundamental of all American decisions prior to entering the war, correct as it might have been at the time, was immediately endangered by hardline opponents of Japan. Secretary of War Henry L. Stimson best exemplified this approach. "The only way to treat Japan," he declared in 1940, "is not to give her anything." Reluctance to compromise with the Japanese was encouraged by Japan's adherence, along with Germany and Italy, to the Tripartite Pact of September 27, 1940, and by the hesitation, after Munich, to do anything which could be interpreted as "appeasement". America was hoping that somehow Asia could return to the situation existing prior to 1937, and this was bolstered by the widespread impression that threats of American military and economic sanctions would easily intimidate the Japanese. In reality, the administration's objectives in the Far East increasingly diverged from America's interests and military power in the region.

The Japanese interpreted American actions and rhetoric as threatening her national security. A more careful examination would have revealed that they were largely bluster. The United States was neither able nor eager to fight Japan. The military recognized that the navy was in no condition, both qualitatively and quantitatively, to challenge Japan in the western Pacific, and it constantly pleaded for more time to prepare for hostilities. Time, however, was the commodity in shortest supply due to the pressures being exerted on Japan. American embargoes on vital natural resources, particularly oil, had made the Japanese desperate. Japan would become self-sufficient in oil and rubber and would be able to continue her war in China indefinitely if she seized the Dutch East Indies and Malaya. The key question was what action would the Americans take if Japan moved southward. Tokyo had concluded that the United States, because of its close relationship with Great Britain and its economic interests in southeast Asia, would declare war immediately. This was, of course, precisely what the United States wanted Japan to presume, believing it would cause Japan to back down. From the Japanese perspective, it made sense to strike at the Americans first at Pearl Harbor and the Philippines in order to eliminate any threat to Japan's lines of communication to the East Indies.

Why had things come to this state? Was there no possibility for compromise? Could concessions to Japan have led to a split between Tokyo and Berlin? Couldn't a case be made for the legitimacy of Japanese objectives? Was there any American national interest worth fighting Japan for, particularly when Washington's priorities lay in Europe? Was it wise to court war in the Far East at a time when Germany's defeat was not yet on the horizon and the military was unprepared? An increasing number of historians are answering these questions in ways which do not cast a favorable light upon the Roosevelt adminstration.

F. C. Jones' Japan's New Order in East Asia: Its Rise and Fall, 1937-1945 (1954) rejects the view that Japan was determined to conquer all of East Asia, while James B. Crowley's important Japan's Quest for Autonomy: National Security and Foreign Policy, 1930-1938 (1966) argues that Japanese leaders pursued traditional and limited goals of security and prosperity, and sympathizes with Japan's refusal to give up its imperial ambitions as long as the western countries showed no inclination to relinquish control over their Asian colonies. Japan, Crowley maintained, did not engage in any imperialistic conspiracy. Rather, as a poor nation whose economic conditions had been exacerbated by the Great Depression, Japan saw no other alternative except geographical expansion and the acquistion of vital natural resources. A Japanese document of the time claimed that American policy aimed to "compel Japan, as in the past, to kowtow to the United States. With the sentinel of the Far East in economic chains, the Orient would once again become the playground of Western economic imperialists."

Gerald K. Haines' incisive essay "American Myopia and the Japanese Monroe Doctrine, 1931-1941," which appeared in the summer, 1981 issue of *Prologue*, draws attention to the seemingly hypocritical American policy of strongly upholding the sanctity of the Monroe Doctrine, and even broadening its scope, while just as vigorously refusing to accept a Japanese Monroe Doctrine for East Asia. Tokyo had proclaimed such a doctrine in the early 1930's, using the original Monroe Doctrine as a model. Haines believes Japan had sufficient legitimate interests in the region to justify such a doctrine, despite the objections of Secretary of State Cordell Hull and others who were unable to see any resemplance between the American and Japanese versions. The Japanese, Haines contended, would have agreed to a modus vivendi with the Americans based on a mutual recognition of each other's Monroe Doctrine. "By refusing to recognize Japan's regional claims," he wrote, "the Roosevelt administration helped harden positions on both sides."

Norman A. Graebner, one of America's leading diplomatic historians, has severely criticized the Roosevelt-Hull Pacific policies.[1] He faulted the administration for failing to recognize that matters of national survival for the Japanese were of little importance for the United States. It was highly unlikely that the threat of economic and military sanctions could change Japan's course. The United States, Graebner contended, had only two options.

[1] Norman A. Graebner, "Hoover, Roosevelt, and the Japanese," in Dorothy Borg and Shumpei Okamoto, eds., *Pearl Harbor as History: Japanese-American Relations 1931-1941* (New York: Columbia University Press, 1973), 45-52; Graebner, "Japan: Unanswered Challenge, 1931-1941," in Margaret F. Morris and Sandra L. Myres, eds., *Essays on American Foreign Relations* (Arlington, Texas: University of Texas Press, 1974), 117-46. She could either recognize Japan's hegemony in the western Pacific because of the primacy of her interests and power, or the United States could oppose Japan's objectives and run the risk of war. Unsympathetic towards Japan's economic plight, oblivious to the psychological and political factors influencing Japanese policies, and confident that Japan could be intimidated, Washington refused to compromise.

The United States did not seek war with Japan.

Quite the contrary, American policies would, it was hoped, force Japan to come to her senses. This underlay the policy recommendations of Stimson, Harold Ickes, Frank Knox, and the other hardliners in the administration. American leadership, despite the warnings of Joseph Grew, our ambassador in Tokyo, failed to appreciate Japan's growing desperation. As late as November 27, 1941, Stanley K. Hornbeck, the chief of the Far Eastern desk in the State Department and a partisan of China, wrote that "he does not believe that this country (i.e., the United States) is now on the immediate verge of war in the Pacific." Graebner claimed that this American "diplomatic inflexibility" aimed at the "unraveling of the whole Japanese empire." For their part, the Japanese found the American policy inexplicable except if it sought to cripple Japan. They could not understand America's commitments in the Far East in view of her limited interests there. The United States, as the Japanese once stated to Washington, "always hold fast to theories in disregard of realities."

Gordon Prange, echoing what other defenders of the Roosevelt administration have contended, wrote that "No one who has examined the great mass of historical evidence on Pearl Harbor can doubt that the United States wanted to maintain peace with Japan as long as possible." This is undoubtedly correct but also irrelevent. The real issue does not involve American intentions but the impact of Washington's actions and words on Tokyo, whether, in fact, these facilitated or obstructed efforts to resolve the conflict short of war. It is impossible to believe, in light of December 7, 1941, that American policies were not viewed by the Japanese as threatening. The exaggeration of America's ability to intimidate the Japanese, the inability to comprehend the sense of desperation permeating the Japanese government and military, and the desire to restore the political situation in the Far East to that which existed prior to 1937, and perhaps even 1931, indicates an unrealistic and dangerous mode of thought. Roosevelt's failure was not due to any diabolical desire to have the Japanese become the instruments whereby the United States could enter the European conflict. Rather, it stemmed from confusion regarding America's interests in the Far East. "Roosevelt," Graebner wrote, "was never able to establish goals in the Far East which reflected the nation's limited interests, its lack of available strength, and its desire to avoid war."

The "revisionist" critique of Roosevelt as exemplified by Infamy is wrong not because it is critical of the president but rather because it posits a conspiratorial theory of history and asks the wrong questions. Roosevelt, Stimson, Knox, Hornbeck, and the rest were men of peace and honor. What can be questioned is their judgment and imagination. The United States in December, 1941 found itself involved in the wrong war, with the wrong enemy, at the wrong time, and in the wrong place. The right war was with Germany not Japan, later not sooner, and in Europe not the Pacific. Only America's industrial might, plentiful natural resources, and large population enabled it to prevail in a two-ocan war. The United States won despite and not because of Rooseveltian diplomacy.

The moral globalism exhibited in 1941 resurfaced exactly two decades later. In January, 1961, a young president told the world that the United States "shall pay any price, bear any burden, meet any hardship, support any friend, oppose any foe, in order to assure the survival and the success of liberty." Four years later we were deeply entangled in the Vietnam War. Neither in 1965 or in 1941 was Washington able to answer satisfactorily the question whether the nation had any vital interests in the Far East worth a major war. Vietnam encouraged some historians to reevaluate America's stakes in the Far East and to take a hard look at the events leading up to Pearl Harbor. These, however, did not include Gordon Prange. He had, after all, first begun serious study in 1943 of the day of infamy.

## ROOSEVELT THE DIPLOMAT

<u>Franklin D. Roosevelt and American Foreign Policy. 1932-1945</u>, by Robert Dallek. New York: Oxford University Press, 1979.

Claire Boothe Luce once remarked that every major world leader had a characteristic gesture. Hitler had the upraised arm and Churchill the V sign. When asked what Franklin Roosevelt's was, she wet her index finger and held it up. In contrast to the bold and experimental nature of the New Deal, Roosevelt's statecraft was marked by a tentativeness and even timidity which has been duly chronicled by historians. James MacGregor Burns' <u>Roosevelt: The Soldier of Freedom</u> noted that FDR "often took bold positions only to retreat from them in subsequent words or actions. He seemed unduly sensitive to both congressional and public opinion. . . . His arresting speeches gave him a reputation as the fearless leader, but he spent far more time feinting and parrying in everyday politics than in mobilizing the country behind crucial decisions." Similarly, Robert A. Divine's <u>Roosevelt and World War II</u> argued that "Roosevelt's claim to greatness must rest on his achievements in domestic affairs. His conduct of foreign policy never equaled his mastery of American politics and his ability to guide the nation through the perils of depression and war."

Robert Dallek's thick volume on Roosevelt the statesman is concerned with discovering the sources of this vacillating, and at times passive, diplomacy. To judge from the earliest evaluations of the book by other Roosevelt scholars, he has largely succeeded. Martin Sherwin of Princeton describes it as "a major contribution to our understanding of the thirty-second president of the United States and an important history of American diplomacy in transition," while William E. Leuchtenburg of Columbia believes it to be "quite simply, the best book that has been written on this important subject."

For Dallek, the inconsistencies and caution of Roosevelt's foreign policy can be explained in large part by his sensitivity to congressional and public opinion. FDR was a superb politician, continually fearful of staking out advanced positions and ending up without a following. This was particularly evident in the 1930's during the debate over neutrality legislation. Although detesting Hitler and eager to do more to help the British, FDR repeatedly backed off from anything that might have eroded his political standing among what he termed "the ladies' peace societies." In the process, he confused both his advisors and our allies. Neville Chamberlain, not usually associated with steadfast policies, concluded after Roosevelt's famous "quarantine" speech in Chicago in October, 1937, that "it is always best and safest to count on nothing from the Americans but words." When Roosevelt grew alarmed in late 1939 over the refusal of the nation to take the European war seriously - "The country," he wrote, "does not yet have any deep sense of world crisis" - he had only himself to blame. His failure to communicate his concern was a prime ingredient in the public's obliviousness to the dangers looming on the horizon. William L. Langer and S. Everett Gleason's The Challenge to Isolation, 1937-1940, the most complete analysis of American policy during this period, concluded that Roosevelt consistently lagged behind public opinion regarding the need to revise the neutrality laws in favor of the democracies. In May, 1941, for instance, Harold L. Ickes described Roosevelt's stance as "innocuous desuetude," and contended that the people, in contrast, were tired of words and wanted action from the president.

For FDR, flexibility was the prime political virtue. He made a habit of surrounding himself with advisors of different persuasions, thereby keeping his options open until action became unavoidable. He once told Henry Morgenthau, Jr., his Secretary of the Treasury, "never let your left hand know what your right is doing." This flexibility was interpreted by his foes as a lack of principles. Infuriated by Roosevelt's position on the tariff during the 1932 campaign, Herbert Hoover said it resembled "a chameleon on a plaid." (On one occasion Roosevelt told his free trade and protectionist advisors to write a speech which would "weave together" their mutually exclusive views.) His advisors never knew where they stood with him, and frequently Roosevelt would blandly discard policies which he had seemingly just approved. A particularly egregious example was his famous "bombshell" message to the 1933 World Economic Conference. Not only did the message virtually destroy the London Conference, but it totally confused the Europeans as well as Roosevelt's advisors who had assumed, based on the President's previous statements, that he favored some form of currency stabilization. "You won't talk frankly even with people who are loyal to you," Ickes once complained. "You keep your cards close up against your belly. You never put them on the table."

Dallek points out that Roosevelt, with the exception of his cousin Theodore, was the most cosmopolitan president since John Quincy Adams. In view of the current disarray of American foreign policy, brought on by a president with no experience beyond the cotton and peanut belts, a familiarity with the world scene is not to be taken lightly. Yet one can legitimately ask whether Roosevelt learned the right lessons from his experience. He had been Assistant Secretary of the Navy during Wilson's administration, and World War I had left an indelible impression on him. He clearly remembered the political disaster which overtook Wilson when he got too far ahead of public opinion, and this reinforced his own cautious political instincts. Furthermore, as Robert Divine has written, FDR's "fundamental aversion to war" resulting from World War I determined his responses to the hostile acts committed by Italy, Japan, and Germany in the 1930's.

Roosevelt's China policy prior to the outbreak of the war was another example of his previous experience leading him astray, in this case his family's long involvement with China. His visceral sympathy for the Chinese, which most Americans shared, led him to exaggerate the importance of China and deflect the nation from a clear perception of its interests in Asia. Dallek notes how Roosevelt responded favorably to the advice of such staunch anti-Japanese advocates as Secretary of War Henry Stimson without questioning whether there was something radically amiss in American Far Eastern policy immediately prior to World War II. As Paul Schroeder argues in The Axis Alliance and Japanese-American Relations, 1941, The United States should have attempted to wean Japan away from the Axis alliance rather than take a categorical anti-Japanese line during 1940 and 1941. There were, after all, no fundamental issues of national interest worth going to war with Japan, especially since the major threat to America and Britain was Germany. Yet while the United States believed Germany was public enemy number one and American military officials were pleading for more time to prepare for military action in the Pacific, the Roosevelt administration adopted a policy designed to force Japan's hand. It is difficult to imagine a more clumsy and ill-conceived strategy than America's Pacific policy of 1941-- speaking loudly while carrying a small stick. One can imagine the results if the American declaration of war against Japan had not been followed by a German declaration of war against the United States. Roosevelt would then had had to ask Congress to declare war against Germany in the absence of any hostile German actions. Either the United States would have been faced with the prospect of fighting Germany with a sizable minority of the public questioning the wisdom of diverting any resources from the Pacific front, or else the United States would have waged war against Japan and only Japan. This truly would have been the wrong war, at the wrong time, in the wrong place, with the wrong enemy.

Roosevelt's tendency to substitute rhetoric for action, his refusal to risk his political capital, is clearly shown by his attitude toward the European refugees. At a time when Americans consuls in Europe were being besieged by unfortunate souls seeking visas, Roosevelt preferred to look the other way. His fears that a more generous immigration policy would lead to a political backlash meant that Breckinridge Long and his ilk would control immigration affairs. "In the refugee crisis," Dallek writes, "Roosevelt allowed domestic and international constraints to limit him to a series of small gestures."

Another of Roosevelt's "small gestures" concerned India. Periodically he would lightly pressure Churchill to grant Indian independence. Churchill, a prototype British imperialist, would hear none of this, not only because he had not become prime minister to preside over the dissolution of the British Empire, but also because he feared Indian independence would lead to religious strife between India's Moslems and Hindus. Roosevelt put Indian independence on the backburner when he discovered Churchill's obduracy. His major concern was a stable and firm American-British alliance, and he was not going to allow friction with Britain over India to interfere with the prosecution of the war. The same thing happened regarding French Indo-China. Roosevelt would have preferred the French leaving Southeast Asia, but French determination to return to the area squelched any American overtures to the Viet Minh.

Roosevelt was confined to lamenting in private the character and results of French colonialism. Roosevelt's "small gestures" has its counterpart in Jimmy Carter's "human rights" buncombe. Neither is effective since both are products of sentiment and domestic politics rather than a clear understanding of the national interest.

Roosevelt's attitude toward the Soviet Union was based on his beliefs that he could form a cordial personal relationship with Stalin, that Russia had legitimate security demands along her western frontiers, and that no agreements could be made with the Soviets until after the 1944 election. Stalin, Roosevelt claimed, "doesn't want anything but security for his country, and I think that if I give him everything I possibly can and ask nothing from him in return, <u>noblesse oblige</u>, he won't try to annex anything and will work with me for a world of democracy and peace." And in March, 1942 Roosevelt told Churchill that he "could personally handle Stalin better than either your Foreign Office or my State Department. Stalin hates the guts of all your top people. He thinks he likes me better, and I hope he will continue to do so." Personal friendship was one thing, but Stalin wanted something more concrete: specifically a Second Front in Europe in 1942, or 1943 at the latest, and western acceptance of Soviet demands in Eastern Europe including the absorption of the Baltic states and the movement of the Soviet's western frontier to the Curzon Line.

Although sympathetic to the idea of territorial changes in Eastern Europe, Roosevelt refused to accept Soviet demands, partially because he feared a backlash among ethnic and Catholic Democrats, and partially because he preferred leaving such issues to the postwar peace conference. He remembered the odious secret treaties of the Allies during World War I as well as the various wartime misunderstandings resulting from Wilson's clear enunciation of America's war aims. Roosevelt thus favored leaving the settlement of territorial and other questions to the postwar period. By the time of the peace conference, of course, the Red Army would be occupying Eastern Europe and the United States would be powerless to influence the future of the region. Yet FDR felt that he could do little in any case regarding Eastern Europe. Roosevelt's "abiding concern" over the Polish issue, Dallek points out, was that it not become a major dispute between the Americans and the Soviets. He tellingly quotes Averell Harriman's recollections of a meeting with the President in November of 1944, during which the President stated that "he wanted to have a lot to say about the settlement in the Pacific, but that he considered the European questions were so impossible that he wanted to stay out of them as far as practicable, except for the problems involving Germany." His mistake, as John Lewis Gaddis argues in The United States and the Origins of the Cold War, 1941-1947, was failing to prepare the American people for Soviet control along her western borders. "Having been led by the President's own rhetoric to expect self-determination everywhere," Professor Gaddis writes, "Americans reacted angrily when the Soviet Union proceeded to extract territorial concessions from its neighbors, and to impose spheres of influence on them."

Roosevelt's willingness to accord the Soviet Union a dominant position in Eastern Europe, his recognition that the Baltic states were probably going to end up controlled by the Russians, his lack of sympathy for the Polish refusal to transfer territory in the east to the Russians in exchange for German lands in the west, his support of military operations designed to beat the Soviets to Hungary and Austria, and his talk about the need for the Big Four to act as international policemen reveals a realistic, and even cynical, element. And yet his anti-imperialism, his hope of salvaging a modicum of independence for the nations of East Europe, his high praise of Stalin, his support for the Morgenthau Plan, and his advocacy of a strong international organization reflects an idealistic and Wilsonian strain of thought. Dallek pictures FDR torn between his commitment to idealistic postwar goals and the wartime need to come to realistic agreements with the Soviets, all the while recognizing that one might make the other impossible. "I dream dreams," Roosevelt once wrote, "but am, at the same time, an intensely practical person." James MacGregor Burns agrees. The president, he contends, was "a deeply divided man--divided between the man of principle, of ideals, of faith, crusading for a distant vision, on the one hand: and, on the other, the man of Realpolitik, of prudence, of narrow, manageable, short-run goals, intent always on protecting his power and authority in a world of shifting moods and capricious fortune." FDR's solution to reconciling the impossible was postponment.

Dallek argues convincingly that much of Roosevelt's wartime diplomacy was designed to avoid a repetition of the isolationist resurgence which followed World War I. Thus he continually reassured the public that the Big Three were laying the basis for a lasting peace free from the rivalries of the past. Never was Roosevelt more carried away by this vision of a brave new world than in the speech he gave to Congress on March 1, 1945 reporting on the Yalta Conference. The Crimea meeting, he asserted, meant "the end of the system of unilateral action, the exclusive alliances, the spheres of influence, the balance of power, and all the other expedients that have been tried for centuries--and have always failed. We propose to substitute for all these, a universal organization in which all peace-loving Nations will finally have a chance to join." These were encouraging words for Wilsonians, but did Roosevelt really believe them? Or did Roosevelt see in the United Nations a means to draw the Soviet Union into extended cooperation with the West and to satisfy internationalist sentiment at home? One hopes that Dallek is right in saying that Roosevelt's verbal support of the United Nations was simply a rhetorical flourish. We do not like to believe that the American people elect fools for presidents, despite our recent history.

Roosevelt's reputation as a diplomatist is not very high today among historians. He has been described as superficial, naive, excessively timid, and devious. While admitting that these criticisms have "some merit," Dallek argues that they ignore the constraints within which FDR had to operate. These included a public supposedly opposed to sustained overseas involvement, a Congress suspicious of bold diplomatic initiatives, and a State Department which Roosevelt believed to be stodgy and rigid. Dallek also asserts that Roosevelt's naivete regarding the Soviets has also been considerably overdrawn. (Dallek describes Roosevelt's approach to the Soviet Union as "equivocal.") He accepted what he did not have the power to change, such as Soviet domination of Eastern Europe, while in other respects he tried to limit the expansion of Russian power. He agreed to station American troops in southern Germany after the end of the war, attempted to acquire air and naval bases in the Pacific and the Atlantic, refused to share the secret of the atomic bomb with the Soviets, and encouraged the illusion of China as a great power so that China could act as a political counterweight to Russia. While not all of these measures were solely directed at the Soviet Union, they certainly go a long way in disproving the popular image of a naive Roosevelt who was the dupe of a cynical Stalin. Had Roosevelt not died in April 1945, Dallek speculates, he would "probably have moved more quickly than Truman to confront the Russians. His greater prestige and reputation as an advocate of Soviet-American friendship would have made it easier for him than for Truman to muster public support for a hard line."

Roosevelt resembles Wilson, Truman, and Johnson in one striking way. All four Presidents were elected for domestic reasons, and yet each one's reputation largely rests on his conduct of foreign affairs. Wilson with his New Freedom, Roosevelt with his New Deal, Truman with his Fair Deal, and Johnson with his Great Society were liberals eager for change in the nation's social and economic fabric, and yet each soon found himself mired in diplomacy. Jimmy Carter shares this experience. Elected because of the public's revulsion from "Watergate" and his own vague promises to restore integrity and trust to government, he soon found himself out of his depth in foreign affairs. None of these five Presidents had any extensive experience in diplomacy before assuming office and, with the exception of Roosevelt, none had evidenced even the slightest interest in it. Robert Divine is undoubtedly correct in maintaining that one of the major lessons of Roosevelt's tenure is that we have a political system "which produces leaders on the basis of their political talents and domestic programs and then confronts them with the responsibility for international issue of enormous complexity." A prediction in 1975 that Jimmy Carter and Andrew Young would, within two years, become two of America's major spokesman on foreign affairs would have elidted incredulity and amazement. And yet our worst fears have come to pass.

# The Military Options to Hiroshima: A Critical Examination of Gar Alperovitz's *Atomic Diplomacy*

## ABSTRACT

Gar Alperovitz's book *Atomic Diplomacy,* published in 1965, purported to be a scholarly analysis of American diplomacy during 1945. One of its arguments was that the dropping of the atomic bomb in August, 1945 was unnecessary to defeat the Japanese and that this was recognized by the American military chiefs at the time. Many readers found *Atomic Diplomacy* convincing, in part because of the growing unpopularity of the Vietnam War. A close examination of the book, however, reveals that it is replete with distortions, and that instead of being a dispassionate historical examination, it is a polemical revisionist tract. At no time was President Truman advised by his military chiefs that Japan was on the verge of surrender or that Japanese capitulation would occur without use of the atomic bomb. While of little value in understanding the circumstances surrounding the dropping of the atomic bomb in 1945, *Atomic Diplomacy* is quite revealing regarding the outlook and methodology of one representative revisionist diplomatic historian.

The publication in 1965 of Gar Alperovitz's *Atomic Diplomacy: Hiroshima and Potsdam* was one of the great events in the wave of radical historiography of that decade. Alperovitz's volume maintained that, after the death of Franklin D. Roosevelt in April, 1945, the United States adopted a hardline, anti-Soviet policy aimed at reversing the Yalta agreements, forcing a Soviet retreat from Central and Eastern Europe, and causing a Japanese surrender prior to any Russian declaration of war against Japan and the entry of Soviet soldiers into North China and Manchuria. According to Alperovitz, leading American policymakers, including the President, the Secretary of State, and the Secretary of War, believed American possession of the atomic bomb could stem the spread of Soviet power and influence. In order for this to occur, however, the bomb's destructive might would have to be demonstrated. The bomb was thus dropped on Hiroshima not to defeat the Japanese but to give pause to the Soviets. The military value of the bomb was slight since Japan was on the verge of collapse anyway, and her surrender would have soon followed the anticipated Soviet declaration of war.[1]

The argument that the use of the atomic bomb was unnecessary to defeat the Japanese, that this was known in the summer of 1945, and that its use was really directed against the Soviet Union was not original with Alperovitz. The British physicist P. M. S. Blackett had claimed this as early as 1948, and it was repeated a decade later by D. F. Fleming and William A. Williams. The importance of *Atomic Diplomacy* lay rather in its copious documentation and aura of scholarly objectivity. Even nonradical scholars were impressed by what one described as Alperovitz's "meticulous use of archival materials." Aside from a few caveats, most notably by Arthur M. Schlesinger, Jr. and Robert James Maddox, historians viewed Alperovitz as working, to quote Christopher Lasch, "in the best traditions of historical

---

[1] Gar Alperovitz, *Atomic Diplomacy: Hiroshima and Potsdam* (New York: Simon and Schuster, 1965), *passim.* The most complete analysis of this topic is Martin J. Sherwin, *A World Destroyed: The Atomic Bomb and the Grand Alliance* (New York: Alfred A. Knopf, 1975).

scholarship." Even some textbooks published after 1965 echoed Alperovitz's conclusions regarding the use of the atomic bomb.[2]

The 1960s were a propitious time for a book such as *Atomic Diplomacy*, a period in which the United States was wracked by racial conflict and involved in an increasingly unpopular war in Southeast Asia. Couldn't comparisons be drawn between the bombing of Hiroshima and Nagasaki and the American bombing of North Vietnam? For those opposed to the course of post-World War II American diplomacy and convinced that it logically lead to Vietnam, what better way was there to shift the burden of responsibility for the Cold War onto American shoulders than by pointing out its poisonous origins in the atomic diplomacy of 1945? And what finer example of American moral insensitivity and racism could there be than the unnecessary explosion of two atomic bombs on a nonwhite nation?

In order to prove that "military considerations were not decisive" in the decision to drop the atomic bomb and that American leaders understood the bomb was neither needed to end the war or to save lives, Alperovitz argued that Japanese capitulation would have occurred prior to the scheduled American invasion of Kyushu Island on November 1, 1945 or shortly thereafter, and that American leaders knew this. So certain was the American military of the imminence of victory, Alperovitz claimed, that they no longer even viewed a Soviet declaration of war against Japan as necessary or desirable. To substantiate this, Alperovitz cited the recollections of Generals Dwight D. Eisenhower and Douglas MacArthur.[3]

In July, 1945, during the Potsdam conference, Eisenhower had a conversation with Secretary of War Henry L. Stimson during which Stimson brought up the question of using the atomic bomb against Japan. Alperovitz quoted Eisenhower's response, found in his memoir *Mandate for Change,* that he opposed dropping the bomb because "Japan was already defeated and that dropping the bomb was completely unnecessary, and secondly because I thought that our country should avoid shocking world opinion by the use of a weapon whose employment was, I thought, no longer, mandatory as a measure to save American lives."

---

[2] P. M. S. Blackett, *Fear, War and the Bomb: Military and Political Consequences of Atomic Energy* (New York: McGraw-Hill, 1948), ch. 10; D. F. Fleming, *The Cold War and Its Origins* (Garden City, New York: Doubleday, 1961), I, pp. 296–308; William Appleman Williams, *The Tragedy of American Diplomacy* (New York: Delta, 1962), pp. 253–55; Barton J. Bernstein, "The Atomic Bomb and American Foreign Policy, 1941–1945: An Historiographical Controversy," *Peace and Change,* II (Spring, 1974), 1–10; Paul Seabury, "Cold War Origins, I," *Journal of Contemporary History,* III (January 1968), 174; Christopher Lasch, "The Explosion That Froze the World," *Nation,* CCI (September 6, 1965), 123–24; Daniel Smith, "The New Left and the Cold War," *University of Denver Quarterly,* IV (Winter, 1970), 81; J. L. Richardson, "Cold-War Revisionism: A Critique," *World Politics,* XXIV (July, 1972), 581; Arthur M. Schlesinger, Jr., "Origins of the Cold War," *Foreign Affairs,* XLVI (October, 1967), 24; Robert James Maddox, *"Atomic Diplomacy:* A Study in Creative Writing," *Journal of American History,* LIX (March, 1973), 925–34; Ralph F. deBedts, *Recent American History: 1933 Through World War II* (Homewood, Ill.: Dorsey Press, 1973), pp. 313–16; Ray Ginger, *People on the Move: A United States History Since 1860* (Boston: Allyn and Bacon, 1975), p. 682.

[3] Alperovitz, *Atomic Diplomacy,* pp. 106–14, 236–39. Alperovitz restated his arguments in a speech, "The Use of the Atomic Bomb," delivered before the 137th Meeting of the American Association for the Advancement of Science in Chicago on December 28, 1970. Parts of the speech are reprinted in Thomas G. Paterson, ed., *The Origins of the Cold War* (Lexington, Mass.: D. C. Heath, 1974, 2nd edition), 51–59.

Alperovitz also quoted Eisenhower's memoir regarding Stimson's response to Eisenhower's doubts. "The Secretary was deeply perturbed by my attitude, almost angrily refuting the reasons I gave [. . .]." Alperovitz concluded that "Eisenhower's searching criticism may well have touched upon a very tender point, namely Stimson's undoubted awareness that Hiroshima and Nagasaki were to be sacrificed primarily for political, not military, reasons." Besides the fact that Stimson in July, 1945 could not have known that Hiroshima and Nagasaki would be the ultimate targets of the atomic bomb raids, what is significant about Alperovitz's use of *Mandate for Change* is what he omitted.[4]

Eisenhower actually began his recollection of the Stimson meeting with a warning that he was hardly the one to give an authoritative opinion regarding the bomb since he had not been concerned with the Pacific theater. "I was not, of course, called upon, officially, for any advice or counsel concerning the matter, because the European theater, of which I was the commanding general, was not involved, the forces of Hitler having already been defeated." Eisenhower's opinion was not a "searching criticism" as described by Alperovitz, but rather uninformed and hastily arrived at. Eisenhower admitted this in the sentence only partially quoted by Alperovitz. "The Secretary was deeply perturbed by my attitude, almost angrily refuting the reasons I gave for my *quick conclusions*." (italics not in original) Eisenhower also discussed the Stimson meeting in his earlier memoir of World War II, *Crusade in Europe*, a book which Alperovitz used in writing *Atomic Diplomacy*. After relating his advice to Stimson that the United States should refrain from using the atomic bomb, Eisenhower recalled, "I did not then know, of course, that an army of scientists had been engaged in the production of the weapon and that secrecy in this vital matter could not have been maintained. My views were merely personal and immediate reactions; they were not based upon any analysis of the subject." Here again there is not a "searching criticism" but instead "personal and immediate reactions" which are "not based upon any analysis of the subject."[5]

Alperovitz's interpretation of MacArthur's thinking regarding the bomb largely rests upon an article in the *New York Times* of August 21, 1963. Here MacArthur noted that he had not been told of the atomic bombing beforehand. Alperovitz contended that the failure of Truman to ask MacArthur, "the military adviser most directly concerned," for his opinion proves that "military considerations were not decisive" in dropping the bomb. MacArthur, however, believed it was normal military practice for him not to have been told of the imminent attack. As quoted in the *New York Times* article, MacArthur declared, "I felt no sense of neglect at all. The whole project was a secret project, and there was absolutely no reason to consult a theater commander 10 000 miles away on such matters." Interestingly enough, Chester W. Nimitz, fleet admiral and commander-in-chief of the Pacific Fleet, and the commanders of the 20th Air Force and the 21st Bomber Command were informed of the bomb since its dropping fell within their bailiwicks. Ironically, one of the sources Alperovitz used to prove that "military considerations were not decisive" since MacArthur had not been told of the bomb was page eighty-nine of the book *No High Ground* by Fletcher Knebel and

---

[4] Alperovitz, *Atomic Diplomacy*, pp. 236–37, 241.

[5] Dwight D. Eisenhower, *The White House Years: Mandate for Change, 1953–1956* (Garden City, New York: Doubleday, 1963), pp. 312–13; Eisenhower, *Crusade in Europe* (Garden City, New York: Doubleday, 1949), p. 443. I have followed the practice in this article of only citing works which Alperovitz used in writing his book.

Charles Bailey, II. This page contains the information that Admiral Nimitz and the air commanders had been notified regarding the bomb.[6]

Alperovitz also used the *New York Times* article to argue that MacArthur believed the atomic bomb to be "completely unnecessary from a military point of view." The only thing MacArthur said on this occasion regarding the bomb's use was "we did not need the atomic bomb here any more than we did [. . .] against Japan." (ellipsis in original) MacArthur was responding here to a charge by former President Truman that the general had proposed using the atomic bomb in Korea. This ambiguous sentence of 1963 should be compared with MacArthur's advice during the summer of 1945. At a crucial meeting on June 18, 1945 at the White House between the Joint Chiefs of Staff and the President a telegram from MacArthur was read. It recommended going ahead with OPERATION OLYMPIC (the invasion of Kyushu) and encouraging Soviet entry into the Pacific War. OLYMPIC, MacArthur declared, "presents less hazards of excessive loss than any other that has been suggested [. . .] its decisive effect will eventually save lives by eliminating wasteful operations of nondecisive character. I regard the operation as the most economical one in effort and lives that is possible." That same month MacArthur told General Henry H. Arnold, Commanding general Army Air Forces, who was then travelling in the Pacific, that although bombing would be helpful, Japan would not surrender until American troops marched into Tokyo. Not only did MacArthur not anticipate a collapse of Japan prior to OLYMPIC, but his advice strengthened the case for using the atomic bomb since the military feared the heavy casualties resulting from any invasion of the Japanese home islands, and saw in the atomic bomb an instrument for securing Japanese surrender prior to any invasion.[7]

Alperovitz was correct in claiming MacArthur believed the atomic bomb to be militarily unnecessary if by "unneccessary" is meant not essential for ultimate victory. This was also true for the other American military leaders since by mid-1945 everyone knew Japan's fate was sealed and her surrender only a matter of time, even without the use of nuclear weapons. Indeed, it had been clear to most Americans and many Japanese from the time of the Battle of the Philippine Sea in June, 1944 that the United States would win the war. The crucial question, however, was not whether Japan would surrender, but when. For the Truman administration the problem was not to secure Japanese capitulation, that was assumed, but to secure it prior to the anticipated bloody invasion of Kyushu. Alperovitz recognized this and so he asserted that *"before the atomic bomb was dropped each of the Joint Chiefs of Staff advised that it was highly likely that Japan could be forced to surrender 'unconditionally,' without use of the bomb and without an invasion."* (Alperovitz's italics) If this was true than Alperovitz is correct in arguing that "military considerations were not primary" in the decision to drop the atomic bombs.[8]

The Joint Chiefs of Staff consisted of General George C. Marshall, Army Chief of Staff and Chairman of the Joint Chiefs of Staff, Admiral Ernest J. King, Chief of Naval Operations, General Henry H. Arnold, Commanding general Army Air Forces, and Admiral William D.

---

[6] Alperovitz, *Atomic Diplomacy*, p. 239; *New York Times*, August 21, 1963, p. 30: Fletcher Knebel and Charles Bailey, II, *No High Ground* (New York: Harper & Brothers, 1960), pp. 73, 89.

[7] Alperovitz, *Atomic Diplomacy*, p. 239; U.S. Department of State, *The Conference of Berlin (The Potsdam Conference), 1945* (Washington: Government Printing Office, 1960), I, 906, II, 1336–37; Henry Harley Arnold, *Global Mission* (New York: Harper & Brothers, 1949), p. 569.

[8] Alperovitz, *Atomic Diplomacy*, p. 237.

Leahy, Chief of Staff to the Commander-in-chief. Of the four, Admiral Leahy was the most critical of the decision to use the atomic bomb. Alperovitz asserted that, from the spring of 1945 on, Leahy consistently opposed dropping the bomb because he believed the war could be ended prior to any invasion of the Japanese home islands.

> Admiral Leahy was absolutely certain there was no need for the bombing to obviate the necessity of an invasion. His judgment after the fact was the same as his view before the bombing: 'It is my opinion that the use of this barbarous weapon at Hiroshima and Nagasaki was of no material assistance in our war against Japan. The Japanese were already defeated and ready to surrender [. . .].'

Leahy was so confident of the imminence of victory, according to Alperovitz, that he even discouraged the entry of the Soviet Union into the Pacific war.[9]

Actually Leahy's opposition to use of the bomb and his advice to the President were not as unequivocal as Alperovitz would have us believe. It is true Leahy never had much confidence in the bomb, partially because he doubted it would in fact work. Equally true is that Leahy, as well as many other naval officials, never believed an invasion of Japan to have been necessary, arguing instead that sea and air blockade would force Japan to her knees. But when did he believe this would occur? Leahy, Alperovitz wrote, "was convinced the war could be ended long before an invasion would have to be launched." Alperovitz's sources for this is the first volume of the Potsdam conference papers issued by the State Department (p. 909) and Leahy's autobiography *I Was There* (pp. 384–85). The only reference to Leahy on page 909 of the State Department volume concerned his opinion regarding the unconditional surrender demand.

> ADMIRAL LEAHY said that he could not agree with those who said to him that unless we obtain the unconditional surrender of the Japanese that we will have lost the war. He feared no menace from Japan in the foreseeable future, even if we were unsuccessful in forcing unconditional surrender. What he did fear was that our insistence on unconditional surrender would result only in making the Japanese desperate and thereby increase our casualty lists. He did not think this was at all necessary.

There is absolutely nothing on this page supporting Alperovitz's contention that Leahy believed the war would be over prior to November 1, 1945, nor do the pages cited from Leahy's autobiography lend any weight to this argument. Here Leahy contended that a modification of the unconditional surrender formula would probably have lead to Japanese surrender before OLYMPIC, a modification which was not acceptable to the President and his diplomatic advisers. What Leahy never stated in his autobiography was that conventional military means alone would have resulted in Japanese capitulation prior to November 1st, and he even admitted that while bombing and blockade would eventually have achieved victory and with fewer American casualties, they might have taken longer than an invasion if the United States had insisted on unconditional surrender.[10]

[9] Alperovitz, *Atomic Diplomacy*, pp. 119, 238.
[10] Jonathan Daniels, *The Man of Independence* (Philadelphia: J. B. Lippincott, 1950), p. 275; Harry S. Truman, *Year of Decisions* (Garden City, New York: Doubleday, 1955), p. 21; William D. Leahy, *I Was There: The Personal Story of the Chief of Staff to Presidents Roosevelt and Truman Based on His Notes and Diaries Made at the Time* (New York: McGraw-Hill, 1950), pp. 245, 286, 384–85, 427; Alperovitz, *Atomic Diplomacy*, p. 108.

Alperovitz also cited the Leahy autobiography to prove that the American military chiefs never really believed OLYMPIC to have been necessary and that planning for it had been on a contingency basis. "Thus, as Admiral Leahy has stressed, *'The invasion itself was never authorized.'*" (Leahy's italics) This must refer to OPERATION CORONET (the proposed invasion of Honshu in March, 1946) and not to OLYMPIC since Leahy also stated that Truman "approved the Kyushu operation and withheld for later consideration a general invasion of Japan." The minutes of the June 18th meeting at the White House make the same point.

> THE PRESIDENT said he considered the Kyushu plan all right from the military standpoint and, so far as he was concerned, the Joint Chiefs of Staff could go ahead with it; that we can do this operation and then decide as to the final action later.

The minutes are also clear that all of the Joint Chiefs of Staff, including Leahy, agreed with this.[11]

The minutes of this meeting also contain a statement by Admiral King, the naval spokesman, that,

> So far as preparation was concerned, we must aim now for Tokyo Plain; otherwise we will never be able to accomplish it. If preparations do not go forward now, they cannot be arranged for later. Once started, however, they can always be stopped if desired.

Alperovitz quoted this passage to show that "prudence, not necessity, dictated military thinking," and that the decision to go ahead with OLYMPIC was, for King, a tentative one. The sentences immediately preceding this passage, however, establish that King was firmly committed to OLYMPIC.

> ADMIRAL KING agreed with General Marshall's views and said that the more he studies the matter, the more he was impressed with the strategic location of Kyushu, which he considered the key to the success of any siege operations. He pointed out that within three months the effects of air power based on Okinawa will begin to be felt strongly in Japan. It seemed to him that Kyushu followed logically after Okinawa. It was a natural setup. It was his opinion that we should do Kyushu now, after which there would be time to judge the effect of possible operations by the Russians and the Chinese.[12]

Here again Alperovitz confused OLYMPIC and CORONET. It should have been obvious from King's reference to the "Tokyo Plain" that any qualms he had concerned the invasion of Honshu and not Kyushu.

Although believing that Japan could be defeated by sea and air power alone, King never gave any assurance this would occur prior to November 1st, and there is some evidence he anticipated this would happen after the scheduled date for OLYMPIC. His assertion at the June 18th meeting that "within three months the effects of air power [. . .] will begin to be felt strongly in Japan" would seem to indicate he did not expect an immediate Japanese surrender. Also, in his autobiography King claimed that had the United States "been willing to wait" the naval blockade would "in the course of time" have forced Japan into submission. Patience would have demonstrated the effectiveness of the "siege operations" King referred to during

---

[11] Alperovitz, *Atomic Diplomacy*, p. 111; Leahy, *I Was There*, pp. 384–85; *Conf. of Berlin*, I, 908–909.
[12] *Conf. of Berlin*, I, 906; Alperovitz, *Atomic Diplomacy*, p. 111.

the June 18th meeting, but this was a virtue in short supply after three and a half years of bloody fighting in the Pacific.[13]

The Air Force of all the services had the most to gain from a Japanese surrender without an invasion since it would seemingly validate the concept of strategic bombing. According to Alperovitz, the official Air Force position as defined by General Arnold was, "Whether or not the atomic bomb should be dropped was not for the Air Force to decide, but explosion of the bomb was not necessary to win the war or make an invasion unnecessary." Arnold did believe Japan would undoubtedly surrender without an invasion or an atomic attack but he did not feel this would take place prior to November 1st. At the June 18th conference Lieutenant General Ira C. Eaker, sitting in for the absent General Arnold, stated that both he and Arnold supported an invasion of Kyushu as "essential, both to tightening our strangle hold of blockade and bombardment on Japan, and to forcing capitulation by invasion of the Tokyo Plain." OLYMPIC, Eaker maintained, would secure the necessary airfields to make the bombing of Japan truly effective. Eaker even denied that air power alone could bring Japan to her knees.[14]

Arnold even made two wagers that Japan would not capitulate prior to November 1st. Lord Ismay, Churchill's chief of staff, recounted in his memoirs that he bet Arnold two dollars during the Potsdam conference that Japan would fall in 1945. Arnold later sent him two silver dollars mounted in a block of polished walnut with the inscription:

> To Pug Ismay from Hap Arnold. Thank God
> I can pay this now.

Arnold mentioned in his own autobiography *Global Mission* another bet at Potsdam, this one with British Air Chief Marshall Sir Charles Portal, that the war would be over closer to December, 1945 than to Valentine's Day, 1946. Both Ismay and Arnold's memoirs are listed in Alperovitz's bibliography.[15]

The Air Force's plans during the summer of 1945 were predicated on the belief that extensive bombing still lay ahead before final victory. Arnold planned to shift eighteen hundred heavy bombers from Europe to the Pacific and to construct twenty airfields in the Ryukus to service them. The Air Force also anticipated establishing two strategic air forces in the Pacific, one of which was not even scheduled to reach minimum force prior to February, 1946. All this was contingent on obtaining bases for the planes, and Arnold was thus overjoyed when he learned during the Potsdam conference that the Soviets would provide the Americans with bases in Siberia for now the American bombers "could literally rip Japan to pieces." Stepping up the bombing, he told the Joint Chiefs at Potsdam, "might cause a capitulation of the enemy, and, in any event, will assure the success of the land campaign in Japan, and reduce the loss of American lives to a minimum."[16]

---

[13] *Conf. of Berlin*, I, 906; Ernest J. King and Walter Muir Whitehill, *Fleet Admiral King: A Naval Record* (New York: W. W. Norton, 1952), p. 621.

[14] Alperovitz, *Atomic Diplomacy*, p. 238; *Conf. of Berlin*, I, 904, 906, 908.

[15] Hastings Ismay, *The Memoirs of General Lord Ismay* (New York: Viking Press, 1960), pp. 401–403; Arnold, *Globald Mission*, p. 583.

[16] Arnold, *Global Mission*, pp. 590, 594–95, 598; Wesley F. Craven and James L. Cate, *The Army Air Forces in World War II*, Vol. V: *The Pacific: Matterhorn to Nagasaki, June, 1944–July, 1945* (Chicago: University of Chicago Press, 1953), pp. 691–95, 700–701, 756.

As for General Marshall, he was the staunchest advocate of the invasion strategy, and he consistently argued that an invasion was essential for achieving victory. According to Alperovitz, however, Marshall *"advised that it was highly likely that Japan could be forced to surrender 'unconditionally,' without use of the bomb and without an invasion,"* and that by mid-June, 1945 Marshall had concluded the Japanese were in such a hopeless military situation that the entry of the Soviet Union into the war might result in their surrender. The invasion plan thus took on a contingency character, although planning for it continued, "especially since General Marshall did not wish to weaken morale by raising possibly false hopes [. . .]." So desperate had the Japanese condition become that "all that was needed was [. . .] in General Marshall's words, 'a terrific shock.'" After the war Marshall would claim, to quote Alperovitz, "that the atomic bombs precipitated the surrender only 'by months' [. . .]."[17]

Marshall's statement regarding the possible impact of Soviet entry into the Pacific war was made at the June 18th meeting. "An important point about Russian participation in the war," he stated, "is that the impact of the Russian entry on the already hopeless Japanese may well be the decisive action levering them into capitulation at that time or shortly thereafter if we land in Japan." The fact that Marshall hedged his assertion regarding Soviet military involvement with a "may" and coupled it with a possible American invasion of Japan indicates his uncertainty regarding the results of a Soviet intervention. Furthermore, throughout the June 18th meeting Marshall stressed his enthusiastic support for the invasion. OLYMPIC, he contended, "is essential to a strategy of strangulation and appears to be the least costly worthwhile operation following Okinawa." At another point in the conference the minutes record that,

> GENERAL MARSHALL said that it was his personal view that the operation against Kyushu was the only course to pursue. He felt that air power alone was not sufficient to put the Japanese out of the war. It was unable alone to put the Germans out [. . .]. He felt that this plan offered the only way the Japanese could be forced into a feeling of utter helplessness. The operation would be difficult but not more so than the assault in Normandy. He was convinced that every individual moving to the Pacific should be indoctrinated with a firm determination to see it through.

One month later, at Potsdam, Marshall again reiterated his support of OLYMPIC, this time at a conference of American, British, and Soviet military leaders.[18]

The "terrific shock" expression of Marshall referred to by Alperovitz is from the general's testimony before the United States Senate Committees on Armed Services and Foreign Relations investigating the circumstances surrounding the firing of General MacArthur from his command in Korea in April, 1951. Marshall outlined for the senators the military thinking during the summer of 1945. As far as achieving victory solely through conventional bombing, "we had no assurance we could get a surrender in the opinion of the Chiefs of Staff who presumably were the best informed in our Government, other than the President [. . .]." Nor did the naval blockade promise victory. The blockade was "a far more expensive procedure and we were not settling the surrender we wanted in China, Burma, Indonesia, and so on." The entry of the Soviet Union into the war would occupy the Japanese army in Manchuria and possibly in Korea. This would still leave untouched the millions of Japanese soldiers in

---

[17] Alperovitz, *Atomic Diplomacy*, pp. 110, 114, 237–38.
[18] *Conf. of Berlin*, I, 904–906; *ibid.*, II, 351–52.

the home islands. The Japanese military still controlled the government and was "preparing to fight to the bitter end just as they had done on all the islands up to and including Okinawa where I think we had to kill 120 000 of them." The chiefs had feared an invasion would result in heavy casualties unless Japan's will to resist could be broken by the atomic bomb.

> [. . .] it was the opinion of the Chiefs of Staff at that time that only a tremendous pressure on Japan itself had any hope of terminating the army dictation, and later, that despite the horrible bombing of Tokyo, some 100 000 lives sacrificed there in flames and explosions, that nothing less than a terrific shock would produce a surrender, particularly a surrender that was carried throughout the Japanese interests from Burma, China, Indonesia down in New Guinea, where we had left them behind, and of course further north.

Marshall's testimony stressed that the bomb was dropped to break the still stiff resistance of the Japanese and not, as Alperovitz would have us believe, to deliver to the faltering Japanese a coup de grace.[19]

Marshall's statement that the atomic bomb precipitated the surrender "by months" is from an article in the November 2, 1959 issue of *U.S. News and World Report*. Here again Marshall emphasized that the only meaningful military alternatives were invasion or "shock". Although the Japanese navy and air force had been destroyed, the army in the home islands was still a potent force and would, based on previous experience, fight to the death to defend the homeland. The United States Army did not believe the naval blockade or aerial bombardment would end the war. "We felt this," Marshall declared, "despite what generals with cigars in their mouths had to say about bombing the Japanese into submission. We had killed 100 000 Japanese in one raid in one night, but it didn't mean a thing insofar as actually beating the Japanese." Fortunately the atomic bomb "precipitated the surrender by months." When Alperovitz referred to this he wrote, "See also Marshall's postwar statement that the atomic bombs precipitated the surrender only 'by months' [. . .]." The inclusion of "only" completely changes the meaning of Marshall's words. The atomic bomb hastened the end of the war "by months', not "only 'by months.'"[20]

Marshall's caution regarding Japanese military capabilites was reflected in American military planning during the summer of 1945. This planning, as a June 29th memorandum of the Joint Chiefs stated, was "premised on the belief that defeat of the enemy's armed forces in the Japanese homeland is a prerequisite to unconditional surrender, and that such a defeat will establish the optimum prospect of capitulation by Japanese forces outside the main Japanese islands." And on July 24th the British and American military chiefs presented to Truman and Churchill at Potsdam a document affirming that "the invasion of Japan and operations directly connected therewith are the supreme operations of the war against Japan; forces and resources will be allocated on the required scale to assure that invasion can be accomplished at the earliest practicable date. No other operations will be undertaken which hazard the success of, or delay, these main operations."[21]

In support of his contention "that the atomic bomb was not needed to force a surrender

---

[19] U. S. Congress, Senate, Committee on Armed Services and Committee on Foreign Relations, 82nd Congress, 1st Session, *Hearings to Conduct an Inquiry into the Military Situation in the Far East* (Washington: Government Printing Office, 1951), pp. 560–65.

[20] John P. Sutherland, "The Story General Marshall Told Me," *U.S. News and World Report*, XLVII (November 2, 1959), 51–53; Alperovitz, *Atomic Diplomacy*, p. 238.

[21] *Conf. of Berlin*, I, 911; *ibid.*, II, 1463ff.

before an invasion," Alperovitz footnoted an article by the military historian Louis Morton. What Morton actually wrote is quite different from what Alperovitz said he wrote. According to Morton,

> It would be a fruitless task to weigh accurately the relative importance of all the factors leading to the Japanese surrender. There is no doubt that Japan had been defeated by the summer of 1945, if not earlier. But defeat did not mean that the military clique had given up; the Army intended to fight on and had made elaborate preparations for the defense of the homeland. Whether air bombardment and naval blockade or the threat of invasion would have produced an early surrender and averted the heavy losses almost certain to accompany the actual landings in Japan is a moot question. Certainly that had a profound effect on the Japanese position. It is equally difficult to assert categorically that the atomic bomb alone or Soviet intervention alone was the decisive factor in bringing the war to an end. All that can be said on the available evidence is that Japan was defeated in the military sense by August 1945 and that the bombing of Hiroshima, followed by the Soviet Union's declaration of war and the bombing of Nagasaki and the threat of still further bombing, acted as catalytic agents to produce the Japanese decision to surrender. Together they created so extreme a crisis that the Emperor himself, in an unprecedented move, took matters into his own hands and ordered his ministers to surrender. Whether any other set of circumstances would have resolved the crisis and produced the final decision to surrender is a question history cannot yet answer.[22]

One of the bits of evidence Alperovitz used to bolster his argument that the military planning for OLYMPIC increasingly took on the character of mere contingency planning was the fact that in late April, 1945, to quote Alperovitz, "the chief United Stated Army planners initiated studies of 'what we do if Japan decides to surrender on V-E Day.'" The quote is from Ray S. Cline's book *Washington Command Post: The Operations Division* and is one of many Alperovitz used to show that during the spring of 1945 "it became more and more doubtful that an invasion would be needed to force Japanese capitulation." Cline's complete statement, however, gives the opposite impression.

> The general philosophy of the possibility of Japanese surrender changed very little in official pronouncements after April. By the end of April the Army planner, General Lincoln, had become convinced that some thinking should be done on 'what we do if Japan decides to surrender on V-E Day,' as he provocatively phrased it. Even though the prospect of an early surrender of Japan began to get a little consideration from Washington staffs in April and May, much more attention was being concentrated on issuing a directive for operation OLYMPIC, scheduled for 1 November 1945. There was no disagreement about the necessity of preparing to launch this initial invasion of the home islands.

Cline, in truth, stressed the extreme caution of the Army planners. When the Joint War Plans Committee in May, 1945 produced its first two studies on operations in the event of sudden Japanese surrender, the Operations Division (OPD) of the War Department responded with great scepticism. The reports were eventually sent to MacArthur, Arnold, and Nimitz with a directive stating, "although there is at present no evidence that sudden collapse or surrender of Japan is likely, the Joint Chiefs of Staff direct that plans be made to take immediate

---

[22] Alperovitz, *Atomic Diplomacy*, p. 238; Louis Morton, "The Decision to Use the Atomic Bomb," *Command Decisions*, ed. Kent Roberts Greenfield (Washington: Department of the Army, 1960), 518. Alperovitz's citation is to page 408 of the Morton article. This is an obvious mistake since the article begins on page 493.

advantage of favorable circumstances, such as a sudden collapse or surrender, to effect an entry into Japan proper for occupational purposes."[23]

What Cline described as "the clearest statements of OPD's attitude on the subject of surrender and the desirability of developing a precise formula for unconditional surrender" appeared in two reports prepared for Secretary of War Stimson in early June. Alperovitz quoted from one of the studies in order to substantiate his argument that the Americans recognized both the extent of the deterioration in the Japanese military position as well as the decisive effect which Russian intervention would have. The part he quoted noted that Japanese "protracted resistance is based upon the hope of achieving a conditional surrender [. . .]. Probably it will take Russian entry into the war, coupled with a landing, *or imminent threat of landing* [. . .] to convince them of the hopelessness of their position." (Alperovitz's italics, not in the original) What Alperovitz did not quote was the first sentence of the paragraph. "The point in our military progress at which the Japanese will accept defeat and agree to our terms in unpredictable."[24]

Alperovitz also quoted from a report of July 8th by the Combined Intelligence Committee which argued that "an entry of the Soviet Union into the war would finally convince the Japanese of the inevitability of complete defeat." What he neglected to mention was that the document also contended that the policy of the Japanese government was "to fight as long and as desperately as possible in the hope of avoiding complete defeat and of acquiring a better bargaining position in a negotiated peace." The report believed the key to Japanese surrender was the position of the Japanese Army. "For a surrender to be acceptable to the Japanese Army," the paper concluded, "it would be necessary for the military leaders to believe that it would not entail discrediting [the] warrior tradition and that it would permit the ultimate resurgence of a military Japan." Peace on these terms was, of course, unacceptable to the American government.[25]

The Army planners remained sceptical of the possibility of imminent Japanese surrender until the latter half of July. Indeed, as late as July 12th OPD completed a paper entitled "Compilation of Subjects for Discussion at Terminal" which recommended adhering to the OLYMPIC-CORONET schedule. Nevertheless, by July 20th Army planners began to think

---

[23] Alperovitz, *Atomic Diplomacy*, pp. 108–110; Ray S. Cline, *Washington Command Post: The Operations Division* (Washington: Department of the Army, 1951), pp. 343–44.

[24] Alperovitz, *Atomic Diplomacy*, p. 109; Cline, *Washington Command Post*, p. 344.

[25] Alperovitz, *Atomic Diplomacy*, p. 109; *Conf. of Berlin*, II, 36–37 fn. The report also claimed the Japanese believed unconditional surrender to be "the equivalent of national extinction. There are as yet no indications that the Japanese are ready to accept such terms. The ideas of foreign occupation of the Japanese homeland, foreign custody of the person of the Emperor, and the loss of prestige entailed by the acceptance of 'unconditional surrender' are most revolting to the Japanese." Furthermore, the report argued the Japanese were far from defeated. They had enough fuel for kamikaze attacks, reserves of ordinance were large except for heavy types of equipment, stocks of ammunition and ammunition production facilities were adequate, there was no serious food problem, and morale within the army was still high. By the end of 1945 Japan's army would number over five million men. The report concluded that the economic situation had not deteriorated to the point where it would influence Japanese strategy, that bombing and naval blockade would not in themselves defeat Japan prior to invasion, and that heavy casualties should be anticipated from the invasions. John Ehrman, *Grand Strategy: October 1944–August 1945* (London: Her Majesty's Stationery Office, 1956), pp. 279–83.

seriously of the possibility of a sudden Japanese collapse, and this new concern increased in intensity over the next three weeks. Cline mentioned that OPD officers worked on a study at Potsdam called "Japanese Capitulation" which spoke of the chance that the Japanese might "capitulate unexpectedly in the next few weeks." But Cline also pointed out that "the insertion of the word 'unexpectedly' revealed a great deal about the background of conservative military planning against which the War Department staffs were attacking this particular problem." On July 30th the Joint War Plans Committee, in response to suggestions received from Potsdam, released a study on the steps necessary to facilitate prompt allied action "in the event of a Japanese collapse or surrender in the immediate future." There was great need for such a study because, as the report clearly stated, "until recently an early surrender by the Japanese was considered improbable. As a consequence the procedures and plans to be followed in the event of an immediate Japanese surrender are indistinct." Cline's volume thus lends little weight to Alperovitz's argument that "as each day of the spring passed, it became more and more doubtful that an invasion would be needed to force Japanese capitulation," and that planning for such an invasion "took on a contingency aspect."[26]

Alperovitz would also have us believe that Stimson, by the summer of 1945, assumed the Japanese were on their last legs. "As Stimson was later to write," Alperovitz stated, "to edge the faltering Japanese into capitulation, all that was needed was 'a tremendous shock,' [. . .]." The "tremendous shock" expression is from Stimson's autobiography, and it is clear from the context in which it was made that a "tremendous shock" was needed because Japan was far from defeated, not because she was on the verge of surrender. "I felt," Stimson wrote, "that to extract a genuine surrender from the Emperor and his military advisers, there must be administered a tremendous shock which would carry convincing proof of our power to destroy the Empire. Such an effective shock would save many times the number of lives, both American and Japanese, that it would cost." Stimson further elaborated on this point in the pages immediately following this statement. He pointed out that there was no indication that the Japanese were willing to accept unconditional surrender, and that Japan was still a potent military force. If Japan decided to fight on rather than accepting unconditional surrender "the Allies would be faced with the enormous task of destroying an armed force of five million men and five thousand suicide aircraft, belonging to a race which had already amply demonstrated its ability to fight literally to the death." Although favoring the OLYMPIC-CORONET invasion strategy, Stimson feared that high casualties would result from such operations. Stimson's memoir contains a memorandum of July 2nd to President Truman in which the Secretary of War claimed there was reason to believe "the operation for the occupation of Japan following the landing may be a very long, costly, and arduous struggle on our part." There is thus sufficient evidence in Stimson's volume that he did not consider Japanese surrender to be imminent as long as American surrender terms remained unchanged. A "tremendous shock" was needed, Stimson concluded, "to end the war in the shortest possible time and to avoid the enormous losses of human life which otherwise confronted us [. . .]. The bomb seemed to me to furnish a unique instrument for that purpose."[27]

Alperovitz's major purpose in writing *Atomic Diplomacy* was to place the major share of responsibility for the Cold War onto the shoulders of Harry Truman and his advisers. Ac-

---

[26] Cline, *Washington Command Post*, pp. 345–50; Alperovitz, *Atomic Diplomacy*, p. 110.

[27] Alperovitz, *Atomic Diplomacy*, p. 114; Henry L. Stimson and McGeorge Bundy, *On Active Service in Peace and War* (New York: Harper & Brothers, 1948), pp. 617–20, 631.

cording to Alperovitz, American fears by the summer of 1945 were primarily focused on the Russians and not the Japanese, and the use of the atomic bomb against Japan actually had the Soviet Union in mind. He ended his book with a rhetorical question. "Were Hiroshima and Nagasaki bombed primarily to impress the world with the need to accept America's plan for a stable and lasting peace – that is, primarily America's plan for Europe?" In order to substantiate this questionable thesis and to demonstrate the military insignificance of the atomic bomb, Alperovitz not only distorted the thinking of the military chiefs but also misquoted their words. It is highly ironic, therefore, that Alperovitz could claim that "the complicated and continuously changing military picture has been misunderstood by almost every important observer." Perhaps the major significance of *Atomic Diplomacy* is its confirmation of the fact that polemics and scholarship generally do not mix well. Its major lesson for historians is to be more vigilant in differentiating between the two.[28]

[28] Alperovitz, *Atomic Diplomacy*, pp. 109, 240–42. On another occasion Alperovitz was even more forthright in presenting his interpretation as to why the atomic bomb was used against Japan. The "over-riding reason for the use of the bomb was that (implicitly or explicitly) it was judged necessary to strengthen the United States's hand against Russia." Truman's relations with the Soviets "rested on the assumption that the combat demonstration of the new weapon would reinforce United States proposals for a peace settlement around the globe." Alperovitz, *Cold War Essays* (Garden City, New York: Anchor Books, 1970), pp. 68, 72.

# Responsibility for the Cold War: A Bibliographical Review

THE history of American historical writing on the Cold War has, up to now, resembled that of the Civil War and World War I. In all three cases the major effort of historians has been in apportioning responsibility for the wars, with the initial interpretations tending to accept the official government explanation for the outbreak of hostilities while later studies often "revised" the "orthodox" analysis.[1] In the case of the Cold War the "orthodox" interpretation, as found in the memoirs of Harry S. Truman, Dean G. Acheson, James F. Byrnes, George F. Kennan, and John R. Deane and in John Spanier's popular book *American Foreign Policy Since World War II* and in Arthur M. Schlesinger, Jr.'s famous essay "Origins of the Cold War," blamed the Cold War on Soviet intransigence, expansionism, and aggression, and praised the course of American diplomacy in the post-World War II period.[2] In the 1960s and 1970s "revisionist" historians endeavored to show partial or complete American culpability for the Cold War. Sympathetic toward the "third world," skeptical of American moral pretensions, dismayed by the Vietnamese War, and convinced that American diplomacy had been the servant of an imperialistic capitalism and of an outmoded political and economic ideology, the revisionists' message found a waiting audience among Americans who were searching for an explanation for America's involvement in Southeast Asia and were convinced that the Cold War had become an anachronism. The revisionists' critique of American foreign policy has been a jumping-off point to censure the supposed conservative and counter-revolutionary character of the American political, economic, and social structure.

Not surprisingly, in view of the radical thrust of much of academia during the late 1960s and early 1970s, many of the basic

---

1. Two studies of the historiography of the coming of the Civil War are Howard K. Beale, "Causes of the Civil War," Social Science Research Council, *Bulletin*, no. 54 (1946), and Thomas J. Pressly, *Americans Interpret Their Civil War* (Princeton, N.J., 1954). Valuable accounts of the historiography of the causes of World War I are Warren I. Cohen, *The American Revisionists* (Chicago, 1966); Richard W. Leopold, "The Problem of American Intervention, 1917: An Historical Retrospect," *World Politics*, II (April, 1950); Daniel M. Smith, "National Interest and American Intervention, 1917: An Historiographical Appraisal," *Journal of American History*, LII (June, 1965); Selig Adler, "The War Guilt Question and American Disillusionment, 1918–1928," *Journal of Modern History*, XXIII (March, 1951); and Ernest R. May, *American Intervention: 1917 and 1941* (Service Center for Teachers of History, Pamphlet 30, 1960).

2. Truman, *Memoirs* (Garden City, New York, 1955 & 1956, 2 vols.); Acheson, *Present at the Creation: My Years at the State Department* (New York, 1969); Byrnes, *Speaking Frankly* (New York, 1947); Kennan, *Memoirs, 1925–1950* (Boston, 1967); Deane, *The Strange Alliance: The Story of Our Efforts at Wartime Cooperation with Russia* (New York, 1947); Schlesinger, "Origins of the Cold War," *Foreign Affairs*, XLVI (October, 1967).

assumptions and conclusions of the revisionists have become widely accepted among historians of American foreign relations. A poll taken several years ago among American historians listed William A. Williams' *The Tragedy of American Diplomacy*, perhaps the most important of all revisionist works, as one of the most influential recently published works in American history. Even historians who are not themselves revisionists have not been immune to the revisionists' arguments. There are some significant differences, for instance, between what Herbert Feis, the leading American historian of World War II diplomacy, wrote in the 1950s and what he said in his 1970 book *From Trust to Terror: The Onset of the Cold War, 1945-1950*. Similarly Gaddis Smith's 1972 study of Dean Acheson of Secretary of State differs considerably from his 1965 volume *American Diplomacy During the Second World War, 1941-1945*. Revisionist Cold War historiography has even influenced the writing of textbooks used in university American history courses.[3]

Recently some historians have attempted to go "beyond revisionism" and to transcend the orthodox-revisionist dichotomy. The reception by diplomatic historians of Robert Maddox's book *The New Left and the Origins of the Cold War* (1973) reveals, however, that the debate over the responsibility for the outbreak and continuation of the Cold War remains intense and even vituperative. Maddox's book examined seven major volumes by revisionist historians—Williams' *The Tragedy of American Diplomacy* (1959), D. F. Fleming's *The Cold War and Its Origins* (1961), Gar Alperovitz's *Atomic Diplomacy* (1965), David Horowitz's *The Free World Colossus* (1965), Gabriel Kolko's *The Politics of War* (1968), Diana Shaver Clemens' *Yalta* (1970), and Lloyd C. Gardner's *Architects of Illusion* (1970)—and concluded that they "are based upon pervasive misusages of the source materials" and that "even the best fails to attain the most flexible definition of scholarship." The books, he claimed, were actually "polemics" and contained countless examples of deliberate falsification and suppression of evidence. Maddox also attacked the publishers of these volumes for printing such shoddy scholarship. "The name of a reputable publisher traditionally has served as a kind of imprimatur for scholarly treatises and . . . and assure(s) the reader that the material has been subjected to (and passed) rigorous critical examination," Maddox wrote. "That assumption may no longer be warranted." Even more lamentable was the failure of historians to bring attention to these books' deficiencies. "Scholars, students and lay readers alike," Maddox contended, "have been poorly served by what can only be regarded as a striking malfunctioning of the critical mechanisms within the historical profession."[4]

Maddox was careful to state that his discrediting of the works of these seven historians did not mean that other revisionist interpretations of the Cold War's origins could not stand up under close scholarly scrutiny. He himself was skeptical that this would occur since the "New Left Seven" had examined the relevant existing source material, and it was doubtful whether valuable additional source material would be uncovered. "Perhaps," Maddox asked, the New Left interpretation could be sustained only "by doing violence to the historical record?"[5]

The seven revisionists were naturally outraged by Maddox's bold claims and fierce attack. Kolko accused him of writing an "intemperate polemic." Clemens

---

3. Two examples of the impact of revisionist historiography on American history textbooks are Ralph F. deBedts, *Recent American History: 1933 Through World War II* (Homewood, Illinois, 1973), pp. 313–316, and Ray Ginger, *People On the Move: A United States History Since 1860* (Boston, 1975), pp. 682–85.

4. Robert J. Maddox, *The New Left and the Origins of the Cold War* (Princeton, N.J., 1973), pp. 10, 159–60.

5. Maddox, *New Left and Origins of Cold War*, p. 164.

likened *The New Left and the Origins of the Cold War* to a McCarthyite "witchhunt" and queried whether Maddox was a scholar or a "certifier of political purity." Gardner described Maddox's volume as a "hatchet job," a "titillating book" which conferred on its author "more notoriety than distinction," Horowitz charged that Maddox was afflicted with "more than an ordinary amount of malice and less than an ordinary quota of intelligence," and that politics and personal motives were responsible for this "slander masquerading as disinterested scholarship." Alperovitz maintained that Maddox's charges were "unwarranted and irresponsible" and flowed from a "blind anti-Communism."[6]

The critiques of the Maddox volume by third parties roughly fall into three categories. Some historians enthusiastically praised the book, others equally damned it, and a third group argued that Maddox had made a valuable contribution by pointing out errors of the revisionists, but that he had vitiated his argument by carrying it to extremes and by making personal attacks on the revisionists. Not surprisingly, the various evaluations of Maddox's book roughly corresponded to the reviewers' attitudes regarding the broader debate as to the responsibility for the Cold War. Thus the dispute over *The New Left and the Origins of the Cold War* provided an opportunity for debating once more the question of culpability for the American-Soviet rivalry.

Cold War traditionalists effusively praised Maddox's book. Herbert Feis had encouraged Maddox to write it in the first place while praise from George Kennan, Eugene V. Rostow, Jr., and Arthur M. Schlesinger, Jr. could be found on the book's dust jacket. Schlesinger, for example, lauded it as "a quiet but devastating indictment of revisionist scholarship." While some other reviewers agreed with Schlesinger that Maddox's interpretation was "devastating," none believed it to be "quiet." Robert Ferrell of Indiana University, whose own contribution to Cold War scholarship was a study of George C. Marshall as Secretary of State, applauded Maddox for revealing the revisionists' footnotes to be "a mosaic of misrepresentation." Daniel M. Smith of the University of Colorado described *The New Left and the Origins of the Cold War* as a "devastating critique" while Charles Burton Marshall contended that it had served "scholarly standards." Bennett Kovrig of the University of Toronto noted that Maddox had uncovered "a depressing degree of deception," "ideological flights of fancy," and manipulation of evidence."[7]

The reviews in conservative journals were particularly laudatory of Maddox's work. Claire Z. Carey entitled her review in *The Intercollegiate Review* "Uncovering an Academic Watergate" and claimed that Maddox had "beyond any doubt, demolished the scholarly pretensions" of the Cold War revisionists. Similarly Jack Chatfield in the *National Review* argued that Maddox's book had uncovered the "intellectual sorcery" of the revisionists and had even "threatened" and "exploded" their historical reputations. While Thomas H. Etzold's critique in *Modern Age* noted that while Maddox's conclusions

---

6. Kolko in *New York Times Book Review*, June 17, 1973, p. 8; Clemens in *ibid.*; Gardner in *ibid.*; Alperovitz in *ibid.* and Alperovitz, "Communications," *Journal of American History*, LIX (March, 1973), 1064; Horowitz, "Historians and the Cold War: the Battle Over America's Image," *Ramparts*, XII (August-September, 1973), 60-61.

7. For Feis' encouragement see Maddox, *New Left and Origins of Cold War*, p. ix; Schlesinger, "Was the Cold War Necessary?" *Wall Street Journal*, November 30, 1972; Ferrell, "Truman Foreign Policy: A Traditionalist View," *The Truman Period as a Research Field: A Reappraisal*, 1972, ed. Richard S. Kirkendall (Columbia, Mo., 1974), pp. 17-20; Smith review of *New Left and Origins of Cold War* in *Journal of Southern History*, XXXIX (November, 1973), 623-24; Marshall, "Historians and the Cold War," *Virginia Quarterly Review*, IL (Autumn, 1973), 624; Kovrig review of *New Left and Origins of Cold War* in *Political Science Quarterly*, CLXXXIX (March, 1974), 202-204.

tended to be one-sided and shot through with *ad hominem* arguments, still his findings were "alarming and devastating."[8]

English historians also commended Maddox. A. E. Campbell of the University of Birmingham claimed Maddox had convincingly demonstrated the casual handling of evidence by the revisionists. The review in the prestigious *English Historical Review* lauded Maddox for "lucidly" showing the tendency of the revisionists "to adjust the facts to suit their conclusions."[9]

The most important favorable review of Maddox's book was by Francis Lowenheim in the *New York Times Book Review*. A professor of history at Rice University and editor of *Roosevelt and Churchill: Their Secret Wartime Correspondence* (1975), Lowenheim characterized *The New Left and the Origins of the Cold War* as "an important book on an important subject." Maddox's harsh indictment of New Left historiography was "fully supported" by his "lucid and impressively detailed account." Maddox's volume, Lowenheim wrote, marked "a milestone in American historical writing" and it demanded the attention of everyone interested in recent American foreign policy, particularly those who had been deceived by the revisionists.[10]

Reviewers sympathetic with the New Left Seven were even more vitriolic than the supporters of Maddox. Richard H. Miller of Newton College published two reviews of the Maddox book. The first, in *Commonweal*, was entitled "A Verbal Mugging" and it described the book as "a curious compound of ignorance, distortion and dedicated nit-picking," while professing to see the book's publication as evidence of a recrudescence of McCarthyism. His second review in the Marxist journal *Science and Society* claimed that "by any criterion of historiographical or ethical judgment," Maddox's volume was "a malicious book." Ronald Radosh, himself a prominent revisionist historian and author of *American Labor and United States Foreign Policy* (1969) and *Conservative Critics of the American Empire* (1974), reviewed the Maddox work for the *Nation*. Not only had Maddox written a "crude polemic," Radosh charges, but his purposes in writing the book had been "to end the dialogue with the revisionists about the origins of the cold war, to take us back to the days when all truth was thought to reside with the State Department, and when only officially approved scholars like Herbert Feis could gain access to government archives for purposes of research." Thomas A. Krueger of the University of Illinois accused Maddox of having written "a gravely deficient volume. Its pretensions to objectivity are disingenuous; its methods defective; its major conclusions invalid; its renditions of the evidence almost always open to question." Robert D. Schulzinger berated Maddox for taking "the low road ... by using hard language." Ronald Steel's review in the leftwing *New York Review of Books* claimed Maddox had committed the same omissions and distortions which he had attributed to the revisionists. "The nastiness that infuses this book," Steel concluded, "makes its tone highly disagreeable."[11]

The most influential attack on Maddox appeared in the *American Historical Review*. Written by Warren F. Kimball, a professor

---

8. Carey, "Uncovering an Academic Watergate," *The Intercollegiate Review*, IX (Winter, 1973-74), 51-53; Chatfield, "Refuting Gauguinism," *National Review*, XXV (August 17, 1973), 904-905; Etzold review of *New Left and Origins of Cold War* in *Modern Age* XVIII (Winter, 1974), 96-98.

9. Campbell, "The Foreign Policy of a Democracy," *The Historical Journal*, XVII, no. 2, 447; W. N. Medlicott, review of *New Left and Origins of Cold War* in *English Historical Review*, XC (July, 1975), 696-97.

10. Lowenheim review of *New Left and Origins of Cold War* in *New York Times Book Review*, June 17, 1973, pp. 6-8.

11. Miller, "A Verbal Mugging," *Commonweal*, XCVIII (August 24, 1973), 457-58; Miller review of *New Left and Origins of Cold War* in *Science and Society*, XXXVIII (Spring, 1974), 90-91; Radosh, "Hot War with the 'New Left,'" *Nation*, CCXVII (July 16, 1973), 55-58; Krueger

at Rutgers University in Newark, New Jersey and author of a study of the lend-lease program and of a history of the Morgenthau plan, it suggested that "historiographical warfare is no substitute for scholarship; dark hints of conspiracy should not replace the awareness that our opinion might be wrong; name-calling and sarcasm must never be confused with careful criticism."[12]

A third group of reviewers took a midway position between Maddox's defenders and critics. For example, John Lewis Gaddis, author of the fine study *The United States and the Origins of the Cold War, 1941-1947* (1973), conceded that Maddox had scored several telling blows, but he also claimed that Maddox's personal attacks on the New Left Seven had weakened his case. Norman A. Graebner of the University of Virginia, one of the country's most prominent diplomatic historians, granted that Maddox had shown that some revisionist writings failed to live up to the highest scholarly standards. He also maintained, however, that the book's brevity made it difficult for the reader to come to any meaningful conclusions as to the accuracy of Maddox's charges, and, in addition, the book was marred by "an unnecessary spirit of vindictiveness." Richard W. Leopold of Northwestern University agreed that Maddox had indeed found some errors within the revisionists' writings but not enough of them to warrant his sweeping conclusions. Leopold was also disturbed by the ferocity of Maddox's attack on the revisionists which, he believed, dismayed those readers desiring a more dispassionate approach to the history of the Cold War.[13]

MY own research in Cold War historiography has convinced me that, at least as far as Gar Alperovitz's *Atomic Diplomacy* is concerned, Maddox's contention that revisionism cannot withstand close scrutiny is warranted. One of Alperovitz's key points was that the atomic bomb was dropped needlessly on Hiroshima in August, 1945 since the Japanese were on the verge of surrender and the United States government was aware of this. On page 105 of *Atomic Diplomacy* Alperovitz wrote that "the State Department was convinced the Emperor was actively seeking a way to stop the fighting." In support of this he footnoted page 15 of Herbert Feis' book *Japan Subdued*. What Feis actually said on that page was that "his selection (*i.e.*, the selection of Kantaro Suzuki as Prime Minister in April, 1945) evoked a hope in the State Department that the Emperor was bent on finding a way to end the war." On page 108 Alperovitz cited Ray S. Cline's book *Washington Command Post* as his source for the statement that "in late April the chief United States Army planners initiated studies on 'what we do if Japan decides to surrender on V-E Day.'" What Cline really said was,

*The general philosophy of the possibility of Japanese surrender changed very little in official pronouncements after April. By the end of April the Army planner, General Lincoln, had become convinced that some thinking should be done on "what we do if Japan decides to surrender on V-E day," as he provocatively phrased it. Even though the prospect of an early surrender of Japan began to get a little consideration from Washington staffs in April and May, much*

---

"New Left Revisionists and Their Critics," *Reviews in American History*, I (December, 1973), 463–66; Schulzinger, "Moderation in Pursuit of Truth is No Virtue: Extremism in Defense of Moderation is a Vice," *American Quarterly*, XXVII (May, 1975), 229–33; Ronald Steel, "The Good Old Days," *New York Review of Books*, XX (June 14, 1973), 34–35.

12. Kimball "The Cold War Warmed Over," *American Historical Review*, LXXIX (October, 1974), 1134–36.

13. Gaddis, "Checking History's Footnotes," *Book World*, May 6, 1973; Graebner review of *New Left and Origins of Cold War* in *Pacific Historical Review*, XLIII (February, 1974), 138–39; Leopold review of *New Left and Origins of Cold War* in *Journal of American History*, LX (March, 1974), 1183–85.

*more attention was being concentrated on issuing a directive for operation OLYMPIC (i.e., the invasion of Kyushu Island) scheduled for 1 November 1945.*

On page 238 of *Atomic Diplomacy* Alperovitz wrote that Louis Morton had argued "that the atomic bomb was not needed to force a surrender before the invasion." Alperovitz cited Morton's article "The Decision to Use the Atomic Bomb." Morton, in fact, had claimed almost the opposite in this essay.

*It would be a fruitless task (Morton wrote) to weigh accurately the relative importance of all the factors leading to the Japanese surrender. There is no doubt that Japan had been defeated by the summer of 1945, if not earlier. But defeat did not mean that the military clique had given up; the Army intended to fight on and had made elaborate preparations for the defense of the homeland. Whether air bombardment and naval blockade or the threat of invasion would have produced an early surrender and averted the heavy losses almost certain to accompany the actual landings in Japan is a moot question.*

These examples of Alperovitz's use of source material are not isolated cases. Countless other similar misuses of evidence are located throughout *Atomic Diplomacy*, and yet the book has been widely praised even by non-revisionist historians as an important contribution to Cold War scholarship. Daniel Smith described it as "well-researched" and "of considerable scholarly value." Paul Seabury complimented Alperovitz for "his meticulous use of archival materials," J. L. Richardson noted its "impressive scholarship," and even Robert Ferrell, in a comment he would later regret, admitted that "Alperovitz makes a good case." Whether the books of the other members of the New Left Seven are as equally vulnerable to close scrutiny as Maddox has charged remains yet to be seen.[14]

WHILE efforts such as Maddox's of tracking down the revisionists' footnotes are certainly a legitimate scholarly enterprise, there are more important tasks ahead for historians of the Cold War. Indeed, one may properly ask whether the attempt to apportion responsibility for the Cold War can ever be truly successful. Louis J. Halle's book *The Cold War as History* (1967), for instance, described the Cold War in virtually fatalistic terms. The proper stance of the historian, Halle contended, as a compassionate and sympathetic attitude towards both the Americans and the Russians. For him the Cold War was caused by historical forces beyond the control of either the West or the East. "In the Cold War," Halle wrote, "various historical circumstances . . . put Russia in the role of challenger—superficially, at least, in the role of aggressor. But the historical circumstances, themselves, had an ineluctable quality that left the Russians little choice but to move as they did. Moving as they did, they compelled the United States and its allies to move in response. And so the Cold War was joined." Halle emphasized that the breakdown of the European and Pacific balances of power occurring as a result of the defeat of Germany and Japan during World War II, combined with the assumption by the United States of a new diplomatic role on continental Europe and in the Far East, made conflict between the

---

14. Smith, "The New Left and the Cold War," *University of Denver Quarterly*, IV (Winter, 1970), 81; Seabury, "Cold War Origins, I," *Journal of Contemporary History*, III (January, 1968), 174; Richardson, "Cold-War Revisionism: a Critique," *World Politics*, XXIV (July, 1972), 581; Ferrell comment in John A. Garraty, *Interpreting American History: Conversations with Historians* (London, 1970), II, pp. 220–21. A detailed refutation of *Atomic Diplomacy* may be had by writing to Edward S. Shapiro, History Department, Seton Hall University, South Orange, New Jersey 07079.

United States and the U.S.S.R. virtually inevitable.[14A]

Ernest R. May, professor of history at Harvard, has also approached the Cold War without attempting to apportion blame and responsibility. In his succinct and pithy *"Lessons" of the Past: The Use and Misuse of History in American Foreign Policy* (1973), May argued that one of the most important influences shaping recent American diplomacy has been the "lessons" American policymakers have learned from their understanding of history. May also maintained that American leaders tended to use history badly and to misapply historical analogies. One of his prime examples was the American perception of and response to the postwar Soviet challenge which, he claimed was molded by the confrontation with another totalitarian nation, Nazi Germany, during the 1930s and World War II. The failure of "appeasement" during the 1930s, the seemingly insatiable appetite for conquest of Hitler and his clique, and the widespread assumption that the only thing totalitarian leaders understand and respect is superior military force were vital in determining the direction of American foreign policy immediately after World War II. Not only did American leaders view the Soviet threat in essentially military terms, but they also believed that Soviet aggression must be stopped as soon as possible (as Germany's aggression had not been stopped in 1935) if World War III was to be prevented. Although May did not discuss the possible use and misuse of history by the Soviet leaders, a case can be made that they too had learned some "lessons" of the past. The intervention of the Western powers, including the United States, in the Soviet Union after World War I, the failure of the United States to recognize the Soviet government until 1933, the pusillanimous policies of the French and British toward Nazi Germany in the 1930s, and the failure of the United States and England to launch an invasion of continental Europe until 1944 undoubtedly convinced the Soviet leaders of the unremitting hostility of the West. Postwar American policies such as the Truman Doctrine, the Marshall Plan, and the North Atlantic Treaty Organization were thus probably interpreted as attempts to destroy the Soviet government rather than as efforts to forestall Russian expansionism. If May is correct in arguing that one must study the historical perceptions of the policymakers as well as the objective social, political, and economic conditions of the 1940s in order to adequately grasp the nature of the Cold War, then diplomatic historians are going to have to know a great deal more about the psychology of perception and cognition.[15]

Historians are also going to have to become more familiar with economics if they are to understand the subtleties of revisionist historiography. Perhaps the most important of the underlying assumptions of the revisionists is that American foreign policy has been mainly determined by the needs of the American economy. For the revisionist, editorials in the business press and the pronouncements of industrialists are every bit as important as the formal papers passed between governments, the interaction between diplomats, and diplomatic incidents. A sophisticated example of the way a diplomatic historian can use economics is Alfred E. Eckes, Jr.'s fine book *A Search for Solvency: Bretton Woods and the International Monetary System, 1941–*

---

14A. Halle, *The Cold War as History* (New York, 1967), pp. xii–xiii.

15. May, *"Lessons" of the Past: The Use and Misuse of History in American Foreign Policy* (New York, 1973), ch. 2. Another attempt to understand the historical perceptions of postWorld War II American diplomats is Les K. Adler and Thomas G. Paterson, "Red Fascism: The Merger of Nazi Germany and Soviet Russia in the American Image of Totalitarianism, 1930s–1950s," *American Historical Review*, LXXV (April, 1970).

*1971* (1975), which also happens to be an effective rejoinder to revisionist attacks on postwar American monetary policies.

Revisionists have tended to discount the role of popular opinion and to emphasize the importance of the financial, industrial, and political "elite" in the formation of American foreign policy. Even the finest of the revisionist studies, however, such as Thomas G. Paterson, *Soviet-American Confrontation: Postwar Reconstruction and the Origins of the Cold War* (1973), Walter LaFeber, *America, Russia and the Cold War, 1945-1971* (1972), and Barton J. Bernstein, ed., *Politics and Policies of the Truman Administration* (1970), have failed up to now to demonstrate adequately the pervasive influence of economic motives in the conduct of postwar American diplomacy. In contrast, one of the more valuable aspects of John Gaddis' *The United States and the Origins of the Cold War* was its emphasis on the importance of domestic politics and public opinion, especially that of Poles and Catholics, in limiting the diplomatic options of the Roosevelt and Truman administrations.[16]

Perhaps the most important contribution of revisionist historiography has been to make more traditional scholars rethink their assumptions and reevaluate their conclusions. The best of the recent nonrevisionist works, including John Gaddis' book, Lisle A. Rose's *Dubious Victory: The United States and the End of World War II*, and George C. Herring, Jr.'s *Aid to Russia 1941-1946: Strategy, Diplomacy, and the Origins of the Cold War* (1973), reflects the influence of the revisionists both in the type of questions asked about American foreign policy and in the refusal to accept the official interpretations of American policies. Undoubtedly the flow of books on the Cold War will continue to pour forth from the university presses, but one may question whether anything startling will appear until the archives of the Soviet Union are opened for inspection by American scholars. When this occurs historians will be better able to apportion blame for the Cold War, or to even decide whether the issue of blame has diverted historians from more fruitful areas of investigation.[17]

---

16. Other prominent revisionist works include William A. Williams, ed., *From Colony to Empire: Essays in the History of American Foreign Relations* (New York, 1972), especially the three essays by Lloyd Gardner; Stephen E. Ambrose, *Rise to Globalism: American Foreign Policy 1938-1970*, (Baltimore, 1971), a rather extreme analysis; and Thomas G. Paterson, ed., *Cold War Critics: Alternatives to American Foreign Policy in the Truman Years* (Chicago, 1971).

17. Besides the Smith and Richardson articles cited above, analyses of revisionist historiography include Harold Wilensky, "Was the Cold War Necessary? The Revisionist Challenge to Consensus History," *American Studies*, XIII (Spring, 1972); Norman Graebner, "Cold War Origins and the Continuing Debate: a Review of the Recent Literature," *Journal of Conflict Resolution*, XIII (March, 1969); Robert Stover, "Responsibility for the Cold War: A Case Study in Historical Responsibility," *History and Theory*, (1972, no. 2); Willard E. Hoogeboom. "The Cold War and Revisionist Historiography." *Social Studies*, LXI (December, 1970); and Philip Jaffe, "The Cold War Revisionists and What They Omit." *Survey*, XIX (Autumn, 1973). Robert W. Tucker, *The Radical Left and American Foreign Policy* (Baltimore, 1971) is a perceptive and important study while Joseph M. Siracusa, *New Left Diplomatic Histories and Historians: The American Revisionists* (Port Washington, New York, 1973), is skimpy, superficial, and of little value.

## "THE UNKNOWN WAR"
### Fairy-Tale Version

On October 7, 1978 a twenty-part series on the German-Soviet War of 1941-1945 entitled "The Unknown War" narrated by Burt Lancaster began on WOR, Channel 9, in New York City. Judging by the first several episodes, the program was designed not simply to refresh our memories of the greatest military conflict in history, but rather to present the communist masters of the Soviet Union in as favorable a light as possible. The series is, as Tom Buckley noted in the New York Times, "a fairy-tale version" and "soft-core propaganda" which "distorts by omission, over-simplification and half truth." "The Unknown War" is the mass media's most important obeisance to date before the idol of detente, and comes at a time when the fabric of detente woven during the early 1970's is coming apart before our eyes in Africa and the Middle East.

The propagandistic character of "The Unknown War" could have been predicted since it is almost entirely a Soviet production. All final editorial decisions rested with Russian film editors working under the distinguished Soviet cinema personality Roman Karmen. Although Isaac Kleinerman is listed as executive producer, both the film editing and the narration were ultimately determined by Soviet officials. Evidently the Soviets were satisfied with the results since, Tom Buckley reported, the series is scheduled to be shown unchanged next year over Soviet television.

The opening segment of "The Unknown War" discusses the events surrounding the German invasion of the Soviet Union on June 22, 1941. It would have us believe that Stalin and the other Soviet leaders shrewdly suspected a Nazi attack and were preparing their people for the blow. Actually, as Barton Whaley has shown in his study Codeword Barbarossa (1973), Stalin was taken completely by surprise, believing that German military preparations were for the purpose of enforcing economic and political demands on the Soviet Union. This segment briefly mentions that the Germans had watched closely the Russian military performance in the Soviet-Finnish War of 1939-1940, a clash which it describes as a border conflict. Not only is the Soviet aggression against Finland ignored, but there is also no attempt to explain the dismal military performance of the Russians during that war or in the early months of the war with Germany.

Particularly noticeable is the complete lack of any mention of the military purges in the Soviet military forces during the 1930s which deprived the Red Army of some of its best military talent and drastically undermined its morale. Of the 80 members of the 1934 Military Soviet only 5 remained in September 1938. Every commander of a military district was executed by late 1938, as were 13 out of 15 army commanders, 57 out of 85 corps commanders, 110 out of 195 divisional commanders, and 220 out of 406 brigade commanders. "When the purges were over," Alan Clark wrote in his book Barbarossa (1965), "the Red Army was obedient to the point of witlessness; dutiful but without experience; stripped of political weight or ambition, at the expense of initiative, experiment, or the desire to innovate."

"The Unknown War" makes no effort to analyze the incredibly inept strategy of Stalin and the Soviet high command (Stavka) during the summer of 1941 or the unprepared condition of the Soviet troops which resulted in a fearful loss of Russian lives. Clark described the disposition of the Russian forces along their western frontier as "idiotic." Approximately 2,500,000 Soviet men and 18,000 tanks were lost by September, 1941. "The Unknown War" emphasizes the importance of the Soviet air force in blunting the German drive eastward. Not mentioned, however, is the Soviet loss of over 2,000 planes during the first two days of conflict which, even taking into consideration the Israeli air strikes during the Six-Day War of 1967, Clark accurately noted was "a casualty rate without precedent." Nor does "The Unknown War" discuss the argument of Seweryn Bailer's Stalin and His Generals (1969) and Albert Seaton's Stalin as Military Commander (1976) that during the opening weeks of the war Stalin emotionally collapsed for a brief time. Stalin, as Buckley wrote, is "no longer the blood-drenched pyschopath of Khrushchev's denunciation, but once again the Man of Steel, the infinitely wise savior of the Motherland." "The Unknown War" prefers to present a picture of Soviet political and military leadership rising to the occasion. Clark instead stressed the great losses suffered by the USSR due to "clumsy, hesitant, and incompetent leadership."

One of the segments of the series entitled "To the East" describes the relocation of Soviet factories from western Russia to the center of the state, and the tremendous production levels achieved by Soviet industry. There is no direct mention of American Lend-Lease aid although there is one oblique reference to aid from "Western Allies." Actually, the Americans provided the Soviets with 40,000 jeeps, almost 150,000 1 1/2-ton trucks, over 180,000 2 1/2-ton trucks, and 7,500 tractors, as well as 380,000 field telephone units and over 1 million miles of field wire. This aid was vital in enabling Soviet factories to concentrate on the production of armaments. "To the East" mentions that over 1,500 factories and ten million people were relocated to the east in the greatest mass movement in history, and it stresses the importance of railroads. "Railroads were Russia's arteries." It is more than likely that many of the railroads involved in this evacuation were pulled by American locomotives since the U. S. shipped to the Soviet Union 1,900 steam locomotives and since the Soviets produced hardly any railway equipment during the war. Needless to say, this is not mentioned in the program.

Especially revealing is the program's treatment of German atrocities. It mentions correctly that Hitler had ordered all Communist officials to be shot immediately on the spot. Incredible as it might sound, however, at no time during the first two segments is there any discussion at all of German attacks on Jews or that the Jews, along with the Communists, had been singled out by Hitler for particularly brutal treatment. In a later segment entitled "The World's Greatest Tank Battle" the battle at Kursk in July, 1943 is examined as well as the liberation of central Russia from the Germans. There is absolutely no discussion of anti-Jewish atrocities. Instead, the program would have us believe that an abstract entity called the Russian people were "violated." It mentions that ten percent of Orel's population was killed and leaves it at that. Actually, the Jewish population of Orel, which totaled approximately 6,000, was almost completely wiped out, and this was well over 50 percent of the city's residents murdered by the Germans.

Why "The Unknown War" chooses to ignore Hitler's war against the Jews can only be surmised. Certainly it conforms to Soviet claims that Jews suffered during

World War II not as Jews but simply as Soviet citizens, and it complies with the Soviet attempt to deemphasize, if not to ignore completely, the Holocaust. "The Unknown War" is thus part of the massive Soviet effort to obliterate Jewish martyrdom from the historical record. This is understandable in view of the Soviet position on the State of Israel and the emigration of Russian Jews. What is troubling is the willingness of Jews, including Isaac Kleinerman, the producer of "Victory at Sea" and "The Twentieth Century," to be associated with this project.

Another possible reason for this blatant ignoring of Jewish suffering during the German invasion is that "The Unknown War" stresses the ideological conflict between communism and nazism. Thus in the opening segment there are scenes of communist leaders haranguing their followers to fight steadfastly against the invaders. This historically warped view of the conflict is responsible for the program's description of the unity and determination of the Soviet people to defend their government and country. Actually when the German armies first crossed the borders they were often greeted as liberators, most notably in the Ukraine and in the Baltic states. The German invasion was viewed by some as an opportunity to escape the hated dictatorship of Stalin and communism, as well as the control of rival ethnic groups. In the second segment entitled "The Battle for Moscow" the citizens of Moscow are pictured as enjoying the summer sun and the ballet in the weeks before the German onslaught, without any mention at all of the attitude of the Soviet people toward their own government.

Not surprisingly, "The Unknown War" does not mention the restiveness of the Soviet population, nor does it call attention to the fact that if Hitler had followed a different policy in Russia he might have been able to capitalize on the internal discontent within the Soviet Union. Hitler's forfeiting of this potential trump card has been fully explained in the memoirs of Captain Wilfried Strik-Strikfeldt, Against Stalin and Hitler (1973).

Stalin himself realized that the Soviet Union needed more than dedicated Communists to defeat the Germans. He deemphasized the antireligious campaign in order to win the enthusiastic support of the Russian Orthodox Church, and he stressed that the fight with Germany was in defense of the holy motherland. The Russian people, by and large, responded heroically to Stalin's call. Yet even when "The Unknown War" directs our attention to the brave stand of the Russian people, it manages to omit some salient facts. A case in point is its discussion of the defense of the city of Brest. Omitted completely is any mention that Brest was the scene of the Treaty of Brest-Litovsk in 1918 when the new Soviet leadership headed by Lenin withdrew Russia from the war with Germany during the First World War. This left the French, British, and Americans to fight the Germans alone in the west. For some reason "The Unknown War" does not feel it appropriate to draw our attention to the Treaty of Brest-Litovsk.

The showing of "The Unknown War" could not have taken place without the advertising dollars of American corporations. The Eaton Corporation of Cleveland and Manufacturers Hanover Bank of New York are picking up the tab for showing the series in the New York area. This also is not surprising since American big business has viewed detente as a wedge to open up the markets of eastern Europe for American products and services. Big business, as Walter Laqueur has recently written, "is usually found in the front line of appeasement. . . . It wants business and politics to be kept strictly apart."

To criticize "The Unknown War" is not to denigrate the heroic stand of the Soviet people against the Nazis. Certainly the defeat of Hitler was due more to the killing of German soldiers between 1941-1945 on the eastern front than to the belated invasion of Normandy by the British and Americans in June, 1944. It was the staunch opposition that Hitler encountered in the Soviet Union which guaranteed first that he would not dominate Europe, and then, second, that his defeat was inevitable. The Soviet contribution to Hitler's defeat included the approximately twenty million Russians who lost their lives during the war, a figure which is over sixty times greater than the total of American deaths due to the war. "The Unknown War," however, by distorting the nature of the conflict in the east, trivializes the ordeal of the Soviet people in the hour of their greatest agony. Most, I imagine, believed they were dying for something other than the bolstering of Stalin's reputation and the glorification of communism and detente.

# The Perjury of Alger Hiss:
# Icon of the Cold War

IN February, 1954 Whittaker Chambers wrote to William F. Buckley, Jr. that "the Hiss Case is a permanent war; and the forces and money behind the enemy effort are formidable. In my opinion, we shall not know how formidable until Alger Hiss leaves prison. Then the guns will begin to go off.... The enemy is tirelessly seeking to discredit me."[1] Alger Hiss was released from prison over two and a half decades ago, as Chambers predicted, the attempt to exonerate him has intensified, beginning with his own apologia, *In The Court of Public Opinion* (1957). The latest battles in the "permanent war" have centered around Allen Weinstein's massive volume, *Perjury: The Hiss-Chambers Case* (1978), and John Lowenthal's movie, "The Trials of Alger Hiss" (1980).

Although never convinced as to Hiss' innocence, Weinstein began his research with serious doubts about Chambers' version of his relationship with Hiss, and, as a liberal Democrat, he expected (and probably hoped) to demonstrate Hiss' guiltlessness. Weinstein, a history professor at Smith College, first discussed the Hiss Case in June, 1970 in *Commentary* magazine. There he argued that Chambers' testimony was "far less credible" than Hiss', containing many contradictions and "significant misstatements," and that the question of Hiss' guilt or innocence "has still to be thoroughly unraveled." Weinstein returned to the permanent war twice in 1972. In the *American Scholar*, he again argued that much of Chambers' evidence was contradictory, and, because of the unreliability of Chambers' testimony, "there appears to be reasonable doubt that Alger Hiss was a member of the Communist party at the time when they knew one another." Weinstein concluded that his findings were "cautious and tentative," and "although Hiss' *guilt* seems to me still unproved beyond a reasonable doubt, it would be equally difficult, in the light of available evidence, to prove him innocent." Weinstein's valuable essay "The Symbolism of Subversion: Notes on Some Cold War Icons" appeared in the August, 1972 issue of the British *Journal of American Studies*. Here he focused on the symbolic dimension of the Hiss case for the political culture of the 1950's. The trial of Alger Hiss, Weinstein wrote, dramatized for Americans the impact of the Cold War with Hiss becoming a political icon to both friends and foes. The Hiss case symbolized the treatment of domestic Communists, the response of radical intellectuals to their past, the role of congressional investigating committees, and the validity of

---

1. William F. Buckley, Jr., ed., *Odyssey of a Friend: Whittaker Chambers' Letters to William F. Buckley, Jr. 1954-1961* (New York: G.P. Putnam's Sons, 1969), p. 50.

the charge of subversive infiltration within the Roosevelt and Truman administrations. Weinstein continued to argue that the evidence failed to substantiate Hiss' membership in the Communist Party or his complicity in espionage.[2]

From 1972 through 1976 Weinstein was busily researching the Hiss case, particularly tens of thousands of pages of records from the FBI, the Justice Department, the OSS, the CIA, the State Department, and the Immigration and Naturalization Service. Many of these documents had been secured as a result of legal action taken under the Freedom of Information Act. Weinstein also interviewed over eighty persons with particular knowledge of the case or of Hiss and Chambers, including Soviet agents, friends and advisors of Hiss and Chambers, members of the Hiss and Chambers families, and congressional investigators. His travels took him to England, Germany, Italy, Israel, Mexico, and Hungary. Weinstein went over the case with Alger Hiss on six different occasions and talked with every major member of the Hiss and Chambers families with the exception of Chambers' widow. Weinstein also examined the records of John Foster Dulles, Allen Dulles, Richard Nixon, Harry Dexter White, and other individuals with special knowledge of the Hiss case. One senses in Weinstein's research "the excitement, the joy, and even the color" of fictional intrigue which, as Robin W. Winks once pointed out, belongs to "the good gray world of professional scholarship." Finally, Weinstein was able to examine the Hiss defense files located in Baltimore, New York, and Boston, undoubtedly because Hiss and his supporters believed Weinstein to be sympathetic to their cause. They were, however, to be sadly disappointed by an essay of Weinstein's in the April 1, 1976 issue of the *New York Review of Book*.[3]

Weinstein answered an emphatic "no" to the question "Was Alger Hiss Framed?" His essay was in the form of a book review of John Chabot Smith's *Alger Hiss: The True Story* which argued for Hiss' innocence. For Weinstein, Smith's volume was unconvincing, contained no new evidence, overlooked the vast bulk of data detailing Hiss' guilt, and depended on several unconvincing conspiratorial theories to account for Hiss' conviction. Weinstein maintained that the American Left had put itself on the defensive by defending Hiss and that it would be to its interest to admit Hiss' guilt and move on to other things.[4]

The response to "Was Alger Hiss Framed?" illustrated the continuing ability of the Hiss case to evoke intense emotions. Weinstein would later note that this partisan exhortation "did little to encourage efforts to analyze the evidence closely. Rather it tended to confirm preconceptions." Critics of Weinstein were impressed by the fact that "Was Alger Hiss Framed?" had been published on April Fool's Day. The essay created a storm of controversy and its author was the center of attention at the April, 1976 meeting of the Organization of American Historians when he delivered a paper repeating many of the points made in the essay. Peter H. Irons, a radical historian, claimed Weinstein's paper reminded him of a "Sally Rand fan dancer's performance" in that it promised far more than it revealed.[5] Weinstein's conclusions were particularly noteworthy since serious doubts had been recently raised by David Levin and Philip Nobile regar-

---

2. Allen Weinstein, "The Witness," *Commentary*, IL (June, 1970), 85-88; Weinstein, "The Alger Hiss Case Revisited," *American Scholar*, XIL (Winter, 1971-72), 132; Weinstein, "The Symbolism of Subversion: Notes on Some Cold War Icons," *Journal of American Studies*, VI (August, 1972), 165-70.

3. Weinstein, *Perjury: The Hiss-Chambers Case* (New York: Alfred A. Knopf, 1978), xvii-xx; Robin W. Winks, ed., *The Historian as Detective: Essays on Evidence* (New York: Harper Torchbooks, 1968), xiii.

4. Weinstein, "Was Alger Hiss Framed?" *New York Review of Books*, XXIII (April 1, 1976), 14-19.

5. Weinstein, *Perjury*, vxi; *New York Times*, April 9, 1976.

ding Hiss' guilt.

Levin, a prominent professor of English at the University of Virginia, had written a lengthy article for the winter, 1976 issue of the *Virginia Quarterly Review* entitled "In the Court of Historical Criticism: Alger Hiss's Narrative" which exonerated Hiss. Nobile published his "The State of the Art of Alger Hiss" in *Harper's* in April, 1976. This was the first of a series of pro-Hiss articles in *Harper's*. Nobile claimed Hiss was innocent, in part because it was inconceivable that any sane person would perpetuate "a quarter-century of deceits, jeopardizing the welfare of family and the reputation of friends, in a doomed attempt to reverse what that person well knows to be the truth."[6]

The response to "Was Alger Hiss Framed?" by Hiss' supporters ranged from Carey McWilliams' comment that Weinstein's conclusions were "premature" to Robert Sherrill's claim that Weinstein was prejudiced. Weinstein's essay also provoked several hostile letters to the *New York Review of Books* by Peter Irons and other Hiss advocates. Weinstein answered the letters in May and September, stepping up his attack on John Chabot Smith's book and providing additional reasons for believing Hiss guilty. This wrangle over "Was Alger Hiss Framed?" was a tempest in a teapot compared to the contention engendered by the publication of Weinstein's *Perjury*.[7]

RARELY has a work in American history been so eagerly awaited or accompanied by so much pre-publication publicity. The anticipation was intensified by the fact that the book had been originally promised for 1976. It did not appear until March, 1978 and then only after *Time* magazine had published a three-page article about Weinstein and *Perjury* in its February 13, 1978 issue. *Time* claimed Weinstein had "carefully and persuasively" documented Hiss' guilt, and quoted his statement that "Alger Hiss is a victim of the facts." In another issue *Time* quoted Weinstein's statement that he originally wanted to believe Hiss innocent, "but I am a historian not an apologist for anyone."[8]

Conservatives and fervent anti-communists echoed *Time*'s analysis of *Perjury*. For George Will, the book was "stunningly meticulous, and a monument to the intellectual ideal of truth stalked to its hiding place." The belief in Hiss' innocence had suffered a "delicate destruction by a scholar's scalpel." Will maintained that *Perjury* had performed "a substantial public service" by undermining Hiss' three-decade "war against truth." Weinstein's book, Will concluded, was "a historic event." Ralph De Toledano, the co-author of the anti-Hiss book *Seeds of Treason*, praised Weinstein for his "encyclopedic research" and conclusive demonstration of Hiss's guilt. After *Perjury*, anyone still believing in his innocence was involved in "an exercise of self-hypnosis." Michael Leeden described the book in *Commentary* as "excellent," "irrefutable," and demonstrating Hiss' culpability "beyond all reasonable doubt." For the *National Review*, *Perjury* was "irrefutable" and "magisterial." It had carefully unearthed Hiss' "frauds and deceits." *Perjury* soon became available both from the Conser-

---

6. David Levin, "In the Court of Historical Criticism: Alger Hiss's Narrative," *Virginia Quarterly Review*, LII (Winter, 1976), 41-78; Philip Nobile, "The State of the Art of Alger Hiss," *Harper's*, CCLII (April, 1976), 67-76.
7. Carey McWilliams, "Post-Mortem on the Hiss Case," *Nation*, CCXXII (April 3, 1976), 389-90; McWilliams, "Battle of the Book Reviews," *ibid.*, (May 1, 1976), 517-19; Robert Sherrill, review of John Chabot Smith, *Alger Hiss: The True Story*, in *New York Times Book Review*, April 25, 1976; Weinstein, et al., "The Hiss Case: An Exchange," *New York Review of Books*, XXIII (May 27, 1976), 32-48; Weinstein, et al., "The Hiss Case: Another Exchange," *New York Review of Books*, XXIII (September 16, 1976), 52-61.

8. *Time*, February 13, 1978, 28-30; *ibid.*, March 29, 1976, 30-31.

**Alger Hiss**

*The Hiss case symbolized the treatment of domestic Communists, the response of radical intellectuals to their past, the role of congressional investigating committees, and the validity of the charge of subversive infiltration within the Roosevelt and Truman administrations.*

vative Book Club, and in a special offer, from The Intercollegiate Studies Institute.[9]

Liberals, especially those who prided themselves on their realism and lack of sentimentility, also praised *Perjury*. This was made easier by Weinstein's distaste for Hiss' enemies. *Perjury* portrayed Nixon as calculating, ambitious, and more concerned with his political future than exposing Hiss, and it described the FBI as a bumbling institution lead by a ranting director. Liberals could accept Hiss' guilt now without becoming partisans of Nixon, Hoover, or the FBI. Thus Arthur M. Schlesinger, Jr. acclaimed *Perjury* as "the most objective and convincing account we have of the most dramatic court case of the century." John Kenneth Galbraith agreed, calling *Perjury* "definitive" and praising Weinstein for going "as far as any historian could to establish the formal validity of the verdict." The *New Republic*, America's leading liberal journal, claimed Weinstein had made a convincing case, while Richard Rovere contended that "Weinstein's finding of culpability is compelling." Congressman Robert F. Drinan of Massachusetts described *Perjury* as "definitive," an "almost monumental book." Garry Wills' review in the *New York Review of Books* claimed Weinstein had conclusively proven Hiss' guilt. According to Wills, Weinstein had been "impeccably fair," showing "no personal or ideological animus of any sort." "So far as any one book can dispel a large historical mystery," Wills concluded, "this book does it, magnificently."[10]

Anti-communist socialists joined in the refrain. Perhaps the most enthusiastic review of *Perjury* was Sidney Hook's. He noted the "immensity" of its achievement and maintained that Hiss' guilt "can no longer be contested on any rational grounds." Irving Howe, the editor of the socialist journal *Dissent*, agreed. He believed *Perjury* conclusively refuted the theories purporting to show a political conspiracy against Hiss. According to Howe, Weinstein's book was "lucidly written, impressively, research, closely argued," a tru-

9. George F. Will, "The Myth of Alger Hiss," *Newsweek*, March 20, 1978, 96; Ralph De Toledano, "Towards a Higher Imperative," *Modern Age*, XXII (Fall, 1978), 412-17; Michael Leeden, "Hiss, Oswald, The KGB, and Us," *Commentary*, LXV (May, 1978), 31; D. Keith Mano, "The Last Traitor," *National Review*, XXX (May 26, 1978), 658, 660; *National Review*, XXX (April 14, 1978), 453-54; see also Hugh Kenner, "Chambers' Music and Alger Hiss," *American Spectator*, XII (June, 1979), 7-11.

10. Weinstein went into Nixon's role in the Hiss case in "Nixon vs. Hiss," *Esquire*, LXXXIV (November, 1975), 73-80, 144-52. He quoted the response of Robert E. Stripling, the House Committee on UnAmerican Activities, chief investigator, to Nixon's self-serving description of his role in the Hiss case in his autobiography *Six Crises*. "*Six Crises* is pure bullshit!" ibid., 147; Schlesinger's comments are on *Perjury*'s book jacket; John Kenneth Galbraith, "Alger Hiss and Liberal Anxiety," *Atlantic Monthly*, CCXLI (May, 1978), 44-47; T.S. Matthews, review of *Perjury*, in *New Republic*, CLXXVIII (April 8, 1978), 27-29; Richard Rovere, "The Case," *New Yorker*, LIV (May 22, 1978), 133-37; Robert F. Drinan, S.J., "Perjury, Piety, Politics," *America*, CXXXIX (August 5, 1978), 65; Garry Wills, "The Honor of Alger Hiss," *New York Review of Books*, XXV (April 20, 1978), 29-30.

ly "formidable book."[11]

THE prediction that, despite Weinstein's copious documentation and careful reasoning, *Perjury* wouldn't silence Hiss' partisans proved accurate. While for liberals and socialists the affirmation of Hiss' guilt was a means of purging the American Left of any taint of subversion, for others on the Left the belief in Hiss' innocence resembled an article of religious faith. "For veterans of the Alger Hiss brigade to give up on him now," Walter Goodman of the *New York Times* wrote, "would call into doubt a deeply held view of the way the world works. Lifetime faiths are at stake." Since 1950 Hiss's innocence had become a matter of dogma for some elements of the American Left for whom nothing good could ever be said of the House Committee on UnAmerican Activities, Richard Nixon, or anti-communism in general. Hiss was elevated into the ranks of martyrs persecuted by the yahoos of the American Right because of involvement with the New Deal and the United Nations. Eleanor Roosevelt, Max Lerner, and other prominent liberals sprang to Hiss' defense during his trial, convinced that New Deal liberalism and internationalism were the ones really on trial. Thus Walter Lippmann could remark, "I know Alger Hiss. He couldn't be guilty of treason."[12]

The belief in Hiss' innocence gained credibility because of Nixon's disgrace in 1974. The President's complicity in a long series of "dirty tricks" and abuse of power made it easier to believe that Hiss had also been victimized by a conspiracy designed to advance Nixon's political fortunes. For the true believers, Hiss became an American Dreyfus. After Watergate, Hiss received a more sympathetic hearing on the college lecture circuit and in the press as Nixon's "first victim" and the personification of the evil effects of McCarthyism. One of Hiss' supporters wrote shortly before Nixon's resignation that the President's career had been based on "fraud, fakery, framing of innocent victims....When we know more about how the Ellsberg case was plotted, we will know how the Hiss case itself was constructed." The exposure during the 1970's of FBI excesses further undermined the belief in Hiss' guilt. Only the gullible could deny that the FBI would not forge documents, plant informers, and frame the innocent. While in the 1950's the Hiss case was a symbol of the malevolence of Communism, in the 1970's it became the symbol of the malevolence of the American government. Hiss was bracketed with the Spocks, Coffins, and Berrigans. He became the first person in history to be readmitted to the Massachusetts Bar after a major criminal conviction, even though no evidence had been presented proving that a miscarriage of justice had taken place. But, as Weinstein stated in *Perjury*, this new sympathy for Hiss was not based on any new data, but rather "on the credulousness of a new generation unfamiliar with the facts in the Case, yet drawn to the notion that Alger Hiss was done in by Richard Nixon."[13]

The most widely disseminated attack on *Perjury* appeared in the June, 1978 issue of *Harper's*. Written by John Chabot Smith, it argued that *Perjury* was a scissors and paste job, offering only circumstantial evidence, lacking any critical analysis, and depending solely on Chambers' unsupported testimony. Smith presented an alternative, and rather far out, explanation for Hiss's conviction. He claimed it resulted from the machinations of J. Edgar Hoover,

---

11. Sidney Hook, "The Case of Alger Hiss," *Encounter* LI (August, 1978), 48-55; Irving Howe, "Alger Hiss Retried," *New York Times Book Review*, April 9, 1978.
12. Walter Goodman, in *New York Times*, April 25, 1978; Weinstein, *Perjury*, p. 516.

13. Merle Miller, "Alger Hiss: Truth and Consequences," *Book World*, April 16, 1978; Weinstein, *Perjury*, pp. 550,562.

James F. Byrnes, and Bernard Baruch who were determined to frame Hiss because of personal motives. The evil plan was then carried out by "Chambers the perjurer and Nixon the popularity seeker."[14]

David Levin's response to *Perjury* was more sensible and tempered. Instead of concocting a fantastic conspiracy, Levin claimed that the volume was less an impartial work of history than "a brief for the prosecution," that it was marked by "selective skepticism and selective reticence," and that it probed only those issues designed to substantiate Hiss' guilt. Levin warned *Perjury*'s potential readers to be alert to "the historian's role in assembling and shaping the evidence."[15]

The most important attack on *Perjury* came, however, not from the ranks of those influenced by the anti-Nixon atmosphere of the 1970's but from those who had never doubted Hiss' innocence in the first place. The best example was the *Nation*, a leftwing journal which had been Hiss' most persistent defender during the 1950's and 1960's. During these two decades it had devoted two special issues to the Hiss Case, had commissioned Fred J. Cook to conduct a fresh investigation of the case, and had published dozens of editorials, articles, and reviews defending Hiss. The *Nation*'s editor at that time was Carey McWilliams who believed the rehabilitation of Hiss was necessary for the revitalization of American radicalism. This and other dissents from the regnant Cold War orthodoxy of the 1950's had lead the conservative poet and historian Peter Viereck to describe the *Nation* in 1956 as "that Last Mohican from the Popular Front illusions of the 1930's," and to contrast "the double standard 'liberalism' of certain *Nation* experts on Russia and the valid liberalism of the *New Republic*." The naming of Victor Navasky as editor of the *Nation* shortly before the publication of *Perjury* did not change the magazine's anti-anti-communism. Navasky was best known for his *Kennedy Justice*, a rather critical portrait of Robert Kennedy's tenure as Attorney General. Now in April, 1978 he embarked upon a full scale offensive againse *Perjury*.[16]

Navasky's initial response appeared in the April 8, 1978 issue where he described Weinstein's book as "false history" which revealed "the pitfalls of scholarship." He lamented the initial praise for the volume, and suggested that the critical comments of Fred Cook, John Lowenthal, and William Reuben were more credible. Reuben was a former journalist for the pro-Communist *National Guardian*, and a self-professed expert on the Hiss Case. Not only did he claim Alger Hiss had been innocent, but he also argued that the FBI had framed the Rosenbergs and that there had never been any conspiracy to steal atomic bomb secrets.[17]

Navasky attempted to refute *Perjury* by charging that Weinstein had misquoted six key persons he had interviewed. Also, he had substituted "his belief for his data," and had exhibited a "selective use and misuse of documents." According to Navasky, Weinstein was "an embattled partisan hopelessly mired in the perspective of one side, his narrative obfuscatory, his interpretations improbable, his omissions strategic, his vocabulary manipulative, his standards double, his 'corroborations' circular and suspect, his reporting astonishingly erratic." Navasky accused Weinstein of being one of the "cold-war intellectuals who presumably sleep better at night secure in the

---

14. John Chabot Smith, "The Debate of the Century (Con't.)," *Harper's*, CCLVI (June, 1978), 81-85.
15. David Levin, "Perjury, History, and Unreliable Witnesses," *Virginia Quarterly Review*, LIV (Autumn, 1978), 725-32.
16. Peter Viereck, *The Unadjusted Man: A New Hero for Americans* (Boston: Beacon Press, 1956), p. 260; see also Viereck, *Shame and Glory of the Intellectuals: Babbitt Jr. vs. the Rediscovery of Values* (Boston: Beacon Press, 1953), pp. 168-83.
17. Victor Navasky, "Pitfalls of Partisanship," *Nation*, CCXXVI (April 8, 1978), 386-88.

knowledge that there *was* an internal Communist espionage menace." While the target of *Perjury* had been Alger Hiss, Navasky concluded, "its temporary victim is historical truth."[18]

The response to Navasky's blast was predictable. John Chabot Smith praised Navasky for his "beautifully documented analysis" while Weinstein was incensed by the accusation of intolerance and unprofessionalism. He appeared on the "Today" television show to rebut Navasky's criticisms, and announced he would be publishing a reply in the *New Republic*. Before that appeared Navasky continued the attack with an editorial accusing Weinstein of being part of the neoconservative intellectual movement, and mocking the "monumental trappings" of scholarship adorning *Perjury*.[19]

"*Perjury*, Take Three," Weinstein's answer to Navasky, appeared in the *New Republic* on April 29th. The article was preceded by an editorial accusing Navasky of "intellectual spuriousness" and reaffirming the *New Republic's* confidence in the scholarship and conclusions of *Perjury*. Weinstein, for his part, denied misquoting anyone, claiming to have three of the interviews on tape as well as corroborating evidence for all six interviews. Navasky's article, he charged, was "a mere accusatory smokescreen" revolving around "trivial allegations of error." At no time, Weinstein showed, had Navasky come to grips with any substantive matters.[20]

Navasky then replied to Weinstein's devastating refutation in a piece entitled "New Republic, New Mistakes." Here he charged the *New Republic* with launching "an *ad hominem* diatribe of their own" and Weinstein with "dishonesty." Weinstein had had enough of Navasky by then and responded in kind, accusing the *Nation*'s editor of "repeated lies and personal slurs."[21]

At first Weinstein believed Navasky's attacks stemmed from a sense of betrayal that a supposed member of the American Left would seek to destroy one of the *Nation*'s sacred cows. Later, however, Weinstein claimed that the *Nation*'s need for publicity was even more important than any differences in historical interpretation. The magazine, he asserted, needed "the attention of the major media in order to survive and prosper." In any case, Navasky's charges had been widely broadcast and had raised doubts in *Newsweek*, the *Village Voice*, and the *New York Times* as to *Perjury*'s accuracy.[22]

Weinstein's fellow historians also responded in diverse ways to *Perjury*. New Left historians such at Athan Theoharis of Marquette University were unconvinced by Weinstein's book and reaffirmed their conviction that Hiss' trial had been unfair. Robert Griffith, the author of the finest book on the career of Joseph McCarthy, was also rather critical of *Perjury*. While praising Weinstein's extensive research and

---

18. Navasky, "Allen Weinstein's *Perjury*: The Case Not Proved Against Alger Hiss," *Nation*, CCXXVI (April 8, 1978), 393-401.

19. John Chabot Smith in *Nation*, CCXXVI (April 22, 1978), 450; Navasky, "Waiting for Weinstein," *Nation*, CCXXVI (April 22, 1978), 451-52.

20. *New Republic*, CLXXVIII (April 29, 1978), 15-16; Weinstein, "*Perjury*, Take Three," *ibid.*, 17-21.

21. Navasky, "*New Republic*, New Mistakes," *Nation*, CCXXVI (May 6, 1978), 523-26; Navasky, '...On Dancer On Prancer on Vixen...," *New Republic*, CLXXVIII (May 13, 1978), 5, 38; Weinstein in *New Republic*, *ibid.*, 38; Weinstein, *et al.*, "Arguments (New & Old) About the Hiss Case," *Encounter*, LII (March, 1979), 84-85.

22. *Newsweek*, April 17, 1978, 92; Weinstein in *Wall Street Journal*, December 13, 1979; Eliot Fremont-Smith, "Will the Real George Crosley Please Stand Up," *Village Voice*, April 17, 1978; Christopher Lehmann-Haupt, review of *Perjury* in *New York Times*, April 7, 1978. Rhodri Jeffreys-Jones also believed Navasky had damaged Weinstein's case against Hiss. See Jeffreys-Jones, "Weinstein on Hiss," *Journal of American Studies*, XIII (number 1, 1979), 123-25. On the other hand, the *National Review* described Navasky's writings as "a frantic search for epistemological loopholes for the sake of those true believers in Hiss's innocence who want to cling to both the ancient faith and intellectual respectability." *National Review*, XXX (May 12, 1978), 577.

his "powerful indictment" of Hiss, he remained unconvinced. "I am inclined," Griffith confessed, "to remain skeptical about sweeping categorical claims" regarding Hiss' innocence or guilt. He did not believe Weinstein had seen all of the important FBI documents, and he was suspicious that the bureau might have doctored the documents that were released. He also censured Weinstein for not closely examining the files of the federal prosecutor or of Chambers' lawyers. Might not an examination of these records, Griffith asked, "expose a series of conflicts and inconsistencies as great as those revealed by the Hiss files?"[23]

In contrast, Stanley I. Kutler, a specialist in American constitutional and legal history, argued that *Perjury* made out a convincing case for Hiss' guilt, and demonstrated that Hiss had been granted a fair trial. David A. Hollinger also praised the book. Although believing that *Perjury* at times was more of a prosecutor's brief than a work of history, Hollinger did admit that no one has come closer than Weinstein to proving "that in the instance of Hiss, the jury's answer is good enough for historians."[24]

Legal scholars generally gave *Perjury* high marks. Iving Younger, a professor of trial techniques at Cornell University Law School and the author of an anti-Hiss essay, portrayed *Perjury* as "magisterial" and "awesome," "the book from which all future students of the matter must start." One exception to the general praise of *Perjury* by lawyers was a review in the *Oklahoma Law Review* by a Stephen Jones,

**Allen Weinstein**

*As Weinstein stated in Perjury, this new sympathy for Hiss was not based on any new data, but rather "on the credulousness of a new generation unfamiliar with the facts in the Case, yet drawn to the notion that Alger Hiss was done in by Richard Nixon."*

identified only as an attorney in Enid, Oklahoma. Jones professed faith in Hiss' innocence, argued that the famous Woodstock typewriter could have been forged, and claimed that the "pumpkin papers" could have been stolen from Hiss. *Perjury*, according to Jones, was based largely on "hearsay, opinion, gossip, and supposition." Nowhere was Jones identified as a member of Jones and Gungall, a law firm which had done extensive work in Hiss' behalf.[25]

While the controversy still swirled around *Perjury*, the National Emergency Civil Liberties Foundation, the Avis of American civil liberties organizations, filed in July, 1978 a petition in the Federal Court for the Southern District of New York for a writ of *error coram nobis* requesting that Hiss' conviction be overturned and a new trial granted. The petition claimed that Hiss' rights under the Fifth and Sixth

---

23. Athan Theoharis, "What the New Hiss Suit Uncovers," *Nation*, CCXXVII (October 7, 1878), 336-40; Robert Griffith, review of John Chabot Smith, *Alger Hiss, The True Story*, Tony Hiss, *Laughing Last*, and Allen Weinstein, *Perjury*, in *Civil Liberties Review*, V (July-August, 1978), 64-71.

24. Stanley I. Kutler, "A Retrial of Alger Hiss," *Progressive*, XLII (September 1978), 39-40; David A. Hollinger, "The Confidence Man," *Reviews in American History*, VII (March, 1979), 134-41.

25. Irving Younger, "Pride and Perjury," *Stanford Law Review*, XXXI (January, 1979), 313-22; Michael D. Hawkins, review of *Perjury*, in *Arizona State Law Journal* (1977), 883-89; Stephen Jones, review of *Perjury*, in *Oklahoma Law Review*, XXI (Summer, 1978), 775-80.

Amendments had been violated by the government prosecutor. It charged that the government had had informers on Hiss' legal staff, that the prosecution had coached two important witnesses and had allowed them to commit perjury, that evidence had been concealed from the court, and that the prosecutor had misrepresented key testimony and evidence. Although unsuccessful as a legal ploy, the supposedly new evidence presented in the petition helped still doubts among Hiss' allies which might have been raised by Weinstein. Others, however, discounted the petition, pointing out that it did not contain any startling new evidence. The fact that the petition, when published in book form, would be accompanied by an introduction by Thomas I. Emerson, a professor of law emeritus at Yale, also raised doubts about the petition. Emerson wrote an introduction also for Michael Tigar's *Law and the Rise of Capitalism*, which had been published by Monthly Review Press, an American Marxist publishing house. Not surprisingly, Emerson argued in the introduction to *In Re Alger Hiss* that Hiss had been unfairly convicted because of the poisonous atmosphere created by the Cold War and McCarthyism.[26]

THE latest battle in Chambers' "permanent war" occurred on March 9, 1980 with the opening of John Lowenthal's two and a half-hour documentary "The Trials of Alger Hiss" in New York City. Prior to producing the film, Lowenthal had worked for Hiss' defense during the 1949 trials, had acted at times as Hiss' attorney, and had written on the Hiss case. His essay "What the FBI Knew and Hid," published naturally in the *Nation* in June, 1976, claimed Hiss had been the victim of anti-communist hysteria and the suppression of vital evidence by the FBI. Hiss, in turned, stated that Lowenthal's essay "knocks out the corroboration of the government case" and demanded a new trial. Those expecting Lowenthal's film to vindicate Hiss would not be disappointed.[27]

Most reviewers believed "the Trials of Alger Hiss" to be an extremely effective documentary, irrespective of the accuracy of its argument. *Cue* magazine called it fascinating, explosive, and compelling, while the *Soho Weekly News* described it as "an engrossing cinematic spectable." The generally astute Stanley Kaufmann, film critic for the *New Republic*, was also impressed by the film's quality. Unfortunately Kaufmann was unfamiliar with Lowenthal's background and came to the zany conclusion that the film "reaches no partisan conclusion." Other reviewers were less concerned with its cinematic value and more with its political message. Robert Hatch's review in the *Nation* was predictably gushing. He portrayed it as an "illuminating," "spellbinding," and "compelling" film with great dramatic appeal. For Hatch, Hiss was "a storybook example of an admirable American and the perfect target for a witchhunt." His accusers were "small, vindictive men" lead by a mentally deranged Chambers. Hatch emphasized that all those accused of being Communists by Chambers were "attractive men, admired by their colleagues, surrounded by friends, good at what they did and happy doing it." Hiss particularly was a person of "dignity and honor." Victor Canby, a restaurant critic for the *New York Times*, used the Lowenthal film to feast on the bones of Whittaker Chambers. Declaring "The Trials of Alger Hiss" to be an "epic documentary," Canby doubted "that it would be possible now to make a film in which Mr. Hiss did not triumph over Mr. Chambers." Canby contrasted the witty, intelligent, and handsome Hiss with the pudgy and pathetic Chambers. While Hiss was a terrifically compelling figure," Canby wrote, Chambers "looks to be

---

26. Edith Tiger, ed., *In Re Alger Hiss: Petition for a Writ of Error Coram Nobis* (New York: Hill and Wang, 1979).

27. John Lowenthal, "What the FBI Knew and Hid," *Nation*, CCXXII (June 26, 1976), 776-82; Hiss in *New York Times*, June 28, 1976.

dangerously deluded. He reminds us of the Son of Sam."[28]

The most extensive review of "The Trials of Alger Hiss" appeared in *Harper's*. William Rodgers' rather absurd essay "Witches and Woodstocks" claimed Hiss had been "harrassed, maligned, pursued," and was the victim of "a prolonged injustice that was born in passions, sustained by fears, and aged by indifference." Rodgers would have us believe that Hiss was convicted of perjury rather than espionage because "a monumental effort" by anti-New Dealers had failed to bring forth any evidence of Hiss' treason. Actually, as any half-informed person knows, Hiss wasn't prosecuted for espionage because the statute of limitations had run out. According to Rodgers, Hiss had gone to jail solely "on the word of one eccentric, suicidal man, an immigrant from the Communist underground, a born-again, come-to-Jesus convert aching for recognition and penance in contrition for a life of sin." Hiss, in contrast, "has enhanced his own life, serving the cause of citizenship more profoundly than he could have been expected to do if his inquisitors had pinioned to the stake some other luckless inheritor of the Roosevelt legacy."[29]

William F. Buckley, Jr., a friend of Chambers, was incensed by Rodger's contemptible essay, particularly its villification of Chambers and mention of the deceased's homosexuality. Buckley attacked Rodgers' lies and distortions, "made more odious by the arrogant sanctimony which is the specialty of the spiteful." John Podhoretz's essay on "The Trials of Alger Hiss" agreed with Buckley regarding the harm done by attempts to whitewash Hiss. For Podhoretz, Lowenthal was the victim of "a self-imposed and suicidal blindness" and his film's anti-anti-communism was an offense against the human spirit.[30]

THREE decades after Alger Hiss was convicted for lying about passing government secrets to Whittaker Chambers a significant element within the American intelligentsia is still in a state of animated agnosticism regarding his guilt. How can this deep concern for a trial which ended over a generation ago be explained? No other incident of that period has been able to sustain the interest of so many people over such a long period of time as Alger Hiss' unsuccessful quest for vindication. Perhaps the key can be found in Leslie A. Fiedler's famous essay of 1951, "Hiss, Chambers, and the Age of Innocence." For Fiedler, Hiss personified a generation, the "popular Front mind at bay." His supporters had all the illusions of the Left, its self-righteousness, its self-deceit, its sentimentality, its belief that it, and it alone, possessed virtue. Not wishing to be Red baiters, Fiedler wrote, the Left "preferred to be fools." American liberals failed to realize that the social and economic principles they highly valued were incompatible with the political techniques of Soviet Russia. Liberals did not understand that Communists were more than extreme liberals. This "half-deliberate blindness of so many decent people" prevented them from recognizing the reality of Alger Hiss. Fiedler called upon liberals to replace a liberalism of innocence with a "liberalism of responsibility."[31]

Shortly before his death Whittaker Chambers noted that the Hiss case had become "an epitomizing drama" in which

---

28. Stanley Kaufmann, "Films: Troubles, Public and Private," *New Republic*, CLXXXII (March 1, 1980), 24-25; Robert Hatch, "Films," *Nation*, CCXXX (March 8, 1980), 283-84; Vincent Canby, review of The Trials of Alger Hiss," in *New York Times*, March 9, 1980.

29. William Rodgers, "Witches and Woodstocks," *Harper's*, CCLX (March, 1980), 80-86.

30. William F. Buckley, Jr., in *Newark Star-Ledger*, April 6, 1980; John Podhoretz, "The Trials of Alger Hiss," *American Spectator*, XIII (May, 1980, 23-24.

31. Leslie A. Fiedler, "Hiss, Chambers, and the Age of Innocence," *Commentary*, XII (August, 1951), 109-119.

he and Hiss were archetypes. This is what, according to Chambers, gave "the peculiar intensity to the struggle." The cause of Alger Hiss has continued to attract a motley group of individuals eager to use the Hiss case to indict the American system of jurisprudence, the conduct of American diplomacy during the Cold War, and private enterprise. A segment of the generation that was on trial in 1949, to paraphrase the title of Alistair Cooke's famous book on the Hiss case, remains unconvinced that Communist subversion was nothing more than a figment of J. Edgar Hoover's imagination, or that Americans were justified in believing that the Soviet challenge must be directly confronted. The *Nation*'s response to *Perjury* resembles Mark Twain's advice in *Pudd'nhead Wilson's Calendar.* "Don't part with your illusions. When they are gone, you may still exist, but you have ceased to live." As Peter Prescott noted in his review of *Perjury*, "too many people have invested too much ego, energy and ideology" in the belief in Hiss' innocence to give up now in the face of seemingly overwhelming evidence. Truth can be so inconvenient, especially for ideologues.[32]

32. Weinstein, *Perjury*, p. 505; Peter Prescott, "The Guilt of Alger Hiss," *Newsweek*, April 3, 1978, 79, 82.

# Revisionism R.I.P.

IN early August, 1980 the *Nation* magazine published a special issue which was then distributed gratis to all delegates to the Democratic National Convention. This was made possible by a grant from The Fund for Tommorrow so that the Democrats could learn "a history lesson" from William Appleman Williams, the dean of America's revisionist diplomatic historians. The lesson consisted of a condensation of Williams's book *Empire as a Way of Life* which was to be published a few weeks later. The *Nation*'s editors described Williams's essay as an "astonishing analysis."[1] "Astonishing" can mean either "surprising" or "amazing." There was nothing surprising in Williams's article since it merely repeated themes he had been expressing over the past two decades. It did, however, continue the amazement of conventional historians who have followed Williams's career since he published *The Tragedy of American Diplomacy* in 1959.

Williams argued that the tragedy of twentieth century American diplomacy had been its consistent subversion of revolutionary ideals by "open-door imperial expansion." This persistent effort to make the world safe for American corporations stemmed from the opposition of American leaders to any socialist domestic program to rectify the failures of capitalism. Chronic overproduction and periodic depressions were to be eliminated solely through the expansion of overseas trade. This necessitated opposing all efforts to close off any areas of the world to American economic penetration, whether originating from Latin America, Nazi Germany, Japan, Great Britain, or the Soviet Union. Thus Williams entitled his chapter on World War II "The War for the American Frontier." American policy-makers supposedly opposed both right-wing autarky and left-wing social revolution in favor of an open-door economic order hospitable to economic penetration. "When combined with the ideology of an industrial Manifest Destiny," Williams wrote, "the history of the Open Door Notes became the history of American foreign policy geared to "an open door for revolutions" accompanied by the reorganization of American society along democratic, economically self-sufficient, and socialist lines.[2]

This was a rather eccentric reading of American diplomatic history. The *American Political Science Review* claimed *The Tragedy of American Diplomacy* "cannot be taken seriously as history," while Foster Rhea Dulles described Williams as "a brilliant but perverse historian," and his

---

1. *Nation*, CCXXXI (August 2-9, 1980).

2. Williams, *The Tragedy of American Diplomacy* (New York: Delta Book, 1962), pp. 45, 307.

book as "argument rather than diplomatic history."[3] The most serious critique of *The Tragedy of American Diplomacy* appeared in 1973 in Robert James Maddox's *The New Left and the Origins of the Cold War*. Maddox's volume was a full-barreled attack on several revisionist historians for falsifying evidence. Its first chapter charged Williams with constructing imaginary speeches and dialogues in *The Tragedy of American Diplomacy*. Maddox said this was particularly reprehensible coming from Williams who had stated in his book that the historian must have "the intellectual and moral courage to acknowledge the facts as they exist without tampering with them." Maddox concluded that *The Tragedy of American Diplomacy* was, indeed, a brilliant volume "but one largely divorced from reality. The "tragedy" is that his book has been taken so seriously by those who ought to have known better."[4]

Williams attempted to answer in the *New York Times* Maddox's accusation that he had spliced together phrases uttered at different times and on diverse subjects. Williams admitted that Maddox was technically correct, but then went on to argue that the analytical technique known as "the chronological ordering of raw data" had its place at the the beginning but not at the end of historical understanding. He lamely claimed that he had gone beyond mere "literal-mindedness" in order to discover the "Weltanschauung" of American policymakers. "If a person uses the idiom of the Open Door Policy...in 1927," Williams asserted, "and then uses it regularly in subsequent years, it is neither mistaken nor misleading to connect the two expressions of the same outlook." Maddox, of course, was not objecting to connecting such statements, but he did protest William's failure to tell his readers that such statements were expressed at different times and in different contexts.[5]

Williams's stature among radical historians during the 1960's was certainly not due to admiration for his historical craftsmanship. Rather, radicals found in *The Tragedy of American Diplomacy* a convincing explanation for the source of America's evil involvement in Southeast Asia, for a Cold War which seemed to be an anachronism, and for our stance as the world's leading counterrevolutionary power. Williams also offered the disaffected of the left with a useful instrumental view of history. "History," Williams believed, "offers no answers per se, it only offers a way of encouraging men to use their minds to make their own history." He was fond of quoting Napoleon: "You commit yourself and then—you see." This was heady stuff for young scholars eager to make a name for themselves and anxious to transform history into a more "relevant" discipline. They agreed with Williams that the role of history was to enable everyone to "formulate relevant and reasoned alternatives and become meaningful actors in making history." They also sympathized with his sense of urgency and his dire warnings of things to come if American imperialism was not reversed.[6]

DURING the 1960's Williams was undoubtedly the most important revisionist historian. This was due not only to *The Tragedy of American Diplomacy*, which even Williams's harshest critics admitted was brilliant, but also because of his being the chief guru of what came to be known as the "Wisconsin School" of diplomatic history. Until he moved to Oregon State University in 1968, Williams taught at the University of Wisconsin a host of diplomatic historians who are now pon-

---

3. Charles A. McClelland, in *American Political Science Review*, LIII (December, 1959), 1195-96; Foster Rhea Dulles in *American Historical Review*, LXIV (July, 1959), 1922-23: see also Robert W. Tucker, in *New Republic*, CXL (May 4, 1959), 19-21.
4. Robert James Maddox, *The New Left and the Origins of the Cold War* (Princeton, N.J.: Princeton University Press, 1973), pp. 13-37.

5. Williams, in *New York Times Book Review*, June 17, 1973, p. 7.
6. Joseph M. Siracusa, *New Left Diplomatic Histories and Historians: The American Revisionists* (Port Washington, N.Y.: Kennikat Press, 1973), pp. 23-48.

tificating in colleges throughout the country on the role of America's capitalist socioeconomic order in fostering imperialism, and on the need for a radical restructuring of our society.

In 1961 Williams published *The Contours of American History*. This broadened the analysis of *The Tragedy of American Diplomacy* to include all of American history. *The Contours of American History* attacked possessive individualism, capitalism, and private property, criticized westward expansion for harming the Indians and Mexico, and claimed that the frontier, by periodically renewing capitalism, had diverted Americans from the possibility of creating the first democratic socialist society in history. Radicals naturally welcomed Williams's new volume. Loren Baritz, writing in the *Nation*, described it as quietly ordered and beautifully reasoned, and congratulated everyone associated with the book's appearance. More dispassionate scholars, however, were not so impressed. Broadus Mitchell criticized the author's tendency to make bold generalizations without a sufficient grounding in the primary sources and without knowing the facts. "If one is to pronounce," Mitchell noted, "he must first be profound." John Braeman claimed Williams had a shallow view of American history, and had merely substituted the myth of economic determinism for other historical myths. Braeman censured Williams's naive faith in socialism, criticized his "willful blindness" in blaming the Cold War on the American desire for markets, and wrote that Williams should be viewed "not as a historian but as a prophet leading the American people to salvation." Frank Freidel believed Williams's economic determinism to be an out-moded oversimplification, and predicted that the impact of *The Contours of American History* was "likely to be that of a novelty not a profundity." Oscar Handlin, Freidel's Harvard colleague, wrote the most critical review of Williams's book. It was so negative that it soon came to be viewed as a skirmish in the historical wars of the 1960's pitting the academic establishment against its youthful critics. Handlin claimed *The Contours of American History* was so absurd that he had initially suspected Williams of playing an "elaborate hoax" on the profession. Large sections of the book were "altogether farcical," while "pervasive wrongheadedness" distorted every page. Furthermore this "total disaster" was written in a literary style reminiscent of "the literary striving of unskilled freshmen." "There has never been anything like it before," Handlin concluded.[7]

Undaunted, Williams three years later published *The Great Evasion: An Essay on the Contemporary Relevance of Karl Marx and on the Wisdom of Admitting the Heretic Into the Dialogue About America's Future*. The new book asserted that America's economic expansion had enabled it to avoid confronting the truths of Marxism. Williams's Karl Marx was not, however, the Marx most of us are familiar with. He ignored Marx's atheism, did not discuss Marx's doctrines of class warfare and the dictatorship of the proletariat, and overlooked Marx's theory of human nature. Robert L. Heilbroner described *The Great Evasion* as "vulgar, self-serving, imprecise, and shallow," while Don Martindale of the University of Minnesota called it misleading and useless except for those interested in the sociology of religion "who could find it an interesting case history of Marxian theology of exegesis."[8]

7. Loren Baritz, "In Search of American," *Nation*, CXCIII (August 26, 1961), 102-104; Broadus Mitchell, in *American Historical Review*, LXVII (April, 1962), 735-36; John Braeman, in *American Political Science Review*, LVI (December, 1962), 1005-1006; Frank Freidel, in *Christian Science Monitor*, August 17, 1961, Oscar Handlin, in *Mississippi Valley Historical Review*, XLVIII (March, 1962), 743-45: see also Irwin Unger, "The 'New Left' and American History: Some Recent Trends in United States Historiography," *American Historical Review*, LXXII (July, 1967), 1247.

8. Robert L. Heilbroner, "Marx and the American Economy," *New York Review of Books*, III (January 14, 1965, 21-22; Don Martindale, in *Annals of American Academy of Political and Social Science*, CCCLVII (March, 1965), 208-209; Milton Cantor, "Inheritor of the Faith," *Nation*, CC (April 5, 1965, 366-68.

*The Great Evasion* equated socialism and community (whereas Robert Nisbet's *The Quest for Community* demonstrated that socialism is antithetical to any true sense of community), called for the decentralizing of political authority into regional communities (as if socialism did not require political and economic centralization), simultaneously supported economic self-sufficiency and opposed nationalism, and equated socialism and "civilization" (even though the most odious crimes against civilization have been committed in the name of national socialism and communism). The book reflected Williams's ambivalence regarding centralization. His hatred of the large corporation accounted for its support of Marxism, while his loathing of imperialism accounted for its suggestion that the federal government be rendered impotent by decentralizing its authority into eight to ten regional groups. *The Great Evasion* was a compendium of much of the radical thought of the 1960's. It asserted that a power elite ran the country and called for participatory democracy, claimed that private enterprise could not prosper except under conditions of hot and cold war, and declared that an increasing number of Americans were being proletarianized. He predicted that a socialist society would lessen the selfishness and alienation resulting from capitalism, and that mental illness as well as juvenile delinquency would also diminish under socialism.[9] Williams also contended in another place that the demise of capitalism would decrease the use of LSD. "It is no wonder at all," he wrote about America's youth, "that many of them contract out of the American empire in the hope of finding a fulcrum for destroying the empire and creating an opportunity to replace it with a democratic American community."[10]

Throughout *The Great Evasion* there are

9. Williams, *The Great Evasion* (Quadrangle Books, Chicago, 1964), *passim*.
10. Williams, "Rise of an American World Power Complex," in Neal D. Houghton, ed., *Struggle Against History: U.S. Foreign Policy in an Age of Revolution* (Clarion Book: New York, 1968), 19.

statements which leave those not initiated into the mysteries of the radical fraternity gasping for a breath of common sense. The assassination of Kennedy was "a classic dramatization of the system's failure to extend its unbelievable largesse to all its citizens." Approximately thirty-five to fifty million Americans "exist under conditions of severe deprivation or outright poverty." And so on. Williams's forecasting ability exhibited this same rhetorical extravagance. He predicted, for example, that another ten years of the Cold War would result in "totalitarian state managerialism." In order to avoid the apocalypse, Williams looked forward to the creation of a political system which would be "democratic in form and social in content." "Democratic socialism," is, of course, oxymoronic. Williams gave the game away when he admitted that the people would have to be educated (*i.e.*, indoctrinated) so that they could "become integrated personalities capable of freeing and using their capacities and powers in a creative manner." It is easy to imagine who will do the educating.[11] In reading *The Great Evasion* one is reminded of Montaigne's statement: "No one is exempt from talking nonsense; the misfortune is to do it solemnly."

WILLIAM'S next book was *The Roots of the Modern American Empire: A Study of the Growth and Shaping of Social Consciousness in a Market-Place Society* (1969). Here he argued that the American expansionism of the late Nineteenth Century could be traced back to the efforts of farm spokesmen of the post-Civil War years to secure foreign markets. Except for the review in the *Nation*, historians found Williams's thesis to be too extreme. Williams, according to Carl Degler, had tried "to prove too much.... There is neither the theoretical need for, nor the possibility of fitting all of politics and foreign policy into that narrow causal explanation." John William Ward agreed, describing the book

11. Williams, *Great Evasion*, pp. 17, 23, 50, 104, 175-76.

**W.A. Williams**

*During the 1970s Williams deserted history for social and econmic prophecy based on a monomaniac obsession with open-door imperialism. (E.S.S.)*

as "tedious," "dull," and "simple-minded."[12]

It was evident by the early 1970's that Williams had run out of ideas, and was merely repeating, in various guises, the same themes which had first appeared in *The Tragedy of American Diplomacy*. Unfortunately, the stylistic and organizational qualities found in that earlier volume were totally lacking in his later efforts. Furthermore, his views had become extensively idiosyncratic and extreme. During the 1970s Williams deserted history for social and economic prophecy based on a monomaniacal obsession with open-door imperialism. This was particularly apparent in *America Confronts a Revolutionary World: 1776-1976* (1976). This volume confirmed Emerson's aphorism that foolish consistency was the "hobgoblin of little minds."

Williams's contribution to the celebration of the bicentennial was induced by a desire to honor "our historical commitment to the revolutionary right to self-determination." He attacked Jefferson's purchase of the Louisiana Territory, praised the Hartford Convention, and censured Lincoln for denying the South the fundamental right of self-determination. William's *bête noire* was James Madison whose *Federalist No. 10* had provided the rationale for believing that the adoption of the Constitution would enable expansion and freedom to exist side-by-side. Williams proposed replacing the Constitution with the Articles of Confederation, creating a federation of democratic Socialist communities, and naming the Northwest community Neahkahnie.[13] The historical profession was aghast at Williams's latest flight of fancy. Edmund S. Morgan of Yale described the book as "eccentric" and "bizarre," while even the reviewer in the *Nation* was forced to admit that it was unfortunate.[14]

*Empire as a Way of Life* is the latest indication of Williams's intellectual and literary degeneration. It is subtitled "An Essay on the Causes and Character of America's Present Predicament Along With a Few Thoughts About an Alternative." The title of chapter three is "A Psychologically Justifying and Economically Profitable Fairy Tale: The Myth of Empty Continents Dotted Here and There with the Mud Huts, the Lean-tos, and the Tepees of Unruly Children Playing at Culture." *Empire as a Way of Life* is a political pamphlet written in the turgid and prolix style familiar to that genre. For some

---

12. Richard W. VanAlstyne, "Beyond the Last Frontier," *Nation*, CCX (February 23, 1970), 214-215; Carl Degler, in *American Historical Review*, LXXV (December, 1970) 1780-82; John William Ward, in *New York Times Book Review*, February 22, 1970 pp. 10, 12, 14; David M. Pletcher, in *Journal of American History*, LVII (June, 1970), 172-74.

13. Williams, *America Confronts a Revolutionary World: 1776-1976* (New York: William Morrow and Company, 1976), pp. 9, 57-108, 183-97.

14. Edmund S. Morgan, "The American Revolution: Who Were 'The People'? *New York Review of Books*, XXIII (August 5, 1976), 29; Michael Zuckerman, "Recasting American Historical Consciousness," *Nation*, CCXIII (September 11, 1976), 214-16; Thomas C. Kennedy, in *American Historical Review*, LXXXII (June, 1977), 724.

reason the Oxford University Press, fresh from celebrating its five-hundredth anniversary, did not believe the volume required proofreading. Thus Lincoln's decision to prevent the South from seceding was because if "he did not zap the Confederacy, then the Devil would call the loan and all hell would break loose." The farmers of the late Nineteenth Century "vented the kind of strident rhetoric about liberty abroad that encouraged an ideology of intervention that enabled those who wanted less liberty at home to justify themselves in the name of an empire abroad that had no primary concern for the welfare or the freedom of the foreigners." Herbert Hoover "was in the position of a father of the 1960s trying to persuade his children that the jazz of the 1920s and 1930s was worth a good listen and a good boogie."[15]

Williams's atrocious prose mirrored his equally sloppy thought. John Lukacs, reviewing *Empire as a Way of Life* in the *New Republic,* characterized Williams as a "vulgarian and a pedant," said the book exhibited a lack of knowledge "which in former times would have debarred him from the lectern of any reputable institution of higher learning," and asserted that his position as the president of the Organization of American Historians reflects "the present state of professional historianship in the United States." For the past two decades, Lukacs concluded, Williams "has learned nothing, and forgotten everything. Truth has further decayed, and lying has become worse."[16]

One would have hoped that *Empire as a Way of Life* would have proven too much even for the ideologues of the *Nation.* That it didn't is a testament to the intellectual halitosis of contemporary radicalism, the left's unwillingness to demand even a modicum of intellectual rigor and literary discipline from its scribblers. *Empire as a Way of Life* is of little historiographical significance, although it does have significant theological value since it proves that there can be life after intellectual death.

Perhaps the most troubling aspect of *Empire as a Way of Life* is that it appeared while Williams was president of the Organization of American Historians, the most important historical society of exclusively Americana specialists. Despite the lofty position Williams has in the historical profession, our most distinguished historians have consistently condemned his views as perverse and outlandish. One suspects that Williams's standing can be explained by the fact that his views have been widely accepted by much of the American intelligentsia and political establishment. Williams noted in February, 1980 that Cold War revisionism had become "the mainstream" of historiography,[17] while making the world safe for democracy and revolution was one of the professed goals of the lamented Carter administration. American historians are overwhelmingly on the left and find Williams's ideology congenial, particularly if their field of specialization is not diplomatic history. Many earned their degrees in the 1960s at a time when there were presumably no enemies to the left. They are now safely ensconced in academia, free to exhibit their knee-jerk leftism. Williams's election as the President of the Organization of American Historians is another reminder of the inability of academicians, when they step outside their areas of expertise, to recognize buncombe.

---

15. Williams, *Empire as a Way of Life* (New York: Oxford University Press, 1980), pp. 93, 121, 181.
16. John Lukacs, in *New Republic,* CLXXXIII (October 11, 1980), 31-33.
17. Williams in *New York Times,* February 8, 1980.

## THE LESSONS OF TEHRAN

Now that the hostages have finally been released, it is time to examine the response of the Carter administration to the entire series of events beginning in November, 1979. It is clear that from the start the administration had two options. The first was to downplay the importance of the hostage seizure, recognizing that the taking of hostages has a long history in the Arab and Moslem world. In fact, during the 1790's and 1800's the United States paid tribute to the rulers of Morocco, Algiers, Tripoli, and Tunis to prevent the enslavement of American sailors or to buy their freedom. Deemphasizing the importance of the hostage seizure would have lessened the ability of the Teheran authorities to humiliate the United States, and would have removed the chief obstacle to the hostages' speedy release. Any incentive the Iranians had to release the captives was diminished by the fact that they possessed something the American government highly valued. Once it became clear that we attached little significance to the lives of the hostages, the Iranians would then have realized that the captives were of slight value. This would have been followed by their speedy release.

The Carter administration, however, both publicly and privately, chose to make the hostage question the overriding concern of its last year in office. The President, by refusing to light the White House Christmas tree and through other symbolic actions, conveyed to the American people the intensity of his commitment to freeing the captives. By emphasizing the hostage issue, Carter provided the Iranian leadership with the opportunity of degrading the American "Satan" and of consolidating their revolution behind a hate-American campaign. The Iranians capitalized upon American humanitarianism and the concern of the Carter administration with "human rights". America's admirable commitment to the sanctity of human life became its Achilles heel.

President Carter's other option was an immediate declaration of war against Iran followed by military action. These measures could have included attacks on oil installations, military bases, highways, and the other targets which American military authorities had brought to the President's attention. The President demurred, hoping for a peaceful resolution to the crisis. It was not until half a year had elapsed that a military response was mounted and that was a dismal and humiliating failure. Military action should have been immediate and should have involved more than a few score troops and several helicopters.

The American government followed the worst course imaginable. It told the American people and the rest of the world that the seizure of the hostages was an unconscionable and unacceptable outrage but refused to do anything about it which involved major military action. The administration simultaneously attached great importance to the hostage issue, and yet refused to take commensurate actions. The result was that the credibility of our military posture as well as our standing as a world power were seriously undermined. Can anyone doubt what the Soviet Union would have done in similar circumstances? The events in Hungary in 1956, Czechoslovakia in 1968, and Afghanistan in 1979 indicate the willingness of the Soviets to protect their national interests, once they conclude they are being seriously threatened.

The source of Carter's failure was his assumption, which he continually conveyed to the nation, that America's major interest was the safe and speedy return of the hostages. Once the issue was defined in this manner the American government was at the mercy of the Iranians since only they had the ability to release the captives. The fate of the hostages, although important to their families, should never have been identified as the crux of the issue. President Carter's major responsibility was not to bring fifty-two hostages home safely, but rather to preserve the best interests of two hundred and twenty million Americans.

The United States had two major interests involved in the hostage question. The first was to demonstrate American determination and power. Other nations must not conclude that the United States was a paper tiger, unwilling or unable to protect its nationals, and unable to punish their captors. American protests must not be viewed as something which can be dismissed with impunity. In this regard, the example of the Israelis is apt. When their citizens were seized and taken to Uganda in July, 1976, the Israelis took immediate military action which not only freed the captives but also inflicted material and personnel damage on the Ugandan military forces. Since then there have been no further hijackings involving Israelis.

The other major American interest was not permanently embittering American-Iranian relations. The current Iranian regime will be replaced within a very few years by a more reasonable government cognizant that the threat to Iran from Moscow should be its major concern. America's long-range interest involves repulsing the spread of Soviet power in the Persian Gulf region, and this demands reestablishing cordial relations with Teheran.

If Washington in 1980 had been most fearful of the undermining of American credibility, then prompt military action should have resulted after the hostages had been seized. If, on the other hand, it was most worried about the increase of Soviet influence in the Middle East, then it could have deemphasized the hostage issue. The Carter administration, in contrast, because of its overriding concentration on the captives' safe release, engaged in a waiting game with Iran which was featured daily on the front pages of the newspapers. The President feared that military action would result in the murder of the hostages, thereby defeating the major purpose of his diplomacy. The administration's failure to recognize what was at stake simultaneously demonstrated American impotence while unduly lengthening the hostages' ordeal.

A similar hostage crisis must never be allowed to occur again. Unfortunately, the Carter's administration's policy of emphasizing the need to free the hostages while refusing to take military action merely encourages such seizures in the future. Potential captors now realize that Americans will not inflict military punishment because of fears for the safety of the hostages. Carter's successors must make it clear that if any Americans are taken captive, the government will consider them prisoners of war and not hostages. Not only will this remove the reward for seizing hostages, but it will increase the potential penalties for such kidnapping. Such a policy to be effective demands a military strike force capable of an immediate and powerful response, an administration willing to contemplate the use of the military option, and a government capable of recongizing America's most fundamental interests. These were sadly lacking between November, 1979 and January, 1981.

# *American Jews and the Business Mentality*

AMERICAN JEWS HAVE HAD AN AMBIVALENT attitude toward financial success and commercial acquisitiveness. On the one hand, their rapid economic mobility over the past seventy-five years, which far exceeds that of any other major American ethnic group during this period, has enabled them to escape from the slums and radically to transform the occupational structure of American Jewry within two or three generations. The fervent desire of the first generation of East European Jews that their children not enter the sweatshops or not live in tenements has been fulfilled beyond their wildest expectations, and much to the surprise of the American Geman Jewish community which initially viewed the East European immigration as largely consisting of *luftmenschen, schnorrers*, and the physically debilitated. While rapid Jewish social, economic, and occupational mobility has become a staple of American sociology, there is, nevertheless, a tendency among many American Jews either to ignore it or to refuse to recognize its source.

Some Jews have even gone out of their way to deemphasize or deny that American Jews are now "haves" rather than "have-nots." Embarrassment over widespread evidence of Jewish affluence lead Jewish spokesmen in the 1960s and 1970s to stress the existence and persistence of Jewish poverty. Not only did many of these seekers after Jewish poverty exaggerate its extent, but they often ignored its transitory character. In contrast to the poverty of other American ethnic groups which has existed over several generations and has created what Oscar Lewis termed a "culture of poverty," Jewish poverty is largely limited to the elderly, to recent immigrants, or to the extremely pious. Jewish poverty is not a social condition which is passed on from generation to generation. Many of the poor Jews of south Miami Beach who are living out their last years on meager social security checks have children who are doctors, lawyers, and professors. Indeed, one of the psychological burdens carried by the elderly Jewish poor is the recognition that they have been largely forgotten by their successful offspring whose concern is limited to a visit or two a year and a phone call once a week.

While most informed American Jews, however, recognize the fact of American Jewish financial success, there is no widespread awareness of the reasons for this success. Perhaps the most generally held explanation is that American Jews took advantage of available educational opportunities, particularly the university and, especially, the fabled City College of New York. CCNY has assumed in American Jewish folklore a position comparable to that of the playing fields of Eton and Harrow. The fact that Russian Jewish immigrants in Latin America, the British Empire, and other areas where educational opportunities were not so easily available also experienced the same rapid economic mobility should have made the CCNY explanation rather suspect. And, in fact, recent historical investigation has demolished the belief that scholastic achievement can account for American Jewish success. Professor Selma Berrol has shown that, prior to World War I, most American Jews did not even finish high school, much less go on to college, and that CCNY was far too small to account for any significant portion of Jewish mobility. In 1913, for example, there were only two hundred and nine graduates of City College, and it was not until the 1930s that the college was large enough to be a route of upward mobility for many Jews. By the 1930s, moreover, Jewish ascent had already been well underway, as seen in the large number of Jews who had been able to move from the Lower East Side. The Jewish population of the ghetto peaked well before World War I, and Jews continued to leave the area throughout the post-World War I era. The Lower East Side housed 353,000 Jews in 1916, but only 121,000 in 1930. The CCNY explanation, therefore, fails to account for the social and economic mobility of the first generation, and it is only a partial explanation for the ascent of the second and third generations.[1]

An alternative, and more reasonable, explanation has been the ability of East European Jews and their descendants to take advantage of the economic and entrepreneurial opportunities offered by American capitalism. The East European Jewish immigrants of the late nineteenth and early twentieth centuries were overwhelmingly oriented toward business. In many areas of East Europe, Jews virtually monopolized commerce. The most frequently voiced criticism of them was their "parasitic" economic character, and many Jewish reformers encouraged the transformation of Jews into "productive" farmers and artisans. While these strictures overlooked the many Jewish artisans and the fact that hundreds of thousands of East European Jews had been proletarianized by the late nineteenth century, they correctly recognized that business was central for them.

The goal of most Jewish immigrants upon settling in America was to open their own business, and it was only as a temporary expedient that they entered the working class. The intense labor union activity in the New York ghetto early in this century was a response, not only to the wretched working conditions of the sweatshops, but, also, to the dissatisfaction of Jewish workers at being workers at all. The Jewish immigrant

---

1. Selma C. Berrol, "Education and Economic Mobility: The Jewish Experience in New York City, 1880-1920," *American Jewish Historical Quarterly*, LXV (March, 1976): 257-71.

working class was, in fact, a bourgeoisie temporarily existing as a proletariat. The social characteristics of the Jewish working class, such as sobriety, temperance, frugality, willingness to defer gratification, and commitment to education, are those generally associated with a mobile middle class.

While the East European Jewish immigrants possessed precisely those traits conducive for success, they would have been for naught if the American economy had not provided them a hospitable environment for exercising their talents. Not only was the American urban economy burgeoning at the turn of the century, but there were no artificial barriers to enterprise. Licensing regulations, minimum wage laws, and other government impediments to enterprise and social advancement did not exist, and the labor movement in the garment industry and other Jewish-oriented industries had not yet achieved its position of strength. As a result of the openness of the economy and their own commercial orientation, East European Jews gravitated toward business to a greater extent than did other immigrant groups.

"The Lower East Side developed a fervent commercial life," writes Moses Rischin, "infused with a vitality that made it something more than a mass of tenements." It was this "fervent commercial life" which, more than anything else, was responsible for Jewish social and economic mobility. "Jews joined the mainstream in seeking success through business," says Professor Thomas Kessner. "And indeed among the first generation immigrants it was not medicine, law or even their vaunted thirst for education that carried them forward. It was business." The same statements could be made of their children and grandchildren. The economic opportunities provided by the sweatshops and a much maligned capitalism have enabled the grandchildren of the immigrants to criticize the economic system from the safety of their homes in Woodmere and Great Neck.[2]

But while the first generation tended to act as capitalists, they tended to think as radicals. The most popular Yiddish newspaper was Abraham Cahan's secular and socialist *Forward*. The Lower East Side was one of only two places ever to send a socialist to Congress, electing Meyer London in 1914. The Jewish labor unions were generally socialist in ideology, and almost all of the first-generation ghetto intellectuals were either anarchists or, more frequently, socialists. To this day, American Jewish social action organizations are to the "left," and support a social and economic program which, it could be argued, has more relevance for Vilna of the 1890s than for contemporary America. Indeed, American Jewry has almost a knee-jerk attitude toward business and capitalism, an attitude

---

2. Moses Rischin, *The Promised City: New York Jews, 1870-1914* (New York: Harper and Row, 1962, 1970). p. 56; Thomas Kessner, *The Golden Door: Italian and Jewish Immigrant Mobility in New York City, 1880-1915* (New York: Oxford University Press, 1977). p. 65.

which has mystified conservatives and been a godsend for countless liberal causes and organizations.

This contempt for business has been a central motif in the recent resurgence of interest in American Jewish history, particularly the nostalgia for the immigrant generation and the old Lower East Side. The movies and books purporting to describe the "world of our fathers" have presented a picture at odds with the perceptions of the Jews who actually lived there. The residents of the Lower East Side, for instance, recognized that they were living in a slum and they expended all possible efforts to escape from it. When Jacob Riis stated that thrift, "the watchword of Jewtown," was "its cardinal virtue and its foul disgrace," he was noting the willingness of Jews to scrimp and save in order to escape from the oppressive overcrowding of the ghetto. They were under no illusions about the Lower East Side. For them it was neither quaint nor colorful.

One of the classic pictures of the Lower East Side as slum was *Jews Without Money*, published in 1930 by Michael Gold, a Communist and resident of the ghetto. His description, when compared to later analyses such as Irving Howe's *World of Our Fathers*, clearly reveals the change in the Jewish radical sensibility. There is no sentimentality or nostalgia in Gold's portrait. Everything about the ghetto disgusted him. Not only did he exaggerate its social misery, but his Marxism prevented him from appreciating the difficult, but yet important and partially successful, struggle of traditional Jewish religious and cultural values to take root in America.

Modern portraits of the East Side and the European *shtetl*, however, are concerned less with condemning them than with recapturing their spirit and outlook. Some of this is an understandable quest for identity on the part of individuals for whom the East Side is, at best, a vague memory. The pithy formula of Marcus Lee Hansen, the historian of American immigration, that what the son wishes to forget the grandson wants to remember, explains some of the current interest in the early years of the East European Jewish settlement. This interest, however, involves something more than an understandable search for roots. The Lower East Side has become not merely a geographical location but also a standard by which to judge, evaluate, and censure modern American Jewry.

This is not the first time that the Lower East Side has been used in this way. At the turn of the century, many native Americans frequented the ghetto ("slumming" we might call it) in search of the excitement and local color which their own culture did not provide. The two most famous were Lincoln Steffens and Hutchins Hapgood who, according to Ronald Sanders, "saw in the life of the Russian Jews a cultural integrity and vitality" lacking in American culture. The modern view of the *shtetl* and the Lower East Side, as presented in *Fiddler on the Roof*, in Mark Zborowski and

Elizabeth Herzog's *Life Is With People*, and in the recently published volumes of photographs of *shtetl* and Lower East Side life is that of an anti-suburb.[3]

Suburbia is, after all, the habitat of the modern Jewish businessman who has "made it." For the modern Jewish intellectual, the memory of the ghetto is a welcome contrast to the ostentatious materialism, spiritual vacuity, and aimlessness which supposedly characterize modern Jewry. The Lower East Side is idealized because of its intellectual intensity, its socialist politics, its working class culture, and because the immigrant generation never completely surrendered to bourgeois values. It has been romanticized to show just how far America's Jews have moved away from the ideals of their immigrant ancestors and have been enveloped within the commercialism and materialism of modern America.[4]

One is struck, in viewing recent films about American Jewry, by their pervasive anti-business sentiments and by their exulting in the world of the ghetto. The ostentatious wedding and Bar Mizvah scenes in *Goodbye, Columbus* and *The Apprenticeship of Duddy Kravitz*, the wealthy but morally flawed uncle in *The Gambler*, and the corrupt businessmen in *Save The Tiger* reflect the distaste for successful Jewish businessmen. When Duddy asks his uncle why he never had time for him, the uncle answers, "Because you're a pusherke. A little Jewboy on the make. Guys like you make me sick and ashamed." Duddy is a caricature of the capitalist hustler.

This animus toward business is perhaps best brought out in the overly praised *Lies My Father Told Me*. The theme of the film is the struggle between the father and the grandfather for the mind of the young boy, David. Harry, the father, is pictured as the quintessential second-generation Jew fleeing from the world of his father-in-law, and especially from Orthodox Judaism. He is the extreme materialist who has made money and social mobility his gods. He is continually thinking up inventions, like expandable cuff links and creaseless pants, which will enable him to escape from the Montreal ghetto. He views his father-in-law's religion as "nonsense," saying to him, at one time, that "for you the world is still waiting for the Messiah." "Zaideh" makes his living by traveling through the narrow alleys of Montreal purchasing rags, clothes, and bottles. David often accompanies his grandfather on these journeys and they frequently discuss religion and the coming of the Messiah. Zaideh personifies the effort of traditional religious and cultural values to survive in the face of the corrosive impact of materialism and the dream of capitalistic success. The film, while sympathetic to the grandfather's world, reluctantly recognizes that the future belongs to the Harrys.

---

3. Ronald Sanders, *The Downtown Jews: Portraits of an Immigrant Generation* (New York: Harper and Row, 1969), p. 219.
4. Marshall Sklare, "The Sociology of Contemporary Jewish Studies," in Sklare, ed., *The Jew in American Society* (New York: Behrman House, 1974), pp. 19-25.

The film, *Hester Street*, also has as its major theme the conflict between the values of traditional Yiddishkeit and the attraction of materialistic America. The movie's central figure is Jake, whose major goal is to be accepted as a "real American fella." Though living in this country for only three years, Jake has been thoroughly Americanized. He has changed his name from Yekl to Jake, he wears a salon derby, he punctuates his conversation with words about the latest happenings in the world of sports, and he spends his evenings at Peltner's Dancing Academy in the company of the beautiful and Americanized Mamie. A cloud, however, comes into Jake's life, with the arrival from Europe of his wife, Gitl, with their son, Yossele. Although Jake does succeed in changing his son's name to Joey and cutting his earlocks, he is unable to do much with Gitl, who holds on tightly to the religious customs and superstitions which she acquired in Europe. Everything about her reminds Jake of his old life, especially the wig which she insists on wearing, despite his strenuous objections. Jake's embarrassment with Gitl soon turns to contempt and then loathing. He is also at odds with his boarder and fellow worker, the Talmudist, Bernstein. Jake teases Bernstein for studying the Talmud, and for being a "greenhorn." Bernstein, in turn, curses Columbus, and says that when a Jewish immigrant leaves for the United States he should cry out to God, "Goodbye, O Lord, I'm going to America." The film ends with Mamie and Jake going to city hall to be married, following Jake's divorce, and with Gitl and Bernstein making marriage plans of their own after Gitl will have fulfilled the waiting period required by Jewish law of a female divorcee. They talk of opening a grocery store which Gitl will operate while Bernstein continues studying Talmud.

Everything about *Hester Street* is designed to portray traditional Jewish immigrant life in as favorable a light as possible, but, to quote Stanley Kaufmann, it is "phony to the eye," since it fails to convey any sense of the poverty, filth, and deprivation of the Lower East Side. As a result, the viewer is unable to comprehend why Jake would choose the meretricious and Americanized Mamie over Gitl, nor is he able to understand, much less sympathize with, Jake's desire to escape the ghetto and become a "Yenkee."[5]

Another important recent attempt to portray immigrant Jewish culture prior to its seduction by materialism is Irving Howe's volume, *World of Our Fathers*. The book's jacket describes the work as an analysis of "the journey of the east European Jews to America and the life they found and made," a rather inaccurate account, since Howe's six hundred and fifty pages of text contain little, if anything, on the petty capitalist outlook of the immigrant generation. There is no mention of a David Sarnoff, but there are long accounts of the labor lawyer, Joseph Barondess, the

---

5. Stanley Kaufmann, "Stanley Kaufmann on Films," *New Republic*, CLXXIII (October 18, 1975): 21; Robert F. Horowitz, "Between a Heartache and a Laugh: Two Recent Films on Immigration," *Film and History*, VI (December, 1976): 75.

socialist politician, Meyer London, and the Yiddish literary critic, Shmuel Niger. According to Howe, the Jewish immigrants found and made a life revolving around Yiddish culture, socialist politics, and the Jewish labor movement. Certainly this is part of the truth, especially in New York City. But, along with this, there was the passion to flee from the ghettos, the hunger to climb the economic and social ladder, and the eagerness to seize the economic opportunities provided by America. Abraham Cahan, that sounding board of East Side life, reflected this immigrant ambivalence. Not only was he editor of the *Forward*, the most important American socialist newspaper, but he was also the author of *The Rise of David Levinsky*, the classic picture of the *parvenu* immigrant Jewish businessman.

American Jews, Howe claims, can look back to the immigrant world for "images of rectitude and purities of devotion." But devotion to what? For Howe, the essence of immigrant Jewish culture was

> a readiness to live for ideals beyond the clamor of self, a sense of plebeian fraternity, an ability to forge a community of moral order even while remaining subject to a society of social disorder, and a persuasion that human existence is a deeply serious matter for which all of us are finally accountable.

If this strikes Jews as a rather extravagant description of the motives of their parents and grandparents, it is because Howe is not writing about the average Jewish immigrant. *World of Our Fathers* is an elitist interpretation of the Lower East Side written by a Jewish intellectual who became a socialist at the age of fourteen and an editor of a socialist weekly when he was twenty-one. Most Jewish immigrants, I maintain, were not overly concerned with what Howe sees as the essence of the Yiddish cultural experience in America: "the messianic impulse of secular Judaism" and the discovery of "modes of conduct" in order to "establish a genuine community." The one overpowering goal for most immigrant Jews was, "My children shall not work in the shops."

Jews can take pleasure, Howe writes, "in having been related to those self-educated workers, those sustaining women, those almost-forgotten writers and speakers devoted to excitements of controversy and thought." Can't Jews also take pleasure in the businessmen and artisans whose enterprise and hard work enabled the immigrant generation to leave the ghettos, and can't Jews be grateful to the immigrant generation for passing on to their descendants middle-class virtues and ambitions which would stand them in good stead? *World of Our Fathers* is an elegy on the old East Side and, like all elegies, it abstracts from our memories those qualities of the deceased that it would most like to be remembered. A history of the world of our fathers, however, must make room for the Sammy Glicks and the David Levinskys as well as for the victims of the Triangle Shirtwaist fire and the pioneers of the Yiddish stage.

Howe's interpretation of the Lower East Side experience is infused with a wistfulness totally lacking in Gold's *Jews Without Money*. While Gold believed that a "garden for the human spirit" could emerge out of the destruction of the ghetto, Howe laments the rapid obliteration of the Yiddish cultural and socialist values occurring as a result of the dissolution of the old East Side. This difference should not, however, obscure Howe's basic agreement with Gold regarding the insignificance of the nonradical aspects of Jewish life on the East Side. A case in point is Howe's virtual ignoring of religion. There is no discussion of the growing and importance of Yeshiva University for the ghetto, nor is there any reference at all to the yeshivot of the Lower East Side, such as Moshe Feinstein's Mesivta Tifereth Jerusalem on East Broadway or the Rabbi Jacob Joseph Yeshiva on Henry Street. In addition to his slighting of religious traditionalism, Howe also passes over the Zionist activity of the ghetto. Indeed, it could be argued that *World of Our Fathers* focuses on the most transitory aspects of Jewish life on the East Side, while disregarding precisely those elements which, since they have been able to weather the migration to suburbia, have proven to be the most lastingly important.

There is something ironic, indeed, about the second and third generation who, safely ensconsed in suburbia, nostalgically yearn to recapture the intellectual intensity, the spirit of community, and even the radical politics which were supposedly the hallmarks of the immigrant ghettos. Seventy-five years ago German Jews in America questioned whether the Jewish immigrants from eastern Europe could make it economically and culturally. Now the descendants of the Russian immigrants question the value of their success and acculturation. The contrast between *Hester Street* and *Lies My Father Told Me*, and films of the 1920s that feature Jews, reveals the extent of this cultural alienation from contemporary America. Movies like *Bleeding Hearts*, *The Heart of the Jewess*, *Child of the Ghetto*, and *The Jazz Singer* associated the ghetto with poverty and ethnic parochialism, and stressed the benefits of assimilation and social mobility. Today, when many have become cynical about mainstream American culture, it is natural to sentimentalize the immigrants who were not yet affluent and had not moved to suburbia. Jews, in particular, have become what Dan Isaac has called "a mythic symbol for ethnic survival."[6]

American Jews will have to come to terms with their history if Jewish identity and cultural pluralism are to rest on more than mere sentimentality. Jews will have to recognize that their history encompasses Inland Steel as well as the I.L.G.W.U., Revlon as well as Delancey Street, and Federated Department Stores as well as Jacob Adler. American Jewish identity will have to rest, in part, on the recognition of American Jewry's persistent middle-class character and on the acknowledgement of the enormous benefit that America's Jews have derived from American capitalism.

6. Dan Isaac, "Some Questions About the Depiction of Jews in New Films," *New York Times*, September 8, 1974; David Weinberg, "The 'Socially Acceptable' Minority Group: The Image of the Jew in American Popular Films," *North Dakota Quarterly*, XL, (Autumn, 1972): 63-65.

## JEWISH LIBERALISM AND JEWISH SURVIVAL

For decades the relationship between liberalism and Jewish survival in America has been considered virtually axiomatic. Jews, it was argued, could be secure only in a society characterized by economic egalitarianism, social reform, and a high degree of tolerance for all forms of cultural and intellectual diversity. The belief that liberalism and Jewish welfare went hand in hand flowed ineluctably from the course of recent Jewish history. A group one or two generations removed from the sweatshops and slums of the Lower East Side and West Chicago naturally looked with favor on individuals and political movements claiming to favor the amelioration of the lot of the urban "masses" in their struggle for social justice. American Jews also had not so fond memories of the relationship between right-wing European governments and anti-Semitism. It was generally the parties of the left which supported the lifting of economic and social disabilities from the European Jews, although the price of Jewish emancipation and equality was often the renunciation of Jewish identity itself.

The belief that the enemies of the Jews were generally on the right lead to the almost automatic, although erroneous, description of the various forms of twentieth century fascism as "conservative" and "rightist". Furthermore, the Holocaust strengthened the conviction of American Jewish spokesmen that anti-Semitism usually resulted from economic and social maladjustments. Had the depression never occurred, so the argument went, Hitler would never had attracted a sizable following. The Holocaust also resulted in a deep sense of pessimism and insecurity among American Jewry for if Germany, the most scientifically and culturally advanced nation in Europe, could succumb to Nazism, what guarantee was there that the same thing could not occur in the United States. Jewish leaders were thus convinced that a liberal political agenda guaranteeing jobs, providing unemployment insurance, constructing public housing, and insuring favorable working conditions was the ultimate bulwark against the emergence of a social and economic environment in which demagogues flourished.

A recent document published by the National Jewish Community Relations Advisory Council entitled "Joint Program Plan for Jewish Community Relations, 1977-78" clearly reveals the extent to which the spokesmen for American Jewry are still committed to the economic and political panaceas of the 1930's and 1940's, despite the widespread evidence that many have been ineffective and counter-productive. Put out by over one hundred local, county, and state Jewish agencies in conjunction with the American Jewish Committee, the American Jewish Congress, the B'nai Brith, the Anti-Defamation League, the Jewish Labor Committee, the Jewish War Veterans, the National Council of Jewish Women, the Union of American Hebrew Congregations, the Union of Orthodox Jewish Congregations, and the United Synagogue, this statement of Jewish purposes has as its major goal the implementation of social changes which will ensure Jewish security and "make the society more conducive to creative Jewish living." "American Jewish life cannot grow, and gather vitality as it grows," the document contends, "unless the Jewish community involves itself in the struggle of the entire society for human decency and justice." In addition, "economic want and deprivation breed discontent, polarize group interests, foster discrimination, play into the hands of demagogues and prepare the soil for scapegoating and anti-Semitism. . . . The most effective assurance of Jewish security and of counteraction against anti-Semitism is the fostering of democratic institutional constraints and adherence to American traditions of equality and social justice." Admitting that most of its social and economic goals require federal action, the document proposes a whole host of reforms which, if enacted, would not only have a catastrophic impact on the economy but would also result in a vast enlargement of the federal bureaucracy. The statement would have us believe that Jewish security and wellbeing are dependent upon the enactment of the Humphrey-Hawkins Full Employment and Balanced Growth Act, an increase in the minimum wage, full federal funding of welfare benefits over the federally-defined poverty level, intensificaton of government efforts to create jobs, an increase in federal funding of public schools, the establishment of a universal and mandatory national health insurance program, the passage of the Equal Rights Amendment, and a drastic increase in the federal government's role in the housing industry. Finally, the document is encouraged by the 1976 elections which resulted in the White House and both houses of Congress being controlled by persons with "compatible social and economic commitments" and opened up the possibility "for early national governmental action directed toward solution or amelioration" of some of the nation's social problems. While the relationship between Jewish survival and Jewish values and the domestic proposals found in this statement are, at best, virtually impossible to discern (there is no mention in the document's forty-eight pages of the problem of intermarriage and only one brief paragraph on Jewish day schools), the relationship between the domestic proposals and the ideology of the liberal faction of the Democratic Party is direct and forthright. It is clear that the standards used by Jewish spokesmen on social issues are those of secular liberalism rather than those of traditional Judaism.

In addition to this strain of liberal collectivism within the ideology of American Jewish leaders, there is also an element of libertarian thought in their social and political outlook. The treatment of Jews by the political, social, economic, and religious authorities in Europe, as well as their exclusion from political decision-making in eastern Europe, has left a lasting impression on contemporary American Jewry. American Jews tend to view authority as alien and threatening, are sceptical regarding the claims of established leadership groups to exercise authority, and are sympathetic toward dissenters who challenge the legitimacy of consituted authority. This tendency to view authority and power as illegitimate and dangerous is reflected in the overrepresentation of Jews in organizations such as the American Civil Liberties Union and the Students for a Democratic Society. This remoteness from political power has also resulted in an unsophisticated understanding of politics marked by stereotypical dichotomies such as the masses versus the classes, the people versus the interests, and the workers versus the bosses.

Jews can thus, at one the same time, support liberal measures resulting in a vast increase in centralized power and also bemoan the threat posed to the rights of the individual by the encroachments of a political leviathan. Most Jewish spokesmen have failed to recognize this contradiction, preferring to believe that any threat posed by the state to civil liberties is due to the abuse of government power rather than its mere expansion. They manage to remain sceptical of government while identifying democracy with political centralization and longing for the economic and social benefits which would supposedly flow from economic planning.

Both the anarchistic and collectivist elements within American Jewish political thinking have made Jews extremely sensitive to any breaching of the wall of separation between church and state. They fear that governmental involvement in religion would increase arbitrary government power and threaten the sanctity of religion. Many also look askance at any effort to help religion because they believe established religions often are politically and socially reactionary. They realize that the only Jewish organizations dissenting from this rigorous interpretation of the separation of church and state are Orthodox, and they remember that in Europe Orthodoxy opposed the Haskalah, the Bund, and secular Zionism. Government aid to Judaism, which would largely be in the form of subsidies to Orthodox educational institutions, would thus benefit what are seen as the most obscurationist elements within American Jewry. Liberal Jews are also fearful that any government help to religion would strengthen Christianity, and the Church was, after all, the ally of some of the most retrogressive European social, economic, and intellectual movements.

The affirmation of the close relationship between liberalism and Jewish security not only ignores the many periods of Jewish history during which Jews prospered under conservative regimes, but it also totally misreads both the nature of the American Jewish experience and the major threat to American Jewish survival. Beginning in the seventeenth century and continuing to the present day, American Jewish identity has been menaced mainly by the attractiveness of an open society and not by the rabble-rousing of cranks and malcontents. For Jews, America has truly been a "golden land". It is revealing that two histories of America's Jews are entitled <u>Adventures in Freedom</u> and <u>Zion in America</u>. The major problem facing American Jews has always been to counter the forces of assimilation and acculturation. This conflict between Yiddishkeit and Americanization has been the central theme of the American Jewish novel beginning with Abraham Cahan's <u>The Rise of David Levinsky</u> and continuing to the works of Philip Roth. Its most explicit expression was in the first talking motion picture, "The Jazz Singer" starring Al Jolson. Some of American Jewry's finest thinkers, including Horace

Kallen and Mordecai Kaplan, have attempted to develop new forms and interpretations of Jewish identity appropriate for the United States. The first priority of American Jewish philanthropists should always have been to establish educational and cultural institutions which would have aided Jews to survive as Jews in an essentially benign society. Instead they created "defense" agencies and organizations to Americanize the immigrant.

It was inevitable that American Jewish leaders would fail to clearly recognize the threat posed to Jewish survival since the American situation was so unique. For the first time in centuries Jews were guaranteed nearly all the rights and opportunities of gentiles instead of being relegated to the role of pariahs. American Jewish leaders continually warned that "it could happen here" despite little evidence that this was, in fact, possible. They persisted in interpreting American Jewish history from the perspective of European history. While it is possible to write a lacrymose chronicle of European Jewry in terms of the rise and fall of anti-Semitism, such is not the case with American Jewry. The United States has never had any Jewish "problem", expulsions and pogroms were unknown, and the major threat to Jewish life has always been cultural assimilation and intermarriage.

This threat is not something to be lightly dismissed. A recent essay in the Jewish monthly Midstream notes that the lack of Jewish commitment in America is "approaching epidemic proportions". "If present trends are not arrested, or reversed," Elihu Bergman writes, "the American Jewish community faces extinction as a significant entity, and by its own hand, during the first half of the 21st century." The sole ray of hope that Bergman, who is the Assistant Director of the Harvard Center for Population Studies, can find is the day school. The Jewish parochial school, he argues, is "the only model capable of providing an effective educational experience within a realistic time span." Similarly, an article in the Wall Street Journal, a paper not generally given to histrionics, discussed "The Crisis in Jewish Identity". It quoted a statement by Rabbi Henry Siegman of the Synagogue Council of America to the effect that "there are massive forces of attrition and hemorrhaging occuring in the Jewish community", and concluded that American Jews could expect a twenty-five per cent reduction in their numbers during the next two and a half decades.

Lying at the core of Jewish secular liberalism is a reluctance to accept the realities of contemporary American Jewish life. In terms of economic and social success, intellectual preeminence, and political influence, American Jewry is today the most powerful and wealthiest Jewish community in the history of the diaspora. By every imaginable indicator, Jews are now part of the American establishment. It was perhaps the embarrassment many liberal Jews felt as a result of this fact that lead to the quest several years ago for the Jewish poor. It was reassuring to know that not all American Jews were among the "haves".

Despite the pockets of poverty still existing within American Jewry and which are largely concentrated among the elderly, there are perhaps no more important domestic tasks facing American Jewish leaders than recognizing that American Jews have made "it", and shaping a domestic social agenda responsive to the real problems facing American Jewry. Jewish organizations need to spend less time drawing up position papers on public housing, the plight of the grape and lettuce pickers of California, and high utility rates, and more time on the growing intermarriage rate, the sorry condition of Jewish education, and the impulses toward acculturation and assimilation, especially among Jews in college. The time is already late.

Jewish leaders must come to realize that their ideology of secular liberalism and their program of political liberalism have very little to do with what ails modern American Jewry. Not only is secular Jewish liberalism out of contact with the real needs of American Jews, but a major threat to Jewish survival emanates from the universalistic values which secularism and liberalism highly esteem. The fact that the major problem facing American Jewry is Judaizing the American Jew and not protecting him from a pogrom, unemployment, or inadequate housing demands a radical reordering of Jewish priorities.

## JEWISH SOCIALISM IN THE UNITED STATES

"By any simple interpretation of the Marxist formula, the United States, by all odds the greatest industrial nation and that in which capitalism is most advanced, should have had long ere this a very strong socialist movement if not a socialist revolution," Norman Thomas lamented in 1950. "Actually in no advanced western nation is organized socialism so weak." The question "Why Is There no Socialism in the United States?", asked by the German sociologist Werner Sombart in his 1906 book Warum gibt es in den Vereinigten Statten keinen Sozialismus?, has continually fascinated historians and sociologists interested in the seeming exemption of the United States from the economic and political patterns familiar to other advanced industrial nations. Marx and Engels, after all, expected the United States to be socialized before any other country.

The interpretations of American "exceptionalism" have fallen into two general categories. Leftists have argued that socialism would have prospered, and perhaps triumphed, were it not for the repressive acts of the defenders of the status quo and the co-opting of potential leaders of the working class by the capitalists. They point to the very large vote for Eugene Debs in 1912, the popularity of socialist literature during the Progressive Era, and the willingness of Americans prior to World War I to elect numerous socialists as mayors and state legislators as evidence of socialism's bright future. These prospects, however, were destroyed by the suppressing of dissident political voices during and immediately after World War I culminating in the Great Red Scare, the theft of the socialist program by such bourgeois reformers as Franklin Roosevelt and the LaFollettes of Wisconsin, and the desertion of their class by some of the proletariat's most promising potential leaders. Thus the failure of socialism, it has been argued, was not due to any intrinsic defects in its ideology or to any misreading of American society.

Most historians and sociologists, in contrast, have asserted that socialism's collapse was caused by a fundamental incompatibility between its message and goals and American social and political conditions. Sombart, for instance, contended that the American high standard of living refuted the socialist argument regarding the inefficiency and injustice of capitalism. "On the reefs of roast beef and apple pie," he wrote, "socialist utopias of every sort are sent to their doom". Another explanation of the failure of American socialism concerns the nation's supposedly fluid social structure. For the majority of Americans, Horatio Alger's gospel of success has more accurately described American society than Marx's growing misery of the proletariat. Believing they can rise above their social origins, Americans assume that their futures will be determined by their individual efforts and talents rather than by the class in which they were born. Americans see themselves as middle-class or, at least, potential members of the middle-class. Other explanations for the poverty of American socialism have stressed the nonideological character of American politics and its emphasis on patronage, personalities, and opportunism, the diverse ethnic, religious, and racial composition of the working class which has hindered proletariat solidarity, the high wages and good working conditions of American workers resulting from a shortage of labor, and the influence of the pragmatic and conservative Samuel Gompers in shaping the character of the American labor movement.

The dismal story of American socialism is particulary painful for the numerous Jews who have been influenced by the working-class, Yiddish-speaking, socialist culture of New York City. For them, socialism has been not merely a political and economic program. It has also been a way to be "Jewish" without being religious and, for some, Zionist. The collapse of the socialist dream has not only ended "the world of our fathers" as portrayed, for example, in Irving Howe's elegy on the secular radical culture of the immigrant generation. It has also forced Jewish radicals into reexamining their own Jewish identity as well as the relevance of socialism to an American Jewish community which seemingly prefers private pleasures to public concern, religiosity to intellectual passion, and economic achievement to political engagement.

The dilemmas of the contemporary American Jewish socialist are highlighted in Arthur Liebman's <u>Jews and the Left</u> (1979), a comprehensive and engrossing history of American Jewish socialism as well as an intensely personal testament to the relevance of political radicalism for contemporary Jews. Liebman, a sociologist at the State University of New York at

Binghamton, argues that American Jewish political radicalism was important during the first half of the Twentieth Century because it was part of a leftwing "subculture". Although the roots of this subculture can be traced back to the Pale of Settlement of eastern Europe, it was in America that there occurred the full flowering of the fraternal orders, labor unions, newspapers, schools and summer camps, and cooperative apartments of the Jewish left. The demise of this subculture, in turn, atrophied the Jewish socialist impulse.

Jewish radicalism in Russia emerged in the late Nineteenth Century because of the impact of what Liebman calls the "natural workings of the capitalist system" on Jewish life. Capitalism drove countless artisans and proprietors to the wall, forced Jews to leave the shtetls for the urban and industrial centers of Lodz, Warsaw, and Bialystok, and caused a "severe deterioration in living standards". Jewish workers now found themselves members of an exploited and impoverished class as well as part of an oppressed religious and ethnic minority. Those socialists who migrated to America encountered a seemingly propitious environment for the dissemination of radicalism. In contrast to Russia, there was no well-respected, anti-radical religious establishment competing for the loyalties of the masses. Although a majority of the first generation were not socialists, there were enough of them to create a viable and legitimate radical subculture, particularly in New York City.

Liebman lists seven reasons for the virtual disappearance of this subculture. The first was the opposition of the rabbinate and the immigrant middle-class to socialism. While the power of the rabbis and bourgeois was weak at first, their numbers and conviction increased rapidly after World War I. Secondly, American social conditions were not conducive to the maintenance of radical loyalties. If the Jewish Left emerged in Russia because of poverty, economic and ethnic exploitation, and compacted living conditions, the Jewish Left in America diminished because of Jewish social and economic mobility, the absence of virulent and official anti-Semitism, and the movement of Jews out of all-Jewish areas of first settlement. A third factor was the waning influence of Yiddish culture. Proletarian solidarity and Yiddish culture had had a symbiotic relationship. The Jewish working class was Yiddish-speaking, and the gradual fading away of the Yiddish-speaking first generation hastened the acculturation of Jews and their integration into the mainstream of American politics. Fourthly, immigrant Jews were mostly employed in the garment trades and petty commerce. Due to the small size of the firms in these fields and their minimum capital requirements, they provided countless opportunities for leaving the working class and becoming a "boss". Jews avidly seized such openings because, despite their seeming workingclass outlook, they were the most bourgeois, entrepreneurial, and capitalist-oriented ethnic group in American history. The very success of the radical subculture in improving the lives of its members was a fifth reason for its demise. Thus the Jewish immigrant press, particularly the <u>Daily Forward</u>, by accelerating the Americanization of the immigrant, diminished the number of Jews looking to the socialist press for political inspiration. Jewish labor unions, by significantly improving the working conditions of its members, demonstrated that capitalism was not the ogre found in socialist tracts. The burial and old-age benefits provided by Jewish benevolent organizations alleviated much of the insecurity associated with an industrial economy, thereby decreasing the hostility felt toward capitalism. In addition, some of the subculture's organizations pursued reformist rather than revolutionary goals. Labor leaders, faced with choosing between working within the system and achieving immediate gains for their people or remaining true to the socialist objective of overthrowing capitalism, generally opted for the former. In this way socialist unions became committed to the status quo and accustomed to working with their supposed class enemies. In time, leaders of these organizations would become more concerned with their survival and their own positions in them than with achieving the goals for which they were originally established.

Sixthly, Jewish socialists were increasingly challenged by leaders of other Jewish movements. Zionism, for instance, became popular among Americans Jews, and socialists were forced to modify their anti-Zionism in order to maintain their influence. Faced with the necessity of being good Jews or good socialists, Jewish socialists generally chose to be good Jews, a tendency intensified by the diminishing size of the natural socialist constituency -- the poor, the immigrants, and the Yiddish-speaking.

Identifying with the American Jewish community, socialists found themselves working closely with rabbis, wealthy businessmen, and other establishment figures. This Judaizing of the socialists was encouraged by the seventh reason -- the growing hostility between socialism and Jewish interests. The anti-Semitism of the Bolsheviks, the hostility of the New Left to Jewish interests, and the sympathy of most "socialist" nations for the Palestine Liberation Organization demonstrated that not all enemies of the Jews were to the right.

Jews and the Left is not merely a long and detailed history of the rise and decline of the American Jewish radical subculture. After reading nearly six hundred pages describing the bankruptcy of American Jewish socialism, the reader encounters the author's incongruous concluding chapter which argues that there will be a revival of socialism among Jews in the near future. It is this prognosis which lead the historian Bernard K. Johnpoll to describe Liebman's book as a "potpourri of simplistic Marxian prophecies with virtually no historical basis." Liebman's claim that the "Jewish community's harsh confrontation with capitalism will result in a renewed Jewish commitment to socialism" is based on the following assumptions: (1) the Jewish position in small and medium-sized businesses is being eroded by the growing power of the giant corporations; (2) this decline in Jewish-controlled businesses will lead to a shrinkage in the income and numbers of Jewish professionals such as lawyers, accountants, and actuaries who have been dependent upon such businesses in the past. With monopoly capitalism undermining the economic position of Jewish businessmen and professionals, the "contours and social physiognomy of the American Jewish community will come to resemble . . . in some (slc!) that of the Russian Jewish community in late nineteenth and early twentieth century czarist Russia." Jews will come to realize once more that "their interests as Jews, downwardly mobile persons, as members of an exploited working class, and as an impoverished, or early impoverished, strata of petty traders and merchants are antithetical to the powerful American bourgeoisie." Jews will then become part of "an ethnically heterogenous socialist movement capable of converting the United States into a humane, democratic socialist society."

All of this is, of course, sheer nonsense. How is one to account for the sharp contrast between the sober historical analysis of Jews and the Left and the rhetorical flight of fancy found in its last chapter? Certainly the author can not expect his readers to take him seriously. At a time when Jews are heading up some of the country's most prominent universities, when Jews are ascending to the very pinnacle of American corporate power, when the barriers against Jews in the most important law firms are disappearing, and when a record number of Jews sit in the United States Senate, Jews and the Left anticipates that "socialism will be on the future agenda of the American-Jewish community." Actually as the Australian W. D. Rubinstein recently pointed out in Midstream magazine, "the world's Jews share disproportionately in the bounties of capitalism and will . . . stand or fall with the fortunes of the Western capitalist democracies."

Liebman's belief in an American Jewish socialist future is a product of something akin to religious faith. It is not faith in God but faith in a political ideology which has proven itself seriously flawed every time it has been put into practice. Nowhere in Jews and the Left is there any acknowledgement of the fact that Jews (and other Americans) might have turned from socialism in part because of the widespread evidence that it is unworkable. Rather than being berated for deserting socialism for the fleshpots of capitalism, Jews should be praised for recognizing their true interests.

Liebman's attempt to reverse the divorce of socialism and the Jews stems from his simultaneous commitment to Jewish identity and socialist theology. While thirty-five years ago the term "Jewish radical" was a legitimate form of American and European Jewish identification, today it has become an oxymoron. The first ninety-five per cent of Jews and the Left convincingly shows why this has taken place.

# THE GOLDEN DOOR

*The Golden Door: Italian and Jewish Immigrant Mobility In New York City, 1880-1915*, by Thomas Kessner. New York: Oxford University Press, 1977.

The Golden Door reflects several recent trends in American historical writing. The first is the attempt to democratize history by focusing on the "inarticulate" and the "grassroots." Secondly, there is the emphasis on urban demography, especially on rates and trends of social mobility, through the collection of quantitative data and the analysis of this data by the use of computers. Finally, there is the growing interest in immigration and ethnic studies, particularly in comparing ethnic and racial differences regarding spatial and social mobility. While Omaha, Newburyport, Poughkeepsie, Birmingham, Atlanta, and other smaller cities have been closely studied, The Golden Door is, I believe, the first analysis to investigate carefully exactly what happened, in social and economic terms, to the hundreds of thousands of impoverished Italian and Jewish immigrants who settled in New York at the turn of the century.

Kessner's book confirms much of what we already knew or suspected about the Italians and the Jews. It is no surprise to read that the rate of expatriation was higher among Italians than Jews, that Jews were more oriented toward business and long-range planning, that Jews tended to migrate as families while the Italian migration consisted primarily of males in the wage-earning years, that Jews came to the United States generally with more skills and with greater business experience than the Italians, that Jews tended to find employment in business and the artisan trades, especially in the garment industries, while the Italians went into unskilled labor in the construction and longshoreman areas, and that there were significant occupational and economic differences among second-generation Jews and Italians. Similiary unstartling are Kessner's findings regarding the differences between the occupational structure of Jewish and Italian women, the greater tendency of Italian children to drop out of school at an early age, and the more intense pressures put on Jewish youth to succeed.

The most important part of The Golden Door discusses the rate of social mobility for the two immigrant groups. While the rapid economic and occupational mobility of the East European Jew has become a staple of American sociology, it is too little recognized that other groups from eastern and southern Europe have also experienced significant social and economic mobility. Kessner argues that New York was truly the "golden door" for Italians as well as Jews. The city, Kessner writes, "offered exceptional possibilities for progress out of the manual classes." "Clearly the statue standing in New York harbor," he contends, "shined her symbolic torch for the poor as well as the rich and well born." One of Kessner's more interesting statistics in behalf of his argument that New York's Italians and Jews progressed rapidly is that an Italian immigrant who lived in New York for ten years had a 32% chance of moving from a blue-collar to a white-collar position (the corresponding figure for Jews was 41%).

The Golden Door is a welcome relief to the bleak portrait of American social history which dominated much of American historiography during the 1960's and early 1970's. The acculturation, integration, and economic and social mobility of European immigrants is one of the great success stories of twentieth century America, and Professor Kessner has performed a real service in showing just how unfounded are the lamentations of the Michael Novaks. The Golden Door is also valuable for pointing out the real hopes and fears of the Jews who settled on the Lower East Side. They were not primarily driven by any desire to create a Yiddish moral community or a socialist commonwealth as Irving Howe's World of Our Fathers would have us believe. The demon which haunted the minds of the Jewish immigrants was economic insecurity, and economic success, more than anything else, was their driving ambition. The Jewish businessman was far more representative of the world of our fathers than the socialist ideologue or the Yiddish poet.

The most important fact about the Jewish Lower East Side is that it has virtually disappeared, destroyed by the aspirations of the immigrants and the opportunities offered by an open and burgeoning commercial and industrial urban economy so ably analyzed by Professor Kessner. Our dismay at the sterility and blandness of so much of Jewish suburbia should not blind us to the very real economic achievements of our parents and grandparents. The price of "making it" was indeed great, as Abraham Cahan's protagonist David Levinsky reminded us over half a century ago, but who can deny the success, and who would favor reclaiming the Lower East Side?

**City College and the Jewish Poor: Education in New York, 1880-1924.** By Sherry Gorelick. New Brunswick: Rutgers University Press, 1981. xii + 269 pp. illustrations. $14.95.

The City College of New York has a place in American Jewish hagiography similar to that of Eton and Harrow in England. The fervent commitment to social justice, the intense political involvement, the heightened intellectuality, and the upward social and economic mobility which have characterized American Jewry were, we have been lead to believe, partially developed in the cafeteria, the library, and the classrooms of the "Jewish Harvard." Recently, however, this argument has been questioned, most notably by Selma Berrol. Now Sherry Gorelick, a Marxist sociologist currently teaching at Rutgers University, has launched a frontal assault on what she terms the "mobility miracle."

Professor Gorelick reminds us that, prior to the Thirties, very few of New York's Jews actually attended City College, and most of these failed to graduate. In 1913, for example, at a time when the Jewish population of New York City was well over a million, the graduating class of CCNY numbered only 209 while that of Hunter College was 240. For the vast majority of Jews from eastern Europe, college was more a matter of mythology than experience. Education was deeply respected within the Jewish community, but it was business and not the university which offered social and economic advancement for most Jews.

The major objective of *City College and the Jewish Poor*, however, is not to examine closely whatever limited impact City College might have had on the city's poor Jews between 1880 and 1924. Rather, most of the volume discusses the college's founding in the mid-nineteenth century, its expansion a half century later, the values permeating the institution, and its curriculum. This enables Gorelick to place CCNY within a Marxist historiographical and sociological framework. She argues that the college's development was part of the national growth of higher education which sought to provide the capitalists with trained and willing employees, to offer a mode of social improvement rivaling that of socialism and the labor unions, and to assimilate the working class into American capitalism.

City College's curriculum, Gorelick argues, was pro-capitalist, racist, and elitist. Courses were offered on business administration but not on union organization, on capitalism but not on socialism, and on English literature but not on Yiddish culture. CCNY's education thus "violated the realities of Jewish workers and ghetto life.

It ignored the vibrant Yiddish socialist culture that was flowering among poets, journalists, artists, and workers at the turn of the century. Jewish students subjected themselves to a world of business assumptions and Anglo-Saxon dominance (134)." CCNY resembled a gigantic social settlement determined to civilize the Jewish young by weaning them away from socialism and from Orthodox Judaism.

The author believes higher education should have stressed working class solidarity, the radical restructuring of the economic and social order, and the liberation of the working class. Not only does she lambast City College for being a reactionary institution in preaching to the Jewish poor the capitalist definition of success, she also questions the very idea of individual social mobility through education, since this separated Jews from their families, culture, history, and especially their class. By being educated along the CCNY pattern, Jews entered a Christian, racist, and conservative culture, and found employment in social welfare and educational bureaucracies which hoped to reform the immigrants rather than to improve their condition.

Gorelick believes this history repeated itself in the 1960's. During that turbulent decade, educational opportunities were enlarged and more social services provided in order to control the disaffected, to furnish business with a better trained labor force, and to offer opportunities for the talented to rise out of the proletariat. *City College and the Jewish Poor* ends with a dedication "to all those who have struggled and who struggle now, at City University and elsewhere, for 'a democratic and free system of higher education for the working masses' – a liberating education (196)." Ironically, Gorelick also professes gratitude to the taxpayers of the city and state of New York for providing most of her elementary, secondary, and college education.

*City College and the Jewish Poor* is thus more of a political tract than a sustained historical or sociological examination of the relationship between CCNY and New York Jewry. This is surprising since the volume originated as a doctoral dissertation at Columbia University. The book is replete with dubious historical statements which accentuate its ideological thrust. A few examples: "Sacco and Vanzetti were murdered by the state for being Italian anarchists (42)." "For the first half century . . . mobility was modest, and affected only a small proportion of Russian Jews (113)." "For the first fifty years, the vast majority of Jewish immigrants remained proletarians. So did a large proportion of their children (114)." This novel approach to American Jewish history evidences little awareness of the most recent findings in American immigration history and American Jewish history regarding rates of social mobility, acculturation patterns, and immigrant educational and social values. Nor is it characterized by the prolonged immersion in primary sources of Thomas Kessner's important volume *The Golden Door: Italian and Jewish Immigrant Mobility in New York City, 1880-1925* (1977), which I reviewed in these pages. Furthermore, *City College and the Jewish Poor* is permeated with a Marxist jargon and an emphasis on conspiracy which most historians will find objectionable.

Lurking behind the scenes, Gorelick asserts, are the ubiquitous capitalists continually conspiring to deprive the working class of the fruits of their labor. Why, for example, did the immigrants from southern and eastern Europe come to America? Because they were recruited by capitalists: "Employers sought to frighten each wave of new workers into sobriety and obedience by importing fresh waves of immigrants (53)." Immigrants are thus transformed into intellectual abstractions, members of an equally abstract "proletariat" which is being continually oppressed by another abstraction, the "capitalists."

Actually immigrants came to the United States because they believed relocation would improve their lives and the lives of their families. And they encouraged their relatives to join them because they concluded that migration, despite all its difficulties, had been the right choice. For Professor Gorelick, the opportunities the immigrants found in America were sparse and meaningless. Those who experienced economic and social mobility through education were actually being victimized by "co-optation." The immigrants knew better. They accumulated capital, took advantage of the schools, including City College, and opened businesses because American opportunities were palpable. Professor Gorelick should know this. Her own life is proof that the economic and social improvements in the lives of the immigrants and their children were hardly insignificant. But to recognize this would require her to see the world from the perspective of a second generation American Jewish academician from a working class family, rather than through the eyes of a radical ideologue.

## THE WAR AMONG THE JEWS

In the spring of 1981 Jacobo Timerman published *Prisoner Without a Name, Cell Without a Number*, a harrowing description of his imprisonment and house arrest by Argentinian military authorities from April, 1977 through September, 1979. Timerman, a prominent Argentinian journalist, recounted in graphic detail the agonies of his confinement, stressing throughout the anti-Semitism permeating the Argentinian military dictatorship, the harsh treatment meted out to him because of the Jewish background, and the pusillanimous attitude of the Jewish leadership of Argentina. *Prisoner Without a Name* also sketched Timerman's biography and his involvement in Jewish affairs. From an early age he had been involved in left-wing Zionist activities, although he had never played any role in the established Jewish community of Argentina. His Jewish identity centered on leftist politics. Proclaiming himself "passionately Jewish," Timerman noted that, "my Judaism was a political act."[1]

*Prisoner Without a Name* created a storm of controversy. Those sympathetic to Timerman used his memoir to indict the Argentinian regime, and to attack the attempts of the Reagan administration to forge better relations with Buenos Aires and to modify the "human rights" theme which had played such a prominent role in the diplomacy of the Carter government. Timerman even appeared as a silent witness at the Senate Foreign Relations Committee hearings to protest the nomination of Ernest Lefever as Assistant Secretary of State for Human Rights and Humanitarian Affairs. Timerman became an instant celebrity, appearing on the Bill Moyers television show, while his book received a front-page review by Anthony Lewis in the *New York Times Book Review*. After his release and deportation from Argentina, Timerman settled in Israel. He soon became a vocal critic of the Begin government's policies regarding the Palestinian issue. "I see that this country is going to totalitarianism and fanaticism. . . . I see very clearly a repitition of what happened in Argentina here," he claimed. In future elections "if there is a good general as a candidate, he will win. There is always a democratic way to elect a fascist government."[2]

Timerman had injected himself into the fervent debate on the Reagan administration's policies regarding violations of human rights by governments sympathetic to the United States. The rationale for these policies had been laid down by Jeanne Kirkpatrick in her famous article "Dictatorships and Double Standards" which had caught the future president's attention when it appeared in <u>Commentary</u> in November, 1979. The essay was prompted by what Kirkpatrick saw as American complicity in the overthrow of the Shah in Iran and the Somoza regime in Nicaragua. She argued that the Carter administration had cooperated in replacing pro-American, moderate autocrats with anti-American revolutionary governments. The United States, she contended, cannot impose democracy and liberalism on governments fighting for their very existence. Any such attempts will merely hasten the coming to power of new regimes which will deprive their people of their remaining rights. Furthermore, it is unrealistic to expect democratic governments in most of the world. Kirkpatrick also maintained that a right-wing autocracy is far more likely to evolve into a liberal regime than a revolutionary government. In addition, right-wing governments are generally more sympathetic to the United States than revolutionary ones. She believed the Carter administration's failures in foreign policy were due in part to a "lack of realism about the nature of traditional versus revolutionary autocracies and the relation of each to the American national interest." Kirkpatrick had provided Reagan with the rationale for changing American policies toward right-wing, pro-American regimes such as those in South Korea, Chile, Taiwan, and Argentina. Kirkpatrick would soon be called upon to defend the new American stance regarding violations of human rights as the Reagan administration's ambassador to the United Nations. One of the things the Reagan government was particularly interested in overturning was the embargo on the shipment of arms to Argentina which had been imposed during the Carter years. Timerman, naturally, vigorously dissented from the American government's new attitude toward Buenos Aires, describing Kirkpatrick, Reagan and Secretary of State Haig as authoritarian, oblivious to the issue of human rights, and monomaniacal regarding communism.[3]

One aspect of the Timerman controversy overlooked by the general public was that Timerman and his book had become matters of serious debate among American

Jews. This debate reflected not only the extreme sensitivity among Jews regarding anything that evoked memories of the Holocaust, but it also highlighted the rightward drift of many American Jewish intellectuals who, it may safely be assumed, are both reflecting and shaping the transformation of American Jewish political and social attitudes. The Jewish response to Timerman probably tells us more about the metamorphosis of the American Jewish community than the status of Argentina's four hundred thousand Jews.

For decades the liberalism of American Jews has been viewed as one of the unchangeables of American politics, having withstood rapid Jewish economic and cultural mobility, the breakdown of the political coalition forged by Franklin Roosevelt in the 1930s, and the intellectual bankruptcy of modern liberalism. Of all ethnic groups, none seemed to ignore with such consistency their economic self-interest as the Jews, and none seemed to be so wedded to the liberal wing of the Democratic Party. "Jews," the radical sociologist Irving Louis Horowitz once wrote, "have proven to be a unique force in American politics in that, despite their class backgrounds or interests, they have exhibited the capacity to vote and act beyond their class and interest group constraints." Jews have been described as having the economic and social profile of Episcopalians and the political profile of Puerto Ricans. Certainly it is no coincidence that New York City is both home to the largest single concentration of Jews in the world and the most liberal city in the nation (and where, it might be added, the results of modern liberalism, including rent control, powerful labor unions, and a bloated civil service bureaucracy, can be most clearly discerned).[4]

Political scientists do not debate the fact of Jewish leftism. Rather, their efforts have focused on exploring the reasons for its existence. Lawrence H. Fuchs argued in his The Political Behavior of American Jews that it could be traced back to the biblical prophets' emphasis on charity and justice for the poor and homeless. Unfortunately Fuchs' thesis foundered on the fact that those Jews who presumably would have been most affected by biblical teachings have been the most reluctant to involve themselves in the causes which have regularly inflamed the imaginations of the American left. The bearded Jews of Brooklyn have not taken part in peace demonstrations, marched in behalf of civil rights, or supported the women's movement.

Conversely, the American Jewish Left has been lead by individuals who, more often than not, were estranged from their ancestral faith, ignorant about Jewish issues and literature, and prone to see in secular liberalism a surrogate religion. Indeed, for many Jews on the left their strongest ties to Judaism and other Jews has been the continuing commitment of organized Jewry to the liberal agenda. They have identified themselves as Jews because to be a Jew meant to be a liberal.

One must instead look to the historical situation Jews found themselves in Europe and the United States during the late nineteenth and twentieth centuries for an explanation of Jewish liberalism. Prior to this period the Jewish political ethic in Europe was relatively passive. Jews feared the state and were detached from political involvement. The Jewish population of eastern Europe, however, beginning in the latter half of the ninteenth century underwent critical economic, social, and intellectual changes. The emergence of the Haskalah (the Jewish enlightenment) undermined the authority of traditional religious leadership and ideas. Orthodox Judaism was challenged by a host of competing ideologies, including secular Zionism, socialist Zionism, socialism, diaspora nationalism, anarchism, and cultural assimilation.

Rapid urbanization and industrialization transformed the overwhelmingly petty bourgeois Jewish population, creating in the process a large and growing industrial working class, particularly in the needles trades. Industrialization has usually improved the conditions of the proletariat. The most poverty-stricken regions of the world today are those in which industrialization has had the least impact. Social and political attitudes, however, are due less to objective factors than to the subjective perceptions of those affected by social and economic developments. By and large the Jews of Russia and the Austro-Hungary Empire, or at least their leading spokesmen, viewed industrialization as a curse, and directed their rage at the supposed sources of their fall in economic and social status--the owning class. Migrating from small towns to burgeoning industrial centers such as Lodz and Minsk, finding employment in dark and unhealthy factories and lofts, and working long hours for what they perceived to be grossly inadequate wages, Jewish workers, students, and intellectuals found convincing the siren call of ideologues arguing that the plight of the Jews (and the rest of mankind) could be resolved only by radical changes in capitalism.

Jewish leftism was also spurred by the increase of anti-Semitism in eastern Europe, particularly within Russia. The socialist emphasis on worker solidarity and class conflict seemed to be immune to the virus of anti-Semitism. In contrast, Judeophobia was most frequently found among the supporters of the economic system and the Czarist regime. Proponents of the status quo in Russia favored a regime which had encouraged forced expulsions, economic and educational quotas, and periodic pogroms. One could have as readily expected the Jews of Russia to be conservatives as one could have expected the blacks of Mississippi during the 1950s to be allies of segregation and discrimination.

This tendency to look to socialist panaceas to rectify the seeming social and economic decline of eastern European Jewry was combined with a deep distrust of authority. Established political and social authority was viewed as hostile to Jewish interests. One recalls the response of the rabbi in "Fiddler on the Roof" after being asked to say a prayer for the Czar. Momentarily taken aback, he cried out: "O God please keep the Czar -- far away from us." Jews were thus sceptical regarding the claims of established leadership groups to exercise authority and sympathetic to dissenters challenging the legitimacy of constituted authority. Ironically Jews have distrusted authority while favoring economic planning and egalitarian economic and social programs which would increase political centralization. Today American Jews are avid supporters of the American Civil Liberties Union, are quick to attack governmental officials if they overstep their bounds, particularly if they are police officers, and often give the benefit of the doubt to the powerless in any conflict with government. At the same time, they vote for liberal Democrats and believe that politics is an arena for the achievement of abstract objectives rather than an opportunity for personal advancement.

The experiences of the first and second generation American Jews reinforced this leftist political outlook. Living in crowded ghettos, working long hours for low wages, and suffering from periodic unemployment, Jews in New York, Philadelphia, Chicago, and Boston at election time stressed the deficiencies rather than the opportunities of American capitalism. The Lower East Side of New York City was a hotbed of socialism prior to 1920, even electing a socialist to Congress. American conditions dissipated most of this support for socialism. What remained was a kneejerk liberalism which flocked to the banner of Franklin Roosevelt in the 1930s and has continued to support the liberal wing of the Democratic Party. Jews, it was said, had three "velten" (worlds): "die velt" (this world); "yene velt" (the future world); and Roosevelt."

Events in Europe strengthened this commitment to liberalism. Jews had traditionally identified anti-Semitism with right-wing governments, and thus they interpreted Nazism as a reactionary movement. They failed to adequately note that the Nazi party professed national "socialism". Furthermore, they attributed the rise of Hitler to the social dislocations and economic misery resulting from the great depression. Liberal reforms which would alleviate social discontent by providing good housing, jobs, unemployment insurance, free health care, and subsidized educational benefits were viewed as barriers against the emergence of anti-semitic demagogues. Hence by the outbreak of World War II Jews in America assumed that liberalism and Jewish welfare went hand-in-hand. A Jewish conservative verged on being a political exotic, if not an oxymoron.

Recently, however, a growing number of Jews have turned rightward, including some of America's most prominent conservative and neo-conservative intellectuals. In April, 1973 Irving Kristol, one of the gurus of the neo-conservatives, declared in <u>Congress Bi-Weekly</u> that the alliance between the Left and the Jews had ended. "This is not a temporary phenomenon. Jewish politics in the decades to come are going to be very different from what Jewish politics have been in the past century and a half." This has been lamented by that small clique of Jewish socialists associated with <u>Dissent</u> magazine.[5]

In the mid-1970s Bernard Rosenberg and Irving Howe published an essay on "Are American Jews Turning to the Right?" They noted that this question had become a matter of great concern since "the overwhelming thrust of Jewish thought and writing in America these past several decades has been liberal, notably more so than in the population at large; and whatever radicalism we have had in America has found disproportionate support among Jews." Although sceptical that the Jewish commitment to the left had been shattered, Rosenberg and Howe pointed to Norman Podhoretz's Commentary magazine, published by the American Jewish Committee, as evidence of a rightward shift among some Jewish intellectuals. They did not believe Commentary was as yet a conservative magazine, preferring to believe that it remained a liberal journal although opposed to the "vulgarizations of liberalism". Commentary's drift to the right, they argued, was symptomatic of a growing Jewish disillusionment with some of the more outlandish aspects of the liberalism of the 1960s, but it would require more than mere disillusionment for a Jewish conservatism to appear. It would demand a positive and coherent ideology.[6]

Howe and Rosenberg admitted there were certain factors with the potential for fostering a Jewish conservatism. These included upward economic mobility, the decline of the Jewish labor movement, cultural assimilation, fear of black anti-Semitism, a greater concern for ethnic survival, and worry for the security of Israel. They surmised that Jewish political attitudes would in the future exhibit a greater emphasis on class and group interests. We are witnessing, Rosenberg and Howe wrote, "a regrouping of forces and ideas within the Jewish world that will bring into existence a stronger conservative wing, which will in time enable the emergence of a conservative Jewish intelligentsia. . . . Certainly, we are witnessing a regrouping of forces within the Jewish world, which will result in a conservatizing of its dominant liberalism." And yet they believed that liberalism had a fighting chance to retain its hold within the Jewish community. This would occur only if the majority of Jews remained faithful to Jewish values of moral compassion and social commitment.[7]

Podhoretz confronted his socialist critics in 1979 when he published Breaking Ranks, his memoir of the intellectual wars of the 1960s. Here he admitted to being a "neo-conservative" and described the socialism of Irving Howe's Dissent as having "no discernible content" and resembling a religious faith. Only the fact that socialism had become a surrogate religion impervious to the realities of contemporary life explained Howe's curious commitment to it. The less socialist content there remained in Howe's thinking, "the more desperate he was to affirm his socialist faith. And since there was so little of a positive nature left to affirm, what he mainly did was to attack other intellectuals for deserting the true faith." Podhoretz also attributed a darker side to Howe's attacks on Commentary. Howe needed to maintain his credentials with the American Left despite the fact that he had ceased being a socialist or even a radical. His personal position depended, Podhoretz wrote, on maintaining his role as a spokesman for socialism. This could be most easily achieved by criticizing Commentary, the most prominent opponent of liberal and socialist pieties.[8]

Dissent's response to Breaking Ranks was not long in coming. The spring, 1981 issue contained a long "special feature" by Bernard Avishai entitled "Breaking Faith: Commentary and the American Jews." Ironically Avishai's title and his twenty pages of turgid prose confirmed Podhoretz's argument that Dissent's socialism had degenerated into a surrogate secularist religion. Avishai contrasted the self-satisfied conservatism of Commentary with the Jewish Daily Forward, the radical labor movement, and the "heroes, sensibilities, moral taste, the civil religion to which we try to make converts" (Avishai's emphasis). Not only had Commentary deserted Jewish interests but it had also rejected both its previous commitment to "social action" as a Jewish "vocation", and its opposition to military adventurism and evangelical anticommunism. Commentary had, in its golden years, believed Jews "belonged with the utilitarians, the socialists and democrats; with people who took the emerging social good and not the individual's sensuous pleasure as the preeminent moral problem."

Avishai attributed Commentary's initial fall from a state of grace to the Six-Day War of 1967. This injected into the magazine a Jewish jingoism which destroyed the intellectual detachment and commitment to radicalism which had been responsible for the magazine's creativity during the early 1960s. Podhoretz had thus broken ranks "with those people who were holding to the radically democratic view of politics with which Commentary had justifiably tried to identify American Jews for a decade". Unfortunately Commentary had become a house organ for the Jewish establishment and a spokesman for its crassest interests. This was accompanied by a "narrow and reckless style of argument" and a mean-spirited attitude toward social reform in general and affirmative action in particular. Commentary, Avishai wrote in prose characteristic of the true believer contemplating the apostate, had been "wrong in the most discreditable way, violating common standards of fairness." It was the responsibility of thinking Jews to "respond in public and repudiate the politics that the magazine claims to be pursuing for our 'own good.'"

Avishai even doubted that Commentary's renowned support for Israel was good for the Jews. By focusing on the strategic value of Israel to America, the journal had weakened the support for the Jewish state among her most reliable allies--"liberal politicians, progressive journalists, labor leaders". They supported Israel because it was democratic and socialist, not because of Israel's importance as a cold-war ally of America. Commentary had thus helped discredit Israel on college campuses, in the liberal press, and wherever there is a well-educated "progressive constituency" opposed to the escalation of the Cold War. Avishai concluded his troglodytic diatribe by accusing Commentary of contributing to "wide-scale disillusionment with democratic humanism", to the growth of the New Right and Christian fundamentalism, and to a decline in federal funding of Jewish philanthropic institutions. Only a return to "the urbane, communitarian values of the left", the same values which were espoused by Podhoretz before turning nasty and which were the authentically American Jewish values, could guarantee the continuing social and intellectual relevance of American Jewry.[9]

As if to answer Avishai's accusation that it did not speak for Jewish interests and values, Commentary published an essay in its December, 1981 issue by Murray Friedman espousing "A New Direction for American Jews." Friedman, the Middle Atlantic Director of the American Jewish Committee, had originally presented his arguments before the annual meeting of the Association of Jewish Community Relations Workers. He called for a radical change in the activities and goals of Jewish community relations organizations such as the American Jewish Congress, the American Jewish Committee, and the Anti-Defamation League of B'nai Brith. Since the New Deal, Friedman noted, Jewish community relations personnel have supported legislation and judicial decisions strengthening civil rights for minorities, a strict secularist interpretation of church-state relations, and the expansion of federal social welfare programs. Possessing a "liberal-left perspective," these professionals believed that the fate of liberalism and Jews were inextricably bound together. Friedman, in contrast, contended that this was out-of-date, and that there was an urgent need for a reshaping of their mission.

Among the factors requiring a change in direction were widespread dismay regarding the growth of government, taxes, and the dependent class, growing concern for the moral fiber of the nation, and fears that America's position in world affairs had been enormously weakened. Friedman also stressed evidence of anti-Semitism and anti-Zionism among radicals and even some liberals, and the increasing use of quotas in employment and education. Friedman hoped Jewish professionals would come to recognize that many aspects of the welfare state were counter-productive, that their previous scepticism regarding the free market had been wrong, that increased expenditures for national defense were mandatory, and that their concern for the separation of church and state should not blind them to the clergy's legitimate fears concerning crime, pornography, abortion on demand, and drugs. The Jewish community, Friedman contended, was threatened far more by the "breakdown of the orderly norms of our society" than by minor breaches in the wall of separation. He was particularly disturbed by the opposition of Jewish spokesmen to tuition tax credits and vouchers for parents electing to send their children to nonpublic schools. In concluding his call for a new direction for American Jews, Friedman argued in behalf of "a moderate conservatism" aimed at bringing inflation under control, reviving the economy, and strengthening social norms and civilized discourse. As of yet Jewish professionals had failed to develop new strategies and policies to meet contemporary circumstances. They had not confronted "some of the implications and consequences of their activities, their policies, and their ideas, let alone to ponder what will be required of them in the years ahead."[10]

Jews such as Friedman recognize that much of their political inheritance is irrelevant, anachronistic, and contrary to American interests in general and

Jewish American interests in particular. The result has been the emergence of what Friedman aptly called "a moderate conservatism" which has been articulated by such leading Jewish neo-conservative intellectuals as Irving Kristol, Nathan Glazer, and Norman Podhoretz. This intraethinc debate between Jewish liberals and neo-conservatives was especially prominent in the reaction to Timerman's Prisoner Without a Name.

The most prominent case for Timerman's volume was Anthony Lewis' review in the New York Times Book Review. Intemperately entitled "The Final Solution in Argentina," the review focused on the anti-Semitic aspect of Timerman's ordeal. Claiming the volume to be "the most important book I have read in a long time," Lewis asserted it provided an unforgettable picture of state terrorism and of a "sophisticated society falling into irrationality and savagery." One week after his review had appeared, Lewis returned to the Timerman case with a Times article asking "What Kind of Country Are We?" Lewis attacked the Reagan administration for making overtures to Argentina where, he wrote, anti-Semitism has become virtually an official policy of the government. He called upon American Jews to make their opposition to any rapprochement with Buenos Aires known. The issue was "one of our own soul. Are things at such a point that we Americans must enlist torturers and murderers as our allies and proclaim their values . . . as ours? . . . How must we appear to ourselves? What kind of country are we?"[11]

Timerman had provided the American Left with a heaven-sent opportunity to savage the Reagan government. If Jacobo Timerman had not existed, the liberal-left would have had to invent him. The distinction of the Reaganites between right-wing authoritarian governments and left-wing totalitarian regimes, which was basic to the outlook of the administration, was for Lewis "pseudo-academic rubbish". Lewis argued in this manner despite the fact that the distinction between totalitarianism and authoritarianism had been familiar to historians and political scientists ever since J. C. Talmon and Hannah Arendt had published their volumes on totalitarianism during the 1950s.[12]

Irving Kristol attempted to answer Lewis' questions in a controversial essay in the Wall Street

Journal. Kristol claimed that Timerman's lofty position in American public opinion was due less to his suffering and more to the fact that he had become a symbol of opposition to Reagan's efforts to mend fences with rightist regimes. Describing Timerman as a "Solzhenitsyn-of-the-left," Kristol was troubled by his failure to discuss his relationship with David Graiver in his book as well as by his analysis of the Argentinian Jewish community. Graiver, a bank swindler on a gigantic scale, had owned forty-five per cent of the stock of La Opinion, Timerman's newspaper. Kristol asserted that the Argentine government had suspected Graiver of being the investment banker for Argentina's left-wing urban terrorists, and had believed that Timerman might have been implicated in this. Thus, Kristol claimed, Timerman was arrested because of his association with Graiver, and the Argentinian publisher knew this. Timerman failed to mention Graiver, Kristol maintained, because he did not want to detract from his role as a martyr to the right-wing government of Buenos Aires. Kristol was also troubled by Timerman's attacks on the leadership of the Argentinian Jewish community for not being more vigorous in protesting violations of human rights and anti-Semitism. Kristol wondered whether these leaders did not have a better appreciation of the situation of Argentinian Jewry than Timerman. Timerman's description of Argentinian Jewry tottering on the edge of another Holocaust was "irresponsible and dishonest demagogy." The Argentinian regime, "for all its ugly aspects, is authoritarian, not totalitarian," and was doing its best to eliminate anti-Semitism. Kristol predicted that the quiet diplomatic attempts of the Reagan administration would prove successful in moving Buenos Aires in the direction of liberalization, contrary to the predictions of Timerman and his leftist supporters.[13]

Suspicions about Timerman's relationship with Graiver were not original with Kristol. They had originally surfaced in December, 1980 when Benno W. Varon, a former Israeli diplomat with four decades of experience in Latin America, published "Don't Reduce Latin American Jews!" in the right-of-center Zionist magazine Midstream. Through this and later writings Varon would become the leading debunker of Timerman. Varon denied that Argentinian Jewry was in any danger or that the Argentine government was a terrorist regime. Jews, in fact, were prospering in Argentina, and their leaders did not share Timerman's paranoia. For Varon, Timerman was neither a Dreyfus nor a Schransky. Rather, he was the hapless associate of Mr. David Graiver.[14]

Varon's essay provoked much comment, both critical and favorable. Morton M. Rosenthal, director of B'nai Brith's Anti-Defamation League's Department of Latin American Affairs, accused Varon of appeasing anti-Semites, of acquiescing in the "suffering of the just," and of writing a piece of "garbage." Rosenthal also described Kristol's essay as "character assassination." Varon responded to Rosenthal by claiming that he had no personal animus against Timerman, that he wished him well, and that he felt he had treated him fairly. It would be difficult to make such claims a few months later after Varon's review of Prisoner Without a Name appeared in Midstream.[15]

The review was entitled "The Canonization of Jacobo Timerman." It accused Timerman of conveying a grotesque caricature of Argentina and Argentinian Jewry, of exaggerating the importance of his ordeal, of deliberately omitting any mention of David Graiver, and of playing fast-and-loose with the truth. Varon was particularly annoyed by Timmerman's comparison of Argentina's Jewish leaders with the subservient Jewish councils established by the Nazis in eastern Europe. Timerman, Varon wrote, "cannot forgive the Jews of Argentina for not considering his tragedy a Jewish tragedy, for not identifying themselves with one who was champion of revolutions and would-be kingmaker, for considering him not their hero but Graiver's victim." Timerman was being used by the American Left for their own purposes. His rise to prominence was sponsored by those who favor "a guerrilla victory in El Salvador, and intend to influence events in all of Latin America."[16]

Varon went over much the same ground in a piece he did for the conservative monthly American Spectator. He titled it "Don't Cry for Jacobo Timerman," or, as the magazine put it, "the weasled words of Prisoner Without a Name." Here Varon described the memoir as "a great book," "a shattering denunciation," "an earpiercing outcry," "an anguished vision," and a "moving description." The book's problem lay in the fact that the author had been elevated into a cultural hero by "the political establishment of America's Left".[17]

Varon was undoubtedly correct in stating that Timerman had assumed mythic proportions within the American Left, particularly among Jewish leftists. Anthony Lewis described the new-conservative attacks on Timerman as mere "pinpricks" and evidence of moral bankruptcy. Alfred Kazin argued in the New Republic that Timerman had become such an embarrassment to the Reagan administration that "right-wing Jewish salesman" had resorted to using "every possible slur" against him. Theodore Solotaroff's review in the Nation described Timerman as a "prophet," "an extraordinary man: reflective, humane, righteous and withal extremely brave, resourceful and hardheaded." He had made Jews "feel proud and protected". Michael Walzer's discussion in the New York Review of Books stressed Timerman's "political and moral stature" and while his suffering which gave the lie to the Reaganite distinction between good authoritarians and bad totalitarians. The neo-conservative critique of Timerman was "beneath contempt", the product of "great simplifiers." "These public statements suggest," Walzer wrote, "that even where there are no royal courts, there are still court Jews."[18]

Dissent's contribution to the discussion of Timerman was Leon Wieseltier's essay, "The Many Trials of Jacobo Timerman." Wieseltier, a graduate student at Harvard, pictured Timerman as a principled foe of all human rights violators, "a democrat, pleading vainly for a return to legality." His memoir was "one of the century's great works of conscience." His critics, in contrast, lacked "political judgment and moral authority," undermined the anti-communist cause, and encouraged fascism and anti-Semitism. "Perhaps the most disgraceful aspect of the campaign against Timerman," Wieseltier went on, "is that it was begun by Jews." This, he claimed, stemmed from the confusion of Jewish intellectuals regarding the Argentinian situation and the nature of anti-Semitism, as well as from their support for the Reagan administration, particularly its foreign policy.[19]

Jewish Frontier, the American organ of the socialist Zionist movement, came to their compatriot's defense in its August/September, 1981 issue. A long editorial by Mitchell Cohen, the magazine's editor, accused Jewish conservatives of willingness to sacrifice Jewish interests in behalf of petty, self-interested politics. Irving Kristol's essay was an "outrageous" effort in character assassination. In contrast, Timerman "does not bow before neo-conservative claptrap." This is his "triumph." Prisoner Without a Name is "a passionate account of the violation of human dignity by the fascists who control and abuse the people of Argentina today." Cohen's editorial accompanied an article by Elliot King, a New York journalist, which asked "Who's Afraid of Jacobo Timerman?" He termed Varon's original Midstream essay "a shameful whitewash of anti-Semitic activity in Argentina," and contended that the critics of Timerman were encouraging Argentinian anti-Semitism.[20]

The Labor Zionists were not the only Jewish group which came to Timerman's defense. The Reform movement honored Timerman for struggling in behalf of human rights. The American Jewish Congress through its publication Congress Monthly strongly attacked Timerman's detractors and the Reagan administration's human rights stance. Timerman was living witness to "the moral bankruptcy of a policy which embraces torturers rather than the tortured." Kristol and other Jewish conservatives have sown "divisiveness and confusion in the Jewish community" and have done "a disservice to Jewish concerns and to human rights." The time had come for Jews to reaffirm their support for human rights which "has long been part of our religious tradition, part of our self-esteem, woven into our history, pursued in causes often unpopular, often perilous."[21]

Moment, a Jewish monthly edited by the liberal political scientist Leonard Fein of Brandeis University, reprinted Lewis' "What Kind of Country Are We?" Fein himself described "The Timerman Conspiracy" as a clique of intellectuals engaged in a "smear" campaign against Timerman. Included among the smearers were Varon, Kristol, and Mark Falcoff, the author of an anti-Timerman essay in the July, 1981 Commentary. The conspirators were supposedly united by the belief that anti-Sovietism should be the overriding goal of American diplomacy. "The stakes here are very large," Fein wrote. If the Reaganites had their way, "both American law and the American soul" would be subsumed under the anti-Soviet banner. Thus Timerman had to be discredited in order to court favor with the anti-Soviet regime in Argentina. "The most eloquent rebuttal to Kristol and his ilk," Fein claimed, "is a renewed commitment to the defense of human rights wherever they are systematically violated, whoever the victim of their abuses." For Fein, Timerman was a courageous "liberal" and thereby deserving of American Jewish support. In truth, "liberal" is a political category with little or no relationship to the Argentinian situation. Timerman was certainly no "liberal". He was either a political opportunist, as his critics charged, or a long-standing socialist and a man of the Left as he described himself in Prisoner Without a Name.[22]

The American Jewish Forum, a conservative organization created by Professor Seymour Siegel of the Jewish Theological Seminary, lent its support to Timerman's foes. Timerman's comparison of Argentina to Nazi Germany, it asserted, was "an error of the grossest sort" since the Argentinian publisher knew he was talking nonsense. The refusal of Argentinian Jews to take their property and leave their country was a more accurate indication of the status of anti-Semitism in Argentina than Timerman's overheated and self-serving imagination. Rabbi Siegel suggested that the American government should support the Argentinian military junta and quietly attempt to move it along the path of democracy and liberty. This, and not the moralizing of the Carter administration or the feverish rhetoric of Timerman, would keep the strategically located and economically powerful Argentinians on the side of the West.[23]

Other important disparaging analyses of Timerman appeared in Contentions and Commentary. Contentions, the organ of the Committee for the Free World, a hard-line anti-communist group headed by Norman Podhoretz's wife Midge Decter, charged that the American Left was less interested in Timerman himself than in using him to indict America's anti-communist allies while diverting attention from the atrocities committed by America's enemies. "Articles employing the man and his book as a stick with which to beat the government of the United States continue to pour from the presses," while "millions suffering far more than Timerman ever did continue to go unchampioned--because they have had the ill fortune to be victims of regimes it does not suit the purposes of the liberal press at this moment to get excited about."[24]

Undoubtedly the most detailed and sophisticated conservative analysis of the Timerman controversy was Mark Falcoff's "The Timerman Case" which appeared in Commentary. Here Falcoff, a professor of Latin

American history at the University of Oregon, predicted that Prisoner Without a Name could be "a propaganda windfall for the foreign-policy establishment of the American Left" if the American people remained ignorant about the political situation in Argentina and the circumstances surrounding Timerman's imprisonment. Falcoff described Argentina as a tolerable place in which to live. Argentinian Jews we're prosperous and had a vibrant cultural community. Buenos Aires might be an authoritarian regime. It certainly wasn't a totalitarian one, nor did it resemble Nazi Germany. Timerman's comparison of Argentina with Hitler's Germany, Falcoff wrote, "cheapens the lives of those exterminated in Central and Eastern Europe, while doing less than nothing to alleviate the suffering of those political prisoners who happen to be Jewish."[25]

It is virtually impossible for nonspecialists and outsiders to evaluate the arguments spawned by the Timerman controversy. Did he exaggerate the extent of Argentinian anti-Semitism and the complicity of Argentinian public officials? Was he arrested because of his association with David Graiver? Is the quiet diplomacy of the Reagan administration more effective than the public chastisements of the Carter regime in ameliorating conditions in Argentina? And yet there has been no reluctance on the part of Timerman's supporters and detractors in uttering categorical and seemingly definitive judgments about these and other questions. Clearly Timerman's saliency within American public opinion was due less to the situation in Argentina and more to the relevance of his experiences to the political circumstances within the United States, including the growing conservatism among American Jews, particularly among American Jewish intellectuals.

The reasons for this are many and complex. Part of the explanation is the gradual acculturation and assimilation of Jews into the American mainstream. Inevitably the political attitudes of Jewish businessmen, workers, intellectuals, and professionals will gradually approximate those of their gentile counterparts. The disparity between the Jewish social and economic profile and Jewish voting patterns could not exist indefinitely, especially when the sources of Jewish liberalism were becoming historically more and more remote. In addition, many Jews have turned away from liberalism because they perceive that some of its manifestations have been hostile to both American and Jewish interests.

The vast majority of American Jews are now professionals or involved in business. It certainly is not in their interest to favor liberal policies which increase their taxes, stifle their opportunities, and regulate their activities. Indeed, it is difficult to see how any American could have benefitted economically from the policies of the past years, except if he or she was part of a strategically located interest group able to sway government in its behalf. Despite the predictions of European Jewish radicals of the nineteenth and early twentieth centuries, Jews and economic leftism have never mixed very well. Jewish welfare and prosperity have been directly proportional to the extent of economic freedom existing in the host society. Countries which underwent socialist revolutions invariably witnessed an exodus of Jews. Conversely, countries where capitalism and economic opportunity predominate, such as Canada and the United States, are precisely those nations with the most stable and prosperous Jewish communities.

Furthermore, Jews, like other Americans, realize that many of the liberal programs of the past, despite the compassionate rhetoric justifying them, have been counter-productive and have actually harmed the very individuals they were designed to aid. This tendency for even the best-intentioned reforms to go astray has been the central motif of Public Interest, the stimulating quarterly begun in the mid-1960s. The majority of Public Interest's editors have been Jewish intellectuals sceptical of liberal panaceas for housing, taxation, crime and punishment, and welfare. Conservative Jews have been especially troubled by the tendency of the modern liberal welfare state to foster dependency. As Rabbi Seymour Siegel has pointed out, the highest form of charity within the Jewish tradition is providing opportunities for the poor "to help themselves escape from the bondage of poverty and dependence."[26]

Jews have also been troubled by the increasingly frequent attempts of the American Left to classify Americans along racial and ethnic lines. Jews clearly remember the anti-Jewish quotas in employment and colleges in Europe and the United States. They are unable to view with equanimity what Nathan Glazer has termed "affirmative discrimination". Conservatives today are more clearly committed than liberals to the merit principle, a principle which has served Jews well in the past.

Finally there are specifically Jewish interests which, it can be argued, are better protected by conservatives than the Left. Insofar as Israel has become a major barrier to the spread of communism and Soviet imperialism in the Middle East, Israel's interests (and those of American Jewry) will be sympathetically viewed by conservatives for whom anti-communism is a key dogma. In contrast, "third world" ideologists and their supporters are now ensconced in the camp of Israel's enemies. Furthermore, as the pages of Commentary indicate, Jews clearly perceive the relationship between a strong American defense posture and the interests of Israel. A large military is, of course, a traditional conservative concern.

Prior to the late nineteenth century Jews were not part of the political Left. Political activity was proscribed for Jews. As a result, they focused their energies within the Jewish community. In time the unique historical circumstances surrounding Jewish emancipation from the ghetto attracted Jews to leftist movements of all sorts. Now exactly one century after the vast migration of Jews from eastern Europe to the United States commenced, the ties binding Jews and the Left have become frayed. The Jews are one of America's most strategically located minority groups. Numbering approximately six million, they reside mainly in the states with the highest number of electoral votes. They turn out in high numbers at election time and are generous in their political contributions. The majority of adult Jews are college graduates employed in business and the professions. Many are in publishing, communications, and academia. Up to now this vocal, affluent, and influential minority has been a vital cog in the liberal coalition. A change in Jewish political orientation to the right would help insure the triumph of conservative ideas for the forseeable future. As of today the signs are propitious.[27]

## FOOTNOTES

[1] Jacobo Timerman, *Prisoner Without a Name, Cell Without a Number* (New York: Alfred A. Knopf, 1981), p. 139.

[2] *New York Times*, June 25, 1981. At a meeting in New York City Timerman called Begin a fascist. *Midstream*, XXVIII (February, 1982), 35. For Timerman's most recent opinion of the Begin government and the Jewish leaders of Argentina and the United States, see his "The Silence of the Jews," *Harper's*, CCLXIII (November, 1981), 20-23.

[3] Jeanne Kirkpatrick, "Dictatorships and Double Standards," *Commentary*, LXVIII (November, 1979), 34-45, Eric F. Saltman, "Torture? On TV?" *New York Times*, May 26, 1981.

[4] Irving Louis Horowitz, *Israel Ecstasies/Jewish Agonies* (New York: Oxford University Press, 1974), p. 109.

[5] Deborah Dash Moore, *At Home in America: Second Generation New York Jews* (New York: Columbia University Press, 1981), ch. viii; Stephen D. Issacs, *Jews and American Politics* (Garden City, N. Y.: Doubleday, 1974); Werner Cohn, "The Politics of American Jews," in Marshall Sklare, ed., *The Jews: Social Patterns of an American Group* (New York: Free Press, 1958), 614-26; Lawrence H. Fuchs, "Sources of Jewish Internationalism and Liberalism," in ibid., 597 ff.; Irving Kristol in *Congress Bi-Weekly*, XL (April 13, 1973), 18-19; Daniel J. Elazar, "American Political Theory and the Political Notions of American Jews: Convergences and Contradictions," in Peter I. Rose, ed., *The Ghetto and Beyond: Essays on Jewish Life in America* (New York: Random House, 1969), 203-27.

[6] Bernard Rosenberg and Irving Howe, "Are American Jews Turning to the Right?" in Lewis A. Coser and Irving Howe, eds., *The New Conservatives: A Critique From the Left* (New York: New American Library, 1977), 64-67.

[7] ibid., 69-89.

[8] Norman Podhoretz, *Breaking Ranks* (New York: Harper & Row, 1979), pp. 63-68.

[9] Bernard Avishai, "Breaking Faith: Commentary and the American Jews," *Dissent*, XXVIII (Spring, 1981), 236-56.

[10] Murray Friedman, "A New Direction for American Jews," *Commentary*, LXXII (December, 1981), 37-44.

[11] Anthony Lewis, "The Final Solution in Argentina," *New York Times Book Review*, May 10, 1981; Lewis, "What Kind of Country Are We?" *New York Times*, May 17, 1981.

[12] Anthony Lewis, "Accomplice to Terror," *New York Times*, March 22, 1981.

[13] Irving Kristol, "The Timerman Affair," *Wall Street Journal*, May 29, 1981.

[14] Benno Weiser Varon, "Don't Rescue Latin American Jews!" *Midstream*, XXVI (December, 1980), 11-16.

[15] Rosenthal quoted in *New York Times*, June 3, 1981. See also Rosenthal and Varon in *Midstream*, XXVII (May, 1981),

62-64. For evidence that Timerman knew his involvement with Graiver was responsible for his incarceration, see Seth Lipsky, "A Conversation with Publisher Jacobo Timerman," Wall Street Journal, June 4, 1981.

[16]Varon, "The Canonization of Jacobo Timerman," Midstream, XXVII (August/September, 1982), 36-44. For reactions to this review and Varon's response, see "Last Word on Timerman," Midstream, XXVIII (February, 1981), 34-42. For the attitude of Mario Gorenstein, the president of the Delegation of Jewish Associations of Argentina, toward Timerman, see New York Times, May 22, 1981.

[17]Varon, "Don't Cry for Jacobo Timerman," American Spectator, XIV (September, 1981), 19-23.

[18]Anthony Lewis, "The Timerman Affair," New York Times, June 14, 1981; Alfred Kazin, "The Solitude of Jacobo Timerman," New Republic, CLXXXIV (June 20, 1981), 32-34; Theodore Solotaroff, review of Prisoner Without a Name, in Nation, CCXXXII (June 13, 1981), 733-36; Michael Walzer, "Timerman and His Enemies," New York Review of Books, XXIX (September 24, 1981), 10-18.

[19]Leon Wieseltier, "The Many Trials of Jacobo Timerman," Dissent, XXVIII (Fall, 1981), 425-35.

[20]Mitchell Cohen, "Bankrupt: A New Chapter," Jewish Frontier, XLVIII (August/September, 1981), 3-5; Elliot King, "Who's Afraid of Jacobo Timerman?" ibid., 6-9.

[21]New York Times, June 3, 1981; Jerome J. Shestack, "Jacobo Timerman: The Perils of Silence," Congress Monthly, (September/October, 1981), 9, 11.

[22]Leonard Fein, "The Timerman Conspiracy," Moment, VI (July/August, 1981), 61-63.

[23]Richard Freund, "Anti-Semitism and Metaphors of the Holocaust," Forum Newsletter, I (Summer, 1981), 2; Seymour Siegel, "Remarks About Argentina," ibid., 2, 7.

[24]"The Use of Jacobo Timerman," Contentions, I (August, 1981), 1-3, 6-8.

[25]Mark Falcoff, "The Timerman Case," Commentary, LXII (July, 1981), 15-23. For letters prompted by Falcoff's essary and Falcoff's response, see Commentary, LXII (December, 1981), 14-23.

[26]Seymour Siegel, "Right Turn," Sh'ma, XI (April 17, 1981), 89-91.

[27]Robert G. Kaiser, "The Jewish Voter: Giving Up on Carter," Washington Post, August 17, 1980.

# THE JEWISH POOR

In the Spring, 1972 issue of the Journal of Jewish Communal Service there appeared an essay by Ann G. Wolfe entitled "The Invisible Jewish Poor." Wolfe, a member of the American Jewish Committee's Social Welfare Division, claimed that Jewish affluence had obscured widespread Jewish poverty. She estimated that the Jewish poor numbered anywhere from 700,000 to 800,000, two-thirds of whom were elderly. She believed that in New York City alone there was at least a quarter of a million poor Jews. Wolfe called upon Jewish communal institutions to raise their "consciousness" regarding poverty, to reexamine their agendas, and to return to their original mandate of caring for those in need.

Wolfe's manifesto was both a cause and an effect of an intensified concern among both Jewish lay and professional leaders regarding poverty within the Jewish community. Within a short time after the appearance of Wolfe's essay the Jewish poor had ceased to be "invisible." A host of articles with such titles as "Jewish Poverty Hurts in South Beach," "Left Behind, Left Alone," "Down and Out in New York," and "Los Angeles is a Shocker" appeared in Jewish magazines. The New York Federation of Jewish Philanthropies established the Metropolitan Coordinating Committee on Jewish Poverty, while the American Jewish Community published The Other Jews: Portraits in Poverty. In 1972 the Office of Economic Development (the "war on poverty" agency) provided the first of several grants to help alleviate Jewish poverty.

Wolfe's article brought forth the inevitable rejoinder from the Jewish establishment. Saul Kaplan, the research director of Chicago's Jewish federation, argued in the pages of the Journal of Jewish Communal Service that Wolfe had greatly exaggerated the extent of Jewish poverty, that poverty was less prevalent among Jews than other ethnic groups, and that organized Jewish philanthropy had not ignored the Jewish poor. Claiming that the poor constituted less than five per cent of the Jewish population, Kaplan contended that effective social planning depended "on realistic, not exaggerated, estimates of the size of the problem in relation to the resources that are or that may become available." Shock treatment was not an effective technique for dealing with the problem.

"The Jewish poor are ill served if their numbers are overstated," he wrote. "The important task is to face up to the responsibilities for the estimated 264,000 Jewish poor."

The attention then being paid to the Jewish poor was an outgrowth of the reformist and collectivist atmosphere of the 1960's. Wolfe praised the socialist Michael Harrington ("a man of insight and vision") in his 1963 book The Other America for awakening Americans to the problem of poverty. The establishment of the "war on poverty" during the Johnson administration provided opportunities for voluntary organizations, Jewish included, to secure federal funds.

This concern with Jewish poverty has continued for some Jews whose politically formative years were the 1960's. Thus Chaim Waxman, a sociologist at Rutgers University and a long-time advocate of intensified governmental efforts to reduce poverty, was still claiming in the late 1970's that approximately one-fourth to one-fifth of the Jews in large metropolitan areas were at poverty or near-poverty levels. In his essay "Bringing the Poor Back In: Jewish Poverty in Education for Jewish Communal Service" (Forum, Spring/Summer, 1979), Waxman berated the six American graduate school programs in Jewish communal service for deemphasizing the sociological roots of Jewish poverty, and for focusing their energies on "the problems of the individual and how that individual might experience growth and change, rather than consideration of institutional and societal changes which would alter his or her plight." By not advocating the cause of the Jewish poor, these schools were betraying "their professed Jewish and professional traditions." This resulted in Jewish communal workers not being sensitized to the needs of the Jewish poor.

Waxman believed this unfortunate situation stemmed from the dominance of middle-class values and goals within contemporary Jewish philanthropy. This, in turn, was a product of a general American middle-class disengagement from the problems of the poverty-stricken. Waxman claimed Jewish social work was dominated by "middle class social work, specifically casework" with "a declining interest in servicing the Jewish poor." He felt there was little likelihood of change, and he predicted that programs already existing for servicing the Jewish poor would be disbanded. This would harm not only the poor but all Jews since Judaism views "the well-being of the nonpoor as integrally related to the well-being of the poor."

Bernard Reisman, director of Brandeis University's Benjamin S. Hornstein Program in Jewish Communal Service, suggested that Waxman's statistics and motivation were due to "nostalgia and a failure to account for changes in the demography and priorities of today's American Jewish Community." This community is largely middle-class, and has "moved beyond the need to highlight the plight of the poor or the orphan as the rationale for Jewish philanthropy." The percentage of poor Jews, Reisman continued, has been continually decreasing during the past several generations, while the major destitution was spiritual and cultural impoverishment rather than material poverty. Combatting assimilation and supporting world Jewry, Reisman concluded, were properly the major priorities of American Jewish philanthropy.

This debate regarding the extent of Jewish poverty mirrored the more general debate concerning American poverty in which poverty estimates were based on figures from the Department of Labor, Bureau of the Census, and the Department of Health, Education, and Welfare regarding family income. Recently, however, a growing number of economists have argued that such statistics greatly inflate the number of poor. Thus Morton Paglin, an economist at Portland State University, claimed in his recent book <u>Poverty and Transfers in Kind</u> that when food stamps, subsidized day-care centers, rent supplements, medicaid, child nutrition programs, public housing, and other transfers, as well as under-reporting of income are taken into consideration, the percentage of poor Americans shrinks to less than 4%. "It is time," Dr. Paglin wrote, "that the statistical veil be lifted so the poverty problem can be seen in its true dimensions." And since Jews are less prone to poverty than the general population, the number of authentically poor Jews must be less than two hundred thousand, and most of these are elderly.

The fact that Jewish poverty has been greatly exaggerated is, of course, little comfort to those Jews who legitimately can be described as poor. It is the human, in contrast to the statistical, dimensions of poverty among the Jewish aged which is the subject of Thomas Cottle's new volume <u>Hidden Survivors: Portraits of Poor Jews in America</u>. Cottle, a Boston clinical psychologist and sociologist, introduces us to Jacob and Millie Portman, residents of a decaying neighborhood in Boston, who are faced with the prospect of having to move from their apartment because of urban renewal. Moving for the elderly, especially if they are poor, is, as Cottle notes, "a terrifying ordeal." Jacob Portman believes society views them as superfluous, nuisances standing in the way of progress. Then there is Ella Crown, living alone in a crowded two-room apartment in which the refrigerator stands alongside the toilet. Ella and her visitors wear sweaters during the winter to ward off the cold. Ella's major problem is that her daughter is too busy to visit her. Her closest acquaintance is Mandy, a Moroccan Jewish prostitute.

Peter Rosenbloom is in his sixties, unmarried, on welfare, and unemployed for years. He embarrasses his brother who once offered to pay his expenses if only he would move away. Peter sees himself as a double bum. "Bum number one because I'm not working like a good Jewish man, and bum number two because I'm not working in the right profession or the right business." A Mr. Klein has also been rejected by his family. "We taught them to study hard and be smart," he says about his children. "They did. They are. What do they want to come around here for."

Anna Leivobitz is sixty-eight, manager of a bakery, and a devout Boston Red Sox fan. She is also consumed by memories of her relatives who perished in the Holocaust. For Anna, baseball is a metaphor of America: "people yelling, shouting, kill the umpire, kill this one, kill that one, people hoping, screaming. It's wonderful. Baseball's wonderful, America's wonderful. The noise is wonderful. But out here, everybody makes noise and nobody gets hurt. That's when I feel peaceful."

Issac Orlovsky, another Holocaust survivor, died at the age of fifty-nine because his wife Rose lacked the money to pay for an ambulance to take him to a hospital after he suffered a stroke and a heart attack. As Rose tells the doctor, "when a man like Issac is brought into this hospital from a poor neighborhood and is taken to emergency instead of to an operating room directly, people know he's not a rich man, so he doesn't get a rich man's medical attention. . . . Do you honestly believe people like us think we get the same treatment as rich people?"

The life stories collected in Hidden Survivors reveal the burden of being poor and elderly in America, particularly if one is Jewish. American culture stresses youth. Our television advertisements, for example, feature the young consuming soft-drinks, wearing designer jeans, and driving the latest automobiles. Little wonder then that the aged often see themselves as extraneous. Note, for example, the widespread concern that Ronald Reagan, at age seventy, might be too old to be president.

Poverty is also a burden in America. In an individualistic and fluid society in which success is attributed to individual qualities (any newborn, we are told, has the opportunity to become president), failure is also attributed to individual traits. The poor are thus deprived of the opportunity of blaming social conditions for their situation. The United States is, after all, the land of Horatio Alger, Dale Carnegie, and the Amway Corporation. It is not the land of John Calvin, Karl Marx, and Thomas Hardy. When "making it" becomes a national passion, those who haven't made it have only themselves to blame.

This emphasis on success is especially found among American Jews who are quintessentially American both in their virtues and their vices. Anti-Semitism and the Jewish respect for schooling pushed American Jews into the professions. Jewish children had to excell in school. Leah Cramer told Cottle that her mother continually stressed that, "In order for us to be like all the others, we have to be better than them. If you don't understand this now, you will. You will." American Jewish folk humor is replete with stories of the newly-born child destined to become "my son, the doctor." And since the Jewish family is quite close, the poor Jew feels more deeply the humiliation for not measuring up to family or ethnic standards.

Poverty is particularly galling for the Jew because the vast majority of American Jews are comfortably middle-class. The poor Jew realizes he is an aberration, and a source of shame and embarrassment to his relatives. The success of other Jews makes his own failure that much more difficult to live with.

Poverty is less onerous if it is the normal way of life. If Hidden Survivors tell us anything it is that the plight of the Jewish poor is primarily psychological, resulting from the rejection by relatives and other Jews. This resentment and self-hatred will not be lessened by the types of social programs popular during the 1960's. Jewish poverty is less a matter of material deprivation and more a matter of an eclipse of a sense of community, an alienation from neighbors and friends, and feelings of powerlessness, inadequacy, and disgrace. Since the Jewish poor is primarily elderly, and since there is little likelihood of a significant immigration of impoverished Jews to America, Jewish poverty is likely to become a casualty of the actuarial tables. This, however, does not lessen the anguished cries of the personae of Hidden Survivors.

# German and Russian Jews in America

America has had its period of Portuguese, Polish, and German settlement. *The Russian period has begun in earnest.* Will its influence prove wholesome or the reverse?[1]

By 1880, the approximately quarter of a million American Jews could look back upon their brief history in the United States with a deep sense of pride and accomplishment. Consisting largely of 19th century immigrants from Germany and their children, they had in the space of a few short decades risen from the ranks of poor peddlers and petty shopkeepers and become substantial and respected businessmen, financiers, and professionals. At this moment of triumph, however, there had begun the mass immigration of Jews from East Europe which was to bring two million Jews to the United States between 1880 and 1920 and increase the Jewish population of New York City from 85,000 in 1880 to over 1,500,000 in 1920. The Germans would increasingly preoccupy themselves with the "Russians" as they called them, and almost immediately perceived the East Europeans as a threat to their pocketbooks, their highly valued status in American society, and even, at times, to their sanity. At the same time, the Germans had a sincere philanthropic regard for the spiritual and physical welfare of the Russians, and they would expend countless hours and millions of dollars in order to make the adjustment of the Russians to American life as painless as possible.

The Germans made it quite clear that they did not want to be associated in the public mind with the Russians. As early as 1872, a German pleaded in a popular magazine for the public not to judge all Jews by the "ignorant . . . bigoted, and vicious" Jews of East Europe who were beginning to arrive in New York. And seventeen years later the United Jewish Charities of Rochester described the East Europeans as "a bane to the country and a curse to the Jews. The Jews have earned an enviable reputation in the United States, but this has been undermined by the influx of thousands who are not ripe for the enjoyment of liberty and equal rights, and all who mean well for the Jewish name should prevent them as much as possible from coming here." The Germans often termed the East Europeans "Asiatics" to contrast them with the westernized and modern German Jews; they frequently described themselves as members of the "Hebrew persuasion" or "Israelites" to differentiate themselves from the Russian "Jews"; and they often used the expression "our co-religionists" when referring to the Russians in order to emphasize that their relationship with the Russians was solely religious and did not involve any cultural, social, or intellectual affinities.

Lying at the basis of the Germans' concern was the fear that the settling of the Russians in large urban ghettos, especially the Lower East Side of New York City which had over half a million Jews in 1910, and the resulting social problems would engender an anti-Semitic backlash that would engulf the Germans and destroy the social acceptibility they had so far secured from non-Jewish Americans. As a Jewish paper in Detroit bluntly stated, "the Jew, being a minority, must elevate his lowest type, if the higher classes are to attain their legitimate place in the popular estimation. . . . It has become a question of self-defense. . . . To the recipients of our help, but also to ourselves, we owe it, because we are a minor element in the community. . . . When there is no lowest type even minorities are safe." The uplifting of the Russian Jew and his assimilation into American culture thus became the major item on the agenda of American German Jewish philanthropy of the late 19th and early 20th centuries.[2]

Probably the most important anxiety of the Germans was that the United States had become the dumping ground for poverty-stricken Jews who would be unable to make a living in America. These destitute Jews, so the Germans believed, disdained physical labor, lacked capital and skills, and had no experience with modern technological and economic methods; consequently, many would be forced to turn to crime, prostitution, and begging to survive. The American Jewish philanthropies would go bankrupt in attempting to meet the needs of the newcomers. The Germans advised European Jewish leaders that only the young, healthy, and skilled should be allowed to migrate to the United States, and that they should tell all Jews anticipating immigration not to expect an easy life. They also attempted to deflect the immigration to western Europe and Latin America, but without any great success. "The Jews of the United States have never, either in their collective or individual capacity, had any organization looking to or aiming at Jewish immigration in any way or manner," the American Jewish leader Simon Wolf testified before a committee of the House of Representatives in 1901. "There has never been on the part of the Jews in the United States any organization that stimulated, encouraged, desired or wished the wholesale influx of their coreligionists. We naturally preferred that they should remain in the countries in which they had been born." Nevertheless, the Germans recognized their religious and moral obligation to help lift out of poverty the Russians who had already migrated to America.[3]

The Germans funded many worthwhile projects to teach vocational skills to immigrant Jews, not only so they would become self-sustaining, but also to "normalize" the occupational structure of the Russians which was seen as too heavily weighted in the direction of the needle trades and commerce. The Hebrew Technical Institute was established in New York to teach East European Jews carpentry, painting, and other skills, while various efforts were made to settle Jews on the land, especially in southern New Jersey in the vicinity of Vineland and Woodbine.

That the Jews of eastern Europe had had little or no experience with agriculture and that millions of native American farmers were leaving rural America and migrating to the factory towns and large cities of the Northeast and Middle West were of less importance to the German philanthropists than the prospect of transforming "sewers of coats" into "sowers of oats," and in so doing disproving the charge that Jews were economic parasites who disdained physical labor and lived off the exertion of others. Jews who choose agriculture would experience "a humanizing school of healthy and honest toil which cannot but leave its unmistakable impression on their characters as well as those of their posterity," declared the *Jewish Exponent* of Philadelphia. "The damning marks of the middleman or the three-balls man will no longer cling to their largely regenerated physiognomies or poison the very vitals of their capable natures." There was something ludicrous about wealthy German Jewish philanthropists, who themselves had begun as peddlers and had become businessmen and financiers, justifying agricultural settlements for East European Jews in part because commerce was somewhat immoral and Jewish involvement in it encouraged anti-Semitism.[4]

The Germans also feared that, as long as the East Europeans lived together in the ghettos, they would remain in the hold of religious and cultural "medievalism" and never absorb American values and adopt American social practices. The New York *Jewish Messenger* suggested that American Jewish missionaries be sent to Russia to first civilize the East European Jews, rather than having the Russians migrate to the United States where they would Russianize American Jewry. The Germans were especially fearful that the Russians would remain loyal to religious Orthodoxy which, the Germans believed, was an atrocious blend of superstition, obscurantism, and narrow-mindedness.

The importing of Rabbi Jacob Joseph from Lithuania in 1888 to serve as the chief rabbi of New York City and the founding of Yeshiva University were opposed by Germans who believed they would be barriers to the assimilation of the Russians. "The Jews of this country do not need a Grand Rabbi and one from a foreign country," declared the Reform journal *Jewish Tidings*, "one who is reared among the prejudices and bigotries of the Eastern countries will certainly provide an obstacle to the people over whom he is expected to exercise control." Throughout, the Germans emphasized the vast gulf separating them from their benighted co-religionists from darkest Europe. "The thoroughly acclimated American Jew . . . has no religious, social or intellectual sympathies with them," the New York *Hebrew Standard* announced in 1894. "He is closer to the Christian sentiment around him than to the Judaism of these miserable darkened Hebrews."[5]

The ideal way to "civilize" the Russians was, as the *Jewish Messenger* wrote, "to pull down the ghetto . . . and scatter its members to the corners of the nation." In 1901, the Industrial Removal Office was founded to encourage Jews to move from New York and settle in the hinterland. Six years later the financier Jacob Schiff contributed $500,000 to finance the Galveston Plan to bring East European Jewish immigrants into the country through the port of Galveston rather than New York, and then to aid the immigrants to make their way into the nation's interior. The Germans also expected the activities of the Jewish Agricultural Society to disperse the Russian Jews away from the large cities. The hoped for decentralization of Jewish population would not only accelerate their Americanization, but it would also get the Russian Jews out of the sweatshops of the garment industries, as well as alleviating the social problems of the ghettos caused by overcrowding.[6]

The attempt to disperse the Russians into the interior was unsuccessful. This was largely because the Russians preferred living in New York, Boston, Baltimore, Chicago, and Philadelphia, rather than in Wichita, Cheyenne, Texarkana, Jefferson City, and Vineland. In addition, German Jews outside of New York City discouraged the migration of Russians to their communities. In 1882, two Jewish leaders in Providence, Rhode Island notified a Jewish charity in New York that "for every new Emigrant you send here we will return two. We have all we can attend to." Similar sentiments were voiced in the same decade by Jews in Milwaukee, Cleveland, Baltimore, Philadelphia, Rochester, and St. Paul.[7]

The refusal of the Russian Jews to leave the big cities made the task of uplifting and civilizing those whom the *Jewish Messenger* described as "slovenly in dress, loud in manners, and vulgar in discourse," and whom Emma Lazarus referred to as "wretched refuse" all that more urgent. The Russians, the *Jewish Messenger* asserted, "must be Americanized in spite of themselves, in the mode prescribed by their friends and benefactors."

The most prominent of the German charitable agencies established to refine the Russians was the Educational Alliance, a settlement house on East Broadway in the heart of New York's Lower East Side. The initial approach of the Educational Alliance to its supposed beneficiaries is indicated by the fact that the speaking of the Yiddish language, which was often referred to by Germans as "piggish jargon," was at first forbidden within the holy walls of the settlement house. Eugene Lyons noted in his autobiography that the Educational Alliance fostered "a disrespect for the alien traditions in our home . . . because they seemed insuperable barriers between ourselves and our adopted land." In 1900, a group of Yiddish intellectuals, dismayed by the thrust of the Educational Alliance, established a rival institution known as the Educational League, declaring that it was time for the Jews of the Lower East Side to "cut away from the apron strings of the German Jews."[8]

The Germans justifiably viewed the ghettos not only as an impediment to the acculturation of the Russian Jews, but also as a threat to their physical and moral well-being. The fact that most impressed the Germans about the Lower East Side, that "desert of degradation and despair" as one described it, was its horrible overcrowding. The German Jews of New York City were among the city's leaders in the important anti-tenement, anti-tuberculosis, and public parks movements, whose purposes were to lessen the population density of the slums and alleviate the unhealthy conditions resulting from overcrowding. The Germans feared that the health of the Russians would degenerate as a result of living on the Lower East Side, and were active in bringing modern medical and sanitary advances to the ghetto. They provided milk, athletic facilities, and summer camps for the children of the Russians, all of which were of great benefit to the downtown Jews. "The importance of physical training for our downtown brethren cannot be overestimated," the first annual report of the Educational Alliance stated. "Our co-religionists are often charged with lack of physical courage and repugnance to physical work. Nothing will more effectively remove this than athletic training." One of the motives behind the establishing of Jewish community centers in the major cities was providing places for physical exercise for those living in tenements and working in sweatshops, as well as furnishing places for wholesome recreational and cultural activities for those surrounded by the temptations of city life.[9]

Even more important than the physical degeneration of the Russians in the ghettos was their anticipated moral deterioration. The Germans were particularly sensitive to accusations that the Lower East Side was a hotbed of crime. The notoriety of such thugs as Yuski Nigger, Big Jack Zelig, Sheeny Mike Kurtz, Sam Schepps, Lefty Louis, Bald Jack Rose, Little Kishky, Dopey Benny, Kid Dropper, Gyp the Blood, Kid Twist, and Abe Grenthal, leader of the Sheeny Gang, as well as the creation of the New York Independent Benevolent Association by Jewish brothel owners led to the founding of several charities to combat crime and juvenile delinquency in the Jewish quarter. The Jewish Protectory and Aid Society, the Hawthorne School, and the Lakeview Home for wayward girls were valuable institutions which grew out of this concern felt by German Jews over ghetto crime. In 1909 the downtown Russian Jews and the uptown German Jews got together to create the New York Kehillah (community) after the city's police commissioner charged in a magazine article that one-half of the city's criminals were Russian Jews. Three years later the Kehillah organized the Bureau of Social Morals which acted as a secret service to fight crime and vice in the ghetto.[10]

Germans correctly attributed the phenomenon of Jewish crime to the poverty and overcrowding of the ghetto, and a weakening of the traditionally strong East European Jewish family. Evidence of this decline was the growth in the ghetto of prostitution, juvenile delinquency, and numerous desertions of families by husbands. The Germans financed a National Desertion Bureau whose function was to track down runaway husbands.

The Germans blamed the general breakdown of moral standards in the ghetto and the weakening of its family life, in part, on the religious functionaries of the Lower East Side. The Germans argued that the refusal of the Orthodox leaders to modify their European ways had destroyed any opportunity they might have had of influencing the Americanized children of the immigrants. Louis Marshall, the unofficial head of the New York German Jewish community, angrily charged the Orthodox rabbinate with having "closed your eyes to the departure of the children of a race, that justly prided itself on the purity of its moral life, to adopt the career of gamblers, thugs, gangsters, thieves, and prostitutes, and to become a byword and a hissing. You have remained silent witnesses to the degradation of Judaism, to the alienation from it of the new generation.... You have clung to the shadow, while the vivifying spirit has departed." Marshall accused the Orthodox rabbis of having made a laughingstock of Judaism among the young. "A heavy responsibility rests upon the heads" of the Orthodox congregations, Marshall argued, "whose sole ideal is to Russianize American Judaism, when all that they can accomplish is to drive their children to atheism." If the children of the immigrants were not to be permanently alienated from Judaism, then the Judaism of the ghetto would have to be Americanized and the grip of the Talmud over the Russian immigrants would have to be loosened.[11]

The major effort of the Germans along this line was financing the Jewish Theological Seminary in order to produce American educated rabbis who would then go back to the ghettos and combat the "anarchistic license," the socialism, the family breakdown, and the crime which, they believed, were rife there. The graduates of the Seminary, it was hoped, would also stem the disaffection of the young from Judaism. "What nobler work than for some of our graduates ... to go to these people and instill into their minds and hearts ... culture, refinement and civilization," the president of the Seminary declared in 1890. "The equipment of such missionaries ... is, indeed, an object that ought to ... secure the support of the Jews, and of every congregation in the United States." In 1902 the Seminary hired the distinguished Cambridge scholar, Solomon Schechter, to be president.

Schechter's goals for the Seminary were of a scholarly nature and he became disturbed by the assumption of the Germans that the Seminary's function was to civilize and westernize the Judaism of the immigrants from East Europe. Schechter wrote to Louis Marshall in December, 1913, two years before his death, that he had not assumed the presidency of the Seminary "for the purpose of converting the downtown Jew to a more refined species of religion."[12]

The final area of concern of the Germans regarding the Russians was their politics. The politically and socially conservative Germans were dismayed by the pro-socialist, pro-anarchist, and pro-labor sentiments of many of the Russian immigrants. They were also fearful that the Russians might become pawns of the urban political machines, especially Tammany Hall, and thereby strengthen bossism and increase political corruption.

Today, one century after the East European Jewish migration began in earnest, it is clear that the response of the German Jews is a classic case of cultural misconceptions. The fears of the Germans that the Russians could not earn a living in the United States, that they could not adjust to American cultural, intellectual, and social patterns, that they would be unable to survive the ghetto physically and morally intact, and that their politics represented a threat to American captialism as well as to the good name of all Jews were all unfounded. Indeed, so rapid has been the economic and social advance of the Russian Jews and so quick has been their cultural integration that what is now problemmatical is not their adaptation to American life but their continued commitment to Judaism.

Of all the fears of the Germans, none has been more disproven than the apprehension that the Russian Jew could not survive economically in the United States. As the sociologist Nathan Glazer wrote in 1955, the "rise in the social and economic position of the Jews has been extremely rapid, far surpassing that which can be shown for any other immigrant group, and indeed surpassing, for the same period, changes in the socio-economic position of long-settled groups." A recent study by the Catholic sociologist Andrew Greeley reveals that real family income of Jews today is higher than that of every other major American religio-ethnic group, including British Protestant, Irish Catholic, and German Catholic.[13]

The German Jews failed to recognize that the economic and social background of the Russians and the occupational skills which they brought with them to the United States were particularly conducive to rapid economic and social advancement. Far more than any other immigrant group from southern and eastern Europe, the Jews had a commercial and middle-class background enabling them to take advantage of the opportunities offered by a burgeoning economy. While not all the Jews in East Europe were businessmen and skilled artisans, in many sectors of Rumania, Poland, and Russia virtually all the businessmen and skilled artisans were Jews. 70 percent of the Jewish immigrants from eastern Europe had been involved in some aspect of industry or commerce in Europe compared to only 13 percent for other immigrants from eastern Europe. Between 1899 and 1910, 67.1 percent of the male Jewish immigrants from Russia were skilled workers, while only 35 percent of the Italians and 13 percent of the Irish came to the United States with skills. The United States Immigration Commission reported that, out of forty-seven trades, Jewish immigrants ranked first in twenty-six. The census of 1900 revealed that 10 percent of the foreign-born in the state of New York were employed at common labor, while only 2 percent of the immigrants from Russia were laborers.[14]

The occupational pattern of first and second generation East European Jewish women also differed dramatically from that of other ethnic groups. The percentage of Russian Jewish women in manufacturing and the artisan fields was the highest of any group. 71 percent of Jewish working girls were employed in manufacturing and the artisan trades, compared to 36 percent for all American women. Conversely the percentage of Jewish working girls in personal services such as servants and waitresses was the lowest of all ethnic groups. In contrast to the Irish, Russian Jews almost invariably avoided domestic work, despite the hopes of some German Jews that they become domestics for German Jewish families. "It is certainly not more menial to sweep out a dwelling than to brush out a store; not near so lowering to be at the call of the young ladies of a family, as to be subjected to the same thing from a merchant employer, his head clerk, and various customers," the *Jewish Messenger* wrote in 1885. "It is surely pleasanter to be hired regularly as a seamstress in a respectable family, than to stitch, stitch, stitch at an endless succession of shirts, or to ruin one's eyesight over an eternal round of button holes. . . .Who could compare the care of happy innocent children, of dimpled laughing babies, with the work of a factory girl — with its never ceasing din and smoke, and its unfortunate, morally unhealthy influences?"[15]

Despite such portraits of the occupational bliss of domestic work, the Russian girls preferred the sweatshops and stores. Nothing could have been more remote from the middle-class, incipient capitalist mentality of the Russian female than becoming a domestic. And when the Jewish girls entered the shops and factories they were far less willing to accept the status of a mere employee than girls from other groups. Jewish working girls were continuously involved in strikes, boycotts, and other activities designed to improve their working conditions.

The economic goal of most Russian Jewish immigrants was to own their own businesses. Nearly one-quarter of the breadwinners on the Lower East Side around the turn of the century were in business. The largely Jewish 8th Assembly District in 1899 had 140 groceries, 131 butcher shops, 62 candy stores, 36 bakeries, and over 2400 peddlers and pushcart vendors. This passion for business and a commercial cunning has been a central theme in American folk humor regarding Jews.

1) What is a *shiksa* (Yiddish for Gentile woman)? Someone who buys retail.
2) Jesus saves, but Moses invests.
3) The new movie "Jews" is about loan sharks.
4) The four shortest books in the world are *Great Irish Cuisine, The Polish Mind, Italian War Heroes,* and *Jewish Business Ethics.*
5) When Billy Graham sang, "All I want is Jesus," 5000 persons became Protestants. When the Pope sang "Ave Maria," 10,000 persons converted to Catholicism. When Pat Boone sang "There's a Gold Mine in the Sky," 100,000 Jews joined the Air Force.
6) God said to Moses, "I have a commandment for you." Moses replied, "How much?" God responded, "They're free." Moses said, "Good, I'll take ten."
7) What do you have when you have a Negro? A janitor. What do you have when you cross a Negro and a Pole? A retarded janitor. And what do you have when you cross that with a Jew? A retarded janitor who owns the building (and is probably sending his son to medical school).

And, of course, the word "Jew" became a commonly used adjective and verb as well as a noun.[16]

Thus while the Russian Jews came to the United States poor in monetary terms, they thought and acted like members of the middle class. In this they resembled the migration of Cubans to the United States in the 1960s. The social characteristics of the Russian Jews were not those generally associated with a proletariat. They were sober, valued education highly and, perhaps most important of all, deferred gratification and saved their money. "Thrift," Jacob Riis wrote, "is the watch-word of Jewtown. It is at once its strength and its fatal weakness, its cardinal virtue and its foul disgrace.". This deferral of gratification combined with the occupational sophistication of the Russian Jews resulted in rapid economic, social, and demographic upward mobility. The Russians were able to take advantage of an open economic and social milieu which placed a premium on commerical enterprise and hard work, and which had few artificial economic barriers such as minimum wage laws, licensing regulations, and restrictive labor union practices.[17]

At the same time the Germans were questioning whether the Jews of the Lower East Side could make it in America, the Russians were leaving the ghetto for better neighborhoods in Brooklyn, the Bronx, and upper Manhattan. While one-half of the city's Jews lived in the ghetto in 1903, less than one-quarter lived there in 1916. The Jewish population of the Brownsville area of Brooklyn increased from 10,000 in 1899 to 60,000 in 1904.[18]

The tendency of Russian Jews to gravitate toward trade was even more pronounced outside of New York City where there was a large Jewish working class. A book entitled *Trenton's Foreign Colonies* published in 1908 noted that over half of Trenton's stores were owned by "thrifty and industrious" Jews, and that the city's Jews had "added more to the material wealth of Trenton than all the other foreign-speaking colonies combined." A demographic study of Trenton's Jewish community revealed that in 1937, 59 percent of the city's 7200 Jews were dependent on trade while less than 14 percent were dependent on manufacturing or the mechanical industries. An analysis of Passaic's (New Jersey) Jews in the same year showed that 43 percent of the city's employed Jews were engaged in trade. The percentage of Jews in trade in Trenton and Passaic was three and a half to four times greater than for non-Jews.[19]

While the first generation of Russian Jews gravitated to trade, their children and grandchildren have moved into the professions. Within two generations the Jewish occupational structure came to resemble that of the Episcopalians, Congregationalists, and Presbyterians, the three highest status Protestant denominations. A third-generation Jewish garment worker is an extreme rarity. As early as 1940, 10 percent of employed American Jews were professionals compared to 7 percent for the general population. By the 1960s, the respective figures were 28 percent and 14 percent. It is estimated that the Jews, who comprise less than 3 percent of the nation's population, make up 10 percent of the country's lawyers. In Camden, New Jersey the percentage of self-employed male Jews declined in one generation from nearly two-thirds to one-third, and by 1964, 87 percent of Camden's employed male Jews were in white collar occupations, compared to 45 percent for the general population. "The shift from unskilled and skilled trades worked at by one generation, to clerical, managerial, and professional occupations in the next," the sociologist Jackson Toby wrote of the Jews, "probably was not duplicated by any other immigrant group."

American humor has also reflected this tendency of Jews to become professionals:

1) What is the difference between the new and old definitions of a C.P.A.? C.P.A. used to stand for Cleaning, Pressing, and Alterations. Now a C.P.A. is a Jewish boy who stutters and can't stand the sight of blood (otherwise he would have become a lawyer or a doctor).
2) A Jewish woman faints in a theater and the call goes out for a doctor. He revives the woman and the first thing he asks him is whether he is married because, if not, she has an eligible daughter.
3) A not too bright Jewish girl was continually advised by her mother to marry a doctor. The daughter could only remember her mother's advice to marry someone with a white coat and she ended up wed to the Good Humor man.[20]

Jewish affluence, which is about the same as that of Episcopalians, has also been a source of American humor. The Cadillac automobile has been referred to as a "Jew canoe." There is also the story of the new family which moves into town. The town's priest, minister, and rabbi decide to pay a visit in order to determine the family's religion. The family is not at home and so the three clergymen decide to peek through the window to see whether they can discover anything. The priest takes a look and says the family isn't Catholic because there is no crucifix on the wall. The minister peers through the window and then says the family isn't Protestant because there is not a King James Bible in the bookcase. The rabbi looks into the window and immediately says the family is one of his. The priest and minister want to know how he can be so sure. "Wall-to-wall carpeting," the rabbi answers. American humor has been a better guide to the economic adjustment of Russian Jews than the apprehensions of the Germans seventy-five years ago.[21]

The Germans also completely underestimated the ability of the Russians to assimilate American culture. There is no coincidence in the fact that the most popular Christmas and Easter songs were written by Irving Berlin, a product of the New York ghetto and also the author of "God Bless America"; or that the classic picture of the American immigrant striving to learn the English language is entitled *The Education of Hyman Kaplan*; or that *The Rise of David Levinsky* is probably the finest portrayal in American literature of the immigrant shedding his European ways. For the Russian immigrant the United States was truly the *goldenah medinah* (the golden land). It was the antithesis of everything he had known in eastern Europe. The Russian immigrant rejoiced in the economic and social opportunities, the religious freedom, the absence of virulent anti-Semitism, and the chance to escape from the intellectually stultifying world of East European Orthodoxy. The greatest humiliation suffered by a Russian Jew was to be called a "greenhorn," while his proudest moments were when he *oysgrien zikh* (ceased being a greenhorn) by cutting his beard, or buying his first American suit, or becoming a citizen, or making his children into regular "Yankees." The Russian immigrants poured into the public schools and libraries to learn more about this culture which offered them so much.

The descendants of the Russian Jews have flocked to the American universities with a vengeance, as if they were out to disprove the fears of the Germans that they could not assimilate the American culture. As early as the 1920s Harvard College was 20 percent Jewish, and president A. Lawrence Lowell publicly voiced concern over the Judaizing of Harvard and the need to restrict Jewish enrollment. The children and grandchildren of penniless Russian immigrants were responsible for the fact that the City College of New York has graduated more persons who eventually earned a doctor of philosophy degree than any other university in the world. Approximately 85 percent of Jewish youth presently go on to college compared with less than 50 percent for the general population. "A college education is becoming virtually universal for the younger segments of the Jewish population," one sociologist has written. "Within the Jewish population itself, the important educational differential will thus be between those who had only some college education and those who went on to postgraduate school." The definition of a Jewish drop-out has become a person with only a B.A. Twice as many Jews are in Phi Betta Kappa than their numbers warrant. The same picture is true of the Jewish entry into academia. At least 9 percent of American professors are Jewish, and 23 percent of Ivy League professors under the age of fifty are Jewish. In no other country in history have Jews been able to do so well academically or have had such intellectual influence as in the United States.[22]

One of the more interesting phenomena of the post-World War II era has been the rise to prominence of Jewish literary critics and novelists, culminating in the awarding of the 1976 Nobel Prize in literature to Saul Bellow who grew up in the Montreal ghetto. During these years the literary values of the nation have, in large part, been determined by such journals as the *Partisan Review*, *Commentary*, and the *New York Review of Books*, most of whose editors have been second and third-generation Russian Jews, and by such critics as Philip Rahv, Alfred Kazin, and Irving Howe. Indeed, a few years ago Truman Capote complained over national television that a New York (i.e., Jewish) literary mafia existed.

Perhaps in retrospect the most ironic fear of the Germans was the supposed inability of the Russians to overcome their pushy and vulgar ways and to act in a respectable and cultured manner. Many of the leading men's and women's clothing stylists and manufacturers who set the standards for what is appropriate to wear in America today are of Russian Jewish background. Similarly, Helena Rubinstein, Revlon, and Max Factor, not to mention Maidenform Bras, companies founded and controlled by Russian Jews, have done much to determine the grooming and appearance of the American female. Strangest of all are the facts that the most important arbiters of proper social behavior in America today are those two apostles to the Gentiles, the Friedman sisters Abigail Van Buren and Ann Landers, and that it was Murray Teichman of the Lower East Side who, after changing his name to Arthur Murray, became the nation's leading authority on the etiquette of proper social dancing.

The fear that the Russian Jew would physically and morally deteriorate under the impact of slum conditions was also unfounded. While the Lower East Side was by far the most crowded area in New York, it had one of the lowest death rates, and this was true even for deaths from tuberculosis. Nor did the areas of Jewish settlement exhibit the classic symptoms of moral deterioration associated with lower-class neighborhoods. The rate of crime in Jewish areas was consistently much lower than that of other ethnic groups. Most Jewish criminality involved white collar crime such as insurance frauds and other commercial chicanery rather than crimes of violence. William McAdoo, the New York City police commissioner, commented that the Russian Jew "is not apt, unless under great pressure, to resort to force to commit crimes of violence .... Among themselves disputes are mostly confined to worldly arguments. They argue with great vigor and earnestness, but the argument ends as it begins." Crime was, by and large, an avenue of social mobility for ambitious Jews, a business which happened to be on the wrong side of the law. The tendency to treat crime as a business is most graphically revealed by the Jewish "Murder Incorporated." Here Jews transformed even murder into a business. Other symptoms of moral deterioration were also lacking in the ghetto. Alcoholism was rare, the divorce rate was low, the juvenile delinquency rate was low, there was less school truancy, and the school children had higher I.Q's. The Germans simply failed to realize that, while the Russians might have been quite poor, they thought of themselves and acted as middle-class. It was only when Jews assimilated into suburban, middle-class life that they began to exhibit evidences of the social pathology found in America. Drug addiction, alcoholism, divorce, and juvenile delinquency resulted from the same processes of acculturation which the Germans so eagerly fostered.[23]

Of all the apprehensions of the Germans, the most accurate proved to be their fear of the strange politics of the Russian Jews. The Russians had a political outlook which contrasted dramatically with that of the Germans as well as with that of the vast majority of other Americans. Because of the oppression they had suffered at the hands of conservative European governments and because of their exclusion from politics, the East European Jews generally viewed official authority as alien, threatening, and illegitimate. For many Russian Jews the whole purpose of political activity was the destruction of officially constituted authority, and they were in the forefront of the various revolutionary movements in Europe during the 19th and 20th centuries. Furthermore, they tended to see the ultimate goal of politics as the establishing of a good and just society, rather than the reconciling of conflicting interest groups. This moralistic and, at times, messianic approach to politics accounts for the large percentage of members of the American Communist Party, the American Socialist movement, and the Students for a Democratic Society with Russian Jewish backgrounds. And yet despite this tendency toward political extremism and utopianism, the vast majority of East European Jews and their descendants have been "liberals" rather than radicals, socialists, and anarchists. And there is an increasing number of second and third generation Russian Jews who are politically to the right. Milton Friedman, a descendant of East European Jews, is the country's most prominent free-market economist and the winner of the 1976 Nobel Prize in economics. Barry Goldwater is of Polish Jewish background on his father's side, although he himself is a Protestant. One of the jokes told by Jews during the 1964 campaign was that they always knew the first Jew to run for President would be an Episcopalian.

Today the major questions Jews ask about themselves are almost exactly the opposite of those the Germans asked. While the Germans wondered whether the Russians could be civilized and Americanized, Jewish leaders today are concerned with Jewish identity, Jewish education, and ways to Judaize Americans. American culture has proven to be so attractive to Jews and its influence so pervasive that serious students of American Jewry have questioned whether, in the face of increasing intermarriage, growing assimilation, and widespread religious indifference, it can long exist without a return to a self-imposed ghetto. Significantly, assimilation is strongest within academia where acculturation has been the greatest.

The confrontation between the German and Russian Jew is not the first time, nor will it be the last, that a supposedly "superior" culture's perceptions of another culture were confuted by the course of history. It should instill in all of us a sense of humility when tempted to make facile generalizations about other cultures and peoples.

*Footnotes*

1. *Jewish Messenger* (New York), March 7, 1884, quoted in Irving A. Mandel, "The Attitude of the American Jewish Community Toward East European Immigration as Reflected in the Anglo-Jewish Press (1880-1890)," *"American Jewish Archives*, III (June, 1950), 15 (italics in original).
2. John Higham, *Send These to Me: Jews and Other Immigrants in Urban America* (New York, 1975), p. 126; Zosa Szajkowski, "The Attitude of American Jews to East European Jewish Immigration (1881-1893)," *Publication of the American Jewish Historical Society*, XL (March, 1951), 232; Robert Rockaway, "Ethnic Conflict in an Urban Environment: the German and Russian Jews in Detroit, 1881-1914," *American Jewish Historical Quarterly*, LX (December, 1970), 135.
3. Szajkowski, "Attitude of American Jews," 222 ff.
4. Joseph Brandes in association with Martin Douglas, *Immigrants to Freedom: Jewish Communities in Rural New Jersey Since 1882* (Phila., 1971), pp. 28-42.
5. Mandel, "Attitude of American Jewish Community," 15; Abraham Karp, "New York Chooses a Chief Rabbi," *Publication of the American Jewish Historical Society*, XLIV (March, 1955), 152-53; Moses Rischin, *The Promised City: New York's Jews, 1870-1914* (Cambridge, 1962), pp. 96-97.
6. Irving Howe, "The Immigrant Glory," *Midstream*, XXII (January, 1976), 16.
7. Szajkowski, "Attitude of American Jews," 238-39.
8. Howe, "Immigrant Glory," 17; Irving Howe, *World of Our Fathers* (New York, 1976), pp. 233-34; Rischin, *Promised City*, pp. 97-98. The unofficial motto of the swank New York German Jewish Harmonie Club was "more polish and less Polish." Similarly, the Phoenix and Eureka Clubs of Rochester, New York refused to admit East European Jews. B'nai Brith, which had been started in the 1840's by poor German Jews living on the Lower East Side, denied a charter to Russian Jews of the Lower East Side in the late nineteenth century.
9. Rischin, *Promised City*, pp. 101-102; Howe, "Immigrant Glory," 17-18.
10. Arthur A. Goren, *New York Jews and the Quest for Community: the Kehillah Experiment, 1908-1922* (New York, 1970), chs ii, vii, viii.
11. Goren, *New York Jews*, pp. 157-58.
12. Howe, "Immigrant Glory," 18; Marshall Sklare, *Conservative Judaism: an American Religious Movement* (New York, 1955, 1972). pp. 163-65.
13. Nathan Glazer, "The American Jews and the Attainment of Middle-Class Rank: Some Trends and Explanations," *The Jews: Social Patterns of an American Group*, ed. Marshall Sklare (New York, 1958), 141; Andrew M. Greeley, "The Ethnic Miracle," *Public Interest*, no 45 (Fall, 1976), 26-28.
14. Howard M. Sachar, *The Course of Modern Jewish History* (New York, 1958), pp. 188-90; Rischin, *Promised City*, pp. 59-68.
15. Rudolf Glanz, *The Jewish Woman in America: Two Female Immigrant Generations, 1820-1929*, Vol. I, *The Eastern European Jewish Woman* (New York, 1976), pp. 19-22.
16. Ed Cray, "The Rabbi Trickster," *Journal of American Folklore*, LXXVII (October-December, 1964), 336-37, 340; Alan Dundes, "A Study of Ethnic Slurs: The Jew and the Polack in the United States," *ibid.*, LXXXIV (April-June, 1971), 193-95; Nathan Hurvitz, "Blacks and Jews in American Folklore," *Western Folklore Quarterly*, XXXIII (October, 1974), 307.
17. Lucy S. Dawidowicz, "From Past to Past: Jewish East Europe to Jewish East Side," *The Jew in American Society*, ed. Marshall Sklare (New York, 1974), 61.
18. Rischin, *Promised City*, pp. 92-93: Thomas Kessner *The Golden Door: Italian and Jewish Immigrant Mobility in New York City, 1880-1915* (New York, 1977) ch. 6.
19. John S. Merzbacher, *Trenton's Foreign Colonies* (Trenton, 1908), pp. 65-69; Sophia M. Robison with the assistance of Joshua Starr, *Jewish Population Studies* (New York, 1943). pp. 13-14, 23-32.
20. Jackson Toby, "Hoodlum or Business Man: an American Dilemma." *The Jews*, ed. Sklare, 549: Dundes, "Ethnic Slurs," 193-95.
21. Hurvitz, "Blacks and Jews," 309; Cray, "Rabbi Trickster," 338.
22. Sidney Goldstein, "American Jewry: A Demographic Analysis," *American Jewish Year Book 1971*, eds. Morris Fine and Milton Himmelfarb, LXXII (Philadelphia, 1971), pp. 60–68.
23. Howe, *World of Our Fathers*, pp. 98, 149-50.

# THE JEWS OF NEW JERSEY

Although Jews have lived in New Jersey from at least the early eighteenth century, a Jewish community did not begin to develop in the state until the middle of the nineteenth century. As late as 1900, there were only 25,000 Jews in New Jersey, and only 21 cities and towns contained an organized Jewish presence whether in the form of a synagogue, a charitable society, or a lodge. Seventy-five years later, New Jersey contained over 400,000 Jews, making up approximately 5.5 per cent of the state's population. Only in New York, of all the states, did Jews comprise a greater percentage of the population.

### Jews in the colonial era

The first Jewish settlers in the colony of New Jersey were descendants of Spanish and Portuguese Jews who had fled the Iberian peninsula in the 1490's. Beginning as peddlers, they soon acquired enough capital to open stores and become landowners. The brothers Aaron and Moses Louzada, for instance, lived in Bound Brook, where they owned a general store, a mill, and large tracts of land. Daniel Nunez resided in Piscataway Township and in 1722 was selected as a Justice of the County Quarter

Sessions Court. He also served as town clerk, treasurer, and tax collector of the township, and was probably the first Jew in America to hold public office.

Occasionally there was mention of New Jersey Jews in colonial newspapers. Thus a notice in the *New York Mercury* in 1760, placed by four Jews and six Christians, offered a reward for the capture of a Myers Levy, who was accused of stealing money and merchandise.

> Whereas Myers Levy, late of Spotswood, in East New Jersey, Trader, is absconded, and being considerably indebted, there's all the Reason to believe he is gone off with intent to defraud his Creditors; this is to request all Persons to exert their Diligence to discover him that he may be secured, and Notify it to the Printer, for which he will pay them 20 Dollars. He is a man of Middle Stature, of a ruddy Complexion, wore his own Hair, is black Bearded, speaks broken English, but perfect in the Dutch; had in Company his Wife, a tall Woman, and five Children; it is conjectured he will go off to some Part of the West Indies.

In another newspaper notice, John Farnsworth of Phillipsburg declared in 1769 that he was no longer responsible for the debts of his wife, Deborah, who had run off with a "Jew shopkeeper" named Nathan Levy. "She likes the said Levy better than me," Farnsworth complained, and "intended to live with him, as he will maintain her as a gentlewoman: I have waited on Mr. Levy respecting the affair, from which I have received no other satisfaction than insolent language." Despite Farnsworth's experience, relations between the colony's two dozen or so Jewish families and their Gentile neighbors were generally harmonious, with no significant incident involving anti-Semitism in New Jersey during the eighteenth century.

New Jersey's Jews easily adapted to colonial life. The fact that they settled in New Jersey rather than in the established Jewish communities of Newport, New York, Philadelphia, Charleston, or Savannah indicates that their Jewish identity was possibly weak to begin with. This, combined with the openness of colonial society, resulted in rapid acculturation. The lack of Jewish identity is perhaps best seen in their response to the Revolution—a response which mirrored the diversity of opinion found among non-Jews. Thus while Asher Levy served as a lieutenant in New Jersey's militia, Jacob Louzada of Bound Brook had to flee to Nova Scotia because of Tory sympathies and had his land seized and sold by the state.

There was always the opportunity for New Jersey's Jews to relate to the Jewish communities of New York and Philadelphia. Because of the rudimentary system of communications and transportation, however, contacts with Jews in these two cities were irregular and infrequent. The colony's sparse Jewish population was unable to sustain a strong sense of Jewish identity.

### The German Jewish immigration

The development of a New Jersey Jewish community did not take place until the immigration of a sizable number of Jews from central Europe beginning in the 1840's. These German-speaking Jews had been mostly merchants and artisans in Europe. Their mercantile and middle-class outlook enabled them to take advantage of the opportunities offered by a rapidly urbanizing and industrializing nation. Beginning as dry-goods and notions peddlers, they advanced rapidly into the ranks of merchants and manufacturers and soon became quite prominent in many sectors of New Jersey commerce and industry. They became particularly significant in cigar manufacturing, the woolen and worsted industry, leather manufacturing, retail and wholesale trade, and the manufacture of ready-made clothing. In Passaic, where woolen manufacturing was to become the city's leading industry, Jacob Basch established its first mill, which eventually became the Passaic Woolen Company.

German Jews were especially important in Newark; as early as the 1860's, the city's two hundred Jewish families dominated its dry-goods trade. An indication of their rapid transformation from peddlers to substantial merchants was the founding in 1872 of the Progress Club, a social club for the German Jewish businessmen of Newark. "The success of the Jews in the commercial, financial and industrial world is phenomenal," wrote William von Katzler in 1913 in his history of Newark's Germans. In "the last fifty years they have gained almost entire control of some industries and a large share of others by their restless ambition; their ability to work almost unceasingly; their frugality and keen judgment." Katzler also noted Jewish dominance of Newark's real estate business, theaters, food stores, restaurants, and professions.

The two most prominent nineteenth-century German Jewish businessmen in the state were Nathan Barnert and Louis Bamberger. Barnert was born near Posen in 1838 and came to America with his parents in 1849. His father settled on the Lower East Side of New York City where he was a tailor. In 1850 the restless son went to California to seek his fortune. Instead of panning for gold, Barnert peddled soap, candles, and other items in the mining camps. Returning to the East in 1856, he opened a clothing and tailoring business in Paterson. He became wealthy during the Civil War as a result of receiving contracts to supply uniforms to the Union Army. After the end of the war, he branched out into real estate and later invested in silk mills, all the while increasing his wealth. Barnert was twice elected mayor of Paterson in the 1880's and gave his entire salary to charity. During his lifetime he gave over one million dollars to charity. He established the Nathan and Miriam Barnert Memorial Temple, the Nathan and Miriam Barnert Memorial Hospital, the Miriam Barnert Hebrew Free School, the Nathan and Miriam Home for the Aged, the Nathan and Miriam Nurses Home, and an orphan asylum in Jerusalem.

Louis Bamberger's father had originally migrated from Bavaria to Baltimore. The son moved to Newark, where, along with his partner and brother-in-law Felix Fuld, he presided over the growth of Bamberger's Department Store into one of the great emporiums of the nation. Bamberger also was a munificent philanthropist. He and Fuld were instrumental in building the Newark Museum, the Young Men's and Young Women's Hebrew Association of Newark, and the Beth Israel Hospital. In 1930, Bamberger and his sister, Fuld's widow, gave five million dollars to establish the Institute for Advanced Study in Princeton.

One future German Jewish mercantile magnate who left New Jersey began his career as a salesclerk for the firm of Ullman and Isaacs, located at Broad and New Streets in Newark. Denied a raise in salary in 1860 after working there for two years, he left for New York, where he established his own business bearing his name, Benjamin Altman.

Business, however, did not completely dominate the life of the first generation of New Jersey's German Jews. They were deeply committed Jews and, settling together in compact communities, they established as soon as possible the religious, social, and cultural institutions they had known in Europe. In Newark, for instance, the German Jews lived in the area of Springfield Avenue and Prince and High Streets, which soon came to be known as *der deutsche Berg*, "the German hill."

Generally the first institution established by the German Jews was a synagogue. New Jersey's first synagogue was Paterson's B'nai Jeshurun, "the children of Israel," founded in 1847. This was followed the next year by B'nai Jeshurun of Newark. In 1858 Trenton's Jews organized Har Sinai, "Mount Sinai," Congregation, and the next year Anshe Emeth, "the people of truth," was created in New Brunswick. The first congregation in Jersey City dates from 1864, while Atlantic City's Beth Israel, "the house of Israel," was organized in 1880 and Elizabeth's B'nai Israel, "the children of Israel," dates from 1882.

These struggling congregations often had to look for financial assistance from Jews in New York and other parts of the country during their initial years. B'nai Jeshurun of Newark in 1855 appealed to Jews in New York and elsewhere to aid them in the construction of a building. "Those who are able to contribute have already expended all their ready funds in the purchase of a lot for the erection of their synagogue and incidental expenses amounting to fifteen hundred dollars," the appeal related, "and they are now compelled to appeal to the benevolence of the community.... Differing in our peculiar views from the Christian people who surround us," the appeal continued, "we rejoice that there are strong points of faith in which we can all agree; and especially in the regard we have for the strict and sober morals and generous feelings of our nature, which are best cultivated in the religious societies to which we respectively belong. We trust our appeal will not be made in vain." Evidently some aid was forthcoming since the building was erected in 1858 on Washington Street at a cost of five thousand dollars. Ten years later, the congregation had grown to such an extent that it constructed another building one block south of the previous location at a cost of seventy-five thousand dollars.

Newark's Jews realized that, ultimately, they would have to depend upon themselves for the support of their institutions. Oheb Shalom, "lover of peace," Newark's third congregation, was organized in 1860 and included in its constitution the stipulation that "Every member is obligated if the synagogue, God forbid, should suffer damage by fire, to contribute $3 towards its repair to cover the loss."

These first congregations reflected not only their members' determination to perpetuate Judaism, but also their wish to maintain their Germanic culture. In the beginning, meetings of the synagogues' boards of trustees were in German, as were the rabbis' sermons. Even the congregations' religious schools conducted their classes in German, and the prayer books and Pentateuch used in religious services usually had German translations alongside of the Hebrew text. Oheb Shalom of Newark also included instruction in German reading and writing in its religious school's curriculum. With the acculturation of the first generation and the emergence of the second generation, the use of German gradually disappeared. In 1882, for example, the rabbi of B'nai Jeshurun of Newark began to deliver his sermons in English.

A more significant adaptation to American norms was the change in the religious ideology of these congregations. At first their outlook was quite traditional, and they attempted to conform to the rituals and religious laws with which they had been familiar in Europe. Hats were worn and men and women were separated during services. The traditional prayers were recited in Hebrew, and the Sabbath was scrupulously observed. In time, the impulse toward assimilation and Americanization proved too strong, and the German congregations changed their religious patterns so as to be more in tune with the temper and style of middle-class American Protestantism. In 1882, the same year its rabbi started preaching in English, B'nai Jeshurun of Newark eliminated the wearing of hats during services. Fourteen years later, it adopted the Union prayer book, which had been developed by Rabbi Isaac Mayer Wise of Cincinnati. Wise was the founder of American Reform Judaism and the foremost proponent of a distinctive American Judaism which would reflect the conditions of American, rather than European, society. Other congregations followed B'nai Jeshurun's example and also embraced Reform. Anshe Emeth, for instance, made the break around 1890.

The evolution of the German congregations mirrored the rapid assimilation of German Jews into American society. Profoundly grateful for the religious freedom and economic and social opportunities of America, they were adamantly opposed to any Jewish or non-Jewish effort to artificially isolate them from the mainstream of American life. Religious practices, such as the observance of Saturday as a complete day of rest, which interfered with their economic and social advancement were gradually eliminated. Other religious rites which made them appear different and unusual in the eyes of their Gentile neighbors, such as the eating of only kosher food, were also dropped.

The almost religious fervor which German Jews exhibited in behalf of the public school system can be explained by their intense desire to "normalize" the status of American Jews, by their zeal to achieve middle-class respectability, and by their fear that the later Russian-Jewish immigrants might segregate themselves in Jewish all-day schools and thereby impede the process of Americanization. When Nathan Barnert gave the land to build the Hebrew Free School of Paterson to serve the children of poor immigrants from east Europe, he stipulated that "no child shall be permitted to attend and be instructed...who shall not be a pupil of a public school." Similarly the Newark benefactors who established and supported the Hebrew Orphan Asylum of Newark insisted that all its residents attend public schools rather than all-day Jewish schools or other private schools.

This rapid adoption of American values and this fervent wish to become part of American middle-class society can also be seen in the development of the charitable institutions founded by New Jersey's German Jews. One of the most important was the Maenner Wohltagket Verein, founded in 1861 and the first prominent Jewish community welfare organization in Essex County. By 1876, it had dropped its German title and become the Hebrew Benevolent and Orphan Asylum Society. At the same time, it also decided to conduct its business in English rather than in German. This institution later developed into the Jewish Counseling and Service Agency, the Jewish family and child care service organization for Essex County. This society was established, not only out of a sincere charitable impulse to help impoverished Jews suffering as a result of the depression of 1857, but also out of a fear that poverty-stricken Jews might become a public charge and prove embarrassing to the rest of the Jewish community.

The insecurity of the Germans is best revealed in their response to the mass immigration of tens of thousands of penniless east European Jews beginning in the 1880's. The Germans had an ambivalent attitude toward this immigration. They recognized that they had a religious and moral responsibility to the "Russians" (as all the immigrants from east Europe were called). But they were also frightened by the strange religious, social, and cultural ways of the newcomers. They feared that, if the Russians were not rapidly Americanized, they themselves would be discredited because non-Jews would associate them with the Russians. As Moses Strauss told fellow members of the Hebrew Benevolent and Orphan Society, the Russians "are not yet accustomed to our free institutions, but we are under the belief that in time, through education and perserverance, they will make honorable and good citizens of this glorious country." To further this transformation, Newark's German Jews established the Hebrew Free School in 1882 for the purpose of insuring that the children of the east European immigrants would be "good, patriotic, law-abiding citizens of the United States."

New Jersey's Jewish rural colonies

The most famous and important effort in New Jersey to aid and "civilize" the Russians was the founding of several Jewish rural colonies in southern New Jersey in the late nineteenth century. The first of these was Alliance, founded three miles west of Vineland in 1882. This was followed by Rosenhayn, Bortmanville, Norma, Carmel, Six Points, Estellville, Hebron, Mizpah, Garton Road, and Woodbine in Salem, Cumberland, Atlantic, and Cape May counties.

These settlements reflected several strands of thought in modern Jewish history. One of these was agrarian idealism, which had a profound impact on Russian Jews during the nineteenth century. Jewish advocates of a return to the soil argued that it would enable the Jews to lead a natural life in which manual labor would be respected, and would disprove the image of the Jew as an unproductive middleman. Agrarianism influenced some Russian Jews to become Zionists and to propose the founding of collective agricultural settlements in Palestine. Other Jews were less sanguine about the possibility of settling in Turkish-controlled Palestine. Loosely grouped in the Am Olam ("eternal people") movement, they favored settlement in the Western Hemisphere, particularly in the United States.

Agricultural colonies also appealed to American German Jewish philanthropists. First of all, such colonies would enable Russian immigrants to move from the slums of urban ghettos to healthier and more wholesome environments. In addition, agricultural settlements would hasten the Americanization of the Russians by diluting the Jewish population of the major cities, particularly New York, and would refute criticisms of the Russians (and Germans) as unproductive economic parasites. As the *Jewish Exponent* of Philadelphia wrote, Jews living in the countryside "will have gone through a humanizing school of healthy and honest toil which cannot but leave its unmistakable impression on their characters as well as those of their posterity.... The damning marks of the middleman or the three-balls man will no longer cling to their largely regenerated physiognomies or poison the very vitals of their capable natures."

It was ironic that affluent German bankers, manufacturers, and merchants counseled the Russians to take up farming—and at a time when millions of native Americans were leaving the countryside for the better opportunities in the cities. Furthermore, the Germans tended to view the most important occupations of the Russians, such as peddling and the garment trades, as not involving honest manual labor when, in fact, many of the Germans themselves had begun as peddlers and some had become quite wealthy through the manufacture of ready-to-wear clothing. The energies of the immigrants, wrote an employee of the Baron de Hirsch Fund, which established Woodbine, "must be directed not to the petty trades, not to the pushcarts, or the pack on the shoulders, not to the tailor shop, but to the free, health-giving, ennobling, invigorating and plenteous farm life."

Germans also feared that a continued growth of the Jewish ghettos of New York, Boston, Philadelphia, and Chicago (and an accompanying increase in urban social and economic problems) could possibly result in an anti-Semitic backlash, which would engulf the Germans as well as the Russians. The alternative to eastern European Jews flocking to the "tenement houses...to disease and a vicious life," the *Jewish Record* argued in 1882, was for the immigrants to become farmers. This would be "the most effectual step to stamp out prejudice against the Jew."

Despite the American trend toward urbanization and the lack of farming experience among east European Jews, agricultural colonies were established in Louisiana, South Dakota, Oregon, Kansas, and other states. Nowhere, however, were they as numerous or as successful as in southern New Jersey. This region became the site of the great experiment in American Jewish agriculture for several reasons. First, the cost of land there was low. Second, it had adequate rail connections to the urban markets of New York and Philadelphia. Finally, it was close enough to these two cities so that wealthy German Jews could supervise and aid the settlements and yet far enough away so that the inhabitants would not be tempted by the attractions of urban life.

The Jewish population of the agricultural colonies reached its pre-1930's peak in 1901, when approximately thirty-three hundred Jews were living in these settlements. The population slowly decreased until the depression decade when over one hundred German Jewish refugee families settled in the Vineland area. Although largely professionals and businessmen, they took up poultry farming with the aid of loans from the Jewish Agricultural Society. The Jewish population of southern New Jersey was further augmented after World War II when approximately one thousand Polish Jews, survivors of the holocaust, settled in such places as Farmingdale, Toms River, and especially Vineland. Many of the Polish Jews also went into poultry farming, and in 1951 they founded the Jewish Poultry Farmers' Association. Vineland became a center of east European Jewish culture. Yiddish programs were broadcast over the local radio station, Yiddish concerts and plays were performed, several new synagogues were built, and a Jewish day school was opened in 1953. Today there are approximately twenty-five hundred Jews in Vineland.

The basic problem of New Jersey's Jewish farmers was their inability to convince their children to stay on the land. This is true whether one is speaking of the pioneers of the 1880's and 1890's, or of the refugees of the 1940's. The children were not attracted to the relatively limited economic opportunities and lower prestige of agriculture as compared to business and the professions. Philadelphia especially became a mecca for young, ambitious Jews from southern New Jersey.

The settlers in the colonies recognized almost immediately that agriculture could not provide enough income and that some industrialization would be necessary. The most significant attempt to create an economy balanced between industry and agriculture was made in Woodbine. This community was established in 1891 by the Baron de Hirsch Fund, a philanthropy founded by a French railroad magnate to subsidize Jewish vocational and agricultural education. "I contend most decidedly against the old system of alms giving which only makes so many more beggars," Baron de Hirsch declared in 1891. "What I desire to accomplish is to give to a portion of my companions in faith the possibility of finding a new existence primarily as farmers, and also as handicraftsmen."

Woodbine soon became the largest and most important of the Jewish colonies in the state. In 1903 it became the first incorporated all-Jewish community in the United States. Even more important was the founding in 1894 of the Baron de Hirsch Agricultural School, the first secondary agricultural school in America. It contained 270 acres of land, stables, and model dairy herds. Rabbi Bernard L. Levinthal of Philadelphia voiced the underlying anti-mercantile philosophy of the school when he spoke at a dedication of a new classroom building in 1900: "Adam was placed in the garden of Eden not to trade or peddle therein, but to till it and to keep it," Levinthal said, "and the greatest of lawgivers, kings, and prophets in Israel came not from merchants, but from the rural population of the farmers." Although the school taught both the mechanical and the agricultural arts, its major focus was on farm education. Its graduates included Jacob Lipman, the dean of Rutgers University's school of agriculture for over two decades; the eminent entomologist Jacob Kotinsky; and Arthur Goldhaft, the founder of the Vineland Poultry Laboratories and a pioneer in the treatment of poultry diseases and the improvement of poultry breeding techniques. Despite their early successes, the trustees of the Hirsch Fund eventually concluded that the school could do a more effective job in New York. In 1919 the school was given to that state, and it became the State Institution for Feebleminded Males.

Jewish farming in the Garden State has not been restricted to the Vineland-Woodbine area. Farm settlements were established in Lakewood, Plainfield, Farmingdale, Bound Brook, New Brunswick, and Monmouth Junction. There was even a New Deal subsistence homestead project known as Jersey Homesteads, which was started in 1933 in Monmouth County five miles south of Hightstown. The project's goal was to provide housing for 200 unemployed garment worker families from New York who would become self-sustaining through subsistence farming and seasonal employment in a cooperative garment factory. Although the 200 houses were built, only 120 families moved to Jersey Homesteads. The garment factory failed, as did the cooperative poultry, dairy, and truck farms. The majority of the settlers were never interested in subsistence agriculture. Critics of the New Deal pointed to Jersey Homesteads as a prime example of the Roosevelt administration's supposed bureaucratic bungling and fiscal extravagance. The most severe critics of Jersey Homesteads were its government administrators themselves, and in 1940 they auctioned off the poultry plant and the farm. After the end of World War II, the government gave up all control of the project by selling the houses to individual families. Shortly thereafter, the residents of Jersey Homesteads changed its name to Roosevelt.

Although the Jewish farm families of New Jersey probably never numbered more than thirty-five hundred, they have made significant contributions to the state's agricultural economy. They took the lead in organizing agricultural credit unions and egg-marketing cooperatives. Undoubtedly the most significant role of New Jersey's Jewish farmers was in developing the state's egg and poultry industry. The economics of poultry farming were such that it allowed Jews lacking capital and farm experience to become successful. Poultry farming did not require large expenditures of money for the purchase of land, and the contacts Jewish farmers had with Jewish businessmen in nearby cities lubricated the process of marketing the eggs and chickens. Furthermore, poultry farming

The predominantly Jewish settlement of Woodbine early in the twentieth century.

could be done on a part-time basis, and some income would be forthcoming soon after beginning farming, important considerations for families lacking adequate outside sources of income. Jews thus naturally gravitated into poultry farming, and Vineland soon became known as the "Egg Basket of the East." Jews also made egg production into a major industry in the Freehold-Lakewood area. By following the recommendations of state and federal farm experts, they transformed egg production into a scientific, mass-production business. The rapid expansion of poultry farming in New Jersey after World War I was largely the work of the Jewish farmer. In 1940, the state ranked nineteenth in egg production, with 805,000,000 eggs. In 1964, the state ranked fourteenth and produced 1,622,000,000. By then, over 75 per cent of New Jersey's Jewish farmers were poultry farmers, and three-fourths of all the state's egg production was by Jewish farmers.

Another important achievement of New Jersey's farm communities was providing a new start in life for refugees from Europe and for residents of New York tenements disillusioned with urbanization and commerce. In 1932, on the fiftieth anniversary of the founding of Alliance, Sidney Bailey, one of Alliance's original settlers, contrasted the life of the Jewish farmers of southern New Jersey during the Great Depression with that of their coreligionists in New York and Philadelphia. Our "farms are all paid for," he noted. "We have a good name, and credit in the bank, befitting industrious and thrifty people. We feel prosperous and can keep our heads up; we are employed steadily; we are our own bosses. We are well and fairly comfortable and happy." After contrasting the condition of the farmers to that of city dwellers, Bailey concluded, "we have less temptations, albeit less luxuries. We lead a natural life." New Jersey's farmers have demonstrated, if it ever needed to have been shown, that a Jew could be the sower of oats as well as the sewer of coats.

### The East European Jewish immigration

New Jersey's Jewish farmers, however, constituted only a tiny minority of the Jewish immigrants from east Europe who settled in the state in large numbers beginning in the late nineteenth century. East European Jews had resided in the state prior to this time. B'nai Abraham, "the sons of Abraham," Newark's second oldest synagogue, had been established as early as the 1850's by Polish Jews. But the great growth of New Jersey's Jewish population did not occur until the mass exodus of Jews from Russia, Hungary, Poland, and Rumania began in the 1880's. In 1880 there were 5,600 Jews in the state. The figure was 25,000 in 1900, 84,000 in 1910, 163,000 in 1920, and 219,000 in 1930. The fifth-largest foreign-born linguistic group in New Jersey during this period consisted of those who spoke Yiddish. In 1910 Yiddish was the mother tongue of

49,000 inhabitants of New Jersey; in 1920, 60,000; and in 1930, 68,000. The percentage of foreign born in New Jersey who listed Yiddish as their mother tongue was 7.5 per cent of all of the state's foreign born in 1910 and 8.1 per cent in 1920 and again in 1930.

This steep population growth resulted in an explosive increase in the Jewish population of the state's major urban centers, the eventual home of the vast majority of the east European immigrants. In 1905 Bayonne had 1,200 Jews, and seven years later it had 10,000. Jersey City had 6,000 Jews in 1905 and 10,000 by 1912. Newark's Jewish population went from 3,500 in 1877 to 30,000 in 1907. There were 37 Jews in Passaic in 1877, and 3,000 in 1907. In Paterson the number of Jews increased from 427 in 1877 to 5,000 in 1907.

The urban orientation of New Jersey's Jews is reflected in the rough correlation between the degree of urbanization of the state's counties and the size of each county's Jewish population. The national census of 1950 revealed a Jewish population of less than 1 per cent in the rural counties of Hunterdon, Sussex, Warren, Burlington, and Gloucester. The relatively sparsely populated counties of Morris, Somerset, and Salem had a Jewish population of between 1 and 2 per cent, while Cape May County's Jewish inhabitants were 2.3 per cent of the total. In Cumberland County, where the Jewish center of Vineland is located, Jews comprised 3.2 per cent of the population.

By contrast, the 1950 Jewish population in the more industrialized and urbanized counties was much larger, both in absolute and relative terms. The percentage of Jews in Camden County was 3.2; in Bergen County, 3.7; in Mercer County, 4.4; in Monmouth County, 4.6; in Hudson County, 4.7; in Union County, 5.3; in Middlesex County, 5.8; in Essex County, 6.3; and in Ocean County, 6.9. The largest concentration was in Atlantic County, whose Jewish population was 8.7 per cent of the total, and in Passaic County, 9.7 per cent of whose people were Jewish.

Today at least three-fourths of New Jersey's Jewish population is located in the most urbanized section of the state, running from Middlesex County north through Bergen County. Other sizable Jewish settlements are in Trenton, Camden, and along the shoreline.

The number of east European Jews in the state increased every decade during the twentieth century. This was due to continued immigration from Europe, to natural increase, and to migration from New York and Philadelphia. The growth of Bergen County's Jewish community began after the completion of the George Washington Bridge in 1931 enabled residents of northern New Jersey to commute easily to their jobs and businesses in New York. Bergen County now has approximately one hundred thousand Jews. The movement of Jews out of Philadelphia's inner city, combined with improvements in transportation from Camden to Philadelphia, contributed to the growth of Camden Jewry. Atlantic

City's Jewish population grew to ten thousand by 1976 as a result of the city's becoming a major resort center.

The first area of settlement of the east European Jewish immigrants was generally in the heart of the city, often in an area previously settled by German Jews. Paterson's Fourth Ward, for example, came to be known as "Jewtown." In Newark, the Russians initially settled in the old Third Ward, which, at one time, was the center of German Jewish settlement. Newark's Prince Street became a thriving shopping area for Newark's east European Jews. Its pushcarts gave the street the atmosphere of a miniature Hester Street and Orchard Street of New York's Lower East Side.

Prince Street mirrored what was perhaps the most significant fact regarding the Russian Jew. Although he came virtually penniless to the United States, he did bring with him a tradition of commercial enterprise and a middle-class mentality. He differed from many of the other immigrant groups from south and east Europe who arrived in the United States at the same time by the extent to which he avoided unskilled and semi-skilled labor and flocked instead to commerce and the professions. John S. Merzbacher analyzed the east European Jew in his 1908 book, *Trenton's Foreign Colonies*. He noted that over 50 per cent of Trenton's stores were owned by Jews, that they were "thrifty and industrious," and that they "added more to the material wealth of Trenton than all the other foreign-speaking colonies combined." Throughout the state, Russian Jews gravitated toward trade, especially in food, clothing and shoes, furniture, and hardware.

This is not to deny, however, that there did exist a first-generation east European Jewish proletariat in New Jersey. Particularly in Paterson's silk factories, Passaic's woolen mills, and the garment factories of Newark and Jersey City there was at one time a Jewish working class. Nevertheless, it differed from the working class of other ethnic groups. First of all, it was relatively small because of the tendency of Jews to enter business and the professions. In Trenton in 1937, for instance, 59 per cent of the city's 7,200 Jews were dependent upon trade, while less than 14 per cent were employed in manufacturing or the mechanical industries. In Passaic in the same year, 43 per cent of the employed Jews were engaged in trade. The percentage of Jews in trade in these two cities was three and a half to four times greater than that for non-Jews. Not only was the percentage of Jews in the laboring class far lower, but the number of years spent in unskilled and semi-skilled work was also much less. In Paterson by the 1920's, 90 per cent of the city's silk factories were owned by the same Polish Jews who two or three decades earlier had begun as workers in these factories. In the clothing factories of Newark and Jersey City, Russian and Polish Jews quickly succeeded German Jews as owners. The Jewish laborer was, at heart, an incipient capitalist who fully anticipated becoming self-employed in the near future. Many laborers achieved this goal; of those who did not hardly any saw their children enter the shops and factories.

The entry of east European Jews into the professions was also quite dramatic. The 10,000 Jews of Passaic made up 16 per cent of the city's 1937 population; yet 50 per cent of Passaic's doctors and 84 per cent of its lawyers and judges were Jewish. In Trenton in the same year, two-thirds of all doctors and 40 per cent of all lawyers and judges were Jews. Twelve per cent of Trenton's employed Jews were in the professions, compared to 5 per cent of the general population.

The large number of Jewish professionals resulted in part from the intense drive for higher schooling exhibited by the east European Jews. A 1964 demographic study of Camden's Jewish population revealed that five times as many Jews as non-Jews had four years of college. Of Jews in the 20 to 24 age group, 59 per cent were still in school, compared to 9 per cent for the rest of the population. The Jewish adult population of New Jersey will, within a few decades, be almost completely college educated.

Jewish college graduates have mostly entered white-collar and professional employment. This trend has led to a rapid decline in the percentage of Jews involved in small business and retail trade. In Camden, for example, the proportion of Jewish men who were self-employed declined in one generation from nearly two-thirds to one-third. By 1964, 87 per cent of Camden's male Jews were in white-collar occupations compared to 42 per cent of the general male population. The same phenomenon was also found in Newark, Passaic, Jersey City, and Trenton, and similar developments have occurred among Jews outside of New Jersey.

The rapid upward economic and social mobility of the east European Jews resulted in their leaving the first areas of settlement for better neighborhoods. In Newark, Jews who had achieved middle-class status began leaving the Third Ward in the 1920's for the Weequahic section, an area which soon had the largest number of Newark's Jews. By 1933, Weequahic's population had grown so quickly that Weequahic High School had to be erected. In contrast, the Third Ward, which in 1924 had over 22,000 Jews, had only 600 twenty years later. Other Jews in Newark left the city entirely prior to World War II and moved to the suburbs. Irvington, for example, had 2,000 Jews in 1927 and 6,600 in 1937. Hillside's Jewish population during these same ten years went from 1,000 to 1,600.

### Jewish suburbanization

This Jewish movement to the suburbs, a statewide occurrence, accelerated rapidly after World War II. The prominent Jewish demographer

Sophia M. Robinson stated, in her 1949 analysis of Trenton Jewry, that "the decentralization of the population, an emptying out of the old Ghettos, following the trend in the general community, suggests another topic of interest not only in the provision of special Jewish services but in the integration of Jews into the general community life and activities as well." Ironically one year before, in her study *The Jewish Population of Essex County*, she had predicted that the Weequahic Jewish community would remain relatively stable. This stability, she contended, "revealed both in the length of residence and the age distribution suggests that it may well provide an integrating and stabilizing force in the community at large." Approximately two decades later, Weequahic was virtually all-black.

Except for several hundred elderly Jews living in two housing projects near the airport, the Jews of Newark have deserted the city for the suburbs. The Jewish population of Essex County (plus the adjoining town of Hillside) numbered 86,000 in 1948. Two-thirds of these Jews lived in Newark. By 1958 the Jewish population of Newark had shrunk to 41,000, while that in Bloomfield had increased from 1,700 to 2,700, in Montclair from 900 to 1,400, in Millburn from 600 to 2,000, and in West Orange from 1,300 to 7,000. In his novel *Goodbye Columbus*, Philip Roth, a product of Newark's Weequahic, described the process whereby Newark's Jews "had struggled and prospered, and moved further west, towards the edge of Newark, then out of it, and up the slope of the Orange Mountains, until they had reached the crest and started down the other side, pouring into Gentile territory as the Scotch-Irish had poured through the Cumberland Gap."

The same thing happened in other parts of the state. In 1958 there were only 15 Jewish families in Wayne; ten years later there were 850. Fairlawn, a suburb of Paterson, had 1,000 Jews in 1948 and 4,000 in 1957. Jersey City's Jewish population declined from 22,000 prior to World War II to 10,000 by 1975. In Camden the center of Jewish population migrated to Cherry Hill, Haddonfield, and Haddon Township. The most dramatic example of Jewish suburbanization in the state took place in Bergen County. In 1950 there were only 20,000 Jews in Bergen County. Two and a half decades later there were 100,000. Englewood contained fewer than 1,000 Jews in 1937, 2,000 by 1948, and 7,000 in 1969. Teaneck had fewer than 1,000 Jews in 1937, 2,100 in 1948, and 12,000 by 1969. Morris County has even acquired a sizable Jewish population as Jews from the metropolitan Newark area continue to push westward.

The movement of Jews from New York City to Bergen and Passaic Counties and, on a smaller scale, from Philadelphia to Camden County has decreased the percentage of the state's Jews who reside in Essex County. Of the 268,000 Jews living in New Jersey in 1937, approximately

88,000 or roughly one-third were in Newark and its suburbs. By 1976, 418,000 Jews were living in New Jersey and only 95,000 or 24 per cent lived in the environs of Newark. The Newark metropolitan area remains, however, the seventh-largest American Jewish community. The flow of Jewish population from Pennsylvania and New York has also increased the numerical importance of New Jersey in the national Jewish community. Whereas, in 1927, the 225,000 Jews of New Jersey comprised 4.5 per cent of the 4,228,000 American Jews, in 1976 the 418,000 New Jersey Jews were 7.3 per cent of the nation's 5,732,000 Jews.

The suburbanization of New Jersey's Jews has resulted in the eclipse of Orthodoxy and the emergence of Conservative Judaism as the major religious denomination of the state's Jews. In 1890 there were no Conservative congregations at all since Conservative Judaism is a product of the twentieth century. Eighty per cent of the congregations were Orthodox, and 20 per cent were Reform. By 1960, there were more Conservative congregations in the state than Orthodox and Reform combined.

The relationship between suburbanization and the growth of Conservatism is best revealed by examining Newark. In 1945 there were forty-eight religious congregations in Newark and the suburbs. Of the thirty-four in Newark, thirty-one were Orthodox. Of the 14 suburban congregations, thirteen were either conservative or "modern" Orthodox. In 1976 there were forty-six congregations in the Newark area, of which eighteen were Orthodox, twenty were Conservative, and eight were Reform. Of the Orthodox congregations, four were in Newark and seven were in the adjoining communities of Hillside and Irvington. Of the seven Orthodox congregations in suburbia, only one had a sizable membership. The Orthodox congregations were, by and large, quite small, and many served merely as places for worship. In contrast, the Conservative congregations were dynamic and active, with memberships in the hundreds of families. There were several Conservative congregations which individually probably had a larger membership than all of the Newark area's Orthodox congregations combined.

The same correlation between suburbanization and growth of Conservative Judaism is found in other parts of the state. In Camden in 1964, 66 per cent of the Jews considered themselves to be Conservative, 22 per cent, Reform, and 8 per cent, Orthodox. Most of these Orthodox were elderly. The growth of Fairlawn resulted in a 300 per cent increase in the membership of the Fairlawn (Conservative) Jewish Center during the 1950's. The (Conservative) Jewish Center of West Orange had 45 families in 1945, 165 families in 1951, and 525 families in 1957.

Conservatism grew in several ways. Some Orthodox congregations became Conservative, such as Congregation B'nai Israel of Elizabeth in 1920. Often this happened when the congregation moved to the suburbs. Or, sometimes new congregations were established, such as Beth El ("house of God") in South Orange in 1946, the Jewish Center of West Orange in 1941, and the Jewish Center of Verona in 1936. Finally, growth stemmed from the movement of existing Conservative congregations to the suburbs, where they were able to attract a larger membership. When Oheb Shalom of Newark moved to South Orange in 1958, its rabbi described the tide of suburbanization as "an almost irresistible, intangible pressure."

The large Conservative synagogue centers with their extensive youth programs and their adult social activities appealed to the new Jewish suburbanites. As Rabbi Morris Werb of the Conservative synagogue of Caldwell wrote, "Suburban life has developed a new form of community organization revolving around the synagogue-center as a focal point of group interest, social activities and for the inculcation of Jewish values for the children." The growing identification of Jews with the suburban Conservative center has not, however, been accompanied by any increase in religious observance or commitment. Synagogue membership is instead the means by which children are socialized within the Jewish community as well as the context within which Jews in suburbia identify themselves as Jews. The Conservative synagogue-center has thus become the major institution of suburban Jews for the preservation of group life.

**The future of Jewish culture in New Jersey**

The greatest challenge to contemporary New Jersey Jewry is maintaining this group life in the face of the very real threat which an open

Aerial photograph of the Jewish Community Center of Trenton, located in suburban Ewing Township. With suburbanization, the Jewish community center movement has played a large role in the lives of New Jersey's Jewry. Courtesy Jewish Federation of Greater Trenton.

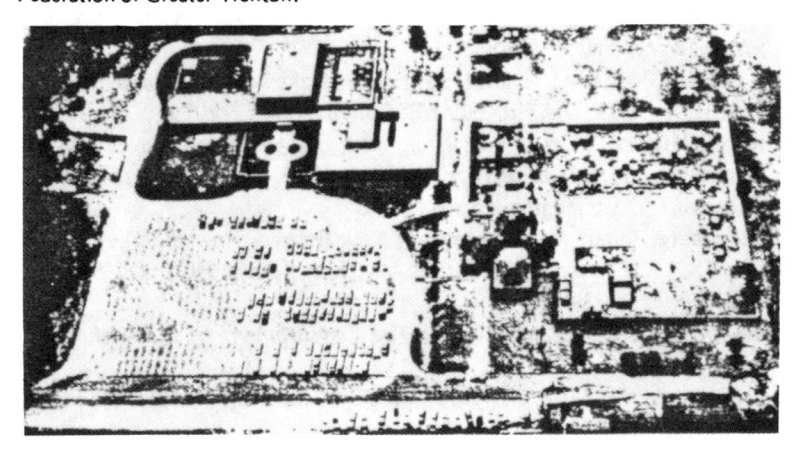

and free society poses to continued Jewish identity. The prognosis for the future is unclear. On the one hand, there is an increasing intermarriage rate, a birth rate lower than that of the general society, and widespread apathy of Jews toward their religion. On the other hand, there is an intense emotional commitment to the state of Israel and a willingness to support a complex of Jewish community centers, old-age homes, hospitals, synagogues, and schools.

Among the most revealing manifestations of the Jewish will to survive are the approximately twenty-five community centers (or Young Men's and Young Women's Hebrew Associations) which have been erected throughout the state. When the Newark "Y" opened in 1924, it declared its purpose to be a community center where "Hebrew men and women in Newark may find a wholesome environment, and where their social, educational, religious and physical standards may be improved." Only time will tell whether the impulse toward cultural and social autonomy and cultural pluralism found in the center movement and within Conservative Judaism will prove stronger than the forces of acculturation, assimilation, and cultural integration.

**Sources and suggestions for further reading**

Baum, Michael T. *Biography of Nathan Barnert: His Character and Achievements Including Histories of Local Institutions.* Paterson, 1914.

Brandes, Joseph, in association with Martin Douglas. *Immigrants to Freedom: Jewish Communities in Rural New Jersey Since 1882.* Philadelphia, 1971.

Conkin, Paul K. "Jersey Homesteads—A Triple Co-Operative." *Tomorrow a New World: The New Deal Community Program.* Ithaca, N.Y., 1959.

*The Essex Story: A History of the Jewish Community in Essex County, New Jersey.* Newark, 1955.

Freedman, Morris. "The New Farmers of Lakewood." *Commentary on the American Scene.* Ed. Elliot E. Cohen. New York, 1953.

Freund, Michael, et al. *Jewish Community Organization in Newark and Essex County: Final Reports and Memoranda Presented to the Survey Committee.* Mimeographed, 1945.

Friedenberg, Albert M. "The Jews of New Jersey from the Earliest Times to 1850." *Publications* of the American Jewish Historical Society, XVII (1909), 33-43.

Gale, Joseph, ed. *Eastern Union: The Development of a Jewish Community.* Elizabeth, 1958.

*Jewish Roots: A History of the Jewish Community of Passaic and Vicinity.* n. p., 1959.

Kohn, S. Joshua. "David Narr of Trenton, New Jersey." *American Jewish Historical Quarterly*, LIII (June 1964), 373-95.

Kussy, Nathan. "Early History of the Jews of Newark." *The Jewish Community Blue Book of Newark*. Ed. Anton Kaufman. Newark, 1926.

Kussy, Sarah. "Reminiscences of Jewish Life in Newark, New Jersey." *YIVO Annual of Jewish Social Science*, VI (1951), 177-86.

Robinson, Sophia M. *A Demographic Study of the Jewish Population of Trenton, N. J., 1949*. New York, 1949.

—. *The Jewish Population of Essex County*. Newark, 1948.

—. "The Jewish Population of Passaic, 1937." *Jewish Population Studies*. Ed. Sophia M. Robinson with the assistance of Joshua Starr. New York, 1943.

—. "The Jewish Population of Trenton." *Jewish Population Studies*. Ed. Sophia M. Robinson with the assistance of Joshua Starr. New York, 1943.

Rosskam, Edward. *Roosevelt, New Jersey: Big Dreams in a Small Town & What Time Did to Them*. New York, 1972.

Newark's Prince Street, circa 1910. Courtesy Newark Public Library.

Seligman, Ben. *The Jewish Population of Passaic, N. J., 1949: A Demographic Study.* New York, n. d.

Stark, Rodney, and Stephen Steinberg. *It Did Happen Here: An Investigation of Anti-Semitism: Wayne, New Jersey, 1967.* Berkeley, Calif., 1967.

*A Study of the Jewish Community of New Brunswick with Special Reference to the Young Men's Hebrew Association.* New York, 1927.

Werb, Morris. "Jewish Suburbia—An Historical and Comparative Study of Jewish Communities in Three New Jersey Suburbs." Unpublished Ph.D. diss., New York University, 1959.

Westhoff, Charles T. *Population and Social Characteristics of the Jewish Community of the Camden Area, 1964.* Cherry Hill, n. d.

## AMERICAN ANTI-SEMITISM RECONSIDERED

The historiography of European Jewry has been quite different from that of American Jewry. European historians have made anti-Semitism the central theme of their narratives, emphasizing pogroms, expulsions and discrimination. Especially has this been true for post-Holocaust historians for whom the murder of six million Jews was the logical culmination of the social, economic, intellectual, and religious currents dominant in Europe during the past 2,000 years. So strong has been this stress on anti-Semitism that a few years ago Salo Baron, the dean of Jewish historians, protested against what he termed the "lachrymose" interpretation of the European Jewish experience.

Historians of American Jewry, in contrast, have tended to view anti-Semitism as an exception, a quirk of fate, an abnormal situation caused by temporary social and economic factors. Whereas for the European historian the glass is half full of anti-Semitism, for the American historian the glass is half full of tolerance and opportunity. Thus Carey McWilliams' 1948 volume, A Mask for Privilege: Anti-Semitism in America, argued that anti-Semitism had been a product of capitalism and would disappear with the socialization of the means of production and distribution. For McWilliams, anti-Semitism had been a capitalist diversion used to distract popular outrage from the capitalists to the Jews. In contrast, the contemporary Harvard historian Oscar Handlin has stressed that anti-Semitism had been a transitory phenomenon resulting from the agrarian discontent of the late nineteenth century. Jews, Handlin asserted, personified the financiers and tradesmen whom farmers believed responsible for their economic plight. John Higham, in a series of perceptive essays written during the past several decades, contended that the anti-Semitism of the late nineteenth century was primarily due to rapid Jewish social and economic mobility which resulted in a backlash among threatened Gentiles eager to preserve islands of exclusivity in a society without traditional signs of status and deference.

The lynching of Leo Frank in Georgia in 1915 was the most prominent anti-Semitic event in American history. Leonard Dinnerstein's The Leo Frank Case, undoubtedly the finest analysis of any American anti-Semitic incident, relates the murder of Frank to southern social and economic tensions caused by rapid industrialization and urbanization. According to Dinnerstein, fundamentalist-oriented southern migrants from the countryside found it extremely difficult to adjust to the urban tempo of Atlanta and other burgeoning southern cities.

Arnold Rose's famous essay, "Anti-Semitism's Root in City Hatred," attributed American anti-Semitism to the Jews' identification with the cities. The Jews' association with political radicalism, economic success and cultural modernism stemmed from their residence in the large cities, especially in "Jew" York. For Rose, Dinnerstein, Handlin and Higham, then, anti-Semitism has resulted from a unique constellation of social and economic factors at a particular point in history, rather than being an ever-present phenomenon taking on various forms. The problem for students of American anti-Semitism thus has been to explain its existence (for students of European anti-Semitism it has been to explain its absence), and to anticipate its eventual demise. Hence, Gordon W. Allport's The Nature of Prejudice (1954) and Gertrude J. Selznick and Stephen Steinberg's The Tenacity of Prejudice: Anti-Semitism in Contemporary America (1969) foresaw the gradual disappearance of anti-Semitism with the spread of education.

Michael N. Dobkowski's The Tarnished Dream: The Basis of American Anti-Semitism challenges the conventional wisdom on two grounds. He claims that anti-Semitism has been far more important and pervasive in our national history than previous scholars were willing to admit, and that the persistence of anti-Semitism within different social and economic contexts throws doubt on the social-economic explanation. Instead, Professor Dobkowski draws our attention to the role of stereotypes in perpetuating negative attitudes towards Jews.

Dobkowski, who teaches Jewish studies at Hobart and William Smith Colleges, argues that most previous studies of anti-Semitism, and particularly of American anti-Semitism, have emphasized its social and economic roots and have underestimated its ideological dimensions. In part this is because most students of anti-Semitism have been sociologists and social psychologists, and in part because of the influence of social and economic interpretations of history.

Whereas previous interpretations of late nineteenth and early twentieth century American anti-Semitism have correlated its ebb and flow with changing economic and social conditions, The Tarnished Dream argues that it was a consistent and widespread element of American life and relatively immune to economic and social changes. Because anti-Semitism resulted from the images Gentiles had of Jews, it could be strengthened but not dislodged by environmental changes. Dobkowski singles out eight images of Jews for consideration: the enemy of Christianity; the criminal; the deceitful money-grubber; the parvenu; the eternal alien; the conspirator; the quintessential capitalist; the radical. These images, Dobkowski claims, were staples of newspaper and magazine articles, plays, and the dime novels of the late nineteenth and early twentieth the centuries.

The Jew as Christ killer was, of course, nothing new. Although the religious image was not as significant in the United States as it had been in Europe, it was important for many Americans, particularly those who identified Americanism with Christianity in general, and evangelical Protestantism in particular. The image of Judaism as narrow, sectarian, superstitious and bigoted had existed prior to the mass immigration of East European Jews to America around the turn of the century, and this immigration merely strengthened Judeophobia. Jewish suffering was attributed to the rejection of the gentle Jesus by a fossilized religion teaching hatred of Gentiles and vengeance on its enemies. Jews were enslaved within a hopeless maze of meaningless formalistic rituals by a Talmudic legal system which blocked out the higher truths of Christianity. Everything about Judaism reeked of the ghetto: its worship of a nationalistic diety; its intolerance of non-Jews; its imperviousness to the spirit of enlightenment. The Jew was a fit subject for American citizenship only because he was a potential Christian.

The image of the Jew as a criminal also predated the mass migration of East European Jewry. Scratch a Jew and you will uncover an arsonist, a white-slaver, a fence, a counterfeiter, a blackmailer, a gambler, and a thief. As one anti-Semite of the time wrote, "the Jewish immigrants have brought us crime, indecency, immorality, filth, and all the other things that have long been associated with that race." Anti-Semites claimed that Jewish involvement in criminal activities stemmed from their hatred of Gentiles, their contempt for physical labor, and their materialism.

Closely associated with the criminal stereotype was the Shylock image. This can be traced at least as far back as Chaucer, centuries before the first Jew set foot in the Western hemisphere. For those Americans dismayed by the growth of factories, banking, and the commercial spirit, the Jews could be viewed as the embodiment of capitalism and commercialism. Jacob Riis, an unsympathetic observer of the Jews of the Lower East Side, noted in How the Other Half Lives that "money is their God. Life is of little value compared with even the leanest bank account." The Jews' major concern seemingly was the accumulation of money. Too cunning and greedy to work with their hands, they profited by manipulating others. Within the Jew, wrote an American magazine in 1899, "the lust for gain is so strongly rooted in his organism, that it extinguishes every other feeling, every other passion." Even Oliver Wendell Holmes claimed that "the principal use of the Jews seemed to be to lend money," while the popular American writer Francis M. Crawford published a novel in 1891 describing the Jews of Prague as "intoxicated by the smell of gold, mad for its possession, half hysteric with the fear of losing it, timid, yet dangerous, poisoned to the core by the sweet sting of money, terrible in intelligence, vile in heart, contemptible in body, irresistible in the unity of their greed." The word "Jew" would become part of the American language as a verb and adjective as well as a noun.

Jews were attacked not only for being avaricious, but also for using their riches to improve their social standing and rectify their cultural failings. The Jew symbolized the parvenu who knew the pride of everything and the value of nothing. Particularly was he resented by those members of the upper class ill-at-ease in the new industrial and urban society of the late nineteenth century and conscious of their displacement from positions of social and political leadership. Henry Adams, for instance, blamed his inability to follow in the footsteps of his father, grandfather, and great-grandfather on the social disintegration resulting from industrialization and materialism. "In a society of Jews and brokers, a world made up of maniacs, wild for gold," he lamented in 1893, "I have no place." This identification of the Jew with materialism, vulgarity, and social disintegration is found in the writings of many of America's leading persons of letters of the time, including Ezra Pound, T. S. Eliot, Ernest Hemingway, and Edith Wharton.

Whereas the Jew as parvenu was resented for his fatuous efforts at social climbing, the Jew as eternal alien was disliked because of his supposed reluctance to become fully assimilated within American society. "What is at the bottom of this antagonism to the Jew today," the pastor of St. Mark's Church in New York City claimed in 1913, was "his race-pride, race-conceit, race-exclusiveness, race-aloofness. . . . He must bury forever all racial self-consciousness, all racial egotism, and be in all things and at all times absolutely and thoroughly American." Evidences of Jewish clannishness were the Zionist movement, the refusal of Jews to convert to Christianity, and their rejection of intermarriage. The magazine World's Week asserted in 1906 that "the reluctance of the Jews to marry outside their race is a survival of a day of a narrower spirit. They have been willing to take advantage of the toleration and of the opportunities given by a democracy, but to the one essential act of a democratic society they have not consented. They are not willing to lose their identity in the people."

The image of the Jews as clannish was closely tied in with the spectre of a Jewish world conspiracy. Jews were suspected of owing ultimate political loyalty to the Jewish people and to a cabal of wealthy Jewish international bankers which controlled the governments of the major industrial world powers, including the United States. This belief in a Jewish worldwide financial conspiracy was particularly popular in the late nineteenth century among farmers suffering economic reverses and currency reformers who blamed the Rothschilds and Jacob Schiff for hard times. The fantasy of a Jewish conspiracy, however, was not limited to farmers. The Quarterly Sentinel of Chicago, in an article entitled "Conquest of the World by the Jews," maintained that "we may say, without exaggeration, that the Jews hold even now in their hands the financial power from one end of the world to the other." Henry Ford was the most influential

American exponent of the myth of the Jewish conspiracy. During the early 1920s the "Flivver King" subsidized the dissemination of the scurrilous Protocols of the Elders of Zion, and his newspaper, The Dearborn Independent, claimed that Jews controlled virtually every major aspect of American life.

Some anti-Semites were less fearful of a Jewish banking conspiracy than of a Jewish radical conspiracy. Radicalism, it was argued, came easy to a people without any sense of American history or tradition. Shortly after the Russian Revolution (which was widely blamed on Jews), Life magazine described the East European Jewish immigrants as having "no real national feeling. They are loyal to Socialism, to Internationalism, to whatever untried ideal of human welfare may be floating in their heads at a given moment, but are not bound by more than the loosest ties to any country or form of government."

The Tarnished Dream asserts that these stereotypes about Jews were the cause, rather than merely the result, of anti-Semitism. "People's minds are shaped by what they hear, see and experience, and in terms of the Jews in the Gilded Age through the Progressive era, this was preponderantly negative." The stereotypes, Dobkowski contends, reveal the presence of much more anti-Semitism than previous scholars believed existed. Jews were attacked for being capitalists and radicals; cliquish and pushy; deracinated and nationalistic; religious and materialistic. The existence of these contradictory and incongruous stereotypes indicates, at least for Dobkowski, that they have a life of their own separate from the social and economic milieu, and that the social and economic environment merely provided the context within which anti-Semitism flourished.

Most historians will dispute Dobkowski's downplaying of the social and economic roots of American anti-Semitism. Some will also argue that he should have spent some space discussing the extent to which the stereotypes accurately mirrored reality and were not merely the products of irrational minds. The Jews during this period were, after all, an upwardly mobile group and one would expect them to have the classic characteristics of nouveaux riches. They did concentrate in the mercantile field and they were predominately on the left politically. Despite these caveats, Professor Dobkowski has performed a real service in reminding us of the influence and persistence of negative images. Social and economic change will lessen anti-Semitism only gradually since the stereotypes tend to outlive the conditions which produced them. The fact that the anti-Semitism behavior of the 1920s and 1930s is no longer around should not make us polyannas as long as the stereotypes exist, and they assuredly are still around.

Although overt anti-Semitism in the U. S. has dramatically declined since the Second World War, one can still see the images at work in the public's perception of Israel and the Middle East conflict. The Israelis, some Americans claim, don't know their place (they are pushy). They refuse to come to terms with their neighbors and become a Levantine people (they refuse to assimilate). American Jews are the chief financial and political mainstays of Israel (Israel is a product of a world Jewish conspiracy). The Israelis are militarists and commit atrocities against the Palestinians (they are criminals). The American taxpayers are paying for Israeli obduracy (Israelis are Shylocks). The Israelis should internationalize the holy city of Jerusalem (Jews are enemies of Christianity). Israel should repeal the Law of Return (Israel considers Diaspora Jews as eternal aliens). Israel is an outpost of western technology and economic interests in an otherwise Arabic world (Israelis are capitalists). Israelis have introduced modern social values in a traditional part of the globe (Israelis are radicals). The wine has remained the same. Now, however, it is being poured into new bottles.

## THE AMERICAN JEWISH ACADEMIC

For centuries Jews have prided themselves on being the people of the book and on their commitment to the life of the mind. In the United States this pride has often focused on the size and quality of the American Jewish professoriate. Jews, it is pointed out, comprise only three per cent of the population and yet are nine per cent of the faculty of American colleges and universities and eighteen per cent of the faculty of the Ivy League schools. The Jewish professor tends to be found in the most abstract and intellectually challenging disciplines such as biochemistry, electrical engineering, psychology, economics, and sociology, while avoiding nursing, agriculture, home economics, and physical education. Jews teach at better universities, do more research, and have more publications than Gentiles. As Seymour M. Lipset and Everett Carll Ladd, Jr. noted in 1971, "by every criterion of academic accomplishment, Jewish faculty as a group have far surpassed their Gentile colleagues."[1]

There is not a major academic discipline which has not been deeply influenced by Jewish academicians, much to the gratification of the Jewish community and also, one must add, often to the acute embarrassment of American Roman Catholics. During the 1950s the criticism of the Catholic university and Catholic intellectuality by Catholic intellectuals became an academic mini-industry. As one asked, where were the Catholic Einsteins, Salks, and Oppenheimers? Monsignor John Tracy Ellis' famous 1955 article "American Catholics and the Intellectual Life", which blamed Catholic anti-intellectualism on a "self-imposed ghetto mentality," was the most famous expression of this Catholic academic inferiority complex.

Jewish preeminence and Catholic lag in Americn universities has been frequently discussed outside of Catholic and Jewish circles. Thus Richard Hofstadter's prize-winning volume <u>Anti-Intellectualism in American Life</u> (1963)

---

[1]Seymour M. Lipset and Everett Carll Ladd, Jr., "Jewish Academics in the United States: Their Achievements, Culture and Politics," <u>American Jewish Year Book, 1971</u> (1972), pp. 99-100.

has a section analyzing the sources of American Catholic intellectual backwardness. While the existence of Catholic-Jewish academic disparities is not questioned, the reasons for these disparities are debated. One explanation quite comforting to Jews is that Catholicism, in contrast to Judaism, is an authoritarian and dogmatic religion which allows little room for that free play of the mind essential for intellectual distinction. Jewish intellectual superiority could thus be expected to continue indefinitely because of the superiority of Judaism as a religion. Not only does this argument ignore the existence of the great European Catholic universities which were the centers of intellectual life during the Middle Ages, but it also overlooks the solid accomplishmenets of Catholic intellectuals throughout Europe during this century.

Any explanation tracing Jewish-Catholic academic differences back to religion would necessarily have to argue that traditional Judaism and the university are basically compatible. In fact, the university has been viewed with great suspicion by Orthodox spokesmen because of the competition it offered to the yeshiva. "How are you going to keep them down in Slobodka after they've seen Heidelberg" could have been the theme song of the European rosh yeshivas of the nineteenth and twentieth centuries. They were, of course, correct in seeing the university as a threat since most of the social and intellectual currents undermining, or at least challenging, the intellectual assumptions of traditional religion emanated from the university. The university is still suspect within the yeshiva realm of American Orthodoxy, and many yeshivas discourage their charges from attending college. Even a university under Orthodox auspices, such as Yeshiva University, is suspect as any reader of Chaim Potok's novel The Chosen knows. If you must go to college for economic reasons, the yeshiva student is often told, then go at night. In this way you won't become involved in the secular and even pagan social, cultural, and intellectual life of the university, and you will still have time for your more important religious studies.

Attributing Jewish academic distinction to Judaism is also contradicted by the fact that the overwhelming majority of Jews attracted to an academic career are generally estranged from Judaism to begin with. In fact, they are far more estranged from their religion than their Christian colleagues. Jewish academics would be amazed to learn that their choice of a career was due to a religion to which they often have only the most attenuated relationship. Early in this century the American economist Thorstein Veblen noted in his essay "The Intellectual Pre-Eminence of Jews in Modern Europe" the tendency of alienated Jews to be attracted to the life of the mind. Only when the Jew escapes from his cultural background, Veblen argued, does "he come into his own as a creative leader in the world's intellectual enterprise. It is by loss of allegiance, or at the least by force of a divided allegiance to the people of his origin, that he finds himself in the vanguard of modern inquiry."

An alternative explanation of Jewish academic distinction is presented in Stephen Steinberg's brief book The Academic Melting Pot, originally published in 1974 and recently reissued in a paperback edition.[2] Steinberg convincingly argues that the sources of Jewish academic success are found in the economic and cultural values of the Jewish immigrants from eastern Europe to the United States during the late nineteenth and early twentieth centuries. American Jews are familiar with photographs of overcrowding and poverty on the Jewish Lower East Side, and every Jewish family is able to recall stories of material deprivation told by their immigrant ancestors. These objective facts of Jewish immigrant life have, however, obscured the even more important subjective characteristics of the great Jewish migration. While the immigrants were unquestionably poor, they generally viewed themselves as middle-class and they certainly possessed middle-class skills and ambitions. Money, which the immigrants lacked, is only one component of a class. More significant are occupational skills and education, and here the Jewish immigrant had a great advantage over the Catholic, and especially the Italian and Polish, immigrant.

Far more literate than Catholics from southern and eastern Europe, eastern European Jews also had much more experience with cities, factories, and business, and had a far higher level of occupational sophistication. The United States Immigration Commission reported in 1911 that two-thirds of the Jewish immigrants to the United States between 1899

[2]Stephen Steinberg, The Academic Melting Pot: Catholics and Jews in American Higher Education (New Brunswick, N. J.: Transaction Books, 1977).

and 1910 were skilled workers. This is by far the highest figure among the major immigrant groups. In contrast, 42% of immigrants from southern Italy were laborers and 35% were farmers; 31% of Irish immigrants were laborers and 46% servants; 45% of Polish immigrants were laborers, 31% farmers, and 17% servants; and 36% of Scandinavian immigrants were laborers, 11% farmers, and 30% servants. Jews ranked first in twenty-six of the forty-seven trades listed by the commission, and they comprised an absolute majority in eight. The Jews were especially prominent as furriers, hat and cap makers, watchmakers, milliners, tinsmiths, tanners, jewelers, glaziers, dressmakers, locksmiths, butchers, printers, bakers, carpenters, and painters.

These figures reflect the economic position of the Jews of eastern Europe. The 1897 Russian census revealed that 38% of the employed Jews in the Pale were artisans, 32% were in manufacturing and commerce, and 19% were in personal services. In contrast, only 18% of non-Jews were in commerce and manufacturing or were artisans. Approximately three-quarters of those involved in commerce in the Pale were Jews, even though they only made up 12% of the Pale's population. Economically and socially the Jews of eastern Europe were prepared to participate in the modern urban and industrial American society. As the director of the Immigration Commission wrote in 1912, the Jews had "the characteristics of a modern people in their economic and social life and in their mentality . . . present a sharp contrast with the peoples among whom they dwell and whose economic and social life are only now taking on modern forms." In contrast, Catholic immigrants from southern and eastern Europe were generally from conservative rural communities, and their backgrounds did not encourage entry into business or taking advantage of the opportunities offered by a burgeoning academia.

The social values the Jewish immigrants transmitted to their children placed a high premium on social mobility, individual achievement, economic success, the deferral of gratification, competition, and entry into the professions. This resulted in a veritable invasion of the university and the emergence of what came to be known as the "Jewish problem". Jewish enrollment at Harvard College, for instance, increased from six per cent in 1908 to twenty per cent in 1922. A. Lawrence Lowell, Harvard's president, argued in his 1922 commencement address that, "To shut the eyes to an actual problem of this kind and ignore its existence, or to refuse to grapple with it courageously, would be unworthy of a university".

A corollary to the social explanation of Jewish-Catholic academic disparities is that these differences will tend to diminish the more Jews and Catholics become fully acculturated within American society. Thus accompanying the decline of ethnicity among Catholic immigrant groups, the near disappearance of anti-Catholicism, and a decrease of Catholic defensiveness has been a slow but steady increase since the end of World War II in the percentage of the professoriate which is Roman Catholic while the Jewish share of academia has levelled off. Furthermore, the post-World War II period witnessed the emergence of outstanding Catholic universities and colleges, most notably Notre Dame and St. John's of Minnesota. George Bernard Shaw's quip that a Catholic university is a contradiction in terms no longer is true, if indeed it ever was true.

One of the more striking facts about American Jewish academics is their politics. While their careers are due to a East European Jewish culture overwhelmingly middle-class in character which stressed competition, social mobility, and individual achievement, their politics are marked by a commitment to egalitarianism, collectivism, and avant-garde social and moral experimentation. Jews are far more to the left than their Gentile colleagues. Less than ten per cent of Jewish professors describe themselves as conservatives while three-quarters believe they are part of the left. While 24% of Protestant academicians voted for Barry Goldwater in 1964, only 2% of Jewish professors did so (even though his famous acceptance speech at the Republican convention was written in part by a Jewish political scientist). In 1968 less than 7% of the Jewish faculty voted for Nixon compared to 25% of Catholics and 42% of Protestants. One would have thought Jewish professors would be sympathetic toward political movements and individuals favoring economic individualism, the free market, and conservative social and moral values, but such has not been the case. Jewish academics tend, for historical reasons, to be critical of the values, social institutions, and economic environment which have been responsible for their achievements in the first place.

The status of Jewish academics is crucial to the future of American Jewry. The fact that they number in the tens of thousands is important in itself, but even more significant is the influence they exert on the approximately 84% of Jewish youth who enter college (the comparable figure for nonJews is under 50%). The vast majority of Jewish professors teach in institutions where there is a large Jewish enrollment, and thus they serve as role models for their Jewish students at precisely the time when many are establishing an identity for themselves and asking what it means to be a Jew in today's America. The answer they are getting from most Jewish professors is that it doesn't mean very much. The university is a miniature society with its own values, traditions, and accepted modes of behavior which, for the majority of Jewish academics, is a rival to, and a surrogate for the Jewish community. Jewish leaders should not remain indifferent in the face of widespread apathy toward Judaism among academicians.

And yet there are signs of a growing Jewish commitment among some Jewish scholars. The founding of American Professors for Peace in the Middle East and the Academic Committee for Soviet Jewry and the creation of academic divisions within both the American Zionist movement and the United Jewish Appeal are hopeful signs. Only time will tell, however, whether these signal a Jewish renaissance among professors or are a brief resurgence of residual ethnicity and the last gasps of Yiddishkeit by academics worried over the future of Israel.

# DOES CONSERVATIVE JUDAISM HAVE A FUTURE?

At first glance the question I have posed appears ridiculous. Contemporary Conservative Judaism is institutionally vibrant: its Solomon Schechter schools are growing rapidly in both numbers and student population; its Ramah camps are an important element within the Jewish summer camp scene; its Jewish Theological Seminary is an outstanding institution and one of the great centers in the world for Jewish study; and its synagogues have become the most important expression of the Jewish religion in the United States. The Conservative "center", with its program of athletic, social, cultural, and spiritual activities, has become the model for Orthodox and Reform congregations. "By choice and by necessity," Ruth R. Wisse has written, "Conservatism remains the proving ground of American Judaism, reflecting its patterns of change and its degree of stability." This seemingly healthy movement is even making inroads in Israeli religious life, as Conservative leaders fervently seek the recognition from the Orthodox Israeli religious establishment which they believe is rightfully theirs because of their contributions to Zion and their status within American Jewry.

And yet despite the glittering achievements of Conservative Judaism, observers both within and outside the movement have questioned its long-range prospects. Wisse, for example, argued that the debate over women becoming Conservative rabbis which erupted in the late 1970s reflected an intellectual emptiness, a flacid willingness to bend before the latest sociological fad. The document recommending the ordination of women evidenced a "defensiveness" and "institutional insecurity", as well as an excessive pragmatism "not very likely to inspire".

Lawrence J. Kaplan, a McGill University colleague of Wisse, is also pessimistic about Conservatism's future. While admitting it has become "the most popular religious movement among American Jews," he noted that Conservative spokesmen were "plagued by self-doubt, disquiet, and gloom." Conservative Judaism, in fact, "has been undergoing a crisis of confidence." Kaplan observed that one indication of this crisis was the division of the Conservative rabbinate into two antagonistic ideological factions, each with its own distinctive position regarding

Jewish law. The Conservative "Left" has repudiated the timetested process of revising the halakhah. Instead of merely interpreting the law, the Left wishes the rabbinate to legislate the law so that it will conform to current social needs. The Conservative "Right", on the other hand, vigorously condemns recent revisions of the halakhah by the Conservative Rabbinical Assembly's Committee on Law and Standards. The Right desires to preserve the halakhah even though parts of it may not conform to contemporary values. Kaplan claimed the two wings of Conservatism are actually closer to Reform and Orthodoxy than to each other. For Kaplan, this conflict within the rabbinate reflects a broader crisis within the Conservative movement whereby its unique ideological posture "has come to seem fragile, ambiguous, and tenuous, and appears now to be in the process of dissolving." It is significant that both Wisse and Kaplan's analyses of the current troubled condition of Conservatism appeared in the prestigious Commentary magazine, American Jewry's most distinguished journal.

Marshall Sklare, the leading authority on the sociology of America's Jews, has provided the most provocative examination of contemporary Conservatism. When he published Conservative Judaism: An American Religious Movement in 1955, Sklare was rather optimistic about Conservatism's future. His concluding chapter "Retrospect and Prospect" claimed Conservatism had "made a notable contribution to survivalism and . . . provides a significant institutional framework for a possible revivified Judaism." He believed there was "no reason why the vitality of Conservatism should not continue for quite some time." Furthermore, it was "unlikely that Conservatism will be confronted with any large-scale defections." Sklare contended that Conservatism could be threatened only by a large-scale religious revival or a further growth of secularism. Neither alternative appeared likely to him. Sklare ended his volume by claiming that Conservatism's "historical mission" of preventing the alienation of the descendants of Eastern European immigrants from Judaism had been completed. "Perhaps Conservatism will not rest upon this accomplishment," he surmised, "but will come to play a new and as yet unforeseeable role in the Jewish life of the future."

In 1972 Sklare published a second edition of *Conservative Judaism* to which he appended a new chapter describing "Recent Developments in Conservative Judaism". In contrast to the 1955 edition, the 1972 version spoke of a "crisis" within the movement. Sklare compared the sagging morale of Conservative spokesmen and their fears for the future with the movement's primary position within American Judaism. Even in the Midwest, which had been a bastion of Reform, Conservatism had become dominant, and yet Conservative leaders were unable to shake off premonitions of doom. Thus Rabbi Max. J. Routtenberg, a Conservative luminary, claimed in 1965 to be "haunted by the fear that somewhere along the way we have become lost; our direction is not clear and . . . (we) are in danger of not having anything significant to say to our congregants, to the best of our youth, to all those who are seeking a dynamic adventurous faith that can elicit sacrifice and that can transform lives."

Sklare attributed this gap between glittering achievement and pervasive dissatisfaction to three things: (1) the post-World War II revival of Orthodoxy; (2) the lack of ritual observance among the Conservative laity; and (3) the inability of the movement to retain the loyalty of the young. Conservative leaders of the pre-World War II years had believed that American Orthodoxy would gradually disappear. This would leave Conservatism, and not ossified Orthodoxy, as the sole and authentic embodiment of traditional Judaism in America. Unfortunately for Conservatism, Orthodoxy has not rolled over and died. Rather, this supposedly fossil religion has experienced a surprising rebirth in numbers, influence, and elan, and has most forcefully rejected the Conservative claim to speak for normative Judaism. Conservative rabbis, who believed they represented tradition, now were confronted by rivals asserting they were religious charlatans betraying traditional Judaism.

Conservative leaders were also dismayed by the lack of religious observance among the Conservative laity for this confirmed the Orthodox charge that Conservatism had undermined, rather than strengthened, traditional Judaism. The founders of Conservatism wished to provide a mode of religious expression which would be traditional and yet free of the practices which had stamped Orthodoxy as European and anachronistic. Only by changing the halakhah to conform to modern conditions, they maintained, could Jews be expected to remain faithful to tradition. Revision of the halakhah was thus a necessary prelude to an intensified observance of the mitzvot. Conservative leaders also hoped that a dignified and decorous religious service would encourage religious observance. This, however, has not occurred. As the Orthodox had predicted, the Conservative effort to modernize tradition and the halakhah has not resulted in increased ritualistic observance. If anything, the Conservative revision of tradition has encouraged the Conservative laity to throw the baby out with the bath water. As Sklare wrote, Conservatism has been "an abysmal failure" in promoting religious observance. "The belief among Conservative leaders that the movement's approach to halachah had the power to maintain observance, as well as to inspire its renewal, has proved illusory."

Very few Conservative Jews are faithful to the tenets of Conservative Judaism. Sabbath observance is infrequent, despite the fact that in 1950 the Rabbinical Assemlby voted to permit automotive travel on the Sabbath for the purpose of attending synagogue services. The Conservative laity use their automobiles on Saturday morning for shopping and recreational activities, not for traveling to the synagogue. Lighting of Sabbath candles, a requirement for Conservative women, is disregarded in most Conservative homes. The situation is the same for kashrut. Only a small minority of Conservative households eat only kosher meat and have separate meat and milk dishes, despite the fact that kashruth is part of Conservative observance. There "is not a Conservative synagogue in the country," Sklare concluded, "where most congregants practice the mitzvoth according to the Conservative regimen." These "religious derelictions" have destroyed the conviction of Conservative Judaism's leaders that they possess the formula for bring American Jewry back to religious observance.

The final source of the Conservative malaise is the fear that the movement is not renewing itself demographically. Sklare mentioned intermarriage and the attraction of exotic religious and political cults as two major reasons for the limited appeal of Conservatism to its youth. The movement's spokesmen are rightly concerned about its inability to attract a sizable segment of the children of Conservative families.

An understanding of the current Conservative perplexity would be incomplete without considering the movement's history. The roots of Conservatism can be traced back to the emergence of the "Historical School" in central Europe and the United States in the Nineteenth Century. The Historical's School's leadership, who included the Americans Sabato Morais, Alexander Kohut, and Marcus Jastrow, believed the spread of Reform sentiment could be checked only if traditional Judaism adopted a more realistic attitude regarding the halakhah and tradition. Judaism, they claimed, had throughout its history exhibited the same change and development characterizing all social phenomenon. But, according to the Historical School, Reform and Orthodoxy both had denied the organic continuity of Jewish experience -- Reform by abruptly breaking with the past, and Orthodoxy by refusing to countenance any change whatsoever.

The founding of Conservative Judaism, however, was due to more than a theological argument about the nature of Judaism. The immediate background for the founding of the Jewish Theological Seminary in the 1880s and its revitalization in the 1900s, as well as the growth of Conservatism in the early Twentieth Century, was the mass migration of eastern European Jews to America and Canada which began in the 1880s. Conservatism's spokesmen believed only a non-European, traditional Judaism could help the immigrants adjust to their new environment and save them for Judaism. They maintained that the immigrants, and particularly their children, would reject European Orthodoxy precisely because it was European and would thus hinder their adaptation to life in America. "Unwilling to foster little enclaves of East-European Jewish Life in America," Moshe Davis wrote in The Emergence of Conservative Judaism, conservative supporters severed all affiliations with Polish-Russian Orthodoxy "because they recognized the inevitability of the occidentalization of the Jew, seeing in the culture of the enlightment and in modern citizenship affirmative values for Jews and Judaism."

The Conservative movement and its struggling seminary would probably have been crushed between Reform and Orthodoxy had not Cyrus Adler in 1902 interested Jacob Schiff in the institution's future.

Schiff then enlisted several members of "Our Crowd" in a campaign to revitalize the Seminary so that it could help "Americanize" the new immigrants. They realized the newcomers were not attracted to Reform, and they believed that European Orthodoxy had nothing to say to the second generation. They feared the "Russians" would become alienated from Judaism itself and left without any moral and religious foundation. This would result in a breakdown of family and moral standards, as well as increasing support for the competing ideologies of socialism and anarchism. The role of the Seminary was to train Americanized and yet traditional rabbis who could then return to the immigrant ghettos and spread enlightenment, morality, and Judaism.

From the beginning, however, there was conflict between the seminary's board of directors and Solomon Schechter who had been brought from England to head the revived institution. Schechter viewed it as a center of higher learning, whereas the board stressed its "missionary" function. At one time Schechter became convinced that his board was more concerned with "civics" than in the training of traditional rabbis. "I must take it out of their minds," he avowed in 1913, "that I came into this country for the purpose of converting the downtown (i.e., Lower East Side) Jew to a more refined species of religion." Schechter's traditionalism was also reflected in the United Synagogue of America, the organization of Conservative synagogues, which he helped found. The USA's constitution declared its purpose to be "the maintenance of Jewish tradition in its historical continuity."

Schechter's goal that the Jewish Theological Seminary's graduates would minister to traditional congregants was frustrated from the beginning. The Seminary's products found pulpits among Jews experiencing rapid acculturation to middle-class American standards. For them, Reform was too "goyish" and Orthodoxy too reminiscent of the neighborhoods and life-style from which they were fleeing. Conservative Judaism provided a vicarious traditional religious experience for the Conservative laity in which the rabbis alone were to observe the Sabbath, kashruth, and the holidays. The Conservative identity of the typical Conservative family was based on the acts and ideology of its rabbi, and not on its own behavior and outlook.

The appeal of Conservative Judaism was thus largely sociological, not theological. Conservatism answered the status needs of an upwardly mobile ethnic groups rather than providing an appealing and distinctive Jewish way of life. Conservatism, as the sociologist Charles Liebman has pointed out, offered middle-class respectability and a modicum of Jewish cultural involvement for those of the second and third generation who were more interested in Jewish survival than in Judaism. Or to put it another way, Conservatism enabled mainly secular Jews to believe they were still somewhat traditional. The relationship between Conservatism and the status needs of the second and third generation explains why the movement's popularity has been limited to the United States and Canada.

Of all the Conservative spokesmen, none grasped the movement's basic thrust more clearly that Mordecai Kaplan. Kaplan taught at the seminary from 1909 through 1963, and is generally considered Conservatism's great heretic. And yet viewed from the perspective of 1981, Kaplan's ideology was prophetic in anticipating the movement's future course. As a naturalist, Kaplan rejected the concepts of a personal God, the Sinaitic revelation, and the covenant, and stressed the cultural aspects of Judaism. He considered Judaism to be more than a religion, and the title of his most important book was Judaism as a Civilization (1934). Kaplan viewed the attenuation of religion among Jews as an inevitable outgrowth of modern secularism, urbanization, and naturalism. Judaism could appeal to modern Jews, he argued, only if it shed much of its excess supernatural baggage, and recognized that for most Jews Jewishness and the Jewish people were more important than Judaism. Kaplan even maintained that an atheist could be a rabbi. "For the Jew who approaches Judaism as a civilization," he wrote, "the test for any form of adjustment will not be whether it conforms to the accepted teachings of revelation. . . . His criterion will be: does that adjustment proceed from the essential nature of Judaism? Will it lead to the enrichment of the content of Jewish life? Is it inherently interesting?" One of Kaplan's books was appropriately titled Judaism Without Supernaturalism (1958). Kaplan articulated a formula whereby Jews could combine their rationalist and survivalist instincts. Despite Kaplan's articulation of the outlook of most of the Conservative laity, he was virtually read out of the Conservative movement. Few Conservative congregations and rabbis were willing to make the radical break with Jewish beliefs demanded by Kaplan. Instead, Conservatism plodded on, while the gap between the teachings of the Seminary and the actions of the laity becoming increasingly divergent.

While refusing to accept Kaplan's theology, the Conservative movement has adopted his sociology. Kaplan wished to turn the synagogue into a "center" in which a continuous round of cultural, educational, religious and social events would express the multi-faceted nature of Jewish civilization. As Professor Liebman noted in his article on Kaplan in the 1970 <u>American Jewish Year Book</u>, Kaplan's naturalism, Zionism, and view of the role of the synagogue have been closer to the operative "folk" religion of Conservative (and nonConservative) Jews than the "elitist" outlook of the traditionalist professors at the Jewish Theological Seminary.

Marshall Sklare has contended that the most important contribution of Conservatism to American Jewry was "offering an acceptable pattern of adjustment to the American environment for many East European-derived Jews." But now that this adjustment has taken place, what purpose does the Conservative movement have? Based on the actions and outlook of its laity, the teachings of the movement have had little influence on its congregants. Jews identify with Conservatism not because of its beliefs but because of inertia, convenience, the personality of the local rabbi, or the attractiveness of the recreational, social, and educational programs sponsored by the local Conservative synagogue. Only a tiny minority of Conservative Jews are faithful to its teachings, while most lead lives indistinguishable from those of Reform Jews. A movement cannot long remain vibrant when its most cherished beliefs are the exclusive possession of a limited number of professors in New York City and some rabbis in the field.

The Conservative movement bears a resemblance to the Communist governments of East Europe. The leaders of both are committed to an ideology which is ignored and even mocked by the masses. Hypocrisy, Voltaire said, is the tribute that vice pays to virtue. Today the Conservative laity is not even hypocritical. Conservative vices, it seems, are not even being distinguished from Conservative virtues.

The decision to allow women to be counted in a minyan and to receive aliyot, as well as the debate regarding their ordination, reveal the extent to which Conservatism has changed from the orginal outlook of Schechter. The effort of some Conservative functionaries to narrow the gap between the rabbinate and the laity by moving to the left is self-defeating since the gap is actually between the laity and Conservatism itself. How far can Conservatism move before it ceases to be Conservative? And if the Conservative movement refuses to give in to the demands of its reformers, what will prevent the disaffected from turning to Reform? What will prevent the Conservative laity from recognizing that, in actuality, they really belong in a rightwing Reform congregation?

The ultimate survival of Conservatism is dependent upon discovering a new raison d'etre which can replace the old one of group survival and immigrant acculturation. In the absence of a new purpose, Conservatism will find it increasingly difficult to meet the challenge of Reform and Orthodoxy. The Conservative left will gradually draw closer to Reform, while its more traditional element will move closer to Orthodoxy. Conservatism then could become the exclusive possession of a few brahmin professors at the seminary. This pessimistic prognosis, however, has not taken one factor into consideration: the possible salutary impact of the Solomon Schechter day schools. Only time will tell whether the graduates of these schools will instill into Conservatism an elan, a new raison d'etre, and a religious commitment which it so desperately needs.

# An Orthodox Recrudescence

*From Suburb to Shtetl: the Jews of Boro Park,* by Egon Mayer. Philadelphia. Temple University Press, 1979. 196 pp. $17.50.

On December 7, 1979 Temple Emanu-El, a Conservative synagogue in the Boro Park section of Brooklyn, was vandalized by a group calling itself TORAH. Although the perpetrators were never apprehended, a call was received from an unidentified person stating that the acronym stood for "Tough Orthodox Rabbis and Hasidim." The hooligans broke the synagogue's stained-glass windows and spray-painted swastikas on its walls. They also painted on one wall a slogan in Hebrew, "May Their Names Be Erased." The spokesman claimed this was to be the first of many attacks against Conservative and Reform congregations throughout New York City to protest the inroads of non-Orthodox religious movements in Israel.

Rabbis of all persuasions were shocked by the incident. Baruch Silverstein of Emanu-El, a refugee from Europe and a former student at the Mirrer Yeshiva and Yeshiva University, remarked on the irony of being hated by both Nazis and Jews, while Alexander Schindler of the Union of American Hebrew Congregations described the attackers as "goons." Nisson Wolpin, editor of the Agudat Israel magazine *Jewish Observer* and a long-time resident of Boro Park, was equally shocked. "This action doesn't represent any responsible group and one can only stand back in horror at acts of vandalism committed in the name of Torah," he asserted.

Two aspects of the vandalism were little noted by the general public. One was that Emanu-El was the only remaining Conservative synagogue in Boro Park, although there was a small Reform congregation in the area. Secondly, exactly one year prior to this incident Orthodox Jews had assaulted the Boro Park police station on a Sabbath afternoon in protest against anti-Semitism and supposedly inadequate police protection.

Jews, and especially Orthodox Jews, are not generally associated with such activities, particularly on the Sabbath (nor are they supposed to throw stones at cars on the Sabbath in Jerusalem). Both events made the pages of *The New York Times*, to the consternation of Jews who dislike such publicity. To this dismay was added bewilderment. Jews were horrified by actions which they associated only with the most extremist elements in Israel. How, they wondered, could these things ever have happened in the United States? Who was responsible? What motivated them? Is there anything in the history and sociology of Boro Park that could explain it? Now, thanks to Egon Mayer, a sociologist at Brooklyn College, we can begin to arrive at some answers to these questions.

Boro Park, located in southwest Brooklyn adjacent to the largely Italian Bay Ridge section of *Saturday Night Fever* fame, houses approximately 55,000 Jews, the great majority of whom are Orthodox. The greatest concentration of Orthodox Jews outside Israel, it contains some 1,700 rabbis, over 30 yeshivas, 150 synagogues, and a host of Hassidic groups. Thirteenth Avenue, the main shopping thoroughfare of Boro Park, has the largest number of kosher restaurants and delicatessens in New York, numerous religious bookstores, and other businesses catering to the religious needs of the Orthodox.

It was not always like this. Boro Park first attracted a large number of Jews during the 1920s with the extension of the New York subway. It was a haven for those escaping the ghettos of the Lower East Side and Williamsburg. Contemporary Boro Park, on the other hand, is a product of the post-World War II migration of pious Jews from other areas in Brooklyn, particularly Crown Heights and Williamsburg, and of refugees from Europe, especially Hungary. In the process, Boro Park was transformed from a "suburb" to which upwardly mobile Jews moved in search of pleasant surroundings to a "shtetl" inhabited by the devout. Jews who felt uncomfortable living among women with wigs and men with skullcaps moved out of Boro Park; it rapidly became America's Jerusalem.

This transformation of Boro Park has contradicted some long-standing sociological assumptions regarding the nature of American Orthodoxy. These argued that Orthodoxy was largely a first-generation phenomenon, that piety and modernity were mutually exclusive, and that upward social and economic mobility was both a cause and a result of assimilation and acculturation. Thus Sidney Goldstein and Calvin Goldscheider's study of Providence, Rhode Island (*Jewish Americans: Three Generations in a Jewish Community*) attributed the decline of Orthodoxy to the social and economic mobility and the acculturation of the second and third generations.

The resurgence of Orthodoxy in Boro Park, however, has occurred within a population containing a large number of professionals and successful businessmen, and a high percentage of college graduates. Furthermore, contrary to the experiences of other communities, Boro Park has retained the loyalty of many of the young, thereby creating a high demand for housing and rapidly escalating property values.

Boro Park has challenged another seemingly iron-clad law of American Jewish sociology, which postulates the irresistible movement of Jews to suburbia. At a time when Jews have been deserting the cities in droves for the suburbs, Boro Park has witnessed an increase in its Jewish population. In addition, the Jewishness of other urban Jewish neighborhoods in Brooklyn, Queens, and Staten Island has been intensified by the settling of Jews seeking a Boro Park life without its high rentals and expensive mortgages.

The example of Boro Park is another piece of evidence that Orthodoxy can "make it" in America. Far from being a transplanted European relic fated to die, Orthodoxy has experienced a renaissance in the United States during the past several decades. Jewish leaders of the late 19th and early 20th centuries would have been amazed by the post-World War II growth of Yeshiva University, the multiplication of Orthodox day schools, and the emergence of an Orthodox intelligentsia. Pre-World War I Orthodox spokesmen were positive that America and Orthodoxy were incompatible. European rabbis continually warned their flocks against migration to the "golden land" where they might prosper, it is true, but only at the expense of their souls.

Thus in 1900 Jacob David Wilowsky, the famous rabbi of Slutsk in Russia, accused a New York audience of being sinners for having migrated to a *trefa* land. "It was not only home that the Jews left behind in Europe," Wilowsky argued, but "their Torah, their Talmud, their yeshivot — in a word, their Yiddishkeit, their entire Jewish way of life." Even Wilowsky, however, was unable to resist the allure of America and in 1903 he settled in Chicago. In 1905, after concluding that his initial impressions of America had been correct, he moved to Safed and established a yeshiva.

Isaac Mayer Wise agreed with Wilowsky that America and Orthodoxy were like oil and water. The founder of the Reform movement in America was invited in 1887 to participate in the dedication of an Orthodox congregation in Cleveland. He proceeded to lecture his hosts on the necessity of renouncing Orthodoxy and becoming Americanized. "You persist in clinging to your old prejudices, your old customs [rather than] searching after noble truths and knowledge to gain the esteem and confidence of your fellow men," he declared. "Judaism is in great danger today owing to uncalled-for Orthodoxy. We will not get the following of our youth: the second generation will desert Judaism." On another occasion he wrote in his paper the *American Israelite* that it was "next to impossibility [sic] to associate or identify ourselves with that half-civilized Orthodoxy which . . . gnaws the dead bones of past centuries."

Fifty years ago a community such as Boro Park would probably have disappeared within one generation due to the pressures of acculturation and economic necessity. Today it has a fighting chance of survival. Thanks to the greater acceptance of ethnic and religious diversity, Americanization no longer demands that religious practices be modeled on those of middle-class Protestantism. The universality of the five-day work week has eliminated the major obstacle to Sabbath observance, while the development of appliances which can be adapted to Sabbath use and the wider availability of kosher food have removed some of the burdens associated with Orthodoxy. As Egon Mayer points out, "the rituals and requirements of Orthodoxy "have been incorporated among the many amenities made possible by the modern world."

Furthermore, Orthodoxy, far from stigmatizing the pious as uneducated and unthinking, is now widely viewed as indicating moral seriousness and intellectual rigor. Most importantly, Orthodoxy is no longer a barrier to social and economic mobility. Boro Park Jewry, as Mayer notes, is "simultaneously growing more 'American,' more middle class, and, religiously, more Orthodox." It is "clearly in the mainstream of the middle class."

Boro Park, Mayer continues, has "evolved under precisely those conditions of modern life that enabled its members to enter successfully into the economic and political arena of the larger society." Its residents have compartmentalized the sacred and secular spheres of their lives, reconciling the demands of Orthodoxy with the desire to succeed financially and professionally. Every community has its own definition of "normality." In Boro Park, the normal Jew is both Torah-observant and moderately prosperous. Backsliders as well as religious fanatics are subjected to subtle pressures to conform.

Boro Park's definition of normality, however, constantly changes: institutions and practices which were "kosher" a decade ago are now viewed with suspicion. This creates a continual state of cultural tension, leading to a rapid multiplication of synagogues and schools. Recently one of Boro Park's yeshivas moved to Flatbush because it had come to be regarded as too modern. Mayer believes "the lack of firm consensus" regarding religiosity results in the Boro Park Jew being uncomfortable since he suspects his neighbors view him as either too religious or too modern.

Another problem for Boro Park is the potential conflict between the values of Orthodoxy and those of general society. How far can Boro Park absorb the values of middle-class America before its religious traditions begin to change? "Technological advances in the kitchen, no matter how kosher," Mayer contends, "tend to liberate the Jewish woman from her traditional chores, and willy-nilly lead to changing sex roles in the family." Unfortunately, the blending of "the artifacts of the modern lifestyle and the two thousand year old sacred normative system inevitably lead to the crystallization of values which are deviant by ancestral standards."

A further threat to Boro Park stems from changing demographic patterns, both internal and external. Boro Park has experienced a serious outmigration of young people unable to find affordable housing. Will Boro Park continue to be a desirable area if it should become populated primarily by the middle-aged and elderly? Furthermore, blacks and Puerto Ricans are becoming more numerous in areas adjacent to Boro Park. Boro Park's Jews are "ringed by an ethnically incompatible population, who are also significantly poorer, less educated, and vastly different in culture and outlook." This would not be the first time that a New York Jewish community disappeared because of shifting ethnic population patterns.

Although quite pessimistic about the future of Boro Park itself, Mayer is encouraged by the fact that Boro Park has spawned several satellite communities in other sections of Brooklyn, Queens, and Staten Island. These neighborhoods ensure that "the communal life which has evolved in Boro Park since the end of World War II will not evaporate into passing history even if Jews should abandon the Boro Park locale. From roots planted in the shtetl, branches are already in bloom elsewhere, and new fruits and seeds are not far behind."

During World War II, Rabbi Aharon Kotler, the leading Talmudist of his day, arrived in America from Lithuania for what he believed would be a short stay prior to settling in Palestine. He was prevailed upon to remain in America and to establish a yeshiva. For Kotler, the essence of Orthodoxy was intensive study of the Talmud which, he argued, could not take place in the midst of the distractions of New York City. Instead, he chose Lakewood, New Jersey. Since that time other Orthodox Jews have come to the same conclusion, leaving the city for Rockland County, New York, and other locations. The Jews of Boro Park, in contrast, have decided to remain in the city and directly confront the challenges of modernity and acculturation. This is what makes their story so interesting and Egon Mayer's brief monograph so engrossing, despite its recurrent lapsing into sociological jargon.

Boro Park is an example of a large and persevering Jewish community that refuses to turn its back upon either Yiddishkeit or the typically American view of social and economic success. One hopes that Mayer is both right and wrong about the future of Boro Park: right about its ability to give birth to satellite communities, wrong about its eventual demise. ∎

# MORE BINTEL BRIEF

A Bintel Brief: Volume II, Letters to the "Jewish Daily Forward," 1950-1980, compiled and edited by Issac Metzker. New York: Viking Press, 1981.

In 1971 Issac Metzker, a staff writer for the Yiddish Jewish Daily Forward edited a marvelous collection of letters entitled A Bintel Brief. "Bintel brief" means bundle of letters, and the bintel brief was the letters-to-the- editor section of the Forward. Here bewildered Jewish immigrants poured out their woes before "Dear Worthy Editor," hoping this august figure would provide instructions for adapting to the new and unsettling conditions they had encountered in America. The 1971 volume of letters spanned the years 1906, when the column began, to 1967, although the great bulk of letters were written prior to the Great Depression. Here are found the real concerns of the Yiddish-speaking immigrants from eastern Europe: their anguish over their inability to control their children, their nostalgia for the old country, the problems of intermarriage, their embarrassment over foreign accents and lack of secular education, and their general befuddlement regarding the strange and harsh environment of New York, Chicago, and Philadelphia. Not surprisingly, the bintel brief soon became the most popular feature of the Forward. There is no better introduction to the "world of our fathers" than the first volume of bintel brief letters which has now been supplemented by a second volume of letters written between 1950 and 1980.

The institution of the bintel brief resulted from the impact of modernization and acculturation on eastern European Jewish immigrants. Problems which would never have arisen in Europe now directly confronted the immigrants and demanded immediate resolution. In desperate need of guidance, the immigrants turned to the impersonal authority of the Jewish Daily Forward, the most important American Yiddish paper. The fact that the immigrants looked to the bintel brief for advice rather than traditional rabbinic authorities indicates their secularism and estrangement from religious orthodoxy. They identified Orthodoxy with Europe, and assumed it was unable to provide relevant answers for American problems. Contemporary Americans, faced with a revolution in manners and morals and sceptical as to the reliability of traditional authorities, support a host of new gurus ranging from Dear Abby and Ann Landers to radio personalities specializing in interpersonal behavior. The immigrants also sensed they were living in the midst of a social and cultural upheaval, and they turned to the bintel brief.

What, for example, could parents, traditionalist teachers, or European rabbis say to a wife who in 1910 wants to go to night school? "When I am alone with my thoughts, I feel I may not be right. Perhaps I should not go to school. I want to say that my husband is an intelligent man and he wanted to marry a women who was educated. The fact that he is intelligent makes me more annoyed with him. He is in favor of the emancipation of women, yet in real life he acts contrary to his beliefs." The editor responded to "The Discontented Wife" that, since her husband "is intelligent and an adherent of the women's emancipation movement, he is scolded severely . . . for wanting to keep his wife so enslaved. Also the opinion is expressed that the wife absolutely has the right to go to school two evenings a week."

And could European wisdom resolve the following dilemma of a young man who in 1908 had not yet freed himself completely from foreign superstitions? "I am a young man of twenty-five, sixteen years in America, and I recently met a fine girl. She has a flaw, however, that keeps me from marrying her. The fault is that she has a dimple in her chin, and it is said that people who have this lose their first husband or wife." The editor answered "The Unhappy Fool" that "the tragedy is not that the girl has a dimple in her chin but that some people have a screw loose in their heads. . . . It's tragic humor to find such superstition in the world today. It's truly shameful that a young man who was brought up in America should ask such questions."

In providing such answers the Jewish Daily Forward was fulfilling the classic role of the immigrant newspaper: acclimating it readers to American conditions. By carrying out this responsibility the paper guaranteed its eventual demise. An acculturated Jewry did not need the Forward when it could turn to CBS, Newsweek, or the New York Times. The Jewish Daily Forward once had the largest circulation of any immigrant or socialist paper in the United States, while its headquarters on East Broadway was the most imposing structure on the Lower East Side. Now the Forward has moved uptown, its building has been sold to Chinese, and it is dependent for survival on telethons and federation bequests.

This comatose situation is clearly revealed in the second volume of bintel brief letters. While the first volume contained dozens of letters from the young and middle-aged regarding love and marriage, employment problems, and anti-Semitism, its sequel is largely given over to the lamentations of the elderly. The exceptions are those letters from readers fortunate enough to have lived through World War II who settled in America in the late 1940's and early 1950's. The problems discussed are typical of the aged. The letters complain of ungrateful children who don't visit and have forgotten the sacrifices made for them by their parents; of living in decaying neighborhoods and fearing youngs toughs; of demoralization after the death of a spouse; of trying to make ends meet on inadequate pensions. Added to the normal tribulations of those in their "golden years" are the elderly's agonies when witnessing their children and grandchildren rejecting Yiddishkeit. One writer described his grandson and granddaughter. "He let his hair grow long, and goes around with a bunch of Christians. He doesn't listen to his parents anymore but does just what he wants to. His sister is no different from him now. She going out with a Christian boy, and it seems that, though there are over four hundred Jewish families in the city, they cannot find any Jewish friends. . . I am very worried about this. I see what is going on and I cannot keep quiet. It is hard for me to observe the actions of the youth in these crazy times. I cannot rest and therefore I am writing to you about this."

The letters' salutations include "Dear Friend Editor," "Worthy Editor," "Esteemed Editor," and Worthy Friend Editor." These indicate the role of the bintel brief editor in the lives of the first generation. He was their psychologist, social worker, marriage counsellor, and sex therapist, and the longevity of the bintel brief attests to the shrewdness and aptness of his advice. The audience for the bintel brief is now rapidly disappearing. There will never be another generation of American Jewry comparable to the immigrant one in its commitment to the continuity of Jewish experience, its passionate quest for social justice, and its unique blend of grasping materialism, soaring idealism, and feverish intellectuality. The bintel brief provides a window into this world for the immigrants' descendants. The reading of the bintel brief is more than a nostalgic journey. It is truly an experience in self-discovery since we are living on the inherited Jewish capital which the immigrant generation bequeathed to us. Issac Metzger's two volumes are thus a notable contribution to strengthening Jewish identity for, as Cicero wrote, "Memory is the treasury of all things and their guardian."

# AMERICAN JEWRY AND THE STATE OF ISRAEL

## PRECIS

For the American Jew the impact of Israel is all-pervasive, with Israel partially filling the vacuum created by the diminishing importance of traditional religious practices and beliefs. Israel has become *the* focal point in the search for Jewish identity, in combating anti-Semitism, and in asserting American patriotism. Support for Israel brings together both the religious and the non-religious Jew, the former seeing Israel as a fulfillment of biblical prophecy, the latter finding Israel a means of expressing Jewish identity or a possible paradigm for a contemporary secular state.

Contemporary pro-Israel sentiment is in marked contrast to the minority position which Zionism held in American Jewry as recently as a decade ago. Reflection on the holocaust experience and the wars of 1967 and 1973 have in large measure been responsible for this change.

American Jews generally perceive Israel as a refuge for the persecuted rather than as a national homeland for all Jews, as the classical Zionist ideology would insist. Brandeis was largely responsible for this American Zionism with its emphasis on charitable and political efforts on behalf of Israel rather than immigration. The result has been a remarkable identification of American Jews with Israel, so much so that for a Jew to be critical of Israel is to be almost outside the pale and for a non-Jew to be either critical or indifferent toward Israel is to risk being labelled anti-Semitic.

While Christians should attempt to see Israel within the context of tragic twentieth-century Jewish events, Jews should refrain from absolutizing the state of Israel.

The greatest challenge confronting contemporary Christian-Jewish relations in the United States concerns the state of Israel. For American Jews anything less than wholehearted Christian backing of Israel is evidence of a lingering anti-Semitism. Many Christians, on the other hand, resent the Jewish demand for all-out support of Israel, seeing it as a form of blackmail in which a pro-Israel attitude is the Jewish price for continuing the Christian-Jewish dialogue. Christians find it difficult to comprehend this intense American Jewish commitment to Israel, while American Jews are often unable to explain the reasons for this commitment or the depth of their concern. What neither American Christians nor American Jews perhaps understand fully is the extent to which Israel has become the religion of an increasingly sizable percentage, perhaps a majority, of American Jews. The most popular way to be Jewish today and to identify with other Jews is by supporting Israel.

Israel has partially filled the vacuum created by the diminishing importance of traditional religious practices and beliefs. Secularism has affected American Jewry more deeply than it has American Protestantism or American Catholicism. Public opinion surveys have revealed that American Jews attend religious services far less frequently than do American Christians, and that a smaller percentage of Jews than Christians accept such basic religious dogmas as the existence of a personal God and an afterlife, and the efficacy of prayer. Various sociological studies have shown that religious observance among second- and third-generation Jews is less frequent than among the immigrant generation. Another indication of the weakening hold of traditional religion on American Jews is an increasing intermarriage rate, a phenomenon which has led many American Jewish leaders to question whether Judaism, in the long run, will be able to survive in the United States.[1]

Even the High Holy Days of Rosh Hashanah and Yom Kippur reflect this growing secularism and acculturation of American Jewry. For many Jews, attending religious services during these days is not to obtain God's forgiveness for their sins but rather to identify physically with the Jewish people. And the nature of that identification is best revealed on Yom Kippur, the Day of Atonement. During this most important day of the Jewish calendar, when more Jews will be at prayer than at any other time of the year, an appeal is made in countless synagogues for the purchase of Israeli bonds. In the modern version of Yom Kippur personal atonement thus involves a financial commitment for the well-being of the state of Israel.[2]

This decreasing traditional religious commitment has been accompanied by a seemingly strong ethnic consciousness. While the ties binding American Jews to Judaism have been attenuated, the ties binding them to one another have remained firm. It is significant that two Jewish rites retaining their popularity in the United States have been the lighting of Chanukah lights and the partaking of the Seder meal during Passover. Both of these celebrate events having a nationalistic as well as a religious dimension. But even more important than the Chanukah lights and the

---

[1] Marshall Sklare, *America's Jews* (New York: Random House, 1971), pp. 110-112; Sidney Goldstein, "American Jewry: A Demographic Analysis," in David Sikorsky, ed., *The Future of the Jewish Community in America* (New York: Basic Books, 1973), pp. 81-89.

[2] Arnold Lasker, "Motivations for Attending High Holy Day Services," *Journal for the Scientific Study of Religion* 10 (Fall, 1971): 241-248.

seder in what the sociologist Charles S. Liebman has called "the celebration and ritualization of communal ties" is the state of Israel.[3]

Israel has become for American Jews a universal screen upon which they project their dreams and aspirations, as well as a universal panacea for relieving their anxieties and frustrations. Israel for American Jewry is all things to all people. For Jews whose major contact with the Jewish community is through the various self-defense organizations, Israel provides the most important opportunity for fighting anti-Semitism. This is due not only to the hostile environment in which Israel finds itself, but also because the diminution of American anti-Semitism since the end of World War II has deprived American Jews who are fearful of anti-Semitism of a domestic focus for their fears.

Israel provides patriotic American Jews an outlet for expressing their patriotism. By portraying Israel as the only democracy in the eastern Mediterranean, as a barrier to the spread of communism and Soviet influence in the Middle East, and as a staunch ally of the United States, Jews are able to view the national interests of Israel and America as essentially congruent. Israel is pictured as a miniature United States in which Western values such as democracy, industrialization, capitalism, and technology predominate. The classical argument against Zionism that it led to dual loyalties and prevented the full acceptance of Jews into American society is thus turned on its head. Zionism now becomes a handmaiden of Americanism, and for a Jew to be a complete American patriot and a defender of American national interests he or she must, by necessity, also be a Zionist.

Support for Israel is found also among both religious and non-religious American Jews. The religious profess to see in Israel's establishment the hand of God, a fulfillment of biblical prophecy regarding the ingathering of the exiles and the coming of the messianic age. To the non-religious, Zionism is a means to express a Jewish identity, although within a secular and even, at times, an anti-religious context. Zionism thus can become "a substitute religion, a surrogate for Judaism."[4]

Radical Jews, although embarrassed by the role of the Israeli religious establishment and fearful of the eventual effect of militarism on Israeli

---

[3] Charles S. Liebman, *The Ambivalent American Jew: Politics, Religion and Family in American Jewish Life* (Philadelphia: Jewish Publication Society of America, 1973), pp. 67, 75, 102; Marshall Sklare and Joseph Greenblum, *Jewish Identity on the Suburban Frontier: A Study of Group Survival in the Open Society* (New York: Basic Books, 1967), ch. 3; Nathan Glazer, "A Jewish Community," *Commentary* 46 (August, 1968): 67-68; Arnold Dashefsky and Howard M. Shapiro, *Ethnic Identification among American Jews: Socialization and Social Structure* (Lexington, MA: Lexington Books, 1974), pp. 46-47; Sidney Goldstein and Calvin Goldscheider, *Jewish Americans: Three Generations in a Jewish Community* (Englewood Cliffs, NJ: Prentice Hall, 1968), pp. 201-204.

[4] Robert Silverberg, *If I Forget Thee O Jerusalem: American Jews and the State of Israel* (New York: William Morrow, 1970), pp. 451-452; Liebman, *Ambivalent American Jew*, pp. 88, 94-108; Sklare and Greenblum, *Jewish Identity*, ch. 6.

society, nevertheless see in Israel the most successful example of a modern democratic and socialist state experiencing rapid economic growth and social modernization. Such is the theme of Irving Louis Horowitz's recent book, significantly entitled *Israeli Ecstasies/Jewish Agonies*. Horowitz, a radical sociologist at Rutgers University, focused in this volume on what he described as "those problems of deepest concern to those of the younger generation possessing a radical persuasion."[5] He was responding especially to those on the left for whom Israel is a capitalistic and militaristic bastion of Western imperialism, as well as reassuring his readers that one can be both authentically radical and pro-Israel at the same time. Not only is Israel "dedicated to principles of social egalitarianism as well as to a higher degree of public ownership of basic means of production,"[6] but it also shares with third-world nations a "deep and desperate sense of national autonomy and national liberation."[7] Israel's natural home, Horowitz claimed, is among the third-world countries, and it is only because of the international situation that it has been forced to forge unnatural economic and military ties with the United States.

Horowitz argued that the close relationship between Israel and the affluent, bourgeois Jewish communities of the West is also artificial and serves to disguise its true character as an increasingly secular and socialistic state whose natural allies are the struggling nations of Africa and Asia. "It is more important," Horowitz contended, "that a Uganda ruler opens up a legation in Jerusalem than that ninety conferences between American Jews and Israeli Jews are held in Israel. The State needs legations more than conferences, needs Africans at least as much as Americans, needs support from poor nations no less than from wealthy Jews."[8] Horowitz proposed that Israel should not only be a model for the proper treatment of oppressed minorities, but that it should also eliminate all vestiges of official religious authority. If these things are not done and if Israel is unable to assume its natural place in the camp of the third-world and socialistic countries, he maintained, "fundamental issues will never be addressed, much less resolved; and thus the unique place of Israel in the covenant of nations will become sheer myth, lost in the rubble of geographical determinism."[9]

The significance of Horowitz's volume lies in part in the extent to which it reveals the tendency of American Jews to project their own values upon Israel. In his discussion of the relationship between Israel and American Jewry, for instance, Horowitz did not stress what American Jews have

---

[5] Irving Louis Horowitz, *Israeli Ecstasies/Jewish Agonies* (New York: Oxford University Press, 1974), p. viii.
[6] Ibid., p. 43.
[7] Ibid., p. 75; see pp. 75-85, 104.
[8] Ibid., p. 79.
[9] Ibid., pp. 84-85.

done for Israel in terms of financial aid and political lobbying. Disdaining the secure, affluent, and complacent American Jewry, Horowitz instead emphasized the example Israel provides American Jews of a socially concerned Jewish community. Thus he recommended closer ties between Israel and the black African states not only because this would aid Israel, but also because it would strengthen "the ties between American Jews and American black people, not automatically, not ipso facto, but it would help to a considerable degree."[10]

One of the interesting things about the ubiquity of this pro-Israel sentiment among American Jews is its relatively recent vintage. Indeed, until forty years ago Zionism was a decidedly minority position within American Jewry, and even ten years ago Israel had a far less important place on the American Jewish agenda than it does today. Prior to the 1930's, Zionism had little appeal in the United States, since what Zionism hoped to achieve for European Jews had already been obtained by American Jews. Zionism emerged as an answer to the problem of European Jews who, in the late nineteenth and early twentieth centuries, found themselves in an increasingly hostile environment. Migration to Palestine offered the European Jew the prospect of a life free from the seemingly endemic anti-Semitism of Europe, a life in which the restrictions placed on one's social, economic, and intellectual advancement would not exist. American Jews, however, already lived in such a nation and thus saw little need for emigration. Little wonder then that when American Jews referred to "the golden land" they had the United States in mind, not Palestine. "The United States is our Palestine," Rabbi David Philipson asserted in 1895, "and Washington our Jerusalem."[11]

The energies of American Jews centered on achieving economic and social mobility and in assimilating into the mainstream of American life, while Zionism was viewed by most as a barrier to the complete acceptance by Gentile Americans of the social and civic equality of Jews. Fearful of being accused of having dual loyalties, American Jews went out of their way to assert their complete commitment to the United States and their rejection of European Zionist ideology. Thus in 1904 the prominent Jewish leader Louis Marshall proclaimed,

> May we never prove recreant to this holy obligation, to this tremendous trust, and may our descendants never forget the debt of gratitude we owe to the God of our fathers, Who has led us out of Egypt into this land of freedom.[12]

---

[10] Ibid., p. 84.

[11] Joseph P. Sternstein, "Reform Judaism and Zionism, 1895-1904," in Raphael Patai, ed., *Herzl Year Book 5* (New York: Herzl Press, 1963), pp. 11-31.

[12] Melvin I. Urofsky, *American Zionism from Herzl to the Holocaust* (Garden City, NY: Anchor Press, 1975), p. 78.

Marshall was merely echoing what a number of Reform rabbis had declared nineteen years previously in the famous Pittsburgh platform:

> We consider ourselves no longer a nation, but a religious community, and therefore expect neither a return to Palestine, nor a sacrificial worship under the sons of Aaron, nor the restoration of any of the laws concerning the Jewish state.[13]

If any one person was responsible for transforming American Zionism into a mass movement it was certainly Adolf Hitler. It is difficult to exaggerate the impact the Holocaust has had on American Jewry. Despite its affluence and influence, the American Jewish community is insecure and fearful of another holocaust, if not in the United States then in the Middle East. Minor as well as major anti-Semitic incidents trigger nightmares among American Jews regarding the possibility of a Hitler coming to power in America. The Jewish calendar in Israel and America is replete with events commemorating the martyrs to the Holocaust; Jewish youths are repeatedly taught the lessons of World War II; an inordinate number of Jewish organizations are continually looking for evidences of anti-Semitism here and abroad; and there is a continual flow of books and motion pictures focusing on the Holocaust. And it is through the prism of the Holocaust that Israel is viewed today by American Jews.[14]

The decimation of the European Jews along with the failure of the Western nations to do anything meaningful to rescue them convinced most American Jews that a Jewish state was a necessity. Israel has become for modern Jewry the answer to Auschwitz. The continued existence of Israel insures that the martyrdom of the six million was not in vain. Israel is the guarantee that Jewish history still has meaning, the answer to those who argue that God died in the gas chambers. Because of World War II, American Jews are psychologically unable to view the situation of Israel and its Arab antagonists as a normal conflict between competing sovereign states. When they talk about the "survival and security" of Israel it is with the memories of the Holocaust still fresh in their minds. The term "survival and security" is not a mere rhetorical flourish; rather, it expresses the fear that what happened in the 1940's can occur again. Thus current American proposals for settling the Middle East crisis arouse concern in American Jewish circles that the United States is going to betray Israel for the sake of Arab oil and American influence in the Arab lands, just as Neville Chamberlain sold Czechoslovakia down the river in 1938. American Jews compare the position of Israel to that of the helpless European Jews of the Holocaust, often overlooking the fact that Israel has on several occasions

---

[13] Ibid., p. 95.
[14] For the impact of the Holocaust on Israelis, see Amos Elon, *The Israelis: Founders and Sons* (New York: Bantam Books, 1971), pp. 258-278.

shown that she is more than a match for her adversaries. What dominates the thinking of American Jewry, however, is not evidence of Israeli military supremacy, but fears regarding the imminent destruction of another Jewish community.

The wars of 1967 and 1973 further accentuated the tendency of American Jewry to see the Middle East situation in apocalyptic terms. Never has American Jewry been as united as it was during June, 1967 and October, 1973, and this was primarily because it perceived the survival of Israel to be at stake. The genocidal rhetoric of the Arabs merely confirmed what American Jews had long correctly suspected to be the Arabs' ultimate objective. The response of American Jewry to the two crises, both in terms of fund-raising and volunteering among the young to work is Israel, surprised both the leaders of the American Jewish establishment and the Israelis. Rabbi Arthur Hertzberg, writing two months after the Six-Day War, noted that the crisis had united American Jews "with deep Jewish commitments as they have never been united before, and it has evoked such commitments in many Jews who previously seemed untouched by them." He concluded, "There are no conventional Western theological terms with which to explain this and most contemporary Jews experience these emotions without knowing how to define them.... Israel may... now be acting as a very strong focus of worldwide Jewish emotional loyalty and thereby as a preservative of a sense of Jewish identity."[15]

In June, 1967, over 7,500 requests were received by various Jewish officials from American Jews volunteering to take over the civilian jobs of those serving in the Israeli armed forces. One official of the Jewish agency was approached on the day the war broke out by a man followed by his two sons who said, "I have no money to give but here are my sons. Please send them over immediately." The outpouring of money by American Jews to help Israel pay for the 1967 war was unprecedented in the history of Jewish philanthropy. Whereas in 1966 $136,500,000 was pledged to the various Jewish community fund drives, in 1967 the figure was $317,000,000. In less than one month $100,000,000 had been raised by the United Jewish Appeal. Money came in faster than it could be tabulated, and individuals, overcome by the urgency of the situation, often insisted on giving cash rather than checks. Numerous persons donated the cash-surrender value of life insurance policies. Contributions were made to the U.J.A. in lieu of anniversary, birthday, graduation, bar mitzvah, and father's day gifts. Jewish youth organizations turned over their treasuries to the U.J.A. In Essex County, New Jersey, the golf course at a Jewish country club was even closed on a Sunday morning so that a fund-raising meeting could take place, while in Washington, DC, a Jewish belly-dancer at an Arabic night club donated several nights' pay to the cause.[16]

---

[15] Arthur Hertzberg, "Israel and American Jewry," *Commentary* 44 (August, 1967): 72.
[16] Lucy S. Dawidowicz, "American Public Opinion," in Morris Fine and Milton Himmel-

The response of American Jews in 1967 was dwarfed by their reaction to the Yom Kippur War of 1973. Once again American Jewry was engulfed by the memories of World War II, and this time over 30,000 persons volunteered for work in Israel. There occurred an outpouring of money the likes of which American philanthropy had never previously witnessed. The sum of $107,000,000 was pledged during the first week of the war, and the total of United Jewish Appeal pledges amounted to $675,000,000. This included $1,000,000 raised by Jewish university students, as well as two gifts of $5,000,000 each.[17]

This solidification of American Jews behind Israel has not, however, been accompanied by any widespread acceptance of classical Zionist ideology. According to David Ben Gurion and other Israeli Zionist spokespersons, Jews living outside the state of Israel were living in exile and should migrate to Israel. The essence of Zionism, Ben Gurion claimed in 1950, is "a complete solidarity with the state and the people of Israel." Although the Israelis have contended that Israel is the homeland of the Jewish people and that every Jew is obligated to become a citizen of the state, relatively few Jews have migrated to Israel for religious or ideological reasons. Migration has generally occurred because persecutions forced Jews to flee their native lands. Few Jews have felt the need to leave the comfort and security of Great Britain, Canada, and the United States and resettle in Israel. Fewer than 60,000 American Jews have emigrated to Israel since the founding of the state, and most of these have returned to the United States. Zionist leaders view this refusal to leave the fleshpots of the West with a mingling of contempt and fright for it not only deprives Israel of the increased Jewish population which is the guarantor of its existence, but it also denies the fundamental tenet of Zionist ideology regarding the abnormality of diaspora life once the Jewish state has been established. The result is, as the Zionist Nahum Goldmann stated in 1954, that Israel is the only state in the world where 90 percent of its people live outside its borders.[18]

Despite their reluctance to exchange Great Neck for Jerusalem and Beverly Hills for Tel Aviv, American Jews do not view themselves as

---

farb, eds., *American Jewish Year Book, 1968* (Philadelphia: Jewish Publication Society of America, 1968), pp. 203-218; Silverberg, *If I Forget Thee*, pp. 1-10, 574-577, 582; Marshall Sklare, "Lakeville and Israel: The Six-Day War and Its Aftermath," *Midstream* 14 (October, 1968): 4-21; S. P. Goldberg, "Jewish Communal Services: Programs and Finances," in Morris Fine and Milton Himmelfarb, eds., *American Jewish Year Book* (Philadelphia: Jewish Publication Society of America, 1972), pp. 238-239.

[17] Norman Podhoretz, "Now, Instant Zionism," *New York Times Magazine*, February 3, 1974, pp. 10-11, 37-39, 42-43; Daniel J. Elazar, "United States of America: Overview," in Moshe Davis, ed., *The Yom Kippur War: Israel and the Jewish People* (New York: Arno Press, 1974), pp. 1-35; Stephen D. Issacs, *Jews and American Politics* (Garden City, NY: Doubleday, 1974), p. 267; Meir Moshe, "The Yom Kippur War in Middle America," *Midstream* 20 (June-July, 1974): 74-79.

[18] Issacs, *Jews and American Politics*, p. 253; Silverberg, *If I Forget Thee*, pp. 467-469.

Zionists manqué. Seeing no reason why they themselves should go on *aliyah*, American Jewry has perceived Zionism as a movement to create a refuge for the persecuted rather than a national homeland for all Jews. As far as American Zionism is concerned, there is much truth to the rather cynical description of Zionism as a movement in which one person gives money to a second person to send a third person to Israel. The implications of the unique American approach to Zionism have been developed since the establishment of the state in 1948, but the basis for it had been laid decades previously, primarily by the greatest of all American Zionists, Louis D. Brandeis.

Brandeis's greatest accomplishment was in Americanizing Zionism—in reconciling the desire of American Jewry to become an integral part of American life with the wish to create in Palestine a refuge for Jews. Brandeis provided a rationale for Zionism which blunted charges of dual loyalty and reassured American Jews fearful of the foreign taint surrounding Zionism. According to Brandeis, both Americanism and Zionism shared common ideals of brotherhood, social justice, democracy, and liberty. For Brandeis the best Americans were those who deeply believed in the universality of these ideals. This meant that American Jews had a patriotic duty to help establish in the Middle East a society based on these American (and Zionist) principles. "To be good Americans," he claimed, "we must be better Jews, and to be better Jews we must become Zionists."[19] Brandeis did not restrict his transnational view of Americanism to Zionism. "Every Irish-American who contributed toward advancing home rule," he maintained, "was a better man and a better American for the sacrifices he made."[20] Brandeis' interpretation of Zionism as a movement to secure freedom and justice for Jews did not require American Jews to settle in Palestine since American Jews were already living in a free and just society. Zionism's *raison d'être* was in providing a refuge for those less fortunate Jews who were being persecuted for racial and religious reasons. Brandeis defined Zionism as

> a movement of freedom, a movement to give the Jew more freedom, not less, to give to him the same freedom which the other peoples enjoy, the freedom to go to the land of his fathers or to remain or go to some land as he may choose, the freedom which is enjoyed by every people and nation practically in all the world, be that nation small or large.[21]

As good Americans, American Jews could not stand aloof from this "movement of freedom."

---

[19] Urofsky, *American Zionism*, p. 129.
[20] Ibid., p. 130.
[21] Ibid., p. 131.

Under Brandeis's leadership American Zionism deemphasized Jewish nationalism and the goal of a Jewish state and stressed instead philanthropic and humanitarian activities in Palestine. The stamp which Brandeis and his followers placed on American Zionism was the only one which could have appealed to large numbers of American Jews, as well as legitimizing Zionism in the minds of non-Jewish Americans. The price that had to be paid for this was the enmity of European Zionists who belittled American Zionism as mere philanthropy and accused the Brandeisians of ignoring the fundamental question of Jewish nationality. Chaim Weizmann, Brandeis' major opponent, accused American Zionists of "lacking in historic understanding of Jewish life and wanting in Jewish soul." They were ignorant of "all those imponderabilia which form a national movement of which Palestine is only a territorial aspect of a national political upheaval."[22]

The failure of Weizmann and his successors to convince American Jewry that Zionism involves something more than political and charitable efforts in behalf of Israel has not, however, diminished the fervor of American Jewry's commitment to the Jewish state. Support for Israel has become the lowest common denominator of American Jewish life, and Israel "provides the major symbolic content for the American Jewish religion today." The impact of Israel on American Jewry is pervasive. Organizations such as the American Jewish Committee, which previously were non-Zionist, today stand in the forefront of Israel's supporters. The Reform Rabbinate, which until the 1930's was a center of anti-Zionism, now requires candidates for ordination to spend at least one year studying in Israel. Even Jewish organizations which are not directly concerned with Israel spend time and money on Israeli-oriented programs and organize tours to Israel because they realize these are necessary if they are to retain and increase their membership. The American Council for Judaism, which was founded in 1943 and has been the major American Jewish anti-Zionist organization, has seen most of its members resign during the past decade and it is now a shell of its former self. It is doubtful today whether any Jew who is not a staunch supporter of Israel could occupy a responsible position in a major American Jewish organization.[23]

This love affair between American Jews and Israel is evident no matter where one turns in American Jewish life. It is seen in the annual mammoth "Salute to Israel" parade up New York City's Fifth Avenue commemorating the establishment of the state. It is found in the gift shops of synagogues and in stores in Jewish neighborhoods where you will see for sale the Israeli art objects which are found in most American Jewish homes, where they assume a quasi-religious character since, after all, they were made in

---

[22] Ibid., pp. 269, 297.
[23] Liebman, *Ambivalent American Jew*, p. vii.

Israel. It is reflected in the emphasis of Hebrew schools on Israeli dances and songs, and in their attempt to inculcate in their students a close identification with Israel. It is revealed by the popularity of Israeli movies and theatrical productions, and by the interest in books about Israel. It is difficult to find an adult American Jew who has not read *Exodus* or seen the movie, a novel which has done for American (and world) Jewry what *Uncle Tom's Cabin* did for the anti-slavery movement. This commitment to Israel is also seen in the round of lectures on Israel and Israeli cultural events which dot Jewish communal calendars. At Jewish communal banquets it is now common to sing the Israeli national anthem "Hatikvah" along with the "Star Spangled Banner." This desire to be a vicarious Israeli provides the clientele for the Israeli night clubs in New York City. American Jewry's romance with Israel is responsible for the numerous college students who spend one or more years in Israeli universities and in the large number of American tourists who go to Israel every year. If an American Jew has not already been to Israel he or she is probably thinking about going and is undoubtedly feeling guilty for not already having done so. Visiting Israel is not a matter of ordinary tourism. Jews feel duty-bound to go to Israel: first, because it helps the Israeli economy; secondly, because it is a form of personal identification with the people of Israel to let them know they are not alone; and thirdly, to see what the Israelis have made out of "our" land. Visiting Israel resembles a religious pilgrimage more than a vacation.[24]

Even the most bizarre events involving American Jews often have a pro-Israel aspect. One such example took place in May, 1974, in New York City. A man named David F. Kamaiko hijacked a helicopter and demanded that $2,000,000 in $10 bills be placed in valises and delivered to him by a bikini-clad girl. The pilot of the helicopter later related that Kamaiko had been quite distraught by the recent massacre of Israeli children at Maalot by Arab terrorists, and that he planned to use the money to buy guns for the Jewish Defense League.[25]

By providing a new image of the Jew to replace the image as martyr and sufferer, Israel has been partially responsible for a new pride among many American Jews in their Jewishness. The Israelis have shown that Jews need not be passive victims who can be slaughtered like sheep. One of the posters produced during the euphoria immediately after the Six-Day War showed a Hassidic Jew stepping into a telephone booth where he takes off his long black coat to reveal a Jewish superman costume underneath. The new image of super-Jew is reflected in the spate of recent novels picturing the Israelis as super-spies and super-counterespionage agents. The back cover of one of these, *Operation Kuwait* by Harry Arvay, has a typical description of the book's scenario.

---

[24] Ibid., pp. 89-92; Sklare, *America's Jews*, pp. 213-222.
[25] *New York Times*, May 24, 1974.

> On the edge of an oil-rich desert, Black September has established X19, a secret base where the art of sky sabotage is taught to paramilitary terror troops. While it operates, no plane can fly anywhere in the world free of fear. But Israel's Security Branch has other ideas. Their daredevil team of counterspy commandos has launched an operation that will smash X19 bullet by bullet, gun by gun, terrorist by terrorist.

The publishers also promised that there would soon be published another novel by Mr. Arvay entitled *The Piraeus Plot* which was described as "another dynamic adventure of the undercover war in the Middle East, matching the crack Israeli Secret Service vs. International Terrorists!"[26]

American Jews have vicariously shared in Israel's military and economic triumphs. The greater the victories, the more pride Americans have in Israel and themselves for, in their opinion, the Israelis are struggling in behalf of Jews throughout the world. This new pride in Jewishness is reflected in the fact that Jews have gone public. No longer do Jewish commedians, singers, and novelists hide their identity; instead they capitalize on it. To be Jewish is to be "in," so much so that a few years ago Truman Capote complained of a Jewish literary mafia. "The creation of the state of Israel," wrote Marshall Sklare, the foremost authority on contemporary American Jewry, "has had a profound effect on the American Jew, particularly on his psychological make-up. It has given him a heightened sense of morale—morale that enables him to abide newer challenges of the American scene to Jewish status and security." The great psychic investment of American Jews in Israel has led some to question whether in the face of the destruction of the state American Jewry could continue to want to continue to exist as a viable community.[27]

This pride in Israel and fear for its security is the spur to the intense American Jewish political activity in its behalf. Statements and actions of prominent American political leaders are carefully scrutinized to insure there is no weakening of the Israeli position in Congress or in the executive branch. Jewish organizations can, at a moment's notice, innundate the President and Congress with a deluge of telegrams and letters. American Jews finance the work of the American Israel Public Affairs Committee, a Washington lobbying organization, to shepherd carefully through Congress legislation favorable to Israel. Many Jewish financial contributions to political candidates are contingent on their positions on Israel. George McGovern found it difficult to finance his presidential campaign in 1972 in part because some Jews were suspicious of his Middle East stance. Conversely, Richard Nixon received an unprecedented amount of money from Jewish sources partially because he was viewed as reliable on the Israeli

---

[26] Harry Arvay, *Operation Kuwait* (New York: Bantam Books, 1975).
[27] Sklare, *America's Jews*, p. 222; Silverberg, *If I Forget Thee*, p. 460.

issue. Jewish political activity in 1972 was so intense and prominent that the journalist Stephen D. Issacs dubbed 1972 the "Year of the Jew."[28]

The most dramatic indication of this American Jewish commitment to Israel is though gifts to the state via the United Jewish Appeal and other organizations, or though the purchase of Israeli bonds. This financial aid has been vital for Israel's economic growth over the past three decades. In the 1950's, for example, 47 percent of Israel's importation of capital represented the loans, investments, and donations of foreign Jews, mostly Americans. American Jewish giving to Israel has shown a tendency to rise, particularly during periods of crisis. In the wake of the emotions engendered by the Yom Kippur War, the sale of Israeli bonds in the United States combined with the charitable contributions of American Jews to Israel totalled nearly one billion dollars. By the 1970's much of Jewish communal work involved raising funds for Israel, and status within the American Jewish community was in part dependent on the size of one's annual gift to the United Jewish Appeal and to the various independent fund-raising organizations such as the American Friends of Hebrew University, the American Technion Society, and the American Committee for the Weizmann Institute.[29]

This intense psychological and financial stake in Israel combined with the fact that support for Israel has become for many the major *raison d'être* of American Jewry makes it difficult, if not impossible, for American Jews to view Israel in a dispassionate manner. It is a truism of social science that people are most intolerant about matters that mean the most to them, and this is confirmed by the attitude toward Israel of the American Jewish community. Deviance among American Jews is now largely defined as something other than a wholehearted enthusiasm for Israel. American Jewry was horrified by the phenomenon of the New Left in the 1960's, largely because some of its most prominent spokespersons were Jews hostile to Israel. That any Jew could be anti-Israel was seen as a major failing of Jewish education in the United States. There is far more criticism of the Israeli government and social system inside Israel than among American Jews, and it is virtually impossible for American Jews to critically examine the nature of their identification with Israel. This identification goes to the heart of the function of religion for many American Jews, and no one is comfortable with a reexamination of his or her fundamental beliefs.[30]

An interesting byproduct of American Jewry's relationship with Israel is a new definition of anti-Semitism. In 1974 two officials of the Anti-

---

[28] Issacs, *Jews and American Politics*, passim.

[29] Silverberg, *If I Forget Thee*, pp. 323, 456-458; Issacs, *Jews and American Politics*, p. 119. For the impact of American philanthropy on the decision-making process within the Zionist movement, see Ernest Stock, "The Reconstitution of the Jewish Agency: A Political Analysis," *American Jewish Year Book, 1972*, pp. 178-193.

[30] Liebman, *Ambivalent American Jew*, p. 94.

Defamation League of B'Nai Brith published a book entitled *The New Anti-Semitism*[31] in which they argued that anti-Semitism today is not restricted to hostile acts and attitudes toward Jews. Indifference and apathy toward Jewish concerns are also anti-Semitic, especially "a widespread incapacity or willingness to comprehend the necessity of the existence of Israel to Jewish safety and survival throughout the world." Among those described as indifferent toward Israel, and hence anti-Semitic, were Senator J. William Fulbright; columnists Jeffrey St. John, Rowland Evans, and Robert Novak; the leaders of the National Council of Churches and the American Catholic Council of Bishops; and the editors of the *Christian Science Monitor*. *The New Anti-Semitism* also singled out for attack a small book published by the American Friends Service Committee in 1970 entitled *Search for Peace in the Middle East*.[32]

This Quaker document was, as one would expect, a rather Olympianlike and politically naïve view of the Middle East conflict. Its authors claimed that the polarized attitudes regarding the Middle East made a dispassionate discussion of the issues quite difficult, and they predicted that their formula for settling the clash would be attacked by both sides as one-sided. The response of American Jews justified these fears. They were particularly disturbed by the gratuitous advice to them to reassess the character of their support for Israel and the nature of their role in American politics.

> As free American citizens members of the American Jewish community have every right to utilize all the instruments of a free society to register their convictions and desires, and to try to influence legislative and executive actions. However, the nature of some of these pressures and their extensiveness have sometimes served to inhibit calm public discussion of the issues in the Arab-Israeli conflict, and, on occasion, to induce public officials to endorse policies concerning Israel in which they do not believe and which they in fact regard as likely to be counter-productive for Israel as well as for the cause of peace. This is not a new phenomenon in American politics, but it is nonetheless disturbing. No one who is truly concerned about the long-term fate of Israel and the long-term threats to inter-faith harmony and brotherhood can be indifferent to these dangers.[33]

Stung by these and other assertions, *The New Anti-Semitism* not surprisingly described the Friends' volume as an unfortunate attempt to rewrite history, "a pro-Arab document masquerading under repeated

---

[31] Arnold Forster and Benjamin R. Epstein. *The New Anti-Semitism* (New York: McGraw Hill, 1974).

[32] Ibid., pp. 18, 127-128, 312-324.

[33] *Search for Peace in the Middle East* (Philadelphia: American Friends Service Committee, 1970), pp. vi-vii.

claims of objectivity."[34] In 1971 a response to the Quaker analysis was published by several Jewish academicians under the title *Truth and Peace in the Middle East: A Critical Analysis of the Quaker Report*. They accused the Quakers of having "displayed a blatant bias, repressed facts, distorted history and presented a slanted and one-sided set of conclusions," and they attributed this to Christian theological anti-Semitism disguised as anti-Zionism. "The basic attitude of some Christians, theologians as well as laymen," the Jewish professors charged, "is still deeply rooted in the postulate that because the Jews refused to accept Jesus as the Messiah, they are eternally damned and condemned to wander the earth as homeless witnesses to their sin."[35]

It is natural, although regrettable, that Christians such as the Quakers fail to comprehend the sources of this fervent American Jewish support of Israel, and are unable to share in American Jewry's concern for the future of the state. Jews were bitterly disappointed and disillusioned by Christianity's seeming indifference to Israel's plight during the crisis in June, 1967. Neither the National Conference of Catholic Bishops nor the National Council of Churches made a forthright statement in Israel's behalf at that time. This was far more important for Jews than the numerous interfaith dialogues and the frequent declarations of Christian good will toward Judaism and Jews which had occurred prior to the Six-Day War. For Jews this was proof that anti-Semitism still infected Christianity, and they failed to realize that for most Christians Israel is simply another country. Jews did not ask themselves how they could expect Christians, who approached Israel from a different perspective, to view Israel in any other way.[36]

As for American Jews, they have frequently allowed their support for Israel to destroy their sense of historical and political perspective. The aid American Jewry has provided Israel is one of the great chapters in American Jewish history, but the price of this has been a tendency to absolutize the state. Israel is, after all, a secular political body. The problem of distinguishing between the sacred and the secular, while recognizing the centrality of Israel for contemporary Jews, was illustrated by an address given at the December, 1974, national conference of the United Jewish Appeal by Rabbi Walter S. Wurzburger, an Orthodox Jew and a professor of philosophy at Yeshiva University. The speech was entitled "The Religious Significance of the State of Israel," and it analyzed the role of Israel

---

[34] Forster and Epstein, *New Anti-Semitism*, pp. 85-88.

[35] Arnold M. Soloway with Edwin Weiss and Gerald Caplan, *Truth and Peace in the Middle East: A Critical Analysis of the Quaker Report* (New York: Friendly House Publishers, 1971), pp. 70-71.

[36] For Christian attitudes toward Israel, see Hertzel Fishman, *American Protestantism and a Jewish State* (Detroit: Wayne State University Press, 1973); and Esther Feldblum, "On the Eve of a Jewish State: American-Catholic Responses," *American Jewish Historical Quarterly* 64 (December, 1974): 99-119.

in modern Jewish faith. While acknowledging that it is impossible to be certain whether the establishment of Israel marks the beginning of the Messianic era, Rabbi Wurzburger refused to rule out the possibility that this might, in fact, be the case. "Granted that for a variety of reasons the State of Israel falls short of Messianic expectations," he argued, "there is no reason why even a purely Jewish State cannot serve as a preliminary phase in the unfolding of the Divine redemption." He then asked:

> Does not the partial return of our people to the Land of Israel strengthen our faith in the feasibility of the ultimate ingathering of all the exiles? Moreover, can we imagine what the spiritual plight of our people would have been after the Holocaust, had the State of Israel not come into being? ... It was because of the invigorating hope, strength, and vitality which the State of Israel has instilled within Jews everywhere, that we were able to witness such unprecedented resurgence of commitment to Jewish survival. Indeed, the breathtaking developments in the Land of Israel have confirmed our belief that the Jewish people will endure, return to Zion and eventually become the vehicle for the Redemption of mankind.

Jews would do well to heed the advice of Reinhold Niebuhr, a Zionist supporter, who wrote in 1944 that "no society ... is great enough or good enough to make itself the final end of human existence.[37] Christians, for their part, must make a greater effort to see Israel within the context of the tragic history of twentieth-century Jewry. Christians in particular should remember the warning of Dante that divine justice weighs the sins of the cold-blooded and the sins of the warm-hearted in different scales, as well as the words of Henri Amiel that "Moral indifference is the malady of the cultivated classes."[38]

### Study and Discussion Questions

1. Would you agree with the author that "the greatest challenge confronting contemporary Christian-Jewish relations in the U. S. concerns the state of Israel"? If not, what is the greatest challenge? Discuss.
2. Discuss whether the author is correct in holding that Israel has become the religion of perhaps a majority of American Jews.
3. In what ways do American Jews equate the national interests of Israel and the U. S.? Do you find the arguments persuasive?
4. What is the thesis of I. L. Horowitz's book, *Israeli Ecstasies/Jewish Agonies*? What significance does Shapiro find in the Horowitz thesis?
5. According to the author, what changes have been introduced into classical Zionism by American Jews and why? Discuss.
6. Discuss in what ways, according to the author, American Jewish support of Israel has been manifested.

---

[37] Reinhold Niebuhr, *The Children of Light and the Children of Darkness* (New York: Charles Scribner's Sons, 1944), p. 133.

[38] *Journal Intime*, October 26, 1870; quoted in *The Macmillan Book of Proverbs, Maxims, and Famous Phrases*, selected and edited by Burton Stevenson (New York: Macmillan Co., 1948).

ABOUT THE AUTHOR

Edward S. Shapiro was born in Washington, D. C. in 1938. He received his B.A. with honors in History from Georgetown University in 1959 and his Ph.D. from Harvard University in 1968. Dr. Shapiro taught at the University of Maryland and St. John's University in Minnesota, and is currently professor of History and director of the American Studies program at Seton Hall University in South Orange, New Jersey. He has been the recipient of grants from Tel Aviv University, the Institute for Ecumenical and Cultural Research, the American Philosophical Society, and the Lucius Littauer Foundation.

## LIBRARY OF DAVIDSON COLLEGE

Books on regular loan may be checked out for **two weeks**. Books must be presented at the Circulation Desk in order to be renewed.

A fine is charged after date due.

Special books are subject to special regulations at the discretion of the library staff.

| MAR 0 6 1991 | | | |
|---|---|---|---|
| | | | |